WRITING WITH SKILL, LEVEL TWO

LEVEL 6 OF THE COMPLETE WRITER

by

Susan Wise Bauer

INSTRUCTOR TEXT

This book is to be **used in conjunction with** *Writing With Skill, Level Two: Level 6 of The Complete Writer, Student Text* (ISBN 978-1-933339-61-0)

Available at www.welltrainedmind.com or wherever books are sold

Cover design by Sarah Park and Justin Moore
Cover illustration by Jeff West

Publisher's Cataloging-In-Publication Data
(Prepared by The Donohue Group, Inc.)

Bauer, S. Wise.
    Writing with skill. Level two, Instructor text / by Susan Wise Bauer.

        p. : ill. ; cm. — (The complete writer ; level 6)

    "This book is to be used in conjunction with *Writing With Skill, Level Two: level 6 of The Complete Writer, Student Text.*"—T.p. verso.
    For instructors of grades 6–8.
    ISBN: 978-1-933339-60-3

    1. English language—Composition and exercises—Study and teaching (Middle school)
2. English language—Rhetoric—Study and teaching (Middle school) I. Title. II. Title: Writing with skill. Level two, Student text.

LB1631 .B384 2012
808/.0712   2012944530

TABLE OF CONTENTS

INTRODUCTION

This is Level Two of the *Writing With Skill* series. It assumes that the student and instructor have both worked through the exercises in Level One. Those exercises lay a vital foundation for the assignments in this text.

If you are working with an older student and need to progress through Level One more quickly, see "Using This Program With Older Students" at the end of the General Instructions.

Although you can review the General Instructions and then progress directly to Week 1, I recommend that you take the time to read the following overview before continuing on.

General Instructions

The directions in this course are targeted at the student. Allow the student to read the instructions and begin to follow them on his or her own before you step in with additional help and guidance. Ultimately, writing is a self-guided activity. This course will continue to develop the student's ability to plan and carry out a piece of writing independently.

Instructions followed by the notation **(Student Responsibility)** are designed to be completed by the student independently, with no help from you. When instructions appear without this notation, the student may need you to help with the assignment or to check his or her work.

When the student sees the symbol ◆, the student should stop and answer the question asked before going on. Encourage the student to answer the questions out loud, in complete sentences; this forces the student to come up with a specific answer rather than a vague formless idea.

NOTE TO INSTRUCTOR: Train the student to read the instructions thoroughly! Students at this level tend to skim instructions and then tell you that they're confused. Your first step, when the student is puzzled, should always be to say, "Read the instructions out loud to me." Often, you'll find that the student has skipped or misunderstood the directions.

Last year, the student put together a Composition Notebook with six different sections in it:

> **Narrations**
> **Outlines**
> *Topoi*
> **Copia**

Literary Criticism
Reference

The student should use this same notebook for this year's work. Although the first section will not be used, the other five will be, and the student may find it useful to look back at the Level One narrations occasionally.

If the student can't find last year's notebook, you may need to help her or him recreate it. Divide a new notebook into five sections, leaving out **Narrations**.

For a new notebook, the student will need to recreate the pages from Level One's **Reference** section. These were:

    Topoi **Chart**
        Chronological Narrative of a Past Event
        Chronological Narrative of a Scientific Discovery
        Description of a Place
        Scientific Description
        Description of a Person
        Biographical Sketch
        Sequence: Natural Process
    Literary Terms
    Sentence Variety Chart
    Time and Sequence Words
    Points of View

You have the information contained in these pages in the appendices of this book.

To recreate the *Topoi* chart, have the student copy out the charts in Appendix One, beginning with Chronological Narrative of a Past Event and ending with Sequence: Natural Process. (Sequence: History is the first new *topos* taught in Level Two.)

To recreate the Literary Criticism chart, have the student copy out everything in Appendix Two, beginning with "hero/heroine" and ending with "ballad." ("Pivot point" is the first term added in Level Two.)

To recreate the Sentence Variety chart, have the student copy out everything in Appendix Three, beginning with "descriptive adjectives ⟷ nouns" and ending with "main verb ⟷ infinitive." ("Adjective ⟷ added adjective" is the first new *copia* skill taught in Level Two.)

You may photocopy Appendix 5 and Appendix 6 and give them to the student to replace the Time and Sequence Words and Points of View charts. The student will create Appendix Four, in the course of this year's work.

It is **highly recommended** that the student copy out the three missing charts, either by hand or with a word processor, rather than simply photocopying them. Copying the charts out will serve as valuable review and will force the student to remember the content of the lost work.

Rubrics (guides for evaluation) are provided in this level, as in Level One. In my opinion, asking the student to revise until the work meets your standards is more useful than giving letter or number grades at this level. If the student has not followed instructions, show the student specifically where the composition falls short and ask for revision. Samples of acceptable answers are given in this instructor text when appropriate. These acceptable answers have the minimum level of complexity and information that you should require from the student; if the student wishes to answer with more detail and subtlety, this is (of course) perfectly fine.

Finally, always remember that the program should serve you and the student— not vice versa. You should always feel free to slow down, to speed up, to skip sections, or to adapt instructions. No skill program can anticipate the needs, strengths, and weaknesses of every student. So be careful to customize this program to your student's needs and abilities.

Using This Program With Older Students

Level Two builds on the skills and vocabulary taught in Level One. However, an older student who is not a reluctant writer and already has good basic skills can progress through Level One in less than one year.

If you wish to accelerate Level One, follow these guidelines:

1) Ask the student to read the General Instructions, the Overview for Weeks 1–3, and the Overview for Weeks 4–15 *carefully.*

2) Ask the student to complete the narration exercises in Day 1 of Week 14 and Day 1 of Week 15. If the student can do this without too much difficulty, you may skip all of Week 1 as well as the Day 1 exercises in Weeks 3–13. If the student struggles, do not skip these exercises.

3) Ask the student to complete the outlining exercises in Day 2 of Weeks 14 and 15. If the student can do this without difficulty, you may skip Week 2, and Day 3 of Week 3. The other outlining exercises serve as models for the *topoi* being taught and should be completed.

4) If the student is already familiar with the concepts of protagonist, antogonist, and conflict, you can skips Days 1–3 of Week 23.

5) If the student is already familiar with rhyme schemes and scansion, you can skip Weeks 32–34.

6) If the student is already a confident writer, you can skip the project in Weeks 35–36.

You may also progress more quickly through any assignments the student finds easy, skipping steps that seem unnecessary. Your goal is to familiarize the student with the *topoi* taught in Level One and with the skills covered in the copia exercises.

Overview of the Year's Sequence

Level One was divided into seven sections: Basic Skills, Building Blocks for Composition, Sentence Skills, Beginning Literary Criticism in Prose and Poetry, Research, and Final Project.

These sections gave step-by-step instructions in the foundational skills needed for writing brief compositions in history, science, and literary criticism.

The first level was divided into sections because the student was learning unfamiliar skills. When you're tackling a new and difficult set of skills, it is usually best to focus on one thing at a time. But now that the student has mastered the basics, the assignments don't need to be separated out into units. Instead, the student will develop flexibility and confidence by going back and forth between compositions in history, science and literary criticism. At the same time, the student will be learning how to make sentences more interesting, research more effective, and note-taking more productive.

In the first level of this course, the student reviewed narrative summaries, learned how to construct one-level outlines, and was introduced to two-level outlines. This year, he will use narrative summaries in his writing, practice two-level outlines, and be introduced to three-level outlines.

In Level One, the student learned the basics of documentation: footnotes, endnotes, note-taking, and avoiding plagiarism. This year, she will put those basics to use in almost everything she writes.

In Level One, the student learned how to write seven kinds of forms: chronological narratives of past events and of scientific discoveries, descriptions of places and persons, scientific descriptions, biographical sketches, and sequences of natural processes. In Level Two, he will practice combining these forms together, and also learn to write sequences in history, as well as explanations by comparison and explanations by definition in both science and history. He will also find out how to round his compositions into fully-formed essays by adding introductions, conclusions, and well-written titles.

In Level One, the student was introduced to thesaurus use and learned how to transform sentences by exchanging nouns and adjectives, active and passive verbs, indirect objects and prepositional phrases, infinitives and participles, and main verbs and infinitives. In Level Two, she will also learn about added and intensified adjectives, using metaphors in place of adverbs, phrase-for-word substitution, and exchanging negatives for positives (and vice versa),

In Level One, the student learned about protagonists, antagonists, and supporting characters in stories; about inversion, surprise stories and idea stories, metaphor, simile, and synechdoche. This year, he will cover stories-within-stories, different points of view, foreshadowing, comparing stories to each other, and writing about longer works of fiction.

In the first level of this course, the student learned about the basics of poetry: rhyme and meter, onomatopoeia and alliteration, sonnet and ballad form, and the relationship between form and meaning. This year, she will learn how to compare poems to each other and how to combine poetry analysis with biographical sketches.

The student wrapped up the last weeks of Level One with an independent final project that used several of the forms learned over the course of the year. This year, he will complete several different independent projects by combining forms together; he will also learn how to find original topics by brainstorming.

Finally, the student will practice a whole new kind of writing by modelling her own work on classic essays.

WEEK 1: SUMMARIES AND OUTLINES

Day One: How (and Why) to Write Summaries

 Focus: Writing brief narrative summaries

The steps that say "Student Responsibility" should be completed by the student with no assistance or feedback from you. Other steps may require you to help the student and/or check the student's work.

The student instructions are reproduced below for your convenience. Texts that the student uses for research and reading are not reproduced; their place is marked with an ★.

STEP ONE: Understand the purpose of writing summaries (Student Responsibility)

Student instructions for Step One:

> One of the most important skills in writing is the ability to sum up a series of events or thoughts in just a few sentences.
>
> Think about it. When you write, you can't just put down *everything* that crosses your mind. Instead, you have to select *which* thoughts fit together and make sense. If you can't do this, your writing simply won't hold a reader's interest.
>
> To see what I mean, read the following two paragraphs from the classic biography *Mary, Queen of Scots*, by Emily Hahn. They describe the murder of Mary's husband, Lord Darnley, and his servant, William Taylor, in 1567.
>
> ★
>
> Emily Hahn was a skilled, well-loved writer, and she knew the importance of summary. Imagine if she had written her two paragraphs without summarizing . . .
>
> ★
>
> All of the details in the second version are taken from contemporary accounts of Darnley's death (accounts written by people who lived at the time). But Emily Hahn chose not to use them. Here are all of the bits of information she intentionally left out:
>
> ★
>
> Can you hear how much more effective and dramatic Emily Hahn's version is? If you can't, read both versions out loud.

Summarizing teaches you to pick out the most important, most fitting, most sense-filled pieces of information. When you write briefly and powerfully, readers believe what you write. They are gripped by it. They are *convinced* by it. Writing summaries gives you the opportunity to practice brief and powerful writing, without putting you under the pressure of coming up with ideas (and information) to write about.

Summaries can also be useful parts of longer papers. When you write about a novel, you'll often need to provide a short summary of part of the plot. And in a science or history paper, you may need to briefly sum up someone else's research or conclusions.

STEP TWO: **Understand how to write a narrative summary (Student Responsibility)**

Student instructions for Step Two:

There are two primary ways to sum up a series of events or thoughts. The first is to write a "narrative summary"—several brief sentences that highlight the most important events or ideas in a passage. The second is to outline the passage (you'll review that skill tomorrow).

Here is a long paragraph describing the arrival of the Armada, the enormous naval force sent by King Philip II of Spain to attack the English. This excerpt from a classic book of stories from history, *The Book of Brave Adventures*, tells how the Armada first came into view of the English shore in late July, 1588.

★

How would you write a brief narrative summary of this paragraph? You would ask yourself: What happens at the beginning of this paragraph? What happens next? What happens at the end?

Here's how you might answer these questions:

What happens at the beginning of this paragraph? The Spanish Armada arrives and the English come out to fight for their country.

What happens next? The English ships were faster than the Spanish ships and rained showers of bullets on them.

What happens at the end? The Spanish Armada retreated towards France.

Your finished summary might sound like this:

When the Spanish Armada arrived, the English came out to fight. Their small, fast ships were quicker than the Spanish ships, and rained so many bullets on them that the Spanish ships retreated towards France.

If you're writing a summary of a science passage with less of a "story" in it, you might need to ask slightly different questions. Read the following paragraph, which describes a scientific process:

★

In this case, you'd need to ask yourself: What exactly does this passage describe? What are the two or three most important parts of that description? What do they do?

What exactly does this passage describe? The circulatory system of a jellyfish.

What are the two or three most important parts of that description? The bell and the canals.

What do they do? The canals of the bell suck up seawater, and the seawater gives the jellyfish oxygen and nutrients.

Your finished summary might sound like this:

The circulatory system of a jellyfish is made up of a network of canals in the "bell." When the bell expands and contracts, the canals suck up seawater. The seawater brings oxygen and nutrients up into the bell.

STEP THREE: **Practice**

Student instructions for Step Three:

Finish today's work by writing brief narrative summaries of the following three paragraphs. Each summary should be two to three sentences long. Try using the two sets of questions suggested below:

What happens at the beginning of this paragraph?
What happens next?
What happens at the end?

What exactly does this passage describe?
What are the two or three most important parts of that description?
What do they do?
(These questions are only tools, so if you don't find them helpful, don't feel obliged to use them.)
If you need help, ask your instructor. When you're finished, show your work to your instructor.

HOW TO HELP THE STUDENT WITH STEP THREE

This exercise has two purposes: to help the student locate the central idea in each paragraph, and to give the student practice in writing a smooth coherent piece of prose.

The first two paragraphs could actually be summed up in a single sentence:

King Louis XV was just as cruel and thoughtless as his father.

The Colorado River is a fast-dropping, erosive river filled with sediment.

The third paragraph could be summed up in two sentences:

Richard Coeur de Lion [Richard the Lionheart] laid siege to the Castle of Chalus because the Viscount of Limoges wouldn't hand over treasure. During the siege, he was killed by an archer.

The suggested questions should help the student find these central ideas. Answers to the questions might resemble these:

Paragraph 1
What happens at the beginning of this paragraph?   Louis XV was a careless and cruel king.
What happens next?   The people hoped that the king's heir would be kinder.
What happens at the end?   Louis XVI was just as unmerciful as the old king.

Paragraph 2

What exactly does this passage describe?   The Colorado River.
What are the two or three most important parts of that description?   The drop of the river,
its erosive power, and the sediment that flows through it.
What do they do?   The drop of the river makes it run faster and increases its erosive power.
The sediment makes the Colorado even more erosive.

Paragraph 3

What happens at the beginning of this paragraph?   The Viscount of Limoges would not
hand treasure over to Richard the Lionheart.
What happens next?   Richard besieged the Viscount's castle.
What happens at the end?   Richard was killed during the siege.

However, a summary should include one or more interesting details to flesh out the narrative, so the student's narrative should resemble one of the following:

After the death of Louis XV, the people of France hoped that Louis XVI would be kinder. But Louis XVI was just as cruel. None of his advisors would help the starving peasants.

The Colorado River drops 13,000 vertical feet in a short distance. It picks up so much sediment that it grinds away the soft rocks it passes through. Before damming, the Colorado carried 235,000 tons of sediment per day through the Grand Canyon.

Richard Coeur de Lion laid siege to the Castle of Chalus because the Viscount of Limoges would not hand over treasure he had found in a field. During the siege, Richard was hit by an arrow. He died 12 days later.

If the student's summary includes the central ideas listed above, the details could vary. The first paragraph, for example, could also be summarized as:

The people of France hoped that Louis XVI would be kinder than his predecessor, but he was just as cruel. His ministers made harsh laws, and his tax collectors demanded even more taxes from the poor.

or

After Louis XV died, his people hoped that the next king would be kinder. But Louis XVI would not listen to their complaints. He even hanged the peasants who asked him for mercy.

The student's final answer should include the central idea and be no longer than three sentences.

Day Two: How (and Why) to Construct an Outline

 Focus: Constructing two-level outlines

In the last day's work, the student learned that there are two primary ways to sum up a series of events or thoughts: narrative summary and outlining. Today, he will review how to construct a two-level outline.

You may need to remind the student that when he sees the symbol ◆, he should stop until he has completed all directions.

STEP ONE: Understand the difference between a two-level outline and a narrative summary (Student Responsibility)

Student instructions for Step One:

> When you write a narrative summary, you are trying to condense a passage of writing into fewer words so that the reader gets the most important facts without having to plow through unnecessary details. When you write an outline, you're doing something different. Instead of summarizing the passage's most interesting information, you're looking for the passage's most central thought—the event or idea that every other sentence in the passage relates to.
>
> Look back again at yesterday's passage about the Spanish Armada.

★

I gave you the following narrative summary of this paragraph:

> When the Spanish Armada arrived, the English came out to fight. Their small, fast ships were quicker than the Spanish ship, and rained so many bullets on them that the Spanish ships retreated towards France.

If I were outlining the paragraph instead of summarizing it, I'd begin by finding the single central event or idea. Instead of writing answers to the questions I suggested in the last lesson ("What happens at the beginning of this paragraph? What happens next? What happens at the end?"), I would ask myself two questions: What is the main thing or person that this passage is about? (The Spanish Armada.) Why is that thing or person important? (It arrived at England, which started the fight between the English and Spanish navies.)

So my outline would begin like this:

I. The Spanish Armada arrives in England

(You should remember from last year that the main points of an outline are given Roman numerals: I, II, III, IV, V, etc.)

Now that I've found the main point of the passage, I need to look for subpoints. Last year, you learned that subpoints give important information about the people, things, or ideas in the main point. In this passage, the subpoints should give only the *most important information* about the Spanish Armada and its arrival in England.

Here's how I would outline the passage:

I. The Spanish Armada arrives in England
    A. The English attack
    B. The Armada retreats to France

You might be tempted to write an outline that looks like this:

I. The Spanish Armada arrives in England
    A. The English all came out to fight
    B. The English fleet surrounded the Armada
    C. The Spanish ships were too slow to get out of the way
    D. The fight went on all the next day
    E. Finally the Armada retreated

But remember that *subpoints are not details.* These are all details of *how* the English attacked. The fact that the English attacked, and the fact that the Armada then retreated, are the most important facts in the passage—and all you need to know to understand what happened when the Spanish Armada arrived in England.

If you were doing a three-level outline (you'll begin practicing these towards the end of this book), those details would go underneath your subpoints, like this:

I. The Spanish Armada
    A. The English attack
        1. Men come from all over England to join the defense
        2. The English navy surrounds the Spanish fleet
        3. The light English ships outmaneuver the Spanish
    B. The Armada retreats to France
        1. Spanish ships are captured
        2. The Spanish admiral orders a retreat

Remember: Narrative summaries can have details in them. Three-level outlines can have details in them. But two-level outlines should simply contain the most important facts.

Let's look at one more example. Here's the narrative summary of the jellyfish passage from the last lesson:

The circulatory system of a jellyfish is made up of a network of canals in the "bell." When the bell expands and contracts, the canals suck up seawater. The seawater brings oxygen and nutrients up into the bell.

Now, read through the passage one more time. Jot down in the box an idea of what the main point might look like. After you've done this (and only after!), look at my answer below.

★

Were you able to come up with a main point?

Since every single sentence in the passage describes some part of a jellyfish's circulation, my main point was:

I. Jellyfish circulation

Now go back through the passage and look for two subpoints. Passages of scientific description, like this one, will often be divided into sections that describe different parts or elements of the main point. You'll see a small vertical line where this division happens. Try to come up with a phrase describing what part of a jellyfish's circulation each section of the passage describes.

Write each subpoint in the box above. Then, look at my answer below.

Here is the outline I came up with:

    I. Jellyfish circulation
        A. The "bell" of the jellyfish
        B. The jellyfish's "blood"

The first part of the description tells how the bell works; the second explains how seawater carries oxygen into the bell as it expands and contracts.

STEP TWO: **Understand the purpose of an outline (Student Responsibility)**

Student instructions for Step Two:

Narrative summaries teach you to write succinctly and powerfully; they can also be used as shorter parts of longer papers. Outlines have different purposes.

An outline helps you understand exactly how a piece of writing is structured—and you can use that knowledge to write your own compositions. Both of the passages in this lesson are forms, or *topoi*, that you studied in the first level of this course; the Spanish Armada passage is a chronological narration of a historical event, and the jellyfish paragraph is a scientific description. You'll continue to use outlining this year to help you understand and master new *topoi*.

Outlining is also an excellent way to remember what you've read. The best way to study a piece of writing is to take notes on it, and outlining is an organized note-taking method. If you needed to study for a history test, this two-level outline:

    I. The Spanish Armada arrives in England
        A. The English attack
        B. The Armada retreats to France

would help you remember that the English beat the Spanish Armada back—exactly the information you'd want to memorize for your test.

A three-level outline will probably be more useful as you study for science exams. If you were taking notes on the jellyfish passage, your outline might look like this:

    I. Jellyfish circulation
        A. The "bell" of the jellyfish
            1. Made up of muscles and nerves
            2. Expands and draws water up into canals
            3. Contracts and squeezes water back up
        B. The jellyfish's "blood"
            1. Seawater carries oxygen and nutrients
            2. Flows through the canals, or "blood vessels"

As you master three-level outlines later this year, you can begin to use them in your science studies as well.

STEP THREE: **Practice**

Student instructions for Step Three:

Finish today's work by writing two-level outlines of the paragraphs from the last lesson. Use your own paper.

Keep three things in mind as you write:

1. To find the main point, ask: What is the main thing, idea, or person that this passage is about? Why is that thing or person important? To find subpoints, ask: What is the most important information about the main point?

2. Be consistent in tense. Look back at the correct and incorrect versions of the Spanish Armada on pp. 9–10. Circle each verb in the incorrect version (the one where all the details have been turned into subpoints). Then, return to this page.

You should have circled the following verbs:

arrives, came, surrounded, were, went, retreated

The first verb is the present tense, but the rest are past tense. You should try to use the same verb tense throughout your outline. (In the correct outlines, I've used all present tense, but you could choose past instead.)

3. Some guides to outlining will tell you that you should use all complete sentences or all complete phrases in your outline. When you're outlining someone else's writing, this doesn't always work. Sometimes a phrase will seem more natural than a sentence, and vice versa. Don't worry about mixing the two.

If you need help, ask your instructor. When you're finished, show your work to your instructor.

NOTE: #2 and #3 are both intended to get you into habits that will make outlines more useful for you in the future. Eventually, you'll want to outline compositions of your own before you write them. It won't matter if your outline is part phrases and part sentences, but if your outline mixes past and present tense, your composition will tend to do the same.

HOW TO HELP THE STUDENT WITH STEP THREE

For each paragraph, the student should pick out one major point and several subpoints.

Paragraph 1
Suggested answers (the student's sentences should resemble the following but don't need to be identical):

I. The beginning of Louis XVI's rule
    A. Louis XV's cruelty
    B. The hopes of the people
    C. Trouble under Louis XVI

OR

    I. Louis XV and Louis XVI
        A. Louis XV was a careless, selfish ruler
        B. The French hoped that Louis XVI would be kinder
        C. Louis XVI was as cruel as the old king had been

Note to Instructor: The passage is primarily about Louis XVI, with Louis XV used for contrast. However, since the first quarter of the paragraph deals with Louis XV, it is not incorrect for the student to mention both kings in the major point. The development of the passage then falls neatly into three sections: Louis XV (sentences 1–4), the troubles and hopes of the people (5–7), and the reality of Louis XVI's rule (8–10). If the student has difficulty settling on subpoints, divide the paragraph into these three sections for him and ask him to come up with one subpoint for each section. You may need to remind him that details (specific incidents, Marie Antoinette, Necker) do not belong in subpoints.

Paragraph 2
Suggested answers:

    I. The Colorado River
        A. Steep drop
        B. Erosive power

OR

    II. The speed and erosion of the Colorado River
        A. The river drops sharply
        B. The river picks up sediment

Note to Instructor: There are really only two parts to this description of the river; the first section of the paragraph describes its drop and speed, while the second talks about its erosive power/the sediment produced by that power. There are many details in the paragraph, which may tempt the student to include too many subpoints. If necessary, point out that drop and speed are related to each other—two different ways to describe the same phenomenon. All of the details about the Southwest, the amount of sediment in the river, and the river's appearance are related to its tendency to pick up massive amounts of sediment. If necessary, divide the paragraph for the student between "mighty Mississippi" and "Because a river's erosive power." Ask him to come up with a subpoint for each section. (You could also divide the paragraph between "any part of the world" and "But in the desert," since the sentence "Because a river's . . . any part of the world" is a transitional sentence between the two parts of the description.)

Paragraph 3
Suggested answers:

> I. The death of Richard Coeur de Lion
>   A. The Viscount of Limoges refused to hand over treasure
>   B. Richard laid siege to the Viscount's castle
>   C. An archer shot Richard in the chest

OR

> I. Richard's siege of the Castle of Chalus
>   A. Demand for treasure
>   B. Siege
>   C. Wound and death

Note to Instructor: Both main points are acceptable, since the death of Richard is the point of the story, but the siege of the castle provides the structure for the chronological narrative about Richard's death. Either way, the story divides into three major events: Richard doesn't get the treasure, Richard besieges the castle, Richard is wounded and dies.

Day Three: Practicing Summaries and Outlines

 Focus: Writing brief narrative summaries and two-level outlines

In later lessons, the student will use both outlining and narrative summary to develop longer papers. Today's assignment is designed to give the student a sense of how the two methods compare.

STEP ONE: **Prepare (Student Responsibility)**

Student instructions for Step One:

> Now that you've reviewed both summaries and outlines, you'll practice writing both.
> Remember, to write a narrative summary, try using one of the following sets of questions:
>   *What happens at the beginning of this paragraph?*
>   *What happens next?*
>   *What happens at the end?*

What exactly does this passage describe?
What are the two or three most important parts of that description?
What do they do?

A narrative summary should give the most important information from the passage along with a couple of interesting details.

A two-level outline should give the central, organizing idea in each paragraph, along with the most essential information about that idea. To write a two-level outline, find the main point by asking:

What is the main thing, idea, or person that this passage is about? Why is that thing or person important?

To find subpoints, ask:

What is the most important information about the main point?

Both your narrative summaries and your outlines should use consistent tense throughout. Make sure that you use complete sentences in the narrative summary, but you can use sentences, phrases, or a mix in the outline.

STEP TWO: **Narrative summary and outline**

Student instructions for Step Two:

The passage below, from *The Emperors of Chocolate,* is about Milton Hershey's attempts, beginning in 1900, to find a new formula for blending milk and chocolate into milk chocolate. Milton Hershey, a native of Pennsylvania, believed that he could discover a way to make milk chocolate that would be better than the methods used for centuries in Europe. But despite trial after trial, he couldn't get the milk and chocolate to combine, consistently, without burning, lumping, or spoiling.

First, write a narrative summary of three to four sentences. Notice that the tense of the selection changes from past tense (when the writer is describing what Milton Hershey did a century ago) to present tense (when he describes current attitudes in Europe). The tense of your narrative summary should remain consistent with the passage—so it's appropriate to shift from past to present when you are summarizing this final section.

After you've finished your narrative summary, put it aside and construct a two-level outline of the passage. You'll notice that the text below is separated into three sections by spaces. Treat each section as if it were a single paragraph. In the last section, the author has begun a new paragraph with each direct quote; this is correct form, but all four of the short paragraphs created by the quotes are related to the same main point. Each section should have one main point and at least one subpoint.

When you've finished both your narrative summary and your outline, show them to your instructor. If you have difficulty, ask your instructor for help.

HOW TO HELP THE STUDENT WITH STEP TWO

The student's narrative should contain three elements:

What happens at the beginning of this paragraph?
Hershey successfully makes milk chocolate.

What happens next?
The chocolate is slightly sour AND Americans like it.

What happens at the end?

Europeans dislike the chocolate.

The narrative should be three to four sentences long and contain one or two supporting details. It should be written in the past tense except for the last sentence(s) about European reactions; this should be in the present tense, consistent with the passage itself. The summary should resemble the following:

Milton Hershey found a way to make milk chocolate by boiling the milk with sugar under low heat in a vacuum. The chocolate had a sour flavor, but the American public loved it. However, Europeans still despise Hershey chocolate as inedible.

OR

Hershey finally figured out how to make smooth milk chocolate. While he was boiling the mixture, though, the enzymes in the milk produced free fatty acids and soured the chocolate slightly. Americans loved the chocolate and bought $2 million worth by 1907. But in Europe, Hershey's chocolate is considered "barnyard" or "cheesy."

The student's outline should have three main points and should resemble one the following:

I. Hershey's solution for milk chocolate
   A. Sugar and milk boiled under low heat in a vacuum
   B. Chocolate was slightly soured
II. The popularity of Hershey's milk chocolate
   A. Sales reached $2 million by 1907
III. European opinions
   A. Europeans do not buy Hershey chocolate
   B. President of Cocoa Merchants' Association despises flavor

OR

I. Hershey chocolate
   A. Milk blended in a vacuum
   B. Enzymes produced sour chocolate
II. Hershey in America
   A. A great success
III. Europeans dislike it
   A. Doesn't sell in Europe
   B. Hans Scheu's opinion

Note to Instructor: Some guides to outlining insist that if you have an A, you should always have a B. That might be a good principle if you're outlining an original argument of your own—but since the writer of another text might have decided to offer only one subpoint, don't force the student to always find a second subpoint. You *can* have an A without a B when you're outlining someone else's work.

As both outlines make clear, the first paragraph is about the milk chocolate itself; the most important supporting information is that Hershey figured out how to blend the chocolate (the first half of the paragraph) and that the chocolate came out sour (the second half). The texture and color of the chocolate are details that do not belong in a two-level outline.

The main idea of the second paragraph is the American reaction to the chocolate. The most important supporting information is that the reaction was a positive one; the student may also include the sales figure, since this is the strongest piece of evidence for the chocolate's popularity. There is only one subpoint to this section.

The main idea of the third paragraph is the European reaction. The reaction falls into two categories; the reaction of Europeans generally, and the reaction of Hans Scheu. The exact flavor of the chocolate is a detail that does not belong in a two-level outline.

If necessary, use the above explanations to prompt the student.

Remember that the student's outline does not need to be identical to the examples. Outlining often involves judgment calls; as long as the student is able to find the central ideas in the selection, you may allow some flexibility in the phrasing and choice of supporting details.

STEP THREE: **Outline and narrative summary**

Student instructions for Step Three:

> Now reverse the order: write your outline first, and your narrative summary second.
>
> Your outline of the following excerpt should have five main points, one for each paragraph. You'll notice that the fourth and fifth paragraphs cover more than one process. It is acceptable for your main points to contain both, like this:

> > IV. Tempering and molding
> >   A. Heating, cooling, reheating
> >   B. Molds in a variety of shapes and sizes

> Alternatively, you could use a more general statement such as

> > IV. After the conching

> in which case your main points would need to be

> >   A. Tempering
> >   B. Molding

> Either is acceptable (and you may copy one of the above when you get to Paragraph 4).
>
> Your narrative summary should be no more than five sentences in length and should list the steps involved in making chocolate.

HOW TO HELP THE STUDENT WITH STEP THREE

The student's outline should have five main points (one for each paragraph) and should resemble the following:

I. Kinds of eating chocolate
    A. Sweet chocolate
    B. Milk chocolate
II. Grinding
    A. Chocolate refined to a smooth paste
III. Conching
    A. Conches knead the chocolate
    B. This develops and modifies the flavor
IV. Tempering and molding
    A. Heating, cooling, and reheating
    B. Molds in a variety of shapes and sizes
V. Cooling and wrapping
    A. Cooling at fixed rate
    B. Wrapping machines

OR

I. Mixing process
    A. Ingredients melted and combined
    B. Mixing into dough
II. Second step
    A. Grinding process
III. Third step
    A. Kneading in conches
    B. Produces different flavors
IV. Fourth and fifth steps
    A. Tempering
    B. Molding
V. Final steps
    A. Cooling
    B. Wrapping

The passage is a step-by-step explanation of the steps involved in making chocolate.

The first paragraph both differentiates between milk and sweet chocolate, and describes the first step in making both: mixing the ingredients into dough. Because the topics are mixed together, either can be chosen as the main point. In Day One, the student was reminded that a paragraph is "a group of sentences that are all related to a single subject." This is true for the first paragraph of the excerpt. All of the sentences are related to the subject of how chocolate is made. However, the author has chosen to cover two aspects of the subject simultaneously: how two particular kinds of eating chocolate are made, and how those kinds are slightly different. Either aspect could serve as the organizing idea of the paragraph.

After the first paragraph, the writer progresses chronologically through the steps of making chocolate. The student may choose to number the steps or to list what actually happens during each, as shown above.

The student's narrative summary should resemble the following:

Sweet chocolate and milk chocolate are both made by melting and combining ingredients in a mixer. The mixture is then ground through heavy rollers. The ground mixture is kneaded by conches, tempered, and poured into molds. Finally, it is cooled, removed from molds, and wrapped for shipment.

OR

Eating chocolate is made from unsweetened chocolate, sugar, cocoa butter, and vanilla. Milk chocolate contains milk as well. The ingredients are mixed into dough and kneaded by machines called "conches." The dough is then tempered (heated, cooled, and reheated) and molded into bars and blocks. The molded chocolate is cooled and then wrapped by wrapping machines.

In both cases the student should list the chronological steps of making chocolate, leaving out unnecessary details.

Day Four: Copia

 Focus: Reviewing skills in sentence writing

Today, the student will begin the year's first exercises in *copia*—rephrasing, rewriting, and rewording sentences.

STEP ONE: **Review basic thesaurus use**

Student instructions for Step One:

> If you're comfortable with thesaurus use, continue on to the exercise. If not, you may need to go back and review Week Three of Level One: Using the Thesaurus.
>
> The simplest way to rewrite a sentence is to choose *synonyms* for the most important words. You've probably learned the basic definition of a synonym: it is a word that means the same, or almost the same, as another word. *Fear* and *terror* are synonyms; they mean almost the same thing. *Run* and *jog* are synonyms. So are *loud* and *noisy*, and *joy* and *happiness*.
>
> But although "word that means the same" is a good definition for an elementary-level

writer, you should remember that "almost the same" is a more accurate definition. No word ever means *exactly* the same thing as another word; if that were the case, you wouldn't need two words. English words may overlap in their basic meaning, but they have different *shades* of meaning. *Joy* is more complete, more overwhelming than *happiness*. *Terror* is more intense than *fear*.

You should always remember shades of meaning when you choose synonyms. Consider the following sentence, from the Sherlock Holmes adventure called *The Speckled Band*:

> Imagine, then, my thrill of terror when last night, as I lay awake, thinking over her terrible fate, I suddenly heard in the silence of the night the low whistle which had been the herald of her own death.

In this sentence, "thrill" stands for the basic meaning of: startling, strong sensation. Look up "thrill" in your thesaurus, and you'll find the following synonyms for startling, strong sensations:

inspiration, satisfaction, frenzy, tumult, tingle

But in *The Speckled Band*, the thrill is a bad thing: terrifying, negative, horrible. A synonym for *thrill* in this sentence has to convey this shade of meaning. So you would not choose one of the following synonyms:

> *Imagine, then, my inspiration of terror when last night, as I lay awake . . .*
> *Imagine, then, my satisfaction of terror when last night, as I lay awake . . .*
> *Imagine, then, my tingle of terror when last night, as I lay awake . . .*

The first two sentences suggest that the strong sensation is pleasant. The third suggests that it isn't all that strong. So if you were to choose a synonym for *thrill*, you'd want to make sure that the essential meaning ("strong, sudden") is combined with an implication of dreadfulness.

> *Imagine, then, my frenzy of terror when last night, as I lay awake . . .*
> *Imagine, then, my tumult of terror when last night, as I lay awake . . .*

The synonyms *frenzy* and *tumult* both work, because both of them have strong negative suggestions to go along with the essential "sudden, strong" meaning of "thrill."

As you complete the following exercise, try to think about shades of meaning.

For each underlined noun, adjective, and verb, find four synonyms in your thesaurus. List those synonyms on the lines provided. Remember that you must provide noun synonyms for nouns, adjective synonyms for adjectives, and verb synonyms for verbs.

After you've found the synonyms, rewrite each sentence twice on your own paper, choosing from among the listed synonyms. Do not repeat any of the synonyms. When you've finished, read your sentences out loud and listen to how the sound and rhythm change with each new set of adjectives, nouns, and verbs.

When you're finished, show your work to your instructor.

HOW TO HELP THE STUDENT WITH STEP ONE

The student has already practiced choosing synonyms, but this year, she will be encouraged to pay more attention to shades of meaning.

As Level One of this course noted, choosing correct synonyms is a skill that takes time, maturity, and plenty of exposure to good writing. The optional Google Books exercise recommended in Level One can continue to help the student understand shades of meaning in particular books.[1]

The student's answers should resemble the following, although other synonyms are certainly acceptable.

Only <u>heaps</u> of stone <u>rubble</u> were left of the whole <u>solid</u> <u>edifice</u>.

Note to Instructor: Heaps is a word that can mean either "piles" or "accumulation, plenty." Since the first shade of meaning is the correct one, you may need to suggest that the student look up "pile" to find additional synonyms. In the same way, "ruins" rather than "trash" is the correct shade of meaning for rubble; "sturdy" rather than "reliable" for solid. In most cases, the original word is the best, but the exercise is meant to emphasize the importance of shades of meaning.

heaps: *piles, hills, masses, mountains, lots, loads, mounds,*
rubble: *remains, debris, fragments, detritus, wreckage, ruins*
solid: *hefty, well-built, sound, stable, strong, sturdy, substantial*
edifice: *building, house, construction, habitation, mansion, domicile*

The student's sentences might resemble the following:

Only masses of stone ruins were left of the whole well-built mansion.
Only mounds of stone debris were left of the whole substantial house.
Only loads of stone fragments were left of the whole sturdy building.

The others would not <u>listen</u> to the <u>pleas</u> of the <u>starving</u> peasants.

Note to Instructor: The student should actually look for synonyms for the verb phrase "listen to"; to "listen to" is to heed, whereas "listen" alone can simply mean that sound enters the ear. She should feel free to use other verb phrases (such as "take notice of") to replace "listen to." "Plea" carries the sense of "entreaty" rather than the more formal "request." "Starving" is a verb form, in this case a present participle, used as an adjective; it can be replaced by a regular adjective. The sense is "hungry" rather than "greedy."

---

1. *Writing With Skill, Level One Instructor Text,* pp. 31–32.

listen: *heed, attend to, give attention to, hear, take into consideration, take notice of*
pleas: *cries, entreaties, supplications, appeals, petitions, prayers*
starving: *hungry, famished, malnourished, underfed, unsatisfied*

The student's sentences might resemble the following:

The others would not heed the cries of the underfed peasants.
The others would not take notice of the petitions of the malnourished peasants.
The others would not attend to the entreaties of the famished peasants.

STEP TWO: Transforming nouns to adjectives and vice versa

Student instructions for Step Two:

In the first level of this course, you learned that descriptive adjectives can be turned into nouns and placed into prepositional phrases that modify the original noun.

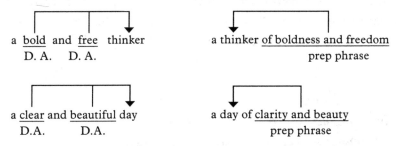

This works in reverse as well. When a prepositional phrase modifies a noun, you can usually turn the noun of the phrase into a descriptive adjective.

In the following sentences, transform as many adjectives into nouns/descriptive prepositional phrases as possible. Don't worry if your new sentences sound strange and awkward. Sometimes, transforming a sentence improves it; sometimes it doesn't. But you won't know until you try!

★

In the following sentences, find any descriptive prepositional phrases and transform them into adjectives.

★

HOW TO HELP THE STUDENT WITH STEP TWO

If necessary, point out to the student the adjectives and phrases (underlined below) that need transformation. They have not been underlined in the student section; the student should try first to figure out which words can/can't be transformed.

The transformed sentences are generally less effective and much more awkward than the originals. Don't worry about this; the purpose of the exercise is to force the student to pay attention to the grammatical structure of sentences. This awareness will pay off in later lessons.

> Hershey's <u>unique</u>, <u>fermented</u> flavor has never sold in Europe.
> Hershey's flavor of uniqueness and fermentation has never sold in Europe.

> In spite of his <u>gentle</u> face and his <u>sweet</u> and <u>kind</u> <u>young</u> wife, the king was unmerciful.
> In spite of his face of gentleness and his wife of sweetness, kindness, and youth, the king was unmerciful.

> A <u>bright</u> moon filled the world with <u>soft</u> light.
> A moon of brightness filled the world with light of softness.

> The sailors and soldiers <u>of the Armada</u> hurried to the guns.
> The Armada's sailors and soldiers hurried to the guns.

> Imagine, then, my thrill <u>of terror</u> when I suddenly heard the whistle in the silence <u>of the night</u>.
> Imagine, then, my terrified thrill when I suddenly heard the whistle in the night silence.

> The Colorado River picks up particles <u>of sediment</u> along the way.
> The Colorado River picks up sediment particles along the way.

STEP THREE: **Rewriting original sentences**

Student instructions for Step Three:

> You'll finish up today's assignment by rewriting two of your own sentences.
> Look back over the work you completed in Days 1–3. Choose two sentences from any of the assignments (they don't have to be from the same project). Make sure that each sentence has at least one noun, one action verb, and one adjective. In one of the sentences, the adjective should be in what's called the "attributive" position—it should come before the noun, not after a linking verb (the "predicate" position).

> attributive position   predicate position
> The <u>fragrant</u> flower was <u>lovely</u> and <u>rare</u>.

> In the sentence with the attributive adjective, turn the adjective into a noun that's part of a descriptive prepositional phrase, as in the exercise above. Using your thesaurus, replace the noun and verb in the sentence with synonyms.
> In the other sentence, replace the adjective (it can be in the predicate position), noun, and verb all with synonyms.
> When you're finished, show your work to your instructor.

HOW TO HELP THE STUDENT WITH STEP THREE

The student's answers will vary, of course. However, the rewritten sentences should resemble the following.

Original sentence with adjective in attribute position:

> Hershey finally <u>figured</u> out how to make <u>smooth milk chocolate</u>.

Rewritten sentence with synonyms for noun and verb plus adjective transformed into noun in prepositional phrase:

> Hershey finally <u>calculated</u> how to make <u>confectionery of smoothness</u>.

Original sentence with adjective in predicate position:

> The <u>people</u> of France hoped that Louis XVI would be kinder than Louis XV, but he was just as <u>cruel</u>.

Rewritten sentence with synonyms for noun, verb, and adjective in predicate position:

> The <u>common folk</u> of France <u>expected</u> that Louis XVI would be kinder than Louis XV, but he was just as <u>callous</u>.

Don't worry too much about the student's synonyms preserving the exact shade of meaning as the original; the purpose of the exercise is to walk the student through the process of analyzing and rewriting his own sentences.

If the student cannot find two sentences with nouns, action verbs, and adjectives in the appropriate places, have him alter his original sentences before rewriting them. For example, the sentence:

> During the siege, Richard was killed by an archer.

contains two nouns (siege, archer) and one action verb (killed), but no adjective. The student might need to add adjectives:

> During the brief siege, Richard was killed by a skilled archer.

before rewriting the sentence.

> During the short blockade, Richard was assassinated by a bowman of skill.

Another example: the student might need to alter a sentence by substituting an action verb for a linking or state of being verb, so that he can then find a synonym for the action verb. The sentence:

> Louis XVI was just as cruel as the old king.

could become

> Louis XVI behaved as cruelly as the old king.

Since the adjective "cruel" has now become the adverb "cruelly," the student would then need to add an attributive adjective:

> Louis XVI behaved as cruelly as his depraved father.

The sentence could now be rewritten with synonyms for *behaved, depraved,* and *father:*

> Louis XVI carried on as cruelly as his harsh progenitor.

or

> Louis XVI carried on as cruelly as his progenitor of depravity.

WEEK 2: NARRATIONS AND SEQUENCES IN HISTORY, PART I

Day One: Review and outline a chronological narration

 Focus: Chronological narrations of past events

Today, the student will review a *topos* (form of writing) from the first level of this course: the chronological narration in history. For this lesson, the student should have the "*Topoi*" section of the Composition Notebook on hand.

STEP ONE: Read (Student Responsibility)

Student instructions for Step One:

Your first assignment is to read the following selection about the siege of Stirling Castle in 1304.

Here's what you should know before you read: Between 1296 and 1328, Scotland and England fought the First War of Scottish Independence. The English king, Edward I, invaded Scotland and claimed to rule it, but the Scots resisted.

The siege of the Scottish Stirling Castle was part of this war. Stirling Castle lay on the River Forth, and protected the north of Scotland. Edward I needed to conquer it before he could control the north.

In the first paragraph, Berwick and Newcastle are both cities in the north of England. Aberdeen, Brechin, and Glasgow are Scottish cities that had already been seized by the English. In the second paragraph, London, Lincolnshire, and Northumberland are all in England; Perth and Dunblane are Scottish cities which had already surrendered. Burgundy is a region in France (Edward I had friends and allies in France).

Sir William Oliphant was the "Constable" of Stirling Castle, meaning that he was the officer responsible for keeping the castle safe.

23

STEP TWO: **Review the form of a chronological narrative**

Student instructions for Step Two:

This passage is a chronological narrative about a past event—the first form you learned in the last level of this course.

A chronological narrative answers the questions: Who did what to whom? (Or: What was done to what?) In what sequence? Before going on, review the definition and format of a chronological narrative. The chart in your notebook should look like this:

Chronological Narrative of a Past Event

Definition: A narrative telling what happened in the past and in what sequence

Procedure	Remember
1. Ask *Who did what to whom?* (Or, *What was done to what?*)	1. Select your main events to go with your theme.
2. Create main points by placing the answers in chronological order.	2. Make use of time words.
	3. Consider using dialogue to hold the reader's interest.

This particular excerpt doesn't use dialogue, but it does follow the rest of the definition. Take a minute now and circle five time words in the passage. You may want to use the Time and Sequence Words appendix from Level One. If you can't find it, your instructor has a copy.

HOW TO HELP THE STUDENT WITH STEP TWO

The following time words could be circled; if the student is able to defend the choice of a word that's not included here, you should accept the choice.

First paragraph: *late, beginning, initial, earlier, began*
Second paragraph: *about to begin, still, immediately*
Third paragraph: *still, last*
Fourth paragraph: *several weeks, still, finally, until, when, last*

STEP THREE: **Two-level outline**

Student instructions for Step Three:

Now go back through the excerpt and try to come up with a two-level outline, with one main point for each paragraph. Each paragraph contains a series of events, but all of those events center on a particular happening, or a specific phase of the siege. The main points should be numbered I, II, III, and IV. They can be either phrases or sentences.

Let's walk through the first paragraph together.

The first sentence of the first paragraph ("It was in late April that the siege began in earnest") is a summary sentence which does *not* state the theme of the first paragraph. In fact, the siege itself is not described until the third paragraph.

So how can you find the theme? Start by listing the main events in the paragraph.

Supplies to castle cut off
Boats seized by the English
Orders for siege issued (a month before)
English ships bring parts of siege engines
Siege engines arrive from Brechin and Aberdeen

All of these events have to do with the first preparations for the siege—the very beginning stages. So you could phrase your main point as

I. Early English preparations for the siege

or

I. The beginning stages of the siege

or

I. The siege of Stirling Castle begins

Now, look back at the list of main events. Your subpoints (the most important pieces of information *about* the preparation for the siege) will be drawn from this list.

Can any of the events be combined under a single heading? If so, the events are actually details that both describe aspects of the same overall thing. "Supplies to castle cut off" and "boats seized by the English" both have to do with the castle being isolated from the outside world at the beginning of the siege, so you could make your first subpoint "Castle cut off." If you were completing a three-level outline, those details would appear like this:

I. Early English preparations for the siege
    A. Castle cut off
        1. Supplies cut off
        2. Boats of garrison seized

For this outline, though, you only need to come up with major subpoints, not details.

The last two events both have to do with the parts of siege engines arriving, so they could be combined as well. The completed outline of your first paragraph might look like this:

I. Early English preparations for the siege
    A. Castle cut off
    B. Orders for siege issued (a month before)
    C. Siege engines arrive

Follow the same procedure and try to come up with main points and subpoints for the next three paragraphs.

If you need help, ask your instructor. Show your completed outline to your instructor.

HOW TO HELP THE STUDENT WITH STEP THREE

The student has been given the outline for the first paragraphs. Her two-level outline for the remaining paragraphs should resemble one of the following:

II. Final preparations for the siege
    A. Raw materials
    B. Workmen and tools
    C. Weapons
III. Stirling Castle holds out
    A. Siege engines ineffective

      B. Edward I's reaction
IV. The end of the siege
      A. Warwolf
      B. The surrender of the garrison

II. English weapons
      A. Lead, stones, iron
      B. Workmen drafted
      C. Tools sent north
      D. Crossbows
      E. Greek fire
III. The siege dragged on
      A. Missiles didn't work
      B. Battering rams ineffective
      C. Edward I frustrated
IV. The Warwolf
      A. Stirling Castle resisted
      B. The Warwolf was assembled
      C. Edward insisted on using the Warwolf
      D. Castle finally surrendered

As you can see, there is more than one way to construct the outline. Outlining isn't always an exact science; it is a tool that is meant to help the student understand paragraph and composition structure.

The student should make a list of the major events in each paragraph before deciding on the main point. The list will help bring the main point into focus. If the student needs help, use the charts below to discuss the student's choices:

PARAGRAPH	LISTED EVENTS	MAIN POINT	EXPLANATION
2	Iron and stones in Glasgow seized Lead stripped from church roofs Workmen drafted Tools sent north Many crossbows delivered Greek fire ingredients prepared Jean de Lamouilly hired	II. Final preparations for the siege OR II. English weapons	Every event in the list is a step in the final preparations for the siege—the last actions taken before real fighting began. However, all of those events have to do with providing the English army with weapons. Either heading is correct.
3	Stirling Castle impervious Missiles didn't work Battering ram ineffective Edward I rode too close to walls Edward I troubled by long siege	III. Stirling Castle holds out OR III. The siege dragged on	The paragraph describes the ongoing siege and Stirling Castle's resistance. The two are dependent on each other—the siege continues *because* the castle holds out—so either phrase may be used.
4	50 men working on *Warwolf* Bigger than other siege engine Still unfinished when Oliphant surrendered Edward refused to accept surrender until *Warwolf* was used The garrison surrendered and was taken prisoner	IV. The end of the siege OR IV. The Warwolf	The listed events can be boiled down to two major occurrences: the assembly of the Warwolf, and the eventual surrender of the garrison (the soldiers defending Stirling Castle). Both of these happen right at the end of the siege, which makes "The end of the siege" a slightly better main point (because it encompasses both themes). However, so much of the paragraph concerns the siege engine that "the Warwolf" is an acceptable alternative.

PARAGRAPH	LISTED EVENTS	SUBPOINTS	EXPLANATION
2	Iron and stones in Glasgow seized Lead stripped from church roofs Workmen drafted Tools sent north Many crossbows delivered Greek fire ingredients prepared Jean de Lamouilly hired	A. Raw materials B. Workmen and tools C. Weapons OR A. Lead, stones, iron B. Workmen drafted C. Tools sent north D. Crossbows E. Greek fire	Iron, stones, and lead are all raw materials; they can either be listed or else summed up with one phrase. It's a judgment call whether to lump workmen and tools together, or to separate them out; neither choice is incorrect. The crossbows can be separated from the Greek fire, or the two can be combined. Either way, Jean de Lamouilly's work should be combined with the Greek fire ingredients, since both are details about the Greek fire's preparation.
3	Stirling Castle impervious Missiles didn't work Battering ram ineffective Edward I rode too close to walls Edward I troubled by long siege	A. Siege engines ineffective B. Edward I's reaction OR A. Castle held out against missiles B. Battering rams ineffective C. Edward I frustrated	The events fall into two parts: the ineffectiveness of the attack, and the reaction of Edward I. However, the writer makes a point of emphasizing the strength and impregnability of the castle, so it is not incorrect for the student to see this as another major subpoint.

PARAGRAPH	LISTED EVENTS	SUBPOINTS	EXPLANATION
4	50 men working on *Warwolf* Bigger than other siege engine Still unfinished when Oliphant surrendered Edward refused to accept surrender until *Warwolf* was used The garrison surrendered and was taken prisoner	A. *Warwolf* B. The surrender of the garrison OR A. Stirling Castle resisted B. The Warwolf was assembled C. Edward insisted on using the Warwolf D. Castle finally surrendered	The events can be reduced to two main headings, or else expanded to separate out the castle's resistance and Edward's insistence on using the siege engine. Neither is incorrect, since all four of the points in the second option are clearly distinct from each other.

Day Two: Historical Sequence

 Focus: Understanding the form of a sequence in history

STEP ONE: **Read (Student Responsibility)**

Student instructions for Step One:

Begin by reading the following passage carefully.

In the second paragraph, you will see several unfamiliar terms: *Balearic fundae, balearic slings,* and *fonevals.* All of these are medieval names for siege engines; historians are still not sure exactly what these siege engines looked like. The *mangonel* mentioned in the third paragraph is a type of catapult.

STEP TWO: **Construct a one-level outline**

Student instructions for Step Two:

Now go back through the excerpt and construct a one-level outline ONLY.

It may be useful to ask yourself the following questions:

I. *What need does this paragraph introduce?*
II. *What background information does this paragraph supply?*
III. *What thing and process does this paragraph describe?*
IV. *What result does this paragraph describe?*

If you have difficulty, ask your instructor for help. When you are finished, show your work to your instructor.

Be sure not to look ahead to the next steps until you are done.

HOW TO HELP THE STUDENT WITH STEP TWO

Today's lesson introduces a new *topos* to the student: the historical sequence. In this passage, the historical sequence (how a trebuchet works) appears in the third paragraph only. The other paragraphs surround and support it.

There are two ways to outline this excerpt. The student could outline it by identifying the function of each paragraph:

I. Introduction
II. Historical development
III. The trebuchet itself
IV. The result

Or the student could identify the central content of each paragraph:

I. Strong castles made sieges difficult
II. Experiments with new siege engines OR Other siege engines
III. Trebuchets
IV. Stronger siege engines

Since the focus in this lesson will be on the third paragraph, don't allow the student to grow frustrated with the rest of the outline; if he cannot figure out what the main points should be, prompt him with the answers above.

STEP THREE: **Construct a two-level outline of the third paragraph**

Student instructions for Step Three:

For the purpose of today's lesson, you will now do a two-level outline of the third paragraph *only*.

Hint: This outline should have two subpoints. The first subpoint covers the first three sentences of the paragraph; the second, the last four.

If you have difficulty, ask your instructor for help. When you are finished, show your work to your instructor.

Do not look ahead at Step Four!

HOW TO HELP THE STUDENT WITH STEP THREE

The historical sequence in the third paragraph should be divided into two subpoints:

III. Trebuchets
    A. What they look like OR Description
    B. How they work

If necessary, provide the student with part of the answer by saying, "The first three sentences describe what a trebuchet looks like. What do the second four sentences describe?"

When the student has come up with the two subpoints above, tell him to continue on to Step Four.

STEP FOUR: **Write down the pattern of the *topos* (Student Responsibility)**

Student instructions for Step Four:

A three-level outline of the third paragraph would resemble the following:

III. Trebuchets
    A. Description
        1. Short and thick end loaded with weights
        2. Long and thin end had a sling
    B. How they work
        1. Thin end winched down
        2. Sling loaded with missile
        3. Arm released
        4. Counterweight dropped
        5. Missile launched

This paragraph is an example of your new *topos:* a sequence in history.

Last year, you learned to write a sequence in science. For your reference, here's what that sequence included:

Sequence: Natural Process

Definition: A step by step description of a cycle that occurs in nature

Procedure	Remember
1. Describe the natural process chronologically, step by step.	
2. Decide which other elements to include.	
a. Introduction/summary	
b. Scientific background	
c. Repetition of the process	

(You should have this in the Reference section of your Composition Notebook.)

When you were introduced to this *topos,* you learned that a sequence is similar to a chronological narrative. Both list a series of events in the order that they happen. But while a chronological narrative tells you about events that happened *once,* a sequence lists events that happen over and over and over again.

Richard the Lionheart was killed only once. The siege of Stirling Castle in 1304 only happened once. But a trebuchet was used over, and over, and over again.

In science, a sequence describes an often-repeated natural process. In history, a sequence describes an often-repeated process as well. A sequence in history might describe the functioning of a historical machine—a trebuchet, a wind-driven grain mill, a Roman aqueduct. Or it might describe a process that was often repeated in the past: the malting of barley into beer, the progress of a typical siege, the steps in the harvesting of an ancient crop.

Looking back at your outline, you will see that the third point contains two distinct parts: a description of the trebuchet, and then a step-by-by step explanation of how it works. These are the most central elements of the historical sequence. If you look at the outline as a whole, you'll see other optional elements in the other paragraphs.

I. Strong castles made sieges difficult	*Introduction*
II. Experiments with new siege engines	*Historical background*
III. Trebuchets	*Sequence itself*
A. Description	*Description*
1. Short and thick end loaded with weights	
2. Long and thin end had a sling	
B. How they work	*Step-by-step explanation*
1. Thin end winched down	
2. Sling loaded with missile	
3. Arm released	
4. Counterweight dropped	
5. Missile launched	
IV. Stronger siege engines	*Result/consequence*

You'll examine this pattern again in the next day's work.

Finish up today's lesson by copying the following onto a blank sheet of paper in the Reference section of your Composition Notebook.

Sequence: History

Definition: A step-by-step description of a process, machine, or cycle in history

Procedure	Remember

1. Provide an introductory description
2. Describe the functioning of the process, step by step
3. Decide which other elements to include
    a. Introduction
    b. Historical background
    c. Results/consequences

Day Three: Practicing the *Topos*

 Focus: Learning how to write a descriptive sequence

Today, the student will make a practice run at the descriptive sequence.

To write a good descriptive sequence in history, she will need to do research, take notes, and document information. Before going through the multiple steps involved in writing a true historical sequence, the student will practice the *form* of the historical sequence—by giving a step-by-step description of a not-so-historical machine in her own house.

Today's work has three purposes: to focus on structure; to force the student to come up with her own topic; and to introduce proofreading skills.

STEP ONE: **Review the pattern of the *topos***

Student instructions for Step One:

> Keep in mind the two central elements of the *topos:* a clear description of the parts of the machine, followed by a step-by-step description of how it works. One or more additional elements might be included: introduction, historical background (a discussion of how the machine developed over time), and results or consequences.
>
> Read the following historical sequence, describing the first metal "submarine." Invented by Robert Fulton, the *Nautilus* was funded by the French government during Napoleon's wars with England. Even though Fulton was English, he built the ship for France because the English were, at first, uninterested in paying for it.
>
> You will need to know the following terms: A "knot" is a measure of speed at sea; a ship going at 20 knots is moving at about 23 miles per hour. A "conning tower" is a raised tower; an officer in the conning tower can see where the ship is going. The "scuttles" are thick glass panes that serve as windows. "Ballast" is heavy material used to weigh the ship down.
>
> ★
>
> In the blanks to the left of the excerpt, identify the paragraphs. One paragraph is a description of parts; identify this as "Description." One explains how the submarine works; identify this as "Step-by-step process." One paragraph contains one of the additional elements of the *topos*. Try to identify it as introduction, historical background, or results/consequences.
>
> When you are finished, show your work to your instructor.

HOW TO HELP THE STUDENT WITH STEP ONE

The student's answers should be:

Description the surface and a two-bladed propeller, rotated by a handwheel, was capable of driving her at one or two knots submerged so long as the muscles of the

Step-by-step process	increasing his intrepid ship's company from one to three, Fulton took the boat down by means of ballast and diving rudders to the bottom at maximum
Results/consequences	government appreciated the dangers of an effective submarine, if one should ever be developed. It might well put the mighty Royal Navy out of business.

The answer to the first paragraph should be clear; this is a very straightforward description of the parts of the first submarine.

The second paragraph is a step-by-step account of how the *Nautilus* first dived beneath the water. The student may notice that the step-by-step process sounds a little more like a chronological narrative than the step-by-step element of the trebuchet excerpt. If necessary, point out the ways in which the paragraph gives details about *how* the submarine works: ballast, diving rudders, compressed air cylinders to provide air.

The third paragraph explains the results/consequences of the dive: the French refused to invest further in the development of the submarine, and Robert Fulton decided to work for England instead.

This is a small section of a much longer book, Richard Compton-Hall's *The First Submarines: The Beginnings of Underwater Warfare.* Compton-Hall also surveys the historical development of submarines *before* the *Nautilus,* and the entire first chapter is an introduction.

STEP TWO: **Choose the topic for the composition**

Student instructions for Step Two:

> Now that you've reviewed another example of a historical sequence, you'll get ready to practice the form yourself.
> Your first task: choose a household appliance or machine.
> Then: Describe the appliance or machine. Then explain, step-by-step, how it works.
> Your finished composition will be three paragraphs long and at least 290 words long. In this particular part of the assignment, you will be writing two paragraphs (you'll add to them in the next step), each paragraph. The total word count for these two paragraphs should be at least 250 but not longer than 500 words.
> Try to finish this assignment independently. You don't need to show your work until the end of Step Three.

HOW TO HELP THE STUDENT WITH STEP TWO

Over the course of this year, the student will be encouraged to use a little more independence in coming up with ideas and content for compositions. Today's exercise is a first step.

The student should choose to describe something with several moving parts. You should insist that the student pick the topic himself. Typical options might include: washing machine, food processor, vacuum cleaner, or refrigerator. A television, computer, DVD player, or iPod is also acceptable, but the student will probably need to do some additional outside research to finish the assignment.

STEP THREE: Add one or more of the optional elements

Student instructions for Step Three:

> Your composition should also include one of the optional elements: an introductory paragraph, a paragraph of historical development, or a paragraph describing the results/consequences of the machine's use.
>
> If you choose development or results, you'll have to make something up. If you decided to write about a blender, for example, you might write,
>
> > *At first, cooks who wanted to blend ingredients together had to use their hands. Eventually, one cook learned how to use a spoon, and many others followed his lead. The invention of the electric motor made it possible to bring power into the blending process.*
>
> (For this exercise, inventing facts is perfectly fine!)
>
> If you don't want to invent a history or a set of consequences, write an introductory paragraph like the one found in the trebuchet excerpt instead.
>
> You must write at least 40 additional words. You may also choose to add more than one of the optional elements.

HOW TO HELP THE STUDENT WITH STEP THREE

Like Step Two, this should be completed independently. However, you may need to encourage the student to brainstorm/be creative/be silly when inventing history or results.

The student may choose to write an introduction, modeled on the first paragraph about trebuchets in Day Two, instead. The introductory paragraph might sound something like this:

> Blenders make life much easier for home cooks. Without a blender to make orange juice, slushies, or milkshakes, cooks would have to work much harder. Soups would be almost impossible. Because of the invention of the blender, a cook can now make smooth purees with very little effort.

This is (obviously) not great prose, but this lesson is designed to highlight structure; the next time the student writes a historical description, she will research actual content.

STEP FOUR: Proofread

Student instructions for Step Four:

> Today, you'll add one more step to your compositions: proofreading them before showing them to your instructor.
>
> You'll be developing your proofreading skills over the course of this year. Here are the basic steps in proofreading that you'll always start with:
>
> 1) Go somewhere private and read your composition out loud. Listen for any parts that sound awkward or unclear. Try to rewrite them so that they flow more

naturally when you're reading out loud. READ OUT LOUD. DO NOT SKIP THIS STEP!

2) Check for spelling by looking, individually, at each word that might be a problem. When you read a word in context, as part of a sentence, your eye often sees what it expects to see: a properly spelled word. Looking at words one at a time, without reading the rest of the sentence, makes it easier to see misspellings. If you're unsure about a word, look it up in a dictionary.

3) Check your commas. Commas are the most frequently misused punctuation mark. Wherever there is a comma, ask yourself: Do I need this?

Commas should primarily be used to:

    a) separate words in a list,

    b) indicate a natural pause or break in a sentence, or

    c) prevent misunderstanding.

(They are also used in dialogue, but that shouldn't be an issue in this composition.)

If you're using a comma for some other purpose, ask yourself if it is really necessary.

When your composition has been proofread, show it to your instructor.

HOW TO HELP THE STUDENT WITH STEP FOUR

Before checking the student's work, make sure that all three of the proofreading steps in the lesson have been completed.

Week 2 Rubric
Sequence: History

Organization:

1   The entire composition should be at least 290 words in length.

2   There should be at least three paragraphs.

    a. One paragraph describing the machine/object.

    b. One paragraph describing its function, step by step.

    c. At least one additional paragraph, containing one or more of the following:

        i.   An introduction of 40 words or more

        ii. Historical background (invented is fine) of the machine's development

        iii. Results/consequences (invented is fine) of the machine's use

Mechanics:

1   Each sentence should make sense on its own when read aloud.

2   There should be no sentence fragments or run-on sentences.

3   All words should be spelled correctly.

4   The first line of each paragraph should be properly indented.

5   Verb tense should be consistent throughout (past tense for the historical background and present tense for the descriptive paragraphs is acceptable).

Day Four: Copia

 Focus: Reviewing skills in sentence writing

Today, the student will review a few more of the sentence-transformation skills learned in the first level of this course: transforming infinitives to participles and main verbs to infinitives.

STEP ONE: Review transforming infinitives to participles (Student Responsibility)

Student instructions for Step One:

> Read the following two sentences out loud.
>
> inf.
>
> In the fortress town of Berwick, the core of the siege train began **to take** shape.
>
> part.
>
> In the fortress town of Berwick, the core of the siege train began **taking** shape.

> In the first sentence, the main verb *began* is followed by an infinitive. An infinitive is a verb form that starts with *to*. Write *inf.* over the bolded **to take** in the first sentence.

> In the second sentence, the main verb is followed by a participle. A participle is a verb form that ends with *-ing*. Write *part.* over the bolded **taking** in the second sentence.

> When a main verb is followed by an infinitive, you can often change that infinitive to a participle. In the next two sentences, underline the main verb twice. Write *inf.* over the infinitive and *part.* over the participle.

> inf.
>
> Milton Hershey could not possibly <u>have intended</u> to invent sour chocolate.
>
> part.
>
> Milton Hershey could not possibly <u>have intended</u> inventing sour chocolate.
>
> ★

In both sentences, you should have underlined the main verb *have intended*. *To invent* is the infinitive; *inventing* is the participle. (Notice that the transformed sentence is not quite as easy to read as the first. One reason to practice copia is to see which version sounds better.)

> You may need to reword slightly or insert additional punctuation.

> A compressed air cylinder was installed **to increase** the endurance to one hour and forty minutes.
>
> A compressed air cylinder was installed, **increasing** the endurance to one hour and forty minutes.

Not every infinitive can be changed into a participle. Read the next two sentences out loud.

The English constable of Edinburgh Castle had been ordered to repair his siege engines.
The English constable of Edinburgh Castle had been ordered repairing his siege engine.

The first sentence makes sense; the second doesn't. Always read your transformed sentences out loud to make sure that they still make sense!

STEP TWO: Review transforming main verbs to infinitives (Student Responsibility)

Student instructions for Step Two:

As you saw in the last step, a main verb can be followed by an infinitive that completes its meaning. But you can also transform a main verb into an infinitive. Read the following two sentences out loud, listening to the differences in sound.

main verb
New siege engines <u>changed</u> the way wars were fought.
main verb   inf.
New siege engines <u>began</u> <u>to change</u> the way wars were fought.

With your pencil, underline the word *changed* in the first sentence twice. Write "main verb" above it. In the second sentence, underline *began* twice. Write "main verb" above it. Then underline *to change* once and write "inf." above it.

In the second sentence, the main verb has been changed to an infinitive. But since that leaves the sentence without a main verb, a new main verb has to be provided. This changes the meaning of the sentence a little bit. If I had decided to use other main verbs, the meaning of the sentence would change yet again.

New siege engines continued to change the way wars were fought.
New siege engines needed to change the way wars were fought.
New siege engines attempted to change the way wars were fought.

When you change the main verb to an infinitive, you have the opportunity to add another level or shade of meaning to your sentence.

Here's one more consideration. When you change the main verb to an infinitive, you'll need to choose a new main verb—and there are certain verbs that go along with infinitives better than others. Here's a short list:

VERBS THAT ARE OFTEN FOLLOWED BY INFINITIVES

agree	aim	appear	arrange	ask	attempt
beg	begin	care	choose	consent	continue
dare	decide	deserve	dislike	expect	fail
forget	get	hesitate	hope	hurry	intend
leap	like	love	ought	plan	prefer
prepare	proceed	promise	refuse	remember	start
strive	try	use	wait	want	wish

STEP THREE: **Practice transformations**

Student instructions for Step Three:

> In the following sentences, decide whether to transform an infinitive into a participle or a main verb into an infinitive. (Remember that you'll need to choose a new main verb if you turn a main verb into an infinitive.) Rewrite each sentence, transformed, on the line that follows.

HOW TO HELP THE STUDENT WITH STEP THREE

More than one correct answer is possible, as noted below.

> The white kitten was purring.
>> The white kitten was beginning to purr.
>>> [Other verbs could be chosen as well; *begin* is the original in *Through the Looking Glass,* from which this sentence was adapted]

> Alice turned the pages to look for some part she could read.
>> Alice turned the pages, looking for some part she could read.
>>> [Infinitive *to look* transformed to participle]
>> Alice began to turn the pages to look for some part she could read.
>>> [Main verb transformed to infinitive, new main verb supplied]
>> Alice began to turn the pages, looking for some part she could read.
>>> [Both transformations made at once—but as long as the student makes one transformation, accept her answer]

> She didn't like to confess that she couldn't make it out at all.
>> She didn't like confessing that she couldn't make it out at all.
>>> [Infinitive *to confess* transformed to participle]
>> She didn't like to confess that she couldn't manage to make it out at all.
>>> [Main verb in clause, *make it out,* transformed to infinitive, new main verb for clause supplied]
>> She didn't like confessing that she couldn't attempt to make it out at all.
>>> [Both transformations made at once]

> Alice did not notice the Rose's last remark.
>> Alice did not choose to notice the Rose's last remark.
>>> [Main verb *notice* transformed to infinitive, new main verb supplied]

> However fast they went, they never passed anything.
>> However fast they attempted to go, they never managed to pass anything.
>>> [Both main verbs transformed to infinitives with new main verbs supplied—if the student transforms only one, that is acceptable.]

STEP FOUR: **Rewriting original sentences**

Student instructions for Step Four:

> You'll finish up today's assignment by rewriting two of your own sentences.
> Look back over the work from this week. Choose two sentences from your own work. In both sentences, try to transform the main verb into an infinitive, adding a new main verb from the list above.
> Then change one other major adjective or noun in each sentence with a synonym. Use your thesaurus to choose new and interesting synonyms.
> When you're finished, show your work to your instructor.

HOW TO HELP THE STUDENT WITH STEP FOUR

Answers will vary.

The student has not been required to change an infinitive to a participle, since his composition would need to include an original sentence with a main verb + infinitive combination that also could be expressed as main verb + participle.

WEEK 3: NOTE-TAKING AND DOCUMENTATION

Day One: Footnotes, Endnotes, In-text Citations, and Works Cited

 Focus: Reviewing proper format for documentation

This week, the student will review last year's lessons on correct documentation. He will also practice taking notes which will be used in Week 4's assignment.

Today's lesson will briefly cover the type of citations learned in Level One of this course, and will also introduce a couple of alternative ways of documenting work. (Last year, this information was provided only to the instructor for reference purposes.)

The first three steps of today's lesson are the student's responsibility. However, you should check to see that the student has read every word carefully.

STEP ONE: Review footnotes and endnotes (Student Responsibility)

Footnotes and endnotes both give essentially the same information; the only difference is where the notes appear in the final draft of the paper.

When you quote from another writer's work, the quote should be followed by a superscript number that comes *after* the closing quotation marks.

In *Beowulf,* the monster Grendel is described as "greedy and grim" and "malignant by nature."[2]

The superscript number refers to the following information:

Seamus Heaney, *Beowulf: A New Verse Translation* (W. W. Norton, 2001), p. 11.

If the information is placed at the bottom of the page where the quote appears, it is called a footnote. If it appears at the very end of the paper, it is called an endnote.

If you use a word processor to write, you can use the program's tools to insert either foot-notes or endnotes (both are correct). If you are handwriting a paper, it is much simpler to use endnotes.

Remember the following rules:

1) Footnotes and endnotes should follow this format:

Author name, *Title of Book* (Publisher, date of publication), p. #.

If there are two authors, list them like this:

Author name and author name, *Title of Book* (Publisher, date of publication), p. #.

If your quote comes from more than one page of the book you're quoting, use "pp." to mean "pages" and put a hyphen between the page numbers.

Author name, *Title of Book* (Publisher, date of publication), pp. #-#.

If a book is a second (or third, or fourth, etc.) edition, put that information right after the title.

Author name, *Title of Book*, 2nd ed. (Publisher, date of publication), p. #.

If no author is listed, simply use the title of the book.

Title of book (Publisher, date of publication), p. #.

All of this information can be found on the copyright page of the book.

2) Footnotes should be placed beneath a dividing line at the bottom of the page.[2] If you are using a word processor, the font size of the footnotes should be about 2 points smaller than the font size of the main text.

3) Endnotes should be placed at the end of the paper, under a centered heading, like this:

ENDNOTES

[2] Seamus Heaney, *Beowulf: A New Verse Translation* (W. W. Norton, 2001), p. 11.

For a short paper (three pages or less), the endnotes can be placed on the last page of the paper itself. A paper that is four or more pages in length should have an entirely separate page for endnotes.

4) The second time you cite a book, your footnote or endnote only needs to contain the follow-ing information:

[2] Heaney, p. 12.

---

2. Like this.

STEP TWO: **Review in-text citations (Student Responsibility)**

In-text citations are often used in scientific writing. Instead of inserting an endnote or footnote, you would write the last name of the author, the date of the book, and the page number in parentheses, after the closing quotation mark but before the closing punctuation mark.

In *Beowulf,* the monster Grendel is described as "greedy and grim" and "malignant by nature" (Heaney, 2001, p. 11).

All of the other publication information about the book goes on the Works Cited page.

STEP THREE: **Review the Works Cited page (Student Responsibility)**

The Works Cited page should be a separate page at the end of your paper. On it, you should list, in alphabetical order by the last name of the author, all of the books you've quoted from.

WORKS CITED

Heaney, Seamus. *Beowulf: A New Verse Translation.* New York: W. W. Norton, 2001.

Remember the following rules:

1) The Works Cited entries should be formatted like this:

Last name, first name. *Title of Book.* City of publication: Publisher, date.

If the work has no author, list it by the first word of the title (but ignore the articles a, an, and the).

2) If the city of publication is not a major city (New York, Los Angeles, London, New Delhi, Tokyo), include the state (for a U.S. publisher) or country (for an international publisher).

Housley, Norman. *Contesting the Crusades.* Malden, Mass.: Blackwell, 2006.

Jackson, Peter. *The Seventh Crusade, 1244–1254: Sources and Documents.* Aldershot, England: Ashgate, 2007.

Generally, you should use standard state abbreviations rather than postal code abbreviations for U. S. states.

If you have difficulty finding the city of publication, visit the website worldcat.org. Type the title and author into the search box. The city of publication will be included in the search results.

STEP FOUR: **Practice correct form in documentation**

Student instructions for Step Four:

> In the spaces provided, write the footnotes, endnotes, or in-text citations for each quote. Use the copyright pages, covers and other details provided to find the information for your notes. Pay attention to where your commas, periods, and parentheses go.
>
> Here's something to keep in mind: When a book has a subtitle (a separate second phrase explaining more about the main title), it is always set off from the main title (the first phrase) with a colon, even if the colon is not on the book cover itself.
>
> Remember that, when handwriting, you indicate italics by underlining the words to be italicized.

HOW TO HELP THE STUDENT WITH STEP FOUR

The student's answers should match the following exactly. Because this is a formatting assignment, correct every mistake in punctuation, capitalization, etc. The student has been asked to handwrite the answers in order to focus his attention on those details. You may choose to have him use a word processor instead; in that situation, the underlined text below would be italicized.

You may need to tell the student that when a book has a subtitle (a separate second phrase explaining more about the main title), it is always set off from the main title (the first phrase) with a colon, even if the colon is not on the book cover itself. This is a punctuation convention that should have been covered in the student's grammar course, but many texts omit it.

---

[1] A. A. Milne, <u>Winnie-the-Pooh</u> (Dutton Children's Books, 2001), p. 235.

---

[2] A. K. Basu Majumdar, <u>Rabindranath Tagore: The Poet of India</u> (Indus Publishing Company, 1993), p. 66.

---

[3] Jane Weir, <u>Max Planck: Revolutionary Physicist</u> (Capstone Press, 2009), p. 14.

---

[4] Geraldine Pinch, <u>Egyptian Mythology: A Guide to the Gods, Goddesses, and Traditions of Ancient Egypt</u> (Oxford University Press, 2002), p. 142.

STEP FIVE: **Understand variants in documentation**

Student instructions for Step Five:

The style described in this lesson is the most common one for student papers. It is known as "Turabian," after Kate Turabian, the head secretary for the graduate department at the University of Chicago from 1930 until 1958. Kate Turabian had to approve the format of every doctoral dissertation and master's thesis submitted to the University of Chicago. These papers were supposed to follow the format of the University of Chicago *Manual of Style,* but the *Manual of Style* is huge and complicated and many students couldn't figure out exactly how to use it. So Kate Turabian wrote a simplified version of the *Manual of Style,* intended just for the use of students writing papers. Known as *A Manual for Writers of Research Papers, Theses, and Dissertations,* her book has sold over eight million copies. Turabian is a streamlined variation of full Chicago Manual style.

Notice that in Turabian, the format in footnotes and on the Works Cited page is slightly different. A footnote uses this format:

First name, last name, *Title* (Publisher, date), page #.

while a Works Cited entry uses this format:

Last name, first name. *Title.* City of publication: publisher, date.

Turabian style is almost always acceptable, but once you begin writing for other teachers and professors, you might find that one of them prefers another style. Just for your information, here is a brief summary of how each of the major styles formats a Works Cited entry. Notice differences in capitalization, punctuation, author's name, and placement of the different elements.

Turabian (most common for students)

Cooper, Susan. *Silver on the Tree.* New York: Atheneum, 1977.

Chicago Manual of Style

Cooper, Susan. 1977. *Silver on the Tree.* New York: Atheneum.

APA (American Psychological Association, the standard for science writing)

Cooper, S. (1977). *Silver on the tree.* New York: Atheneum.

Harvard

COOPER, S. (1977). *Silver on the tree.* New York, Atheneum.

MLA (Modern Language Association, more often used in the arts and humanities)

Cooper, Susan. *Silver on the Tree.* New York: Atheneum, 1977. Print.

Using the above as your model, compose three different Works Cited pages for the following two books. Use your own paper, centering the title WORKS CITED at the top of the page. First, create a Works Cited page in Turabian format. Second, create a Works Cited page in APA format. Third, create a Works Cited page using any of the other three formats (the same format for the whole page, please!). When you are finished, you will have three Works Cited pages in three different formats (Turabian, APA, and your choice), each with two citations.

When you are finished, show your work to your instructor.

HOW TO HELP THE STUDENT WITH STEP FIVE

The first set of answers is for the Turabian Works Cited page; the second, for the APA Works Cited page. The student may need to go to the publisher websites or to worldcat.org to find the city of publication.

If she uses worldcat.org, she will see that Harcourt is listed as Harcourt, Harcourt Brace, and Harcourt Brace Jovanovich. Any one of those names is acceptable on the Works Cited page.

If the student's work is handwritten, the italicized words should be underlined.

WORKS CITED [Turabian]

Estes, Eleanor. *The Middle Moffat*. New York: Harcourt, 2001.

Preston, Richard. *Panic in Level 4: Cannibals, Killer Viruses, and Other Journeys to the Edge of Science*. New York: Random House, 2008.

WORKS CITED [APA]

Estes, E. (2001). *The middle moffat*. New York: Harcourt.

Preston, R. (2008). *Panic in level 4: cannibals, killer viruses, and other journeys to the edge of science*. New York: Random House.

WORKS CITED [Chicago]

Estes, Eleanor. 2001. *The Middle Moffat*. New York: Harcourt.

Preston, Richard. 2008. *Panic in Level 4: Cannibals, Killer Viruses, and Other Journeys to the Edge of Science*. New York: Random House.

WORKS CITED [Harvard]

ESTES, E. (2001). *The middle moffat*. New York, Harcourt.

PRESTON, R. (2008). *Panic in level 4: cannibals, killer viruses, and other journeys to the edge of science*. New York, Random House.

WORKS CITED [MLA]

Estes, Eleanor. *The Middle Moffat*. New York: Harcourt, 2001. Print.

Preston, Richard. *Panic in Level 4: Cannibals, Killer Viruses, and Other Journeys to the Edge of Science*. New York: Random House, 2008. Print.

NOTE TO INSTRUCTOR:

Citation of periodical articles, ebooks, and other sources will be covered when necessary. For a complete handbook of how to cite numerous authorities (newspaper articles, websites, textbooks, etc.), I highly recommend that you buy and keep on hand Kate L. Turabian's *A Manual for Writers of Research Papers, Theses, and Dissertations,* 7th ed., rev. Wayne C. Booth et al. (Chicago: University of Chicago Press, 2007). A quick guide to the most common source types can be found at:

https://www.library.georgetown.edu/tutorials/research-guides/turabian-footnote-guide

Day Two: Common Knowledge and Plagiarism

 Focus: Reviewing the definition of plagiarism

As with the last day's work, make sure that the student reads carefully.

STEP ONE: Understand common knowledge (Student Responsibility)

Student instructions for Step One:

> By this point, you should know that every direct quote in your writing must be documented with a footnote, endnote, or in-text citation.
>
> In the last level of this course, you also learned that you should add a note or citation anytime you use someone else's words and ideas—even if you change the words around or use your own phrasing. Borrowing words and ideas without giving proper credit is *plagiarism*—literally, "kidnapping" someone else's work and taking it for yourself.
>
> Read the following passage carefully. It comes from my book *The History of the Renaissance World,* published by W. W. Norton, and it describes the invasion of the Chinese empire, ruled by the Song dynasty, by the northern tribes known as Jurchen. The Jurchen had been nomads not long before—they had barely begun to think of themselves as a people—so the Song government despised them as barbarians. But they were strong fighters, and by AD 1130, the Jurchen army had pushed its way into China all the way to Kaifeng, which was the Song capital city.
>
> ★
>
> The first footnote is there because of the direct quote in the first paragraph. I took those words from Yuan-Kang Wang's book, so I needed to give him credit.
>
> There are no direct quotes in the third paragraph. So why is there a footnote to Peter Allan Lorge's book *War, Politics, and Society in Early Modern China?*
>
> As I was researching the Jurchen invasion of the Song, I found that many historians describe the Jurchen invasion of the southern Song land—an invasion that ultimately failed. But I took the explanation for the failure directly from Peter Allan Lorge's book. He suggested that the Jurchen failed because 1) they had no experience with fighting over water, and 2) they were growing more comfortable, so less willing to fight hard.
>
> Those were Peter Allan Lorge's ideas, so, even though I put them into my own words, I needed to give him credit.

What about the second paragraph?

The statement that the Jurchen were mounted soldiers with no experience of running a country is simply a statement of fact. Anyone could conclude this by looking at the history of the Jurchen. I saw a mention of this fact in every history of the Jurchen I consulted.

This is "common knowledge"—a piece of information widely known by a large group of people. You don't have to footnote common knowledge.

Generally, the following are considered to be common knowledge:

Historical dates	"The Jurchen conquered Kaifeng in 1127."
Historical facts	"The Jurchen were nomads."
Widely accepted scientific facts	"The Yangtze River floods during the rainy season."
Geographical facts	"The source of the Yangtze is in the Tanggula Mountains."
Definitions	"Nomads move from place to place instead of settling down in one area."
Proverbs and sayings	"A watched pot never boils."
Well-known theories and facts	"Flooding makes farmland more fertile because the floods leave silt behind."
Anything that can be learned through the senses	"Silt is black, thick soil."
	"A boiling pot emits large clouds of steam."

How about the conclusions that the Jurchen "did not want vassals" and "wanted to conquer China, not run it as an occupied land"? I came up with that on my own after reading multiple books about the Jurchen. If another historian uses that idea after reading *The History of the Renaissance World*, I hope she gives me credit.

When I write, I don't use footnotes for broad statements of fact that can be found in many books, like "Walter Tyrrel shot King William II with an arrow in 1100." That piece of information can be found in dozens of books about English history. But if I then write, "After shooting the king, Walter Tyrrel jumped on his horse, struck it with his spurs, and galloped away without anyone in pursuit," I would insert a footnote. Those details come from one specific source: William of Malmesbury's twelfth-century history, *The Deeds of the Bishops of England*.

It isn't always easy to distinguish common knowledge from information that should be footnoted. If you're in doubt, footnote.

STEP TWO: **Practice**

Student instructions for Step Two:

Mark each sentence CK (for "common knowledge") or NF (for "needs footnote"). When you're finished, check your answers with your instructor. Don't worry if you have trouble deciding. Your instructor will provide explanations for each answer, if necessary.

HOW TO HELP THE STUDENT WITH STEP TWO

Explanations for each answer are in brackets. Give the student any help necessary.

CK   Motion sickness is caused by a conflict between what the eye sees and what the inner ear feels. [Widely accepted scientific fact]

__NF__   "Conditioned motion sickness" can strike a student pilot at the mere sight of an airplane, if the student has suffered from motion sickness during every previous flight. [This is not widely known and has been discovered only through very specific scientific studies]

__CK__   Tibet has been a Buddhist country since the fifth century. [Historical fact]

__NF__   Buddhism came to Tibet during the rule of the 28th king of the Yarlung Dynasty, King Thori Nyatsen. [Historical fact found only in particular well-researched histories of Tibet]

__CK__   The peak of Mount Everest is 29,029 feet above sea level. [Geographical fact]

__CK/NF__   The Indian mathematician Radhanath Sikdar was the first surveyor to discover that Mount Everest is the highest mountain on earth. [This is a judgment call. I would tend to footnote it, since it is a specific detail. However, it is also a historical fact noted in many books about Everest. Accept either answer as long as the student can explain his reasoning.]

__NF__   Studies suggest that it takes 45.6 days for the human body to adapt to life at an altitude of 13,000 feet above sea level. [Specific scientific detail discovered in particular scientific studies]

__NF__   Only one percent of the names of the feudal lords in the *Domesday Book* are Anglo-Saxon; the rest of the names are Norman. [Specific historic detail known only through examination of the *Domesday Book* itself or through the work of other historians]

__CK__   William II's heir was his brother Robert, Duke of Normandy. [Historical fact]

__CK__   California bedrock was often very rich in gold. [Geographical fact]

__CK__   Neil Armstrong walked on the moon on July 21, 1969. [Historical date and fact]

__NF__   Right before he walked on the moon, Neil Armstrong said, "I'm going to step off the LEM now." [Specific detail that would have to be learned from an eyewitness]

STEP THREE: **Research**

Student instructions for Step Three:

> Using an Internet search engine, find and read at least two articles about three of the people on the list (that's a total of *six* articles). Search for each name, with quotes around it, plus the word *plagiarism*.

Fareed Zakaria
Jonah Lehrer
Stephen Ambrose
Doris Kearns Goodwin
Chris Anderson

When you are finished, report back to your instructor. Explain orally (and briefly—a couple of sentences is fine) why each public figure was accused of plagiarism.

HOW TO HELP THE STUDENT WITH STEP THREE

This assignment is intended to raise the student's awareness of the need to be *careful* about documentation. A caution: Anytime a younger student is using an Internet search engine, you should be supervising. The searches for these names and terms should not bring up anything inappropriate. In our experiments at Well-Trained Mind Press, we found that by the third and fourth pages of results, we began to get blog posts (etc.) about the issues that contained some profanity (although relatively mild). To avoid this, stay on the first two pages of results.

The student's explanations should sound something like the following. After he has told you about his two selected examples, show him the comparisons below. Have him read them aloud to hear the similarities.

Fareed Zakaria: Copied the organization and exact information from a paragraph from Jill Lepore's 4/23/12 column ("Battleground America") in *The New Yorker* and used it without attribution in his own 8/20/12 column ("The Case for Gun Control") in *Time*.

Zakaria's column	Lepore's column
Adam Winkler, a professor of constitutional law at UCLA, documents the actual history in Gunfight: The Battle over the Right to Bear Arms in America. Guns were regulated in the U.S. from the earliest years of the Republic. Laws that banned the carrying of concealed weapons were passed in Kentucky and Louisiana in 1813. Other states soon followed: Indiana in 1820, Tennessee and Virginia in 1838, Alabama in 1839 and Ohio in 1859. Similar laws were passed in Texas, Florida and Oklahoma. As the governor of Texas (Texas!) explained in 1893, the "mission of the concealed deadly weapon is murder. To check it is the duty of every self-respecting, law-abiding man."	As Adam Winkler, a constitutional-law scholar at U.C.L.A., demonstrates in a remarkably nuanced new book, "Gunfight: The Battle Over the Right to Bear Arms in America," firearms have been regulated in the United States from the start. Laws banning the carrying of concealed weapons were passed in Kentucky and Louisiana in 1813, and other states soon followed: Indiana (1820), Tennessee and Virginia (1838), Alabama (1839), and Ohio (1859). Similar laws were passed in Texas, Florida, and Oklahoma. As the governor of Texas explained in 1893, the "mission of the concealed deadly weapon is murder. To check it is the duty of every self-respecting, law-abiding man."

Jonah Lehrer: Between 2010 and 2012, copied material from press releases, other writers, and his own past work (which is not necessarily plagiarism, if the student asks, but Lehrer had certified the work as "not previously published"). Lehrer also made up quotes and facts for his articles, which some reports are calling "plagiarism" as well. That's not plagiarism, just fraud. The plagiarized material appeared in his columns for *Wired,* in articles for *The New Yorker,* and in three published books. One interesting example, first pointed out by Michael C. Moynihan on Twitter (http://www.twitlonger.com/show/illeo6), follows. Notice that Lehrer *did* insert a footnote—but he apparently made it up, copying the words directly from Haynes's lecture instead. That is plagiarism because it steals Haynes's words without his permission.

Jonah Lehrer, in *How We Decide*	Public lecture given by Al Haynes, 5/24/91
"For most of my career, we kind of worked on the concept that the captain was the authority on the aircraft," says Al Haynes, the captain of Flight 232. "And we lost a few airplanes because of that. Sometimes the captain isn't as smart as we thought he was." Haynes freely admits that he couldn't have saved the plane by himself that day. "We had 103 years of flying experience there in the cockpit [on Flight 232], trying to get that airplane on the ground. If I hadn't used CRM, if we had not had everybody's input, it's a cinch we wouldn't have made it." (footnote: "Al Haynes, interview with the author, January 21, 2008")	"Up until 1980, we kind of worked on the concept that the captain was THE authority on the aircraft. What he said, goes. And we lost a few airplanes because of that. Sometimes the captain isn't as smart as we thought he was. And we would listen to him, and do what he said, and we wouldn't know what he's talking about. And we had 103 years of flying experience there in the cockpit, trying to get that airplane on the ground, not one minute of which we had actually practiced, any one of us."

Stephen Ambrose: In 2002, accused of taking word-for-word passages from a World War II history called *Wings of Morning,* by Thomas Childers, and using them in his book *The Wild Blue.* Although Ambrose did credit Childers, he didn't enclose the borrowed passages in quotation marks, so he didn't make clear that the exact words belonged to Childers. Later, many other passages in other books were also called into question.

Ambrose, *Wild Blue*	Childers, *Wings of Morning*
"Up, up, up he went, until he got above the clouds. No amount of practice could have prepared the pilot and crew for what they encountered—B24's, glittering like mica, were popping up out of the clouds over here, over there, everywhere."	"Up, up, up, groping through the clouds for what seemed like an eternity . . . No amount of practice could have prepared them for what they encountered. B-24s, glittering like mica, were popping up out of the clouds all over the sky."

Doris Kearns Goodwin: Copied sentences and paragraphs from three other books and used them without attribution in her 1987 book, *The Fitzgeralds and the Kennedys: An American Saga.* Much of the plagiarism came from Lynn McTaggert's *Kathleen Kennedy: Her Life and Times.* McTaggart claimed that Goodwin took exact phrases and language from 91 of the 248 pages of her book; even though the phrases and sentences were often shuffled around, the sheer volume of the borrowed language meant that Goodwin had plagiarized. Three examples, publicized by the Associated Press and by the *New York Times,* follow.

Goodwin's book	McTaggart's book
"During weekends at country houses, the imminence of war was discussed with a certain detachment, as though it were merely a topic of intellectual interest."	"At country house weekends the imminence of war was discussed with a certain detachment, as though it were merely a topic of intellectual interest."
"Hardly a day passed without a newspaper photograph of little Teddy taking a snapshot with his camera held upside down, or the five Kennedy children lined up on a train or on a bus."	"Hardly a day passed by without a photograph in the papers of little Teddy taking a snapshot with his Brownie held upside down, or the five Kennedy children lined up on a train or bus."
"One summer day, a photographer on the Daily Mail in London photographed Kathleen in her blue-gray uniform on a bicycle pedaling to work. The photograph was snapped up by the Boston Globe and reproduced all over the States as a symbol of the all-American girl coming to the aid of the GIs abroad."	"One summer day a photographer on the Daily Mail in London photographed Kathleen in uniform on a bicycle pedaling to work. The photograph was promptly snapped up by The Boston Globe and reproduced in papers across the country as an apt symbol of the all-American girl coming to the aid of the boys abroad."

Chris Anderson: In 2009, admitted that he had copied Wikipedia entries word-for-word in his new book *Free: The Future of a Radical Price.* The comparisons on the next page were originally reported by Waldo Jaquith in *The Virginia Quarterly Review,* who also pointed out similarities with two other published books.

Anderson's book	Wikipedia
"In 1179, the Third Council of the Lateran decreed that persons who accepted interest on loans could receive neither the sacraments nor Christian burial. Pope Clement V made the belief in the right to usury heresy in 1311 and abolished all secular legislation that allowed it. Pope Sixtus V condemned the practice of charging interest as 'detestable to God and man, damned by the sacred canons and contrary to Christian charity.' "	"Lateran III decreed that persons who accepted interest on loans could receive neither the sacraments nor Christian burial. Pope Clement V made the belief in the right to usury a heresy in 1311, and abolished all secular legislation which allowed it. Pope Sixtus V condemned the practice of charging interest as 'detestable to God and man, damned by the sacred canons and contrary to Christian charity.' "
"This chestnut is known as the TANSTAFL in the economics world and was a favorite rejoinder of Milton Friedman, the Nobel-Prize winning former University of Chicago economics professor. It simply states that a person or a society cannot get something for nothing. Even if something appears to be free, there is always a cost to the person or to society as a whole, even though that cost may be hidden or distributed."	"TANSTAAFL, on the other hand, indicates an acknowledgment that in reality a person or a society cannot get 'something for nothing.' Even if something appears to be free, there is always a cost to the person or to society as a whole even though that cost may be hidden or distributed. . . . TANSTAAFL was a favorite rejoinder of Milton Friedman, the Nobel Prize-winning former University of Chicago economics professor."

Day Three: Taking Notes

Focus: Practicing note-taking

The student now has one more skill to review: taking notes.

The first step in writing is selecting a topic, something we'll address a little later this year. The second step is to find out more about the topic through reading and taking notes.

While taking notes, the student must write down all the information he will need to construct footnotes later on. He should never trust his memory! This note-taking assignment is separated from the connected writing assignment so that the student can practice using notes after the memory of the original source has faded slightly.

Depending on the student's comfort level with note-taking, you may want to expand this assignment over two days.

STEP ONE: Review the rules for taking notes (Student Responsibility)

Student instructions for Step One:

Last year, you learned four rules for note-taking.

1. Always write down the full bibliographical information of your source (author, full title, city of publisher, publisher, date) as if you were entering it on a Works Cited page.
2. Always quote directly and use quotation marks around the exact words of your source. You can combine this with brief paraphrases that sum up information you're not going to quote directly.
3. Always write the page number of quotes right next to the words themselves.
4. If you are reading a book or resource online, never copy and paste words into your notes. Type them out yourself (this will force you to pick only the most important information).

You can take your notes onto 3x5 (index) cards and then arrange the cards in order when you start to write. Use a different card for each quote, write the full bibliographical information about the source on the first card, and then just write the author's last name at the top of each remaining card.

Or, create a document in your word processor for your notes. Type the full information for each book before you start to take notes on it. Then, make a list of important quotes (with page numbers!) under each book's title.

STEP TWO: Take notes about the California Gold Rush

Student instructions for Step Two:

Next week, you'll write an essay that combines a chronological narrative about a past event with the new form you've just learned, the descriptive sequence in history. Today's assignment is to take notes on the information you'll need to write that composition.

The chronological narrative will be about the California Gold Rush, and the descriptive sequence will explain exactly how panning for gold works.

Rather than telling you how many notes to take on each source (as I did last year), I'll tell you that the chronological narrative should be at least 200 words long, but not longer than 400 words. It should cover at least four major events of the Gold Rush. The descriptive sequence should be 75-150 words in length. It *must* contain both a physical description of the tools used in panning gold, and a step-by-step explanation of the process itself.

Before you begin to take notes, read through all of the sources from beginning to end.

The photos are provided for your reference. You'll want to look at them as you write your descriptive sequence, but you don't need to make notes about them. The following excerpts have been slightly condensed; ignore the gaps in the text, which contained irrelevant information.

When you're finished taking your notes, show them to your instructor.

The first resource has no author; the editors of *Life* decided to publish it anonymously. When there is no author, list the resource alphabetically in your works cited by the first main word in the title ("Gold") and simply omit the mention of an author completely.

HOW TO HELP THE STUDENT WITH STEP TWO

In the first level of this course, the student was given a guided introduction to the skill of note-taking. This second level is designed to have less hand-holding. The student has not been told how many notes to take, or what kinds of information to look for.

Insist that the student read through the material, all the way to the end, before taking notes. This will give him an initial idea of what sorts of information to look for.

He should end up with perhaps 5–15 notes per source. More than 15 means that he's not picking out the most useful information—he's just copying everything down. Fewer than five notes may mean that he's struggling with the assignment.

A sample of acceptable student notes on the first source might resemble the following (since the entire selection is on the same page, no page numbers are necessary):

"The Gold Country." *Life*, Feb. 2, 1948, p. 44

James Wilson Marshall worked at a sawmill owned by John Sutter.
On Jan. 24, 1848, he saw "a yellow speck" and then "another yellow flake."
He said to the other workmen, "Boys, I think I've found a gold mine."
The next day, he found "a full three ounces" of gold.
He took the gold to John Sutter's fort.
The two men tested it and found that "It was 23-carat gold."
Sutter "tried to keep the discovery secret."
The news spread and Californians "stampeded toward Sutter's mill."
"By spring of the next year thousands of . . . forty-niners were headed west."
This was the beginning of the Gold Rush.
The Gold Rush made California into first a territory and "then a state."
James Marshall "died, penniless and all alone in a shack not far from Sutter's mill."

If the student has difficulty, suggest that he begin by making a simple chronological list of events in the source, and then deciding which of the items on the list he would like to expand by including more details and direct quotes from the piece itself.

If the student uses 3x5 cards, each one should say "The Gold Country" at the top. Sample acceptable notes on the second source might resemble the following:

White, Stewart Edward. *The Forty-Niners: A Chronicle of the California Trail and El Dorado.* New Haven: Yale University Press, 1920.

James Marshall discovered gold right at the end of the Mexican War. (55)
Many young men needed to find "a way out of their financial difficulties." (55)
At first, interest in the discoveries was "rather tepid." (56)
Sam Brennan "rode down from Sutter's Fort" with "gold-dust and nuggets," shouting "Gold! Gold! Gold from the American River." (57)

Brennan's announcement created a stampede. (57)

People came from all over the state. Soldiers, sailors, and "able-bodied" men came. (58)

At first, gold could be picked up from the ground or "from the veins in the rocks." (60–61)

There was so much gold that "it was much easier to dig it than to steal it." (61)

A Baltimore paper "published a short item" about the discovery. (62).

An official letter to the War Department said that there was much more gold. (62)

The song *Oh, Susannah* was sung "in every quarter of the world." (63)

"Every man with a drop of red blood in his veins wanted to go to California." (63)

Clubs were formed "for the purposes of getting at least one . . . of their members" to California. (55)

The notes for the third and fourth sources should follow the same pattern:

Behme, Bob. "Pan for gold this summer—here's how and where." In *Popular Mechanics,* July 1974 (Vol. 142, No. 1), pp. 82–85.

Usually settles to the bottom of a stream. (83)

Most likely to be found in: "roots and grasses along a bank, in bedrock crevices, behind boulders, in sandbars" (83)

"Fill a pan half full of sand and clay" and put it under the water. Break up clods of dirt, take out large rocks. Swirl water in the pan in "a quick circular motion." Let water "flow gently over the lip of the pan" until "only the heavier materials" remain. (84)

Rohrbough, Malcolm J. *Days of Gold: The California Gold Rush and the American Nation.* Berkeley, Calif.: University of California Press, 1997.

"Found in the nooks and crannies of old, dry streambeds and in the bottoms of existing watercourses" (12)

"Moving water flowing through a pan would separate the lighter sand and gravel . . . from the heavier gold particles" (12)

Gold would sink to the bottom, sand and gravel be "carried off" (12)

All you needed to pan for gold was "a shovel and a pan" (12)

Day Four: Copia

Focus: Reviewing skills in sentence writing

Today's copia exercise completes the review of last year's sentence skills.

STEP ONE: **Review transforming active into passive verbs (Student Responsibility)**

Student instructions for Step One:

> Look carefully at these sentences, drawn from this week's readings:
>
> Song Gaozong's plea was rejected.
>
> Gold was discovered at Sutter's Mill by James Marshall.

Underline the subject of each sentence once and the complete verb (main verb plus helping verbs) twice.
> You should have underlined:

>> <u>plea</u>   <u>was rejected</u>
>> <u>gold</u>   <u>was discovered</u>

Both of these verbs are in the passive voice, which means that the subject receives the action of the verb. The plea didn't do anything. Neither did the gold. In both sentences, someone or something else *did* the action of rejecting and discovering.
> In a sentence with a verb in the active voice, the subject does the action of the verb. Most sentences can be rewritten so that the voice changes from passive to active. Read the next two sentences out loud:

>> subject active verb   direct object
>> The <u>Jurchen</u> <u>rejected</u> Song Gaozong's plea.
>>   subject   active verb direct object
>> <u>James Marshall</u> <u>discovered</u>   gold   at Sutter's Mill in 1848.

> In the original version of the first sentence, you are not given any information about *who* or *what* performed the action of the verb. Sometimes, sentences are written in the passive voice because the author doesn't have this information. In the case of Song Gaozong and the Jurchen, we don't actually know which official, general, or ruler decided to ignore Song Gaozong's request. To rewrite my original sentence in the active voice, I have to choose a new subject, someone who's actually *doing* the rejecting. My only choice is the broad, vague subject "the Jurchen."
> Other times, the actor in the sentence is found in a prepositional phrase following the passive verb. In the second sentence, James Marshall does the actual discovering. If you wanted

the focus of the sentence to be on the gold, you would write, "Gold was discovered by James Marshall." If you wanted the focus to be on James Marshall, you would write, "James Marshall discovered gold."

To sum up: Passive verbs can be transformed into active verbs by supplying a new subject. Sometimes you'll need to invent this subject; sometimes, you can locate it in the prepositional phrase after the passive verb.

STEP TWO: Review transforming indirect objects into prepositional phrases (Student Responsibility)

Student instructions for Step Two:

In the first level of this course, you also learned how to transform an indirect object into an object of a preposition.

Remember: an indirect object is a word that is indirectly affected by an action verb. In the sentence:

<pre>
          S   V   IO   DO
</pre>
The discovery of gold brought California a host of new settlers.

"host" is the direct object; it receives the action of the verb "brought" (meaning that the host of settlers was the thing brought). "California" is the indirect object. California didn't get "brought" somewhere. But the action of bringing did affect California; it ended up with a whole lot of new residents.

Indirect objects can be taken out of their place (between the verb and the direct object), and paired up with a preposition to express the same meaning:

<pre>
          S   V   DO   PREP OP
</pre>
The discovery of gold brought a host of new settlers to California.

In this transformed sentence, the indirect object has become the object of the preposition "to."

STEP THREE: Practice transformations

Student instructions for Step Three:

Read each of the following sentences and decide whether it contains a passive verb that could be active, or an indirect object that could become the object of a preposition. In the blank next to each sentence, write "p" for "passive verb" or "io" for "indirect object."

Then rewrite each sentence on your own paper.

For the sentences with passive verbs, decide whether you can find a new subject in a prepositional phrase. If not, make a new subject up from your imagination.

For the sentences with indirect objects, simply transform each indirect object into the object of a preposition.

When you're finished, read both the original sentences and your sentences out loud. Sometimes, the revised sentence will sound better—and sometimes the original will be much clearer than the rewritten sentence! Place a checkmark by any of your sentences that sound like improvements on the original.

Show your completed work to your instructor.

HOW TO HELP THE STUDENT WITH STEP THREE

The filled-in blanks should read:

1. More people in Africa are killed by hippos than by lions. _____P_____
2. The hippopotamus's sudden grunt gave the young boy quite a scare._____IO_____
3. Hippos were hunted by Egyptians because the large animals damaged their crops. _____P_____
4. Only one small animal is allowed near the hippo. _____P_____
5. The white sandpiper bird offers the hippo relief from parasites. _____IO_____
6. The formidable hippo guarantees the bird safety. _____IO_____
7. This relationship between two animals is called symbiosis. _____P_____
8. You will be taught about symbiosis when you study biology. _____P_____

The student's rewritten sentences should resemble the following, although he may choose different subjects for sentences 7 and 8.

1. Hippos kill more people in Africa than lions [do].
2. The hippopotamus's sudden grunt gave quite a scare to the young boy.
3. The Egyptians hunted hippos because the large animals damaged their crops.
4. The hippo allows only one small animal near [it].
5. The white sandpiper bird offers relief from parasites to the hippo.
6. The formidable hippo guarantees safety to the bird.
7. We call this relationship between two animals symbiosis.
8. Your textbook will teach you about symbiosis when you study biology [OR] You will learn about symbiosis when you study biology [although this doesn't exactly fulfill the directions, it is natural to change "teach" to "learn"].

WEEK 4: NARRATIONS AND SEQUENCES IN HISTORY, PART II

Day One: Review and Outline a History Narration and Sequence

 Focus: Constructing a two-level outline

Note to Instructor: For today's work, the student will need to use his reference materials from Level 1: the Points of View chart (Appendix II), the Time and Sequence Words and Space and Distance Words (Appendix I), and the *topoi* section of the Composition Notebook (Appendix I in the Instructor Text).

STEP ONE: **Read (Student Responsibility)**

Student instructions for Step One:

Read the following description of kangaroo-hunting, written in the nineteenth century by a man who was visiting the British colonies in Australia.

As you may already know, in the late eighteenth century, the British government decided to send convicted prisoners to the continent of Australia in order to make British prisons less crowded. These prisoners were given the task of establishing a British colony in Australia. The colony was known as New South Wales. In 1803, the colony spread to the southern island of Tasmania, which the British called Van Diemen's Land.

Sir William Denison was the governor of New South Wales from 1855 until 1861. A *lurcher* is a type of hound.

STEP TWO: **Analyze**

Student instructions for Step Two:

Using the text on the following page, try to identify the three different *topoi* that make up this composition. Consult the *topoi* section of your Composition Notebook as you work.

The first two paragraphs serve as an introduction and are already labelled for you.

The first *topos* is made up of the five paragraphs in bold print. Write the name of the *topos* in blank 1.

The second *topos* is found in the italicized paragraph. Write its name in blank 2. (Ignore blank 3 for right now.)

The third *topos* is found in the paragraph written in regular type. Write its name in blank 4.

When you are finished, show your work to your instructor.

HOW TO HELP THE STUDENT WITH STEP TWO

See below for the completed assignment. The student's final text should be marked up in the same way.

Now, go through the steps on pages 63-65 with the student.

"Kangaroo-Hunting in the New Australian Colonies"

Introduction

I have not yet, in this veritable record, described any of our kangaroo-hunts, and what is Van Diemen's Land without a kangaroo-hunt?

Sometimes, when Sir William Denison comes to the country for "high hunting," with his aides-de-camp and secretaries, I am told he hunts with a pack of beagles, and a great field of horsemen; but this is not our style, nor indeed the usual style. The proper dog for this sport is a kind of powerful greyhound bred for the purpose; and two of them are enough.

1. Chronological narrative of a past event

One day, <u>not long ago</u> John Knox and I rode out with Mr. Reid and his two dogs, one a small thorough-bred greyhound, the other a large strong kangaroo dog, very like what is called in England a lurcher, but of finer make and taller stature.

2. Description of a place

We take the direction of the Blue Hill, westward, and soon find ourselves <u>in</u> a hilly, rocky, desolate and thickly-wooded region, littered by dead, prostrate trees, and cut up <u>by</u> hundreds of precipitous gullies running <u>in</u> all directions. The little hills are all so like one a place *another, that to fix a landmark is impossible. Save by the position of the sun, you cannot tell <u>towards</u> what point of the compass you are going. The trees are so dense <u>on</u> the <u>sides</u> of all the hills, and the ground is so rough <u>with</u> broken and burned stumps, rocks, and holes, that fast riding is out of the question.*

3. Moving through or around

The dogs keep close to our horses' feet, as we slowly penetrate this wilderness, until <u>at last</u>, from behind a huge decaying log, with a shrill chirrup of terror, bounds a kangaroo. In three huge leaps, springing on hind legs and nervous tail, he is out of our sight, and away behind the bushes and down the rocky gorge.

But <u>from the moment</u> his mouselike ears appear, as he rises to his first bound, the dogs are on his trail. The hounds also are out of sight in an instant; and we hold in our horses, and stand motionless, awaiting the result.

4. Sequence: History

In five or ten minutes they will have either worried him, or lost him altogether. In either case they will come straight back to where they left us; and, the moment they appear, we shall know by their expression whether they have done their business. If the kangaroo has got away, they will slink back with drooping ears and penitent eyes, and lie down to pant at our feet. If they have slain the enemy, they will come bounding through the trees, with their heads high and their jaws bloody, and before coming quite up to us, they will turn and trot off, and so bring us to the spot where he lies dead.

We listen, and <u>for a while</u> can hear the crash of the dead branches as the dogs rush on—and <u>then</u>, occasionally, a short angry bark—and then dead silence. <u>Presently</u>, shame-faced, they come panting along. They do not dare look us in the face, but approach in a zig-zag manner and lie down on their sides, heaving as if their ribs would burst. We do not reproach them; their own failure is punishment enough.

We proceed still farther amongst the hills, and presently another kangaroo breaks cover. <u>Again</u>, the dogs disappear in a twinkling. We hear a sharp, angry, almost constant barking. Then there is silence. And then, from the distance of a mile, rings the loud yell of one of the dogs. They are worrying the enemy. We dare not move in that direction, lest we should miss the dogs among the winding gullies, but wait impatiently. <u>Finally</u> they appear, with slow steps and trailing tails, but with triumph in their eyes.

1. Identifying the *topoi*

If the student has difficulty identifying the *topoi,* prompt him with the following questions:

1. Do the events of the kangaroo hunt occur in chronological order?
2. What is the writer describing?
3. Does the paragraph give you the steps that occur during the process of a kangaroo hunt?

Although the chronological narrative and description should be fairly easy, the student may have difficulty identifying the Sequence: History (line #4 on his text). You may need to explain that the writer has moved from the chronological account of a *particular* kangaroo hunt to describing how kangaroo hunts *in general* might unfold. That is the difference between a narrative and a sequence.

Remind the student of what he read in Week Two, Day Two:

When you were introduced to this topos, you learned that a sequence is similar to a chronological narrative. Both list a series of events in the order that they happen. But while a chronological narrative tells you about events that happened once, a sequence lists events that happen over and over and over again.

Richard the Lionheart was killed only once. The siege of Stirling Castle in 1304 only happened once. But a trebuchet was used over, and over, and over again.

In science, a sequence describes an often-repeated natural process. In history, a sequence describes an often-repeated process as well. A sequence in history might describe the functioning of an historical machine—a trebuchet, a wind-driven grain mill, a Roman aqueduct. Or it might describe a process that was often repeated in the past: the malting of barley into beer, the progress of a typical siege, the steps in the harvesting of an ancient crop.

This particular sequence describes what might happen in two different scenarios. Show the student the following flow chart:

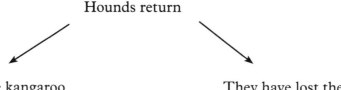

Hounds return

They have worried the kangaroo   They have lost the kangaroo
They return triumphant   They slink back
They lead the hunters back to the prey   They lie down

After describing the steps that happen over and over again in kangaroo hunts, the writer returns to the chronological narrative and tells what happened in one specific past hunt.

2. Point of view

After the student has filled out blanks 1, 2, and 4, ask him to identify the point of view of the description. His point of view chart for place descriptions gives four options:

1. From above (impersonal)
2. From inside
3. From one side or angle
4. Moving through or around

The chronological narrative clearly reveals that the writer is moving through the landscape (on horseback).

3. Space and distance words

Ask the student to find and underline at least two space and distance words or phrases used in the description.

4. Time and sequence words for chronological narratives

Ask the student to find and underline at least three time and sequence words in the chronological narrative.

5. Tense

Ask the student to write the words TENSE SWITCH next to the place in the chronological narrative where the writer changes from past to present tense. This happens in the line "*We take the direction of the Blue Hill, westward, and soon find*".

The student has learned that tense should be consistent throughout. Explain to the student that, in this case, the writer uses only one past verb ("We rode") to establish that the event took place in the past. He then switches to present tense to create a sense of immediacy—a feeling that the hunt is actually going on, right now. Because he stays in the present tense for the rest of the selection, he is using consistent tense.

STEP THREE: **Review the *topos* Sequence: History**

Student instructions for Step Three:

> The sequence you identified in the last assignment only had one element from your *topoi* chart: the step-by-step process of a kangaroo hunt. Because the sequence was part of a longer composition, the chronological narrative served as both introduction and historical background.
>
> Here is a sequence in history that contains both the step-by-step process and two other elements from your chart. Identify each element and label it in the margin of your paper.
>
> "Aborigines" are the native peoples of Australia, who lived on the continent before the British colonists arrived.

HOW TO HELP THE STUDENT WITH STEP THREE

The student's labels should read:

Introductory description

The stone axe of the aborigines resembles the stone axes found in Europe. This useful and indispensable implement is of various sizes. It is made chiefly of green stone, shaped like a wedge, and ground at one end to a sharp edge. At the other end it is grasped in the bend of a doubled piece of split sapling, bound with kangaroo sinews, to form a handle, which is cemented to it with a composition of gum and shell lime.

Step by step process

This cement is made by gathering fresh wattle gum, pulling it into small pieces, masticating it with the teeth, and then placing it between two sheets of green bark, which are put into a shallow hole in the ground, and covered up with hot ashes till the gum is dissolved. It is then taken out, and worked and pulled with the hands till it has become quite stringy, when it is mixed with lime made of burnt mussel shells, pounded in a hollow stone—which is always kept for the purpose—and kneaded into a tough paste.

Results/ consequences

This cement is indispensable to the natives in making their tools, spears, and water buckets.

—James Dawson, *Australian Aborigines* (Melbourne: Walker May & Co., 1881), p. 24.

Day Two: Review Notes and Write the Narration

 Focus: Writing a chronological narration from notes

Over the next two days, the student will write a composition of at least 250 but not more than 500 words. This composition will contain a chronological narrative and a descriptive sequence in history.

Today, the student will write a draft of the chronological narrative. Tomorrow, he will write the descriptive sequence, combine the two parts of the composition into one whole essay, and proofread his work.

The student will be reviewing and re-using the methods taught in Week 29 of Level One. Later this year, he will learn to streamline this method and take several short-cuts.

STEP ONE: Read back through notes (Student Responsibility)

Although the student should complete this work independently, you may need to check and make sure that he reads last week's notes carefully rather than just skimming through (or skipping the step altogether).

Student instructions for Step One:

> Open the document containing last week's notes on the Gold Rush. (Or pull out your notecards.) Read carefully through your notes.

STEP TWO: Arrange your notes in chronological order

Student instructions for Step Two:

> First, separate out your notes about how gold panning works. You'll use these tomorrow when you write your sequence.
>
> Now, arrange your notes in chronological order.
>
> You learned how to do this in Week 29 of last year, when you wrote a chronological narrative about Julius Caesar. Here's a very quick review of what you were told to do:
>
> > **You took notes about Caesar's actions from two books,** The Delphian Course **and Caesar's Commentaries on the Gallic War.** *In this step, you'll put the notes from both books together into one chronological list, cutting out unnecessary repetition.*
> >
> > **From Caesar's Commentaries,** *you might have written down the following three events:*
> >
> > > *Caesar found out about the senate's decree "at Ravenna, on the 10th of January, 49 BC." (xiii)*
> > >
> > > *Caesar "crossed the Rubicon . . . and advanced into Italy." (xiii)*
> > >
> > > *As he marched through Italy, "town after town threw open its gates" to him. (xiii)*

***From* The Delphian Course,** *you might have written down:*

    Caesar "completed his Gallic campaign" in 49 BC. (480)

    The senate was afraid of Caesar and "asked him to disband his soldiers." (480)

    Caesar refused and "crossed the Rubicon, the stream north of Rome." (480)

Put those two lists together so that all of the events are in order, and then cross out notes that repeat the same information:

    Caesar "completed his Gallic campaign" in 49 BC. (480)

    The senate was afraid of Caesar and "asked him to disband his soldiers." (480)

    Caesar found out about the senate's decree "at Ravenna, on the 10th of January, 49 BC." (xiii)

    Caesar refused and "crossed the Rubicon, the stream north of Rome." (480)

    ~~*Caesar "crossed the Rubicon . . . and advanced into Italy." (xiii)*~~

    As he marched through Italy, "town after town threw open its gates" to him. (xiii)

If you're using a word processor, create a new document and cut and paste information from both lists of events into it. If you're using note cards, simply arrange the cards in order and set aside the ones that have repeated information.

Repeat these same steps for your information about the Gold Rush.

If you need help, show your work to your instructor. If not, go on to the next step.

HOW TO HELP THE STUDENT WITH STEP TWO

It isn't necessary for the student to show you his work, but if he needs assistance, go carefully through the instructions with him.

His answers might resemble the following (because there are page numbers only after the White notes, it should be simple to remember which source is which):

James Wilson Marshall worked at a sawmill owned by John Sutter.

James Marshall discovered gold right at the end of the Mexican War. (55)

On Jan. 24, 1848, he saw "a yellow speck" and then "another yellow flake."

He said to the other workmen, "Boys, I think I've found a gold mine."

The next day, he found "a full three ounces" of gold.

He took the gold to John Sutter's fort.

The two men tested it and found that "It was 23-carat gold."

Sutter "tried to keep the discovery secret."

Many young men needed to find "a way out of their financial difficulties." (55)

At first, interest in the discoveries was "rather tepid." (56)

Sam Brennan "rode down from Sutter's Fort" with "gold-dust and nuggets," shouting "Gold! Gold! Gold from the American River." (57)

Brennan's announcement created a stampede. (57)

~~The news spread and Californians "stampeded toward Sutter's mill."~~

People came from all over the state. Soldiers, sailors, and "able-bodied" men came. (58)
"By spring of the next year thousands of . . . forty-niners were headed west."
This was the beginning of the Gold Rush.
At first, gold could be picked up from the ground or "from the veins in the rocks." (60–61)
There was so much gold that "it was much easier to dig it than to steal it." (61)
A Baltimore paper "published a short item" about the discovery. (62).
An official letter to the War Department said that there was much more gold. (62)
The song *Oh, Susannah* was sung "in every quarter of the world." (63)
"Every man with a drop of red blood in his veins wanted to go to California." (63)
Clubs were formed "for the purposes of getting at least one . . . of their members" to
    California. (55)
The Gold Rush made California into first a territory and "then a state."
James Marshall "died, penniless and all alone in a shack not far from Sutter's mill."

There is little overlap between the two sources.

STEP THREE: Divide notes into main points

Student instructions for Step Three:

> Here's one more review from Week 29 of Level One:
>
> *Before you can write your chronological narrative about Caesar, you need to make yourself an outline. You're going to do this by dividing your list of events up into groups and giving each group a phrase or sentence that explains what it's about.*
>
> *Imagine that these are the first eight notes that you have on your list.*
>
> > Caesar "completed his Gallic campaign" in 49 BC. (480)
> > The senate was afraid of Caesar and "asked him to disband his soldiers." (480)
> > The senate told Caesar "to resign the governorship of both Gauls and disband his army." (xiii)
> > Caesar found out about the senate's decree "at Ravenna, on the 10th of January, 49 BC." (xiii)
> > Caesar refused and "crossed the Rubicon, the stream north of Rome." (480)
> > As he marched through Italy, "town after town threw open its gates" to him. (xiii)
> > Caesar reached the capital "sixty days after the edict of the senate." (xiii)
> > Caesar entered Rome and "brought order instead of turmoil to the city." (480)
>
> *The first four events are all leading up to the senate's decree, so you can group them all together and describe them like this:*
>
> > I. The senate's decree to Caesar
> > > Caesar "completed his Gallic campaign" in 49 BC. (480)
> > > The senate was afraid of Caesar and "asked him to disband his soldiers." (480)
> > > The senate told Caesar "to resign the governorship of both Gauls and disband his army." (xiii)

*Caesar found out about the senate's decree "at Ravenna, on the
10th of January, 49 BC." (xiii)*

**Give each group a title or description. If you're using a word processor,
give the titles Roman numerals and type them into your document, using
the same format as above:**

II. *Title for second group of notes*

event

event

event

**and so on. If you're using note cards, write each title on a separate note
card and place it in front of the group of cards that it describes.**

When you've finished this step, you'll have a two-level outline that you can use to write
your narrative.

Aim for four or five main groups of events.

If you need help, show your work to your instructor. If you feel comfortable with your
outline, go on to the next step.

HOW TO HELP THE STUDENT WITH STEP THREE

As with Step Two, it isn't necessary for the student to show you his work, but if he needs assistance, go carefully through the instructions with him.

His answers might resemble the following:

I. James Wilson Marshall's discovery

James Wilson Marshall worked at a sawmill owned by John Sutter.

James Marshall discovered gold right at the end of the Mexican War. (55)

On Jan. 24, 1848, he saw "a yellow speck" and then "another yellow
flake."

He said to the other workmen, "Boys, I think I've found a gold mine."

The next day, he found "a full three ounces" of gold.

He took the gold to John Sutter's fort.

The two men tested it and found that "It was 23-carat gold."

II. The beginning of the Gold Rush

Sutter "tried to keep the discovery secret."

Many young men needed to find "a way out of their financial
difficulties." (55)

At first, interest in the discoveries was "rather tepid." (56)

Sam Brennan "rode down from Sutter's Fort" with "gold-dust and nuggets,"
shouting "Gold! Gold! Gold from the American River." (57)

Brennan's announcement created a stampede. (57)

III. The arrival of the Forty-Niners

People came from all over the state. Soldiers, sailors, and "able-bodied"
men came. (58)

"By spring of the next year thousands of . . . forty-niners were headed west."
This was the beginning of the Gold Rush.

IV. The gold
   At first, gold could be picked up from the ground or "from the veins in the
      rocks." (60–61)
   There was so much gold that "it was much easier to dig it than to steal it." (61)

V. The results of the Gold Rush
   A Baltimore paper "published a short item" about the discovery. (62).
   An official letter to the War Department said that there was much more gold. (62)
   The song "Oh, Susannah" was sung "in every quarter of the world." (63)
   "Every man with a drop of red blood in his veins wanted to go to California." (63)
   Clubs were formed "for the purposes of getting at least one . . . of their members" to
      California. (55)
   The Gold Rush made California into first a territory and "then a state."
   James Marshall "died, penniless and all alone in a shack not far from
      Sutter's mill."

If the student struggles, you may suggest the main points to him, and then ask him to group events beneath them. Other possible groupings might include:

   I. Marshall finds gold
   II. The news spreads
   III. The gold
   IV. The Gold Rush itself
   V. Marshall's fate

OR

   I. The discovery
   II. The news spreads
   III. The miners arrive
   IV. The results

STEP FOUR: **Write the narration**

Student instructions for Step Four:

   Take a minute to review the Chronological Narrative of a Past Event chart in the Reference section of your notebook.
   Using the outline you have created, write one paragraph about each group of events. Your narrative should be at least 200 words but not longer than 400. If you use an idea that is not common knowledge, be sure to use a footnote even if you put the idea into your own words.

The *Life* article has no listed author and is also a magazine article. Here is how you should format it for a footnote:

"The Gold Country" (*Life,* Feb. 2, 1948), p. 44.

The second time, just call it "The Gold Country."

On your Works Cited page, it should be alphabetized as if "Gold" were the author's name, like this:

"The Gold Country." In *Life,* Feb. 2, 1948, p. 44.

In your composition, include at least one line of dialogue (something one of the characters actually said). If you didn't include dialogue in your notes, go back to the sources and choose a line. (Often, when you write, you will find yourself returning to the sources to find something that you didn't know you needed.)

When you are finished, show your composition to your instructor.

HOW TO HELP THE STUDENT WITH STEP FOUR

You will not be grading the student's chronological narrative; he has not yet proofread it. However, you do need to check that the composition:

1. Is in chronological order
2. Has at least 200 words
3. Contains at least one line of dialogue
4. Has footnotes to the White and *Life* articles.

Apart from this, do not evaluate the narrative until the end of Day Three.

Day Three: Write the Sequence and Complete the Composition

 Focus: Writing a sequence describing a historical process

The student should work independently today until the final draft is submitted for your review. If necessary, you may use the sample composition and rubric at the end of the lesson to prompt the student.

STEP ONE: **Read back through notes (Student Responsibility)**

As with the last day's work, you may need to check that the student has thoroughly reviewed the material.

Student instructions for Step One:

Go back through the notes you took about panning for gold. Look carefully at the photographs in last week's lesson.

STEP TWO: **Write the sequence (Student Responsibility)**

Student instructions for Step Two:

> Write a sequence that includes
>
> > 1) a description of the pan used for panning gold and
> > 2) a step-by-step description of the gold panning process
>
> This sequence should be at least 50 words long, but no longer than 100 words. (It's a pretty simple process, so 100 words would have to be a flowery and elaborate sequence!)

If the student asks you for help, here is a sample of what the descriptive sequence might sound like:

> A gold pan was a wide, flat pan, usually made out of metal. The pan was filled halfway up with sand and clay, and then the rest of the way with water. When the water was swirled around and around, the heavier gold sank to the bottom of the pan. The sand and silt then poured out of the pan along with the water. The miner collected the gold from the bottom of the pan and put it in a sack.

Notice that I have not footnoted this passage. The steps in panning for gold are definitely common knowledge—anyone with a pan can figure it out, and numerous authors describe it. I was very, *very* careful not to use any exact phrases from the sources in my description. Here's how the paragraph might look if I used the language of either Rohrbough or Behme:

> A gold pan was a wide, flat pan, usually made out of metal. The pan was filled halfway up with sand and clay, and then the rest of the way with water. When the water was swirled around and around, **churning up the contents,** the heavier gold sank to the bottom of the pan.[1] The sand and silt then poured out of the pan along with the water. The miner **easily retrieved** the gold from the bottom of the pan and **stored** it in a **small** sack.[2]

---

[1] Bob Behme, "Pan for gold this summer—here's how and why" (*Popular Mechanics,* July 1974, Vol. 142, No. 1), p. 84.

[2] Malcolm J. Rohrbough, *Days of Gold: The California Gold Rush and the American Nation* (University of California Press, 1997), p. 12.

STEP THREE: **Combine the narration and sequence into a full composition (Student Responsibility)**

Student instructions for Step Three:

> Now, decide where to insert the sequence into your chronological narrative. Look for a place where you mention gold miners, discuss their daily routines, or talk about gold found in a stream.

You may need to write a transitional sentence to go at the beginning of your sequence; something like "Panning for gold was difficult work" or "Many gold miners used gold pans to search for gold." (If you can't come up with your own sentence, you can use one of mine.)

Place a title at the top of your first page. You'll work on writing good titles a little later this year, when we talk more about selecting topics. This composition can just be titled "The Gold Rush."

Insert a Works Cited page at the end of your document.

STEP FOUR: **Proofread**

Student instructions for Step Four:

Repeat the basic steps of proofreading from Week 2 (Day 3):

1) Read your composition out loud. Listen for awkward or unclear sections. Rewrite them so that they flow more naturally.
2) Check spelling by looking, individually, at each word that might be a problem.
3) Check your commas.

Add the following step:

4) Check the punctuation and capitalization on your footnotes, your Works Cited page, and any direct quotes (including your required line of dialogue).

When you are confident that your composition is finished, show it to your instructor.

HOW TO HELP THE STUDENT WITH STEP FOUR

Before checking the student's work, make sure that all three of the proofreading steps in the lesson have been completed.

Week 4 Rubric
Chronological Narrative And Sequence: History

Organization:

1 The entire composition should be at least 250 words in length.
2 The events of the Gold Rush should be in chronological order.
3 There should be at least five paragraphs.
    a. At least four paragraphs should describe the major events of the Gold Rush.
    b. One paragraph should describe the process of panning for gold.
        i. One sentence should describe the pan itself.
        ii. The other sentences should describe, step by step, the panning process.
4 There should be at least one line of dialogue.

Mechanics:

1 Each sentence should make sense on its own when read aloud.
2 There should be no sentence fragments or run-on sentences.
3 All words should be spelled correctly.
4 The first line of each paragraph should be properly indented.
5 Verb tense should be consistent throughout (past tense for the historical background and present tense for the descriptive paragraphs is acceptable).
6 Specific information should be properly footnoted.
7 A Works Cited page should be attached.

An acceptable sample composition might resemble the following. Note that it is fine for the paragraphs to be short.

THE GOLD RUSH

On January 24, 1848, a workman named James Wilson Marshall discovered gold at a sawmill owned by John Sutter. He told the other workmen, "Boys, I think I've found a gold mine."[1] Then, he and John Sutter tested it. It was 23-carat gold.

John Sutter wanted to keep the gold secret, but a man named Sam Brennan rode through town with gold dust, shouting, "Gold! Gold! Gold from the American River."[2] Many young men were in financial trouble at the time, and they came to dig for gold.

They were known as Forty-Niners. They came from all over California. That was the beginning of the Gold Rush.

At first, there was so much gold that it was just as easy to dig it as to steal it. It could be picked up from the ground and dug out of rocks with pocket-knives. [3]

Many miners used gold pans to search for gold. A gold pan was a wide, flat pan, usually made out of metal. The pan was filled halfway up with sand and clay, and then the rest of the way with water. When the water was swirled around and around, the heavier gold sank to the bottom of the pan. The sand and silt then poured out of the pan along with the water. The miner collected the gold from the bottom of the pan and put it in a sack. [4]

After an official letter to the War Department announced that there was gold in California, many more people came from all over the country. [5] The Gold Rush made California into a territory, and then, into a state. But James Marshall, who had made the first discovery, died "penniless and all alone" in a ruined house near Sutter's Mill. [6]

----

[1] "The Gold Country" (*Life*, Feb. 2, 1948), p. 44.

[2] Stewart Edward White, *The Forty-Niners: A Chronicle of the California Trail and El Dorado* (Yale University Press, 1920), p. 57.

[3] White, pp. 60–61.

[4] Malcolm J. Rohrbough, *Days of Gold: The California Gold Rush and the American Nation* (University of California Press, 1997), p. 12

[5] White, p. 62.

[6] "The Gold Country," p 44.

WORKS CITED

"The Gold Country." In *Life*, Feb. 2, 1948, p. 44.

Rohrbough, Malcolm J. *Days of Gold: The California Gold Rush and the American Nation.* Berkeley, Calif.: University of California Press, 1997.

White, Steward Edward. *The Forty-Niners: A Chronicle of the California Trail and El Dorado.* New Haven, Conn.: Yale University Press, 1920.

If the student quotes from the Bob Behme article, here is how it should appear in a footnote:

Bob Behme, "Pan for gold this summer—here's how and where" (*Popular Mechanics*, July 1974, Vol. 142, No. 1), p. 84.

Here's how it should appear in the Works Cited:

Behme, Bob. "Pan for gold this summer—here's how and where." In *Popular Mechanics*, July 1974 (Vol. 142, No. 1), pp. 82–85.

Show the student the examples and allow him to copy; proper citation of articles will be covered in detail in a later lesson.

Day Four: Copia

 Focus: Added and intensified adjectives

STEP ONE: Understand the purpose of added and intensified adjectives (Student Responsibility)

Student instructions for Step One:

Although the student should complete this step independently, you may need to check to see that he has underlined the correct adjectives (marked below).

So far, you've reviewed five kinds of sentence transformation learned in Level One of this course:

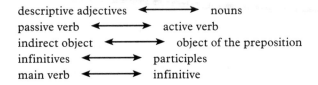

descriptive adjectives ⟷ nouns
passive verb ⟷ active verb
indirect object ⟶ object of the preposition
infinitives ⟷ participles
main verb ⟷ infinitive

Today, you'll learn a new skill: transforming a sentence by adding and intensifying adjectives. Read the following two sentences.

My heart stood still, stopped dead short by a terrible cry, by the cry of great triumph and of severe pain.

My heart stood still, stopped dead short by an exulting and terrible cry, by the cry of inconceivable triumph and of unspeakable pain.

The second sentence is from the novel *Heart of Darkness*, by Joseph Conrad. Compare the first version of the sentence (which just says that the narrator heard a cry of triumph and pain) with Conrad's version of the sentence. In Conrad's sentence, underline each adjective.

by a   cry, by the cry of   great triumph and of   severe pain.
by an <u>exulting</u> and <u>terrible</u> cry, by the cry of <u>inconceivable</u> triumph and of <u>unspeakable</u> pain.

Joseph Conrad uses two methods to make his sentence gripping and colorful.

First, he *intensifies* his adjectives. "Great" and "severe" are both useful adjectives, but Conrad chose to think: What is the most intense kind of greatness there is? A greatness that is *so* great that it is . . . *inconceivable*. What is the most intense pain possible? A pain so severe that it is . . . *unspeakable*.

Second, he *adds* adjectives. The cry isn't just terrible. It is both terrible *and* exulting.

Conrad often uses intense and added adjectives. Here is another sentence from *Heart of Darkness*:

I had blundered into a place of <u>cruel</u> and <u>absurd</u> mysteries.

Underline the adjectives that Conrad uses to describe the mysteries.

Once again, notice that he uses not just one adjective, but two. And both are *intense* adjectives. *Cruel* is a stronger description than *unkind* or *bad*. *Absurd* is a stronger word than *silly*.

How do you know if one adjective is more intense than another? That's a judgment call, so often there's not a clear right or wrong answer. Intense adjectives are more specific and less common than milder adjectives.

You shouldn't add adjectives that are exact synonyms. If Conrad had written "cruel and harsh mysteries" or "horrible and terrible cry," his sentences would be less powerful (and less interesting). But "exulting" and "absurd" add different shades of meaning.

STEP TWO: **Practice intensifying adjectives**

Student instructions for Step Two:

Using your thesaurus, write two intensified adjectives for each of the following words.

Possible answers might include:

frightening	dreadful, mind-blowing, shocking, sinister, malevolent
large	colossal, immeasurable, massive, stupendous, vast
enjoyable	thrilling, compelling, scrumptious, enticing, enchanting
embarrassed	mortified, shamed, stunned, humiliated, crushed

As long as the student chooses words which are more specific or more evocative than the original, accept his answers.

STEP THREE: **Add to the Sentence Variety chart (Student Responsibility)**

Student instructions for Step Three:

Add the following principle and illustration to the Sentence Variety chart.

adjective $\longrightarrow$ intensified adjective   The sun was bright.

The sun was incandescent.

adjective ———⟶ added adjective

He leaped into the cold water.
He leaped into the cold and murky water OR
He leaped into the cold, murky water.

STEP FOUR: **Practice sentence variety**

Student instructions for Step Four:

> Using your own paper or a word processing document, rewrite the following sentences by intensifying each adjective and adding a second adjective. Each sentence is adapted from Charles Dickens' classic novel *Oliver Twist*.
>
> Use your thesaurus to find intense adjectives. You can also use your thesaurus to find second adjectives, but try to introduce adjectives that have different shades of meaning. For example, given the sentence:
>
> > The boy was poor.
>
> you would look up "poor" in your thesaurus. "Penniless" is a more intense synonym for poor:
>
> > The boy was penniless.
>
> But you don't want to choose another synonym of "poor" for your second adjective. Instead, pick one of the synonyms and look up the entry for *that* word. Another synonym for "poor" is "destitute." Under the entry for "destitute," you would find the synonym *exhausted*. So your sentence could now read
>
> > The boy was penniless and exhausted.
>
> The two adjectives go together, but don't mean exactly the same thing.
>
> When you are finished, show your work to your instructor, who has the original versions of the sentences for you to compare to your own.
>
> > The girl fixed him with a sharp look.
> > At that time of day, the streets were quiet.
> > He was a nice gentleman.
> > The alley was dirty.
> > Oliver was in high spirits.

HOW TO HELP THE STUDENT WITH STEP FOUR

The original Dickens adjectives are:

> The girl fixed him with a keen and searching look.
> At that time of day, the streets were silent and deserted.
> He was a pleasant and respectable gentleman.
> The alley was narrow and muddy.
> Oliver was in elated and honored spirits.

Accept any reasonable answers.

WEEK 5: EXPLANATION BY COMPARISON, PART I

Day One: Two-Level Outline

 Focus: Constructing a two-level outline of a comparison in nature

NOTE TO INSTRUCTOR: Today's assignment introduces one of the most useful *topoi*: the comparison. It also introduces a more sophisticated (and useful) way to think about outlines, encouraging the student to focus on the overall structure of an essay instead of individual paragraphs. Provide as much handholding as necessary!

STEP ONE: **Read (Student Responsibility)**

Student instructions for Step One:

> Read the following brief essay about tigers and cats (written by by novelist Boris Fishman).

STEP TWO: **Begin the two-level outline**

Student instructions for Step Two:

> Your assignment is to make a two-level outline of this passage, but today, you'll approach the outline a little differently.
>
> Up until now, you've been told to outline by finding the main point of each paragraph and then looking for subpoints within the paragraph. But in this passage, the paragraphs *are* the subpoints.
>
> Look at the first four paragraphs and finish the following statement: "Each paragraph tells you how cats and tigers are _____."
>
> Your answer to this question should help you find the first main point of the passage—the point that the first four paragraphs *all* relate to. Each of the first four paragraphs is a *subpoint*, giving more information about the main point. So your outline should look like this:
>
> I. (Main point that all four paragraphs relate to)
>   A. (Main point of Paragraph 1)

B. (Main point of Paragraph 2)
C. (Main point of Paragraph 3)
D. (Main point of Paragraph 4)

On your own paper, try to complete this outline.
Check your work with your instructor when you are
finished.

HOW TO HELP THE STUDENT WITH STEP TWO

The student's answer to the question should have been,
"Each paragraph tells you how cats and tigers are the same." So the outline should resemble the
following:

I.   How cats and tigers are the same OR Similarities between cats and tigers
     A. Same scientific family OR Both belong to Felidae
     B. Fierce hunters OR Both are fierce hunters

     [The details—strong bodies, sharp claws and teeth, similar methods of killing—would
     belong in a three-level outline. They would only go in a two-level outline if the student
     were giving each paragraph a Roman numeral. In this assignment, the student is focus-
     ing on the larger overall structure of the passage.]

     C. Sharp senses OR Both have sharp senses
     D. Kept as pets OR Both are kept as pets

It is fine for the student to mix sentences and phrases; she should use whichever is clearer and
more natural.

   If necessary, use the following questions to prompt the student:
      A. "What name do tigers and cats share?"
      B. "Both do the same thing fiercely. What is it?"
      C. "Both have sharp what?"
      D. "Both are kept as . . . ?"
(Most students should be able to do this assignment without prompting.)

STEP THREE: **Finish the two-level outline**

Student instructions for Step Three:

Now that you've gotten the idea, finish the outline of the passage.
Here's a hint for you: It should follow this pattern.

   II.
      A. (Main point of Paragraph 5)
      B. (Main point of Paragraph 6)
   III.
      A. (Main point of Paragraphs 7 AND 8 combined)

B. (Main point of Paragraph 9)

You might find II.A. (the main point of Paragraph 5) and III. (the overall main point that Paragraphs 7–9 all relate to) particularly challenging. Give it a good try first, but then don't be reluctant to ask your instructor for help.

You've done something difficult and important today—you've outlined a piece of writing as a *whole*, rather than just approaching it paragraph by paragraph. That's a huge step. You probably deserve some chocolate. (Hershey's, if you like barnyard flavors—Godiva, if you don't!)

HOW TO HELP THE STUDENT WITH STEP THREE

The student's answer should resemble the following:

II. How cats and tigers are different OR Differences between cats and tigers
   A. Obvious differences OR Size, sound, and water
   B. Number in existence OR More serious difference
III. How they are perceived OR What people think about cats and tigers
   A. In mythology OR Cats and tigers in mythology
   B. Popularity OR Which is more popular

Because the student is being asked for the first time to outline the structure of an entire passage, she may find this challenging. Give as much help as necessary.

If the student needs help, use the following questions and explanations.

II. How cats and tigers are different OR Differences between cats and tigers
Since the first section described similarities, it should be obvious that this section describes differences. If the student draws a blank, you can always say, "Is the writer still talking about similarities? What, then?"

A. Obvious differences OR Size, sound, and water
This answer may be difficult, since the writer lumps three differences together into one paragraph. The best answer is "Obvious differences," because this is a single topic that all three described differences relate to—and the writer provides that phrase in the first sentence. You can prompt the student by asking, "What do all of these differences have in common?" (They are obvious.)

If the student independently comes up with an answer resembling "Size, sound, and water," accept it. However, point out that "Obvious differences" is a simpler and more straightforward way to phrase it.

B. Number in existence OR More serious difference
"More serious difference" is parallel to "Obvious difference." If the student has difficulty coming up with this answer, say, "Is this also an obvious difference, or does the writer use another adjective to describe it?" An answer summing up the *essence* of the difference (it has to do with numbers, population, or scarcity) is also acceptable.

III. How they are perceived OR What people think about cats and tigers

To reach this main point, the student needs to answer the question, "What do human mythology and popularity have in common?" That's a tough question (the answer is, "They both have to do with what people think and perceive"), so try using the following questions to move the student in the right direction:

"Who comes up with mythologies? I don't mean a particular person—where do mythologies come from?" *People invent them, groups of people.*

"Popularity has to do with 'how many people like something.' What's the word that 'People invent them' and 'how many people like something' have in common?" *People.*

"What do people think about cats and tigers?" *[Allow the student to answer using the information in the passage.]*

"All of these answers have to do with how people perceive, or think about, cats and tigers. Use that as your main point."

A. In mythology OR Cats and tigers in mythology

Both paragraphs have to do with how cats and tigers are portrayed in myths—what they represent.

B. Popularity OR Which is more popular

This paragraph deals only with popular perceptions.

Day Two: Analyzing the *Topos*: Explanation by Comparison in Science

Focus: Learning the form of comparison/contrast

STEP ONE: Examine model passage

Student instructions for Step One:

> Read the following passage:
>
> ★
>
> Like the passage you read in the last day's work, this excerpt discusses the similarities and differences between two natural phenomena (in both cases, living things).
>
> The comparison begins in the first paragraph: People fear both reptiles and amphibians. This is a similarity—maybe not between the animals themselves, but in the reactions people have to them. On the first line, write "Similarity: People fear them."
>
> The first sentence of the second paragraph contains a second similarity. On line 2, write, "Similarity: They are _____" and fill in the blank.

The authors then use the last sentence of the second paragraph to transition from similarities to differences. On line 3, write "Transition." (You'll learn much more about transitions later in this course.)

The third paragraph begins to highlight the differences between reptiles and amphibians by describing the skin, feet, and young of reptiles (scales, claws, and miniature versions). On the fourth line, write "Differences: Scales, claws, miniature young."

The final paragraph finishes the contrast by describing the skin, feet, and young of amphibians (moist skin, no claws, larvae). On line 5, write "Differences: Moist skin, no claws, larvae."

HOW TO HELP THE STUDENT WITH STEP ONE

Although this step is really the student's responsibility, you may need to glance at the student's workbook and make sure that the lines are filled in as follows:

1. **Similarity: People fear them.**
2. **Similarity: They are cold-blooded.**
3. **Transition**
4. **Differences: Scales, claws, young**
5. **Differences: Moist skin, no claws, larvae**

STEP TWO: Write down the pattern of the *topos* (Student Responsibility)

Student instructions for Step Two:

Like the passage that you outlined in the last lesson, this passage explains what two living creatures are by comparing them to each other.

This form of writing is called *explanation by comparison and contrast*. It is one of the most useful *topoi* you will learn. Comparison and contrast gives the reader a clear, straightforward picture of what two things are like by explaining how they are the same and how they are different.

When you set out to write an explanation, you'll have to decide how to organize your comparisons (similarities) and contrasts (differences). In the comparison of cats and tigers, Boris Fishman used the *point-by-point* method. He listed one quality after another and, for each, compared cats and tigers.

Scientific family?	Cats, yes.	Tigers, yes.
Fierce hunters?	Cats, yes.	Tigers, yes.
Sharp senses?	Cats, yes.	Tigers, yes.
Kept as pets?	Cats, yes.	Tigers, yes.
Size?	Cats, small.	Tigers, bigger.
Sound?	Cats, purr.	Tigers, roar.
Water?	Cats, hate.	Tigers, love.
Numbers?	Cats, millions.	Tigers, 2,000

The authors of *Peterson First Guide* started out by using the same method for comparisons.

People fear them?	Amphibians, yes.	Reptiles, yes.
Coldblooded?	Amphibians, yes.	Reptiles, yes.

But when they began to give contrasts, they changed to the *subject by subject method*. They described three things about reptiles, and then the same three things, in the same order, about amphibians.

Reptiles	Skin
	Feet
	Young
Amphibians	Skin
	Feet
	Young

The point-by-point method is very clear and easy to write, but it can get monotonous (like a very long tennis match, where the ball goes back . . . and forth . . . and back . . . and forth . . . and back . . .). The subject-by-subject method gives your writing a better forward flow, but requires the reader to keep all of the points of the first subject in mind while reading the second—so you wouldn't want to list more than three or four points of comparison for one subject before going on to the next.

Alternating methods, as in *Peterson First Guide,* can give your composition variety and hold the reader's interest.

Copy the following onto a blank sheet of paper in the Reference section of your Composition Notebook.

Explanation by Comparison/Contrast

Procedure	Remember
1. Decide which aspects of the subjects are the same, and which are different.	1. Use both methods to give variety.
2. Choose a method for comparing and contrasting.	
a. Point-by-point	
b. Subject-by-subject	

STEP THREE: **Read**

Student instructions for Step Three:

You'll finish today's assignment by taking notes on the following information. In the next day's work, you'll use it to write a comparison of your own.

This is less complicated than the Gold Rush assignment. Tomorrow's comparison can be brief, and because all of the information in the sources below comes under the heading of common knowledge (widely accepted scientific facts, well-known theories, and things learned through the senses), you don't have to worry about documentation.

Instead, divide a sheet of paper into two columns. Label one "platypus" and the other "beaver." In each column, jot down facts about these two animals, using the source material below. Aim for 12–15 notes per animal.

The first set of notes is done for you, just to give you a sense of what kinds of facts you're looking for. Read the excerpt from *The International Wildlife Encyclopedia* carefully before looking at the notes. Then, take your own notes using the pattern I've provided, or else copy my notes into your column.

★

SAMPLE NOTES
PLATYPUS

Mammal
Monotremes—egg-laying mammals
Lays two soft-shelled white eggs
Eggs stick together
Female lays eggs in a tunnel
Young is naked and blind
Eyes open in 11 weeks
Weaned at nearly 4 months

Notice that you don't need to note down the authors, books, and page numbers as long as you are jotting down scientific facts.

Now, continue to take notes on the following sources on your own.

HOW TO HELP THE STUDENT WITH STEP THREE

If the student works slowly, you may allow her to complete this assignment over two days; she can also finish taking notes as part of the next day's lesson, before writing. The student should have no fewer than 12–15 notes per animal. Her answers should resemble some of the following:

Platypus	Beaver
Mammal	Eats twigs and bark
Monotremes—egg-laying mammals	Eats skunk cabbage, grasses, berries
Lays two soft-shelled white eggs	Needs 1 1/2 to 2 pounds per day
Eggs stick together	Digs bank burrows
Female lays eggs in a tunnel	Uses claws to dig a tunnel
Young is naked and blind	Excavates chamber in bank
Eyes open in 11 weeks	Has a cloaca
Weaned at nearly 4 months	Young stay with parents 2 years
Eats worms and crayfish	Monogamous
Has a bill like a duck	Yearlings stay with parents
Soft and rubbery beak	Kits are fully furred
Uses claws to dig burrows	Eyes open, incisors present
Amphibious	12 inches long, 1 pound
Has a cloaca	Soft fluffy fur, no guard hair
Produces milk/mammary glands	Cannot get out of lodge
Monotremes (one opening in body)	4-9 in a litter
Streamlined	Largest North American rodent
Smaller than beavers	Large, scaly, paddle-like tail
Webbed front limbs	Reddish brown to blackish brown
Uses front limbs to swim	Short rounded ears
Dense waterproof fur	Hind legs longer than front legs
Four-chambered heart	Massive skull and teeth
Single bone in lower jaw	
Three bones in middle ear	
Extra bones in shoulders	
Beaver-like tail	

Day Three: Practicing the *Topos*

 Focus: Writing an explanation by comparison/
contrast

STEP ONE: **Organize platypus notes**

Take the notes from the last day's work and organize them into groups, by topic. Give each group a title.

Start with the platypus notes. For example, if I were organizing the notes I took on the very first source, I would divide them up like this:

CLASSIFICATION

Mammal

Monotremes—egg-laying mammals

BABIES

Lays two soft-shelled white eggs

Eggs stick together

Female lays eggs in a tunnel

Young is naked and blind

Eyes open in 11 weeks

Weaned at nearly 4 months

If necessary, you may borrow my two topics to get you started.

Cut and paste (or rearrange) your notes so that all the notes that belong to a single topic are grouped together. You should be able to find at least four different topics.

When you are finished, show your work to your instructor.

HOW TO HELP THE STUDENT WITH STEP ONE

The student's answers might resemble the following:

CLASSIFICATION

Mammal

Monotremes—egg-laying mammals

Amphibious

Has a cloaca

Monotremes (one opening in body)

Four-chambered heart

Single bone in lower jaw

Three bones in middle ear

Extra bones in shoulders

BABIES

Lays eggs

    Produces milk/mammary glands
    Lays two soft-shelled white eggs
    Eggs stick together
    Female lays eggs in a tunnel
    Young is naked and blind
    Eyes open in 11 weeks
    Weaned at nearly 4 months
FOOD
    Eats worms and crayfish
APPEARANCE
    Has a bill like a duck
    Soft and rubbery beak
    Streamlined
    Smaller than beavers
    Webbed front limbs
    Dense waterproof fur
    Beaver-like tail
HOME
    Uses claws to dig burrows
ACTIVITIES
    Uses front limbs to swim

Accept any reasonable division topic names and divisions. For example, my category "Babies" above could also be divided as "Reproduction" and "Young":

REPRODUCTION
    Lays eggs
    Produces milk/mammary glands
    Lays two soft-shelled white eggs
    Eggs stick together
    Female lays eggs in a tunnel
YOUNG
    Young is naked and blind
    Eyes open in 11 weeks
    Weaned at nearly 4 months

"Uses claws to dig burrows" and "Uses front limbs to swim" could both be grouped together under "Habits." I have listed the details about bones and the four-chambered heart under "Classification," but those details could also go under a separate topic such as "Characteristics."

    If the student is unable to come up with groupings or topics, you may either divide the notes for her and then tell her to come up with topic names, or else supply her with the topic names above and tell her to divide the notes underneath them.

STEP TWO: **Organize beaver notes**

Student instructions for Step Two:

> Now take your beaver notes and organize them into the same categories. If you have additional beaver notes that don't fall into those groupings, put them under the heading "Other." When you are finished, show your work to your instructor.

HOW TO HELP THE STUDENT WITH STEP TWO

Using the same headings, the beaver notes might be organized like this:

CLASSIFICATION
    Has a cloaca
    Largest North American rodent
BABIES
    Young stay with parents 2 years
    Yearlings stay with parents
    Kits are fully furred
    Eyes open, incisors present
    12 inches long, 1 pound
    Soft fluffy fur, no guard hair
    Cannot get out of lodge
    4–9 in a litter
FOOD
    Eats twigs and bark
    Eats skunk cabbage, grasses, berries
    Needs 1 1/2 to 2 pounds per day
APPEARANCE
    Large, scaly, paddle-like tail
    Reddish brown to blackish brown
    Short rounded ears
    Hind legs longer than front legs
    Massive skull and teeth
    Internal reproductive organs
HOME
    Digs bank burrows
    Uses claws to dig a tunnel
    Excavates chamber in bank
ACTIVITIES
OTHER
    Monogamous

STEP THREE: **Choose topics for your comparison/contrast (Student Responsibility)**

Student instructions for Step Three:

Now that you've organized your notes, you should be able to figure out the similarities and differences between the two animals.

Remember that you're writing an explanation by comparison and contrast—that means that your composition needs to be structured around 1) what is similar and then 2) what is different.

In your notes, underline, highlight, or circle the things that are *the same*—that both animals have in common.

Then, choose *two* topics or groupings that contain *differences* between the two animals.

You won't use the rest of the material. Any time you write a comparison and contrast, you will need to pick and choose among the material, deciding to use only the facts that make your composition flow easily forward. So pick the topics that you think will be the easiest to write about.

STEP FOUR: **Write the comparison**

Student instructions for Step Four:

Now you'll write the actual comparison and contrast, using the directions below.
If you are confused at any point, ask your instructor for help.

DIRECTIONS

First, write a paragraph explaining how the two animals are the same. Do this before you move on.

Second, using one of the topics/groups you selected, write a paragraph explaining how the two animals are *different*. Make use of the point-by-point method.

This paragraph will have three parts—read a), b), and c) below before you write!

a) Begin the paragraph with a sentence that says, in your own words, "Beavers and platypuses[1] are different in _____ [fill in the blank with the topic]."

b) Continue by addressing the facts in the group that apply to both platypuses and beavers. For example, if you are writing about appearances, you might write:

The platypus has a bill like a duck, but the beaver has massive front teeth. The platypus is smaller than the beaver.

c) Conclude by describing the facts that apply only to platypuses, and then the facts that apply only to beavers. You will never find *exact* parallels between two living things, so you will need to give yourself room to finish out the paragraph without finding perfect, point-by-point contrasts for every fact.

Finish the paragraph before you move on.

Third, using the second topic/group selected, write a paragraph explaining how the two animals are *different,* using the subject-by-subject method.

a) First, write several sentences describing the platypus, fact by fact.

b) Then, write several sentences describing the beaver, fact by fact.

---

[1] Scientists differ on what the plural of "platypus" should be. "Platypuses" is used by many; others just use "platypus" (in the same way that "one deer" and "many deer" have the same form). Some even use "platypi," because the Latin plural ends in -i (even though the word "platypus" is derived from the Greek). You may choose any of these options when you write.

HOW TO HELP THE STUDENT WITH STEP FOUR

Sample answers for each paragraph should resemble the following:

> **First**, write a paragraph explaining how the two animals are the same. Do this before you move on.

Both beavers and platypuses are mammals. Both also have *cloaca*—a single opening in the body. They have four-chambered hearts and nurse their young. Beavers have thick, waterproof fur. So do platypuses. And both animals have large, flat tails and use claws to dig out their burrows.

OR

The beaver and the platypus both belong to the mammal family. They have fur and nurse their young. Both beavers and platypuses dig out burrows for their homes, using their claws. And, unlike other mammals both have a single opening in their body, called the *cloaca.*

> **Second,** using one of the topics/groups you selected, write a paragraph explaining how the two animals are *different*. Make use of the point-by-point method.

Despite their similarities, beavers and platypuses are different in the way they eat. Platypuses eat worms and crawfish. On the other hand, beavers eat twigs, bark, skunk cabbage, grasses, and berries. Beavers need almost two pounds of food per day to survive.

OR

The beaver and the platypus look very different. Beavers have long incisors, and platypuses have soft, rubbery beaks, like ducks. Platypuses are much smaller than beavers. Platypuses are streamlined, with webbed front limbs. Beavers have short, round ears, and their hind legs are longer than their front legs.

> **Third,** using the second topic/group selected, write a paragraph explaining how the two animals are *different*, using the subject-by-subject method.

The platypus lays two white, soft-shelled eggs in its tunnel. The eggs often stick together. When the eggs hatch, the young platypuses are blind and have no fur. Their eyes open when they are 11 weeks old, and they are weaned when they are four months old. Beaver babies are born with fur. Their eyes are open, and their incisors are already growing. At first, they are soft and fluffy and cannot even swim out of the beaver lodge.

OR

Platypuses have duck-like beaks and are streamlined and small. Their front limbs are webbed, and their fur is waterproof. Beavers have reddish or blackish brown fur. Their skulls and teeth are large, and their ears are rounded. Their hind legs are longer than their front legs.

NOTE TO INSTRUCTOR: Don't worry if the composition sounds abrupt or stops and starts suddenly. The focus in this lesson is on planning and constructing the comparison and contrast; introductions and conclusions will be studied in the next week's work.

Not all details need to be included in each paragraph.

Also, notice that where there are similarities (for example, the beaver and platypus both have flat paddle-like tails), those are covered in the first part of the composition and left out of the second part. The student is learning how to organize her thoughts so that *all* similarities come in one part of the composition, *all* differences in another.

STEP FIVE: **Proofread**

Student instructions for Step Five:

> Repeat the basic steps of proofreading:
>
> 1) Read your composition out loud. Listen for awkward or unclear sections. Rewrite them so that they flow more naturally.
> 2) Check spelling by looking, individually, at each word that might be a problem.
> 3) Check your commas.
>
> When you're finished, show your work to your instructor.

HOW TO HELP THE STUDENT WITH STEP FIVE

Make sure that the student reads the composition out loud as part of the proofreading.

The final composition should resemble the following:

> The beaver and the platypus both belong to the mammal family. They have fur and nurse their young. Both beavers and platypuses dig out burrows for their homes, using their claws. And, unlike other mammals, both have a single opening in their body, called the *cloaca*.
>
> Despite their similarities, beavers and platypuses are different in the way they eat. Platypuses eat worms and crawfish. On the other hand, beavers eat twigs, bark, skunk cabbage, grasses, and berries. Beavers need almost two pounds of food per day to survive.
>
> The platypus lays two white, soft-shelled eggs in its tunnel. The eggs often stick together. When the eggs hatch, the young platypuses are blind and have no fur. Their eyes open when they are 11 weeks old, and they are weaned when they are four months old. Beaver babies are born with fur. Their eyes are open, and their incisors are already growing. At first, they are soft and fluffy and cannot even swim out of the beaver lodge.

Use the following rubric to evaluate the student's work.

Week 5 Rubric
Explanation By Comparison/Contrast

Organization:

1   The entire composition should be 100–300 words in length. NOTE: The student has not been assigned a dictated length. The student's focus should be on the form of the composition, which should take at least 100 words to develop properly.
2   There should be three paragraphs.
     a.   The first paragraph should describe *only* similarities.
     b.   The second paragraph should describe differences, going back and forth between beavers and platypuses as it compares them fact for fact.
     c.   The third paragraph should describe differences, first covering all the facts for platypuses, and then covering similar facts for beavers.

Mechanics:

1   Each sentence should make sense on its own when read aloud.
2   There should be no sentence fragments or run-on sentences.
3   All words should be spelled correctly.
4   The first line of each paragraph should be properly indented.
5   Verb tense should be consistent throughout.

Day Four: Copia

 Focus: Introduction to simile

Today, the student will begin to build the skills needed for a more complex set of sentence transformations.

Last year, the student was introduced to similes as part of descriptions. This year, he will begin to work more directly on choosing evocative, effective similes.

STEP ONE: **Understanding simile (Student Responsibility)**

Student instructions for Step One:

Read the following sets of sentences out loud.

He was very large and very fat.
He looked, in fact, very much like a colossal bowl of jelly, without the bowl.

There was an ominous stillness.
For an instant there was an ominous stillness, as if even the air was holding its breath.

The higher they went, the darker it became.
The higher they went, the darker it became, though it wasn't the darkness of night, but rather more like a mixture of lurking shadows and evil intentions which oozed from the slimy moss-covered cliffs and blotted out the light.

The second sentence in each pair is from Norman Juster's classic adventure *The Phantom Tollbooth*. Each one of Norman Juster's sentences contains a *simile*.

In the second sentence of each pair, find and underline the word *like* or *as*.
Then, circle the set of words that follow each underlined word.
Here's what you should have circled . . .

a colossal bowl of jelly, without the bowl
if even the air was holding its breath
a mixture of lurking shadows and evil intentions

Each one of these phrases is a *simile*.

You studied similes very briefly in the first level of this course. Let's review: **A simile is a comparison between two things, introduced by the words *like* or *as* (or *as if*).** In the first sentence, a fat man is compared to a bowl of jelly. In the second, stillness is compared to a living creature holding its breath. In the third, darkness is compared to shadows and evil intentions.

In a good simile, the comparison reminds the reader of the most important, or most striking, or most interesting thing about the subject. Norman Juster wants you to focus in on how formless, quivering, and bulgy the fat man is . . . so he chooses *jelly* (which is formless, quivering and bulgy). He wants you to *feel* the stillness, so he reminds you of how it feels to hold your breath and be completely motionless. And he wants you to *sense* just how threatening and scary the darkness is, so he compares it to "lurking" shadows and "evil intentions."

NOTE TO INSTRUCTOR: Although this step is the student's responsibility, you may need to check that the following words have been circled and underlined:

He looked, in fact, very much <u>like</u> a colossal bowl of jelly, without the bowl.

For an instant there was an ominous stillness, <u>as</u> if even the air was holding its breath.

The higher they went, the darker it became, <u>though it wasn't the darkness of night</u>, but rather more <u>like</u> a mixture of lurking shadows and evil intentions which oozed from the slimy moss-covered cliffs and blotted out the light.

STEP TWO: **Identifying simile**

Student instructions for Step Two:

> In the following sentences, underline the simile. Draw an arrow from the simile back to the subject—the word the simile describes by comparison.

HOW TO HELP THE STUDENT WITH STEP TWO

The student's answers should be:

Oh, my Luve's like a <u>red, red rose,</u>
That's newly sprung in June
        (Robert Burns)

[The door] was opened by another footman in livery, with a round face,

and large eyes <u>like a frog.</u>
        (Lewis Carroll, *Alice in Wonderland*)

[Meg] tried to get rid of the kitten, which had scrambled up her back and stuck
<u>like a burr just out of reach.</u>
        (Louisa May Alcott, *Little Women*)

As Anne sits at the window, she can look down on the sea, which this morning is
calm <u>as glass.</u>
        (Charlotte Bronte, *Letters*)

The wrath of the monarch's eye dazzled <u>like the lightning in the sky.</u>
        (Jean Racine)

The sun to me is dark, and silent <u>as the moon.</u>
        (John Milton, *Samson Agonistes*)

He squeaks <u>like a hurt chicken.</u>
        (Alexander Wilson) [Although "he" is the subject, the "hurt chicken" sound
        actually refers back to the squeaking sound, so you can accept "squeaks"]

The vast clouds fled, countless and swift <u>as leaves on autumn's tempest.</u>
(Percy Bysshe Shelley) [Although "clouds" is the subject, the "leaves" simile refers back to the swift movement of the clouds, so you can accept "swift"]

Yellow butterflies flickered along the shade <u>like flecks of sun.</u>
(William Faulkner, *The Sound and the Fury*)

STEP THREE: **Invent new similes**

Student instructions for Step Three:

Now it's your turn to find similes.

On your own paper, rewrite the sentences from Step Two by finding your own simile. Try to choose a simile that expresses the meaning in the brackets below. So, for example, a good answer to

Oh, my Luve's like [something fresh, beautiful, and new].

would not be

Oh, my Luve's like rain after a long drought.

It's very nice to say that your love is like rain after a long drought, but that simile doesn't convey *fresh, beautiful,* and *new.* It might convey

Oh, my Luve's like [something that saves me when I'm desperate].

but that's a whole different set of ideas.

Oh, my Luve's like the first grass of spring.

would be a better simile (although perhaps not quite as good as Robert Burns's!).

As you're working on your similes, use the following meanings:

Oh, my Luve's like [something fresh, beautiful, and new].

The door was opened by another footman in livery, with a round face, and large eyes
like [something rather stupid].

Meg tried to get rid of the kitten, which had scrambled up her back and stuck like [something uncomfortable and annoying].

As Anne sits at the window, she can look down on the sea, which this morning is calm
as [something smooth].

The wrath of the monarch's eye dazzled like [something frightening and destructive].

The sun to me is dark, and silent as [something very distant].

He squeaks like [something powerless and silly].

The vast clouds fled, countless and swift as [something passing, temporary, soon gone].

Yellow butterflies flickered along the shade like [something incredibly bright].

When you are finished, show your sentences to your instructor.

HOW TO HELP THE STUDENT WITH STEP THREE

Answers on this exercise will vary widely.

Although similes were introduced last year, this year's exercise takes a step forward, introducing the student to the idea that some similes fit better than others.

A few suggested similes are offered below, but you should accept any simile that the student can defend.

As suggested last year, the public-domain *Dictionary of Similes,* by Frank Jenners Wilstach (full text available online from books.google.com and elsewhere) is a useful reference.

Oh, my Luve's like [something fresh, beautiful, and new]
morning breeze, fruit or berries, sunrise, dew, April, spring

The door was opened by another footman in livery, with a round face, and large eyes like [something rather stupid]
stone, a hog, wood, a dog, monkey

Meg tried to get rid of the kitten, which had scrambled up her back and stuck like [something uncomfortable and annoying].
leech, a cold, something in your eye, an itch you can't scratch, a tag in your clothes, a seam in your sock

As Anne sits at the window, she can look down on the sea, which this morning is calm as [something smooth]
brass, china, linen, oil, silver, a jetstream, ice, mirror, marble

The wrath of the monarch's eye dazzled like [something frightening and destructive]
hail, fire, meteor, thunder, bomb

The sun to me is dark, and silent as [something very distant]
north pole, deep sleep, distant galaxy, far horizon, death, dreams

He squeaks like [something powerless and silly]
a calf, a baby, a grub, a cricket, a kitten

The vast clouds fled, countless and swift as [something passing, temporary, soon gone]
moths, wind or breezes, flies, dust, ghosts, visions, shadows, dew

Yellow butterflies flickered along the shade like [something incredibly bright]
diamonds, flame, fire, ice, candles, star, mirror, pearl, gold, snow

WEEK 6: INTRODUCTIONS AND CONCLUSIONS

Day One: How to Write an Introduction

 Focus: Learning the structure of introductions

NOTE TO INSTRUCTOR: You may wish to check that the student has completed the Student Responsibility steps carefully.

STEP ONE: Understand three types of introduction (Student Responsibility)

Student instructions for Step One:

> When you wrote last week's composition about the beaver and the platypus (the comparison/contrast), you were told to begin with a paragraph explaining how the two animals are the same. Your composition probably started something like this . . .
>
>> The beaver and the platypus both belong to the mammal family. They have fur and nurse their young. Both beavers and platypuses dig out burrows for their homes, using their claws. And, unlike other mammals, both have a single opening in their body, called the *cloaca*.
>
> That's a perfectly good paragraph about similarities. But it's missing something: an *introduction*.
>
> Today, you'll return to your comparison and give it an introduction.
>
> In order to understand what a good introduction does, let's look at three different introductions to three different essays about animals. We'll start with the first paragraph of Boris Fishman's comparison of cats and tigers.
>
>> A cat snoozing on a couch may not remind you of a tiger, but in many ways the two animals are almost identical. In the scientific system that classifies all living things, cats and tigers belong to the same family, *Felidae*, which also includes lions and leopards, who are technically known as "big cats."
>
> The first sentence of this paragraph *introduces* Fishman's first set of comparisons by telling you, ahead of time, what the conclusion of his entire essay will be: Although there are important

97

contrasts between cats and tigers, their *similarities* are much more important than their differences. The *introduction by summary* provides one or two sentences at the beginning of a composition that tell the reader exactly what the composition is about and what its most central conclusion will be.

Introduction by summary is one of the simplest forms of introduction. Here's a second kind, from the comparison of reptiles and amphibians you looked at last week:

> Time was when the only good snake was a dead one. Fortunately, as we have come to understand that every species has a place in the global environment, that attitude is almost a thing of the past.[3]

This kind of introduction, the *introduction by history,* looks back in time, telling you something about the subject's history: In the past, snakes were usually just killed, but now that attitude has changed.

An introduction by history gives you a snippet of information about past attitudes, an idea of how the subject has developed over time, or a brief scene from history. Here's another *introduction by history,* this one about beavers [*extirpate* means "to remove" or "to destroy completely]":

> Two beaver species inhabit our world: the North American and the Eurasian beaver. Both had been extirpated over large areas by the beginning of the 20th century. But during the past 50 years . . . each of the species has traveled along a different trajectory. In the United States, reintroduction of the North American beaver in its former range has been so successful that burgeoning populations have no choice but to move into developed land . . . In Europe, meanwhile, reintroductions have given some countries their first beavers in decades. Still small in numbers, these new populations are being carefully nurtured.[4]

This introduction by history tells how the beaver population has developed over time: Fifty years ago, beavers were uncommon. Then they were reintroduced. Now there are almost too many beavers in North America, and the population in Europe is starting to grow. The introduction tells you how beaver populations have developed over time.

Here's one more introduction from history, this one using a brief scene from history to introduce an essay about scientific controversy over the platypus:

> It all began harmlessly enough. Nearly 10 years after settlement, in November 1797, at Yarramundi Lagoon just north of Sydney, Governor John Hunter watched an Aboriginal guide wait patiently to spear a platypus as it surfaced. Hunter sent the skin and a sketch to the Literary and Philosophical Society in Newcastle-upon-Tyne . . . [5]

The third type of introduction, *introduction by anecdote,* starts by telling a story. This story might be drawn from personal experience, as in the introduction to *Reptiles and Amphibians for Dummies:*

> Most reptile and amphibian owners can point with unerring accuracy to the moment they got hooked on these animals. For me, it was when I walked across the street at age 6 to the open lots west of my home in Albuquerque, New Mexico. The lots were filled with tumbleweeds, tufts of scrub

---

3. Conant, Stebbins, and Collins, p. 4.

4. Dietland Muller-Schwarze, *The Beaver: Natural History of a Wetlands Engineer* (Comstock, 2003), p. ix.

5. Penny Olsen, *Upside Down World: Early European Impressions of Australia's Curious Animals* (National Library of Australia, 2010), p. 14.

grass, and a few (very few, thank goodness) scraggy, low cholla cactus. Dashing from clump to clump were blue-tailed skinks. Less active but lying quietly amidst concealing gravel patches were the sand lizards. I never knew what occupied the fist-sized tunnels, but imagined they might be rattlesnakes. I spent most of my summers exploring those lots . . . [6]

An *introduction by anecdote* can also take the form of an invented scene—a story that you make up, based on what you know about the subject. Here are two examples, both taken from books that compare and contrast animals.

You wake up one morning and are walking sleepily toward the kitchen when all of a sudden, your pet cat rubs against your leg. She seems cute and friendly, but what your pet is really doing is acting like a wild cat![7]

It is feeding time. In the dense Indian jungle, an enormous Bengal tiger drags his fresh kill to a hiding place. Thousands of miles away on a dusty African plain, a male lion takes the first bite of a zebra that his lionesses have just killed. No animal dares to get in his way.[8]

There are many other ways to introduce a composition, but these three are the most common (and the most useful).

STEP TWO: **Create an Introduction reference page (Student Responsibility)**

Student instructions for Step Two:

Keep this information on hand as you write by adding it to the Reference section of your Composition Notebook.

At the top of a sheet of paper, center the word INTRODUCTIONS. Beneath it, write the following information:

1. Introduction by Summary
   One or more sentences that tell the reader what the composition is about and what its most central conclusion will be

2. Introduction by History
   a. Information about past attitudes towards the subject
   b. Description of how some aspect of the subject has changed or developed over time
   c. Brief scene from history

3. Introduction by Anecdote
   a. A story drawn from personal experience
   b. An invented scene, based on your knowledge of the subject

6. Patricia Bartlett, *Reptiles and Amphibians for Dummies* (Wiley, 2003), p. 1.
7. Jenni Bidner, *Is My Cat a Tiger? How Your Pet Compares to its Wild Cousins* (Lark Books, 2007), p. 7.
8. Isabel Thomas, *Lion vs. Tiger* (Heinemann Library, 2007), p. 4.

STEP THREE: **Practice**

Student instructions for Step Three:

Finish today's work by writing three brief introductions to your platypus and beaver comparison: one introduction by summary, one introduction by history, and one introduction by anecdote. Each introduction can be as short as one sentence or as long as three or four.

If you have difficulty with any of these introductions, ask your instructor for help.

1. Introduction by Summary

In one or more sentences, tell the reader whether the beaver and the platypus are more alike than they are different—or vice versa.

2. Introduction by History

Using the following information, write one or more sentences (you'll probably need at least two) describing past attitudes towards the platypus.

Ever since the first specimen (a dried skin) of the platypus arrived in Britain from Australia in about 1798, the species has been surrounded by controversy. This first specimen was thought to be a fake animal which a taxidermist had made by stitching together the beak of a duck and the body parts of a mammal! Even when it was found to be real, the species was not accepted as actually being a mammal.[9]

When the first platypus specimens from Australia were sent back to England in 1798, people thought they were two unrelated animals sewn together. A faked-up mermaid (which was commonly fabricated from monkey remains and fishtails) was more understandable. At least mermaids were well-known mythical creatures. But who would believe an otter-and-duck combination?

In the end, scientists discovered that the platypus was not only real, but even weirder than was immediately apparent.[10]

3. Introduction by Anecdote

Write a description, one sentence or more, set in the present tense, of both a platypus and a beaver carrying out some daily activity. Your end result should resemble the lion-and-tiger introduction in Step Two.

Alternately, if you've ever seen a platypus, write one or more sentences about your reactions. (If you feel creative, you could *pretend* that you've seen a platypus and write about your *possible* reaction.)

When you've finished your three introductions, show them to your instructor. Together, decide which one is the most effective introduction to your composition.

---

9. Tom Grant, The Platypus (Sydney, Australia, University of South Wales Press, 1995), pp. 2, 5.

10. Margaret Mittelbach and Michael Crewdson, *Carnivorous Nights: On the Trail of the Tasmanian Tiger* (Random House, 2005), p. 225.

HOW TO HELP THE STUDENT WITH STEP THREE

1. Introduction by Summary

The student's introduction should resemble one of the following:

Although beavers and platypuses share a very strange characteristic, they are different in many ways.

Beavers and platypuses are both mammals, but they eat and reproduce very differently.

Beavers and platypuses look very different, but they are alike in many important ways.

The beaver and the platypus have very different ways of reproducing. However, they are the same in one strange and interesting way.

The introduction by summary may sound stilted and unnecessary; for such a short composition, summaries are usually too repetitious. However, it is still important for the student to practice the skill.

2. Introduction by History

The student may come up with a single sentence, like this:

At first, scientists did not believe that the platypus was a real animal.

Depending on the student's skill level, you may choose to accept this. However, you may also choose to encourage the student to write a slightly more fleshed-out introduction by saying, "Why don't you add details about where and when the platypus was first seen by British scientists?" or "Where was the platypus discovered, and when?" The student's answer would then become:

The platypus is an Australian animal. When British scientists first saw it in 1798, they didn't believe it was real.

OR

When scientists first saw the platypus, in 1798, they didn't believe it was a real animal. They though that someone had sewn and otter and a duck together for a joke!

3. Introduction by Anecdote

The student's answer can be very simple:

On a riverbank in North America, a beaver is chewing on a piece of bark. Meanwhile, in Australia, a platypus is digging up worms.

If the student has difficulty, say, "Write a sentence describing a beaver eating. Where is the beaver and what is it eating? Then write a sentence describing a platypus eating. Answer the same questions."

A more complex answer would contain more descriptive details, such as:

It is a sunny morning on the bank of a river. A shiny brown beaver is sitting on its hind legs, clutching a piece of bark between its claws. Far away, a furry platypus is digging in the mud with its own claws, looking for a crawfish to eat.

If the student chooses to write a personal anecdote, it might sound like this:

When I was eleven, I visited the zoo and saw a platypus. It was a little bit like a very small beaver—but with an odd, rubbery beak. It was the strangest creature I had ever looked at!

Day Two: How to Write a Conclusion

 Focus: Learning the purpose and structure of conclusions

STEP ONE: Understand three types of conclusion (Student Responsibility)

Student instructions for Step One:

When you first meet someone, you say "hello." When you leave, you say "goodbye." An introduction is a composition's "hello" to the reader. Today, you'll learn how to say "goodbye" by writing a strong conclusion.

There are many ways to conclude an essay, but let's look at three of the most common.

First, you can summarize your conclusions. *Conclusion by summary* is similar to *introduction by summary*; the difference is that, by the end of the essay, you've given the reader plenty of specific details. So when you write a conclusion by summary, you should use a couple of those details.

How would *conclusion by summary* work for Boris Fishman's essay on cats and tigers? You could simply write,

Despite their many differences, cats and tigers are very much alike.

But using a few of the details from the essay would make this a much more effective conclusion.

Cats and tigers may be very different in size, in the way they sound, and in their love of water. But as their hunting habits and their sharp senses show us, they have just as many similarities as differences.

Notice how I went back and mentioned specifics: size, sound, love of water, etc.

Here's another example of *conclusion by summary*. Reread this excerpt from *Peterson First Guide to Reptiles and Amphibians* (you saw this in Day Two of last week's lesson). Notice the bolded sentences I have added to the end.

★

Despite their cold-blooded nature, amphibians and reptiles are actually quite different. Scales and claws set reptiles apart, and young amphibians look nothing like young reptiles!

(One consideration: At the end of a short composition, conclusion by summary can sound repetitive. After all, the reader *just* learned those details two minutes ago! You'll probably find it useful for slightly longer compositions.)

Second, you can end with a personal statement or opinion—your own reaction to what you've just written. The *conclusion by personal reaction* tells the reader what *you* think. So Mr. Fishman's composition might have ended:

I can understand why so many people like tigers—but give me a cat any day. I'd far rather have a cat sleeping on the end of my bed than a pet tiger caged in my backyard!

Telling the reader which animal is *your* favorite brings the composition to a nice, neat end.

A *conclusion by personal reaction* to the reptile and amphibian comparison might sound like this:

Even though amphibians and reptiles are different in many ways, they seem very much alike to me. I'd be happy to have either a frog or a turtle for a pet, and snakes and salamanders both give me the shivers.

Here again, the reader finds out what *you* think: In your opinion, the similarities are a lot more obvious important than the differences.

Another way to write a personal reaction would be to mention your own experience with the subject (very much like the *introduction by anecdote,* except at the end of the composition instead of the beginning). The reptile-amphibian comparison could end like this:

I have kept both turtles and frogs as pets. Both of them needed to be kept warm during the winter. But I have to say that I find baby turtles much more appealing than frog larvae!

Third, you can end by posing a question to the reader. The *conclusion by question* asks the *reader* to react—so in a way, it's similar to the *conclusion by personal reaction.*

The cat-tiger comparison might end like this:

Tigers may be noble, but remember: they can eat over ninety pounds of meat in a single meal! If you had a choice between a tiger or cat for a pet, could you afford to feed it?

or

Even though tigers are magnificent animals, the number of pet cats in the world tells me that most people actually prefer the tiger's smaller relative. What would your preference be—tiger or cat?

Both conclusions take the last part of the comparison and contrast (how people react personally to cats and tigers) and ask the reader to have an opinion about it.

Keep this in mind as you write: All of these sample conclusions have more than one sentence. A conclusion written as a separate paragraph should have a minimum of two sentences.

Sometimes, you may find it more natural to write a single-sentence conclusion. In that case, attach that sentence to the last paragraph of the essay, like this:

> The two animals have a little sibling rivalry going on when it comes to popularity. Though one recent poll found cats to be the most popular domestic pet, another poll found tigers to be the most beloved animal overall. One animal specialist explained why this way: "We can relate to the tiger, as it is fierce and commanding on the outside, but noble and discerning on the inside."[1] **Tigers may be noble and discerning—but I'd rather have a pet cat snoozing on *my* sofa!**

[1]David Ward, "Humankind's favourite animal is a tiger" (*The Guardian*, Dec. 5, 2004, www.guardian.co.uk)

STEP TWO: **Create a Conclusion reference page (Student Responsibility)**

Student instructions for Step Two:

Keep this information on hand as you write by adding it to the Reference section of your Composition Notebook.

At the top of a sheet of paper, center the word CONCLUSIONS. Beneath it, write the following information:

GENERAL: A paragraph of conclusion should contain at least two sentences. Single-sentence conclusions should be written as the last sentence of the final paragraph.

1. Conclusion by Summary
   Write a brief summary of the most important information in the passage, including specific details

2. Conclusion by Personal Reaction
   a. Personal statement
   b. Your opinion about the material
   c. Your own experience with the subject

3. Conclusion by Question
   Ask the reader to react to the information

STEP THREE: **Practice**

Student instructions for Step Three:

Finish today's work by writing three brief conclusions to your platypus and beaver comparison: one conclusion by summary, one conclusion by personal reaction, and one conclusion by question.

One of these conclusions (you can choose which one!) may be a one-sentence conclusion attached to your last paragraph. However, the other two *must* be separate paragraphs (so should have at least two sentences each).

If you have difficulty with any of these introductions, ask your instructor for help.

1. Conclusion by Summary

Come to a decision: Are they more alike or more different? Which details will make this clear to the reader? (This may sound very much like the introduction by summary you wrote in the last day's work—that's perfectly fine.)

2. Conclusion by Personal Reaction

Which would you rather have for a pet? Or, which animal is more interesting? Or, have you ever seen a beaver or platypus? If so, what did you think about it?

3. Conclusion by Question

Ask the reader a question. Which animal does the *reader* like better? Can you think of another question to ask?

HOW TO HELP THE STUDENT WITH STEP THREE

1. Conclusion by Summary

A one-sentence conclusion added to the final paragraph might resemble the following:

Although their young are very different, adult beavers and platypuses are actually quite similar in many ways.

OR

Even though the beaver has a cloaca like the platypus, the two animals have more differences than similarities.

Such a short composition doesn't really need a conclusion by summary, as the student has already learned, so the conclusion may sound awkward. It is fine for it to sound similar to the *introduction by summary*, but it should have at least one specific detail that the introduction doesn't have.

A paragraph-long conclusion might sound like this:

The beaver and the platypus have similar fur and body structures, and both dig burrows. But because the platypus lays eggs while the beaver has live babies, they are very different animals.

OR

Platypuses lay eggs; beavers have babies with fur, eyes, and incisors. Despite this huge difference, both animals are mammals, and they share the odd single opening called a *cloaca*.

2. Conclusion by Personal Reaction

A one-sentence conclusion added to the last paragraph should resemble one of the following:

Personally, I find the platypus much more fascinating than the beaver—even if it is a much weirder animal.

OR

I hope one day to see a platypus, even though I'll have to travel to Australia!

A paragraph-length conclusion might sound like

After reading about both animals, I think that the greatest difference between the platypus and the beaver has to do with the ability to build. I have seen beaver dams, and they are amazing structures. The platypus may be fascinating, but the beaver is a far more useful animal.

OR

The platypus is such a fascinating animal that I wondered whether I'd be able to see one in a zoo. After searching for the nearest zoo with a platypus, I learned that platypuses can't be exported from Australia to other countries. On the other hand, beavers live in rivers all across the United States.

3. Conclusion by Question

The most straightforward one-sentence conclusion by question is simply:

Now that you've read about both animals, which do you prefer—the beaver or the platypus?

A longer conclusion by question might resemble one of the following:

Since the platypus is found only in Australia, you've probably never seen one. But beavers are found all across North America. Have you ever seen a beaver lodge, built on the edge of a river?

OR

Scientists may have decided that the platypus and the beaver belong to the same classification, but the platypus still has many things in common with a duck. What do you think of the platypus—is it more bird, or more mammal?

Day Three: Introductions and Conclusions: Further Practice

 Focus: Practicing introductions and conclusions

STEP ONE: **Analyze**

Student instructions for Step One (the entire essay is provided for your reference):

Read the following essay, taken from *Mark Twain's Autobiography*. Mark Twain's real name was Samuel Clemens. He lived 1835–1910 and is best known as the author of *The Adventures of Tom Sawyer* and *The Adventures of Huckleberry Finn*.

This essay uses comparison and contrast to describe the Mississippi River.

"Two Ways of Seeing a River"

Now when I had mastered the language of this water and had come to know every trifling feature that bordered the great river as familiarly as I knew the letters of the alphabet, I had made a valuable acquisition. But I had lost something, too. I had lost something which could never be restored to me while I lived. All the grace, the beauty, the poetry had gone out of the majestic river!

I still keep in mind a certain wonderful sunset which I witnessed when steamboating was new to me. A broad expanse of the river was turned to blood; in the middle distance the red hue brightened into gold, through which a solitary log came floating, black and conspicuous; in one place a long, slanting mark lay sparkling upon the water; in another the surface was broken by boiling, tumbling rings, that were as many-tinted as an opal; where the ruddy flush was faintest, was a smooth spot that was covered with graceful circles and radiating lines, ever so delicately traced; the shore on our left was densely wooded, and the somber shadow that fell from this forest was broken in one place by a long, ruffled trail that shone like silver; and high above the forest wall a clean-stemmed dead tree waved a single leafy bough that glowed like a flame in the unobstructed splendor that was flowing from the sun. There were graceful curves, reflected images, woody heights, soft distances; and over the whole scene, far and near, the dissolving lights drifted steadily, enriching it, every passing moment, with new marvels of coloring.

I stood like one bewitched. I drank it in, in a speechless rapture. The world was new to me, and I had never seen anything like this at home. But as I have said, a day came when I began to cease from noting the glories and the charms which the moon and the sun and the twilight wrought upon the river's face; another day came when I ceased altogether to note them. Then, if that sunset scene had been repeated, I should have looked upon it without rapture, and should have commented upon it, inwardly, in this fashion: "This sun means that we are going to have wind to-morrow; that floating log means that the river is rising, small thanks to it; that slanting mark on the water refers to a bluff reef which is going to kill somebody's steamboat one of these nights, if it keeps on stretching out like that;

those tumbling 'boils' show a dissolving bar and a changing channel there; the lines and circles in the slick water over yonder are a warning that that troublesome place is shoaling up dangerously; that silver streak in the shadow of the forest is the 'break' from a new snag, and he has located himself in the very best place he could have found to fish for steamboats; that tall dead tree, with a single living branch, is not going to last long, and then how is a body ever going to get through this blind place at night without the friendly old landmark?"

No, the romance and the beauty were all gone from the river. All the value any feature of it had for me now was the amount of usefulness it could furnish toward compassing the safe piloting of a steamboat. Since those days, I have pitied doctors from my heart. What does the lovely flush in a beauty's cheek mean to a doctor but a "break" that ripples above some deadly disease? Are not all her visible charms sown thick with what are to him the signs and symbols of hidden decay? Does he ever see her beauty at all, or doesn't he simply view her professionally, and comment upon her unwholesome condition all to himself? And doesn't he some-times wonder whether he has gained most or lost most by learning his trade?

When you have finished reading the essay, ask your instructor for directions.

HOW TO HELP THE STUDENT WITH STEP ONE

Although the structure of this essay is very straightforward, Twain's sentences are long and his vocabulary is slightly archaic. If the student has difficulty following the essay, ask him to read it out loud (or read it out loud as he follows along).

After reading the essay, the student should discuss it with you. Talking about a piece of writing is one of the best ways to appreciate its structure. The goal of this exercise is simply to begin to expand the student's awareness of how good writing works.

Use or adapt the suggested dialogue and information below.

INSTRUCTOR: In this essay, Mark Twain is comparing two different ways of looking at the Mississippi River. After his introductory paragraph, he begins by describing a sunset that he saw when the river was still new to him. What adjective does he use to modify *sunset*?

Student: Wonderful.

Instructor: The second paragraph describes the sunset over the river with almost completely positive words—nouns and modifiers that have good connotations for us. Can you find three positive adjectives, adverbs, or nouns?

Possible answers: gold, sparkling, graceful, delicately, silver, flame, splendor, soft, marvels.

Instructor: Then things change for Twain. What changes?

Student: He begins to see all the dangers of the river OR He becomes more familiar with the river OR He knows what all of the signs of the river mean now.

NOTE: Give the student a chance to try to answer independently. If he needs help, you can ask, "Does he lose himself in the beauty of the river? When he sees the slanting mark on the water, does he think how lovely it is? What does he think about what might happen?"

Instructor: As Twain becomes more familiar with the river, he doesn't see the beauty any more—he just sees all of the dangers and problems that steamboat pilots will face. This essay is another type of comparison. It compares how Twain sees the river at two different points in time—when he was young, and after he became an experienced pilot. Now look at the introduction and the conclusion. What kind of introduction does Twain write?

Student: Introduction by summary OR Introduction by anecdote

NOTE: Discuss the following with the student.

This is primarily an introduction by summary: Point out to the student that Twain sums up the comparison when he says, "I had made a valuable acquisition. But I had lost something too." The comparison itself simply illustrates this point. The student may say that this is an introduction by anecdote, because Twain begins by explaining that he had "mastered the language of this water" and become familiar with it. Tell the student that the introduction actually has elements of both, so this is not an incorrect answer, but then guide him into seeing the summary as well.

Instructor: Now look at the last paragraph. What kind of conclusion does Twain write?

Student: Conclusion by question

NOTE: Discuss the following with the student.

In this conclusion, Twain is actually doing two interesting things simultaneously. He is using the rhetorical structure *conclusion by question*, but he is tying this structure together with another form—the closing metaphor. This metaphor has a series of parallels:

beautiful woman = river

doctor = river pilot

red flush on her cheeks = river "break" signifying a dangerous shallow place and so on.

Without the metaphor, the series of questions would just repeat the information in the essay itself. It might sound something like this:

What does the silver streak in the water mean, but a "break" that ripples above some deadly shallow place? Are not all the visible beauties of the river simply signs and symbols of hidden danger? Does the pilot ever see the river's beauty at all, or doesn't he simply see it professionally and comment on its dangers all to himself? And doesn't he sometimes wonder whether he has gained most or lost most by learning his trade?

STEP TWO: **Review the Introduction and Conclusion charts in your Reference Notebook (Student Responsibility)**

Student instructions for Step Two:

> In the last step of this lesson, you'll write an introduction and conclusion to a brief essay. Prepare for this assignment by going back to your Reference Notebook and reviewing the three types of introduction and the three types of conclusion.

STEP THREE: **Write an introduction and conclusion**

Student instructions for Step Three (all text is included for your reference):

> Read the following comparison/contrast essay carefully.
>
> When you're finished, write an introduction and a conclusion. Choose the type you prefer from your charts. Both should be separate paragraphs, at least two sentences in length.
>
> Introduction by summary and conclusion by summary are very similar. DO NOT CHOOSE TO WRITE BOTH! If you write an introduction by summary, pick another kind of conclusion (and vice versa).
>
> Introduction by anecdote and conclusion by personal reaction are also similar. Don't write both!
>
> If you have difficulty coming up with an introduction and conclusion, ask your instructor for ideas.

> If you were to look at Venus and Earth side by side, they might appear to be twins. Earth's diameter (measured at the equator) is 12,756 kilometers (7,926 miles) compared to Venus's 12,100 kilometers (7,518 miles). The difference in their diameters is less than the width of Texas, which for a planet is barely noticeable. Earth and Venus have very similar masses as well, meaning that the surface gravity on each planet is nearly the same. If you stood on Venus, you would weigh about 90% of what you weigh on Earth, and you probably wouldn't notice much of a difference.
>
> However, Venus is much hotter than Earth. The average surface temperature on Earth is 14 degrees Celsius (57 degrees Fahrenheit), or the temperature of a cool autumn day. But on Venus the average surface temperature is 462 degrees Celsius (864 degrees Fahrenheit), making it the hottest planet in our solar system. Even Mercury, which is closer to the sun than Venus, has an average temperature of only 167 degrees Celsius (332 degrees Fahrenheit).
>
> How did Venus get so hot? The thick atmosphere of Venus is composed mostly of carbon dioxide. Once sunlight passes through the atmosphere, it is trapped by the atmosphere and continues to heat the planet. This is called the greenhouse effect. Just like the glass roof of a greenhouse, which allows sunlight to come in but not go out, the atmosphere of Venus traps the sun's heat. Earth doesn't suffer from this horrendous heat because the planet's atmosphere is less than 1% carbon dioxide, allowing it to "breathe" better than Venus.

> Here is additional information that you might find useful:

Neil F. Comins and William J. Kaufmann, *Discovering the Universe* (New York: W. H. Freeman, 1996), pp. 206–207.

Unlike Mercury, Venus is intrinsically bright because it is completely surrounded by light-colored, highly reflective clouds. Because visible light telescopes cannot penetratethis thick, unbroken layer of clouds, we did not even know how fast Venus rotates until 1962. In the 1960s, however, both the United States and the Soviet Union began sending probes there. The Americans sent fragile, lightweight spacecraft into orbit near the planet. The Soviets, who had more powerful rockets, sent more durable spacecraft directly into the Venusian atmosphere.

. . . Finally, in 1970, the Soviet probe *Venera* (Russian for "Venus") *7* managed to transmit data for 23 minutes directly from the Venusian surface. Soviet missions continued until 1985, measuring a surface temperature of 750 [degrees] K[elvin] (900 F) and a surface air pressure of 90 atm, among other things. This value is the same pressure you would feel if you were swimming 0.82 km (2700 ft) underwater on Earth.

In contrast to Earth's present nitrogen- and oxygen-rich atmosphere, Venus's thick atmosphere is 96% carbon dioxide, with the remaining 4% mostly nitrogen . . . Soviet spacecraft also discovered that Venus's clouds are confined to a 20-km-thick layer located 48 to 68 km above the planet's surface.

Kenneth R. Lang and Charles A. Whitney, *Wanderers in Space: Exploration and Discovery in the Solar System* (Cambridge: Cambridge University Press, 1991), p. 72.

Venus has boiled dry, like a kettle left too long on a stove. And there are no seasons such as we know on Earth. Her terrain is gloomy; 98 per cent of the sunlight is captured at higher levels in the dense, cloudy atmosphere. As a result of the atmosphere's peculiar filtering action, the rocky surface of Venus is bathed in the dim light of an orange sky.

Vicki Cameron, *Don't Tell Anyone, But—: UFO Experiences in Canada* (Burnstown, Ont., Canada: General Store Pub. House, 1995), p. 147

Venus holds the prize for Most Frequently Seen as a UFO.

Venus normally appears brighter than any other star, low in the western sky after sunset or just above the eastern horizon in the early morning. Like all planets, Venus seems to wander about the sky during the year, although it's really travelling a known path.

About every two years, Venus appears extremely bright, in the evening and in the morning. It's so bright it remains visible after the sun rises. Various effects in the atmosphere make it ripple in rainbow colours, dance, or appear to head right for you on a collision course.

HOW TO HELP THE STUDENT WITH STEP THREE

Because introduction by summary and conclusion by summary are so similar, the student has been directed *not* to write both. The same holds true for introduction by anecdote and conclusion by personal reaction.

Part One: Introduction

The student's introductions might resemble the following (note that he has to write only ONE of the following, but that it should be a separate paragraph of at least two sentences).

1. Introduction by Summary

Accept the student's introduction if he is able to produce it without help. But if he struggles, encourage him to avoid the summary introduction (or conclusion). For such short essays, summaries always sound repetitive and stiff.

The additional information provided in the lesson should help guide the student towards introduction by history or introduction by anecdote.

Possible introductions by summary would be:

Venus and Earth are very similar in size and mass. But the planets differ in their temperature and atmosphere.

OR

Although Venus and Earth have many similarities, their differences are even more striking. Only Earth is able to support life.

2. Introduction by History

The planet Venus was a mystery to scientists until the 1960s, when the Americans and Soviets sent probes to investigate it. The American probes stayed in orbit, but the Soviet probes went into the atmosphere to measure temperature, pressure, and many other things.

OR

In 1970, a Soviet probe was able to send data from the surface of Venus. For the first time, scientists were able to understand how Venus was different from the Earth.

The student could also write a more dramatic scene, such as:

The date is 1970. A Soviet probe hovers over the surface of the planet Venus, sending back a stream of information to earth. For the first time, scientists begin to understand just how different this planet really is.

If the student struggles, prompt him with the following questions:
Did scientists always know about Venus's mass, diameter, heat, and atmosphere?
When did scientists find out?
What did they have to do to get this information?

3. Introduction by Anecdote

The student may choose to write two or more sentences about his own experience viewing Venus.

If he has no personal experience, he could imagine viewing Venus, or else think about what it would be like to stand on the surface. (This information has been provided for him.)

His introduction might be:

> I am standing outside on a cool, clear fall night. There are stars above me, but I see something on the horizon that doesn't look like a star. It's far too bright, and it seems to be heading straight for me. Is it a UFO—or just the planet Venus?

OR

> Imagine standing on the surface of Venus. The rocky ground is drier than the driest desert on Earth. You are surrounded by dim orange light. The air presses down on you. Of course, you can't really be standing on Venus—because if you were, your blood would be boiling in the 864-degree heat.

If the student struggles, prompt him with the following questions:

Have you ever looked at the planet Venus? What did you see?
Imagine that you're standing on the surface of Venus. What does it look and feel like?
Imagine that you're outside at night, looking at Venus. What do you see?

Part Two: Conclusion

1. Conclusion by Summary

This would resemble the introduction by summary, only with a little more specific detail:

> Venus and Earth are alike in size and mass. But Venus's heat, carbon dioxide, and pressure make it a very different planet from our own.

OR

> Although Venus and Earth have many similarities, their differences are even more striking. Venus's average temperature of 864 degrees, compared to the Earth's 57 degrees, means that no human could ever stand on its surface.

As before, if the student struggles, encourage him to write a different kind of conclusion using the information provided.

2. Conclusion by Personal Reaction

This conclusion could resemble the introduction by anecdote, either this anecdote:

> Imagine standing on the surface of Venus. The rocky ground is drier than the driest desert on Earth. You are surrounded by dim orange light. The air presses down on you. Of course, you can't really be standing on Venus—because if you were, your blood would be boiling in the 864-degree heat.

or the student's personal experience of seeing Venus.

It could also sound like this:

> I have always been fascinated by the planet Venus and how different it is from Earth. I hope to study astronomy so that I can learn more about Venus's atmosphere and surface. Maybe I'll even help discover whether or not there is any kind of life on Venus!

You could prompt the student by asking:

> *Have you ever viewed Venus? What did you see?*
> *Can you imagine standing on the surface of Venus? What do you see?*
> *Can you contrast what it would be like to stand on Venus and what it is like to stand on Earth?*
> *Would you like to study Venus more in the future?*

3. Conclusion by Question

> The heat and poisonous air of Venus makes it completely hostile to human life. Can you imagine standing on the surface of Venus? What kind of space suit would you need to protect you?

> OR

> Have you ever stood outside at night and looked at the horizon? Could you see Venus? It would be the brightest star on the horizon. Did it seem to dance as you watched it?

Note that a conclusion by question might need to include a few details.

If the student struggles, prompt him by saying:

> *Ask the reader to imagine standing on Venus.*
> *Ask the reader to imagine looking at Venus at night.*

Day Four: Copia

 Focus: Introduction to Metaphor

STEP ONE: Understanding metaphor

Student instructions for Step One:

> Last week, you worked on similes. This week, you'll advance to metaphors. And next week, you'll be doing an exercise that will draw on both sets of skills.
> Similes and metaphors are two related types of figurative language. Like a simile, a metaphor is a comparison between two things, but a metaphor does not use the words "like" or "as."

In *King Lear,* William Shakespeare wrote,

> Methought his eyes were two full moons.

This sentence contains a metaphor, because it directly compares eyes to full moons. If the sentence read, "Methought his eyes were <u>like</u> two full moons," it would be a simile, because it uses the word "like." The metaphor says, instead, that the eyes *were* moons.

You studied metaphors briefly in the first level of this course. Let's review: **A metaphor is a comparison that does not use "like" or "as." It simply describes one thing in terms of another.**

Of course, when you read this metaphor, you realize that eyes are not moons. Your brain inserts a "like" or "as" somewhere in there. But the metaphor itself is more powerful than a simile, because it is so much more direct.

Sometimes metaphors are found with linking verbs, as in this sentence. Other times metaphors can follow action verbs. Those metaphors are sometimes more difficult to identify.

Each of the following sentences describes rain by comparing it to another object. Practice identifying metaphors by circling each comparison that you see. (If you have trouble, ask your instructor.)

★

After circling the comparisons, underline each main verb twice. Write "l.v." above the linking verbs and "a.v." above the action verbs. Check your answers with your instructor before going on.

★

As you can see from the above sentences, metaphors don't always have to follow linking verbs.

Good metaphors give the reader a picture of the subject. Roe wanted to describe rain as soft and pleasant, so he compared it to a "gentle lullaby," whereas Bagnold wanted to describe rain as sharp and piercing so she compared it to "long knitting needles." Metaphors describe an unfamiliar subject by comparing it to a different familiar thing.

HOW TO HELP THE STUDENT WITH STEP ONE

The student should have marked the sentences as follows:

l.v.
The rain <u>was</u> a curtain of silver needles.
(Shirley Rousseau Murphy, *Unsettled*)

l.v.
The patter of rain <u>was</u> a gentle lullaby to Amy.
(Edward Payson Roe, *Nature's Serial Story*)

a.v.
The rain <u>came</u> down in white sheets, making a mighty roar.
(Victor Villaseñor, *Rain of Gold*)

a.v.
Thc rain came down in long knitting needles.
(Enid Bagnold, *National Velvet*)

l.v.
Where in the world was the rain? Those blinding cataracts she had endured day after day?
(Ann Patchett, *State of Wonder*)

STEP TWO: **Identifying metaphor**

Student instructions for Step Two:

> In the following sentences, underline the metaphor. Draw an arrow from the metaphor
> back to the subject—the word the metaphor describes by comparison. There may be more than
> one metaphor. If you're unsure, ask your instructor for help.

HOW TO HELP THE STUDENT WITH STEP TWO

The student's answers should be:

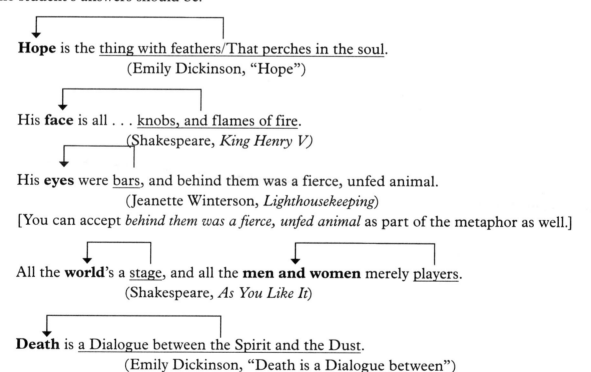

Hope is the thing with feathers/That perches in the soul.
(Emily Dickinson, "Hope")

His **face** is all . . . knobs, and flames of fire.
(Shakespeare, *King Henry V*)

His **eyes** were bars, and behind them was a fierce, unfed animal.
(Jeanette Winterson, *Lighthousekeeping*)
[You can accept *behind them was a fierce, unfed animal* as part of the metaphor as well.]

All the **world**'s a stage, and all the **men and women** merely players.
(Shakespeare, *As You Like It*)

Death is a Dialogue between the Spirit and the Dust.
(Emily Dickinson, "Death is a Dialogue between")

CHALLENGE ASSIGNMENT (Optional)

Student instructions for Challenge Assignment:

> Now you know the basics about metaphor. If you'd like to go further, complete the next assignment too.
> Read the passage below from *Lighthousekeeping* by Jeanette Winterson. The author and Pew are caretakers for the lighthouse. A sou'wester is a waterproof hat with a floppy brim.
>
> ★
>
> There are many descriptions of the darkness in this passage. Some use figurative language, and some do not. For example, look in the last paragraph. *The first night, Pew cooked the sausages in darkness. No, Pew cooked the sausages* with *darkness.* One of these sentences is a metaphor, and one is not. Can you tell which one is the metaphor?
>
>
>
> The second sentence is a metaphor, because it compares darkness to a food that you could eat with sausages. The first sentence is not a metaphor, because it simply tells you that it was dark when Pew was cooking the sausages.
> Read through the passage again, and underline each metaphor and simile. If it is a simile, circle the word *like* or *as*. If an entire sentence is a metaphor, you can underline the whole sentence.

HOW TO HELP THE STUDENT WITH THE CHALLENGE ASSIGNMENT

Because students at this level vary widely in their ability to think abstractly, the following should not be required from struggling students. Some of the sentences from it will be used in Step Three, however.

Use the following answers and explanations to prompt the student:

In this passage, the student must distinguish between mere descriptions, and figurative language that uses comparisons. Sometimes the entire sentence is a metaphor. For those, the student can underline the entire sentence or only the comparative words.

> Above me was the kitchen where Pew cooked sausages on an open cast-iron stove. Above the kitchen was the light itself, <u>a great glass eye with a Cyclops stare</u>.
> Our business was light, but we lived in darkness. The light had to be kept going, but there was no need to illuminate the rest. Darkness came with everything. It was standard. <u>My clothes were trimmed with dark</u>. When I put on a sou'wester, the brim left a dark shadow over my face. When I stood to bathe in the little galvanised cubicle Pew had rigged for me, <u>I soaped my body in darkness</u>. Put your hand in a drawer, and <u>it was darkness you felt first</u>, as you fumbled for a spoon. Go to the cupboards to find the tea caddy of Full Strength Samson, and the hole was <u>**(as)**</u> <u>black **as** the tea itself</u>.

Our business was light is not a metaphor because they run a lighthouse.

Standard is not a metaphor; it is only a description. If the student identifies it as a metaphor, ask her what the darkness is being compared to.

My clothes were trimmed with dark is a metaphor, because it compares dark to clothing, something that it is not. However, the sentence about the sou'wester is not a metaphor, because hat brims actually leave dark shadows on your face. It is just a description.

> The darkness had to be brushed away or parted before we could sit down. Darkness squatted on the chairs and hung (like) a curtain across the stairway. Sometimes it took on the shapes of the things we wanted: a pan, a bed, a book. Sometimes I saw my mother, dark and silent, falling towards me.

The first two sentences in this paragraph contain two metaphors and a simile. The darkness is being compared to a curtain and an animal. The third sentence is trickier. If the student underlines *a pan, a bed, a book*, that is acceptable. This sentence can be interpreted as a straightforward description of the pan, bed, and book in the dark (not a metaphor, not underlined), or as a comparison of the darkness to the pan, bed, and book (a metaphor, underlined).

The last sentence is also tricky. Again, it could be interpreted as a metaphor, in which the darkness is compared to the mother (underlined), or simply as if the author were imagining her mother in the dark (not underlined). If the student underlines the sentence, ask her if she thinks the darkness is being compared to the mother. It is important that the student understands that metaphors are comparisons.

> Darkness was a presence. I learned to see in it, I learned to see through it, and I learned to see the darkness of my own.

In fact, *the darkness of my own* may be a metaphor for the author's sadness, but the student is not expected to identify this at this level.

> Pew did not speak. I didn't know if he was kind or unkind, or what he intended to do with me. He had lived alone all his life.

> The first night, Pew cooked the sausages in darkness. No, Pew cooked the sausages *with* darkness. It was the kind of dark you can taste. That's what we ate: sausages and darkness.

STEP THREE: **Invent new metaphors**

Student instructions for Step Three:

> Now it's your turn to write metaphors.
> Look back at the metaphors you identified in Step One.
> On your own paper, rewrite these two metaphors about rain.

> The rain came down in [something sharp and stabbing].

> The patter of rain was [something quiet and soothing].

> Now, read (or reread) the following lines from the optional exercise. In this, the author describes the darkness as something you can feel, something that is a part of everyday life, such as soap or clothing.

It was the kind of dark you can taste.

Darkness squatted on the chairs and hung like a curtain across the stairway.

Our business was light, but we lived in darkness. The light had to be kept going, but there was no need to illuminate the rest. Darkness came with everything. It was standard. My clothes were trimmed with dark. When I put on a sou'wester, the brim left a dark shadow over my face. When I stood to bathe in the little galvanised cubicle Pew had rigged for me, I soaped my body in darkness. Put your hand in a drawer, and it was darkness you felt first, as you fumbled for a spoon. Go to the cupboards to find the tea caddy of Full Strength Samson, and the hole was as black as the tea itself.

On your own paper, rewrite the following metaphors for darkness.

It was the kind of dark you can [sense or experience].

Darkness [did something a house pet might do].

I [did some everyday task] with darkness.

Darkness was [something alive].

When you are finished, show your metaphors to your instructor.

HOW TO HELP THE STUDENT WITH STEP THREE

Answers on this exercise will vary widely.

A few suggested metaphors are offered below, but you should accept any metaphor that the student can defend.

Encourage the student to build these metaphors without reverting to *like* or *as* (which would turn the metaphors into similes).

The rain came down in [something sharp and stabbing].
knives, skewers, tent pegs, ice picks . . .

The patter of rain was [something quiet and soothing].
a whisper, a murmur, a bedtime story, a prayer

It was the kind of dark you can [sense or experience].
smell, feel, hear, hold . . .

Darkness [did something a house pet might do].
crept through the halls, purred in the corners, clawed at the carpet . . .

I [did some everyday task] with darkness.

    brushed my teeth, tied my shoes, washed the dishes, combed my hair . . .

Darkness was [something alive].

    my sister, a houseplant, my companion, my pet, the butler . . .

WEEK 7: EXPLANATION BY COMPARISON, PART II

Day One: Three-Level Outline

 Focus: Completing a three-level outline of a comparison in history

NOTE TO INSTRUCTOR: Next week's lesson will introduce the skill of topic selection. Try to plan a library visit early in the week so that the student can browse through resources. If a library visit is not possible, the student will need to browse online, using Google Books, Project Gutenberg, or another online database.

STEP ONE: Read (Student Responsibility)

Student instructions for Step One:

> Read the following excerpt from *Collapse: How Societies Choose to Fail or Succeed*, by Jared Diamond. Here, he is comparing the nations of Haiti and the Dominican Republic, both of which occupy the island of Hispaniola in the Caribbean.

★

STEP TWO: Find four areas of comparison

Student instructions for Step Two:

> Jared Diamond starts his comparison of Haiti and the Dominican Republic with an introductory question. As you can see, *introduction by question* is another method of beginning an essay. Unlike conclusion by question, which asks the reader to react, this kind of introduction asks a question that you will then answer in the essay.

★

> After this introduction, he compares and contrasts the two countries in *four different ways*. On your own paper, list the four areas of comparison.
> Here's a hint: The first comparison is found in paragraphs 2 and 3 combined. The second comparison is in the fourth paragraph, the third comparison in the fifth, and the fourth comparison is contained in the last paragraph.

If you have difficulty, ask your instructor for help. When you are finished, show your work to your instructor.

HOW TO HELP THE STUDENT WITH STEP TWO

The four areas of comparison are:

Paragraphs 2 & 3	**Environment OR Rain and soil OR The landscape**
Paragraph 4	**Colonial history OR History OR Spanish and French colonies**
Paragraph 5	**Population OR Population density OR Number of people**
Paragraph 6	**Trade OR Trade with other countries OR Economy**

Although the comparisons are fairly obvious, the student may have trouble coming up with the right vocabulary words (such as "environment" and "economy"). If necessary, prompt him using the following questions:

Paragraphs 2 & 3

"These paragraphs compare the amount of rainwater and the thickness of the soil. Complete this sentence: Rain, mountains, valleys, and soil are all part of the natural *what*?"

Paragraph 4

"Both Haiti and the Dominican Republic were both claimed by European nations. What name do we give to a place where settlers go from another country? The U.S. and Canada started out this way too."

Paragraph 5

"The number of people in any one country is called the country's . . . what?"

Paragraph 6

"This paragraph tells us that the Dominican Republic did something that the Haitians got no help with. What is that thing?"

STEP THREE: **Complete a three-level outline**

Student instructions for Step Three:

In this essay, Jared Diamond does a point-by-point comparison of Haiti and the Dominican Republic. Here's the overall structure:

I. Introduction
II. Environment
    A. Dominican
    B. Haitian
III. Colonial history
    A. Haiti
    B. Dominican Republic

        IV. Population
            A. Haiti
        V. Trade
            A. Haitians
            B. Dominicans

Notice that Diamond avoids monotony by changing the order in which he gives the comparisons: first the Dominican environment and then the Haitian; the reverse order when he discussions colonial history. When he talks about population, he only addresses Haitian population directly, just referring to the Dominican Republic in passing.

The actual comparisons are found in the details of the paragraphs, which belong in the third level of an outline.

Study the following outline carefully. Compare the details listed in the second main point (II. Environment) to the second and third paragraphs. Then, try to complete the outline by filling in the details for main points III, IV, and V.

When you are finished, show your work to your instructor. Ask for help if you need it.

HOW TO HELP THE STUDENT WITH STEP THREE

The student will not be asked to make three-level outlines independently until later in the course. However, this lesson serves as an introduction to three-level outlining, as well as giving the student a close look at how a best-selling author constructs a comparison/contrast.

The student's completed outline should resemble the following:

I. Introduction
II. Environment
    A. Dominican
        1. More rain
        2. Higher rates of plant growth
        3. Higher mountains
        4. Rivers flow eastward
        5. Broad valleys, plains, plateaus
        6. Much thicker soil
    B. Haitian
        1. Drier
        2. Barrier of high mountains
        3. Less flat land
        4. More limestone
        5. Thinner, less fertile soil
III. Colonial history
    A. Haiti
        1. Colony of France
        2. Most valuable French colony
        3. Slave-based plantation agriculture
        4. More slaves imported

    B. Dominican Republic
        1. Colony of Spain
        2. Neglected by Spain
        3. No slave-based agriculture
        4. Fewer slaves imported
IV. Population
    A. Haiti
        1. Seven times higher than Dominican Republic
        2. Still has larger population today
        3. Smaller area
        4. Double the Republic's density
V. Trade
    A. Haitians
        1. Owned their own land
        2. Fed themselves
        3. No help developing trade
    B. Dominicans
        1. Export economy and overseas trade

Outlining is not an exact science, and the student may depart slightly from this pattern (for example, under III.A., "colony of France" and "most valuable French colony" could be combined into a single detail). Accept reasonable combinations or additions.

If the student struggles, show him the completed outline. Allow him to read it, and then take it away and ask him to try again to complete his own outline while looking at the excerpt.

Day Two: Note-Taking

 Focus: Taking notes for a comparison of two people

As you can see from yesterday's excerpt, comparisons and contrasts can be used for many different subjects—in history as well as in science. You can compare and contrast countries (as Jared Diamond did in *Collapse*), people, rivers, castles, fortresses, villages, or mountains. You can compare and contrast events in history—battles, discoveries, or crises of various kinds. You can even write a comparison/contrast between something in its present form, and how it was at an earlier point in time ("In the sixteenth century, Cairo had 150,000 people living in it and covered only two square miles. Today, Cairo has 1.3 million residents and occupies over 62 square miles").

Now that the student has practiced writing a comparison in science and seen an example of a history comparison, she'll begin work on a historical comparison of her own.

STEP ONE: **Add to the Introduction chart (Student Responsibility)**

Student instructions for Step One:

Before you start work on your comparison, make an addition to your Introduction chart. On it, write:

4. Introduction by Question
Ask a question that you will answer in your essay.
Example: "Since X and Y are so similar in _____, why are they so different in _____?"

Jared Diamond used this method to introduce his comparison of Haiti and the Dominican Republic.

STEP TWO: **Taking notes**

Student instructions for Step Two:

You'll spend the rest of today taking notes for a comparison of two historical figures—the brothers Wilbur and Orville Wright.

Take your notes in a way that will help you organize your composition when you return to it tomorrow. Divide a sheet of paper into two columns. Write "Similarities" and "Differences" over the columns.

If a piece of information applies to both brothers, put it in the "Similarities" column. If it only applies to one, list the brother's name and then put the information after it.

Use the last name(s) of the author and the page numbers to identify your source. You can refer back to the full publication information in this book when you construct your footnotes and works cited page.

The first notes have been done for you. Read the following excerpt carefully *before* you examine the chart that follows. (In the excerpts, the numbers in parentheses are page numbers.)

Tara Dixon-Engel & Mike Jackson, *The Wright Brothers: First in Flight* (New York: Sterling Publishing Co., Inc., 2007), pp. 2–7.

(2) They weren't always two serious-looking men in starched collars and dark hats. In fact, as boys, Orville and Wilbur Wright were typical brothers, teasing each other, disagreeing on any and all topics, and dreaming of new experiences and distant horizons. They both enjoyed tinkering with mechanical devices and it was this early interest in "how things worked" that would lead them into the bicycle business and, later, fuel their dream of flight . . .

(6) As Wilbur and Orville aged, their personalities began to gel. In fact, they complemented each other in strengths and weaknesses. Orville was an outgoing student, and somewhat of a mischief-maker, while Wilbur had inherited his mother's shyness. Will's tendency toward daydreaming did not win him any points in school, but it was the sign of a sharp mind

that was always in motion, always exploring questions and seeking answers. Wilbur found a home as an athlete and gymnast, while Orville was a (7) budding businessman from the age of six onward. In addition to collecting scrap metal to sell to a junkyard, the young man built and sold kites to his neighborhood friends. Neither brother especially enjoyed schoolwork or, perhaps, being tied to a disciplined classroom setting. Both were curious and loved to learn, but they preferred to choose the subject themselves.

Now, compare the following notes to the excerpt:

Similarities	Differences
"typical brothers, teasing each other, dis- agreeing . . . dreaming of new experiences and distant horizons." (Dixon-Engel & Jackson, p. 2) "both enjoyed tinkering with mechanical devices" (D-E & J, p. 2) "Neither brother especially enjoyed school- work" but "Both were curious and loved to learn" (D-E & J, p. 7)	Orville: outgoing, mischief-maker (D-E & J, p. 6) Wilbur: shy, daydreaming, "sharp mind that was always in motion" (D-E & J, p. 6) Wilbur: "athlete and gymnast" (D-E & J, p. 6) Orville: "budding businessman from the age of six," collected scrap metal and sold kites (D-E & J, p. 7)

(Notice that I abbreviated the authors' names after the first note—as long as you can identify where the material came from, you don't need to write the same names over and over again.)

Now take your own notes on the first excerpt (or copy mine, if you want!). Continue on by taking notes on the following excerpts. When you are finished, show your work to your instructor.

HOW TO HELP THE STUDENT WITH STEP TWO

The student's finished chart should resemble the following:

Similarities	Differences
"typical brothers, teasing each other, disagreeing . . . dreaming of new experiences and distant horizons." (Dixon-Engel & Jackson, p. 2)	Orville: outgoing, mischief-maker (D-E & J, p. 6)
"both enjoyed tinkering with mechanical devices" (D-E & J, p. 2)	Wilbur: shy, daydreaming, "sharp mind that was always in motion" (D-E & J, p. 6)
"Neither brother especially enjoyed schoolwork" but "Both were curious and loved to learn" (D-E & J, p. 7)	Wilbur: "athlete and gymnast" (D-E & J, p. 6)
	Orville: "budding businessman from the age of six," collected scrap metal and sold kites (D-E & J, p. 7)
Didn't attend college or graduate from high school (Wright & Kelly, p. 3)	Wilbur four years older (Wright & Kelly, p. 3)
	Wilbur studied Greek and trigonometry (W & K, p. 3)
Interested in bicycle racing, started Wright Cycle Co. together (W & K, p. 3)	Orville studied Latin (W & K, p. 3)
	Wilbur was an intellectual who wanted to go into a profession (M & G, p. 27)
Joint bank account (W & K, p. 3)	Wilbur wanted to ponder philosophy (M & G, p. 27)
Remained bachelors (McPherson & Gardner, p. 26)	Orville: wanted to build horseless carriages (M & G, p. 28)
	Wilbur: "laughed at horseless carriages" (M & G, p. 28)
Enjoyed being uncles (M & G, p. 26)	Wilbur: suffered from "a period of extended illness and depression." (Crouch, p. 50)
Longed for "broader opportunities" (M & G, p. 27)	Wilbur wrote letters to his father (Crouch, p. 50)
	Orville wrote to his sister Katharine (Crouch, p. 50)
Started making bicycles in 1896 (M & G, p. 27)	Wilbur: "older, balder," wrote more letters, "more visionary" (Kirk, p. 19)
Wilbur says that they "lived together, played together, worked together . . . thought together" (Crouch, p. 49)	Wilbur depressed, three-year withdrawal after an injury (Kirk, p. 19)
	Wilbur died at 45 from typhoid (Kirk, p. 19)
Owned toys together, talked constantly (Crouch, p. 49)	Orville closer to Katharine (Kirk, p. 19)
	Orville shy but "more of a prankster" (Kirk, p. 19)
Fought with each other, decided to "present all their ideas as joint conceptions" (Kirk, p. 18)	Orville "dapper dresser," mustache, vain (Kirk, p. 19)

Day Three: Practicing the *Topos*

 Focus: Writing a comparison/contrast of two historical figures

STEP ONE: **Organize the similarities and differences**

Student instructions for Step One:

Today, you'll use the notes you took on Wilbur and Orville Wright, inventors of the first working airplane, to write a comparison and contrast between the two men.

Look back at the reference notes in your Composition Notebook. Reread the description of "Explanation by Comparison/Contrast." The first step is to decide which aspects of the subjects are the same, and which are different. You've already begun to organize your notes in similarities and differences. Now, you need to group those similarities and differences into larger categories. For example, the excerpts talk about Wilbur and Orville being bachelors, enjoying being uncles, and writing to their father and to their sister Katharine. You probably noted that Orville was closer to his sister, Wilbur to his father. All of those have to do with *family relationships*.

Go through the rest of your similarities and differences and try to organize them into three or four additional categories. If you have trouble, ask your instructor for help.

When you're finished, show the categories to your instructor. Don't go on to the next step until then!

HOW TO HELP THE STUDENT WITH STEP ONE

In addition to *family relationships,* the student might come up with three or four of the following categories:

education OR school
intellect
bicycles
personality
goals OR dreams OR aspirations
aptitudes OR talents
appearance OR personal qualities
habits
relationship with each other

If the student comes up with other categories, accept them as long as two or three notes can be organized under them. Your goal is to steer the student away from having multiple *narrow* categories with only one or two notes, towards wider categories. If necessary, suggest a few of the categories above and encourage the student to organize her notes into them.

STEP TWO: **Plan the composition**

Student instructions for Step Two:

Now that you've taken notes and organized them into larger categories, you've essentially already come up with an outline for your composition. For each category, discuss first the similarities between the two brothers, and then the differences. Here's an example of how you might organize the aspect/category "family relationships":

II. Family relationships
A. Similarities between the two brothers
"typical brothers, teasing each other, disagreeing" (Dixon-Engel &
Jackson, p. 2)
Remained bachelors (McPherson & Gardner, p. 26)
Enjoyed being uncles (M & G, p. 26)
B. Differences between them
1. Orville
Orville wrote to his sister Katharine (Crouch, p. 50)
Orville closer to Katharine (Kirk, p. 19)
2. Wilbur
Wilbur wrote letters to his father (Crouch, p. 50)

Now choose four categories that you'll write about in your composition. Give each category a Roman numeral. Organize the appropriate notes under each category, following the pattern above. (You can use my outline above if you choose to write about family relationships!)
If one category contains *only* similarities or *only* differences, that's fine.

HOW TO HELP THE STUDENT WITH STEP TWO

For each category, the student should end up a set of similarities and a set of differences.

NOTE TO INSTRUCTOR: The way in which the student organizes the differences is modeled on Jared Diamond's essay. He followed this pattern:

II. Environment *(aspect/category)*
A. Dominican *(first subject)*
(details)
B. Haitian *(second subject)*
(details)
III. Colonial history *(aspect/category)*
A. Haiti *(second subject)*
(details)
B. Dominican Republic
(details)
and so on.
But notice that Jared Diamond's essay is almost entirely about *differences* between the two countries. Since there are so many similarities between the Wrights, the student needs to also place these on the outline.

You may choose to discuss this with the student if you think it will be useful.

The students' categories/organization might resemble the following:

II. Education
    A. Similarities
        "Neither brother especially enjoyed schoolwork" but "Both were curious
            and loved to learn" (D-E & J, p. 7)
        Didn't attend college or graduate from high school (Wright & Kelly, p. 3)

    B. Differences
        1. Orville
            Orville studied Latin (W & K, p. 3)
        2. Wilbur
            Wilbur studied Greek and trigonometry (W & K, p. 3)

III. Personality
    A. Similarities
        "dreaming of new experiences and distant horizons" (Dixon-Engel &
            Jackson, p. 2)
        Wilbur says that they "lived together, played together, worked
            together . . . thought together" (Crouch, p. 49)
        Owned toys together, talked constantly (Crouch, p. 50)
    B. Differences
        1. Orville
            Orville: outgoing, mischief-maker (D-E & J, p. 6)
            Orville shy but "more of a prankster" (Kirk, p. 19)
            Orville "dapper dresser," mustache, vain (Kirk, p. 19)
        2. Wilbur
            Wilbur: shy, daydreaming, "sharp mind that was always in
              motion" (D-E & J, p. 6)
            Wilbur: suffered from "a period of extended illness and
              depression." (Crouch, p. 50)
            "more visionary" (Kirk, p. 19)
            Wilbur depressed, three-year withdrawal after an injury (Kirk, p. 19)

IV. Bicycles
    A. Similarities
        Interested in bicycle racing, started Wright Cycle Co. together (W & K, p. 3)
        Started making bicycles in 1896 (M & G, p. 27)

V. Goals
    A. Similarities
        Longed for "broader opportunities" (M & G, p. 27)
        "dreaming of new experiences and distant horizons" (Dixon-Engel &
            Jackson, p. 2)
        Fought with each other, decided to "present all their ideas as joint
            conceptions" (Kirk, p. 18)
    B. Differences
        1. Orville
            Orville: "budding businessman from the age of six," collected scrap
                metal and sold kites (D-E & J, p. 7)
            Orville: wanted to build horseless carriages (M & G, p. 28)
        2. Wilbur
            Wilbur: "laughed at horseless carriages" (M & G, p. 28)

STEP THREE: **Write the body of the composition**

Student instructions for Step Three:

> Using your outline as a guide, write one or two paragraphs to describe each aspect. Depending on how much information you have, you can either write a paragraph about similarities and then a second about differences, or write a paragraph combining the two.
>
> The facts about Orville and Wilbur Wright are found in many biographies. If you use your own words, you don't need to footnote. But be sure to use quotation marks and to insert a footnote if you use the exact words from *any* of the sources!
>
> The paragraph does not need to say specifically, "They were the same in . . . " or "They were different because . . . " Instead, you can simply write about the similarities and then the differences. For example a paragraph based on the outline above might sound like this:

> > As children, Wilbur and Orville Wright teased each other and argued with each other. Neither man ever got married, and both of them enjoyed being uncles. But Orville was closest to his sister Katharine and wrote her many letters. Wilbur was closer to his father than to his sister.

> (If you need to use this paragraph to get you started, go ahead. But try to change at least a few of the words to make it more your own.)
>
> Instead of working towards a minimum number of words, try to produce a minimum of six paragraphs.
>
> When you're finished, show your work to your instructor.

HOW TO HELP THE STUDENT WITH STEP THREE

Since the student will not proofread until tomorrow, do not check his work for spelling, grammar, or accuracy. Instead, simply check to see that the student has written about four aspects, has followed the outline, and has produced at least six paragraphs (they can be short paragraphs, but each should have at least two complete sentences).

If the student struggles, you may show him one of the sample paragraphs for an aspect he is *not* writing about.

The student's paragraphs might resemble the following:

As children, Wilbur and Orville Wright teased each other and argued with each other. Neither man ever got married, and both of them enjoyed being uncles. But Orville was closest to his sister Katharine and wrote her many letters. Wilbur was closer to his father than to his sister.

Wilber and Orville were very similar students. Neither one of them "enjoyed schoolwork,"[1] and neither one graduated from high school—or attended college. But they had different specialties. Orville took Latin; Wilbur took trigonometry and Greek.

---

[1] Tara Dixon-Engel & Mike Jackson, *The Wright Brothers: First in Flight* (Sterling Publishing Co., 2007), p. 6.

In many ways, the brothers were alike in personality. They were daydreamers, always hoping for "new experiences" and looking towards "distant horizons."[1] They did most things together—playing, working, talking, and thinking. They even owned the same toys when they were children.

However, Wilbur was much shyer than his brother. He was smart, but after a long sickness he became depressed and withdrawn. Orville, on the other hand, was outgoing. He liked to play tricks on people, and he was a little bit vain about his appearance.

---

[1] Tara Dixon-Engel & Mike Jackson, *The Wright Brothers: First in Flight* (Sterling Publishing Co., 2007), p. 2.

[Note that the sources seem to disagree, one of them saying that Orville was shy and the other that he was outgoing. If the student points this out, ask which one seems more likely. Given that Orville was a prankster and that Wilbur was clearly very shy, I would choose to describe Orville as the outgoing one, Wilbur as the retiring brother.]

The brothers worked together building bicycles. Both of them were interested in bicycle racing, and in 1896 they started the Wright Cycle Company together and began manufacturing bicycles.

[Note that this section contains only similarities and no differences]

The brothers were daydreamers. They had the same goals—they wanted to find "broader opportunities"[1] for themselves. And even though they fought with each other, they chose to make all of their ideas "joint conceptions."[2]

But sometimes they differed on how to get to their goals. Orville, who was good at business even when he was a child, wanted them to build cars—"horseless carriages."[3] Wilbur thought this was ridiculous.

---

[1] Stephanie Sammartino McPherson & Joseph Sammartino Gardner, *Wilbur and Orville Wright: Taking Flight* (Lerner Publishing Group, 2004), p. 27.

[2] Stephen Kirk, *First in Flight: The Wright Brothers in North Carolina* (R. R. Donnelly & Sons, 2003), p. 18.

[3] McPherson & Gardner. p. 28.

Day Four: Practicing the Topos, Part II

 Focus: Completing a comparison/contrast of two historical figures

Today, the student will finish the comparison and contrast of Wilbur and Orville Wright by writing an introduction and a conclusion.

STEP ONE: **Write an introduction**

Student instructions for Step One:

> Look back at the Introductions page in the Reference section of your Composition Notebook. Decide which kind of introduction you will use.
>
> You may write a one-sentence introduction rather than writing a separate paragraph—but if you do, remember that your conclusion (see Step Two) *must* be a separate paragraph of two sentences or more.
>
> You may need to look back over the sources listed on Day Two. Some of the information there will be helpful if you decide to write an introduction by history or an introduction by anecdote—and might not have made it onto your chart of similarities and differences.
>
> If you need help, ask your instructor.

HOW TO HELP THE STUDENT WITH STEP ONE

The student's completed introduction might resemble one of the following. Note that the student does not need to show you the introduction before incorporating it into the composition. But if he struggles, you may wish to show him one or more of the sample answers.

1. Introduction by Summary

Wilbur and Orville Wright, inventors of the first working airplane, had very similar experiences in school and in relationships. But their personalities were very different.

2. Introduction by History

At age 45, Wilbur Wright died of typhoid. His death brought an end to his partnership with his brother Orville—a partnership that had lasted their entire lives.

3. Introduction by Anecdote

In the city of Dayton, three men are arguing about the horseless carriage. One of them, Cordy Ruse, has just bought the brand-new invention. The other two, brothers Wilbur and Orville Wright, are disagreeing. "We should build those," the older brother, Orville, tells his younger sibling. "If we don't, we might lose our bicycle business!" But Wilbur just laughs. "That's way too hard," he objects. "We might as well just try to build a flying machine!"

[This introduction would need footnoting, since it draws on the actual dialogue in McPherson and Gardner's biography.]

4. Introduction by Question

Wilbur and Orville Wright kept a joint bank account, took joint credit for all their ideas, and ran a joint business. But were they really alike?

STEP TWO: **Write a conclusion**

Student instructions for Step Two:

> Look back at the Conclusions page in the Reference section of your Composition Notebook. Decide which kind of conclusion you will write. If you wrote a one-sentence introduction, your conclusion should be a separate paragraph.
> Look back at the sources if necessary.
> If you need help, ask your instructor.

HOW TO HELP THE STUDENT WITH STEP TWO

The student's completed introduction might resemble one of the following. He does not need to show you the conclusion before incorporating it into the composition. If he struggles, you may wish to show him one or more of the sample answers.

1. Conclusion by Summary

Even though the Wright brothers were very different in personality, they chose to remain close together.

OR

Despite the close similarities in their relationships, their education, and their goals, Wilbur and Orville were clearly very different people. Wilbur's illness, his depression, and his shyness set him apart from his more extroverted, easygoing brother.

2. Conclusion by Personal Reaction

I visited Kitty Hawk on vacation last year and had the opportunity to see the Wright Museum. I was amazed by the accomplishments that these two brothers, despite their disagreements, managed to achieve together.

3. Conclusion by Question

Despite their differences, Orville and Wilbur decided to remain close. If they had allowed themselves to drift apart, would we be able to take a plane across the world today?

STEP THREE: Assemble the Works Cited page

Student instructions for Step Three:

> If your composition contains any footnotes, put the sources used on a Works Cited page, using the correct format.

HOW TO HELP THE STUDENT WITH STEP THREE

The correct format for the works cited page (either ampersands or the word "and" can be used):

Crouch, Tom D. *The Bishop's Boys: A Life of Wilbur and Orville Wright.* New York: W.W. Norton, 1989.

Dixon-Engel, Tara & Mike Jackson. *The Wright Brothers: First in Flight.* New York: Sterling Publishing, 2007.

Kirk, Stephen. *First in Flight: The Wright Brothers in North Carolina.* Chicago: R.R. Donnelley & Sons, 2003.

McPherson, Stephanie Sammartino & Joseph Sammartino Gardner. *Wilbur & Orville Wright: Taking Flight*. Minneapolis: Lerner Publishing Group, 2004.

Wright, Orville & Fred C. Kelly, *How We Invented the Airplane: An Illustrated History*. New York: David McKay, 1953.

STEP FOUR: **Proofread**

Student instructions for Step Four:

Add the introduction, conclusion, and Works Cited page to the body of your essay.
Repeat the basic steps of proofreading:

1) Read your composition out loud. Listen for awkward or unclear sections. Rewrite them so that they flow more naturally.
2) Check spelling by looking, individually, at each word that might be a problem.
3) Check your commas.

Today, add one additional step:

4) As you read, listen for repeated nouns, verbs, and modifiers. If you find yourself using the same noun or verb more than twice, use your thesaurus to find an alternative. If you use a modifier (adverb, adjective, or prepositional phrase acting as an adjective or adverb) more than once, find another word. (Phrases like "In the same way" or "In contrast" tend to be overused in comparisons!)

When you're finished, show your work to your instructor.

HOW TO HELP THE STUDENT WITH STEP FOUR

Evaluate the essay using the following rubric.

Week 7 Rubric
Explanation By Comparison/Contrast In History

Organization:

1 The entire composition should be at least seven paragraphs in length.
2 At least four aspects/categories of the brothers should be discussed.
3 For each aspect discussed, the student should first cover similarities, and then should explain differences, first for one brother and then the other. (Note that the bicycle category has *only* similarities).
4 The composition should contain both an introduction and a conclusion. At least one of these must be a separate paragraph of two sentences or more.
5 The conclusion and introduction should not *both* be summaries.
6 All direct quotes should be footnoted.
7 All sources mentioned in footnotes should be placed on a Works Cited page.

Mechanics:

1 Each sentence should make sense on its own when read aloud.
2 There should be no sentence fragments or run-on sentences.
3 All words should be spelled correctly.
4 The first line of each paragraph should be properly indented.
5 Verb tense should be consistent throughout.
6 No noun or verb should be used more than twice (with the exception of state-of-being verbs, linking verbs, and the verb "said").
7 No modifier or prepositional phrase acting as a modifier should be used more than once.

Week 8: Finding a Topic

This week, the student will begin to research her own project on a topic that she chooses herself.

At the end of *Writing With Skill: Level One,* the student was given her first independent project. She was given a list of the seven *topoi* studied last year along with the job of combining at least two of them into a composition.

That was an elementary exercise in choosing a topic. Over the next two weeks, the student will complete a similar (but shorter) assignment. But in this assignment, she will be introduced to a more advanced skill: choosing a subject area and then allowing the subject area to determine the appropriate *topos.*

This week's assignment focuses on finding a topic. Next week, the student will complete note-taking and write the composition.

The student should work independently as much as possible, but she should show her work at the end of Day One and Day Two.

The second half of this week should be dedicated to a library visit and reading.

Day One: Brainstorming in History

 Focus: Finding a topic in history

NOTE TO INSTRUCTOR: The student's brainstorming instructions involve using an Internet search engine. Be sure that the appropriate safeguards and parental controls are in place, and consider having the student do the assignment in a place where you are able to glance at the screen to make sure that she stays on track.

The student may need to use a history atlas or encyclopedia to generate ideas.

Student instructions for Day One:

> Instead of beginning with particular *topoi,* you'll start by brainstorming topics that might interest you in history and in science.
> You'll need five blank sheets of paper for today's work.

STEP ONE: **Use the four Ws to find broad subjects**

Turn your first piece of paper sideways. Along the top, write the words WHEN, WHERE, WHAT, and WHO, like this:

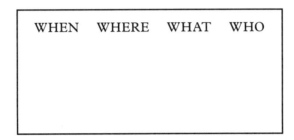

Now you're ready to begin brainstorming.

Under the heading WHEN, write at least three words or phrases describing a period in time: a century, a decade, a year, or a period (like "The Roaring Twenties").

Under the heading WHERE, write at least three geographical designations: countries, cities, rivers, mountains, etc. (such as "Mount Everest").

Under the heading WHAT, write down at least four events or things from history: inventions, discoveries, explorations, wars, languages, customs, etc. ("The Civil War" or "smallpox")

Under the heading WHO, write down at least three names of famous people from history—anyone from Julius Caesar to Margaret Thatcher.

If necessary, flip through the index of a history encyclopedia or atlas for ideas.

STEP TWO: **Use the other 3 Ws to narrow a subject**

Look back over your paper. Circle one name or phrase in each column that seems potentially the most interesting to you.

What did you circle in the "When" column? Write it in the center of your second blank sheet of paper. Now ask yourself: Where? What? Who? And try to come up with at least two answers for each question. Three or four answers are much better.

Here's an example.

Imagine that you chose "The Roaring Twenties." Now ask yourself: Where did the Roaring Twenties happen?

You probably won't know the answer to that. So to help yourself brainstorm, use the Internet. Enter the terms "Roaring Twenties" and "where" into a search engine such as Google, Bing, or Yahoo.

When I do this, the first link that comes up is the "Roaring Twenties" entry on Wikipedia. You might remember this paragraph from the first level of *Writing With Skill*:

> You may *not* use Wikipedia. Wikipedia is not professionally edited or fact-checked. Anyone can post anything on Wikipedia. Usually, other users will identify and remove mistakes—but if you happen to use Wikipedia five minutes after someone has posted bad information (which people sometimes do just for fun), you won't realize that you're writing down false facts.[11]

---

11. Susan Wise Bauer, *Writing With Skill, Level One Student Text* (Well-Trained Mind Press, 2012), p. 478.

That's still true! But you're not doing research right now—you're just trying to come up with as many connected ideas and bits of information as possible. If there's a mistake in the information, you'll discover it as soon as you start taking notes. So go ahead and use Wikipedia if your search engine turns it up.

When I click on the Wikipedia link, I discover that the Roaring Twenties was centered at large cities: Chicago, New Orleans, Los Angeles, New York, Philadelphia, Paris, and London. That certainly gives me plenty of answers to the question "where."

Write your newly-discovered words or phrases around the word at the center of your brainstorming paper, like this

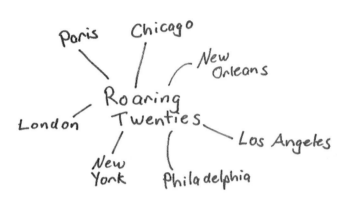

Now do the same for "what" and "who." Remember to put quotes around words or phrases that belong together. Your answers to "what" will probably be phrases or even short sentences; when I search for "Roaring Twenties" and "what," I come up with "decade following World War I", "time of unprecedented prosperity," "jazz," and "speakeasies." For "who," I find "flappers," "Sinclair Lewis," "Edith Wharton," and "suffragettes." (Notice that "who" can be answered with either proper names or categories of people.)

If possible, use a different color of pencil or pen for the "what" answers, and a third color for the "who" answers.

Here's how my brainstorming map looks now. You can't see the colors, but I used a regular pencil for "where," a purple pencil for "what," and a green pencil for "who."

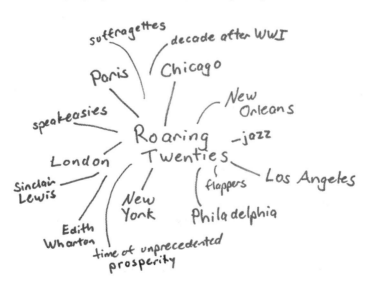

You should now have a completed brainstorming map for your chosen entry in the "When" column.

STEP THREE: **Complete the brainstorming maps**

Now finish your remaining three maps. For your chosen entry in the "where" column, ask, "When? What? Who?" For the "what" entry, ask "When? Where? Who?" And you can figure out on your own what to ask for the "who" entry!

Remember to use different colored pens or pencils for the answers to each of the "W" questions.

STEP FOUR: **Finish defining the subject area**

Now you'll take the final step in defining your subject.

Choose your favorite brainstorming map. Pick one answer each from *two* of the categories (this will be easier if you've used different colors) and put them together with your central subject.

For example: I asked "Who? What? Where" about the Roaring Twenties. So I need to pick a "who" answer and a "where" answer and put them together with "Roaring Twenties":

Suffragettes in Paris during the Roaring Twenties

or

Flappers in Philadelphia during the Roaring Twenties

I could also pick one of the "what" answers to go with a "where" answer:

Jazz in New Orleans during the Roaring Twenties
Unprecedented prosperity in Chicago during the Roaring Twenties

or a "who" and a "what":

Suffragettes and speakeasies during the Roaring Twenties

Using your own map, try to come up with three different phrases or clauses defining subject areas. Jot them down on the edges of your map.

You may need to use your search engine to look up a little more information. For example, if I came up with the subject area definition "Edith Wharton in Paris during the Roaring Twenties," I would want to find out whether Edith Wharton had ever *been* in Paris. If I enter "Edith Wharton," "Paris," and "Roaring Twenties" into Google.com, I find out that Edith Wharton actually received an award in Paris for work that she did there during World War I. So "Edith Wharton in Paris during the Roaring Twenties" is a perfectly good subject. (I don't know what her work was or what the award was called, but that's OK; I'm not doing research yet.)

When you are finished, show your work to your instructor.

HOW TO HELP THE STUDENT WITH DAY ONE

Check to make sure that the student has four completed brainstorming maps. Each one of the maps should contain a central topic. The words and phrases around the central topic should be written in three different colors of pen or pencil.

Day Two: Brainstorming in Science

 Focus: Finding a topic in science

The student will need five more sheets of paper for today's work. She may also find it useful to glance through the index of a science reference work such as an atlas, general textbook, or visual guide.

Student instructions for Day Two:

STEP ONE: Use the four Ws to find broad subjects

Turn your first piece of paper sideways. Along the top, write the words WHAT, WHERE, WHO, and WHY. "When" is a good question for history, but since science is about *explanation,* "why" is a more useful question for you to ask.

Under the heading WHAT, write down at least six names or phrases describing scientific phenomena, natural objects, or occurrences. As you do so, think about the major fields of scientific research: biology, chemistry, physics, astronomy, and geology. If you have trouble, browse through the index of a science encyclopedia or glance through the table of contents of a science survey textbook. Examples might include: frogs, the atom, the speed of light, supernovas, and continental drift.

Under the heading WHERE, write at least three physical places, such as outer space, the ocean (deep or shallow?), the Sahara desert, or just "deserts." (You can use one of mine, but you have to come up with the other two on your own.)

Under the heading WHO, write down at least four names of famous scientists.

Under the heading WHY, write down the names of at least two scientific theories. (Here's an example: Johannes Kepler's "Laws of Planetary Motion.") If you can't think of any scientific theories, enter "scientific theory" and "example" into your Internet search engine and skim through the results.

STEP TWO: Use the other three Ws to narrow a subject

Look back over your paper. As you did yesterday, circle one name or phrase in each column that seems potentially the most interesting to you.

What did you circle in the "What" column? Write it in the center of your second blank sheet of paper. Now ask yourself: Where? Who? Why? Try to come up with at least two answers for each question; three or four answers is much better. Use different colored pens or pencils to write the answers in a brainstorming map around your central term.

Here's how I would do this.

In my "What" column, I circled "space dust." (I've always thought "space dust" was a fascinating phrase.) I entered "space dust" and "where" into my Internet search engine, and after that entered "space dust" and "who" and "space dust" and "why." Here's what my completed map looks like. The single-underlined words are in answer to "where" (places space dust is found), the double-underlined words are in answer to "who" (scientists who have made discoveries about space dust), and the plain words are in answer to "why" (observations and theories about space dust).

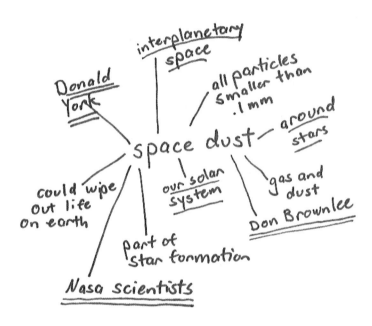

STEP THREE: Complete the brainstorming maps

Now create brainstorming maps for your favorite entries under the Where, Who, and Why headings. When you're finished, you should have four finished maps.

STEP FOUR: Finish defining the subject area

Choose your favorite brainstorming map. Using the same method as yesterday, come up with three different phrases, sentence fragments, or sentences, defining subject areas that you might do further research in. Jot them on the edge of your map.

Using the map above, I chose the "why" answer "could wipe out life on earth" and the "where" answer "interplanetary space" to come up with:

Space dust is in interplanetary space and could wipe out life on earth.

Using a "who" and "where" answer, I googled "Donald York," "space dust," and "around stars" to make sure that Donald York's experiments had something to do with dust around stars. They do, so I came up with

Donald York and space dust around stars

Other subject area definitions might be:

NASA scientists and space dust in our solar system
Space dust, star formation, and our solar system

When you are finished, show your work to your instructor.

HOW TO HELP THE STUDENT WITH DAY TWO

Check to make sure that the student has four completed brainstorming maps. Each one of the maps should contain a central topic. The words and phrases around the central topic should be written in three different colors of pen or pencil.

Days Three and Four: Pre-Reading

 Focus: Initial research

The student should spend the next couple of days doing general reading about one of your subject areas. Plan a library visit.

If a library visit is impossible, the student can make use of the e-texts at Google Books (books.google.com). Supervise the student if she uses this website, since some of the books contain adult content.

She should search for the keywords, as suggested below, but using books.google.com instead of the library website. After the search results come up, click on "Preview Available" on the left-hand side of the page. This will allow the student to then click on each individual book and read a certain amount of text.

Each step has a suggested amount of time for you to spend on it. This is only a very general guideline; you may decide to change it.

Student instructions for Days Three and Four

You should have two completed brainstorming maps with tentative subject areas written on them, one in history and one in science. Choose one.

You haven't yet picked a *topos*, so you don't know whether you'll be writing a chronological narration, a biographical sketch, a comparison and contrast, or some other form. You'll make this decision *after* you finish your general reading. The reading will give you an idea of what sorts of information are available about your subject; that will help you choose the appropriate *topoi*.

STEP ONE: **Prepare for the library visit**   **30–60 minutes**

Your goal is to end up with five sources that tell you something helpful about your general subject area.

With your instructor, plan a library visit. Before the visit, prepare by making an initial list of titles to look for by using your local library's online catalog. (Most local libraries have online catalogs now, but if yours doesn't, you'll have to perform this step at the library.)

Visit the library's website and look for the link "Catalog" or "Library Catalog." Once you're on the catalog page, you should see a dropdown menu that gives you an option of searching title keywords, subject area keywords, author names, etc. Generally, start off by searching for "title keyword." If that doesn't bring you any results, search for "subject keyword" instead.

Start by typing in the word or phrase at the center of your brainstorming map. For me, that would be "Roaring Twenties" (from the map I did for Day One). When I search by "title keyword," I instantly see at least six nonfiction books, shelved in the young adult section, about different aspects of the Roaring Twenties. That's a good sign—it means there are plenty of resources available.

Make a quick list of the titles and call numbers that you might want to investigate. Then, choose one of the subject area definitions that you jotted down on your map. Do a similar search for the keywords in the definition.

For example, I jotted down "Suffragettes and speakeasies during the Roaring Twenties." A title keyword search for "Suffragettes" only brings up one book, *33 Things Every Girl Should Know About Women's History: From Suffragettes to Skirt Lengths to the ERA*. But the catalog page for that book also contains a link to the subject area "Women's rights—History—Juvenile literature." When I click on the link, I find nine more books. So I've learned that books about suffragettes are more likely to be under the heading "Women's rights—History."

When I search for "speakeasies," the same thing happens. I only find one title. But there is a link on the page to the subject heading "Prohibition—United States—History," which leads me to more books.

Searching for these titles before going to the library will save you frustration. If you're unable to find more than one or two books, you should choose another subject area definition and try using its keywords for your search. And if *none* of your subject area definitions are giving you good keywords for searching, you might consider choosing another brainstorming map.

STEP TWO: **Collect resources**   **1–3 hours**

Now it's time for your library visit. Be sure to take your brainstorming map with you!

You should already have a preliminary list of titles to locate. Ask the reference librarian for help finding the books, if necessary. Glance on either side of the titles to see whether nearby books might also have something interesting to say about your subject area.

Pull at least 10–12 books off the shelf and take them to a place where you can examine them more closely. Using the index, make sure that at least one of the keywords in your subject area appears in the book!

For example, if I am researching "Suffragettes and speakeasies during the Roaring Twenties" and I pull a book called *The Roaring Twenties* off the shelf, I want to make sure that the word "suffrage" or the word "speakeasies" appears in the index. If I can't find anything about speakeasies *or* suffrage in any of the books about the Roaring Twenties, I might need to pick another subject area from my brainstorming map.

Try to bring home at least six books that relate to your subject. (You'll only need five sources, but one will probably turn out to be unhelpful.)

STEP THREE: **Do initial reading**   **At least 3 hours**

Your last task this week is simply to read.

Read the chapters or sections of each book that relate to your topic. Don't take notes yet—you don't know what information you'll need. But be sure to use bookmarks (torn slips of notebook paper are fine) or Post-It Notes to mark pages where you find interesting information.

You'll return to these pages next week as you settle on a final form for your composition.

HOW TO HELP THE STUDENT WITH DAYS THREE AND FOUR

Do your best to get the student to the library.

Make sure that the student returns with at least six useful books.

Provide the student with Post-It Notes, if possible, so that she can mark useful pages.

Make sure that the student spends at least three hours reading on her chosen topic.

Check each book as she finishes to make sure that she is marking pages with bookmarks or Post-It Notes. Next week's work will be much simpler if she is able to return directly to the useful pages in her resources.

WEEK 9: COMPLETING THE COMPOSITION

Last week, the student worked on the new skill of finding, defining, and reading about a subject area for a composition. This week, he'll decide which *topoi* best fit the subject, take notes, and complete his composition.

Encourage the student to work as independently as possible this week. However, he may need help reading the instructions carefully. If he seems confused, ask him to read the instructions out loud. If he's still puzzled, give any help needed.

You will want to check at the end of each day to make sure that the student has completed the assignment. However, do not criticize or evaluate until the end of Day Four.

As always, suggested word lengths are just that—suggestions. Feel free to tailor the requirements to your own student's style and maturity level.

Depending on the student's reading speed and the complexity of the chosen topic, you may decide to take more than four days to finish this assignment.

Day One: Choosing the Right Topos

 Focus: Matching form to content

Student instructions for Day One:

STEP ONE: Review the *topoi*

Before you can begin taking notes, you'll need to make a tentative decision about the form of your composition. Your composition will need to be at least 500 words in length (that includes your introduction and conclusion, but not your Works Cited page). It can be just one *topos,* or it can combine two or three.

Last year, you learned the following forms:

> *Chronological narrative of a past event*
> *Chronological narrative of a scientific discovery*
> *Description of a place*
> *Scientific description*
> *Description of a person*

Biographical sketch
Sequence: Natural process

So far this year, you've added:

Sequence: History
Explanation by comparison/contrast

Turn to the Reference section of your Composition Notebook and review the details of each form by reading *carefully*. Then, think back through your preliminary reading. Which *topoi* seem to fit the information best?

Here are some questions to ask yourself:

Does the reading tell you about a series of events? If so, you may want to write a chronological narrative.

Does the reading contain lots of visual details? If so, you may want to write a description—of a place, person, or scientific phenomenon.

Does the reading give you information about the character and life of a particular person? If so, you may want to write a biographical sketch—either alone, or combined with a chronological narrative of some important part of the person's life.

Does the reading explain a series of events that happened, or happens, more than once? If so, you may need to write a sequence.

Does the reading draw comparisons? If so, you may be looking at a comparison/contrast. But remember that comparison/contrast is a very flexible form. By doing a little additional research, you can turn almost any set of details into a comparison and contrast. You can compare a chronological narrative (say, the events leading up to and during the Battle of Hastings) to another chronological narrative (by researching another historic battle, you could describe how the two battles are the same and how they are different). You can compare one person to another, one series of events to another, or one description to another.

STEP TWO: **Make a preliminary plan**

Now that you've made a tentative decision about the form of your composition, make a preliminary plan. Decide what sorts of details you'll need to fill out your composition, so that you don't take lots of unnecessary notes.

For your chosen *topoi*, jot down the answers to the questions below on a piece of a paper. (Don't just answer the questions in your head!) If necessary, go back to the lessons listed to review the forms of each *topos*.

Chronological narrative of a past event
WWS1, Week 4, Days 3–4; Week 6, Days 3–4
   What is the theme of the narrative—its focus?
   What are its beginning and ending points?
   Will you use dialogue? Who will speak?

Chronological narrative of a scientific discovery
WWS1, Week 5, Days 3–4; Week 7, Days 3–4
   Will you need a background paragraph explaining the circumstances before the
      discovery?
   Can you quote from the scientist's own words?

Description of a place
WWS1, Week 8, Days 3–4; Week 9, Days 3–4; Week 10, Days 3–4
> What purpose will this description fulfill?
> What is your point of view?
> What metaphors or similes will make the description more vivid?

Scientific description
WWS1, Week 12, Days 3–4; Week 13, Days 3–4; Week 14, Days 3–4
> What are the parts of the object or phenomenon?
> What is your point of view? Will you use more than one?
> What figurative language can make the description more visual?

Description of a person
WWS1, Week 16, Days 2–3; Week 17, Days 2–3; Week 18, Days 2–3
> What aspects will be included?
> Will you slant the description in a positive or negative direction?
> Will you use an overall metaphor to give clues about the person's character?

Biographical sketch
WWS1, Week 19, Days 2–3; Week 20, Days 2–3
> What will the focus be—life events, or the subject's accomplishments/work?
> > If life events, which ones will be included?
> > If accomplishments/work, will they be listed chronologically or by topic?
> What aspects from the Description of a Person chart should be included?

Sequence: natural process
WWS1, Week 21, Days 2–3; Week 22, Days 2–3
> What other elements will you include?
> > Introduction/summary?
> > Scientific background?
> > Repetition of the process?

Sequence: History
WWS2, Week 2, Days 2–3; Week 4, Days 1–3
> What other elements will you include?
> > Introductory paragraph?
> > Historical development?
> > Results/consequences?

Explanation by comparison/contrast
WWS2, Week 5, Days 2–3; Week 7, Days 1, 3–4
> Will point-by-point or subject-by-subject comparison work better?
> Can you use both?
> Will you need to do additional research to complete your comparison?

STEP THREE: **Begin taking notes**

Finish today's work by taking notes on one of your sources. If you need to review the proper format, review Week 3, Day 3.

Choose the source that you think will be the most helpful. The number of notes that you will take will vary. However, for a short composition you should try never to take more than 20 notes from any individual source.

After you've finished taking your notes, you should have some idea of how well the details in your source will fit into your chosen *topos*. If necessary, go back to the list of *topoi* and adjust your plan. (You may realize, for example, that what you thought were events in a sequence actually fit better into a chronological narrative—or that the details you intended to use in a place description are actually better suited to a comparison or contrast.)

When you're finished, tell your instructor which *topos* you've chosen, and show your notes.

HOW TO HELP THE STUDENT WITH DAY ONE

Doing basic research first and then finding a *topos* that fits the material is a new skill. Don't let the student get hung up on picking the *topos* that's *exactly right*. If necessary, explain that this can be a back-and-forth process: choose a tentative *topos*, start taking notes, and then (if you realize you're not finding the right information), go back and pick another *topos*. The goal is to help the student avoid taking unnecessary notes by giving him an idea of what *sorts* of information he needs to collect.

If necessary, go back to the previous lessons listed and review the forms taught.

At the end of the lesson, check to make sure that the student has written down the correct bibliographical information for his first source. Also check to see that all notes taken are clearly identified by author/title.

Day Two: Finish Taking Notes

 Focus: Gathering information

Student instructions for Day Two:

Today's assignment is simple: Take notes from your remaining sources.

You should have done preliminary reading from about six books. When you did this reading, you probably found at least one or two books that weren't particularly helpful. Choose three of the remaining books and take notes from them.

Try not to create duplicate notes—if you've learned a fact from one book, there's no need to note it again when you find it in another. You may end up only taking two or three notes from the last book that you use.

HOW TO HELP THE STUDENT WITH DAY TWO

Today's work can be extended over two days if the student needs additional time.

Check to make sure that the notes are properly identified by author/title.

Day Three: Draft the Composition

Focus: Writing an initial draft from notes

Student instructions for Day Three:

STEP ONE: Place your notes in order and divide them into main points

Take your notes from yesterday and arrange them in order.

This order will depend on the form you've chosen for your composition. Here's a quick review. You don't have to read all of the following, just the section that deals with the *topos* you've chosen:

This year, you've already reviewed arranging notes in chronological order for a **chronological narration** (Week 4, Day 2) and writing a **sequence in history** from notes (Week 4, Day 3). You have also practiced arranging notes in the correct order to write a **comparison/contrast** (Week 5, Day 3 and Week 7, Day 2).

You used notes to write a **personal description** and a **description of a place** in Week 29 of Level 1. You organized the personal description by reading through your notes and using scratch paper to jot down aspects from the Description of the Person chart that the notes described; you then organized your notes so that they were grouped together by aspect. For the place description, you followed the same procedure, using the Description of a Place chart. (If you need a more detailed review, go back to Level 1, Week 29 and reread the instructions for Day 3 and Day 4.)

You used notes to write a **sequence of a natural process** and a **scientific description** in Week 30 of Level 1. You organized them by placing them so that all of the events in the sequence were listed in order, eliminating the notes that simply repeated information. You divided them so that each group covered a different stage of the sequence. (If you need more review, go back to Level 1, Week 30, Days 2–3.)

You used notes to write a **biographical sketch** in Week 31 of Level 1. You had the choice of organizing them chronologically (for a listing of major life events), or else organizing them into a brief summary of life events followed by a survey of the subject's accomplishments and achievements.

STEP TWO: Write the *topos* (or *topoi*)

Using your ordered notes, write your composition. In most cases, you'll probably want to write one paragraph for each group of notes, but if it seems more natural to combine groups or to use more than one paragraph, that's fine.

Be sure to quote directly from at least two of your sources. Make sure that all direct quotes and anything which is not common knowledge is footnoted.

Check your *topoi* chart one more time to make sure that you have included the required elements.

Since your complete composition, including introduction and conclusion, should be at least 500 words long, aim to have at least 450 words in this initial draft.

STEP THREE: **Write an introduction and conclusion**

Review the Introductions and Conclusions chart in the Reference section of your Composition Notebook.

Choose one kind of introduction and another kind of conclusion. (That means you can't do an introduction by summary *and* a conclusion by summary, and you should be careful that your introduction by anecdote and conclusion by personal reaction don't sound too similar.)

Write a draft of your introduction and a draft of your conclusion. Assemble the entire composition. Make sure that you have 500 words or more.

Now put your composition away until tomorrow at the earliest. You should show your instructor that the composition is finished, but your instructor shouldn't offer suggestions or criticisms until you've had a chance to complete Day Four's work.

HOW TO HELP THE STUDENT WITH DAY THREE

If the student has difficulty dividing his notes into groups (essentially, creating a two-level outline for his composition), go back with him to the lessons noted above. Review the procedure for organizing notes.

Check the student's composition for the following elements: length (suggested: at least 450 words); at least two direct quotes, properly footnoted; and the required elements of his chosen *topoi*. However, do not edit or critique for content until the student has had a chance to do the proofreading and revising steps in Day Four.

The student has practiced writing introductions and conclusions for comparisons and contrasts. If he needs to see further examples of introductions and conclusions, you may show him the examples below, written to go along with Week 4's assignment (chronological narrative and sequence in history about the Gold Rush).

First, ask the student to read the following sample composition:

THE GOLD RUSH

On January 24, 1848, a workman named James Wilson Marshall discovered gold at a sawmill owned by John Sutter. He told the other workmen, "Boys, I think I've found a gold mine."[1] Then, he and John Sutter tested it. It was 23-carat gold.

John Sutter wanted to keep the gold secret, but a man named Sam Brennan rode through town with gold dust, shouting, "Gold! Gold! Gold from the American River."[2] Many young men were in financial trouble at the time, and they came to dig for gold.

They were known as Forty-Niners. They came from all over California. That was the beginning of the Gold Rush.

At first, there was so much gold that it was just as easy to dig it as to steal it. It could be picked up from the ground and dug out of rocks with pocket-knives.[3]

Many miners used gold pans to search for gold. A gold pan was a wide, flat pan, usually made out of metal. The pan was filled halfway up with sand and clay, and then the rest of the way with water. When the water was swirled around and around, the heavier gold sank to the bottom of the pan. The sand and silt then poured out of the pan along with the water. The miner collected the gold from the bottom of the pan and put it in a sack. [4]

   After an official letter to the War Department announced that there was gold in California, many more people came from all over the country. [5] The Gold Rush made California into a territory, and then, into a state. But James Marshall, who had made the first discovery, died "penniless and all alone" in a ruined house near Sutter's Mill. [6]

[1] "The Gold Country" (*Life*, Feb. 2, 1948), p. 44.

[2] Stewart Edward White, *The Forty-Niners: A Chronicle of the California Trail and El Dorado* (Yale University Press, 1920), p. 57.

[3] White, pp. 60–61.

[4] Malcolm J. Rohrbough, *Days of Gold: The California Gold Rush and the American Nation* (University of California Press, 1997), p. 12

[5] White, p. 62.

[6] "The Gold Country"

Then, allow him to read the sample introductions and conclusions below.

1. Introduction by Summary

One or more sentences that tell the reader what the composition is about and what its most central conclusion will be

James Wilson Marshall was the first man to find gold at Sutter's Mill. But although his discovery led many others to find great riches, Marshall himself did not benefit at all.

2. Introduction by History

a. Information about past attitudes towards the subject

For thousands of years, men and women have prized gold. Even though it is too soft for tools and less useful than bronze or copper, gold has always been a symbol of status, wealth, and power.

b. Description of how some aspect of the subject has changed or developed over time

The California Gold Rush began with the simple discovery of a single nugget of gold. But within a few years, it had become a massive movement that changed the course of American history.

c. Brief scene from history

It is a cool California morning. The sun is barely up. The American River flows peacefully in the dim morning light. And a workman is on his way to check the newly-built tailrace of a mill. He has no idea that he is about to change history.

3. Introduction by Anecdote

a. A story drawn from personal experience

Panning for gold is hard work. At the recent State Fair, I had the chance to try panning for gold at one of the historical exhibits. I worked for what seemed like hours to get just a tiny fleck of gold. After that, I gave up—unlike the miners of the California Gold Rush.

b. An invented scene, based on your knowledge of the subject

A young man dressed in ragged cotton clothes and a wide-brimmed hat leans over a cold California stream. He has been panning for gold for six hours. His hands are blue with cold and his knuckles are chapped and bleeding. He hasn't seen a single fleck of gold yet—but he can't stop yet. He's too sure that great riches are within his grasp.

1. Conclusion by Summary

Write a brief summary of the most important information in the passage, including specific details

Hundreds of thousands of men had benefited from Marshall's discovery—but he had gained nothing at all.

2. Conclusion by Personal Reaction

a. Personal statement

Gold may not be the most useful metal in the world—but I think it is the most beautiful. If I had been given the chance to leave home and pan for gold in California, I would certainly have taken it.

b. Your opinion about the material

Marshall's tragic end shows just how dangerous it is to pursue riches, no matter what—and how many pitfalls lie in the way of those who think of nothing but profit.

c. Your own experience with the subject

At the recent State Fair, I had the chance to try panning for gold at one of the historical exhibits. I worked for what seemed like hours to get just a tiny fleck of gold. After that, I gave up—unlike the miners of the California Gold Rush. I had no idea just how hard it was to pan for gold!

3. Conclusion by Question

Ask the reader to react to the information

The Gold Rush changed California forever. But did Marshall wish, during his last days, that he had never seen those flecks of gold?

Day Four: Finalize the Composition

 Focus: Revising and proofreading

Student instructions for Day Four:

STEP ONE: **Title**

Begin today's work by reading carefully through your composition from beginning to end (silently is fine; see Step Two).

Now it's time to give the essay a title.

When you finished your composition at the end of Level 1, you were asked to give it a very simple title—just the name of an event, person, place, or process. But you should now begin to work towards more complex titling.

What is the event, person, place, or process that your composition discusses? Jot it down on a scratch piece of paper. Now, think about the *topos* (or *topoi*) that you used to write your paper. Can you come up with a phrase that includes both the event/person/place/process *and* a description of the *topos*?

Here are a few examples to help you out.

If you wrote about Abraham Lincoln and decided to do a chronological narrative of a past event, you'd want to combine Abraham Lincoln and the event:

The Assassination of Abraham Lincoln

or perhaps

Abraham Lincoln Declares War.

A biographical sketch might be titled

Who Was Abraham Lincoln?

or even

A Character Sketch of Abraham Lincoln.

But if you planned to compare and contrast Abraham Lincoln with another historical figure, you could title your paper:

The Similarities between Abraham Lincoln and George Washington

or

The Differences between Abraham Lincoln and Chairman Mao.

The chronological narrative of a scientific discovery could be titled, very simply:

The Discovery of the Polio Vaccine

or

How a Vaccine for Polio was Discovered.

A scientific description could be titled:

How Polio Vaccines Work

or

The Polio Vaccine and How It Functions.

You can title the description of a place by using your final evaluation of it:

The Beauties of the Grand Canyon

or

The Dangers of the Grand Canyon.

And finally, sequences can be titled with the name of the sequence itself:

How Galaxies Are Formed

or

The Formation of Galaxies.

If you have chosen to use two or more *topoi* in your composition, choose the *topos* that seems most important or central for your title.

When you have come up with your title, center it at the top of your first page. Use initial capitals, but do not put your title in all caps.

STEP TWO: **Revise**

Using your *topoi* chart, check to make sure that all of the required elements of your chosen *topos* are included in your paper. If you are missing one, return to your notes (or sources if necessary) and add it in.

Now read your composition out loud. Listen for awkward or unclear sections. Rewrite them so that they flow more naturally.

Finally, read your composition out loud a second time. Listen for repeated nouns, verbs, and modifiers. If you find yourself using the same noun or verb more than twice, use your thesaurus to find an alternative. (This doesn't include the name of your actual subject, of course!) If you use a modifier (adverb, adjective, or prepositional phrase acting as an adjective or adverb) more than once, find another word.

STEP THREE: **Assemble the Works Cited page**

Put the sources used in your footnotes on a Works Cited page, using the correct format.

STEP FOUR: **Proofread**

1. Read through the paper one more time, looking for sentence fragments or run-on sentences.

2.   Check the format of your footnotes and Works Cited page. (If necessary, look back at Week 3, Day 1.)

3.   Check your spelling by looking, individually, at each word that might be a problem.

When you have finished proofreading and corrected any errors, give your paper to your instructor for evaluation.

HOW TO HELP THE STUDENT WITH DAY FOUR

When the student has completed all of the steps in the lesson, evaluate his paper using the following general rubric. Note that you will need to use the *topoi* chart to evaluate whether all required elements are present.

Week 9 General Rubric

Organization:

1   The entire composition should be around 500 words in length.

2   The required elements of the selected *topoi* should be present.

3   The composition should contain both an introduction and a conclusion. At least one of these should be a separate paragraph of two sentences or more.

4   The conclusion and introduction should not *both* be summaries.

5   The composition should contain at least two direct quotes.

6   All direct quotes should be footnoted.

7   All sources mentioned in footnotes should be placed on a Works Cited page.

8   The composition should have a title, centered at the top of the first page. This title should include both the event/person/place/process and a word or phrase describing or defining the purpose of the paper.

Mechanics:

1   Each sentence should make sense on its own when read aloud.

2   There should be no sentence fragments or run-on sentences.

3   All words should be spelled correctly.

4   The first line of each paragraph should be properly indented.

5   Verb tense should be consistent throughout.

6   No noun or verb should be used more than twice (with the exception of the name of the paper's subject, state-of-being verbs, linking verbs, and the verb "said").

7   No modifier or prepositional phrase acting as a modifier should be used more than once.

8   Footnotes and the Works Cited page should be properly formatted.

WEEK 10: THE EMBEDDED STORY

Introduction to Weeks 10-11

In the first level of *Writing With Skill,* the student spent eight weeks working on skills in beginning literary criticism: identifying protagonists, antagonists, and conflicts; learning basic vocabulary for literary techniques; and writing brief literary analysis essays about fiction and poetry.

In this second level, he will build on those basic skills and develop a few new ones. Instead of spending an entire month writing about fiction and another month on poetry, he will work on these intermediate skills for a couple of weeks at a time, interspersed with other writing assignments; this will improve his flexibility and his ability to come up with topics across the curriculum.

You will need the Level 1 list of literary terms for reference. You can find these in Appendix II.

You should read the stories yourself before the student does. They are short! (And entertaining.)

Day One: Read

Focus: Reading

This week, the student will be asked for the first time to think about what fiction *does*—how it creates a new and different world and asks the reader to step inside. He will also review some of the basic terms and skills from Level One.

STEP ONE: **Learn about the author (Student Responsibility)**

Student instructions for Step One:

"The Open Window" was written by a British author named Hector Hugh Munro. He was actually born in Burma in 1870, because his father was an English official in

British-controlled India. But he grew up in England, because his mother died and his father sent him to live with two aunts back at home.

He began to write short stories, essays, and newspaper articles when he was in his twenties. He published his short stories under the pen name Saki, which he borrowed from a very popular book of Persian poems called *The Rubaiyat of Omar Khayyam.*

When World War I began in 1914, Munro lied about his age in order to join the British army (he was 44, too old for regular enlistment). He fought for two years before he was killed by a German sniper in November of 1916.

"The Open Window" was first published early in 1914, in a collection of short stories called *Beasts and Superbeasts.*

Before you read, you should know that the word "romance" in the last line is not used in the modern sense of "boy meets girl." It has the older sense of "tales of daring, excitement, and brave deeds."

STEP TWO: **Read (Student Responsibility)**

Student instructions for Step Two:

Get in a comfortable place and read the story from beginning to end. Enjoy yourself. Eat a cookie.

STEP THREE: **Re-read**

Student instructions for Step Three:

Now read through the story a second time.

Why do you think you were told to do a second reading? Tell your instructor why you think this second reading was assigned. If you don't know, your instructor will explain. (Hint: it has to do with the genre of the story, which you should be able to recognize.)

HOW TO HELP THE STUDENT WITH STEP THREE

This is a *surprise story.* It uses inversion (an unexpected revelation that reverses the meaning or action of the story) to change the reader's point of view. "The Necklace" by Guy de Maupassant and "The Ransom of Red Chief" by O. Henry (both studied in Level 1) are also surprise stories that make use of inversion.

If the student is able to identify "The Open Window" as a surprise story, remind him of the previous two stories. If not, point out the definitions of "surprise story" and "inversion" in Appendix II. Ask him, "At what point did you realize that the niece, Vera, had made up the whole story about her uncle and cousins being lost in the bog?" Explain that this is the inversion point which changes the reader's point of view—now, you know that the entire story was an elaborate hoax.

The student was asked to read the story a second time because the inversion at the story's end changes the reader's point of view on everything that has happened. Once the reader knows that Vera is making up her story, everything she says, all of Mr. Nuttel's reactions, and the way Mrs. Sappleton behaves all seem different.

Day Two: Think

 Focus: Finding the story within the story

As you learned last year, the student will find it easier to write about a story if she has talked about it first. In the steps below, you will need to direct the lesson by carrying on the suggested dialogue with the student. At the end of each dialogue, the student will write a brief observation; these will be used in tomorrow's brief essay.

For each step, if the student has trouble coming up with the appropriate answers, prompt her using the suggested dialogue.

STEP ONE: **Identify the protagonist and antagonist**

Instructor: Last year, you learned that the first question to ask about a story is: *Who* is the story about? Who is the central character—the protagonist? Read me the definition of "protagonist" from your list of literary terms.

Student: The character who wants to get, become, or accomplish something.

Instructor: Who do you think is the protagonist in "The Open Window"?
NOTE TO INSTRUCTOR: You can make an argument for either main character as the protagonist—so there is no "right" answer! It is possible for the student to answer with either of the options below. If the student wavers between options, say, "Choose either Vera or Mr. Nuttel and let's see what happens when we talk about it."

If the student answers with "Mr. Nuttel," carry on the following dialogue:
*Instructor: In some stories, the protagonist has a very strong want. In others, the want is much weaker—but the character is still a protagonist. Why does Framton Nuttel pay a visit to Mrs. Sappleton and her niece?

Student: His sister told him to OR He had a letter of introduction to Mrs. Sappleton OR It is part of the "nerve cure" he is undergoing.

Instructor: So Framton Nuttel is there because he wants to do the right thing—the polite thing. He doesn't *really want* to sit and visit with these strangers—but he knows he needs to be courteous. That is a pretty weak "want," but it is still something he wants to accomplish. He is determined to sit and visit politely with people he doesn't know—to have a perfectly normal, trivial, polite visit. But one of the characters acts as an *antagonist* and makes this very difficult. Who is it?

Student: Vera.

Instructor: Vera makes Mr. Nuttel so uncomfortable that he can't manage a polite social visit. Read what Mrs. Sappleton says about him in the third paragraph from the end of the story.

Student: "A most extraordinary man, a Mr. Nuttel, could only talk about his illnesses, and dashed off without a word of goodbye or apology when you arrived. One would think he had seen a ghost."

Instructor: Of course, Mr. Nuttel talked so much about his illnesses because he wanted his hostess to think about "a less ghastly topic"! So while he was trying to be a polite and courteous guest, he actually made himself *less* polite and courteous—all because of Vera and her story. Now, let's think about this from another angle. For most of the story, you think that Mr. Nuttel is the main character, and that the story is all about his reaction to an impossible situation—stuck in a drawing room with a deluded woman who thinks her dead husband and brothers will return at any moment. But at the end of the story, what do you discover?

Student: None of the story was true OR Vera was making the whole thing up.

Instructor: So while Framton Nuttel appears to be the protagonist for most of the story, at the end of it you discover that Vera has actually been acting like a protagonist all along.

[Continue on with the dialogue below.]

If student answers with "Vera," carry on the following dialogue:
Instructor: What does Vera want? Hint: look at the last line of the story.

Student: She wants romance OR She wants to make up exciting tales OR She wants excitement.

Instructor: How does she make this happen?

Student: She makes up a convincing story to tell Mr. Nuttel.

Instructor: Remember, the *antagonist* is the character, force, or circumstance that opposes the protagonist. Vera doesn't have an actual enemy in this story—but what force or circumstance might keep her from getting what she wants?

Student: Her aunt might tell the truth OR Her aunt might find out that she's been telling a made-up story OR Mr. Nuttel might not believe her.

Instructor: Vera wants to create a much scarier, more exciting, more interesting world than the one she actually lives in—so she has to be *very* convincing. But no matter how convincing her story is, when her uncles appear, the excitement will all be over. Read the paragraph describing her reaction—the one beginning, "Framton shivered slightly."

Student: "Framton shivered slightly and turned towards the niece with a look intended to convey sympathetic comprehension. The child was staring out through the open window with a dazed horror in her eyes. In a chill shock of nameless fear Framton swung round in his seat and looked in the same direction."

Instructor: Vera is working very hard to keep the illusion she has created alive. That's what a protagonist does—works to get something she wants.

If the student answered "Vera," now use the following dialogue and then go back to the ★ above. The goal is that the student will discuss both Vera and Mr. Nuttel as protagonists.
Instructor: When you first read the story, you probably thought that it was about Mr. Nuttel. Mr. Nuttel could also be considered the protagonist of the story—particularly before the inversion at the end.

After you have discussed both choices of protagonist, ask the student to decide whether Vera or Mr. Nuttel is the main protagonist of the story. (Either choice is fine—this is a judgment call.) Ask the student to jot down in her workbook the names of both possible protagonists and what each one wants.

STEP TWO: **Find the story within the story**

Carry on the following dialogue with the student. If she has trouble coming up with the appropriate answers, prompt her using the suggested dialogue.

Instructor: This story seems to have two different protagonists. There is a good reason for that—there are actually two different stories here. The first story is about Framton Nuttel. Look through the story now and write down the main *events* of Framton Nuttel's visit. Don't include any of the content of the conversations—just write down the things the the characters do.
NOTE TO INSTRUCTOR: The student's answers should resemble the following:

> Framton Nuttel goes to visit Mrs. Sappleton
> Vera tells him a story
> Mrs. Sappleton arrives
> Nuttel tries to carry on conversation
> The husband and brothers return
> Framton Nuttel dashes away

If necessary, prompt the student by asking:
> "Whom does he go visit?"
> "What occupies most of his time while he's there?"
> "Who finally arrives in the room with Nuttel and Vera?"
> "How does he act towards her?"
> "What new characters then arrive?"
> "How does he react?"

Instructor: That is the first story Saki is telling. The second story is contained within the first one. It's the story Vera tells about her uncles. What are the main events in that story? List them now. This is a shorter story—you will probably have only three or four events.
NOTE TO INSTRUCTOR: The student's answers should resemble the following:

> Mrs. Sappelton's husband and brothers go shooting
> They fall into a bog
> Mrs. Sappleton keeps the window open
> She still thinks they will return

If necessary, prompt the student by asking:
"What do the three men set out to do?"
"What happens to them?
"What does Mrs. Sappleton do in response?"

Instructor: The author, Saki, has written this story so that it is actually two stories in one. Framton Nuttel's story is a *frame story* that surrounds the tale Vera tells. In the margin next to your notes for Story #1, write "frame story."

Instructor: Now read out loud the quote from your workbook.

> Student: "Not only does the unfortunate Mr. Nuttel fall victim to the story's joke, but so does the reader. The reader is at first inclined to laugh at Nuttel for being so gullible. However, the reader, too, has been taken in by the story and must come to the realization that he or she is also inclined to believe a well-told and interesting tale."[12]

Instructor: The story-within-a-story structure makes "The Open Window" entertaining, but it also makes a point about fiction—about storytelling. The point is that it can be very hard to tell what is true and what is not. A well-told story can deceive any reader—even you.
NOTE TO INSTRUCTOR: More advanced students may enjoy thinking about the connection between the open window and the "story within a frame story" structure of the narrative. The open window "frames" the outdoors—which is where the death of Vera's uncles might/ might not have happened. In the same way, the narrative about Mr. Nuttel "frames" the story about the death—which might/might not have happened.

STEP THREE: **Examine the author's language**

Instructor: Throughout the story, the author uses word choice very carefully to make his story more effective. Let's start with the names of the three major characters. Write them down in your workbook in the order they appear in the story.

#1 **Vera**   =
#2 **Framton Nuttel** =
#3 **Mrs. Sappleton** =

---

12. Nozar Niazi and Rama Gautam, *How to Study Literature: Stylistic and Pragmatic Approaches* (PHI, Ltd., 2010), p. 164.

Instructor: Do you happen to know what the name "Vera" means?
NOTE TO INSTRUCTOR: If necessary, explain to the student that the name "Vera" comes from the Latin word "veritas," or *truth*.

Instructor: Write "truth" next to Vera's name.
  #1 Vera = truth

Instructor: Vera's name is an example of *ironic language*. Does Vera tell the truth?

  Student: No.

Instructor: Listen carefully to the definition of "ironic language": *when words are opposite to the reality they describe*. Write that definition in your workbook.
NOTE TO INSTRUCTOR: Repeat the definition as often as necessary.

Instructor: Look at Framton Nuttel's name. What does it remind you of? Hint: look at the *last* name only.

  Student: Nut

Instructor: When Mr. Nuttel bolts out of the drawing room at the end of the story, he looks like a nut case. But he isn't *really* a nut. He's acting perfectly reasonably—given what he thinks he knows about the family. So his name is also ironic. Write "nutty" next to his name.
  #2 Framton Nuttel = nutty

Instructor: Now, look at Mrs. Sappleton's name. What does it remind you of?
NOTE TO INSTRUCTOR: If necessary, explain to the student that "Sappleton" is derived from *sapientia,* the Greek word for "wisdom." (Only the most advanced students will know this!)

Instructor: Is Mrs. Sappleton a wise woman?

  Student: No.

NOTE TO INSTRUCTOR: Point out to the student that a wise woman would realize Vera's tendency to tell huge elaborate lies. Mrs. Sappleton is not at all "wise"; she has no idea that her niece makes up stories, and she has no understanding of why Mr. Nuttel has suddenly run out of her house. Write "wise" next to her name.
  #3 Mrs. Sappleton = wise

Instructor: All of these names are ironic. There are several other places in the story where Saki's word choice is opposite to the reality described. Look at the paragraph beginning "In the deepening twilight three figures were walking across the lawn." Circle the following words: "noiselessly," "hoarse," and "chanted." Then, go up two paragraphs and circle the phrase "muddy up to the eyes." All of these words and phrases suggest that the three men are ghosts—and that they drowned in a swamp. But are they ghosts?

Student: No.

Instructor: The language is ironic because it suggests they are ghosts—and, in reality, they aren't. Look at one other example. In the paragraph beginning "Framton shivered slightly," circle the following words and phrases: *shivered, dazed horror, chill shock,* and *nameless fear.* All of these suggest that Framton Nuttel has a very good reason to be terrified by the sight of the three men. *He* thinks he has a good reason to be terrified. But does he *really* have good reason to be afraid?

Student: No.

Instructor: This language is ironic because it is opposed to reality; in reality, Framton Nuttel has absolutely no reason to fear the three men. But in his imaginary world—the world created by the story—he has *plenty* of reason to be afraid. On the lines in your workbook, write down two examples of ironic language from the story, along with the reason why that language is opposite to reality.

NOTE TO INSTRUCTOR: Sample answers might look like this:

EXAMPLE	OPPOSITE TO REALITY BECAUSE . . .
Vera	Means truth, but Vera tells lies
dazed horror	No reason to be horrified—the men are alive

Day Three: Write

Focus: Writing about the story

Today, the student will write a brief essay following the pattern learned in Level One of this course: a brief summary of the story, followed by two or three paragraphs explaining the most central issues with the story's structure and function.

STEP ONE: **Write the summary**

Student instructions for Step One:

> Begin by writing a brief narrative summary of the story. This summary should be five to ten sentences in length, and may be either one or two paragraphs.
> You should be comfortable writing summaries by now, but if you need help, ask your instructor.

HOW TO HELP THE STUDENT WITH STEP ONE

The student's summary should resemble the following:

> In "The Open Window," by the British writer Saki, Framton Nuttel pays a visit to the home of a stranger. The stranger, Mrs. Sappleton, has a niece named Vera. While Framton Nuttel is waiting to see Mrs. Sappleton, Vera tells him that Mrs. Sappleton's husband and brothers drowned in a bog three years ago, and that the French windows of the house are open because she is waiting for them to come back.
>
> When Mrs. Sappleton arrives in the room, Nuttel tries to avoid the topic of the dead husband and brothers by talking about his own ailments. But while he is talking, the three men appear in the yard and walk towards the window. Terrified, Nuttel runs away. But then the men walk through the window—alive. Vera had made the entire story up.

If the student has difficulty, allow him to read the following summaries from published critical guides to short stories. Then, ask him to write his own summary without looking at the models.

> Framton Nuttel, a nervous young man, is waiting to pay a courtesy call on Mrs. Sappleton. He has a letter of introduction from his sister, who was determined that he would not be lonely during his country rest-cure. Until Mrs. Sappleton comes downstairs, her niece, Vera, a self-possessed fifteen-year-old, is "entertaining" the visitor. Having made certain that Nuttel is unacquainted in the neighborhood, she tells him of her aunt's great tragedy: Three years before, her husband and two young brothers had gone through the new open French doors, off on a hunting trip from which they never returned. When Mrs. Sappleton finally appears, she is cheerful enough, but the reappearance of her husband and brothers completely unnerves Nuttel, who takes an abrupt leave.
>
> —Aileen M. Carroll, *150 Great Short Stories: Teaching Notes, Synopses, and Quizzes* (J. Weston Walch, 1989), p. 127.

> Framton Nuttel is a young man in the country on a rest cure. He has been given letters of introduction by his sister, and as he waits in the sitting room of a country estate for the woman of the house to see him, he is entertained by the woman's niece, who explains to Nuttel why the large French window that looks out onto the lawn is open even in October. It seems that Mrs. Sappleton's husband and her two brothers were lost in a bog during a hunt three years to the day before Nuttel's arrival. The woman cannot bear to imagine them dead, so she leaves the window open in the hope that they will return.
>
> When Mrs. Sappleton joins the two, she cannot talk of anything else but the imminent return of the men. Nuttel is at first touched by the pathetic scene, thinking the woman mad for believing that the men are not dead, and then horrified when the three hunters wander out of the mist and into the house. In his haste to leave the house, Nuttel is nearly hit by a cyclist.
>
> —Patrick A. Smith, *Thematic Guide to Popular Short Stories* (Greenwood, 2002), pp. 244–245.

STEP TWO: **Write the analysis**

Student instructions for Step Two:

Now you'll write an analysis of how the story works. This analysis should have four parts:

1. A description of the story-within-a-story structure (two to three sentences),
2. The way that the central story fools both the reader and Mr. Nuttel (two to three sentences),
3. The way Saki uses word choice to make the ghost story more effective, and
4. The way Saki uses irony to hint at the trick he is playing on us.

You can combine these into two or three paragraphs or else write a separate short paragraph for each.

Remember that you should use either present tense ("Saki structures this story by telling *two* stories") or past tense ("Saki structured this story by telling *two* stories") throughout.

Be sure to quote directly from the story at least twice. You do not need to footnote these quotes, since it is very clear that you are using "The Open Window" as your source.

If you have trouble getting started, you can use my opening sentence above ("Saki structures this story by telling *two* stories") as your first sentence. If you're still stuck, ask your instructor for help.

HOW TO HELP THE STUDENT WITH STEP TWO

The student's analysis should resemble the following:

Saki structures this story by telling two stories. The first is the story of Mr. Nuttel's visit to Mrs. Sappleton. This story acts as a frame for the second story, which Vera tells to Mr. Nuttel while he is sitting in the drawing room waiting to see her aunt. This second story tricks Mr. Nuttel into believing that the three men are actually ghosts—but it also tricks the reader. We have no idea, until the very end of the frame story, that Vera has told an elaborate lie!

The author uses very carefully chosen words to keep us believing in Vera's story. When the three men appear on the lawn, he tells us that they are "muddy up to the eyes," just as they would be if they had drowned in a bog. He also describes the reactions of both Vera and Mr. Nuttel with words that suggest they are really seeing ghosts—they are struck with "dazed horror" and "nameless fear."

But he also uses ironic language to tell us that he is playing a trick on us. "Vera" means truth, but Vera is making up her entire story. Mr. Nuttel reacts to the story in a reasonable way, but that makes him look like a nutcase. And Mrs. Sappleton (the name comes from the word for "wise") is completely fooled by her niece.

The student may assume that this assignment is more complicated than it actually is. If she seems blocked, try prompting her sentence by sentence as follows:

1. A description of the story-within-a-story structure (two to three sentences)
    "What is the first story?"
    "How does it relate to the second story?"
2. The way that the central story fools both the reader and Mr. Nuttel (two to three sentences)
    "What effect does the second story have on Mr. Nuttel?"
    "What effect does it have on the reader?"
3. The way Saki uses word choice to make both stories more effective
    "How does he make us believe in Vera's ghost story? Give two examples."
4. The way Saki uses irony to hint at the trick he is playing on us
    "Explain each one of the characters' names."

STEP THREE: **Proofread**

Student instructions for Step Three:

> Before you give your essay to your instructor, proofread it using the following steps:
>
> 1. Read your composition out loud. Listen for awkward or unclear sections. Rewrite them so that they flow more naturally.
> 2. Read your composition out loud a second time. Listen for repeated nouns, verbs, and modifiers. If you find yourself using the same noun or verb more than twice, use your thesaurus to find an alternative. If you use a modifier (adverb, adjective, or prepositional phrase acting as an adjective or adverb) more than once, find another word.
> 3. Look for sentence fragments or run-on sentences. Correct them if you find them.
> 4. Check to make sure that you have quoted directly from the story at least twice.
> 5. Make sure that all five required elements are present—narrative summary plus the four parts listed above.
> 6. Check your spelling by looking, individually, at each word that might be a problem.

HOW TO HELP THE STUDENT WITH STEP THREE

Evaluate the student's paper using the following rubric. Refer back to the model summary and analysis in Steps Two and Three if necessary.

Week 10 Rubric

Organization:

1 The entire composition should have at least three paragraphs: narrative summary (first paragraph) and at least two paragraphs covering the analytical elements. It can be as long as five paragraphs.
2 The analysis should cover all four of the required topics:
   a. Two to three sentences about the story-within-a-story structure
   b. Two to three sentences about the way the central story fools Mr. Nuttel *and* the reader
   c. How word choice makes the ghost story more effective
   d. How Saki uses irony in the choices of the names
3 The composition should contain at least two direct quotes.

Mechanics:

1 Each sentence should make sense on its own when read aloud.
2 There should be no sentence fragments or run-on sentences.
3 All words should be spelled correctly.
4 The first line of each paragraph should be properly indented.
5 Verb tense should be consistent throughout.
6 No noun or verb should be used more than twice (with the exception of state-of-being verbs, linking verbs, and the verb "said").
7 No modifier or prepositional phrase acting as a modifier should be used more than once.

Day Four: Literary Language

 Focus: Understanding point of view

Today, the student will be introduced (on a very basic level) to the complicated subject of *point of view* in fiction.

Point of view is not easy to grasp, and there are many subtle variations on the definitions given below. The goal of today's lesson is to provide the student with a not-too-overwhelming first look at the topic. Because the subject itself is difficult, the student will not be required to write—just to read, think, and then discuss.

STEP ONE: **Review point of view (Student Responsibility)**

Student instructions for Step One:

In the first level of this course, you were introduced to *point of view*. Take a minute now to review what you've already learned.

1. First-person point of view uses the pronouns *I, we, my,* and *mine.* You learned about this when you read from Helen Keller's autobiography in Level 1, Week 3:

> **We** walked down the path to the well-house, attracted by the fragrance of the honeysuckle with which it was covered. Someone was drawing water and **my** teacher placed **my** hand under the spout. As the cool stream gushed over one hand, she spelled into the other the word *water,* first slowly, then rapidly. **I** stood still, **my** whole attention fixed upon the motions of her fingers.
> —Helen Keller, *The Story of My Life* (Doubleday, Page & Company, 1903), p. 24.

2. In the same lesson, you learned that third-person point of view uses third-person pronouns and names. You were given the following third-person version of the same paragraph:

> **Helen and Miss Sullivan** walked down the path to the well-house, attracted by the fragrance of the honeysuckle with which it was covered. Someone was drawing water and **Helen's** teacher placed **her** hand under the spout. As the cool stream gushed over one hand she spelled into the other the word *water,* first slowly, then rapidly. **Helen** stood still, **her** whole attention fixed upon the motions of her fingers.

3. In Weeks 9 and 13, you learned that when writing a description, you need to think of your *point of view* as a narrator—where are you in relation to the thing being described? You were given four options:

1. From above, as though you were hovering over the place. This is sometimes called the "impersonal" point of view, because you're not directly involved in the place itself; you're looking over it as a detached observer.

2. From inside it, as though you were part of the place, standing still in the middle of it at a particular point and looking around.

3. From one side, as though you were standing beside the place looking at it from one particular angle.

4. Moving, as though you were walking through the place, or around it.

STEP TWO: **Understand first, second, and third-person point of view in fiction**

Student instructions for Step Two:

In short stories and novels, "point of view" has a very particular meaning. "Point of view" has to do with who the narrator of the story is and how much that narrator knows.
Read the following descriptions and examples carefully.

1) First-person point of view ("I") gives a very immediate, but limited, perspective. First-person allows you to hear a character's most private thoughts—but in exchange, you can only see what happens within the character's line of sight, and you can only know those facts that the character is herself aware of.

> I could only look upwards; the sun began to grow hot, and the light offended my eyes. I heard a confused noise about me; but in the posture I lay could see nothing except the sky. In a little time I felt something alive moving on my left leg, which advancing gently forward over my breast, came almost up to my chin; when bending my eyes downward as much as I could, I perceived it to be a human creature not six inches high, with a bow and arrow in his hands, and a quiver at his back.
> —Jonathan Swift, *Gulliver's Travels*

2) Second-person ("You walk down the street and open the door . . .") is unusual. It is generally found only in experimental literary works and in adventure games. Like first-person point of view, second-person keeps the reader intimately involved with the story. But second-person also tends to limit the writer to the present tense, cutting off any reflection on the past.

> You are about to begin reading Italo Calvino's new novel, *If on a winter's night a traveler*. Relax. Concentrate. Dispel every other thought. Let the world around you fade. Best to close the door; the TV is always on in the next room.
> —Italo Calvino, *If on a winter's night a traveler*

3) Third-person tells the story using third-person pronouns—he, she, it, they—and proper names. There are four kinds of third-person stories, but these three are the most common:

a) Third-person limited. This tells the story from the viewpoint of one particular character, delving into that character's mind, but using the third-person pronouns (he or she) rather than the first-person pronouns. This allows the writer to gain a little bit of distance from the story, but still limits the writer to those events that the viewpoint character can actually see and hear.

> With this excellent resolve for the future, Goodman Brown felt himself justified in making more haste on his present evil purpose. He had taken a dreary road, darkened by all the gloomiest trees of the forest, which barely stood aside to let the narrow path creep through, and closed immediately behind. It was all as lonely as could be . . . [H]e passed a crook of the road, and, looking forward again, beheld the figure of a man, in grave and decent attire, seated at the foot of an old tree.
>
> —Nathaniel Hawthorne, *Young Goodman Brown*

b) Third-person multiple. This point of view allows the writer to use the third-person viewpoints of several different characters, jumping from the "inside" of one character to the "inside" of another in order to give multiple perspectives.

> Clutching his broken glasses to his face, Harry stared around. He had emerged into a dingy alleyway . . . Feeling jumpy, Harry set off, trying to hold his glasses on straight and hoping against hope he'd be able to find a way out of here.
>
> Peeves was bobbing overhead, now grinning wickedly, surveying the scene; Peeves always loved chaos.

> "Don't be silly, Ron, I've got to keep up," said Hermione briskly. Her
> spirits were greatly improved by the fact that all the hair had gone from her
> face and her eyes were turning slowly back to brown.

—J. K. Rowling, *Harry Potter and the Chamber of Secrets*

c) The omniscient point of view—the most popular until the nineteenth century—puts the writer in the place of God. He can see and explain everything—events, thoughts in anyone's head, secrets. The narrator can even give opinions and ideas and talk directly to the reader ("Gentle reader, what depths of guilt such a man must feel!" is an example of the omniscient point of view.)

Here is an example of the omniscient point of view in which the narrator knows what's going on in both character's heads better than they do:

> Aunt March put on her glasses and took a look at the girl, for she did
> not know her in this new mood. Meg hardly knew herself, she felt so brave
> and independent, so glad to defend John and assert her right to love him, if
> she liked. Aunt March saw that she had begun wrong, and after a little pause,
> made a fresh start . . .

—Louisa May Alcott, *Little Women*

HOW TO HELP THE STUDENT WITH STEP TWO

Although this step is structured for the student to complete independently, most students will probably find it easier either to read it aloud to you, or to follow along as you read. This will slow the student down, make the contrasts between the point of views more obvious, and help you to be sure that the student has read *carefully* rather than simply skimming.

STEP THREE: **Understand the point of view of "The Open Window"**

Student instructions for Step Three:

> Now look back at "The Open Window" and try to decide which point of view the narrator of the story uses.
> As you do, think particularly about the following lines:

> Privately he doubted more than ever whether these formal visits on a succession of total strangers would do much towards helping the nerve cure which he was supposed to be undergoing.

> "Do you know many of the people round here?" asked the niece, when she judged that they had had sufficient silent communion.

> Romance at short notice was her specialty.

> When you've decided, tell your instructor your conclusions.

HOW TO HELP THE STUDENT WITH STEP THREE

This story uses the omniscient point of view. The narrator goes back and forth between what Mr. Nuttel is thinking and what Vera is thinking. But he also adds his own editorial comments about Vera at the end. If the student concludes that the story is third-person multiple, ask him to reread the last line and answer the question, "Who is thinking this?"

To conclude this lesson, point out to the student that Saki's choice of point of view is a little bit of a trick—just like the story itself. Although he uses the omniscient point of view, he holds back information from you. He tells you everything Mr. Nuttel is thinking—but he certainly doesn't tell you everything that Vera is thinking! And he tells you *nothing* that Mrs. Sappleton is thinking, because then you would know that her husband and brothers are actually alive. Omniscient point of view means that the narrator *can* tell you what's in everyone's minds—but it doesn't mean that the narrator will choose to do so!

Week 11: Comparing Stories

Day One: Read

 Focus: Reading

STEP ONE: **Learn about the author (Student Responsibility)**

Student instructions for Step One:

"The Monkey's Paw" was written by William Wymark Jacobs. Born in 1863, Jacobs grew up in London. He worked for the British postal service and wrote stories in his spare time. His first book of short stories was published in 1896; by the time he died in 1943, he had written over 150 stories and published 12 different story collections. Many of Jacobs's stories feature British colonials (residents in British colonies in India and other countries) who have just returned home.

You may find some unfamiliar vocabulary in the story. "Rubicund" means "ruddy, flushed, red." "Fakir" was the name that British officers in India often used for local Muslim and Hindu monks, particularly those who claimed to be able to do miracles. An "antimacassar" is a decorative drape that goes on the back of a sofa or chair to help keep it clean. "Simian" means "monkey-like."

Something that is "prosaic" is everyday, ordinary, comfortable. Someone who is "credulous" believes tall tales easily. "Bibulous" means "having to do with drink."

A "fusillade," often used to describe a whole collection of gunshots let off at once, means a "general discharge" or all-at-once outpouring.

STEP TWO: **Read (Student Responsibility)**

Student instructions for Step Two:

Get in a comfortable place and read the story from beginning to end. Enjoy yourself. Eat a cookie.

HOW TO HELP THE STUDENT WITH STEP TWO

Provide cookies.

Day Two: Think

 Focus: Understanding story structure, story climax, and foreshadowing

In each of the steps below, you will carry on a dialogue with the student. At the end of each dialogue, the student should write a brief observation on the lines provided. These observations will help the student construct a brief essay at the end of the week.

STEP ONE: Identify the protagonist

Instructor: Let's start with the most basic question: Who is the protagonist—the central character of the story?

Student: Mr. White

NOTE TO INSTRUCTOR: If necessary, ask, "Who ends up making the wishes?" This is the action that causes the plot of the story to develop; the person making the wishes is the protagonist.

Instructor: What does Mr. White want? This might be a little bit hard to figure out. After all, in the first part, he actually says, "It seems to me I've got all I want." So why does he wish for the two hundred pounds?

Student: His son tells him to.

NOTE TO INSTRUCTOR: The student may answer "because he wants to clear the house" [pay off the mortgage]—but his son also suggests this to him. Both are Herbert's ideas, not Mr. White's.

Instructor: So if he doesn't want anything, why does he take the monkey's paw from the soldier to begin with? Here's a hint: The story refers two times to his "credulity"—his willingness to believe.

NOTE TO INSTRUCTOR: Mr. White is fascinated by the *idea* of the three wishes. He wants to find out if the paw works. He really *wants* to believe that the paw has power—that's why he took it, and why he insisted on paying Morris for it. (Herbert, on the other hand, doesn't believe in the paw at all.) If the student has difficulty coming up with this answer (it is not the most obvious "want" a character could have), simply present the idea to him.

Instructor: Write the name of the protagonist and what he wants down in your workbook.

STEP TWO: **Examine the structure of the story**

Instructor: How many parts is the story divided into?

Student: Three parts

Instructor: Why do you think it is divided into three?

Student: The paw grants three wishes.

NOTE TO INSTRUCTOR: If necessary, ask, "How many wishes does the paw grant?"

Instructor: There are three wishes and three sections to the story. At the beginning of the story, how many people are in the villa?

Student: Three

Instructor: Their world remains the same until the fourth person arrives, Sergeant-Major Morris—and the arrival of the fourth person is what sets the whole tragedy in motion. How many people will be able to have three wishes granted?

Student: Three

Instructor: Can you find something else that happens three times in Part I?

Student: Morris has three glasses of whiskey before he begins to tell stories.

NOTE TO INSTRUCTOR: You could also argue that he gives three warnings about the paw: "Better let it burn," "Pitch it on the fire," and "I warn you of the consequences."

Instructor: Can you find something that happens three times in Part II?

Student: The man from Maw & Meggins walks by the gate three times.

Instructor: The fourth time, when he comes in, changes the lives of the old couple. The author is telling you in several different ways that the number three is important. In your workbook, write down three examples of how the author highlights the number three. (Don't include the division of the story into three parts.)

NOTE TO INSTRUCTOR: These examples could resemble the following:

The paw grants three wishes

Three people get three wishes

Morris has three drinks

Man from Maw & Meggins walks by gate three times

STEP THREE: **Understand the pivot point**

Instructor: Over the course of a story, the protagonist's goal—what he *wants*—can change and develop. Sometimes, what a character wants at the beginning of the story is very different from what he or she wants at the end.

NOTE TO INSTRUCTOR: If possible, discuss how this happens in a story that the student is already familiar with to illustrate this point. For example:

> HARRY POTTER (J. K. Rowling)
>> Beginning: Harry wants to get away from his uncle and aunt
>> End: Harry wants to destroy Voldemort
> THE LORD OF THE RINGS (J. R. R. Tolkien)
>> Beginning: Frodo wants to destroy the Ring
>> End: Frodo wants to be at peace
> A LITTLE PRINCESS (Frances Hodgson Burnett)
>> Beginning: Sarah Crewe wants to be served hand and foot
>> End: Sarah Crewe wants to belong to a family/be loved for herself

Instructor: In the first part of "The Monkey's Paw," Mr. White wants to find out if the paw can actually grant wishes. In the second part of the story, does he get his wish for two hundred pounds?

Student: Yes.

Instructor: Why does he get the two hundred pounds?

Student: Because his son has been killed.

NOTE TO INSTRUCTOR: Provide this answer to the student if necessary.

Instructor: So in the second part of the story, Mr. White has actually gotten what he wanted—he now knows that the monkey's paw can indeed grant wishes. But is he glad for the money?

Student: No.

Instructor: Some stories are about a protagonist reaching his goal—getting what he wants. But in other stories, the protagonist gets what he wants—and then realizes that he doesn't want it after all. The point at which the protagonist changes his direction is often called the *pivot point*. After his son is killed, does Mr. White believe that the paw has power?

Student: Yes.

NOTE TO INSTRUCTOR: If necessary, point out that Mr. White doesn't want to make the second wish because he believes it *will* work—and he doesn't want to.

Instructor: In the third part of the story, what does Mr. White's wife suddenly realize?

Student: They can use the monkey paw to get her son back.

Instructor: What does Mr. White want? Hint: it's a negative want—something he wants to *avoid.*

Student: He wants to avoid using the paw.

Instructor: So in the middle of the story, Mr. White's goal completely changes direction. He now wants the opposite of what he wanted before. Use the lines in your workbook to write two sentences describing the pivot point of "The Monkey's Paw."
NOTE TO INSTRUCTOR: The student's sentence[s] should resemble the following:

After his son dies, Mr. White no longer wants to know if the monkey's paw has power. Instead, he wants to avoid using it.

OR

Mr. White's wish is granted when he receives 200 pounds after his son's death. After that, all he wants is to not use the monkey's paw.

STEP FOUR: **Identify the climax of the story**

Instructor: At the end of the story, Mr. White makes his one final wish—because he is afraid of his wife. He wishes Herbert alive again. At first, nothing happens. Then, what do he and his wife hear?

Student: A knock on the door.

Instructor: What does his wife do?

Student: She goes down to answer the door.

Instructor: Is she able to get it open?

Student: No.

Instructor: While she is struggling with the door, what is Mr. White doing?

Student: Looking for the monkey's paw.

Instructor: What does he hope to do with it?

Student: Make the third wish.

Instructor: So at the very end of the story, Mr. White is forced to do the one thing he is trying to avoid—in order to keep something much worse from happening. The scene where he searches for the paw while his wife struggles to open the door is the climax of the story. Read the definition of story climax from your workbook.

Student: Story climax: the point of greatest tension or conflict

Instructor: What is the conflict between Mr. White and his wife?

Student: She wants to open the door and he doesn't OR She wants Herbert back and he is afraid of what Herbert will look like.

Instructor: There is also a tension here between Mr. White and whatever it is on the porch. Mrs. White doesn't feel that tension—she just wants her son back. But Mr. White is afraid of what he will see if that door opens. There is also a third level of tension. Mr. White has been trying to avoid the monkey's paw. But now, what does he have to do?

Student: Use it.

Instructor: So there are three levels of conflict and tension in the story climax—between Mr. White and his wife, between Mr. White and the thing on the porch, and between what Mr. White really wants, and what he has to do. A good story climax has more than one level of conflict and tension in it. In your workbook, write down the three kinds of tension present in the climax of "The Monkey's Paw."

STEP FIVE: **Learn about foreshadowing**

Instructor: There's one more literary term you should know. Read me the definition of *foreshadowing* from your workbook.

Student: Foreshadowing: giving the reader clues about what will happen later in the story.

Instructor: There are two examples of foreshadowing in Part I of "The Monkey's Paw." The first comes when Herbert White asks Sergeant-Major Morris why he hasn't had three wishes. Morris says, "I have." Look back at the story now. What happens to his face when he says that?

Student: His face whitens.

Instructor: This tells you that something horrible happens on the third wish. You never find out what happened to Morris—but now you're prepared for something bad to happen at the third wish. Now, look down three lines. Sergeant-Major Morris says that the first man who had the paw also had three wishes. What was his third wish for?

Student: Death

Instructor: This tells you that something even worse must have happened on the second wish. Now you're prepared for the second wish on the paw to be awful as well. This is foreshadowing. The author is preparing you for what happens to Mr. White. What horrible thing happens on his second wish?

Student: His son comes back.

Instructor: This forces him to do something dreadful on the third wish. What does he do?

Student: He wishes his son away.

Day Three: Compare

 Focus: Comparing similarities and differences

Beginning in Week 5, the student practiced writing comparisons—using similarities and differences to organize compositions in history and in science. Today, she will do the same in literature, listing the similarities and differences between "The Monkey's Paw" and "The Open Window."

The sentences and paragraphs the student writes today will become part of this week's composition, which will be finished in tomorrow's assignment.

STEP ONE: **Add to the Literary Terms chart (Student Responsibility)**

Student instructions for Step One:

> Review what you learned in Day Two by adding the following definitions to your Literary Terms chart:
>
> pivot point: the moment at which the main character changes goals, wants, or direction
> story climax: the point of greatest tension or conflict
> foreshadowing: giving the reader clues about what will happen later in the story

STEP TWO: **Compare structure**

Student instructions for Step Two:

> Using your own scratch paper (or word processing program) write two to four sentences describing the structure of "The Open Window." If necessary, glance back at Week 10, Day Three and the work you did in Step Two.
> Then, write three to six sentences describing the structure of "The Monkey's Paw." Be sure to discuss the pivot and the parts into which the story is divided.
> When you are finished, show your work to your instructor.

HOW TO HELP THE STUDENT WITH STEP TWO

The student's work should focus more on the structure than on the content of the two stories, although she'll need to include some plot details as she writes. Her answers should resemble the following:

> "The Open Window" is a story-within-a-story. Framton Nuttel goes to visit a neighbor. While he is there, he meets the neighbor's niece. She tells him the second story, about the neighbor's husband and brothers drowning in a bog.

OR

The first story in "The Open Window" is Mr. Nuttel's visit to Mrs. Sappleton. This is a frame around the second story, which Mrs. Sappleton's niece Vera tells to Mr. Nuttel while they are waiting for her aunt.

AND

"The Monkey's Paw" is divided into three parts, reminding us of the three wishes the monkey's paw is supposed to grant. The second part of the story acts as the pivot. After his son is killed, Mr. White no longer wants to test the power of the paw.

OR

"The Monkey's Paw" is divided into three parts. In the first part, Mr. White wants to find out if the paw has power. He wishes for two hundred pounds, but this leads to his son's death in the second part of the story. This is the pivot point. After this, Mr. White has a different want—to avoid using the paw at all.

STEP THREE: **Compare story climaxes**

Student instructions for Step Three:

> Write two to three sentences describing what happens at the climax of "The Open Window."
> Then, write three to four sentences describing what happens at the climax of "The Monkey's Paw."
> When you are finished, show your work to your instructor.

HOW TO HELP THE STUDENT WITH STEP THREE

The student's answers should resemble the following:

The story climax of "The Open Window" comes when Mr. Nuttel sees Mrs. Sappleton's husband and brothers coming across the lawn. He thinks they are ghosts, so he runs away in terror.

OR

At the climax of "The Open Window," Vera's uncles come walking across the lawn towards the house. Because of Vera's story, Mr. Nuttel thinks they are ghosts. He leaps up and dashes away.

AND

The story climax of "The Monkey's Paw" comes in the third part of the story. Mr. White wishes for Herbert to come back to life, but then is afraid of what he will see. While his wife is trying to open the door, Mr. White uses his last wish to send Herbert back to his grave.

OR

Mr. White uses his second wish to bring Herbert back to life, but when he hears his son knocking on the door, he is terrified. At the climax of the story, Herbert is on the porch and Mrs. White is trying to let him in. Mr. White is searching frantically for the paw. When he finds it, he wishes Herbert away just in time.

STEP FOUR: **Compare language**

Student instructions for Step Four:

> Write three to four sentences describing how Saki uses word choice in "The Open Window" to create suspense and to fool the reader. You can choose to use sentences from the essay you wrote last week, or write new sentences.
>
> Then, write three to four sentences describing how W. W. Jacobs uses word choice to make his story more effective. Discuss his use of repeated threes, but also look for vocabulary that heightens the sense of horror, especially towards the end of the story. If you have difficulty, ask your instructor for help.
>
> When you are finished, show your work to your instructor.

HOW TO HELP THE STUDENT WITH STEP FOUR

The student's answers should resemble the following:

In "The Open Window," Saki describes the three men as "muddy up to the eyes," just as they would be if they had drowned in a bog. He also describes the reactions of both Vera and Mr. Nuttel with words that suggest they are really seeing ghosts—they are struck with "dazed horror" and "nameless fear."

But he also uses ironic language to tell us that he is playing a trick on us. For example, "Vera" means truth, but Vera is making up her entire story.

OR

Saki uses phrases such as "dazed horror" and "nameless fear" to suggest that the three men walking across the lawn are actually ghosts. But he also uses ironic names for his characters to tell us that we should not take them seriously. "Vera" means truth, but Vera tells lies. And although Mrs. Sappleton's name comes from the word for "wise," she is completely fooled by her niece.

AND

In "The Monkey's Paw," W. W. Jacobs uses the number three to remind us of the three wishes the paw grants. Three different people get three wishes each. Sergeant-Major Morris has three glasses of whisky, and the man from Maw & Meggins walks past the gate three times. He also chooses words that make us feel horror over Mr. White's wishes. When his wife tells him to wish Herbert alive again, Jacobs describes her as feverish and with an "unnatural look." She has "burning eyes," and while she is looking out the window, a candle throws "pulsating shadows" on the ceiling and walls.

OR

> Jacobs points out the importance of the number three right at the beginning of the story, when three people are gathered together in the villa. When Morris arrives, he has three drinks, and then tells them that the monkey's paw will grant three wishes each to three different people.
>
> Jacobs also uses word choice carefully. He describes the monkey's paw as dirty and shriveled, and tells us that Mr. White shivers and wipes his hand after touching it. Later, he calls it an "unwholesome thing." He also makes us fear Herbert by telling us that Herbert's knocks are a "fusillade," like gunshots going off.

The paragraph does not have to display a sophisticated grasp of how language is used to heighten the atmosphere of the story—the goal is for the student to try, independently, to reflect on how words are used to bring about the story's effect.

If the student has trouble with "The Monkey's Paw," ask her to go back to the paragraph beginning "He went down in the darkness," in Part III of the story, and to underline every word that makes her think of fear, terror, horror, or suspense. Then, ask her to do the same for the paragraphs beginning "He sat until he was chilled with the cold" and "Neither spoke, but lay silently." Her paragraphs might then look like this:

> He went down in the <u>darkness</u>, and felt his way to the parlour, and then to the mantelpiece. The talisman was in its place, and a <u>horrible fear</u> that the unspoken wish might bring his <u>mutilated</u> son before him ere he could escape from the room <u>seized</u> upon him, and he caught his breath as he found that he had lost the direction of the door. His brow <u>cold</u> with sweat, he felt his way round the table, and groped along the wall until he found himself in the small passage with the <u>unwholesome</u> thing in his hand.
>
> He sat until he was <u>chilled</u> with the cold, glancing occasionally at the figure of the old woman peering through the window. The candle-end, which had burned below the rim of the china candlestick, was throwing <u>pulsating shadows</u> on the ceiling and walls, until with a <u>flicker</u> larger than the rest, it <u>expired</u>. The old man, with an unspeakable sense of relief at the failure of the talisman, <u>crept</u> back to his bed, and a minute afterward the old woman came silently and apathetically beside him.
>
> Neither spoke, but lay silently listening to the <u>ticking</u> of the clock. A stair <u>creaked</u>, and a squeaky mouse scurried noisily through the wall. The <u>darkness</u> was <u>oppressive</u>, and after lying for some time screwing up his courage, he took the box of matches, and striking one, went downstairs for a candle.

Then ask her to choose from the underlined words as she writes her sentences.

Day Four: Write

Focus: Writing a comparison and contrast of two stories

Today, the student will write a brief essay comparing the structure, story climaxes, and language of "The Monkey's Paw" and "The Open Window."

For this comparison, the student won't need to write a narrative summary. Instead she will concentrate on writing a point-by-point comparison with an introduction and conclusion.

STEP ONE: **Write the first point-by-point comparison**

Student instructions for Step One:

> Look at the two sets of sentences you wrote about the structure of the two stories. Ask yourself: What is similar about the structure of the stories? Try to sum up this similarity in one sentence. Then, combine the sentences into a paragraph describing what is different about how each story is put together.
>
> If you have difficulty, ask your instructor for help.
>
> When you're finished, show your work to your instructor (just to make sure that you're on the right track).

HOW TO HELP THE STUDENT WITH STEP ONE

The most obvious similarity between the structure of the two stories is that both have more than one section, part, or element: "The Open Window" has two elements (Vera's story and the frame story) and "The Monkey's Paw" has three sections.

The student's paragraph should resemble the following:

> Both stories are made up of more than one section. However, the stories are structured differently. "The Open Window" is a story-within-a-story. Framton Nuttel goes to visit a neighbor. While he is there, he meets the neighbor's niece. She tells him the second story, about the neighbor's husband and brothers drowning in a bog. "The Monkey's Paw" is divided into three parts. In the first part, Mr. White wants to find out if the paw has power. He wishes for two hundred pounds, but this leads to his son's death in the second part of the story. This is the pivot point. After this, Mr. White has a different want—to avoid using the paw at all. However, in the third part of the story, he is forced to use the paw for two more wishes.

If the student is stumped, tell her, "The similarity is that they both have more than one section." If she is still frustrated, let her read the sample paragraph above; she may need to see an example before she understands what she's being asked to do.

STEP TWO: **Write the second and third comparisons**

Student instructions for Step Two:

> Use the same strategy to write about the story climaxes. Write a sentence telling what is the same about the climaxes. Then, describe the differences by telling what happens in each one.
>
> Now finish your comparison by describing what is the same about the way both authors use language. Then, describe precisely what each one does—and how they are different.
>
> Remember that you should use either present tense or past tense throughout.
>
> You should quote each story at least once in your section comparing the language that the two authors use. You do not need to footnote the quotes as long as you clearly indicate which story you are quoting.
>
> If you need help, ask your instructor. If you are comfortable with your work, you do not need to show it until the composition is finished and proofread.

HOW TO HELP THE STUDENT WITH STEP TWO

The story climaxes are the same in that both involve "ghosts." The student could also conclude that both climaxes are intended to scare the reader, and that both of them involve a terrified protagonist (Mr. Nuttel and Mr. White). Both of them also involve the "ghosts" approaching or trying to come through a door. The difference, of course, is that the ghosts in "The Open Window" are actually living men, while the ghost in "The Monkey's Paw" is "real."

Both authors create suspense, a feeling of spooky supernaturalism, and a sense of fear through their choices of language. The difference is that Jacobs intends to create *actual* fear, while Saki is playing a game with the reader. It may help to point out to the student that while Saki makes heavy use of irony, Jacobs is not ironic at all.

Discuss the above with the student if necessary.

The student's paragraphs should resemble the following:

> Both stories end with the appearance of a ghost. In "The Open Window," the ghosts are pretend. At the climax of "The Open Window," Vera's uncles come walking across the lawn towards the house. Because of Vera's story, Mr. Nuttel leaps up and dashes away—but the men are actually still alive. On the other hand, the ghost in "The Monkey's Paw" is real. Mr. White uses his second wish to bring Herbert back to life, but when he hears his son knocking on the door, he is terrified. At the climax of the story, Herbert is on the porch and Mrs. White is trying to let him in. Mr. White is searching frantically for the paw. When he finds it, he wishes Herbert away just in time.
>
> Both authors choose their words carefully to create a sense of horror. In "The Open Window," Saki describes the three men as "muddy up to the eyes," just as they would be if they had drowned in a bog. He also describes the reactions of both Vera and Mr. Nuttel with words that suggest they are really seeing ghosts—they are struck with "dazed horror" and "nameless fear." But he also uses ironic language to tell us that he is playing a trick on us. For example, "Vera" means truth, but Vera is making up her entire story.
>
> W. W. Jacobs is not playing tricks on the reader. His words are meant to convey real

fear! He also chooses words that make us feel horror over Mr. White's wishes. When Mr. White's wife tells him to wish Herbert alive again, Jacobs describes her as feverish and with an "unnatural look." She has "burning eyes," and while she is looking out the window, a candle throws "pulsating shadows" on the ceiling and walls. Jacobs also uses the number three to remind us of the three wishes the paw grants. Three different people get three wishes each. Sergeant-Major Morris has three glasses of whisky, and the man from Maw & Meggins walks past the gate three times.

STEP THREE: **Write an introduction and conclusion**

Student instructions for Step Three:

> Finish your composition by writing an introduction by summary and a conclusion by personal reaction. If you need to review these forms, go back to Week Six, Days One and Two.
> Your introduction by summary should say whether you think the stories are more alike or more different, and what the greatest similarity or difference is. It should also include the titles and authors of both stories.
> Your conclusion by personal reaction should say which story you prefer and why.
> The introduction and conclusion should each be an independent paragraph.

HOW TO HELP THE STUDENT WITH STEP THREE

The student's introduction should resemble the following:

"The Open Window," by Saki, and "The Monkey's Paw," by W. W. Jacobs, are both ghost stories. However, "The Monkey's Paw" is actually supposed to be scary, while "The Open Window" plays a joke on the reader instead.

OR

"The Monkey's Paw" by W. W. Jacobs and "The Open Window" by Saki are very different in structure and in language. Both stories end with the appearance of a ghost—but only one of the ghosts is real.

If necessary, allow the student to read one of the above examples—but then require him to write his own introduction using different similarities and differences.

The student's conclusion should resemble the following:

The first time I read "The Open Window," I was just as fooled by Vera's story as Mr. Nuttel was. I prefer it to "The Monkey's Paw" because of the clever ending.

OR

"The Monkey's Paw" is a genuinely scary story. When I first read it, I could feel the hair on the back of my neck standing up. I found it much more compelling than "The Open Window," which was a funny story but not frightening at all.

STEP FOUR: **Proofread**

Student instructions for Step Four:

Before you give your essay to your instructor, proofread it using the following steps:

1. Read your composition out loud. Listen for awkward or unclear sections. Rewrite them so that they flow more naturally.
2. Read your composition out loud a second time. Listen for repeated nouns, verbs, and modifiers. If you find yourself using the same noun or verb more than twice, use your thesaurus to find an alternative. If you use a modifier (adverb, adjective, or prepositional phrase acting as an adjective or adverb) more than once, find another word.
3. Pay special attention to your transitions. When you are writing a comparison/contrast paper, it is very easy to overuse the words "but," "however, "on the one hand," and "on the other hand." If necessary, look up "however" and "but" in your thesaurus to find substitutes.
4. Look for sentence fragments or run-on sentences. Correct them if you find them.
5. Check to make sure that you have quoted directly from each story.
6. Make sure that your composition includes introduction, three sets of comparison/contrasts, and conclusion.
7. Check your spelling by looking, individually, at each word that might be a problem.

HOW TO HELP THE STUDENT WITH STEP FOUR

Evaluate the student's paper using the following rubric. Refer back to the models in the first three steps if necessary.

Week 11 Rubric

Organization:

1 The entire composition should have at least five paragraphs but can be as long as seven to eight paragraphs.
2 The introduction should include the titles of both stories and authors, and should summarize the most compelling similarity or difference between the stories. It should be the first independent paragraph of the paper.
3 The comparison and contrast section of the paper should be at least three paragraphs in length. It should compare and contrast three elements:
   a. story structure
   b. story climax
   c. language
   Each comparison and contrast should begin by describing similarities and then should describe differences.
4 The paragraph[s] on language should contain direct quotes from both stories.
5 The conclusion should be the last paragraph of the paper. It should give the student's personal opinion about the stories.

Mechanics:

1 Each sentence should make sense on its own when read aloud.
2 There should be no sentence fragments or run-on sentences.
3 All words should be spelled correctly.
4 The first line of each paragraph should be properly indented.
5 Verb tense should be consistent throughout.
6 No noun or verb should be used more than twice (with the exception of state-of-being verbs, linking verbs, and the verb "said").
7 No modifier or prepositional phrase acting as a modifier should be used more than once.
8 "However" and "but" should not be used more than twice each. "One the one hand" and "on the other hand" should not be used more than once.

WEEK 12: EXPLANATION BY DEFINITION: ESSENTIAL AND ACCIDENTAL PROPERTIES

This week the student will begin to investigate a new *topos: explanation by way of definition*.

This is a major *topos* with three separate elements; it can serve as the basis for an entire extended essay. The student will learn each element separately. First he'll work on answering the question, "What is it?" In another week, he will address the question, "How does it work?" Finally, he'll study how to answer the question, "Where does it belong?" In technical language, he'll be learning to define the *properties, function,* and *genus* of an object or phenomenon.

First, the student will practice this in science. Then, he will exercise those same skills on a topic in history.

Day One: Essential Properties and Accidental Properties

 Focus: Answering the question "What is it"?

The student has been told to complete today's steps ***slowly and carefully.*** You may want to repeat that to him, out loud, before he begins.

STEP ONE: **Review scientific description (Student Responsibility)**

Student instructions for Step One:

> You've already practiced the first part of *explanation by way of definition*. Last year, you learned to write a *scientific description*—a visual and structural description of an object or phenomenon. A description is one of the building blocks you'll use when you write full definitions.
>
> Take a minute now to review the form of the scientific description. Read the following chart out loud.

Scientific Description

Definition: A visual and structural description of an object or phenomenon

Procedure	Remember
1. Describe each part of the object or phenomenon and tell what it is made from.	1. Consider using figurative language to make the description more visual.
2. Choose a point of view.	2. Consider combining points of view.

When you first learned about scientific descriptions, back in Week 12 of Level One of this course, you learned how to describe the parts of an object and tell what each part is made of, while also giving the reader a clear picture of what the object looks like. Among the examples given was this excerpt from Bill Bryson's *A Short History of Nearly Everything:*

★

This description gives you the parts of the cell (membrane, nucleus, cytoplasm, skeleton) and tells you what they are made of (genetic information, lipids). It also uses figurative language (peas, basketballs, and bullets) to give you a sense of what the cell *looks* like.

Your assignment in Week 12 was to describe the parts of a volcano and explain what each part was made from, using at least one metaphor (figurative language). (If you can find that description, you should read back through it now. But if it's lost forever, I understand.)

The following week, you added one more element to your description. You learned that, when writing a scientific description, you can use either a *removed* or *present* point of view.

You were given two examples. Review them now.

The first is written from a *removed* point of view. The narrator of this paragraph knows a lot about volcanoes, but he isn't actually *there* as the volcano erupts.

★

The second is an eyewitness description written by the Roman lawyer Pliny the Younger after he lived through the eruption of Mount Vesuvius in the year 79.

★

A description written from the present point of view tells the reader what the narrator is seeing, hearing, feeling, smelling, and/or tasting.

STEP TWO: **Understand essential properties and accidental properties**

Student instructions for Step Two:

When you write a scientific description, you give the reader basic answers to two important questions:

What is it?

How does it work?

Those questions, asked even more carefully, can also help you to write a definition—an explanation of the nature of a scientific object. To them, you'll add a third question: "Where does it belong?"

For this week, you'll just concentrate on "What is it?"

When you answer this question for the reader, you are describing the *properties* of an object. You can write perfectly serviceable descriptions without understanding exactly what a property is, but it's time to stretch your mind (and to prepare yourself for the upper-level writing you'll be doing later in your student years). So take a few minutes now to think about properties.

A property is something that belongs to the object. The philosopher Aristotle said that there are two different kinds of properties: essential and accidental. What's the difference? Here's how one philosopher puts it:

> *Essential properties are those that define a thing as the sort or kind that it is; accidental properties are all other properties of a thing.*[13]

Think about cows for a minute. All cows chew a cud, have a four-part stomach, and contain cow DNA. These are "essential properties" of cows. If an animal doesn't chew its cud, have a four-part stomach, and contain cow DNA, it isn't a cow. These essential properties *make* a cow a cow.

Many cows are brown. But being brown is not necessary to being a cow. It is an "accidental property." Some cows may be black or white.

Sometimes, cows are outfitted with sunglasses. The sunglasses are not an essential part of being a cow. In Aristotle's language, they are also "accidental properties."

When you answer the question "What is it?" you're describing the essential and accidental properties of a scientific object or phenomenon.

In the following list of properties, underline *only* those that are **essential properties.** When you're finished, show your work to your instructor. (The first one should be easy. The second might be a little harder—consult an encyclopedia or online resource if necessary. For an exercise like this, Wikipedia is perfectly acceptable.)

HOW TO HELP THE STUDENT WITH STEP TWO

The answers to the exercise are:

father	**tornado**
thirty-seven	visible
blond	wedge-shaped
<u>male</u>	black
protective	<u>rotating</u>
accountant	<u>touching ground</u>
<u>parent</u>	noisy
tall	form in afternoon
	destructive

STEP THREE: Examine the questions about properties

Student instructions for Step Three:

> When you define an object, you start out by describing its essential properties and its accidental properties. Asking the following questions will help you identify these.
>
> Read these questions out loud to your instructor. If any of them are unclear, ask for explanations.

---

13. Richard Cross, "Duns Scotus: *Ordinatio.*" In *Central Works of Philosophy, Volume 1: Ancient and Medieval,* ed. John Shand (McGill-Queens, 2005), p. 230.

HOW TO HELP THE STUDENT WITH STEP THREE

The student should read the questions out loud to you; this forces him to slow down and pay attention. Brief explanations are provided below in case the student needs them.

1. Essential Properties and Accidental Properties

What does it look like?

This is visual appearance—basically, what the student learned in Level One when writing scientific descriptions.

How does it behave?

This has to do with appearance but will inevitably overlap with the second question about function, "How does it work?" If the student asks why, tell him that he'll learn more about this when he studies function.

What senses come into play as you observe it?

Sight, hearing, smell, touch, taste.

What do those senses reveal?

Is your observation passive (watching/listening) or active (experimenting/collecting/probing)?

The basic division between active and passive observation is very important in science. Interacting with an object or phenomenon can change its accidental properties—behavior, appearance, etc.

What sorts of measurements (temperature, quantity, time, etc.) are necessary to your observation?

Size measurements are length, height, and width/breadth. Other measurements include mass (weight), time (how long something has existed/behaved in a certain way), temperature, and pressure.

What does it resemble?

This could either be a straightforward comparison (a wolf looks like a dog) or a metaphor (a storm cloud looks like a mountain range in the sky).

What is it made of?

This could include both the large and small building blocks of an object: a person is made of bone, muscle, and blood; a person is made up of cells; a person is made up of molecules.

What sort of structure does it have?

How many parts does it have? How are those parts related to each other?

What is its extent in space?

Measurement of size and mass are used to define extent in space—how big something is.

What is its extent in time?

Time measurement is used to determine how long something has been in existence.

Which properties are essential?

Which are accidental?

These are explained in the lesson.

STEP FOUR: **Practice the questions**

Student instructions for Step Four:

Now you'll identify the answers to these questions for a scientific object or phenomenon close to you—someone who lives in your house.

Choose a sibling, your parent, or (if necessary) a family pet. On your own paper, jot down phrases or sentences answering each of the "properties" questions, using the additional guidelines below. You won't be writing an essay about the person (or pet) you're describing—right now, you're just practicing thinking about essential and accidental properties.

1. Essential Properties and Accidental Properties

What does it look like?

Size (height, weight), color (hair, skin, fur), outline (arms and legs? how many?), clothes (or fur), features . . .

How does it behave?

Expressions, characteristic behaviors, habits, bad habits . . .

What senses come into play as you observe it?

Sight, hearing, smell, touch, taste . . .

What do those senses reveal?

. . . ?

Is your observation passive (watching/listening) or active (experimenting/collecting/probing)?

Which of your observations so far happen when you're not actually talking to the person/pet? Which come from the person/pet doing his/her/its own thing while you just watch?

What sorts of measurements (temperature, quantity, time, etc.) are necessary to your observation?

You're probably using measurements for height and weight . . . are there any others?

What does it resemble?

Do you know another person/pet that your subject looks like?

What is it made of?

You don't have to go into too much detail here . . . but describe basic blood/bone/ hair or fur . . .

What sort of structure does it have?

How many arms, legs, toes/fingers/claws? How about the face—eyes, nose, mouth, or muzzle?

What is its extent in space?

How much physical space does it take up?

What is its extent in time?

How long has it been alive?

Which properties are essential?

What makes the person or pet it??

Which are accidental?

What could be different about other siblings/parents/pets, and yet make them still siblings/parents/pets?

HOW TO HELP THE STUDENT WITH STEP FOUR

The student's answers might resemble the following (although, obviously, the specifics will be very different). If the student struggles, allow him to read through the answers below. Notice that some answers will overlap.

Essential Properties and Accidental Properties of Mars, the German Shepherd

What does it look like?

> About two feet high at the shoulder, weighs 75 pounds. Light brown with black muzzle and legs; four legs; very large, pointed ears. Enormous tail, strong enough to knock things off shelves when he wags it. Strong, sharp, white teeth, white blaze in front.

How does it behave?

> Curls up in the middle of the floor while I do schoolwork, watches me. Every time I get up, he gets up too and follows me, even if I just go across the room. He likes to sit underneath the shelf where we keep the dog biscuit bowl and stare at it. When I rub his belly he turns all the way over on his back and makes grunting noises.

What senses come into play as you observe it?

> Sight, hearing, smell, touch

What do those senses reveal?

> He looks and sounds fierce—he has very sharp teeth and a loud, frightening bark. He smells like swampy pond water today because he's been in the pond and he needs a bath. His fur is coarse on the outside, but when I push my fingers closer to his skin it is soft and downy.

Is your observation passive (watching/listening) or active (experimenting/collecting/probing)?

> All of my observations are active. When I am watching Mars, he is always watching me too, and reacting to me.

What sorts of measurements (temperature, quantity, time, etc.) are necessary to your observation?

> So far, mostly size measurements. I could also use time measurements. Mars is four years old.

What does it resemble?

> Mars has the same basic features (head, tail, legs and paws) as our border collie. He is as large as a wolf, though, and his coloring is a lot like a wolf.

What is it made of?

> Muscles over a bone skeleton, with a thick coating of fur.

What sort of structure does it have?

Four legs, four paws. Large head with sharp teeth and strong jaw. Very large alert ears. Enormous tail.

What is its extent in space?

See above.

What is its extent in time?

Four years old.

Which properties are essential?

Canine teeth, four legs, two ears, muzzle.

Which are accidental?

Color, behavior, smell, size.

Day Two: Analyze

 Focus: Studying a model answering the question "What is it?"

STEP ONE: **Read (Student Responsibility)**

Student instructions for Step One:

> Carefully read the following paragraphs from *A Naturalist's Guide to the Arctic*, by E. C. Pielou.

★

STEP TWO: **Answer the questions**

Student instructions for Step One:

> This is the first part of an explanation by definition. It answers many of the questions you practiced in the last lesson.
>
> Your task now: to identify which questions the paragraph answers.
>
> Using the list of questions from Step Three of Day One, go back through the paragraphs about the *aurora borealis*. On the worksheet below, answer each question. If the paragraphs do not provide you with an answer, draw a line through the question and continue on. The first one is done for you.
>
> When you are finished, show your work to your instructor.

HOW TO HELP THE STUDENT WITH STEP TWO

The student's answers should resemble the following. He should have at least two answers for each question, but doesn't need to have every answer provided.

If he needs help, use the explanations below.

What does it look like? pale green, occasionally red or violet, glowing, shimmering, flickering, pulsating patches of light

How does it behave? shimmers, flickers and pulses [paragraph 1, the only actions performed by the lights]

What senses come into play as you observe it? sight [hearing is also mentioned, but you may want to point out that the author is describing a lack of sound]

What do those senses reveal? colors and lack of sound [paragraphs 1 and 3]

Is your observation passive (watching/listening) or active (experimenting/collecting/probing)? passive [the author describes what the aurora looks and (doesn't) sound like. There is no experimenting in this observation.]

What sorts of measurements (temperature, quantity, time, etc.) are necessary to your observation? size-height [it is also correct for the student to mention the movement of the particles and the "liberation" of energy as light.]

What does it resemble? arcs, bands, rippling draperies, patches, neon sign [paragraph 1]

What is it made of? electrically charged particles, subatomic particles, oxygen and nitrogen OR light [paragraph 3][Either answer is acceptable, since the student will not necessarily have a sophisticated understanding of the construction of the borealis]

What sort of structure does it have? it is made up of the interaction between subatomic particles and atoms and molecules [in this case, the structure is described in terms of an ongoing process, since the aurora borealis is a phenomenon rather than an object]

What is its extent in space? 100 to 300 km above the ground, only in the arctic [answers to "where" questions describe extent in space]

What is its extent in time? when the sky is totally dark, not high summer [answers to "when" questions describe extent in time]

Which properties are essential? atoms and molecules struck by electrically charged particles [the actual makeup of the borealis]

Which are accidental? color, shape, height

STEP THREE: **Two-level outline**

Student instructions for Step Three:

> Now that you've seen how the author E. C. Pielou describes the essential and accidental properties in an essay, look a little more closely at the way in which he organizes his thoughts.
> Complete the following two-level outline of the passage. If you have trouble, ask your instructor for help.

HOW TO HELP THE STUDENT WITH STEP THREE

The student's outline should resemble the following:

   I.   Appearance
        A. Shape
        B. Color
   II. Sound
        A. Silent
        B. Accompanying sounds
   III. Causes
        A. The aurora itself OR Light
        B. Colors

If necessary, use the following questions to prompt the student:

I.   "Everything in the first paragraph can be seen with the eye. What do we call something that can be seen with the eye?"
     A. "What do arcs, bands, draperies, and patches all describe?"
     A. "What does the last sentence of the paragraph describe?"
II. Sound
     A. "The lack of something is described. What is it?"
     B. "What can actually be heard?"
III. "The *aurora borealis* is actually a phenomenon. This paragraph describes what makes the phenomenon happen. What is another word for this?"
     A. "The second half of the paragraph describes how the colors are caused. In the first half of the paragraph, what is being caused?"
     B. Colors

Day Three: Write About Essential and Accidental Properties

Focus: Writing answers to the question
"What is it?"

Today the student will prepare to write an explanation by definition that answers the questions about essential and accidental properties. The finished composition will be at least 150 words in length (but can be longer).

The student will write about volcanoes and volcanic eruptions—the same topic you covered in Level One when you wrote scientific descriptions. But this week's composition will be much more closely focused on the properties of the volcano.

If you can locate last year's composition, the student might enjoy comparing the two at the end of the week.

STEP ONE: **Read (Student Responsibility)**

Student instructions for Step One:

> Read back through the questions you'll be asking one more time. Then, read through the following passages without stopping to take notes.

★

STEP TWO: **Take notes**

Student instructions for Step Two:

> Now you'll take notes for your own description. The description should cover both the volcano and the volcanic eruption, since the eruption answers the question "How does it behave?"
>
> Today, try a slightly different method of taking notes.
>
> On your own paper, write each question and then look for the answers to that question in the passages provided. Jot down the answers. Be sure to record the author and page number of the passage where you found the information.
>
> Here's an example of how some of your answers might look:
>
> Question: What does it resemble?
> Answer: A "safety valve in the earth's crust" (Dineen, p. 10)
> > Rocks might be "as large as houses" (Clarkson, p. 8)
> > Eruption has flames "like lightning, but bigger" (Pliny, p. 534)
> > Cloud of ash "like a flood poured across the land" (Pliny, p. 535)
> > Dark "like the black of closed and unlighted rooms" (Pliny, p. 535)
>
> Question: What sorts of measurements (temperature, quantity, time, etc.) are necessary to your observation?
> Answer: Size, quantity, time, temperature

You would not need to have all of these answers, but you should aim to have at least two answers for each question. Some of the questions may not be addressed at all. If you find no answers, draw a line through the question and continue on.

> Writers work in different ways. Some writers find it easier to take many notes and then go back through them, looking for a theme to emerge. Others find it easier to settle on a tentative theme first and then take very specific notes supporting it. As you continue to write, you'll find out which method suits you best.
>
> Before you move on to the next step, show your work to your instructor.

HOW TO HELP THE STUDENT WITH STEP TWO

The student's answers should resemble the following. He should have at least two answers for each question unless the question is marked through; most possible answers have been provided, for your use only.

Notice that there may be overlap between answers.

What does it look like?

Opening in the earth's surface (Dineen, p. 6)

Clouds of steam and dust "thousands of feet high" (Dineen, p. 10)

"Surges of red-hot lava" (Dineen, p. 10)

Steep-sided depression: caldera (Dineen, p. 10)

"Bubbling springs of boiling mud" (Clarkson, p. 7)

Exploding geysers, streams flowing under glaciers (Clarkson, p. 7)

Columns of smoke, burning streams of lava, blanket of ash (Clarkson, p. 8)

Dark clouds covering everything, flames (Pliny, p. 534)

Thick darkness that can't be seen through (Pliny, p. 535)

Layers of ash on everything (Pliny, p. 535)

How does it behave?

Magma and gases are forced to the surface and escape (Dineen, p. 6)

Gases "escape explosively in a huge cloud of steam and dust" (Dineen, p. 10)

"Surges of red-hot lava flood out of the volcano's crater" (Dineen, p. 10)

Volcano collapses into itself after eruption (Dineen, p. 10)

Mud boils, hot pools explode, streams flow from glaciers (Clarkson, p. 7)

Ash and rock and steam explode when waves flow into the craters (Clarkson, p. 7)

Clouds rise "several miles" (Clarkson, p. 8)

Streams of lava burn "everything in their paths" (Clarkson, p. 8)

Rocks thrown into the air, blanket of ash settles (Clarkson, p. 8)

Ground shifts back and forth, sea "sucked backwards" (Pliny, p. 534)

"Dense cloud" of dust and ash shuts everything out (Pliny, p. 535)

What senses come into play as you observe it?

Sight, hearing, touch [neither smells nor tastes are mentioned]

What do those senses reveal?

Sights of the lava, dust, fire, geysers, dust clouds

Sound of explosion

Feeling: warmth (Clarkson, p. 7)

Feeling: shifting earth back and forth (Pliny, p. 534)

Is your observation passive (watching/listening) or active (experimenting/collecting/probing)?

Passive

What sorts of measurements (temperature, quantity, time, etc.) are necessary to your observation?

Size, quantity, time, temperature, speed (600 feet per second, Dineen, p. 10)

What does it resemble?

A "safety valve in the earth's crust" (Dineen, p. 10)
Rocks might be "as large as houses" (Clarkson, p. 8)
Eruption has flames "like lightning, but bigger" (Pliny, p. 534)
Cloud of ash "like a flood poured across the land" (Pliny, p. 535)
Dark "like the black of closed and unlighted rooms" (Pliny, p. 535)

What is it made of?

Magma and gases
Magma chamber
Ash and rock

What sort of structure does it have?

Opening at plate margins, "crack or weakness in the earth's crust" (Dineen, p. 10)
Crater with lava flowing from it

What is its extent in space?

At surface of the earth
Where "rising magma finds a way through a crack or weakness in the earth's crust" (Dineen, p. 6)

What is its extent in time?
Which properties are essential?

Magma and gas pushed out by pressure

Which are accidental?

Caldera
Violence of eruption
Mud, hot pools, streams, cones of ash
Thrown rocks, columns of smoke
Earthquake
Ash blanket

STEP THREE: **Organize**

Student instructions for Step Three:

Finish up today's work by organizing your answers into groups.

You should be able to divide your answers into two main groups—because there are actually two separate (but related) objects/phenomena described. Volcanoes are described, but so are volcanic eruptions.

Organize your answers into the following two groups:

I. Volcano

II. Eruption

When you're finished organizing your answers, show your work to your instructor.

HOW TO HELP THE STUDENT WITH STEP THREE

The student's division should resemble the following:

I. Volcano

What does it look like?

    Opening in the earth's surface (Dineen, p. 6)

    Steep-sided depression: caldera (Dineen, p. 10)

    "Bubbling springs of boiling mud" (Clarkson, p. 7)

    Exploding geysers, streams flowing under glaciers (Clarkson, p. 7)

How does it behave?

    Magma and gases are forced to the surface and escape (Dineen, p. 6)

    Volcano collapses into itself after eruption (Dineen, p. 10)

    Mud boils, hot pools explode, streams flow from glaciers (Clarkson, p. 7)

Is your observation passive (watching/listening) or active (experimenting/collecting/probing)?

    Passive

What does it resemble?

    A "safety valve in the earth's crust" (Dineen, p. 10)

What is it made of?

    Magma and gases

    Magma chamber

    Ash and rock

What sort of structure does it have?

    Opening at plate margins, "crack or weakness in the earth's crust" (Dineen, p. 10)

What is its extent in space?

    At surface of the earth

    Where "rising magma finds a way through a crack or weakness in the earth's

        crust" (Dineen, p. 6)

Which properties are essential?

    Magma and gas pushed out by pressure

II. Volcanic eruption

What does it look like?

    Clouds of steam and dust "thousands of feet high" (Dineen, p. 10)

    "Surges of red-hot lava" (Dineen, p. 10)

    Steep-sided depression: caldera (Dineen, p. 10)

    Columns of smoke, burning streams of lava, blanket of ash (Clarkson, p. 8)

    Dark clouds covering everything, flames (Pliny, p. 534)

Thick darkness that can't be seen through (Pliny, p. 535)
Layers of ash on everything (Pliny, p. 535)
How does it behave?
Gases "escape explosively in a huge cloud of steam and dust" (Dineen, p. 10)
"Surges of red-hot lava flood out of the volcano's crater" (Dineen, p. 10)
Volcano collapses into itself after eruption (Dineen, p. 10)
Ash and rock and steam explode when waves flow into the craters (Clarkson, p. 7)
Clouds rise "several miles" (Clarkson, p. 8)
Streams of lava burn "everything in their paths" (Clarkson, p. 8)
Rocks thrown into the air, blanket of ash settles (Clarkson, p. 8)
Ground shifts back and forth, sea "sucked backwards" (Pliny, p. 534)
"Dense cloud" of dust and ash shuts everything out (Pliny, p. 535)
What senses come into play as you observe it?
Sight, sound, touch [neither smells nor tastes are mentioned]
What do those senses reveal?
Sights of the lava, dust, fire, geysers, dust clouds
Sound of explosion
Feeling: warmth (Clarkson, p. 7)
Feeling: shifting earth back and forth (Pliny, p. 534)
Is your observation passive (watching/listening) or active (experimenting/collecting/probing)?
Passive
What sorts of measurements (temperature, quantity, time, etc.) are necessary to your
observation?
Size, quantity, time, temperature, speed (600 feet per second, Dineen, p. 10)
What does it resemble?
Rocks might be "as large as houses" (Clarkson, p. 8)
Eruption has flames "like lightning, but bigger" (Pliny, p. 534)
Cloud of ash "like a flood poured across the land" (Pliny, p. 535)
Dark "like the black of closed and unlighted rooms" (Pliny, p. 535)
What does it look like?
Opening in the earth's surface (Dineen, p. 6)
Clouds of steam and dust "thousands of feet high" (Dineen, p. 10)
"Surges of red-hot lava" (Dineen, p. 10)
Steep-sided depression: caldera (Dineen, p. 10)
"Bubbling springs of boiling mud" (Clarkson, p. 7)
Exploding geysers, streams flowing under glaciers (Clarkson, p. 7)
Columns of smoke, burning streams of lava, blanket of ash (Clarkson, p. 8)
Dark clouds covering everything, flames (Pliny, p. 534)
Thick darkness that can't be seen through (Pliny, p. 535)
Layers of ash on everything (Pliny, p. 535)
How does it behave?
Magma and gases are forced to the surface and escape (Dineen, p. 6)

Gases "escape explosively in a huge cloud of steam and dust" (Dineen, p. 10)

"Surges of red-hot lava flood out of the volcano's crater" (Dineen, p. 10)

Volcano collapses into itself after eruption (Dineen, p. 10)

Mud boils, hot pools explode, streams flow from glaciers (Clarkson, p. 7)

Ash and rock and steam explode when waves flow into the craters (Clarkson, p. 7)

Clouds rise "several miles" (Clarkson, p. 8)

Streams of lava burn "everything in their paths" (Clarkson, p. 8)

Rocks thrown into the air, blanket of ash settles (Clarkson, p. 8)

Ground shifts back and forth, sea "sucked backwards" (Pliny, p. 534)

"Dense cloud" of dust and ash shuts everything out (Pliny, p. 535)

What senses come into play as you observe it?

Sight, sound, touch [neither smells nor tastes are mentioned]

What do those senses reveal?

Sights of the lava, dust, fire, geysers, dust clouds

Sound of explosion

Feeling: warmth (Clarkson, p. 7)

Feeling: shifting earth back and forth (Pliny, p. 534)

Is your observation passive (watching/listening) or active (experimenting/collecting/probing)?

Passive

What sorts of measurements (temperature, quantity, time, etc.) are necessary to your observation?

Size, quantity, time, temperature, speed (600 feet per second, Dineen, p. 10)

What does it resemble?

A "safety valve in the earth's crust" (Dineen, p. 10)

Rocks might be "as large as houses" (Clarkson, p. 8)

Eruption has flames "like lightning, but bigger" (Pliny, p. 534)

Cloud of ash "like a flood poured across the land" (Pliny, p. 535)

Dark "like the black of closed and unlighted rooms" (Pliny, p. 535)

What is it made of?

Magma and gases

Magma chamber

Ash and rock

What sort of structure does it have?

Opening at plate margins, "crack or weakness in the earth's crust" (Dineen, p. 10)

Crater with lava flowing from it

What is its extent in space?

At surface of the earth

Where "rising magma finds a way through a crack or weakness in the earth's crust" (Dineen, p. 6)

~~What is its extent in time?~~

Which properties are essential?

Magma and gas pushed out by pressure

Which are accidental?
    Caldera
    Violence of eruption
    Mud, hot pools, streams, cones of ash
    Thrown rocks, columns of smoke
    Earthquake
    Ash blanket

Day Four: Write About Essential and Accidental Properties

Focus: Writing answers to the question
"What is it?"

STEP ONE: **Write (Student Responsibility)**

NOTE TO INSTRUCTOR: Make sure that the student reads and pays attention to the final paragraph of instructions. You might want to ask him to read it out loud to you.

Student instructions for Step One:

> Now that your answers have been organized into the proper order, write the description. Keep the following rules in mind:
>
> 1) The description should have at least two paragraphs and be at least 150 words in length. Longer is just fine.
> 2) Cite each source at least one time. When you cite Pliny's letter in your footnote, use the following format:
>
>> Pliny the Younger, "Pliny to Tacitus," trans. Cynthia Damon, in Ronald Mellor, ed., *The Historians of Ancient Rome: An Anthology of the Major Writings*, second ed. (Routledge, 2004), p. 534–535.
>
> When you cite a work from a larger collection, you put the name of the work being cited in quotation marks and the name of the larger collection/book in italics.
> 3) Use at least one metaphor or simile—either from your sources, or from your own imagination.
>
> Remember: you do not have to use all of the quotes and answers you've collected! Nor is it necessary for you to answer every question. For example, there's no reason in this particular description to explain to the reader that your observation of the volcano is passive, or that you are using the sense of sight. These questions will be much more useful to you when you do your own scientific observation instead of basing your work on what other people have written. Right

now, you are just practicing the skill of sorting through details and putting them together into readable prose.

STEP TWO: **Assemble the Works Cited page (Student Responsibility)**

Student instructions for Step Two:

> Title a separate piece of paper "Works Cited." List your sources in alphabetical order. The letter by Pliny should be listed in the same format as in your lesson. Alphabetize Pliny under "P."

STEP THREE: **Title your description**

Student instructions for Step Three:

> Now choose a title for your description.
> In Week 9 you learned the following steps for choosing a title:
>
> 1. What is the event, person, place, or process that your composition discusses? Jot it down on a scratch piece of paper.
> 2. Now, think about the *topos*: explanation by definition, with a focus on the essential and accidental properties of a scientific object or phenomenon.
>
> Can you come up with a phrase that includes both the event/person/place/process and a description of the *topos*?
> Center your title at the top of the first page of your composition. Double-space between the title and the top line of your first paragraph.
> If you need help, ask your instructor.

HOW TO HELP THE STUDENT WITH STEP THREE

Titling is a new skill for the student; he may think that this is a more complicated assignment than it actually is. Any of the following titles would be acceptable:

> "Defining a Volcano and a Volcanic Eruption"
> "What Is a Volcano?"
> "How a Volcano Works"
> "What Happens When a Volcano Erupts"

The student should not simply title the paper, "Volcanoes" or "Volcanoes and Eruptions." The point of the exercise is to push the student towards more specific and definite titles (even though the title of this particular paper may sound a little stilted.)

If the student is complete stuck, say, "Complete the following title. 'What Happens When . . .'"

STEP FOUR: **Proofread**

Student instructions for Step Four:

Before handing your paper to your instructor, go through the following proofreading steps.

1) Read your paper out loud, listening for awkward or unclear sections and repeated words. Rewrite awkward or unclear sentences so that they flow more naturally.
2) Read through the paper one more time, looking for sentence fragments, run-on sentences, and repeated words. Correct fragments and run-on sentences. If you used the same noun or verb more than twice, pick an alternative from the thesaurus. If you used a modifier (adverb, adjective, or prepositional phrase acting as an adjective or adverb) more than once, find another word.
3) Check the format of your footnotes and Works Cited page.
4) Check your spelling by looking, individually, at each word that might be a problem.

When you are finished, give your paper to your instructor for evaluation.

HOW TO HELP THE STUDENT WITH STEP FOUR

Evaluate the paper using the rubric at the end of this lesson.

The student's paper should resemble the following:

HOW A VOLCANO WORKS

A volcano is an opening in the earth's surface at a "plate margin," a weakness in the earth's crust.[1] A volcano is made up of a chamber that contains magma and gas that has been pushed to the surface by pressure. After the magma and gas erupts, the volcano sometimes collapses inward and forms a caldera. Volcanoes are like "safety valves" in the crust of the earth.[2]

When the pressure of the magma and gas gets too intense, the volcano explodes into an eruption. Columns of smoke and streams of fiery lava pour out of the opening of the volcano. A thick blanket of ash may fall all around. Dust and thick clouds cover the nearby land. Sometimes, huge rocks are thrown into the air.[3] The lava can burn everything in its path. The earth can shake, and the dust and ash can turn even daylight completely black. The flames coming from the lava can look like lightning, only larger.[4]

WORKS CITED

Clarkson, Peter. *Volcanoes*. Stillwater, Minn.: Voyageur Press, Inc., 2000.

Jacqueline Dineen, *Natural Disasters: Volcanoes*. Mankato, Minn.: The Creative Company, 2005.

Pliny the Younger, "Pliny to Tacitus," trans. Cynthia Damon. In Ronald Mellor, ed., *The*

Historians of Ancient Rome: An Anthology of the Major Writings, second ed. New York: Routledge, 2004, pp. 534–535.

_____

[1] Jacqueline Dineen, *Natural Disasters: Volcanoes* (The Creative Company, 2005), p. 10.

[2] Dineen, p. 10.

[3] Peter Clarkson, *Volcanoes* (Voyageur Press, 2000), p. 7.

[4] Pliny the Younger, "Pliny to Tacitus," trans. Cynthia Damon, in Ronald Mellor, ed., *The Historians of Ancient Rome: An Anthology of the Major Writings*, second ed. (Routledge, 2004), p. 534.

Week 12 Rubric

Organization:

1 The entire composition should be two paragraphs and at least 150 words in length.
2 The first paragraph should describe what a volcano is. The second should describe a volcanic eruption.
3 All three sources should be cited.
4 All sources mentioned in footnotes should be placed on a Works Cited page.
5 The composition should have a title, centered at the top of the first page. This title should *not* be simply "Volcano" or "Volcanic Eruption." (See Step Three.)
6 At least one metaphor or simile should be included.

Mechanics:

1 Each sentence should make sense on its own when read aloud.
2 There should be no sentence fragments or run-on sentences.
3 All words should be spelled correctly.
4 The first line of each paragraph should be properly indented.
5 Verb tense should be consistent throughout.
6 No noun or verb should be used more than twice (with the exception of state of being verbs, linking verbs, and the verb "said").
7 No modifier or prepositional phrase acting as a modifier should be used more than once.
8 Footnotes and the Works Cited page should be properly formatted.

WEEK 13: EXPLANATION BY DEFINITION: FUNCTION

This week, the student will work on the second part of an explanation by way of definition.

A fully-developed definition answers three questions:

What is it? [Essential and accidental properties]

How does it work?

Where does it belong?

Last week, the student described the essential and accidental properties of an object or phenomenon. This week, he will learn to answer the second question: "How does it work?" (What is its *function*?)

Day One: Function

Focus: Answering the question
"How does it work?"

The student has been told to complete today's steps **slowly and carefully.** You may want to repeat that to him, out loud, before he begins.

STEP ONE: Understand function (Student Responsibility)

Student instructions for Step One:

> When you answered the question "What is it?", you painted a picture of what the object looks like—its essential and accidental properties. But you need more than this to really understand what an object or phenomenon *is*.
>
> Read the following definition of a machine:
>
>> There in the flickering light of the lamp was the machine sure enough, squat, ugly, and askew; a thing of brass, ebony, ivory, and translucent glimmering quartz. Solid to the touch—for I put out my hand and felt the rail of it—and with brown spots and smears upon the ivory, and bits of grass and moss upon the lower parts, and one rail bent awry.

213

This tells you what the machine looks like, what it resembles, what it is made of, its structure and extent in space—but your understanding of the machine is still incomplete, because you don't know what it *does*. Until the reader can understand the **function** of the machine, it remains mysterious.

Now read on:

> I gave it a last tap, tried all the screws again, put one more drop of oil on the quartz rod, and sat myself in the saddle . . . I took the starting lever in one hand and the stopping one in the other, pressed the first, and almost immediately the second. I seemed to reel; I felt a nightmare sensation of falling; and, looking round, I saw the laboratory exactly as before. Had anything happened ? For a moment I suspected that my intellect had tricked me. Then I noted the clock. A moment before, as it seemed, it had stood at a minute or so past ten; now it was nearly half-past three!
>
> I drew a breath, set my teeth, gripped the starting lever with both my hands, and went off with a thud. The laboratory got hazy and went dark . . . I pressed the lever over to its extreme position. The night came like the turning out of a lamp, and in another moment came tomorrow. The laboratory grew faint and hazy, then fainter and ever fainter. Tomorrow night came black, then day again, night again, day again, faster and faster still . . . I saw trees growing and changing like puffs of vapor, now brown, now green; they grew, spread, fluctuated, and passed away. I saw huge buildings rise up faint and fair, and pass like dreams. The whole surface of the earth seemed changing— melting and flowing under my eyes. The little hands upon the dials that registered my speed raced round faster and faster. Presently I noted that the sun belt swayed up and down, from solstice to solstice, in a minute or less, and that, consequently, my pace was over a year a minute; and minute by minute the white snow flashed across the world and vanished, and was followed by the bright, brief green of spring.

Now that you've read about how the machine works, do you have a better idea of what it is? The answer follows . . . so if you want to answer the question on your own, think of an explanation before you go on.

Both passages come from the *The Time Machine* by H. G. Wells.[14] The machine is a time machine that shoots into the future, stopping at AD 802,701—hundreds of thousands of years away. The answer to "How does it work?" often overlaps with the answer to "How does it behave?" (one of the "essential and accidental properties" questions). But "How does it work?" is a much more specific question. It also encompasses, "How does it interact with other things?" In the case of the time machine, you discover the effect that the time machine has on the person who uses it. When you define the function of a living thing, such as a wildcat or a cell or a cactus, you talk about how it grows and thrives in nature and how it is used or affected by other objects. When you define the function of a phenomenon, such as a volcanic eruption or the aurora, you explain not only what conditions cause it and what it does, but what is affected by it.

Read the following definition of *soil*. Notice that the first two paragraphs tell you about the properties of soil, while the third paragraph describes how soil behaves—and how it interacts with both the person examining it, with plant roots, and with water and air.

★

---

14. H.G. Wells, *The Time Machine: An Invention* (Kettering: Manor House, 1895), p. 210.

STEP TWO: **Examine the questions about function**

Student instructions for Step Two:

> When you define the function of an object or phenomenon, you have to answer three major questions:
>> *How does it work or behave?*
>> *Who/what needs it or uses it?*
>> *For what purposes?*
>
> To give good, complete answers to these larger questions, you'll probably need to ask a series of more focused questions:

★

> Although you wouldn't need to ask *all* of these questions for any one object or phenomenon, a selection of them may help you decide what details belong in your definition.
>
> Read these questions out loud to your instructor now. If any of them confuse you, ask your instructor for help.

HOW TO HELP THE STUDENT WITH STEP TWO

The student should read the questions out loud to you; this forces him to slow down and pay attention. Most of these questions should be self-explanatory, but brief explanations or examples are provided below in case the student needs them.

How does it work or behave?

Will a descriptive sequence help the reader understand how it works? What would the sequence describe?

> *The sequence of a natural process, first studied in Weeks 21–22 of Level One of Writing With Skill, is one of the building blocks of this explanation by definition. If the student needs a reminder, you may wish to go back and reread the steps in these lessons.*

Is its behavior predictable or unpredictable?

> *Does it always do the same thing? Or can its behavior suddenly shift?*

Does it work/behave differently under different circumstances?

> *Plants, for example, act differently during the winter and the summer.*

At different times?

> *Even during summer, a plant might function differently during the day and at night.*

Can its behavior be divided into phases?

> *The moon is an obvious example; another might be a butterfly, which goes through several stages (larva, cocoon, etc.) and behaves differently in each.*

Is there a cause or trigger for its behavior?

> *Cause and trigger are not the same. The phases of the moon are caused by the changing relationship between the moon and the earth as the moon orbits. A trigger is an event which suddenly changes the behavior of an object. A volcano is caused by upswelling magma, but the trigger for a volcanic eruption could be an earthquake.*

What is the time frame for its behavior?

Does it have a life cycle of a few days, a few years, a few centuries? How long has it existed? How long will it continue to take place?

Where does the behavior take place?

Does it move in space, or stay in the same place?

Who/what needs it or uses it?

Is anything dependent on it?

For example, flowers are dependent on bees.

Is it dependent on anything else?

Who/what affects its working/behavior?

For what purposes?

Is there more than one purpose?

Bees use flowers for food. Do they use flowers for anything else?

Does the purpose change at different times?

For example, winter and summer, morning and evening, day and night . . .

Is the purpose dependent on any other conditions?

Bees use flowers for food, but the flowers have to be producing pollen. So what are the conditions under which flowers produce pollen?

STEP THREE: **Practice the questions**

Student instructions for Step Three:

> Now, you'll identify the answers to these questions for a scientific object or phenomenon right outside your window: a tree.
>
> Choose a tree that you can see outside (or, if you can't see any trees, a kind of tree that you already know something about). On your own paper, jot down phrases or sentences answering the "function" questions above. You can skip questions that don't seem to apply—but be sure to answer at least five of the work/behavior questions, and at least two out of the three questions under "*Who/what needs it or uses it?*" and *"For what purposes"?*
>
> As you did last week, you'll just practice *thinking* about this category. You won't be writing an essay about the tree.
>
> When you are finished, show your answers to your instructor.

HOW TO HELP THE STUDENT WITH STEP THREE

The student's responses might resemble the following (based on a peach tree). If the student finds the assignment too frustrating, you can choose to allow him to read the answers below instead and then ask him to redo the assignment using another natural object (or even just another kind of tree).

How does it work or behave?

> *Will a descriptive sequence help the reader understand how it works? What would the sequence describe?*

Possible sequences might be the way the tree takes in nutrients or the way the peach fruit develops.

Is its behavior predictable or unpredictable?

Predictable

Does it work/behave differently under different circumstances?
    At different times?

During winter and summer; during spring when the fruit is forming

Can its behavior be divided into phases?

Dormant and active (winter and summer), or fruiting/non-fruiting

    What separates the phases?

Time

Is there a cause or trigger for its behavior?

Temperature and amount of daylight

What is the time frame for its behavior?

Peach trees have fruit every spring/can live 15–20 years

    Where does the behavior take place?

In one place (the garden)

Who/what needs it or uses it?

    People, bees, squirrels, birds, insects, fungi, wood lice, mosses . . .

    Is anything dependent on it?

    Not on peach trees alone, but fruit trees generally are necessary for bees

    Is it dependent on anything else?

    It needs insects to pollinate it.

    Who/what affects its working/behavior?

    Insects, various fruit tree diseases, sunlight, rain, temperature

For what purposes?

    Is there more than one purpose?

    People eat the fruit and use the wood for carpentry.

    Squirrels and birds eat the fruit.

    Birds make nests in the tree.

    Bees pollinate the blossoms.

    Fungi grow on the leaves.

    Wood lice live in the trunk.

    Mosses grow in the shade.

    Does the purpose change at different times?

    Yes

    Is the purpose dependent on any other conditions?

    See above

Day Two: Take Notes About Function

Focus: Taking notes in answer to the question
"How does it work?"

Today the student will prepare to write an explanation by definition that answers the questions about function. The finished composition should be at least 150 words in length (but can be longer).

The student will write about Venus flytraps, how they work, and how they fit into the ecosystem.

STEP ONE: Read (Student Responsibility)

Student instructions for Step One:

Read back through the questions on function one more time. Then, read through the following passages without stopping to take notes.

STEP TWO: Taking and organizing notes

Student instructions for Step Two:

Now you'll take notes for your own description.

As you did last week, organize your notes as you take them. On your own paper, write each question, and then look for the answers to that question in the passages provided. Write down the answers. Be sure to record the author and the page number of where you found specific pieces of information. If there is no page number provided, record only the author's name.

You do not have to answer every question! For example, the passages don't really tell you whether the behavior of the Venus flytrap is predictable or unpredictable. You can deduce that it is predictable, but since the passages don't address this question directly, it's not an important or useful one for this particular topic.

When you're working through the descriptive sequence (under the main question "How does it work/behave?"), you may find it helpful to number the steps of the process by which the flytrap catches and eats its prey. Your notes would resemble the following:

Will a descriptive sequence help the reader understand how it works?

1. The flytrap produces "a sweet-smelling nectar" (Gollon, p. 78)
2. A fly is tempted by "the scent of nectar" (Zimmer, p. 82)
3.
4.
5 . . .

and so on.

As you answer the second and third questions (*Who/what needs it or uses it?* and *For what purposes?*) you might find it useful to put your notes into two columns, like this (one example of an answer is provided):

Who/what needs it?	For what purpose(s)?
Who/what uses it?	For what purpose(s)?
Aphids, grasshoppers, raccoons, rodents, caterpillars	Food (Anderson)
Is anything dependent on it?	For what purpose(s)?
Is it dependent on anything else?	For what purpose(s)?
Who/what affects its working/behavior?	How?

HOW TO HELP THE STUDENT WITH STEP TWO

The student's notes should resemble the following:

How does it work or behave?

Will a descriptive sequence help the reader understand how it works? What would the sequence describe?
1. The flytrap produces "a sweet-smelling nectar" (Gollon, p. 78)
2. A fly is tempted by "the scent of nectar" (Zimmer, p. 82)
3. The legs of the fly "brush against tiny hairs on the trap" (Anderson)
4. If only one hair is touched, nothing happens (Anderson)
5. The fly may touch "two trigger hairs or the same hair twice within about 20 seconds" (Gollon, p.78)
6. Then, the trap closes, "locking their spiky teeth together" (Anderson)
7. The leaf makes enzymes, not nectar, "that eat away at the fly's innards" (Zimmer, p. 82)
8. "The plant releases the exoskeleton" (Gollon, p. 78)
9. After about two weeks, "the trap reopens" (Anderson)

Can its behavior be divided into phases?
   What separates the phases?
The trapping phase is followed by a digesting phase (two weeks) (Anderson)

Is there a cause or trigger for its behavior?
   Cause: The flytrap is carnivorous because the soil it grows in "cannot provide all its nutrients" (Gollon, p. 78)
   Trigger: Insects landing on the leaves brush at least two of the trigger hairs "or the same hair twice within about 20 seconds" (Gollon, p. 78)

What is the time frame for its behavior?
About two weeks for digestion (Anderson)

Where does the behavior take place?
   Where the plant grows, in the "swampy pine savanna within a 90-mile radius of Wilmington, NC" (Zimmer, p. 82)

Who or what needs/uses it?	*For what purposes?*
Raccoons, rodents, caterpillars	Eat the flytrap
Aphids and grasshoppers	Eat the flytrap
Humans	Make the drug Carnivora® from the "steril-ized fresh juices" of the flytrap to treat cancer (Tierra, p. 157) Carnivora® "has no effect on non-solid can-cers" (Tierra, p. 157) Carnivora® "stimulates the immune system" (Tierra, p. 157)

Day Three: Write About Function

 Focus: Writing answers to the question
"How does it work?"

STEP ONE: Write (Student Responsibility)

Student instructions for Step One:

Now, use your notes to write a definition of the Venus flytrap that focuses on the *function* of the plant. Follow the basic order of your notes:

1) First, answer the question "How does it work/behave?"

2) Second, answer the questions "Who/what needs it or uses it? For what purpose?" Follow these additional guidelines:

3) The description should have at least two paragraphs and be at least 150 words in length. Longer is just fine.

4) Be sure to cite each source at least one time. You will be citing two unusual sources this time, one from a magazine article (the Zimmer article), and one source written especially for this textbook (the Anderson passage). Use the following format for your footnotes:

> Carl Zimmer, "Fatal Attraction," *National Geographic* (March 2010, Vol. 217:3), p. 82.
> Audrey Anderson, "The Venus Flytrap's Circle of Life." In *Writing With Skill, Level Two* (Well-Trained Mind Press, 2013), pp. 176–177.

Remember, when you cite a work from a larger collection, which includes an article in a magazine, you put the name of the work being cited in quotation marks and the name of the larger collection/book in italics.

5) Use at least one metaphor or simile from your own imagination.

6) Use transitional words such as "first," "next," or "finally" when you describe the sequence of the Venus flytrap's function.

Remember: you do *not* have to use all of the quotes and answers you've collected! Although you should give a detailed description of function, you do not need to answer all questions—as long as your finished composition is the proper length.

Note that correct spellings of the plant include *Venus flytrap, Venus Flytrap, Venus' flytrap, Venus Fly Trap,* and *Venus's Fly-trap.* Choose one spelling and stick with it.

STEP TWO: **Assemble Works Cited page (Student Responsibility)**

Student instructions for Step Two:

Title a separate piece of paper "Works Cited." List your sources in alphabetical order.
The Anderson piece should be listed as:
Anderson, Audrey. "The Venus Flytrap's Circle of Life." In *Writing With Skill, Level Two.*
Charles City: Well-Trained Mind Press, 2013, pp. 176–177.
The Zimmer piece should be listed as:
Zimmer, Carl. "Fatal Attraction." In *National Geographic,* March 2010, Vol. 217, Issue 3, pp. 80–82.

STEP THREE: **Title your description**

Student instructions for Step Three:

Now choose a title for your essay. You may look back at Day Four, Step Three of last week if you need to review.
Remember to center your title at the top of the first page of your composition. Double-space between the title and the top line of your first paragraph.
As always, if you need help, ask your instructor.

HOW TO HELP THE STUDENT WITH STEP THREE

Any of the following descriptive titles would be acceptable:

How a Venus' Flytrap Works
The Function of a Venus' Flytrap
How Does a Venus' Flytrap Function?

The student should *not* just title the composition "Venus' Flytraps." The point of this step is to encourage the student to write descriptive and specific titles.

STEP FOUR: **Proofread**

Student instructions for Step Four:

Before handing your paper to your instructor, go through the following proofreading steps.
1) Read your paper out loud, listening for awkward or unclear sections and repeated words. Rewrite awkward or unclear sentences so that they flow more naturally.
2) Read through the paper one more time, looking for sentence fragments, run-on sentences, and repeated words. Correct fragments and run-on sentences. If you used the same noun or verb more than twice, pick an alternative from the thesaurus. If you used a modifier

(adverb, adjective, or prepositional phrase acting as an adjective or adverb) more than once, find another word.

    3) Check the format of your footnotes and Works Cited page.

    4) Check your spelling by looking, individually, at each word that might be a problem.

When you are finished, give your paper to your instructor for evaluation.

HOW TO HELP THE STUDENT WITH STEP FOUR

Evaluate the paper using the rubric at the end of this lesson.

    The student's paper should resemble the following:

HOW A VENUS' FLYTRAP WORKS

    A Venus' flytrap is an unusual plant that catches flies and eats them. First, a fly is attracted to the smell of nectar in the flytrap. The Venus' flytrap has six little hairs on the trap.[1] If only one hair is touched, nothing happens. But if the fly touches two hairs, the trap closes "like the teeth of a jaw trap."[2] The fly is trapped. Then, the plant produces enzymes that digest the fly. The flytrap does not eat the exoskeleton; it discards it when it is finished digesting the fly.[3] Two weeks later the trap opens again, and the process starts over.[4]

    The Venus' flytrap has many uses. They are well known for what they eat, but they also are food for many animals. Raccoons and mice and even some insects eat the plant. Most of these animals prefer to eat other plants, though.[5] Humans use the "sterilized fresh juices" of the flytrap to make a medicine called Carnivora®. This drug is used to treat cancer and help the immune system.[6]

WORKS CITED

Anderson, Audrey. "The Venus' Flytrap's Circle of Life." In *Writing With Skill, Level Two.* Charles City: Well-Trained Mind Press, 2013, pp. 176–177.

Gollon, Matilda, ed. *The Big Idea Science Book.* New York: DK Publishing, 2010.

Tierra, Michael. *Treating Cancer with Herbs: An Integrative Approach.* Twin Lakes, Minn.: Lotus Press, 2003.

Zimmer, Carl. "Fatal Attraction." In *National Geographic*, March 2010, Vol. 217, Issue 3, pp. 80–82.

---

[1] Matilda Gollon, ed., *The Big Idea Science Book* (DK Publishing, 2010), p. 78.

[2] Carl Zimmer, "Fatal Attraction," in *National Geographic* 217:3 (March 2010), p. 82.

[3] Gollon, p. 78.

[4] Audrey Anderson, "The Venus' Flytrap's Circle of Life," in *Writing With Skill, Level Two* (Well-Trained Mind Press, 2013), pp. 176-177.

[5] Ibid.

[6] Michael Tierra, *Treating Cancer with Herbs: An Integrative Approach* (Lotus Press, 2003), p. 157.

Week 13 Rubric

Organization:

1 The entire composition should be two paragraphs and at least 150 words in length.
2 The first paragraph should describe how a Venus' flytrap works. The second should describe what creatures use a Venus' flytrap and for what purposes.
3 All three sources should be cited.
4 All sources mentioned in footnotes should be placed on a Works Cited page.
5 The composition should have a title, centered at the top of the first page. This title should *not* be simply "Venus' Flytraps." (See Step Three.)
6 At least one metaphor or simile should be included.

Mechanics:

1 Each sentence should make sense on its own when read aloud.
2 There should be no sentence fragments or run-on sentences.
3 All words should be spelled correctly.
4 The first line of each paragraph should be properly indented.
5 Verb tense should be consistent throughout.
6 No noun or verb should be used more than twice (with the exception of state-of-being verbs, linking verbs, and the verb "said").
7 No modifier or prepositional phrase acting as a modifier should be used more than once.
8 Footnotes and the Works Cited page should be properly formatted.

Day Four: Copia

Focus: Understanding and using phrase-for-word substitution

STEP ONE: **Understanding phrase-for-word substitution (Student Responsibility)**

Student instructions for Step One:

When you were introduced to the first *copia* exercises, back in Week 16 of Level One, you were also introduced to the Renaissance scholar and theologian Desiderius Erasmus, who took

the sentence "Your letter pleased me greatly" and rephrased it 195 different ways.
Among those sentences were:

> The words from your pen brought joy.
> The pages I received from you sent a new light of joy stealing over my heart.
> Your pearls of wisdom gave me pleasure.

All three of these sentences have the same basic structure as the original—there's a subject, an action verb, and a direct object. But in each of them, Erasmus has substituted a phrase (or clause)[37] for the noun "letter."

S	V	DO	
letter	pleased	me	
S	V	DO	
words from your pen	brought	joy	
S	V	DO	
pages I received from you	sent	light	
S	V	IO	DO
pearls of wisdom	gave	me	pleasure

In each sentence, the phrase acts in exactly the same way as the original subject noun.

The first two sentences use very literal phrases in place of the noun "letter." What is a letter made up of? Words written on paper. "Words written on paper" could be substituted for "letter." Where did the words come from? Well, your brain ("Words from your brain" might work too), but in a very basic sense, the words came from the end of your pen. In the same way, the letter is, physically, pages that arrived because they were sent.

The third sentence uses a metaphor. You reviewed metaphors back in Week 6 (and if you don't remember the difference between a metaphor and a simile, go back and review Day Four of Week 5 *and* Day Four of Week 6 now). A metaphor describes something by comparing it to something else. Wise words from a loved one's letter are treasured. Pearls are treasured. So the letter can become "pearls of wisdom."

A third way to substitute a phrase for a word is to use a *kenning*—a method common in Norse and Old English poetry. A *kenning* substitutes a description of some quality that the noun possesses, or some function that it performs, for the noun itself. So, for example, an *arrow* might become a "slaughter shaft," or blood a "hot battle-sweat." Instead of *body,* a Norse poet might use the phrase "house for the bones." The *sea* becomes the "whale road," ships become "wave floaters."

Sometimes, using a phrase for a word can make a sentence too complicated and wordy, but phrase-for-word substitution can also make your writing more vivid, poetic, and engaging.

---

37. Just for your information: A phrase is a grouping of words that has a single grammatical function. A clause is different from a phrase in that it contains a verb. "Words from your pen" is a phrase (with no verb in it). "I received from you" is a clause that describes "pages" (verb is underlined).

STEP TWO: **Changing whole phrases to words**

Student instructions for Step Two:

> Each one of the following sentences contains an underlined phrase that has been substituted for a noun. Write a plain noun that could be used in place of each phrase on the blank line.

HOW TO HELP THE STUDENT WITH STEP TWO

The student's answers should resemble the following:

Be sure to get up before the lighting of the sky candle. **dawn** or **sunrise** or **daybreak**

The groaning board was piled with cakes, cookies, and pies. **table**

He peeled the elongated yellow fruit thoughtfully. **banana**

The vitamin-laden liquid comes from cows. **milk**

I was just admiring the fringed curtain of your eye. **[your] eyelashes**

He drove away in his shiny new status symbol. **car**

Harry Potter's greatest enemy is He Who Must Not Be Named. **Voldemort**

Just let me turn on the darkness destroyer. **light**

I'm going to see a performance of the Scottish play. **Macbeth**

STEP THREE: **Add to the Sentence Variety chart (Student Responsibility)**

Student instructions for Step Three:

> Add the following principle and illustration to the Sentence Variety chart.

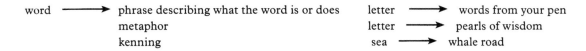

word ⟶	phrase describing what the word is or does	letter ⟶	words from your pen
	metaphor	letter ⟶	pearls of wisdom
	kenning	sea ⟶	whale road

STEP FOUR: **Inventing and substituting new phrases for words**

Student instructions for Step Four:

> The following sentences are taken from "The Lady Who Put Salt in Her Coffee," the first chapter of Lucretia P. Hale's classic novel *The Peterkin Papers*. For each underlined word, come up with two phrases that you can substitute for the original noun. One phrase should be based on the word's literal meaning; the other should involve a metaphor.
>
> When you are finished, read the sentences aloud to your instructor, substituting the new phrases. Which versions of the sentences do you prefer?

HOW TO HELP THE STUDENT WITH STEP FOUR

The student's answers will vary; possible answers are suggested below. If the student has difficulty coming up with phrases, encourage her to think about the *function* of the noun to come up with the literal phrase; then, ask her to think about something *else* that functions in the same way in order to create the metaphor. So, for example, a "mistake" is an action that causes things to go wrong. What else causes things to go wrong? Well, electrical storms can make the power go off. So the "mistake" could also be an "electrical storm of misfortune."

It was a <u>mistake</u>.

"action that caused unpleasantness" or "thunderstorm of misfortune."

She had poured out a delicious cup of coffee, and, just as she was helping herself to cream, she found she had put in <u>salt</u> instead of <u>sugar</u>.

"crystals of flavor" or "essence of change"

"seasoning of delight" or "a child's daydream"

The <u>family</u> came in; they all tasted, and looked, and wondered what should be done, and all sat down to think.

"gathering of her relatives" or "garden of her flesh and blood"

At last Agamemnon, who had been to <u>college</u>, said, "Why don't we go over and ask the advice of the chemist?"

"place of learning" or "assembly of minds"

First he looked at the <u>coffee</u>, and then stirred it.

"bitter breakfast beverage" or "potion of alertness"

The <u>herb-woman</u> lived down at the very end of the street; so the boys put on their india-rubber boots again, and they set off.

"grower of plants" or "cultivator of secrets"

As soon as the little old woman came, she had it set over the <u>fire</u>, and began to stir in the different herbs.

"open flame" or "shining nest of heat"

The <u>children</u> tasted after each mixture, but made up dreadful faces.

"small humans" or "dwellers in nurseries"

WEEK 14: EXPLANATION BY DEFINITION: GENUS

A fully-developed definition answers three questions:

What is it? [Essential and accidental properties]

How does it work? [Function]

Where does it belong?

This week, the student will work on the third and final part of a definition: "Where does it belong?"

NOTE TO INSTRUCTOR: Next week, the student will be assigned the job of researching and writing an original explanation by definition on an object or phenomenon in nature. He'll be allowed to choose the general subject. Be sure to allow time for him to read and research; you will also want to plan a library trip if at all possible.

If the student can link next week's assignment to one of his other subjects, the project can also fulfill a science requirement.

Remember that you can allow assignments to take up more than one week, if necessary. At this stage, students work at very different speeds.

Day One: Introduction to Genus

Focus: Answering the question "Where does it belong?"

STEP ONE: Understand genus (Student Responsibility)

Student instructions for Step One:

> When you answer the question "Where does it belong?" you are describing the *genus* of the object or phenomenon you're defining.
>
> You may have come across the word "genus" in your science studies. In modern biology, living things are divided up first into one of five *kingdoms* (protist, fungus, plant, bacteria, animal); then, each of the kingdoms is divided up into different *phyla* (so, for example, the plant

kingdom is divided into five *phyla*—algae, mosses, ferns, trees with cones, and flowering trees and plants); then, each of the phyla is further divided into classes . . . and so on. You may have seen the following chart in your biology book:

Kingdom
Phylum
Class
Order
Family
Genus
Species

For the biologist, a *genus* is a class that contains several different species (so, for example, the Scots Pine tree is a species of pine tree that belongs to the genus *Pinus,* along with the species Red Pine, Japanese Black Pine, Arizona Pine, and others).

When Aristotle talked about *genus,* he meant something a little bit less scientific. For Aristotle, finding the *genus* of something was a way of grouping it together with things that were like it—and different from it. When he spoke of *genus,* he wanted to know: What larger group does it belong to?

So when you determine the genus of something, you look back at its essential and accidental properties, and you think about its function. And then you ask yourself: What other objects or phenomena have these properties, or function in this way?

There is often more than one way to answer this question. Think back to Week 12, when you studied essential and accidental properties. You listed the properties of a volcano. What other objects or phenomena have these properties, or function in this way?

Volcanoes and earthquakes both happen at plate margins, when tectonic plates shift—so you could identify volcanoes as belonging to the larger group "Phenomena caused by shifting tectonic plates." If you then investigated what other phenomena are caused by shifting tectonic plates, you'd discover that both mountains and oceanic trenches belong to the same group.

On the other hand, volcanoes also explode—a quality that earthquakes, mountains, and oceanic trenches don't share. What other objects in nature explode? Supernovas and solar flares are both explosions. Avalanches are a type of natural explosion. So are meteor impacts—and lightning strikes.

What's the purpose of identifying *genus*?

Grouping your object (or phenomenon) together with others forces you to think about *why* you're defining it—what the ultimate point of your essay will be. When you write about volcanoes, are you focusing in on a volcano as just one of the many things that happen at the edges of the earth's plates—simply another example of what shifts in the earth's crust bring about? Or will you present the volcano as one of the most destructive forces in nature—an explosive phenomenon that destroys everything it touches?

Like the questions you've asked about properties and function, questions about genus force you to think more deeply about what you're writing. (And that's why writing is such hard work—because you have to *think* in order to do it well.)

STEP TWO: **Examine the questions about genus**

Student instructions for Step Two:

Asking the following questions will help you think more deeply about genus.
You'll start by asking three basic questions:

What other objects or phenomena can it be grouped with?
What are the qualities that lead you to group them together?
What name can you give this group?

In the case of the volcano, if you grouped it along with lightning, meteor strikes, and avalanches, you would be thinking about the volcano's explosion and its destructive power as the central qualities of the volcano—as opposed to its location at the edge of the earth's tectonic plates.

What name would you give this group? You don't have to get complicated: "Things That Explode in Nature" or "Destructive Natural Phenomena" would work.

You would then need to ask one more question:

In what significant ways is it different from the others in its group?

Aristotle thought that finding genus also involved finding what he called "divisions"—differences between your object and other objects in the same group. If you were to group a volcano along with lightning, meteor strikes, and avalanches, you would also include in your description of genus the information that the volcano, unlike the other three, spews molten lava. Explosive, destructive power *groups* the volcano *together* with lightning, meteor strikes, and avalanches; lava *differentiates* it from the others.

Now read all three questions out loud to your instructor (this forces you to slow down and think).

HOW TO HELP THE STUDENT WITH STEP TWO

The student should read aloud the following questions:

What other objects or phenomena can it be grouped with?
What are the qualities that lead you to group them together?
What name can you give this group?
In what significant ways is it different from the others in its group?

If he has struggled with the previous weeks of explanation by definition, you may want to ask him to read the entire lesson out loud to you; this will force him to slow down and pay close attention.

STEP THREE: **Practice the questions**

Student instructions for Step Three:

Now you'll practice these questions.

Go back to Week 12, Day Two. Reread the description of the *aurora borealis* and look back through your answers to the question about its properties.

Now, jot down on your own paper answers to the following questions:

What other objects or phenomena can it be grouped with?
What are the qualities that lead you to group them together?
What name can you give this group?
In what significant ways is it different from the others in its group?

To answer these questions, you might need to do some investigation.

You can start with an encyclopedia or with Wikipedia. Although you should be suspicious of information found on Wikipedia (see Week 8, Day One, if you don't remember why), Wikipedia can be a good starting place when you're unfamiliar with a subject—particularly if you're reading up on subjects that don't arouse strong emotions in people. (For example, I'd be more inclined to trust Wikipedia's information about the chemical composition of fool's gold than its entry on the aims of the Republican Party or the responsibilities of the Pope.)

You can then follow up by doing an online book search for terms you find in the encyclopedia or Wikipedia.

Identifying genus often takes a little bit of additional research, since your original source materials may not include the information about *other* objects and phenomena that you need. Remember this—and make sure to allow time for it in future projects.

Ask your instructor for assistance if you need it. And when you're finished, show your work to your instructor.

HOW TO HELP THE STUDENT WITH STEP THREE

The *aurora borealis* has been assigned for two reasons: the student has already listed its properties; and it belongs to a very clear and simple larger group.

The student's answers should resemble the following:

What other objects or phenomena can it be grouped with?

The aurora australis

What are the qualities that lead you to group them together?

They are light displays in the sky caused by the collision of particles with atoms.

What name can you give this group?

Aurora

In what significant ways is it different from the others in its group?

It only happens in the northern latitudes.

The student may be tempted to overcomplicate the assignment. Keep an eye on him as he works; if he seems frustrated, say, "There's really only one other phenomenon to group with it."

The student can actually complete these exercises perfectly well without going beyond Wikipedia. However, don't discourage him from doing additional reading. If necessary, point him towards the book search function at books.google.com.

Day Two: Take Notes on Properties or Function

Focus: Preparing to answer the question "Where does it belong?"

Today the student will prepare to write an explanation by definition that answers last lesson's questions.

Before he can assign an object or phenomenon to a larger group, he'll have to know something about it. His preparation: answering either the questions about properties, or the questions about function. Tomorrow, he will work on genus.

STEP ONE: **Prepare**

Student instructions for Step One:

> Start out by reviewing the questions about properties and function. Read these out loud to your instructor now.

HOW TO HELP THE STUDENT WITH STEP ONE

The student should read the following questions out loud to you:

Essential Properties and Accidental Properties
    What does it look like?
    How does it behave?
    What senses come into play as you observe it?
    What do those senses reveal?
    Is your observation passive (watching/listening) or active (experimenting/collecting/probing)?
    What sorts of measurements (temperature, quantity, time, etc.) are necessary to your observation?
    What does it resemble?
    What is it made of?
    What sort of structure does it have?
    What is its extent in space?
    What is its extent in time?
    Which properties are essential?
    Which are accidental?
Function
    How does it work or behave?
    Will a descriptive sequence help the reader understand how it works?

What would this sequence describe?

Is its behavior predictable or unpredictable?

Does it work/behave differently under different circumstances?

    At different times?

Can its behavior be divided into phases?

    What separates the phases?

Is there a cause or trigger for its behavior?

What is the time frame for its behavior?

Where does the behavior take place?

Who/what needs it or uses it?

    Is anything dependent on it?

    Is it dependent on anything else?

    Who/what affects its working/behavior?

For what purposes?

    Is there more than one purpose?

    Does the purpose change at different times?

    Is the purpose dependent on any other conditions?

STEP TWO: Read (Student Responsibility)

Student instructions for Step Two:

> Now that you've reviewed the questions, read through the following passages without stopping to take notes.

★

STEP THREE: Take notes

Student instructions for Step Three:

> Decide whether you'd rather take notes about properties or about function. Answering either set of questions will give you enough information to assign bamboo to a genus (that will be tomorrow's project).
>
> Whichever category of questions you decide on, go back through the readings now and use them to jot down answers to the questions on your own paper. Use the same method as last week; write down each question, and then note the answers, recording the author and page number of specific pieces of information. Here's an example from last week:

> *Is there a cause or trigger for its behavior?*
> **Cause: The flytrap is carnivorous because the soil it grows in "cannot provide all its nutrients" (Gollon, p. 78)**
> **Trigger: Insects landing on the leaves brush at least two of the trigger hairs "or the same hair twice within about 20 seconds" (Gollon, p. 78)**

> *What is the time frame for its behavior?*

About two weeks for digestion (Anderson)

Where does the behavior take place?
Where the plant grows, in the "swampy pine savanna within a 90-mile radius of Wilmington, NC" (Zimmer, p. 82)

If you need help, ask your instructor.

HOW TO HELP THE STUDENT WITH STEP THREE

The student's notes should resemble one of the following sets:

Essential Properties and Accidental Properties

What does it look like?

> Canes called "culms" are wrapped in "papery tan" sheaths that give them "a hyphenated look." The rest of the cane is covered with "6- to 12-inch long, bright green, lance-shaped leaves that alternate" (Cullina, p. 131)

How does it behave?

> Tough—"sprouted new shoots just days after the blast" at Hiroshima (Wallin, p. 6)
> "tensile or bending strength and flexibility that surpasses that of most trees"
> The culms "simply expand like a telescope as they fill with water" instead of growing "cell by cell," incrementally, like other grasses (Cullina, p. 131)
> "not a tree but a primitive member of the grass family" (Wallin, p. 6)

What senses come into play as you observe it?

What do those senses reveal?

Is your observation passive (watching/listening) or active (experimenting/collecting/probing)?

What sorts of measurements (temperature, quantity, time, etc.) are necessary to your observation?

What does it resemble?

> Some species look "like the protective shells turtles carry with them" (Goldberg, p. 14)
> "giant grasses aspiring to be woody plants" (Cullina, p. 131)

What is it made of?

> "cellulose fibers with lignin and silica" (Goldberg, p. 14)
> "strong, resilient perennial stems composed primarily of lignin and cellulose" (Cullina, p. 131)

What sort of structure does it have?

> Hollow stems with joints, hollow stem is called "culm" (Wallin, p. 6)
> "not a tree but a primitive member of the grass family" (Wallin, p. 6)
> Rhizomes "spread out horizontally . . . form an interlocking web underground" (Wallin, p. 6)
> Some are hollow, some are solid; some tall and straight, others irregular

(Goldberg, p. 14)

"each aerial stem, or culm, grows from a creeping rhizome" (Cullina, p. 131)

What is its extent in space?

"120 feet in height, with hollow stems a foot in diameter" (Wallin, p. 6)

Different species, from six inches high to more than a hundred feet (Goldberg, p. 14)

From "pencil-thin" to "diameters of nearly a foot" (Goldberg, p. 14)

Rhizomes "two to three feet below the soil's surface" (Goldberg, p. 14)

Leaves are 6 to 12 inches long and "bright green" (Cullina, p. 131)

What is its extent in time?

"World's fastest growing plant" (Wallin, p. 6)

Which properties are essential?

Which are accidental?

Function

How does it work or behave?

Tough—"sprouted new shoots just days after the blast" at Hiroshima (Wallin, p. 6)

"World's fastest growing plant" (Wallin, p. 6)

Rhizomes "spread out horizontally . . . form an interlocking web underground" (Wallin, p. 6)

The culms are "nearly fully formed, compressed canes that simply expand like a telescope as they fill with water" (Cullina, p. 131)

Will a descriptive sequence help the reader understand how it works?

What would this sequence describe?

the rhizomes spreading and "popping up almost overnight" (Cullina, p. 131)

Is its behavior predictable or unpredictable?

Does it work/behave differently under different circumstances?

At different times?

Can its behavior be divided into phases?

What separates the phases?

Is there a cause or trigger for its behavior?

What is the time frame for its behavior?

Rhizomes spread "up to ten feet a year" (Wallin, p. 6)

"base of the culm is wrapped by sheaths" that "take a few months to fall off" (Cullina, p. 131)

Inflation of the culms is "much faster than the incremental cell-by-cell growth seen on most grasses" (Cullina, p. 131)

Where does the behavior take place?

"native to every continent except Europe and Antarctica" (Wallin, p. 6)

Who/what needs it or uses it?

Japanese kitchens, for baskets—zaru, "simple woven bamboo basket-trays",
used to "drain and rinse" and also display soba noodles (Bess, p. 65)
Bamboo scoops, trays 'for steaming," storage baskets (Bess, p. 65)
Farmers (Lewis and Miles, p. 2)

Is anything dependent on it?

"More than half the human race" (Wallin, p. 6)

Is it dependent on anything else?

Who/what affects its working/behavior?

For what purposes?

Food, poles, livestock feed and silage, "screen the farm from roads," shade,
"catch dust," "protect riparian zones," prevent erosion, manufacturing
(Lewis and Miles, p. 2)

Is there more than one purpose?

"over 1,500 products from medicines to scaffoldings" (Wallin, p. 6)

Does the purpose change at different times?

"Web of rhizomes" makes earth safe during an earthquake (Wallin, p.
6)

Is the purpose dependent on any other conditions?

Earthquake

These notes are simply examples. Some of the pieces of information answer multiple questions
and can be placed elsewhere; also, the student's notes do not need to be as thorough and complete as the above. However, encourage the student to answer at least six of the questions in his
chosen group.

If the student struggles, allow him to read one set of the answers above, and then ask him
to work at answering the other set.

This exercise has two purposes. It prepares the student for tomorrow's short composition,
but it also gives him additional practice in note-taking skills.

If the student does not include the information that bamboo is a grass rather than a tree,
point out that this fact is necessary in order to place the bamboo into a scientific group.

Day Three: Write About Genus

 Focus: Writing answers to the question "Where
does it belong?"

Today, the student will write two separate (brief) answers to the question "Where does it
belong?"

In an explanation by definition, the descriptions of properties and functions will take up
most of the paper. Identifying genus will be the briefest part of the composition. Today, the

student will simply write a couple of paragraphs that could be added to a longer paper. She won't have to come up with a title (although she will still have to proofread and format her footnotes properly).

STEP ONE: **Examine examples (Student Responsibility)**

NOTE TO INSTRUCTOR: Although this step is designed to be completed independently, you may need to check up behind the student to make sure that she is reading carefully.

Student instructions for Step One:

When you define the genus of an object or phenomenon, you try to answer the following questions:

What other objects or phenomena can it be grouped with?
What are the qualities that lead you to group them together?
What name can you give this group?
In what significant ways is it different from the others in its group?

Before you write, look at the brief examples below.

The first is from *Protozoans, Algae & Other Protists*, by Steve Parker.

★

In just a few sentences, the author identifies the quality that groups protists together into a single genus: they are one-celled organisms. He then tells you some of the ways in which protists differ: protozoans eat food, protophytans use sunlight; some protists are smaller than a letter of the alphabet, others bigger than human beings.

Here's a second example of identifying genus, this one about (once more) volcanoes.

★

The authors tell you briefly *two* qualities that group all volcanoes together. One is a property ("holes connecting the exterior and interior of the earth") and the other is a function ("eject materials at a high temperature"). Then, they tell you the differences between the different kinds of volcanoes.

Here's one final example, from the book *A Journey into a Wetland,* by Rebecca L. Johnson.

★

This third excerpt shows how a discussion of genus might fit into a larger context. The author has spent most of the chapter talking about swamps—what they are, what's in them, how they function, what they look like, and so on. She then puts swamps into a genus—the larger group *wetlands,* which includes not just swamps but also bogs, marshes, sloughs, and other wet areas.

STEP TWO: **Answer the question "Where does it belong?"**

Student instructions for Step Two:

Now that you've seen examples of how to write about genus, it's your turn.

Rather than just answering this question one time, you'll do it twice—briefly.

Your first assignment: Write a single paragraph, at least three sentences long, explaining what larger group, scientifically speaking, bamboo belongs to. Also explain how bamboo is different from other members of that group. If you use exact words from your sources, or comparisons or ideas unique to those writers, be sure to footnote.

Optional: you can also include some information about how different types of bamboo differ from each other.

If you can't find the information you need in your notes, glance back at the passages about bamboo from the last lesson.

When you're finished, proofread your paragraph. By now, you should know what to look for—awkward sentences, misspelled words, incorrect punctuation, missing required elements. Don't forget to read your paragraph out loud.

Show your work to your instructor.

HOW TO HELP THE STUDENT WITH STEP TWO

The student's composition should resemble one of the following:

Paragraph placing bamboo into the grass family and describing how it is different from other grasses:

Bamboo can grow a hundred feet high, but bamboo is actually a member of the grass family. Most grasses grow one cell at a time. Instead, bamboo grows when rhizomes spread underground. Spears called culms pop up quickly and fill with water. This helps them grow quickly, unlike other grasses that grow cell by cell.

Paragraph including the optional comparison of different kinds of bamboo with each other:

Although bamboo can look like a tree, bamboo actually belongs to the grass family. However, unlike other grasses, new bamboo shoots (called culms) expand by filling with water, instead of growing one cell at a time.[1] Some bamboo plants are only six inches long and as broad as a pencil.[2] Others can grow to more than a hundred feet high and their canes can be a foot across.

---

[1] William Cullina, *Native Ferns, Moss, and Grasses: From Emerald Carpet to Amber Wave* (Houghton Mifflin, 2008), p. 131

[2] Gale Beth Goldberg, *Bamboo Style* (Gibbs Smith, 2002), p. 14.

NOTE TO INSTRUCTOR: Note that in the second paragraph, the information about expansion by filling with water is footnoted; the wording of that sentence is very close to the original source, so even though this is common scientific knowledge, it seems wisest to footnote it. The second footnote is included because Goldberg offers the comparison with a pencil, which is not common knowledge (although "1/4 inch in diameter" would be, since anyone measuring a bamboo stalk could come up with this figure).

If the student needs additional help, allow him to read the first sample paragraph. Then ask him to write his own paragraph that also includes comparisons between different types of bamboo.

STEP THREE: **Answer the question "Where does it belong?" in another way**

Student instructions for Step Three:

> Bamboo belongs to the grass family—but not every object or phenomenon you'll describe will fit easily into a scientific classification. Remember our illustration about volcanoes: they can be grouped together with other natural explosions, or with other events taking place at the edge of a tectonic plate.
>
> Choosing a genus for your object can be a little more creative than just finding out how it is classified. Look back through your notes now. Decide which aspects of bamboo you would like to draw attention to. Then, choose a group of objects that have similar properties, or similar functions, to bamboo. (You may need to consult an encyclopedia or browse websites in order to do this.)
>
> If you need help brainstorming, your instructor can help you out.
>
> When you've done this, write two paragraphs, each one at least two sentences long. The first paragraph should explain what qualities the group has, what the group is called, and why bamboo belongs in it. The second paragraph should explain how bamboo *differs* from the other objects or phenomena in the group.
>
> When you're finished with your two paragraphs, proofread them and then show them to your instructor.

HOW TO HELP THE STUDENT WITH STEP THREE

This assignment will force the student to think creatively about a nonfiction assignment—something that's essential to good writing.

Her first task is to assign bamboo to a group. For students who answered the questions about properties, possible answers might be:

Plants that spread through rhizomes
Plants that grow to more than hundred feet high
Things that grow very quickly

Groups drawn from the answers about function could include:

Plants that spread through rhizomes
Living things native to five continents
Plants that can be used for both food and building
Materials used for kitchen implements
Materials used for medicines

If the student has difficulty finding a group, ask one of the following questions:
"How does bamboo spread?"
"What is unusual about the speed with which bamboo grows?"
"What two widely different uses can bamboo fulfill? What are they?"

If the student comes up with another group, accept it as long as she can find at least two other things to group with it.

As part of this assignment, the student will need to make use of an encyclopedia, Wikipedia, or Google book search. You should not expect her to come up with the answers unassisted!

The student's final composition should be at least two paragraphs long, with at least two sentences in each paragraph. A rubric is not necessary; as long as the paragraphs are the correct length and grammatical, accept them.

Sample paragraphs might resemble the following:

> Bamboo is only one of a number of plants that spread through rhizomes. Others include strawberries, Venus flytraps, asparagus, and wiregrass.
>
> Bamboo spreads much more quickly than any of these other plants. In fact, the rhizomes of bamboo can spread up to ten feet every year.

OR

> Bamboo is only one material used to make kitchen trays and other kitchen implements. Other common materials are Teflon, plastic, cedar, and china.
>
> Unlike these other materials, bamboo can be eaten—not just used to serve other kinds of food! People in many countries eat bamboo leaves and young bamboo canes. Bamboo can also be used as livestock feed.

You may want to point out to the student that this is very similar to a comparison-contrast exercise. The student is comparing bamboo to other objects in the group, explaining how they are similar, and then highlighting how they differ.

If the student struggles, allow her to read one of the examples above. Then, ask her to write a similar set of two paragraphs, using another genus.

Day Four: Copia

 Focus: Substituting similes for adverbs

STEP ONE: Understanding simile-for-adverb substitution (Student Responsibility)

Student instructions for Step One:

> In your copia exercise last week, you studied how to substitute descriptive phrases for words. Today you will study a specific way of doing this: substituting similes for adverbs.
> Recall the definition of a **simile** from Week 5, Day Four: **A simile is a comparison**

between two things, introduced by the words *like* or *as* (or *as if*).

Today you will practice seamlessly working similes into your writing, by substituting them for adverbs. Erasmus did this in his own examples of copia. Examine his sentences below:

S   V   DO ADV
Your <u>letter</u> <u>pleased</u> me **greatly.**

S   V   DO   SIMILE
Your <u>letter</u> <u>pleased</u> me **as food does a glutton.**

In both sentences, the bolded words tell you more about the verb **pleased.** How much did the letter please Erasmus? Greatly; just like food pleases a glutton.

When you substitute a simile (a phrase or clause beginning with like or as) for an adverb, always think about what the adverb implies. For Erasmus, the sensation of getting a letter from his loved one was just as satisfying as a plateful of delicious food to a greedy man.

STEP TWO: **Changing whole phrases to adverbs**

Student instructions for Step Two:

Each one of the following sentences contains a simile. Write an adverb that could be used in place of each. Think carefully about the exact shade of meaning, sensation, and feel of the underlined simile. Try to choose an adverb that has that same shade of meaning. The first sentence has been done for you.

You may want to use a thesaurus.

When you are finished, show your work to your instructor.

HOW TO HELP THE STUDENT WITH STEP TWO

The student's answers may differ from the suggestions. If he gets stuck as he tries to think of an adverb, read him one of the suggested adverbs and ask him to find a related one.

He smiled, <u>like I do when Mom finds out about something I did that I shouldn't have done.</u>

guiltily

—Jonathan Safran Foer, *Extremely Loud and Incredibly Close*

Past him, ten feet from his front wheels, flung the Seattle Express <u>like a flying volcano.</u>

wildly, explosively, thunderously, dangerously, terrifyingly

—Sinclair Lewis, *Arrowsmith*

All day Tarzan followed Kulonga, hovering above him in the trees <u>like some malign spirit.</u>

creepily, spookily, silently, weirdly, eerily

—Edgar Rice Burroughs, *Tarzan of the Apes*

The silence overtook me <u>like a cancer.</u>

quickly, completely, utterly, entirely, powerfully, forcefully

—Jonathan Safran Foer, *Extremely Loud and Incredibly Close*

Then fear, disguised in the garb of mild-mannered doubt, slips into your mind <u>like a spy</u>.
sneakily, silently, cunningly, subtly, artfully, deviously
—Yann Martel, *Life of Pi*

The calm sea opened up around me <u>like a great book</u>.
broadly, welcomingly
—Yann Martel, *Life of Pi*

They nodded and smiled and kept on scrubbing me <u>as if I were the deck of a ship</u>.
industriously, vigorously, busily, diligently, thoroughly
—Yann Martel, *Life of Pi*

Doctors and nurses cared for me <u>as if I were a premature baby</u>.
tenderly, conscientiously, vigilantly, anxiously, carefully
—Yann Martel, *Life of Pi*

He must face infection <u>as a soldier must face bullets</u>.
bravely, fearlessly, courageously, boldly, heroically
—George Bernard Shaw, *Candida*

Rustling about the room, his softly-slippered feet making no noise on the floor, he moved <u>like a refined tiger</u>.
majestically, powerfully, grandly, impressively, mightily
—Charles Dickens, *A Tale of Two Cities*

There could not be fewer than five hundred people, and they were dancing <u>like five thousand demons</u>.
wildly, crazily, madly, frantically, passionately
—Charles Dickens, *A Tale of Two Cities*

He was afraid of things, and skipped and dodged and scrambled around <u>like a woman who has lost her mind on account of the arrival of a bat</u>.
eccentrically, insanely, illogically, witlessly, frantically
—Mark Twain, *Personal Recollections of Joan of Arc*

STEP THREE: **Inventing and substituting similes for adverbs**

Student instructions for Step Three:

Now, you will practice writing your own similes to substitute for adverbs. The following sentences were taken from *Tarzan of the Apes*, by Edgar Rice Burroughs.

When you are finished, read the sentences aloud to your instructor, substituting the similes for the adverbs. Which version sounds better to you?

HOW TO HELP THE STUDENT WITH STEP THREE:

Answers on this exercise will vary widely.

A few suggested similes are offered below, but you should accept any simile that the student can defend.

In the meantime the lion had approached with quiet dignity to within ten paces of the two men, where he stood <u>curiously</u> watching them. like a nosy neighbor peeping through the blinds, as if they were a puzzle

He suffered <u>terribly</u> to see her so. like a dying man, as if he were being eaten alive

<u>Carefully</u> he lifted Tarzan to the cot. Like a mother with a newborn baby, as if he were carrying a priceless vase

Tarzan of the Apes would have felt cold lead once again had not D'Arnot cried <u>loudly</u> to the man with the leveled gun. like a howler monkey, as if he were stuck in a well

Arrows and bullets flew <u>thick and fast</u>. like sleet in a winter storm, as a stampede

He traveled <u>very slowly</u>, sleeping in the jungle at night. like a sloth with a gimpy knee, as if he were on a leisurely stroll

He beat <u>furiously</u> upon the heavy portal. like a fierce warlord, as if trying to pound a hole

As Tarzan moved <u>steadily</u> onward, his mind was occupied with many strange and new thoughts. like salmon swimming upstream in the fall, as if he were on autopilot

Jane Porter shuddered and looked <u>fearfully</u> up at the giant figure beside her. like a frightened bird, as if she were being hunted

<u>Gently</u> the door opened until a thin crack showed something standing just without. Like a whisper, As if it were blown by a soft gust of wind

WEEK 15: EXPLANATION BY DEFINITION PROJECT

This week, the student will choose her own object or phenomenon in nature and will write a 500-word explanation by definition that covers properties, function, and genus.

At this point in the *Writing With Skill* sequence, the student will begin to apply her skills to independent projects more frequently. When possible, try to create overlap between her independent writing assignments and her other subjects. If she can write on a topic related to her science study, the time spent on this composition (which will probably be more time than she normally spends on her *Writing With Skill* assignment alone) can be drawn from her science study time as well.

In this week's work, a number of skills covered in the first fourteen weeks of this course are revisited. If necessary, give her additional time to go back and review.

The assignment has been broken down into steps, with suggested amounts of time for each. These are *suggestions only*. Change, adapt, and even skip steps if appropriate. The overview is:

Step One: Review the *topos*	20–30 minutes
Step Two: Brainstorm a topic	45–60 minutes
Step Three: Pre-reading	Time for library visit, plus 1–3 hours for reading
Step Four: Take notes	2–4 hours
Step Five: Draft the composition	2–4 hours
Step Six: Finalize the composition	1–3 hours

Make sure that the student reads through the ***entire lesson*** before beginning to work.

Although the student does not need to show her work after each step, help tips have been provided for every one. You can always show the student my examples if she can't figure out what to do next.

You may also require that she show her work whenever you think it is appropriate.

STEP ONE: **Review the *topos* (20–30 minutes)**

Student instructions for Step One:

> Before you start to look for a topic, review the questions you'll be trying to answer.
> On a sheet of paper, copy down the following *topos* and place it into the Reference section of your Composition Notebook.

HOW TO HELP THE STUDENT WITH STEP ONE

The student's completed chart should resemble the following:

Explanation by Definition: Natural Object or Phenomenon
Definition: An explanation of properties, function, and genus

Procedure
1. Answer the following questions:
Essential Properties and Accidental Properties
    What does it look like?
    How does it behave?
    What senses come into play as you observe it?
    What do those senses reveal?
    Is your observation passive (watching/listening) or active
        (experimenting/collecting/probing)?
    What sorts of measurements (temperature, quantity, time,
        etc.) are necessary to your observation?
    What does it resemble?
    What is it made of?
    What sort of structure does it have?
    What is its extent in space?
    What is its extent in time?
    Which properties are essential?
    Which are accidental?
Function
    How does it work or behave?
        Will a descriptive sequence help the reader
            understand how it works? What would the
            sequence describe?
        Is its behavior predictable or unpredictable?
        Does it work/behave differently under different
            circumstances?
            At different times?
    Can its behavior be divided into phases?

Remember
1. Not all questions need to be answered.
2. Selection of genus can be based on either properties or function.

What separates the phases?

Is there a cause or trigger for its behavior?

What is the time frame for its behavior?

Where does the behavior take place?

Who/what needs it or uses it?

Is anything dependent on it?

Is it dependent on anything else?

Who/what affects its working/behavior?

For what purposes?

Is there more than one purpose?

Does the purpose change at different times?

Is the purpose dependent on any other
conditions?

Genus

What other objects or phenomena can it be grouped with?

What are the qualities that lead you to group them
together?

What name can you give this group?

In what significant ways is it different from the others in its
group?

STEP TWO: **Brainstorm a topic (20–30 minutes)**

Student instructions for Step Two:

To choose an object or phenomenon for study, you'll carry out a slightly simplified version of the brainstorming you learned in Week 8.

Back then, you learned to ask four questions for topics in science: What? Where? Who? Why? You'll follow the same procedure, but you won't ask *who*. "Who?" is a question that usually leads you in the direction of a biographical sketch (which you'll review later this year), or possibly towards a narrative of scientific discovery.

Here's a reminder of the sequence you'll follow as you brainstorm. If you need more explanation, go back to Week 8 and read through the instructions for Day Two.

1. Write the words WHAT, WHERE, and WHY along the long side of a piece of paper.

Under WHAT, write six names or phrases describing scientific phenomena,
natural objects or occurrences. (Keep in mind: Biology, chemistry, physics,
astronomy, geology!)

Under WHERE, write at least three physical places.

Under WHY, write down the names of at least two scientific theories.

2. Circle one name or phrase in each column that seems potentially the most interesting to you. Write the circled term from the WHAT column in the middle of a second blank sheet of paper. Now ask yourself: Where? Why? Try to come up with at least two answers for each question. Use different colored pens or pencils to write the answers in a brainstorming map around your central term.

3. Repeat #2 for the circled terms in the WHERE and WHY columns

4. Because you are writing a definition, you do not need to complete the final brainstorming step of defining the subject area. It's already defined: you're writing a definition! But these

brainstorming maps should give some idea of which object or phenomenon is best suited to an explanation by definition. Pick the map that turned out the best—the one that you found the most information on, or that you found the most interesting. You will end up covering a number of the different topics on this brainstorming map. Remember that your paper will be easier to write if you pick something with a clear *function* as well as *properties*.

HOW TO HELP THE STUDENT WITH STEP TWO

The student may instantly know what object or phenomenon she wants to research, particularly if she's been studying something in science that interests her. If you need to condense the assignment, you may choose to give her permission to skip this step.

However, if you can make time for it, have her go through this brainstorming process even if she thinks she already has a topic. This year's independent projects are designed to give the student repeated practice in going through the steps of researching and writing a paper. Every time the student goes through the entire sequence of steps, they will seem easier and more natural.

In addition, brainstorming for an explanation by definition paper is slightly different than general brainstorming, so the student will benefit from the practice.

Remember that the student will probably need to use the Internet for help in brainstorming. For your review, here are the instructions given to the student back in Week 8 when she first learned how to brainstorm:

> So to help yourself brainstorm, use the Internet. Enter the terms "Roaring Twenties" and "where" into a search engine such as Google, Bing, or Yahoo.
>
> When I do this, the first link that comes up is the "Roaring Twenties" entry on Wikipedia. You might remember this paragraph from the first level of *Writing With Skill:*
>
> You may *not* use Wikipedia. Wikipedia is not professionally edited or fact-checked. Anyone can post anything on Wikipedia. Usually, other users will identify and remove mistakes—but if you happen to use Wikipedia five minutes after someone has posted bad information (which people sometimes do just for fun), you won't realize that you're writing down false facts.[15]
>
> That's still true! But you're not doing research right now—you're just trying to come up with as many connected ideas and bits of information as possible. If there's a mistake in the information, you'll discover it as soon as you start taking notes. So go ahead and use Wikipedia if your search engine turns it up.
>
> When I click on the Wikipedia link, I discover that the Roaring Twenties was centered at large cities: Chicago, New Orleans, Los Angeles, New York, Philadelphia, Paris, and London. That certainly gives me plenty of answers to the question "where."
>
> ★
>
> Remember to put quotes around words or phrases that belong together. Your answers to "what" will probably be phrases or even short sentences;

Here is an example of how the first and second instructions might look, completed. If necessary, you can show these brainstorming maps to the student (but then she has to make her own).

---

15. Susan Wise Bauer, *Writing With Skill, Level One Student Text* (Well-Trained Mind Press, 2012), p. 478.

#1

WHAT   WHERE   WHY

Enzymes   Deep sea   ⟨germ theory⟩
              trenches
Butterflies   ⟨The Arctic⟩   Climate
                             change
⟨Amber⟩   High altitude

The speed of sound

Dust explosions

Supernova

In the following map, done for Step #2, the answers for WHERE are underlined and the answers for WHY are not, just so that you can tell the difference.

I wanted to find out more about amber, but when I entered "amber" and "why" in my search engine, I got lots of information about reality TV stars named "Amber." So I entered "amber" AND "resin" AND "why." Because the term has more than one meaning, I had to borrow "resin" from the Wikipedia entry to narrow down my search.

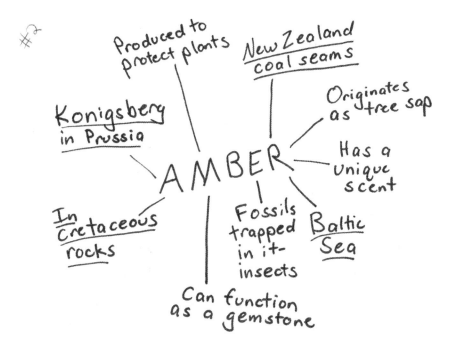

When I write my definition of amber, I will end up talking about its origins as tree sap *and* its ability to serve as a gemstone *and* its location in Königsberg, Prussia. The brainstorming step has now given me lots of different topics to search for when I go to the library in Step Three.

STEP THREE: Pre-reading (Time for library visit, plus 1–3 hours for reading)

Student instructions for Step Three:

Now you'll use your brainstorming map to help you locate titles for prereading.

The pre-reading you do for your definition by explanation won't need to be quite as extensive as the pre-reading you did for your independent project in Weeks 8–9. You should aim to end up with three sources that give you valuable information about your topic. You'll follow the same sequence as in Week 8; if you need reminders, go back to Day Three of Week 8 and read back through the lesson.

1. Make an initial list of titles to look for, using your local library's online catalog. Search for several different terms from your brainstorming map.

2. Take your brainstorming map with you and visit the library. Locate your chosen titles. Glance at the titles on either side on the shelf to see if they look useful. Pull six to eight books off the shelf and examine them. Use the indices to make sure that each book addresses your topic. Remember: you need information about properties *and* function. You can determine an appropriate genus yourself.

3. Try to bring home at least four books that relate to your subject.

4. Read the chapters or sections of each book that relate to your topic. Don't take notes yet; instead, use bookmarks or Post-It Notes to mark pages that you might want to use.

HOW TO HELP THE STUDENT WITH STEP THREE

The brainstorming map should help the student design a productive library catalog search.

When I searched my local library for my central term *amber,* I only found one book:

Ake Dahlstrom and Leif Brost, *The Amber Book*

But when I searched for "insect fossils" I found the additional title:

Christa Bedry, *Insects*

which covers fossils in amber as well as living insects. And when I searched for "gemstones" I found:

Sandra Friend, *Earth's Hidden Treasures*

which has a chapter on amber. I would put all of these on my library list.

Remember that the student can also use Google Books to find sources, particularly if a library visit is impractical. Google searches are best done with the central term plus at least one of the other terms on the page. When I searched for "amber" plus "fossil" plus "insects," I found:

Andrew Ross, *Amber*

George Poinar, Jr. and Roberta Poinar, *What Bugged the Dinosaurs? Insects, Disease, and Death in the Cretaceous*

both of which allowed me to read several chapters online.

STEP FOUR: **Take notes (2–4 hours)**

Student instructions for Step Four:

> Using proper form (see Week 3, Day Three if you need a refresher), take notes from at least three of your books. The number you will take will vary; try not to take more than 20 notes from any one book.
>
> Take notes in the way suggested in Day Three of Week 12 and Day Two of Week 13: As you take your notes, organize them by the question that they answer. If you don't remember how this works, read back through the instructions for both days now.
>
> As you take your notes, you will constantly need to refer back to your Explanation by Definition chart. Look for answers to the questions on the chart, and note the answers underneath each question.
>
> This is a different method of note-taking than the method used in Weeks 8–9, when you chose both your own subject and your own *topoi*. There are two different ways of preparing to write a paper: knowing ahead of time what kind of paper you'll write (as in this assignment), and deciding after you look at the available information what kind of paper you'll write (as in the Weeks 8–9 assignment). You'll be given both kinds of assignment in college, so you need to practice both.
>
> Be sure that your notes answer at least four of the questions under Properties, and at least three to four of the questions under Function.
>
> Whenever you find a piece of information that might help you place your subject into a group, list it under Genus. You'll probably want to put the *same* information into either Properties or Function; it's perfectly fine to duplicate your notes for Genus.

HOW TO HELP THE STUDENT WITH STEP FOUR

For the purposes of this exercise, the student will need to organize her notes as she takes them, rather than taking notes on a single source and organizing them later.

Although this takes a little more time at the beginning, because the student has to constantly refer back to the questions as she takes notes, it saves time when the student begins to write, because an additional "Organize your notes" step is unnecessary.

You may need to reinforce the final paragraph in the instructions: that notes taken for Genus (information that helps put the subject into a group) will probably be copied directly from the notes on Properties and Function. It's fine to have the same note reproduced, word for word, in the Genus section and in another section as well.

For example, I might put the following notes under Properties:

What is it made of?

"this warm, organic gem began as resin slowly oozing down the bark of an ancient tree" (Poinar, p. 12)

"amber is completely polymerized, has no volatiles, and is inert" (Ross, p. 3)

"Amber generally consists of around 79% carbon, 10% hydrogen and 11% oxygen, with a trace of sulphur" (Ross, p. 4)

"Baltic amber commonly contains hairs from the flowers of oak trees and black cracks filled with tiny pyrite crystals" (Ross, p. 4)
What sort of structure does it have?
"ranged in size from teardrops to walnuts, and many were encrusted with a dark oxidized covering" (Poinar, p. 12)

Then, under Genus, I would put:

Genus
"this warm, organic gem began as resin slowly oozing down the bark of an ancient tree" (Poinar, p. 12)
"turpentine is a volatile liquid obtained from tree resin and is often used as a solvent"

because, as I take notes, I realize that I can group amber together with "Other things made out of tree resin"—such as turpentine.

If necessary, show the above example to the student.

NOTE TO INSTRUCTOR: Some students may wish to take all notes from a book first, and then divide the notes into properties and functions. This curriculum is designed to expose students to a number of methods of researching and writing, so that they can find the ones that seem most natural. Encourage the student to try to stick to the instructions, so that she can practice this particular method. But if she seems unnecessarily frustrated, it means that this method isn't going to work for her; let her take notes in the way she prefers.

STEP FIVE: **Draft the composition (2–4 hours)**

Student instructions for Step Five:

Using your notes, write your composition. Follow these guidelines:

First, describe the properties of your subject (in any order that you choose). Then, describe the function. Finally, identify the genus.

Aim for at least two to three paragraphs each for properties and function, one to two paragraphs for genus.

Quote directly from at least two of your sources. Make sure that all direct quotes and anything which is not common knowledge is footnoted.

Check your *topoi* chart one more time to make sure that you have included the required elements.

Since your complete composition, including introduction and conclusion, should be at least 500 words long, aim to have at least 450 words in this initial draft.

HOW TO HELP THE STUDENT WITH STEP FIVE

The student may find it helpful to read the following examples, describing properties, function, and genus.

Properties of a volcano (what does it look like? how does it behave? what is it made of? what does it resemble? what sort of structure does it have?)

> *A volcano is an opening in the earth's surface at a "plate margin," a weakness in the earth's crust.[16] A volcano is made up of a chamber that contains magma and gas that has been pushed to the surface by pressure. After the magma and gas erupts, the volcano sometimes collapses inward and forms a caldera. Volcanoes are like "safety valves" in the crust of the earth.[17]*

> *When the pressure of the magma and gas gets too intense, the volcano explodes into an eruption. Columns of smoke and streams of fiery lava pour out of the opening of the volcano. A thick blanket of ash may fall all around. Dust and thick clouds cover the nearby land. Sometimes, huge rocks are thrown into the air.[18] The lava can burn everything in its path. The earth can shake, and the dust and ash can turn even daylight completely black. The flames coming from the lava can look like lightning, only larger.[19]*

Function of a Venus' flytrap (How does it work or behave? Who uses it, for what purpose?)

> *A Venus' flytrap is an unusual plant that catches flies and eats them. First, a fly is attracted to the smell of nectar in the flytrap. The Venus' flytrap has six little hairs on the trap.[20] If only one hair is touched, nothing happens. But if the fly touches two hairs, the trap closes "like the teeth of a jaw trap."[21] The fly is trapped. Then, the plant produces enzymes that digest the fly. The flytrap does not eat the exoskeleton; it discards it when it is finished digesting the fly.[22] Two weeks later the trap opens again, and the process starts over.[23]*

> *The Venus' flytrap has many uses. They are well known for what they eat, but they also are food for many animals. Raccoons and mice and even some insects eat the plant. Most of these animals prefer to eat other plants, though.[24] Humans use the "sterilized fresh juices" of the flytrap to make a medicine called Carnivora®. This drug is used to treat cancer and help the immune system.[25]*

---

16. Jacqueline Dineen, *Natural Disasters: Volcanoes* (The Creative Company, 2005), p. 10.
17. Dineen, p. 10.
18. Peter Clarkson, *Volcanoes* (Voyageur Press, 2000), p. 7.
19. Pliny the Younger, "Pliny to Tacitus," trans. Cynthia Damon, in Ronald Mellor, ed., *The Historians of Ancient Rome: An Anthology of the Major Writings,* second ed. (Routledge, 2004), p. 534.
20. Matilda Gollon, ed., *The Big Idea Science Book* (DK Publishing, 2010), p. 78.
21. Carl Zimmer, "Fatal Attraction," *National Geographic,* March 2010, p. 82.
22. Gollon, p. 78.
23. Audrey Anderson, "The Venus' Flytrap's Circle of Life," in *Writing With Skill, Level 2* (Well-Trained Mind Press, 2013), pp. 176-177.
24. Ibid.
25. Michael Tierra, *Treating Cancer with Herbs: An Integrative Approach* (Lotus Press, 2003), p. 157.

Genus of bamboo (What other objects can it be grouped with? How is it different from other members of this group?)

Bamboo can grow a hundred feet high, but bamboo is actually a member of the grass family. Most grasses grow one cell at a time. Instead, bamboo grows when rhizomes spread underground. Spears called culms pop up quickly and fill with water. This helps them grow quickly, unlike other grasses, that grow cell by cell.

You may need to point out that the question "How does it behave?" overlaps with function.

STEP SIX: **Finalize the composition (1–3 hours)**

Student instructions for Step Six:

> 1. Review the Introductions and Conclusions chart in the Reference section of your Composition Notebook. Choose one kind of introduction and another kind of conclusion. Write your introduction and conclusion. Make sure that you have at least 500 words total.
> 2. Choose a title. If necessary, look back at Week 9, Day Four to review the process.
> 3. Assemble your Works Cited page, using the correct format.
> 4. Proofread, using the four-part process described in Week 13, Day Three, Step Four.

> When your composition is finished, show it to your instructor.

HOW TO HELP THE STUDENT WITH STEP SIX

If the student has difficulty with the introduction and conclusion, tell him to read back through Days 1–2 of Week Six. For help with titling, look back at Week Nine, Day 4. The student's title can be as simple as "A Definition of Amber" or "What Amber Is and How It Functions."

Check the student's composition, using the following rubric.

Week 15 Rubric

Organization:

1   The entire composition should be at least six paragraphs and at least five hundred words in length.
2   The first two to three paragraphs should describe the properties of the object or phenomenon and should answer at least three of the questions about properties.
3   The next two to three paragraphs should describe function and should answer at least two of the questions about function.
4   The next one to two paragraphs should place the object or phenomenon into a group and explain what qualities define the group. It can also say how the object differs from the others in the group, but this is optional.
5   The composition should have both an introduction and a conclusion. One of these should be a separate paragraph. The introduction and conclusion should be of different types.
6   The composition should have a title, centered at the top of the first page. This title should *not* be simply the name of the object or phenomenon.
7   At least two sources should be cited.
8   All sources mentioned in footnotes should be placed on a Works Cited page.

Mechanics:

1   Each sentence should make sense on its own when read aloud.
2   There should be no sentence fragments or run-on sentences.
3   All words should be spelled correctly.
4   The first line of each paragraph should be properly indented.
5   Verb tense should be consistent throughout.
6   No noun or verb should be used more than twice (with the exception of state-of-being verbs, linking verbs, and the verb "said").
7   No modifier or prepositional phrase acting as a modifier should be used more than once.
8   Footnotes and the Works Cited page should be properly formatted.

WEEK 16: COMPARING TWO POEMS

Day One: Read

 Focus: Reading

Overview of Weeks 16–18

The student has spent the last four weeks writing about science. Now he'll change directions and do something completely different: write about poetry.

In the first level of this course, the student wrote three different beginning literary analysis essays about three different poems: "The Bells," by Edgar Allan Poe; "Ozymandias," by Percy Bysshe Shelley; and "The Charge of the Light Brigade," by Alfred, Lord Tennyson. This second level also spends three weeks on poetry analysis, but the focus will be on bringing together skills that have already been learned. The student will begin by writing a one-week comparison/contrast of two poems. Then, he will spend the next two weeks working on a combined poem analysis/biographical sketch.

Today's reading work will be done independently. However, check to make sure that the student has looked up unfamiliar words in the dictionary and has also followed the reading directions closely.

Student instructions for Day One:

> Turn to Appendix II. The first two poems in the appendix, "The Armful" and "The Road Not Taken," are by the American poet Robert Frost.
> Robert Frost (1874–1963) grew up in California and Massachusetts; he also lived in New Hampshire, England, Vermont, and Florida. He worked as a farmer, teacher, and writer. He won four Pulitzer Prizes for his poetry and published over thirty volumes of poetry, plays, and essays.
> "The Road Not Taken" was originally published in 1916; "The Armful" was published in 1928.
> Read each poem four times in a row, closely following these instructions.
> STEP ONE: **Read silently**
> Read the poem silently and slowly. Stop and look up the meanings and pronunciations of all words you don't know.

STEP TWO: **Read out loud**

Go to a private place and read the poem out loud, at a normal pace. Pronounce each word clearly. Pause at the end of each line so that you can hear the sound of each individual line.

STEP THREE: **Read for punctuation**

Read the poem out loud a second time. This time, ignore the line endings. Instead, pause at each comma; pause for a longer time at semicolons and colons; make the longest pause of all at periods. If there is no punctuation at the end of a line, read on without pausing. Use your voice to indicate exclamation points.

STEP FOUR: **Read for rhyme**

Read the poem out loud one last time, emphasizing the last syllable of every line. Listen for repeated rhymes.

Day Two: Examine Form

 Focus: Understanding meter, rhyme scheme, and stanza arrangement

STEP ONE: **Review meter**

Student instructions for Step One:

When you wrote about poetry in the first level of this course, you learned that *meter* is the rhythmical pattern of a poem. Poems written in regular meter have a repeating pattern of stressed and unstressed syllables. Each set of stressed and unstressed syllables is known as a *foot*.

In these lines from "Ozymandias," each *foot* is surrounded by parentheses. Within each foot, an accent mark is over each stressed syllable. A circumflex is over each unstressed syllable.

˘ ´ ˘ ´ ˘ ´ ˘ ´ ˘ ´

(My name) (is O) (zyman) (dias, King) (of Kings):

˘ ´ ˘ ´ ˘ ´ ˘ ´ ˘ ´

(Look on) (my works), (ye migh) (ty, and) (despair)!

Read those two lines out loud to your instructor. Use your voice to emphasize each stressed (marked with an accent) syllable.

Each line of this poem has five feet. Each foot has the same pattern: one unstressed syllable, followed by a stressed syllable. Last year, you learned that this meter is called **iambic pentameter**. An **iamb** is a foot with the pattern "unstressed-stressed." **Pentameter** means that there are five feet per line.

You also learned that in **trochaic** meter, each foot has the pattern "stressed-unstressed." **Anapestic** meter follows the pattern "unstressed-unstressed-stressed." And **dactylic** meter follows the pattern "stressed-unstressed-unstressed."

Label each line below as iambic, trochaic, anapestic, or dactylic. When you're finished, show your work to your instructor. Remember—reading poetry out loud is the very best way to hear the meter!

HOW TO HELP THE STUDENT WITH STEP ONE

When the student reads the lines from "Ozymandias" out loud to you, he should emphasize each bolded syllable:

> My **name** is **Ozyman**dias, **King** of **Kings,**
> Look **on** my **works,** ye **migh**ty, **and** de**spair!**

If the student has difficulty finding the answers below, read the lines out loud to him, stressing the bolded syllables.

'Twas the **night** before **Christ**mas, and **all** through the **house**   Anapestic
    (Moore)
Be**cause** I **could** not **stop** for **Death,**/ He **kind**ly **stopped** for **me**   Iambic
    (Emily Dickinson)
Decked them **with** their **bright**est **fea**thers   Trochaic
    (Longfellow)
Shall **I** com**pare** thee **to** a **sum**mer's **day?**   Iambic
    (Shakespeare)
Bubble, **bu**bble, **toil** and **trou**ble.   Trochaic
    (Shakespeare)
Black were her **eyes** as the **ber**ry that **grows** on the **thorn** by the **way**side   Dactylic
    (Longfellow)
    [NOTE: this line contains an incomplete dactyl; the very last foot is missing the final
syllable]

STEP TWO: **Understand the meter of each poem**

Student instructions for Step Two:

> Begin by marking the meter of "The Armful," which is very regular. On the copy of the poem below, mark stressed syllables with accents and unstressed with circumflexes. (Ignore the blanks to the right for the moment.)
>
> ★
>
> When you are finished, circle each foot in the first two lines. What is the name of the poem's meter? Write the answer on the line below.
>
> _____
>
> When you are finished, show your work to your instructor. If you need help, ask for it!

HOW TO HELP THE STUDENT WITH STEP TWO

The student may find this step tedious. Marking the meter of a poem has two benefits, though. It forces the student to pay close attention to the words, which will make it simpler to think about meaning; and it improves the student's sensitivity to the rhythms of the English language.

The student's markings should follow the pattern below:

The Armful
by Robert Frost

For every parcel I stoop down to seize

I lose some other off my arms and knees,

And the whole pile is slipping, bottles, buns—

Extremes too hard to comprehend at once,

Yet nothing I should care to leave behind.

With all I have to hold with, hand and mind

And heart, if need be, I will do my best

To keep their building balanced at my breast.

I crouch down to prevent them as they fall;

Then sit down in the middle of them all.

I had to drop the armful in the road

And try to stack them in a better load.

The meter is iambic pentameter, five iambic (unstressed-stressed) feet per line.

Continuing student instructions for Step Two:

Now look carefully at the first stanza of "The Road Not Taken." See if you can mark the stressed and unstressed syllables in the first stanza. Here's a hint: there is one *irregular foot* in each line. Can you find it?

When you've done your best, show the stanza to your instructor. (You'll use the blanks to the right of the poem in the next step.)

★

After discussing the meter with your instructor, go on and mark the rest of the lines. When you're finished, write the name of the meter on the line below.

_____

HOW TO HELP THE STUDENT WITH STEP TWO

The meter is marked below.

The student has been encouraged to mark the first stanza independently. If he needs assistance, mark the first line for him while he watches. Ask him to try to complete the rest. Each line in the first stanza follows the same pattern: four iambic feet (unstressed-stressed) plus one additional unstressed syllable.

After the student has marked the first stanza, tell him that there are two different ways to think about the meter of the poem.

1) It is *iambic tetrameter,* four iambic feet per line, but many of the lines are *hypermetric*— have one extra syllable.

2) It has three iambic feet and one anapestic foot (unstressed—unstressed—stressed) per line.

Point out that the anapestic foot doesn't always occur in the same place—in the first three lines, it is the third foot, but then in the fourth line, it shifts suddenly to the last foot. The change in rhythm continually pushes the reader off balance.

Now ask the student to mark the rest of the poem. Tell him that three lines are completely regular iambic tetrameter, with no anapestic foot; he should underline those three lines. Also warn him that there is one line with two anapests and two iambs. He should circle this line when he finds it.

At the end of the poem, the student should write either "Hypermetric iambic tetrameter" or "Three iambic feet and one anapestic foot."

Two roads diverged in a yellow wood,

And sorry I could not travel both

And be one traveler, long I stood

And looked down one as far as I could

To where it bent in the undergrowth;

Then took the other, as just as fair,

And having perhaps the better claim

Because it was grassy and wanted wear,

<u>Though as for that the passing there</u>

Had worn them really about the same,

And both that morning equally lay

<u>In leaves no step had trodden black.</u>

Oh, I marked the first for another day!

Yet knowing how way leads on to way

I doubted if I should ever come back.

I shall be telling this with a sigh

Somewhere ages and ages hence:

Two roads diverged in a wood, and I,

<u>I took the one less traveled by,</u>

And that has made all the difference. OR difference. [if pronounced "diffrance"]

STEP THREE: **Understand the rhyme scheme of each poem**

Student instructions for Step Three:

Go back to "The Armful" and mark the rhyme scheme, using the blanks to the right of the poem.

Remember: a rhyme scheme is a pattern of repeating rhymes. You find a rhyme scheme by giving each line-ending sound a different letter of the alphabet, like this:

"Will you walk a little faster?" said a whiting to a snail,	A
"There's a porpoise close behind us, and he's treading on my tail.	A
See how eagerly the lobsters and the turtles all advance!	B
They are waiting on the shingle—will you come and join the dance?"	B

"You can really have no notion how delightful it will be	C
When they take us up and throw us, with the lobsters, out to sea!"	C
But the snail replied "Too far, too far!" and gave a look askance—	B
Said he thanked the whiting kindly, but he would not join the dance.	B

(Those are two stanzas from a poem by Lewis Carroll called "The Lobster Quadrille.") The same ending sound always gets the same letter—that's why "advance," "dance," and "askance" are all given the letter B.

Show your work to your instructor. Answer the following question: Is the rhyme scheme regular or irregular?

Now do the same thing for "The Road Less Travelled." Show your work to your instructor. Answer the following question: Is the rhyme scheme regular or irregular?

HOW TO HELP THE STUDENT WITH STEP THREE

Rhyme scheme for "The Armful":	AABBCCDDEEFF
Rhyme scheme for "The Road Not Taken":	ABAAB
	CDCCD
	EFEEF
	GHGGH

Both rhyme schemes are regular. However, point out to the student that "The Armful" is much simpler—almost more like a nursery rhyme. "The Road Not Taken" has a more complex, less predictable rhyme scheme. Ask the student whether any rhymes in "The Road Not Taken" reoccur in later stanzas (the answer is no).

STEP FOUR: **Complete the comparison chart**

Student instructions for Step Four:

Sum up your conclusions about meter and rhyme by completing the following chart.

HOW TO HELP THE STUDENT WITH STEP FOUR

The student's completed chart should resemble the following:

	"The Armful"	"The Road Not Taken"
Name of meter?	Iambic pentameter	Hypermetric iambic tetrameter OR 3 iambic feet and 1 anapestic foot
Which poem's meter is more regular? More irregular?	Very regular meter	More irregular meter
Do any lines break the metrical pattern? If so, write them here.		Though as for that the passing there In leaves no step had trodden black I doubted if I should ever come back I took the one less traveled by
What is the rhyme scheme?	AABBCCDDEEFF	ABAAB CDCCD EFEEF GHGGH
Is the rhyme scheme regular or irregular?	Regular	Regular
Which rhyme scheme is simpler? More complex?	Simpler	More complex

Day Three: Think

 Focus: Connecting form and meaning

In the first two steps of today's lesson, carry on the following dialogues with the student. During these dialogues, the student will write brief answers to be used in tomorrow's essay.

Prompt the student as necessary, using the answers below.

STEP ONE: **Discuss "The Armful"**

Instructor: Is the poem written in first, second, or third person?

Student: First person

Instructor: Tell me what happens in the poem—taking everything that the narrator says literally. What is the narrator doing? What happens? And how does he (or she) react?

Student: The narrator is carrying a pile of things and they keep slipping off. He tries to keep them from falling, but he drops them all. Then he has to sit down and try to stack them up into an armful again.

Instructor: Where is the narrator?

Student: On a road.

Instructor: In a way, this poem tells a straightforward story. But there are hints that the poet is actually describing something more complicated than dropping an armload of stuff in the middle of a road.

NOTE TO INSTRUCTOR: Depending on the student's comfort level with poetry, you might choose to give her the chance to make independent observations before carrying on the rest of the dialogue.

Instructor: Three things that the narrator is carrying are specifically named. What are they?

Student: Parcels, bottles, buns

Instructor: Bottles and buns are shaped differently, but are they really "extremes too hard to comprehend at once"?

Student: No.

Instructor: The parcels, bottles, and buns are metaphors—they stand for something else. Here's another hint: the narrator says he has to hold his pile of things with "hand and mind and heart, if need be." Do you normally carry things with your heart?

Student: No.

Instructor: So the narrator is trying to juggle a whole stack of things that don't fit well together—but they aren't actual parcels, bottles, and buns. What do you think he's trying to juggle?

Student: Choices OR priorities OR situations

NOTE TO INSTRUCTOR: The purpose of this lesson is to teach the student to *write* about poetry, not to force her to have great insights into poems. If she cannot come up with an answer, provide one for her. It may help to read her this excerpt from *The Robert Frost Encyclopedia:* "One plausible application is that Frost is recalling the frustration of balancing diverse personal responsibilities . . . while wishing for unencumbered attention to his poetry . . . As with 'bottles' and 'buns,' so with activities and commitments."[26]

Instructor: Last year, you learned that most poems don't begin and end in the same place. Something happens, or changes, during the poem. At the beginning of the poem, the narrator is trying to juggle a slippery pile of things. What has changed, at the end?

Student: He is trying to rebalance them.

Instructor: So the poem is about the search to try to keep lots of different responsibilities and tasks balanced. Does the narrator decide to give up any of the things in the pile? Leave them behind?

Student: No.

Instructor: Instead of solving his problem by eliminating things, he finds it by rearranging them into a better balance. The poem is all about finding a balance. How does the meter and rhyme relate to the theme of finding balance?

Student: The meter and rhyme are very regular and "balanced."

Instructor: Now that you've talked about the poem, answer the questions in your workbook. Brief phrases are fine.

The student's answers should resemble the following:

What is the literal meaning of the poem?   The narrator is trying to balance a lot of different things in a pile and keeps dropping them.

Where does the poem take place?   On a road

What do the things in the pile represent?   Choices OR Situations OR Responsibilities

What changes between the beginning and end of the poem?   The narrator decides to rebalance all of the things in the pile so that they are easier to carry.

How do the meter and rhyme relate to the meaning of the poem?   The meter and rhyme are very balanced.

---

26. Nancy Lewis Tuten and John Zubizarreta, eds., *The Robert Frost Encyclopedia* (Greenwood Press, 2001), p. 11.

STEP TWO: **Discuss "The Road Not Taken"**

Instructor: Is the poem written in first, second, or third person?

Student: First person

Instructor: Tell me what happens, literally, in the poem.

Student: The narrator comes to a crossroad. He looks down one road as far as the bend, and then decides to take the other road.

Instructor: Where is the narrator?

Student: Standing at the crossroad OR On a road

Instructor: Can you find a place where the poem suggests that the narrator is talking about something bigger and more important than two literal roads in an actual wood? Here's a hint: look at the last stanza.

Student: The narrator is "telling this with a sigh," "ages and ages hence." Also, his choice "made all the difference."

Instructor: In "The Armful," the narrator doesn't have to leave any of the things in his pile behind. But in "The Road Not Taken," the narrator does have to give something up. What does he give up—or choose not to do?

Student: He chooses not to take one of the roads.

Instructor: So in this poem, what changes for the narrator between the beginning stanza and the ending stanza?

Student: His choice is made.

Instructor: Does the narrator think that his choice was an important one? How do you know?

Student: Yes, because he says that it "made all the difference."

NOTE TO INSTRUCTOR: Remember not to frustrate the student if she has difficulty figuring out the answers to these questions! Prompt her as much as you need to. You may want to read her the following paragraph from a study of Frost's work: "The human condition is that we can travel only one road at a time. What makes all the difference in the end, we are left to ponder. And what difference it makes . . . we are also left to wonder. Frost purposefully leaves many of the questions raised by the poem unanswered . . . [I]t is not about taking both roads or about which road was taken but about having to choose only one."[27]

Instructor: The rhyme scheme of this poem is regular—but it is more complicated than the rhyme scheme of "The Armful." That should tell you something about the choice the narrator is making—that it is more complicated than the choice in "The Armful." Frost also uses the

---

27. Deirdre Fagan, *Critical Companion to Robert Frost: A Literary Reference to His Life and Work* (Facts on File, 2007), p. 295.

irregular meter of "The Road Not Taken" to convey a message to you: This poem isn't quite as clear and straightforward as "The Armful." Look back at your chart. You should have written down four lines that break the metrical pattern of the poem. What is the first line?

Student: Though as for that the passing there.

Instructor: At the end of the poem, the narrator says that he took the road less traveled by. But that irregular line warns you that he might not be remembering correctly. Finish the thought: "Though as for that, the passing there" did what?

Student: Had worn them really about the same.

Instructor: So even though he says at the end of the poem that one road was less traveled by, when he is actually *looking* at the roads, they look about the same. Now look at the second irregular line. What is it?

Student: In leaves no step had trodden black.

Instructor: Both roads are covered in leaves that no one had trampled. Was one less trampled than the other?

Student: No.

Instructor: So you can see that Frost uses changes in the meter to keep the reader alert—to warn you that the poem's story is not as simple as it first sounds. What is the next irregular line?

Student: I doubted if I should ever come back.

Instructor: But in a way, the narrator *has* come back—in his memory, over and over again, to the moment when he made the choice to take one road instead of the other. What's the very last irregular line?

Student: I took the one less traveled by.

Instructor: But was it really less traveled by? No—because "the passing there/Had worn them really about the same," and both of them "equally lay/In leaves no step had trodden black." The complicated structure of the poem tells you that the narrator's conclusion ("that has made all the difference") is too simple.

NOTE TO INSTRUCTOR: Use the next section only if the student is following the lesson so far without difficulty. It is an optional advanced topic.

Instructor: Here's one last thing to consider: I keep calling those lines "irregular" because they break the pattern of all the other lines. But the truth is that these "irregular" lines are the most regular in the whole poem. Three of them are straight iambic tetrameter without the extra syllable. Which three? Read them out loud, emphasizing the stressed syllables.

Student: Though **as** for **that** the **pass**ing **there**, In **leaves** no **step** had **trod**den **black**, I **took** the **one** less **trav**eled **by**.

Instructor: The fourth irregular line is also regular, in its way. Listen: *I **doubted** if **I** should **ever** come **back.*** It repeats the pattern unstressed-stressed, unstressed-unstressed-stressed twice in a row. This creates a very catchy rhythm, like a horse galloping. In this poem, the regular rhythms become irregular—and the irregular rhythm with the extra syllable becomes the "regular," or normal meter. This is just another way in which Frost tells you that the narrator's conclusion might need to be turned inside out.

Instructor: Now that you've talked about the poem, answer the questions in your workbook. Brief phrases are fine.

The student's answers should resemble the following:

What is the literal meaning of the poem?   The narrator is standing at a crossroad, trying to decide which road to take. He chooses one instead of the other.

Where does the poem take place?   On a road OR At a crossroad

What do the roads represent?   A choice that the narrator needs to make

What changes between the beginning and end of the poem?   He makes his decision and then looks back and says that it "made all the difference."

How do the meter and rhyme relate to the meaning of the poem?   The rhyme is regular, but it is more complicated—like the choice the narrator makes. The meter tells us that the narrator's conclusion might be the wrong one.

STEP THREE: **List similarities and differences**

Student instructions for Step Three:

Finish up today's work by making a list of the similarities and differences between the two poems.

Using your own paper, begin by listing every similarity between the two poems, like this:

SIMILARITIES

Written in the first person

You can use phrases, not complete sentences. Try to come up with at least four similarities.

Next, list the differences. Be specific and use the following format:

DIFFERENCES

"The Armful"	**"The Road Not Taken"**
Narrator doesn't have to leave anything behind	**Narrator has to make a choice between two things**

If you have trouble, ask your instructor for help. Try to come up with at least three differences.

You can use the examples above to start your lists.

HOW TO HELP THE STUDENT WITH STEP THREE

The student's answers should resemble the following. She should have at least four similarities and three differences.

SIMILARITIES

Written in the first person
Take place on a road
Regular rhyme scheme
Same theme: both about making choices
Uses iambic feet

DIFFERENCES

"The Armful"	"The Road Not Taken"
Narrator doesn't have to leave anything behind	Narrator has to make a choice between two things
Simple rhyme scheme	Complicated rhyme scheme
Regular meter	Irregular meter
One stanza	Five stanzas
Trustworthy narrator	Narrator might be wrong

If the student has trouble, ask the following questions:

What person is each poem written in?
Where do both poems take place?
What is the same about the rhyme scheme?
What theme do the poems share?
What type of foot does each poem use?

What is different about the choice that the narrator has to make in each poem?
How are the rhyme schemes different?
How are the meters different?
How many stanzas does each poem have?
Does each narrator come to the correct conclusion?

Day Four: Write

Focus: Writing about the poem

Today, the student will write about "The Armful" and "The Road Not Taken," using a *topos* that was covered a few weeks ago: explanation by comparison and contrast.

Make sure that the student reviews the following chart (reproduced in her workbook) carefully:

Explanation by Comparison/Contrast

Definition: A comparison of similarities and differences

Procedure	Remember
1. Decide which aspects of the subjects are the same, and which are different.	1. Use both methods to give variety.
2. Choose a method for comparing and contrasting.	
a. Point-by-point	
b. Subject-by-subject	

The student has already finished the first part of the procedure—deciding which aspects of the subjects are the same and which are different. Now, she will use a point-by-point method to compare and contrast them.

The final composition should be at least 250 words long.

Make sure that the student carefully reviews the following rules for quoting poetry:

Identify clearly which poem you're quoting.

Place the line number of the poem in parentheses after the closing quotation marks of the quote, like this: "In leaves no step had trodden black" (12)

If you quote two or three consecutive lines from a poem, use a forward slash mark followed by a space to show the division between the lines. Use exactly the same punctuation as in the original, except for the last line quoted; drop the punctuation of the last line completely, like this: "Two roads diverged in a wood, and I,/ I took the one less traveled by" (18–19).

If you quote four or more lines from a poem, double-space down, indent twice, and reproduce the lines exactly as they appear in the poem. This is called a "block quote." No quotation marks are needed.

NOTE TO INSTRUCTOR: The student can complete the first three steps independently. If she needs help, show her the appropriate paragraph from the sample composition at the end of the lesson.

STEP ONE: **Write about similarities (Student Responsibility)**

Student instructions for Step One:

> Begin by writing a paragraph describing the similarities between the two poems. The paragraph should be 60–100 words long and should quote directly from at least one of the poems.

STEP TWO: **Write about differences (Student Responsibility)**

Student instructions for Step Two:

> Now write three short paragraphs, each one describing a difference between the two poems. Quote from each poem at least one time. Altogether, your three paragraphs should be at least 125 words long.
>
> You can use the following phrases/words, but don't use any phrase/word more than once:
>
> > **on the one hand . . . on the other hand**
> >
> > **by contrast**
> >
> > **however**
> >
> > **but**
>
> Also, make sure that each one of your paragraphs has a different opening (in other words, don't begin each paragraph by saying, "In 'The Armful' . . . but in 'The Road Not Taken' . . . "). If you need help, ask your instructor.
>
> You do not need to show your work to your instructor until it is proofread, but you may ask your instructor whether or not you're on the right track (or road!).

STEP THREE: **Write an introduction and conclusion (Student Responsibility)**

Student instructions for Step Three:

> Finish your composition by writing an introduction and conclusion.
>
> Last year, you learned that an introduction should include the name of the poem, the name of the author, and the main topic, idea, or theme of the poem. For this comparison/contrast, you can begin by stating either a topic, idea, or theme that the poems have in common, or else by describing a difference between them.
>
> Which should you pick? It depends on whether you think the poems are more alike, or more different. This type of introduction is very much like the Introduction by Summary you studied in Week 6:
>
> > 1. Introduction by Summary
> >
> > > One or more sentences that tell the reader what the composition is about and what its most central conclusion will be.
>
> In the case of a literature paper, you also have to be sure to identify the works that you'll be writing about.
>
> Your introduction should be a separate paragraph. It can be either a single sentence long, or more than one sentence.
>
> Now, choose one of the following conclusions that you studied in Week 6:

2. Conclusion by Personal Reaction
    a. Personal statement
    b. Your opinion about the material
    c. Your own experience with the subject
3. Conclusion by Question
    Ask the reader to react to the information

Write a conclusion for your paper. Remember that a paragraph of conclusion should contain at least two sentences. Single-sentence conclusions should be written as the last sentence of the final paragraph.

STEP FOUR: **Title and proofread your essay**

Student instructions for Step Four:

Give your essay a title. It should include both poem titles and a phrase explaining that you are comparing and contrasting the two poems. (Ask your instructor if you need help.)
Now proofread your essay, using the following checklist:

1) Make sure that your paper is at least 250 words long
2) Check for the required elements: introduction, one paragraph describing similarities, three paragraphs describing differences, and a conclusion.
3) Make sure that you quote directly from each poem at least once.
4) Read your paper out loud, listening for awkward or unclear sections and repeated words. Rewrite awkward or unclear sentences so that they flow more naturally.
5) Read through the paper one more time, looking for sentence fragments, run-on sentences, and repeated words. Correct fragments and run-on sentences. If you used the same noun or verb more than twice, pick an alternative from the thesaurus. If you used a modifier (adverb, adjective, or prepositional phrase acting as an adjective or adverb) more than once, find another word.
6) Check your spelling by looking, individually, at each word that might be a problem.
7) Make sure that your paper has a title. The title should include both poem titles.

When you're finished proofreading, show your paper to your instructor.

HOW TO HELP THE STUDENT WITH STEP FOUR

If the student needs assistance with titling, show her the following two titles and ask her to come up with her own, based on the models:

How "The Armful" and "The Road Not Taken" Are Similar
Differences Between "The Armful" and "The Road Not Taken"

The student's composition can resemble the sample below. This is fairly simple—completely appropriate for the student's first attempt at comparison and contrast. Some students will be able to produce much more complex and detailed comparisons, but you should not require this on the first try.

Differences Between "The Armful" and "The Road Not Taken"

In his poems "The Armful" and "The Road Not Taken," Robert Frost writes about making choices.

"The Armful" and "The Road Not Taken" are both written in the first person and use a regular rhyme scheme. Both poems take place on a road; in "The Armful," the narrator drops his pile of things on a road, and in "The Road Not Taken," the narrator stands on a crossroad deciding which path to take. "The Armful" ends with the narrator making a choice to "try to stack" everything he's carrying "in a better load" (12). In "The Road Not Taken," the narrator also makes a choice—to take one road instead of another.

In "The Armful," the narrator doesn't have to leave anything in his pile behind. Instead, he has to "sit down in the middle of them all" (10) and work on rebalancing them. However, in "The Road Not Taken," the narrator is forced to choose one road and leave the other behind.

The rhyme scheme of "The Armful" is quite simple. Each pair of lines rhymes, and no rhyme is repeated. "The Road Not Taken" has a more complex rhyme scheme. Each stanza has the pattern ABAAB, and none of the rhymes are repeated.

The narrator of "The Armful" comes to a simple conclusion: he has to restack everything he's carrying so that it is easier to keep the pile balanced. But in "The Road Not Taken," the narrator says that he chose the road less traveled by. The rhythm of the poem tells us that he might not be remembering correctly. Irregular lines remind us that the roads were worn "about the same" (10) and that they "equally lay/In leaves no step had trodden black" (11–12).

Like the narrator of "The Road Not Taken," I have looked back at choices and thought to myself, "If only I had made another choice, my whole life would be different." But Robert Frost's poem reminds us that what we see in hindsight might not be accurate.

Check the student's essay, using the following rubric.

Week 16 Rubric
Brief Poem Essay

Organization:

1   The entire composition should be at least five paragraphs and 250 words in length, but can be longer.
2   The introduction should include the names of both poems and a major similarity or difference between them.
3   One paragraph should describe similarities. At least three additional paragraphs should describe differences.
4   Each poem should be quoted directly at least once.
5   The conclusion should be either a conclusion by personal reaction or a conclusion by question.
6   The title should be centered at the top of the page. It should include the names of both poems.

Mechanics:

1   Each sentence should make sense on its own when read aloud.
2   There should be no sentence fragments or run-on sentences.
3   All words should be spelled correctly.
4   The first line of each paragraph should be properly indented.
5   Verb tense should be consistent throughout.
6   No noun or verb should be used more than twice (with the exception of state-of-being verbs, linking verbs, and the verb "said").
7   No modifier or prepositional phrase acting as a modifier should be used more than once.
8   Poem citations should be properly formatted.

WEEK 17: COMBINING LITERARY ANALYSIS AND BIOGRAPHICAL SKETCH, PART I

Over the next two weeks, the student will work on combining a previously learned *topos* (biographical sketch) with literary criticism of a poem. The aim: to show how some aspect of the poem relates to the writer's life.

Note that the student will be reading "The Highwayman," by Alfred Noyes. "The Highwayman" has been chosen because it is Noyes's best-known, most-anthologized poem; it also is a story poem that illustrates his conservative, traditional style and allows the student to review terms and techniques first covered last year. This classic ballad is traditionally taught in middle school. However, it does involve one suicide and one death. If you are working with a younger student, you may wish to preview the student's reading.

Day One: Read

Focus: Reading

NOTE TO INSTRUCTOR: Although today's assignment is the student's responsibility, you may need to check and make sure that the student is reading the poem four full times, three of them out loud. It is tempting for students to take shortcuts and just skim over the poems silently. Reading out loud is a necessary step in understanding poetry!

Student instructions for Day One:

> Turn to Appendix II. The third poem in the appendix, "The Highwayman," is by the British poet Alfred Noyes, who was born in 1880 and died in 1958. You'll learn more about Noyes when you take notes for your biographical sketch. "The Highwayman," one of his earlier works, was published in 1907.
> As before, you'll read the poem four times in a row. It's a long poem, so this may take you a while.
> Closely follow these instructions.
> STEP ONE: **Read silently**
> Read the poem silently and slowly. Stop and look up the meanings and pronunciations of all words you don't know.

STEP TWO: **Read out loud**

Go to a private place and read the poem out loud, at a normal pace. Pronounce each word clearly. Pause at the end of each line so that you can hear the sound of each individual line.

STEP THREE: **Read for punctuation**

Read the poem out loud a second time. This time, ignore the line endings. Instead, pause at each comma; pause for a longer time at semicolons and colons; make the longest pause of all at periods. A dash is a pause that's just a little bit longer than a comma but shorter than a semicolon. A dash shows that the action of the line is still moving energetically forward, even though you're pausing slightly.

If there is no punctuation at the end of a line, read on without pausing. Use your voice to indicate exclamation points.

Be sure to change the tone of your voice slightly when reading direct quotes. Use a slightly different voice for the Highwayman and for the soldiers.

STEP FOUR: **Read for drama**

In your final reading, try to wring every drop of drama out of this poem. You'll read out loud once again. And unless you are a born actor, you'll probably want to do this reading VERY privately.

Here are a few suggestions . . .

Use a creepy, horror-movie voice for lines like "The moon was a ghostly galleon" and for the last two stanzas.

Sway back and forth in rhythm for the lines about the highwayman's skills on horseback (for example, "Riding—riding—riding" and "Tlot-tlot; tlot-tlot!"). March in place when King George's men come marching.

Shriek when the highwayman shrieks.

Use a low ominous voice when Tim the ostler appears on the scene.

Use a syrupy, sappy voice when the highwayman starts kissing Bess's hair.

Add anything else you can think of. Try to throw yourself into the poem as fully as possible—even if you feel a little silly.

Day Two: Examine Form

 Focus: Understanding meter, rhyme, and overall structure

In each step of today's work, the student will work independently at first and then will discuss his work with you.

STEP ONE: **Identify the genre of the poem**

Student instructions for Step One:

Look back at the list of literary terms that you made during Level One of this course. (If you no longer have it on hand, your instructor has a copy.) Can you find the term that identifies the genre of "The Highwayman"?

When you've identified the genre, tell your instructor what it is. (And if you need help, ask your instructor.)

HOW TO HELP THE STUDENT WITH STEP ONE

If the student cannot find his Level One list of literary terms, give him Appendix II.

"The Highwayman" is a *ballad*.

If the student has trouble identifying the genre, say, "Does the poem tell a story? Is it a tragic story?" (The answer to both questions is "yes.") Then say, "What term describes a poem that tells a tragic story?"

Make sure that the student writes "ballad" on the line in his workbook.

After the student identifies the genre (with or without your help), go through the following dialogue with him.

Instructor: You first learned about ballads in Level One. A ballad is a poem that tells a story, usually a heroic or tragic one. Ballads don't have one particular form, but many ballads are written in quatrains—four-line stanzas. Does "The Highwayman" have quatrains?

Student: No.

Instructor: Many ballads also have a refrain—a line that is repeated exactly, or with slight variation, throughout the poem. Does "The Highwayman" have a refrain?

NOTE TO INSTRUCTOR: This is a trick question, intended to help the student think. Both "Yes" and "No" are appropriate answers.

If the student says, "I don't know," say, "This is a tricky question. Pick whichever you think is closest to the truth, *yes* or *no*, and then we'll talk about it."

If the student says, "No," use the following dialogue:

Instructor: It's true that the poem as a whole doesn't have a line that repeats all the way through. But there are repeated lines, or parts of lines, within each stanza. In the first stanza, the word "riding" in the fourth line is repeated twice more to make a fifth line. In the second, "twinkle" is repeated from the fourth line as part of the fifth line—*and* the sixth line. So each stanza has a partially repeated line that helps form a kind of refrain. What is repeated in the third stanza?

Student: Daughter

Instructor: In the fourth stanza?

Student: Daughter

Instructor: How about in the fifth stanza?

Student: By moonlight

Instructor: The sixth stanza repeats a whole phrase. What is it?

Student: Waves in the moonlight

Instructor: So Alfred Noyes uses a *kind* of refrain, but it's a little different from what you've seen before.

If the student says, "Yes," use the following dialogue:

Instructor: There is a *kind* of refrain in this poem. There isn't one line that repeats all the way through. But there are repeated lines, or parts of lines, within each stanza . . .

Then repeat the dialogue above from the words "In the first stanza" onward.
　　When you are finished, tell the student to write "Repeated words and lines within each stanza form a refrain" in his workbook.

> Genre of "The Highwayman": Ballad
> Features: Repeated words and lines within each stanza form a refrain

STEP TWO: **Understand the meter of the poem**

Student instructions for Step Two:

> Your next task is to examine the meter of "The Highwayman."
> Go through the first stanza now. Try your best to mark each stressed and unstressed syllable, using accent marks and circumflexes the same way you did last week.
> Once you've done this, put parentheses around each foot. (Hint: there may be more than one kind of foot in these lines!)
> After you finish the first stanza, show it to your instructor.

HOW TO HELP THE STUDENT WITH STEP TWO

The student's metrical notations should resemble the following:

```
   ˘     ´       ˘    ´      ˘      ´       ˘     ´      ˘    ´      ˘     ´
(The wind) (was a tor) (rent of dark) (ness among) (the gus) (ty trees,)

   ˘     ´       ˘    ´     ˘    ´       ˘     ´       ˘     ´      ˘    ´
(The moon) (was a ghos) (tly gal) (leon tossed) (upon clou) (dy seas,)

   ˘    ´      ˘     ´     ˘    ´       ˘    ´      ˘    ´       ˘    ´
(The road) (was a rib) (bon of moon) (light o) (ver the pur) (ple moor,)

   ˘     ˘    ´      ˘     ´      ˘    ´      ˘
(And the high) (wayman)  (came rid) (ing—)

        ´     ˘      ´    ˘
     (Riding—) (riding—)

   ˘    ´      ˘     ´      ˘    ´      ˘    ´     ˘    ´      ˘    ´
(The high) (wayman) (came rid) (ing, up to) (the old) (inn-door.)
```

If he has difficulty with the assignment, show him the first line and its notations (cover the rest of the poem) and then ask him to do the rest.

After the student finishes marking the stanza, go through the following dialogue with him.

Instructor: How many feet does the first line have?

Student: Six

Instructor: Each line in this stanza has six feet. The fourth line looks like it only has four, but the fifth line, which only has two feet, is really just the end of the fourth line. Because the author decided to break that line, the repeated words "Riding, riding" would stand out as a refrain. A poem with six feet per line is written in *hexameter*. As you can see, each line mixes different kinds of feet. What are the two kinds of feet used? You can look back in your workbook if necessary.

Student: Iambs and anapests OR Iambic and anapestic

Instructor: So the meter of the poem is mixed iambic and anapestic hexameter. Write that in your workbook now.

Meter: Mixed iambic and anapestic hexameter

Instructor: Alfred Noyes does other unusual things with the meter of this poem. I want you to mark the stressed and unstressed syllables and put parentheses around the feet in the fifth stanza, printed in your workbook.

("One kiss,) (my bon) (ny sweet) (heart, I'm af) (ter a prize) (to-night,)

(But I) (shall be back) (with the yel) (low gold) (before) (the mor) (ning light;)

(Yet, if) (they press) (me sharp) (ly, and har) (ry me through) (the day,)

(Then look) (for me) (by moon) (light,

Watch) (for me) (by moon) (light,

I'll come) (to thee) (by moon) (light, though hell) (should bar) (the way.")

Instructor: How many feet does the second line have?

Student: Seven

Instructor: You should also see something strange happening with the feet at the end of the fourth and fifth lines. Each foot is divided; the first syllable comes at the end of the line, and then the rest of the foot comes at the beginning of the next line. Alfred Noyes uses a very loose interpretation of the meter and changes it whenever it suits his story. Go back and add the words "loosely interpreted" to your description of the meter.

Meter: Mixed iambic and anapestic hexameter, loosely interpreted

STEP THREE: **Understand the rhyme scheme of the poem**

Student instructions for Step Three:

The rhyme scheme of "The Highwayman" is very regular. Go back to the stanzas in Step Two. Mark the rhyme scheme for both stanzas and then show them to your instructor.

HOW TO HELP THE STUDENT WITH STEP THREE

The rhyme scheme for almost every stanza is regular: AABCCB. The exception is in the fifth stanza, which has the rhyme scheme AABAAB.

STEP FOUR: **Identify the techniques used in the poem**

Carry on the following dialogue with the student.

Instructor: The fifth stanza of Part One has irregularities in both meter and rhyme scheme. This warns you that something is going to happen in the moonlight. What ends up happening in the moonlight?

Student: Beth dies.

Instructor: Noyes gives you another clue in the third stanza of Part Two. How many lines does this stanza have?

Student: Seven

Instructor: This stanza also repeats the words "in the moonlight." So throughout the poem, the author uses irregularities to point out that something is about to happen. Write that down in your workbook.

Purpose of irregularities: They point out that something is about to happen.

Instructor: In Level One of this course, you learned about two poetic techniques: onomatopoeia and alliteration. Read me the definition of onomatopoeia from your appendix now.

Student: Onomatopoeia: when a word sounds like its meaning

Instructor: Using the copy of the poem in the appendix, circle the examples of onomatopoeia.

NOTE TO INSTRUCTOR: The student should circle the following words:

Part One
  Stanza III: clattered, clashed
Part Two
  Stanza VI: Tlot-tlot (four times)
  Stanza VII: Tlot-tlot (twice)

Instructor: Write those words on the blank in your workbook. Now, read me the definition of alliteration.

Student: Alliteration: when words begin with the same sound or sounds

Instructor: Using the copy of the poem in the appendix, underline the examples of alliteration that occur within the same line. Do not include repetitions of the same word.

NOTE TO INSTRUCTOR: The student should underline the following words. He should not get too caught up in identifying *every* alliteration (for example, her/his/he in the same line). It is not necessary for him to find *every* example listed below, but he should find at least ten of them.

Part One
  Stanza I: ghostly galleon
  Stanza II: coat of the claret, breeches of brown
  Stanza III: clattered and clashed, whistled/window/who/waiting
  Stanza IV: deep in the dark, hollows/hair/hay, loved the landlord's, dumb as a dog
  Stanza VI: burnt like a brand, black/breast
Part Two
  Stanza I: did/dawning
  Stanza II: bound/bed, road/ride
  Stanza III: bound/beside/barrel/breast, keep/kissed
  Stanza IV: stretched/strained, tip/touched/trigger
  Stanza V: tip/touched, barrel/breast, blank/bare
  Stanza VI: distance/deaf/did, stood/straight/still
  Stanza VII: drew/deep, moved/moonlight, musket/moonlight
  Stanza VIII: died/darkness
  Stanza IX: spurred/shrieking/sky, down like a dog, blood/bunch
  Stanza X: ghostly galleon
  Stanza XI: cobbles/clatters/clangs

Instructor: In your workbook, write two examples of alliteration from "The Highwayman." Pick the two that you find most interesting or effective.

Alliteration: down like a dog, ghostly galleon [answers may vary]

Instructor: You're almost finished. Your last job today is to identify at least two metaphors and two similes in the poem. Read me the definition of simile and the definition of metaphor from your literary terms appendix.

Student: Simile: a comparison that uses "like," "as," or similar words. Metaphor: a comparison that speaks of one thing in terms of another.

Instructor: Find two similes and two metaphors in the poem. Write them on the lines in your workbook.

Possible answers:

Similes: hair like mouldy hay, dumb as a dog, face burnt like a brand, hours crawled by like years, face was like a light, like a madman, down like a dog

Metaphors: wind was a torrent of darkness, moon was a ghostly galleon tossed upon cloudy seas, road was a ribbon of moonlight, jewelled sky, eyes were hollows of madness, black cascade of perfume, road was a gypsy's ribbon, looping the purple moor, there was death at every window, hell at one dark window, ribbon of moonlight, brow of the hill, white road smoking behind him, blood-red were his spurs, wine-red was his velvet coat

Day Three: Think

 Focus: Connecting form and meaning

Carry on the following dialogues with the student. During these dialogues, the student will write brief answers to be used in next week's essay.

Prompt the student as necessary, using the answers below.

STEP ONE: **Analyze the poem's use of color**

Instructor: From the very beginning of the poem, the author hints to you that Bess and the highwayman are doomed. One of the ways he does this is through his use of the color red. The first mention of red comes in the description of the highwayman's "coat of claret velvet." Claret is a deep, blood-red. What is the next mention of the color red?

Student: The dark red love-knot

Instructor: What is the third mention?

Student: Red-lipped daughter

Instructor: All three of those are positive images. They are meant to convey richness and beauty. Write those three images down underneath the heading "Positive occurrences." Then, look at the next mention of a red color—the tawny sunset. Tawny is the reddish-orange color of a beautiful sunset—but what comes marching out of that beautiful sunset?

Student: King George's men

Instructor: Write "tawny sunset" as the last positive occurrence of the color red. Now, the poet will use the color red the same number of times—four times—but all in a negative context. Can you find the next four mentions of red? List them under "negative occurences."

POSITIVE OCCURRENCES OF RED	NEGATIVE OCCURRENCES OF RED
Coat of claret velvet	Red-coat troop
Dark red love-knot	Red blood
Red-lipped daughter	Blood-red spurs
Tawny sunset	Wine-red velvet coat

Instructor: Red is a beautiful color—but red is also the color of blood. From the first stanza, Alfred Noyes is hinting that both Bess and the highwayman will shed their blood.

STEP TWO: **Understand the reversals in the poem**

Instructor: Halfway through the poem, Alfred Noyes reverses his use of the color red so that it becomes tragic, rather than beautiful. "The Highwayman" uses several different kinds of reversals throughout. Let's start with the highwayman himself. What is a highwayman? Hint: the poem tells you directly in the fourth stanza.

Student: A robber

Instructor: A robber is not a hero. But who is the hero of this poem?

Student: The highwayman

Instructor: The poem takes a thief, a criminal, and makes him into the good guy. How about King George's soldiers? In the world of the poem, are they good or bad?

Student: They are bad.

Instructor: They actually end up robbing—they come into the landlord's house and do what?

Student: Steal his ale and tie up his daughter.

Instructor: But they are actually supposed to be the forces of law and order, out to capture criminals—like the highwayman. In the poem, their role is reversed. Instead of capturing the highwayman so that he can be put on trial, what do they do?

Student: They shoot him.

Instructor: In your workbook, write two or three sentences describing how the highwayman and King George's soldiers play reversed roles—become the opposite, in the poem, of who they really are.

NOTE TO INSTRUCTOR: The student's sentences might resemble the following:

Although the highwayman is a robber and a criminal, in the poem he is a hero. King George's soldiers are supposed to be on the side of good, but they actually act like criminals. They steal from the landlord and also commit murder.

Instructor: Let's look at another reversal. The fourth stanza in Part I describes Tim, the ostler. "Ostler" is another word for "stableman." Tim looks after the horses—and he is in love with Bess. What similes does the poem use to describe him?

Student: Hair like mouldy hay, dumb as a dog

Instructor: Both of those are animal metaphors. The highwayman is dashing and elegant, but Tim is like an animal. The poem doesn't directly state it, but we can assume that Tim is the one who told the soldiers that the highwayman would be coming back to the inn. When the soldiers shoot the highwayman, what simile does the poet use for his death?

Student: He is shot down like a dog.

Instructor. The highwayman has changed places with Tim. Tim has disappeared—just like the highwayman rides off and disappears. And the highwayman has become the one who is like animal. In your workbook, write two or three sentences describing how Tim and the highwayman change places.

NOTE TO INSTRUCTOR: The student's sentences might resemble the following:

At the beginning of the poem, the highwayman is elegant and handsome but Tim is described as "dumb like a dog." But then the two men reverse their positions. At the end of the poem, the highwayman dies "like a dog" on the highway.

Instructor: Normally, what would be the safest time to be up and about—day or night?

Student: Day

Instructor: At what time of day does most of this poem take place?

Student: At night

Instructor: You know that it's night because the poet tells you over and over again that Bess and the highwayman are meeting in the moonlight. They only see each other at night. When does the highwayman die?

Student: During the day OR At noon

Instructor: As long as he only rides at night, the highwayman is safe. But when he hears about Bess's death, he comes riding back at "the golden noon." The poem tells you that the road is no longer a ribbon in the moonlight; it is a "white road smoking behind him." Now, the sun is up. So in this poem, love flourishes at night—and the day brings death. In your workbook, write a couple of sentences describing how the poem reverses the meanings of day and night.

NOTE TO INSTRUCTOR: The student's sentences might resemble the following:

In the poem, night is a safe time when love can flourish. The day brings death. This is opposite to what a reader might expect.

Instructor: The biggest reversal happens between the first two stanzas of the poem and the last two stanzas. The final two stanzas are almost the same as the first two. But what is the difference?

Student: Bess and the highwayman are dead.

Instructor: They're carrying out all the same actions—but now they are ghosts! Write that final observation in your workbook.

NOTE TO INSTRUCTOR: The student's sentence might resemble the following:

At the end of the poem, Bess and the highwayman carry out the same actions, but now they are dead.

Day Four: Review

 Focus: Reviewing the elements of a biographical sketch

Next week, the student will work on writing a brief analysis of "The Highwayman." The analysis will be combined with a form learned in the last level of this course: the biographical sketch.

Today, the student will prepare for next week's work by reviewing the elements of a biographical sketch and then reading about the life of Alfred Noyes.

STEP ONE: Review the *topos* (Student Responsibility)

Student instructions for Step One:

Last year, you practiced writing biographical sketches. Read through the elements of a biographical sketch now.

Biographical Sketch

Definition: A chronological summary of the important events in a person's life combined with description of aspects of the the person

Procedure	Remember
1. Decide on the life events to list in the chronological summary. 2. Choose aspects from the Description of a Person chart to include.	1. The main focus can be on the subject's work/accomplishments. a. Listed chronologically b. Listed by subject/topic

A biographical sketch includes elements from another *topos*—the Description of a Person. Read carefully through the elements of personal description now.

Description of a Person
Definition: A description of selected physical and non-physical aspects of a person

Procedure	Remember

1. Decide which aspects will be included. They may include:
   Physical appearance
   Sound of voice
 	
   What others think
   Portrayals
   Character qualities
   Challenges and difficulties
   Accomplishments
   Habits
   Behaviors
   Expressions of face and body
   Mind/intellectual capabilities
   Talents and abilities
   Self disciplines
   Religious beliefs
   Clothing, dress
   Economic status (wealth)
   Fame, notoriety, prestige
   Family traditions, tendencies
	1. Descriptions can be "slanted" using appropriate adjectives.
	2. An overall metaphor can be used to organize the description and give clues about character.

Last year, you practiced writing a biographical sketch of Marie Antoinette. You'll follow a similar process next week: taking notes, organizing them, and writing. You'll need to make a chronological list of the events in Alfred Noyes's life; you will also need to decide which physical and non-physical aspects of Noyes you will describe.

STEP TWO: **Prepare to take notes**

Student instructions for Step Two:

Prepare now by reading through the following articles and descriptions of Alfred Noyes and his life. Refer back to the Description of a Person *topos* as you read. Make a tentative decision about which aspects (at least three, but not more than six) of Noyes you will write about. When you have decided, tell your instructor what aspects you have chosen.

HOW TO HELP THE STUDENT WITH STEP TWO

The student should have selected at least three of the following aspects:

Physical appearance
What others think
Accomplishments
Habits
Mind/intellectual capabilities
Talents and abilities
Religious beliefs
Fame, notoriety, prestige

The source material does not provide sufficient information on the other aspects.

WEEK 18: COMBINING LITERARY ANALYSIS AND BIOGRAPHICAL SKETCH, PART II

Day One: Take Notes

Focus: Note-taking

Today, the student will prepare to write a biographical sketch of Alfred Noyes.

The biographical sketch, studied in detail last year, is a combination of character description and chronological narrative. The sketch will give chronological details of Alfred Noyes's life, but also will include paragraphs that are organized around aspects of Noyes's character, personality, appearance, and accomplishments. Later this week, the student will work on writing a critical analysis of "The Highwayman." Finally, she will combine the two together into a single composition.

STEP ONE: **Make up working bibliography**

Student instructions for Step One:

You've practiced taking and organizing notes in several different ways. Today, you'll learn another variation on taking and organizing your notes.

Start out by making a working bibliography. Go through all of the sources in Day Four of Week 17 and list them on a sheet of paper, just as if you were making a bibliography for a finished paper.

Newspaper articles are cited in the following format:

Author last name, author first name. "Title of Article." *Name of newspaper,* date of publication, page range of article.

You will notice that the obituary of Alfred Noyes has no author. The *New York Times* traditionally publishes obituaries anonymously. The obituary should be cited like this:

"Title of Article." *Name of newspaper,* date of publication, page range of article.

and alphabetized by the first word of the title.

Journal articles are cited in the following format:

Author last name, author first name. "Title of article." *Title of journal* volume: number (date): page range.

When you are finished, show your work to your instructor. If you need help, ask.

HOW TO HELP THE STUDENT WITH STEP ONE

A useful online guide to citation forms can be found at http://www.chicagomanualofstyle.org /tools_citationguide.html.

The student's list should resemble the following:

"Alfred Noyes Dead; British Poet was 77." *New York Times*, June 29, 1958, pp. 1, 68.

Davison, Edward. "The Poetry of Alfred Noyes." *The English Journal* XV:4 (April 1926): pp. 247–255.

Ray, Mohit K., ed. *Atlantic Companion to Literature in English*. New Delhi: Atlantic Publishers, 2007.

Stade, George and Karen Karbiener, eds. *Encyclopedia of British Writers, 1800 to the Present*, Volume 2. New York: Facts on File, 2009.

Van Gelder, Robert. "An Interview With Mr. Alfred Noyes." *New York Times*, April 12, 1942, p. BR2.

STEP TWO: **Take notes on chronological events**

Student instructions for Step Two:

Now, go through the sources from Week 17, Day Four, and use them to construct a list of chronological events in Alfred Noyes's life. For every event, note the last name of the author. For example:

Born in Wolverhampton, England (Stade)
Married Garnett Daniels (1907) (Ray, 401)

Since all of the information from Stade is on a single page, you don't need to list the page number.

If you use the exact phrasing of one of your sources, use quotation marks.

Visited the U.S. for the first time in 1913 and "was heralded widely for the fact that he supported himself by poetry alone" ("Alfred," 1)

Even though Stade uses the exact phrasing "Born in Wolverhampton, England," this is common knowledge—and also a phrase that any writer would use to express this common knowledge. So it is not necessary to put it in quotation marks. "Heralded widely for the fact that he supported himself by poetry alone," on the other hand, is a sentence that is unique to the article "Alfred Noyes Dead."

You will probably find it easier to do this with a word processing program, since you will need to rearrange events as you go from source to source.

Aim to list at least fifteen but no more than twenty events from Noyes's life.

If you need help, ask your instructor. When you are finished, show your work.

HOW TO HELP THE STUDENT WITH STEP TWO

The student's list of events might resemble the following; she will need to pick and choose from the source material, so you will see some differences. If she has difficulty, show her the first five events on the list as an example.

Born in Wolverhampton, England (Stade)

Grew up in Wales (Stade)

Wrote first poetry at age 9, first epic by 14 ("Alfred," 68)

Went to Exeter College, Oxford, but "did not finish his degree" (Stade)

First book of poetry published 1902 (Stade)

"Hailed as England's leading poet" ("Alfred," 68)

Married American, Garnett Daniels, in 1907 (Stade)

Visited the U.S. for the first time in 1913 and "was heralded widely for the fact that he supported himself by poetry alone" ("Alfred," 1)

Professor of Modern English Literature at Princeton (Ray, 401)

Became a Commander of the Order of the British Empire, 1918 ("Alfred," 68)

Converted to Catholicism 1925 ("Alfred," 68)

Wife died 1926 (Ray, 401)

Married Mary Angela Mayne Weld-Blundell, 1926 (Ray, 401)

Moved to Isle of Wight, 1929 (Ray, 401)

"Was a strong advocate of the Allied effort" (Ray, 401)

"Continued to write until his death" (Stade)

Suffered from "failing eyesight" ("Alfred," 1)

"Changing fashions in poetry" began to exclude him "from the ranks of major poets" ("Alfred," p. 68)

Died June 28, 1958, aged 77 ("Alfred," 1)

STEP THREE: **Take notes on aspects**

Student instructions for Step Three:

Your final composition must describe at least two aspects of Alfred Noyes, but no more than five. Now, you will complete your research by taking notes on the aspects you have decided to highlight as part of your biographical sketch.

List each aspect (chosen at the end of last week's work) at the top of a separate sheet of paper. Beneath the aspect, write the notes that give more information about it. You can do this one of two ways:

1) Go through the sources one time each, placing each relevant bit of information beneath the appropriate aspect as you come across it. For example:

Physical appearance	What others think	Mind/intellectual capabilities
	Critics rebuked his "resistance to change and literary evolution" (Stade)	Detested modernism for its "haphazardness" (Stade)
"sturdy, active man" ("Alfred," 68)	Poetry "still stirs to tears readers of all ages" ("Alfred," 68)	"Intense loyalty to Britain's romantic past" ("Alfred," 68)
"more like a healthy business man than a devotee of the arts" ("Alfred," 68)	"early volumes were well received" ("Alfred," 68)	"outspoken critic of his contemporaries" ("Alfred," 68)

2) Go through each source, looking for information about one particular aspect. Then, turn to the next aspect and go through each source a second time (and so on).

Some writers find it easier to research one narrow subject at a time, even if that means you have to reread sources multiple times. Others would rather read each source once, looking for multiple kinds of information. Pick whichever style suits you.

In your final composition, you must describe at least two (and not more than five) aspects of Alfred Noyes. So you'll want to research at least three aspects, in case you don't find enough information to support one of your choices. If you decide to describe Noyes's physical appearance, you can also choose to describe one or both of his portraits. As you are taking notes, also jot down your observations about his portraits. (You can use my sample notes to get you started.)

Take at least four but no more than ten notes on each aspect.

If you need help, ask your instructor for assistance. When you are finished, show your work.

HOW TO HELP THE STUDENT WITH STEP THREE

The student's answers should resemble the following. She does not need to have all of the notes listed, but she should have at least four and no more than ten notes for each aspect. Some notes could be assigned to multiple aspects.

If the student needs help, allow her to read one of the sample answers below (preferably, for an aspect she will not be researching).

Physical appearance

"sturdy, active man" ("Alfred," 68)

"more like a healthy businessman than a devotee of the arts" ("Alfred," 68)

From portrait of Noyes as older man: thick glasses, hair white on the sides but still dark on top, combed over a bald spot, heavyset, heavy jowls

"In his sixties, a tall man with thin sandy hair slicked across his head and a most noticeable cupid's bow mouth" (van Gelder)

What others think

"out of step with the modernist movement of the 20th century" (Stade)

Critics rebuked his "resistance to change and literary evolution" (Stade)

Poetry "still stirs to tears readers of all ages" ("Alfred," 68)

"early volumes were well received" ("Alfred," 68)

In early thirties, "hailed as England's leading poet" ("Alfred," 68)

"Succeeding appraisals . . . found his work unable to meet the challenging standards of imaginative technique and philosophical insight set by other poets" ("Alfred," 68)

During visit to U.S. in 1913, "I was heralded as a poet who had succeeded in making poetry pay, and had proclaimed the—the commercial spirit. It was all a mistake . . ." (van Gelder)

By 1906, many reviewers "were referring to him as the new Tennyson" (Davison, 247)

"captured the popular ear" (Davison, 248)

Other poets "did not take Alfred Noyes half so seriously" as the public (Davison, 248)

"poems were crowded with gratuitous roses, moons, and galleons" (Davison, 249)

Accomplishments

Hailed as "new Tennyson" by 1906, after publication of epic "Drake" (Davison, 247)

"Captured the popular ear" (Davison, 248)

By 1920, "The Highwayman" was "in more and more school books" (van Gelder)

"one of the most prolific, most popular and most traditional of English poets" ("Alfred," 1)

Visited the US 15 times, lectured in "more than 1,000 American cities and towns" ("Alfred," 1)

"The Highwayman" "still stirs to tears readers of all ages" ("Alfred," 68)

"In his early thirties . . . hailed as England's leading poet" ("Alfred," 68)

Published "two dozen" volumes of poetry, as well as theology, history, biography ("Alfred," 68)

"first-class oarsman during his college days" ("Alfred," 68)

Wrote first poetry at 9, first epic by age 14 ("Alfred," 68)

Taught at Princeton University from 1914–1923 ("Alfred," 68)

Made Commander of the Order of the British Empire, 1918 ("Alfred," 68)

Habits

"continued to write until his death" (Stade)

"wrote mostly of the sea and the country in ballad form" ("Alfred," 1)

"awaits the call of the Muse" every morning in his study (van Gelder)

reads books by "the men who have carried on civilization for us" (van Gelder)

Mind/intellectual capabilities

"educated at Exeter College, Oxford, but did not finish his degree" (Stade)

Detested modernism for its "haphazardness" (Stade)

"Intense loyalty to Britain's romantic past" ("Alfred," 68)

"outspoken critic of his contemporaries" ("Alfred," 68)

"Succeeding appraisals . . . found his work unable to meet the challenging standards of imaginative technique and philosophical insight set by other poets" ("Alfred," 68)

"consistently decried the trend toward naturalism in literature" ("Alfred," 68)

Wrote first poetry at 9, first epic by age 14 ("Alfred," 68)

Talents and abilities

"one of the most prolific, most popular and most traditional of English poets" ("Alfred," 1)

"two dozen volumes of his poetry published during the first three decades of his career" ("Alfred," 68)

"works of theology, history and biography" ("Alfred," 68)

"first-class oarsman . . . sturdy, active man" ("Alfred," 68)

"pleasant and appealing" poetry (Davison, 247)

"the verse . . . never failed to sing" (Davison, 249)

Religious beliefs

Converted to Catholicism (Ray, 401)

Buried in the Roman Catholic cemetery at Freshwater, Isle of Wight (Ray, 402)

"Works of theology, history and biography . . . showed the influence of his conversion to the Roman Catholic Church in 1925" ("Alfred," 68)

"did much of his later writing on Catholicism," including editing "The Golden Book of Catholic Poetry," a book about Horace, and a biography of Voltaire ("Alfred," 68)

Revised biography of Voltaire to gain church acceptance ("Alfred," 68)

Fame, notoriety, prestige

By 1920, "The Highwayman" was "in more and more school books" (van Gelder)

"one of the most prolific, most popular and most traditional of English poets" ("Alfred," 1)

Visited the US 15 times, lectured in "more than 1,000 American cities and towns" ("Alfred," 1)

In early thirties, "hailed as England's leading poet" ("Alfred," 68)

Many of his "works had greater success in the United States than in Britain" ("Alfred," 68)

"The Highwayman" "still stirs to tears readers of all ages" ("Alfred," 68)

"In his early thirties . . . hailed as England's leading poet" ("Alfred," 68)

"the reputation of a practical craftsman in a generally unprofitable field continued to haunt him" ("Alfred," 68)

By 1906, many reviewers "were referring to him as the new Tennyson" (Davison, 247)

"captured the popular ear" (Davison, 248)

Other poets "did not take Alfred Noyes half so seriously" as the public (Davison, 248)

Day Two: Write the Biographical Sketch

 Focus: Writing a biographical sketch that includes aspects of personal description

Over the next two days, the student will work on the rough draft of her composition.

STEP ONE: Draft the chronological narrative

Student instructions for Step One:

Using your list of chronological events, write a chronological narrative describing Alfred Noyes's life. You do not have to use every event, but your composition has to be at least three paragraphs and 150 words long. It should not be longer than 300 words.

You must quote directly from at least one of your sources. Also footnote (or endnote) information that does not seem to be common knowledge. There is some room for interpretation here, but (for example), you would want to footnote the information that he wrote his first major epic poem at the age of 14, because that information is only found in one source and does not seem to be widely known. That Noyes married Garnett Daniels, didn't graduate from Exeter, and visited the U.S. for the first time in 1913—all of those facts are common knowledge.

In a footnote, newspaper articles should be cited like this:

"Title," [or Author, "Title,"], *Name of newspaper* (Date), p. #.

Journal articles should appear as

Author name, "Title," in *Name of journal* volume:number (Date), p. #.

Remember two additional rules about footnotes:

1. The first time you cite a source, you write out its information in full; the second time, you just need to use the last name of the author (for the Alfred Noyes obituary, just refer to it as "Alfred Noyes Dead" the second time you use it.)

2. If you cite the exact same source and the exact same page number twice **in a row**, the second time you should just write "Ibid." This is an abbreviation for the Latin word *ibidem*, which means "in the same place."

If you need help, ask your instructor. When you are finished, show your paragraphs to your instructor.

HOW TO HELP THE STUDENT WITH STEP ONE

This is only a rough draft. The student will work on writing an introduction and conclusion on Day Four of this week's work, so it is perfectly fine for the student's work to begin with "Alfred Noyes was born."

An acceptable draft might resemble the following:

Alfred Noyes was born in Wolverhampton, England, in 1880. He grew up in Wales, where he first began writing poetry (at age nine) and wrote his first major epic poem by the age of fourteen.[1]

Although he attended Exeter College, Oxford, Noyes did not graduate. Instead, he began to work on his first book of poetry, published in 1902. Before long, Alfred Noyes was known as one of England's greatest poets.[2]

Noyes visited the United States for the first time in 1913. He married an American woman, Garnett Daniels, and became Professor of Modern English Literature at Princeton University. After Garnett died in 1926, Noyes remarried and moved back to Britain, to the Isle of Wight.[3]

For the rest of his life, Alfred Noyes continued to write poetry. He struggled with his eyesight, and "changing fashions in poetry" began to make his poetry less and less popular.[4] But he worked right up until his death in June of 1958, aged 77.

---

[1] "Alfred Noyes Dead; British Poet was 77," *New York Times* (June 29, 1958), p. 68.

[2] "Alfred Noyes Dead," p. 68.

[3] Mohit K. Ray, ed., *Atlantic Companion to Literature in English* (Atlantic Publishers, 2007), p. 401.

[4] "Alfred Noyes Dead," p. 68.

When the student shows you her work, do not check it as if it were a finished composition (she will not proofread and finalize it until Day 4). However, *do* check to make sure that the composition has at least three paragraphs and is between 150 and 300 words in length.

You may also want to check and see that the student has formatted her footnotes properly.

If the student has trouble, show her *only* the first and last paragraphs of the sample composition above.

STEP TWO: **Draft the paragraphs describing the aspects of Alfred Noyes**

Student instructions for Step Two:

Now, write one paragraph for each aspect of Alfred Noyes that you have chosen to describe.

You must write at least two paragraphs, each one describing a separate aspect. Each paragraph must be at *least* 35 words long, but no longer than 150 words. You must cite at least one source in each paragraph (although you do not necessarily need to quote directly).

You may do as many as five paragraphs if you're feeling very ambitious—five different aspects!

When you are finished, show your work to your instructor. Your instructor can help you if you have trouble.

HOW TO HELP THE STUDENT WITH STEP TWO

As with Step One, do not check the composition as if it were finished. Make sure that the student has written at least two separate paragraphs about two separate aspects. (The student may choose to do as many as five aspects.) Each paragraph should be between 35 and 150 words in length.

The paragraphs might resemble the following (but could be longer and more complex).

If the student has difficulty, show her one or two of the sample paragraphs below, and ask her to compare them with the sample notes provided at the end of Day One. Choose aspects that she will *not* be writing about herself!

Physical appearance

Noyes was an active, healthy man who had once been a college rower. One interviewer described his mouth as shaped like a "cupid's bow."[1] In his seventies, he used thick glasses because of his bad eyesight. He wore his hair, white on the sides but dark on the top, combed over his bald spot. He had gained weight and had jowls and a sizeable belly.

---

[1] Robert van Gelder, "An Interview With Mr. Alfred Noyes," *New York Times* (April 12, 1942), p. BR2.

What others think

At the beginning of his career, Alfred Noyes was one of England's most popular poets. Some reviewers called him the "new Tennyson."[1] He was even more popular in America than in Britain; in fact, he made fifteen different tours of the U.S. His most famous poem, "The Highwayman," was published in many different school texts. But many critics did not take Noyes seriously. As he grew older, he was condemned for his "resistance to change" and his refusal to accept modern styles of poetry.[2]

---

[1] Edward Davison, "The Poetry of Alfred Noyes, in *The English Journal* XV:4 (April, 1929), p. 248.

[2] George Stade and Karen Karbiener, eds., *Encyclopedia of British Writers, 1800 to the*

Present, Volume 2 (Facts on File, 2009), p. 356.

Accomplishments

Alfred Noyes was not only a highly accomplished writer, but a Princeton professor and a Commander of the Order of the British Empire. He was called the "new Tennyson," and his poem "The Highwayman" is still popular.[1] As well as two dozen volumes of poetry, Noyes wrote books of theology, history, and biography. He toured the United States fifteen different times and spoke in over a thousand cities.

---

[1] Edward Davison, "The Poetry of Alfred Noyes," in *The English Journal* XV:4 (April, 1929), p. 247.

Habits

Alfred Noyes wrote regularly—almost every single morning, right up until his death. He most often wrote about the sea and about the country of England.[1] When he was not writing, he was reading classic books.

---

[1] Robert van Gelder, "An Interview With Mr. Alfred Noyes," *New York Times* (April 12, 1942), p. BR2.

Mind/intellectual capabilities

Noyes got an early start; he wrote his first poetry at the age of 9 and his first epic at 14.[1] As an older poet, he criticized his contemporaries who wrote modernist and naturalist poetry. In return, he was criticized for being less imaginative and less insightful than other poets.

---

[1] "Alfred Noyes Dead; British Poet was 77," *New York Times* (June 29, 1958), p. 68.
[2] Ibid.

Talents and abilities

Alfred Noyes was "one of the most prolific, most popular and most traditional of English poets," according to his obituary. As one critic remarked, his poems "never failed to sing."[1] He wrote over twenty books of poetry, but his talents went beyond poetry. He also wrote books of theology, history and biographies; and in college, he was a champion rower.

---

[1] "Alfred Noyes Dead; British Poet was 77," *New York Times* (June 29, 1958), p. 68.

Religious beliefs

In 1925, Noyes converted to Catholicism. His Catholic faith is evidenced in his writing. His books of theology, history and biography were influenced by his Catholicism, and he even edited a book of Catholic poetry and changed a biography so that it would be approved by the Catholic Church.[1] When he died, he was buried in a Catholic cemetery.

---

[1] "Alfred Noyes Dead; British Poet was 77," *New York Times* (June 29, 1958), p. 68.

Fame, notoriety, prestige

Alfred Noyes became so famous that many reviewers called him "the new Tennyson."[1] He was a popular lecturer in the United States; in fact, he was even more famous in the U.S. than he was in England. His most famous poem, "The Highwayman," was included in more and more school texts and is still read today.[2] But despite this popularity, many other poets did not take Alfred Noyes seriously. They thought of him as no more than a "practical craftsman."[3]

---

[1] Edward Davison, "The Poetry of Alfred Noyes," in *The English Journal* XV:4 (April, 1929), p. 248.
[2] Robert van Gelder, "An Interview With Mr. Alfred Noyes," *New York Times* (April 12, 1942), p. BR2.
[3] "Alfred Noyes Dead; British Poet was 77," *New York Times* (June 29, 1958), p. 68.

STEP THREE: **Combine the narrative and the aspects (Student Responsibility)**

Student instructions for Step Three:

> Your final step today is to combine the chronological narrative and the paragraphs describing aspects of Noyes into one composition.
> You can choose one of two methods:
> 1. Put the paragraphs describing the aspects at the end of the chronological narrative.
> 2. Place each paragraph describing an aspect after a paragraph of the chronological narrative that mentions that aspect.
> Once your composition is assembled, you're done for the day. Tomorrow, you'll work on the last major element of the composition—the analysis of "The Highwayman."

Day Three: Write the Analysis

 Focus: Writing about the poem

Today, the student will write a brief critical analysis of "The Highwayman." The analysis will have three parts: a brief summary of the plot; a description of the poem's structure; and at least one paragraph that deals with a major critical aspect of the poem.

The student can work independently unless she becomes stalled. You may show her the examples at the end of the lesson if necessary.

STEP ONE: Write a brief summary of the poem's plot (Student Responsibility)

Student instructions for Step One:

> Begin by writing a summary of the action in the poem.
> Writing a narrative summary is something you practiced again and again in the first level of this course. Treat the poem as a story and summarize its action in 6–10 sentences. Aim for 80–140 words.
> Remember that a narrative should have consistent tense throughout.

STEP TWO: Write a brief description of the poem's structure (Student Responsibility)

Student instructions for Step Two:

> The second part of the critical analysis should deal with the structure of "The Highwayman." Using your notes from Day Two of Week 17, write a paragraph describing at least four of the following structural elements:
>> genre
>> stanza structure
>> refrain
>> meter
>> rhyme scheme
>> irregularities
>> onomatopoeia
>> alliteration
> Quote directly from the poem at least once in your paragraph.
> Aim for a total of 100–150 words for this paragraph.

STEP THREE: Describe one major critical aspect of the poem (Student Responsibility)

Student instructions for Step Three:

> Now, add the final element to your composition by discussing how the form and meaning of the poem interact.
>
> Using your notes from Day Three of Week 17, explain how either the color red or reversals work in the world of the poem. Aim for 75–100 words.

STEP FOUR: Read through your completed analysis

Student instructions for Step Four:

> Now assemble the three parts into one completed analysis. It should be at least three paragraphs long, around 250 to 400 words in length. Read the analysis out loud to yourself. You will proofread it again tomorrow, but take the time now to cut out any sentences that unnecessarily repeat the same information.
>
> When you are finished, show your work to your instructor.

HOW TO HELP THE STUDENT WITH STEP FOUR

Examples of each of the sections of the critical analysis are provided below. The student can, of course, write more complex paragraphs; the examples are meant to show what is acceptable.

When you check the composition, look to make sure that it is the correct length (three paragraphs, 250 to 400 words) and that it contains all three elements: narrative summary, description of at least four technical aspects, and discussion of either the color red or the reversals in the poem. Keep any other comments until the student has finished proofreading tomorrow.

Two examples of narrative summary

> "The Highwayman" tells the story of Bess, a landlord's daughter, and the Highwayman. At the beginning of the poem, the Highwayman tells Bess that he is going out robbing—but that he will return in the moonlight. He is overheard by the stableman, Tim, who is also in love with Bess. Apparently Tim tells the king's soldiers that the Highwayman will visit Bess. They arrive at the landlord's inn, intending to shoot the Highwayman when he returns. They also tie Bess up with a musket against her chest. When she hears the Highwayman returning, she shoots herself in order to warn him. The Highwayman escapes, but when he hears of Bess's death, he rides back and is shot down by the soldiers.

> In "The Highwayman," a robber visits the beautiful daughter of a landlord and tells her that he will return to her by moonlight. But while he is away, a band of the king's soldiers arrive. They steal the landlord's ale, tie Bess up next to a musket, and wait for the highwayman to return. Bess knows that they intend to kill the highwayman, so she manages to shoot

off the musket. This warns the highwayman—but it also kills Bess. When the highwayman realizes that Bess is dead, he returns to the inn for vengeance. But the soldiers shoot him down instead. At the poem's end, both Bess and the highwayman are back at the inn—but both of them are ghosts.

Two examples of technical discussion
Addresses genre, refrain, meter, stanzas, and irregularities

"The Highwayman" is a ballad. Like many ballads, it has a refrain, but the refrain isn't the same throughout the poem. Instead, certain words and lines are repeated within each stanza. The meter of the poem mixes iambs and anapests together. Each line is a hexameter (six feet). Alfred Noyes uses irregularities in the meter and in the lines of each stanza to warn the reader that something is about to happen. In Part 2, the third stanza has seven lines instead of six—the only time this happens in the poem. The extra line means that the poet can repeat "by moonlight" three times as a refrain. This warns the reader that something bad is going to happen in the moonlight.

Addresses alliteration, genre, meter, rhyme scheme, and irregularities

In "The Highwayman," Alfred Noyes uses alliteration in almost every stanza. The first stanza calls the moon a "ghostly galleon"; in Stanza IX of Part 2, the Highwayman "spurred like a madman, shirking a curse the sky." When the soldiers shoot him, he lies "down like a dog" (l. 91). The alliteration makes the poem even more rhythmic. It is a ballad, written in mixed anapestic and iambic hexameters, with a very regular rhyme scheme of AABCCB. This rhyme scheme only changes once, in the fifth stanza of Part One. The irregularity warns the reader that something tragic will happen "in the moonlight."

Three examples of the final paragraph
The color red

The poem uses the color red to tell you that Bess and the Highwayman are doomed. At first, the color red is beautiful. Bess has a red love-knot in her hair and red lips, and the High-wayman wears a red velvet coat. But in the middle of the poem, red-coated soldiers march out of a reddish sunlight. After this, all of the mentions of the color red are negative. When Bess shoots herself, she is drenched in red blood. When the Highwayman returns to the inn, his spurs are "blood-red," and when he is shot down, his velvet coat is soaked in blood.

The reversals in the poem

In "The Highwayman," Alfred Noyes uses reversals. The hero of the poem, the Highway-man, is actually a thief and a criminal. King George's soldiers are supposed to be the keepers of law and order. Instead, they are thieves and murderers. Another reversal happens when the Highwayman dies. The stableman Tim, who is also in love with Bess, is described as "dumb as a dog," while the Highwayman is elegant. But when the Highwayman is shot down, he also becomes like a dog.

In "The Highwayman," the hero is actually a thief and a criminal. King George's soldiers, who are supposed to enforce the laws, steal and kill instead. In the world of the poem, night—which is usually dangerous—is the only time when Bess and the Highwayman are safe. When day comes, the Highwayman dies. The biggest reversal happens at the end of the poem, when Bess and the Highwayman carry out the same actions as at the beginning of the poem—but as ghosts!

Day Four: Finalize the Composition

 Focus: Finishing and proofreading a composition

STEP ONE: **Put the entire composition together (Student Responsibility)**

Student instructions for Step One:

> Now it's time to put all of the elements of the composition together.
>
> Insert the three paragraphs of the critical analysis into your biographical sketch. You may decide whether to put it at the end, or whether to insert it after a mention of "The Highway-man" in the sketch. You may also need to add a transition to the first paragraph. Something as simple as adding the phrase, "Alfred Noyes's best-known poem, 'The Highwayman' . . ." to the first sentence may be all that is necessary.
>
> Attach your working bibliography as the Works Cited page. Cut any source that you did not cite in the paper.

STEP TWO: **Write an introduction and conclusion (Student Responsibility)**

Student instructions for Step Two:

> Your composition still needs an introduction and a conclusion.
>
> When you first learned about biographical sketches in Level One, you also learned that a biographical sketch should begin with an introductory sentence that gives an overview of who the subject is and why he or she is important. You should recognize this now as an Introduction by Summary: One or more sentences that tell the reader what the composition is like and what its most central conclusions will be. Write an introduction by summary now and attach it to the first paragraph of the composition.
>
> This assignment is long enough so that you can also write a conclusion by summary. You may also choose to write a conclusion by personal reaction. Either conclusion may be a sentence attached to the last paragraph, or a separate closing paragraph.

STEP THREE: **Choose a title**

Student instructions for Step Three:

> Title your composition, using the following pattern:
>
> Alfred Noyes: ___ _____
>
> In the blank, write a phrase that you think best describes Alfred Noyes. If you have trouble, ask your instructor for help.

HOW TO HELP THE STUDENT WITH STEP THREE

If the student draws a blank, say, "What famous poem did Alfred Noyes write?" When the student answers, "The Highwayman," say, "Does that make him the author of 'The Highwayman'? There's your title."

Alfred Noyes: Author of "The Highwayman"

Other possible titles might be:

Alfred Noyes: A Popular Poet
Alfred Noyes: An Old-Fashioned Romantic
Alfred Noyes: More Popular with the People than with Critics
Alfred Noyes: Loved by the People

STEP FOUR: **Proofread**

Student instructions for Step Four:

> Now proofread your essay, using the following checklist:
>
> 1) Make sure that your paper is at least 500 words in length (about 2 1/2 double-spaced typed pages)
> 2) Check for the required elements: introduction, chronological narrative, description of at least two aspects of Alfred Noyes, critical analysis of "The Highwayman," conclusion, title.
> 3) Read your paper out loud, listening for awkward or unclear sections and repeated words. Rewrite awkward or unclear sentences so that they flow more naturally.
> 4) Listen for information that is repeated more than once. Eliminate repetition of ideas.
> 5) Read through the paper one more time, looking for sentence fragments, run-on sentences, and repeated words. Correct fragments and run-on sentences. Listen for unnecessary repetition. (You will have to repeat the words "poem," "highwayman," "Noyes," etc. multiple times. But listen for other nouns and verbs that you could vary.) If you used a modifier (adverb, adjective, or prepositional phrase acting as an adjective or adverb) more than twice, find another word.

6) Check your spelling by looking, individually, at each word that might be a problem.

7) Check the formatting of your footnotes and your Works Cited page.

When you're finished proofreading, show your paper to your instructor.

HOW TO HELP THE STUDENT WITH STEP FOUR

The student's finished composition might resemble the following:

ALFRED NOYES: LOVED BY THE PEOPLE

The British poet Alfred Noyes was so popular with common readers that his poems are still read and loved today. He was born in Wolverhampton, England, in 1880. He grew up in Wales, where he first began writing poetry (at age nine) and his first major epic poem by the age of fourteen.[1]

Although he attended Exeter College, Oxford, Noyes did not graduate. Instead, he began to work on his first book of poetry, published in 1902. Before long, Alfred Noyes was known as one of England's greatest poets.[2]

Noyes visited the United States for the first time in 1913. He married an American woman, Garnett Daniels, and became Professor of Modern English Literature at Princeton University. After Garnett died in 1926, Noyes remarried and moved back to Britain, to the Isle of Wight.[3]

At the beginning of his career, Alfred Noyes was one of England's most popular poets. Some reviewers called him the "new Tennyson."[4] He was even more popular in America than in Britain; in fact, he made fifteen different tours of the U.S. His most famous poem, "The Highwayman," was published in many different school texts. But many critics did not take Noyes seriously. As he grew older, he was condemned for his "resistance to change" and his refusal to accept modern styles of poetry.[5]

For the rest of his life, Alfred Noyes continued to write poetry. He struggled with his eyesight, and the "changing fashions in poetry" began to make his poetry less and less popular.[6] But he worked right up until his death in June of 1958, aged 77.

Alfred Noyes was "one of the most prolific, most popular and most traditional of English poets," according to his obituary. As one critic remarked, his poems "never failed to sing."[7] He wrote over twenty books of poetry, but his talents went beyond poetry. He also wrote books of theology, history and biographies; and in college, he was a champion rower.

He is best remembered for a single poem, "The Highwayman." This poem tells the story of Bess, a landlord's daughter, and the Highwayman. At the beginning of the poem, the Highwayman tells Bess that he is going out robbing—but that he will return in the moonlight. He is overheard by the stableman, Tim, who is also in love with Bess. Apparently Tim tells the king's soldiers that the Highwayman will visit Bess. They arrive at the landlord's inn, intending to shoot the Highwayman when he returns. They also tie Bess up with a musket against her chest. When she hears the Highwayman returning, she shoots herself in order to warn him. The Highwayman escapes, but when he hears of Bess's death, he rides back and is shot down by the soldiers.

"The Highwayman" is a ballad. Like many ballads, it has a refrain, but the refrain isn't the same throughout the poem. Instead, certain words and lines are repeated within each stanza. The meter of the poem mixes iambs and anapests together. Each line is a hexameter (six feet). Alfred Noyes uses irregularities in the meter and in the lines of each stanza to warn the reader that something is about to happen. In Part 2, the third stanza has seven lines instead of six—the only time this happens in the poem. The extra line means that the poet can repeat "by moonlight" three times as a refrain. This warns the reader that something bad is going to happen in the moonlight.

In "The Highwayman," the hero is actually a thief and a criminal. King George's soldiers, who are supposed to enforce the laws, steal and kill instead. In the world of the poem, night—which is usually dangerous—is the only time when Bess and the Highwayman are safe. When day comes, the Highwayman dies. The biggest reversal happens at the end of the poem, when Bess and the Highwayman carry out the same actions as at the beginning of the poem—but as ghosts!

Even though Alfred Noyes was considered old-fashioned by the end of his life, "The Highwayman" still gave me the chills. It is a frightening and tragic story, and it is still scaring readers over sixty years after Alfred Noyes's death.

---

[1] "Alfred Noyes Dead; British Poet was 77," *New York Times* (June 29, 1958), p. 68.

[2] "Alfred Noyes Dead," p. 68.

[3] Mohit K. Ray, ed., *Atlantic Companion to Literature in English* (Atlantic Publishers, 2007), p. 401.

[4] Edward Davison, "The Poetry of Alfred Noyes," in *The English Journal* XV:4 (April, 1929), p. 248.

[5] George Stade and Karen Karbiener, eds., *Encyclopedia of British Writers, 1800 to Present*, Vol. 2 (Facts on File, 2009), p. 356.

[6] "Alfred Noyes Dead," p. 68.

[7] Ibid.

WORKS CITED

"Alfred Noyes Dead; British Poet was 77." *New York Times*, June 29, 1958, pp. 1, 68.

Davison, Edward. "The Poetry of Alfred Noyes." *The English Journal* XV:4 (April 1926): pp. 247-255.

Ray, Mohit K., ed. *Atlantic Companion to Literature in English*. New Delhi: Atlantic Publishers, 2007.

Stade, George and Karen Karbiener, eds. *Encyclopedia of British Writers, 1800 to Present*, Vol 2. New York: Facts on File, 2009.

Check the student's essay using the following rubric:

Week 18 Rubric
Biographical Sketch And Critical Analysis

Organization:

1   The entire composition should be at least five paragraphs and 500 words in length, but can be longer.
2   The composition should include an introduction, a chronological narrative of events in the life of Alfred Noyes, at least two different paragraphs describing at least two different aspects of Noyes's life, a brief critical analysis, and a conclusion.
3   The critical analysis should be at least three paragraphs in length. It should include a plot summary of "The Highwayman," a paragraph discussing the structure of the poem, and a final paragraph describing either Noyes's use of the color red or else the reversals in the poem.
4   The composition should include at least one direct quote from "The Highwayman" and at least one direct quote from another source.
5   The title should include the name of Alfred Noyes and a phrase describing him.
6   The introduction should summarize why Noyes is important.
7   The conclusion should either summarize Noyes's importance or give a personal reaction to Noyes or his work. If the conclusion summarizes, it should not be identical to the introduction.
8   No single piece of information or quote should be repeated from one section to the next.

Mechanics:

1   Each sentence should make sense on its own when read aloud.
2   There should be no sentence fragments or run-on sentences.
3   All words should be spelled correctly.
4   The first line of each paragraph should be properly indented.
5   Verb tense should be consistent throughout. The narrative summary may be in either the past or the present tense.
6   No modifier or prepositional phrase acting as a modifier should be used more than twice.
7   Poem citations, footnotes, and works cited should be properly formatted.

WEEK 19: EXPLANATION BY DEFINITION IN HISTORY: PROPERTIES AND FUNCTION

Day One: Shared and Unique Properties

Focus: Answering the question "What is it?"

In Weeks 12 through 14 of this course, the student learned *explanation by way of definition:* how to explain the nature of a scientific object or phenomenon. Over the next two weeks, he will learn to do the same for a historical object, place, event, or group of people.

For scientific definitions, the student asked three questions:

What are its properties?

How does it function?

Where does it belong?

He will ask the same three questions for historical definitions, but he will need to learn a slightly different approach to answering them.

STEP ONE: Understand shared and unique properties

Student instructions for Step One:

> Let's start with essential and accidental properties.
>
> In science, you learned that essential properties are those things that *define a thing as the sort or kind that it is*; accidental properties are all of the others. Look at the following properties of a star:
>
> —ball of gas
> —nuclear fusion at its core
> —held together by gravity
>
> Those are *essential*. If an object in space isn't a ball of gas, or doesn't have nuclear fusion at its core, or isn't held together by gravity, it's not a star. It's something else.
>
> But the star Rigel, in the constellation Orion, is 62 times bigger than our sun, while Proxima Centauri, in the constellation Centaurus, is only 15% of our sun in size. Both of them are still stars, though. Size is *accidental*. It can change from star to star.

How does this work with history?

There is only one *Titanic* or War of 1812. But the *Titanic* shares many qualities with other passenger liners, and even more qualities with ships in general. The War of 1812 was an armed conflict—which means that it is like many, many other wars.

What makes the *Titanic* the *Titanic*, instead of another passenger liner? Size—she was the biggest ship in the world (in 1912). What made the War of 1812 unlike any other of the thousands of wars fought? Time, place, and goals—all of those things were different than the time, place, and goals of other wars.

When you write about history, you will find it more useful to think about properties as *shared* or *unique*. Always try to focus in on the properties that belong to *that particular phenomenon alone* and are not shared with others. Of course you'll also need to discuss properties that are shared—for example, the three-engine system of the *Titanic* (which had been used on an earlier passenger liner) or the combatants in the War of 1812 (the United States and the British Empire, two countries which had fought wars before). But even then, you'll always be asking yourself: What is *unique* about this? What made the *Titanic*'s engines different? What was *new* about the conflict between the United States and Britain?

Remembering this will help your writing to be vivid, engaging, and interesting. Continually asking yourself about the unique properties of a historical phenomenon will keep you from writing boring, bland, generic compositions.

As you look for the shared and unique qualities of a historical phenomenon, you will ask the questions below. Read them out loud to your instructor now. If any of them are unclear, ask for explanations.

What did it look like?
How did it behave?
What did it resemble?
What was it made of?
What sort of structure did it have?
What was its extent in space?
Where did it take place or exist?
What was its extent in time?
Did it repeat or continue into modern times?
    How has it changed over time?

Of course, not all questions will apply to all historical phenomena. For example, the questions "What is it made of?" and "What sort of structure does it have?" would help you in writing a definition of the *Titanic,* but not the War of 1812.

HOW TO HELP THE STUDENT WITH STEP ONE

The student will read these questions out loud to you. Brief explanations are provided below in case the student needs them.

What does it look like?

This is visual appearance and applies to all of the categories: objects, events, places, and groups of people. You might want to ask the student: If it's an object in history, who is looking at it? Are you thinking about how it might have looked to a person in the past? Who is that person?

How does it behave?

For objects, this will overlap with function and answer the question "How does it work?" For groups of people, this will refer to culture and tradition. It does not usually apply to places or events.

What does it resemble?

This could be a straightforward comparison for objects, but encourage the student to use similes and metaphors in answering this question.

What is it made of?

For objects and manmade places, what are its physical components?

What sort of structure does it have?

For objects and manmade places, how many parts does it have? How do those parts relate to each other?

What is its extent in space?

How big is it? What area of land does it cover? For groups of people, how many are/were there? For events, what geographical extent does the event encompass?

Where did it take place or exist?

What is its physical location?

What is its extent in time?

When did it take place or exist? For how long?

Did it repeat or continue into modern times?

How has it changed over time?

Did it happen or exist only once, or did it repeat or continue over time? Are later versions different from earlier ones? How so?

STEP TWO: **Practice the questions about properties**

Student instructions for Step Two:

Read the following description of the ancient Incan city of Machu Picchu, which still exists in ruins today.

★

This passage answers many of the questions about properties that you just studied—but not all of the questions. Some of the questions in your list don't really work if you're asking them about a place rather than an object, or a group of people rather than a place.

Determine which of the questions the passage answers, and then answer the relevant questions on the worksheet below. If the question is not answered in the passage, draw a line through it. Otherwise, answer the question.

When you are finished, show your work to your instructor.

HOW TO HELP THE STUDENT WITH STEP TWO

The student's answers should resemble the following:

What does it look like? Two large temples near the top of the ridge. *[paragraph 1]*
       The land was carved into terraces *[paragraph 2]*
       Simple stone houses on the other section of the ridge, and fountains were designed with channels to natural springs *[paragraph 3]*

~~**How does it behave?**~~

What does it resemble? The terraces look like giant steps covered with soil. *[paragraph 2]*

What is it made of? Stone, soil, spring water *[paragraphs 2 and 3]*

What sort of structure does it have? *This question overlaps with the first question, "What does it look like?" The student may have crossed out this question, or her answers may be the same as Question 1.*

What is its extent in space? Two peaks in the Andes Mountains *[paragraph 1]*

Where did it take place or exist? It lay northwest of Cuzco, the capital of the great Inca Empire, between two peaks in the Andes Mountains of Peru in South America. *[paragraph 1]*

What is its extent in time? Built in the AD 1400s *[paragraph 1]*

Did it repeat or continue into modern times? How has it changed over time? Yes, it still exists today.
It was deserted by the Inca in 1573 *[paragraph 4]*
. . . and lay undisturbed for four centuries *[paragraph 5]*

STEP THREE: **Practice the Qualities Diagram**

Student instructions for Step Three:

> As you think about shared and unique qualities, you should add three more questions to the list above. Read these questions out loud now:
>
> > What large group of other phenomena can it be assigned to?
> > What smaller group of other phenomena can it be assigned to?
> > What qualities does it share with *no other* phenomena?
>
> A historical phenomenon has qualities that are shared with almost all things of its type. The *Titanic* is a boat—so it has many qualities in common with a rowboat tied up at the pier of a fishing pond! (For example: It floats. It has a hull and a bow. It carries people.)

A historical phenomenon also has qualities that are shared with a much smaller group of things. The *Titanic* shares some of its qualities with other ocean liners—but those qualities aren't shared by canoes, submarines, or aircraft carriers. (For example: It was designed to carry paying passengers and to offer luxurious surroundings.)

Finally, a historical phenomenon has qualities that belong only to itself. The *Titanic* was the only ship of its size in the world—it was 882.9 feet long, 92.5 feet across, and 175 high (from the keel to the top of its funnels).

So here's how you would answer these questions:

What large group of other phenomena that can be assigned to? *Boats.*
What smaller group of other phenomena can it be assigned to? *Ocean liners.*
What qualities does it share with *no other* phenomena? *Size.*

To help you think through the relationships between these groups, examine the diagram below.

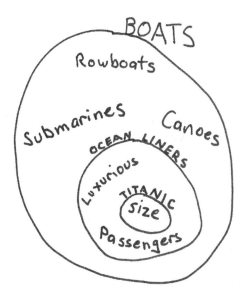

The biggest circle represents the large group *boats*. Ocean liners (like the *Titanic*) are boats. So are rowboats, submarines, and canoes.

The next circle represents the smaller group *ocean liners*. Written within the circle are three characteristics of ocean liners: they are luxurious, they carry passengers, and they are very large in size.

The *Titanic* shares these characteristics with other ocean liners, but in one area the *Titanic* is unique: in her size. The smallest circle represents the unique properties of the *Titanic*.

Why should you draw out a diagram like this? It will help you focus in on the details that should be highlighted in your composition. Obviously, you can't *only* talk about the *Titanic*'s size. You'll also need to focus in on the qualities that the *Titanic* shares with other ocean liners. You'll want to describe the luxurious fittings of the ship, and talk about the number of passengers it could carry. But you won't want to spend very much time in your composition talking about characteristics that the *Titanic* shares with other boats generally. That would produce a bland, uninteresting composition.

There is, of course, more than one way to assign a historical phenomenon to groups. In the diagram above, the large group "boats" is divided into *types* of boats. But you could also divide "boats" according to where they are used, like this:

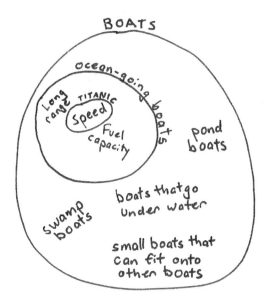

In this diagram, the *Titanic* belongs to the smaller group "ocean-going boats." Ocean-going boats share certain characteristics: they have a long range, they have large fuel capacity, and they are fast. Which quality is unique to the *Titanic*? Speed: the *Titanic* had the ability to get across the ocean and arrive in New York faster than another ocean-going boat. If you were to use this diagram to organize your composition, you would be able to talk not only about speed, but also about the *Titanic's* range and how much fuel the ship carried.

The purpose of these diagrams is to help you focus in on the most important, most distinctive properties of a historical phenomenon. Now, practice drawing up a diagram yourself. Look back at the passage about Machu Picchu. Answer these three questions:

What large group of other phenomena can it be assigned to?
What smaller group of other phenomena can it be assigned to?
What qualities does it share with *no other* phenomena?

Then, construct a diagram like my *Titanic* diagrams illustrating the relationship between the larger and smaller groups.

If you need help, ask your instructor. When you're finished, show your work.

HOW TO HELP THE STUDENT WITH STEP THREE

The student's answers might resemble the following:

What large group of other phenomena can it be assigned to? Ancient cities

What smaller group of other phenomena can it be assigned to? Ancient cities built by the Inca

What qualities does it share with no other phenomena? On a ridge between the mountains and the Urubamba River

Or, possibly:

What large group of other phenomena can it be assigned to? Cities of the Inca

What smaller group of other phenomena can it be assigned to? Mountain cities of the Inca

What qualities does it share with no other phenomena? Never visited by the Spanish

If necessary, ask the student leading questions to guide him to the answers above.

His diagrams might resemble the following. NOTE: The words in parentheses are implied, not explicitly provided in the paragraph. They are there to provide context for what is in the passage. The student is not required to come up with these, but when he is finished his diagrams, show him the suggestions below.

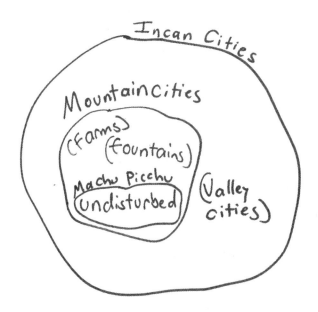

Because this kind of diagramming is a brainstorming tool, not an outlining tool, the

diagrams above show what the authors might have chosen to leave out and what to focus on.

The author clearly chose not to focus on the cities of other ancient cultures. We can assume that temples and stone houses were part of other Incan cities as well, but we can also be sure that Machu Picchu was the only city located on that particular mountain ridge.

In the same way, we can assume that the Incas also had valley cities—but the author chose not to focus on them, since they are part of the largest group that Machu Picchu belongs to. And since farms and fountains are mentioned, we can assume that these were part of other Incan mountain cities. But the author focuses in on one particular aspect of Machu Picchu— that its ruins were undisturbed by the Spanish. In this passage, that quality is unique to Machu Picchu.

Day Two: Take Notes on Properties

Focus: Taking notes to answer the question "What is it?"

Today the student will take notes and prepare to write an explanation by definition that answers the questions about properties of the Inca people. The finished composition will be at least 120 words, but can be longer if the student wants.

STEP ONE: Read (Student Responsibility)

Read back through the questions from Day One that you will be answering.
What did it look like?
How did it behave?
What did it resemble?
What was it made of?
What sort of structure did it have?
What was its extent in space?
Where did it take place or exist?
What was its extent in time?
Did it repeat or continue into modern times?
How has it changed over time?
What large group of other phenomena can it be assigned to?
What smaller group of other phenomena can it be assigned to?
What qualities does it share with *no other* phenomena?

Then, read through the following passages without stopping to take notes.

★

STEP TWO: **Take notes**

Student instructions for Step Two:

> Now you'll take notes for your own description. On your own paper, write each question and then look for the answers to that question in the passages provided. You can change the word *it* to *they* or *he* in the question since you are studying a group of people rather than an object or event. Jot down the answers, and be sure to record the author and page number of the passage where you found specific pieces of information.
>
> Only try to answer the first ten questions. Leave the last three questions for the next step. Here is an example of how some of your answers might look:
>
> ***What did they resemble?***
>> **clothing "gave them the appearance of Romans or medieval pages," or "rather Grecian" (Hemming, p. 61)**
>
> If the question does not apply to your topic, you do not need to write it down or answer it. For every other question, you should aim to have at least two answers. Take at least three notes from each author.
>
> When you are finished, show your work to your instructor.

HOW TO HELP THE STUDENT WITH STEP TWO

The student's notes should resemble the following. It is not necessary for his notes to be as complete as this, but he should have at least two answers for each question.

What did they look like?
"Men wore a breechclout" (Hemming, p. 60)

"women wore a long belted tunic" (Hemming, p. 61)

High forehead, aquiline nose, firm chin and mouth, face "majestic, refined, and intellectual," hair "carefully arranged" (Markham, p. 121)

Wool tunic and mantle, mantle tied "over the left shoulder or round the waist" (Markham, p. 122)

Wore golden breastplates, later Incas wore brocade belts (Markham, p. 122)

How did they behave?
"society was based on sharing. People did not work for money." (Kalman, p. 8)

They used quipu to record information. It was "a fringe consisting of a main cord with other cords of various colors hanging from it. In the fringe knots of different kinds were tied" (Mead, p. 59)

Spoke a language called Runa-simi, "human speech" (Markham, p. 137)

Tried to establish a single language in the empire (Markham, p. 137)

What did they resemble?

clothing "gave them the appearance of Romans or medieval pages," or "rather Grecian" (Hemming, p. 61)

~~What was it made of?~~
~~What sort of structure did it have?~~

What was their extent in space?

"The land of the Incas was 250 miles in length by 60 in width" (Markham, p. 78)
Bounded on the west by the Apurimac river, on the east by the Vilcamayu river (Markham, p. 78)

Where did they take place or exist?

The empire "included areas in modern-day Peru, Ecuador, Chile, Bolivia and Colombia" (Underwood, p. 7)
"lived in the Cuzco region of Peru as early as the 1100s" (Kalman, p. 8)

What was their extent in time?

"lived in the Cuzco region of Peru as early as the 1100s, but historians have recorded 1438 as the beginning of their empire" (Kalman, p. 8)
"conquered by the Spanish in 1532" (Kalman, p. 8)

Did they repeat or continue into modern times? How have they changed over time?

"45 percent of the population of the Andes region" are Incan descendants (Underwood, p. 6)
Many traditional Incan religions and customs "managed to survive" (Underwood, p. 8)

STEP THREE: **Diagram**

Student instructions for Step Three:

Now, return to the last three questions and try to answer them.
What large group of other phenomena can the Inca be assigned to?
What smaller group of other phenomena can the Inca be assigned to?
What qualities do the Inca people share with *no other* phenomena? (You can provide more than one answer to this question.)

When you've answered the questions, try to construct a diagram showing the larger group, the smaller group, and the qualities that only the Inca have.
If you get frustrated, ask your instructor for help. When you're finished, show your work.

HOW TO HELP THE STUDENT WITH STEP THREE

The student's answers might resemble the following:

What large group of other phenomena can the Inca be assigned to? Ancient peoples

What smaller group of other phenomena can the Inca be assigned to? Peoples conquered by Spain

What qualities do the Inca people share with *no other* phenomena? Used quipu AND/OR spoke Runa-simi

    OR

Conquered nations

Conquered nations whose descendants have survived

Empire centered at Cuzco

The student's diagram might resemble the following:

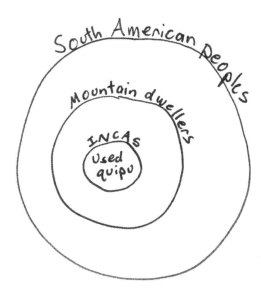

NOTE TO INSTRUCTOR:

Some students find a graphic representation of the answers to be helpful. Others won't see the point of drawing the diagram and will just find it frustrating. The usefulness of this exercise depends on the student's particular method of processing information.

If the student simply can't figure out how the diagram works, show him the answer above and then cut the diagram assignment from any future lessons. If the diagram forces him to organize his information better, leave the assignment in. Remember that writing is a skill area, and that different brains may need different tools when mastering a skill.

The end goal here is to force the student away from vague, general observations towards sharp and specific ones.

Day Three: Write About Properties

Focus: Writing answers to the question
"What is it?"

Today the student will write a composition about the Inca people, based on Day Two's notes. The composition will be two paragraphs long and at least 120 words.

Although the student may check his work with you at any time, he does not need to show you his composition until it has been proofread (Step Five). Helps have been provided for you in each of the steps below in case the student needs assistance.

STEP ONE: **Organize**

Student instructions for Step One:

You may choose to organize your composition in one of the following ways:

Paragraph I. The Inca Empire (where, when, etc.)
Paragraph II. The Inca people (appearance, behavior, etc.)
OR
Paragraph I. Incan people in the past
Paragraph II. Incan influence in modern times

Whichever organization you choose, be sure to spend at least three sentences discussing the property or properties that you identified as unique to the Inca.
Divide your notes now so that they fall into two groups.

HOW TO HELP THE STUDENT WITH STEP ONE

If the student needs help, use the following to help him organize each question and the notes attached to it into the appropriate paragraph.

Paragraph I. The Inca Empire (where, when, etc.)
What was their extent in space?
Where did they take place or exist?
What was their extent in time?

Paragraph II. The Inca people (appearance, behavior, etc.)
What did they look like?
How did they behave?
What did they resemble?
Did they repeat or continue into modern times?

OR

Paragraph I. Incan people in the past
What did they look like?
How did they behave?
What did they resemble?
What was their extent in space?
Where did they take place or exist?
What was their extent in time?

Paragraph II. Incan influence in modern times
Did they repeat or continue into modern times?

STEP TWO: **Write**

Student instructions for Step Two:

Now use your organized notes to write a description of the Inca people. Follow these guidelines:

1) The description should have at least two paragraphs and be at least 120 words in length. Longer is just fine.
2) Cite at least three of your sources.
3) Answer at least five of the questions.
4) Use at least one direct quote.
5) Use at least one simile or metaphor from your own imagination.
6) Write at least three sentences dealing with the quality or qualities you've identified as unique to the Incas.

Remember: you do *not* have to use all of the quotes and answers you've collected! Nor is it necessary for you to answer every question.

HOW TO HELP THE STUDENT WITH STEP TWO

See sample composition, below.

STEP THREE: **Assemble the Works Cited page**

Student instructions for Step Three:

Title a separate piece of paper "Works Cited." List the sources you used in alphabetical order.

HOW TO HELP THE STUDENT WITH STEP THREE

The student only needs to include the sources that he actually cites in the paper. A comprehensive list of all the sources, formatted properly, is below.

WORKS CITED

Hemming, John. *The Conquest of the Incas*. New York: Harcourt, Inc., 1970.

Kalman, Bobbie. *Peru: The People and Culture*. New York: Crabtree Publishing Company, 2003.

Markham, Clements Robert. *The Incas of Peru*. New York: E. P. Dutton and Co., 1910.

Mead, Charles Williams. *The Musical Instruments of the Incas*. Washington, D.C.: The American Museum of Natural History, 1903.

Underwood, Gary. *Spirit of the Incas*. Clayton South, Australia: Blake Education, 2006.

STEP FOUR: **Title your description**

Student instructions for Step Four:

> Now choose a descriptive title for your composition. The title should *not* simply be "The Incas"! If you need to review, look back at Week 12, Day 4.

HOW TO HELP THE STUDENT WITH STEP FOUR

If the student struggles with titling her description, ask her to write down her main topic, which should be "Incas" or "Inca People." Next, ask her to list one major property of the Incas, such as location or time period. Then have her combine them into a title, such as "The Inca People from 1438 to 1532."

Below are a few more suggestions:

The Inca People from 1438 to 1532
The Incas of South America
Peru's Inca People
The Inca: A Lost Civilization
The Inca: An Ancient People

STEP FIVE: **Proofread (Student Responsibility)**

Student instructions for Step Five:

> Before handing your paper to your instructor, go through the following proofreading steps.
>
> 1) Check to make sure that your paper has followed the guidelines in Step One.
> 2) Read your paper out loud, listening for awkward or unclear sections and repeated words. Rewrite awkward or unclear sentences so that they flow more naturally.

3) Read through the paper one more time, looking for sentence fragments, run-on sentences, and repeated words. Correct fragments and run-on sentences. Replace repeated words that sound monotonous; use your thesaurus if necessary.
4) Check the format of your footnotes and Works Cited page.
5) Check your spelling by looking, individually, at each word that might be a problem.

When you are finished, give your paper to your instructor for evaluation.

HOW TO HELP THE STUDENT WITH STEP FIVE

Check the student's work, using the following rubric.

Week 19 Rubric
Properties Of A Historical Phenomenon

Organization:

1 The entire composition should be at least two paragraphs and 120 words in length, but can be longer.
2 The composition should be organized in one of the following ways:
    Paragraph I. The Inca empire (where, when, etc.)
    Paragraph II. The Inca people (appearance, behavior, etc.)
        OR
    Paragraph I. Incan people in the past
    Paragraph II. Incan influence in modern times
3 At least five of the questions about properties should be addressed.
4 The composition should include at least three sentences discussing the property or properties that the student identified as unique to the Inca.
5 The composition should include at least one direct quote and should cite at least three sources.
6 The composition should include at least one simile or metaphor.
7 The title should include the word "Inca" plus another descriptive word or phrase.

Mechanics:

1 Each sentence should make sense on its own when read aloud.
2 There should be no sentence fragments or run-on sentences.
3 All words should be spelled correctly.
4 The first line of each paragraph should be properly indented.
5 Verb tense should be consistent throughout.
6 No modifier or prepositional phrase acting as a modifier should be used more than twice.
7 Footnotes and the Works Cited page should be properly formatted.

The student's composition might resemble the following, which uses the second option for organization. Note how much shorter the second paragraph is. The first organizational option would produce a composition with two paragraphs of more equal length.

The sample composition answers the questions, "How did they behave? What was their extent in space? Where did they take place or exist? What was their extent in time? Did they repeat or continue into modern times?" The unique property covered is the use of the *quipu*. The simile is "As if they were family."

The Incas of South America

Around 1100, the ancestors of the Inca people settled in Cuzco, Peru. Eventually, the Inca empire spread to cover much of modern Peru, Ecuador, Chile, Bolivia, and Colombia.[1] It was 250 miles long and 60 miles wide.[2] Rather than money, the Incas used a system of sharing as if they were family.[3] They did not have written language, but they used a knot system called the quipu to record information. The quipu was made up of "a main cord with other cords of various colors hanging from it." Knots in the cords stood for different facts.[4]

The Spanish conquered the Incan empire in 1532. But today, around 45% of the population in the Andes is descended from the Incas. Traditional Incan religious practices and customs still survive.[5]

WORKS CITED

Hemming, John. *The Conquest of the Incas.* New York: Harcourt, Inc., 1970.

Kalman, Bobbie. *Peru: The People and Culture.* New York: Crabtree Publishing Company, 2003.

Markham, Clements Robert. *The Incas of Peru.* New York: E. P. Dutton and Co., 1910.

Mead, Charles Williams. *The Musical Instruments of the Incas.* Washington, D.C.: The American Museum of Natural History, 1903.

Underwood, Gary. *Spirit of the Incas.* Clayton, Australia: Blake Education, 2006.

---

[1] Gary Underwood, *Spirit of the Incas* (Blake Education, 2006), p. 7.

[2] Clements Robert Markham, *The Incas of Peru* (E. P. Dutton & Co., 1910), p. 78.

[3] Bobbie Kalman, *Peru: The People and Culture* (Crabtree Publishing Company, 2003), p. 8.

[4] Charles Williams Mead, *The Musical Instruments of the Incas* (The American Museum of Natural History, 1903), p. 59.

[5] Underwood, pp. 6, 9.

Day Four: Understand Function

> Focus: Answering the question, "How does it work?"

A fully-developed definition answers three questions:

What is it? [Shared and unique properties]

How does it work? [Function]

Where does it belong? [Genus]

Now that the student has learned how to write about the properties of a historical phenomenon, she will wrap up the week by learning about function.

STEP ONE: Understand how to explain function in history

Student instructions for Step One:

When you learned how to write about the function of a scientific phenomenon, you answered three major questions:

How does it work or behave?

Who/what needs it or uses it?

For what purposes?

For a historical phenomenon, you have to add one more question:

What was its significance?

When you explain *significance*, you explain how a historical object, event, place, or people group affected the world around it and after it.

Read the following description of the submarine *Turtle,* built in 1775 by the American submarine inventor David Bushnell. (Notice the mention of the *Nautilus* in the last paragraph of the reading; you may remember reading about the *Nautilus* back in Week 2 of this course.)

⭐

This passage answers all four questions about function. It gives a detailed description of how the *Turtle* worked. It explains who/what used it—the Americans, during the Revolutionary War. It tells the reader what purpose the *Turtle* served: it was intended to help break the British blockade of New York harbor. And, finally, it tells you what the significance of the *Turtle* is. The *Turtle* was "the first American submarine." And not only was the *Turtle* the first American submarine, but its design led to the work of later submarine inventors and, finally, to the establishment of the Naval Torpedo Station.

Historical significance often involves superlative words such as "first," "last," "largest," "greatest," and "most influential." You may also see phrases such as "led to," "inspired many," "changed the course of," and "is still." Read the statements of historical significance below:

⭐

Each statement is part of a discussion of *function.*

Underline the phrases that point to the historical significance of the phenomenon discussed. When you are finished, show your work to your instructor.

HOW TO HELP THE STUDENT WITH STEP ONE

The student's work should resemble the following:

OBJECT

Magna Carta <u>is still</u> invoked today by politicians, and <u>is still sometimes</u> cited in judgements in courts of law.

> Claire Breay, *Magna Carta: Manuscripts and Myths* (London: British Library, 2002), p. 48

EVENT

The second siege of Constantinople <u>changed the course of history.</u>

> M. P. Cosman and L. G. Jones, *Handbook to Life in the Medieval World* (New York: Facts on File, 2003), p. 47.

PLACE

Odessa was probably the <u>most influential</u> place for the development of modern Hebrew literature.

> Marcel Cornis-Pope and John Neubauer, *History of the Literary Cultures of East-Central Europe* (Philadelphia: J. Benjamins Pub., 2006), p. 194.

PEOPLE

The Athenians, rather than the Egyptians, were the <u>greatest</u> artists, the <u>bravest</u> soldiers, and the creators of the "<u>noblest</u> polity" in the ancient world.

> Lynn Parramore, *Reading the Sphinx* (New York: Palgrave Macmillan, 2008), p. 3

STEP TWO: **Examine the questions about function**

Student instructions for Step Two:

> When you studied function in science, you found good, complete answers to the questions about function by asking a series of more focused questions. The same is true for function in history.
>
> Of course, you wouldn't ask *all* of these questions for any one phenomenon. But a selection of them will help you find the details that belong in your definition.
>
> Read these questions out loud to your instructor now. If any of them confuse you, ask your instructor for explanations.
>
> > How did it work, behave, or unfold?
> > > Will a descriptive sequence help the reader understand how it worked?
> > > > What would the sequence describe?
> > > Was its behavior predictable or unpredictable?
> > > Did it work/behave differently under different circumstances?
> > > > At different times?
> > > Can its behavior or sequence be divided into phases?
> > > > What separates the phases?

Was there a cause or trigger for the event?
What was the time frame for its behavior or significance?
Where did the behavior take place?
Who/what needed it, used it, or was affected by it?
What effects did it have on the surrounding events/people?
What events led up to it?
What events occurred because of it?
For what purposes or reasons?
Is there more than one purpose or reason?
Did the purpose or reason change at different times?
Was the purpose or reason dependent on any other conditions?
What is its significance? Why do we remember it?
What did it change?
What did it cause?
Did it create/become a major turning point?
Did later phenomena use it or depend on it?

HOW TO HELP THE STUDENT WITH STEP TWO

You may need to emphasize to the student that these questions are designed to *comprehensively* cover function for historical events, objects, places, and groups of people. The questions will not apply to every topic, and will often overlap depending on the specific topic. They are designed as a brainstorming tool.

If the student needs additional explanation, use the following.

How did it work, behave, or unfold?
Will a descriptive sequence help the reader understand how it works?
What would the sequence describe?
The historical sequence covered in Week 2 is one of the building blocks of this explanation by definition. If the student needs a reminder, you may wish to go back and reread the steps in these lessons.
Was its behavior predictable or unpredictable?
Did the event unfold in a surprising manner? Did the objects/people involved behave in a consistent or regular manner, or did their behavior suddenly shift?
Did it work/behave differently under different circumstances?
At different times?
Can its behavior or sequence be divided into phases?
For example, the American Revolution has been divided into the New England Phase, the Middle Atlantic Phase, and the Southern Phase.
What separates the phases?
For events, this could be timing, location, or effects.
Was there a cause or trigger for the event?
A trigger is a single or discrete event that suddenly changes the behavior of something or the unfolding of events. The cause of World War I was a combination of conflicts among European powers, but the trigger was the assassination of Archduke Ferdinand.

What was the time frame for its behavior or significance?

When did it exist or unfold? When did it have its effect on history?

Where does the behavior take place?

This question will overlap with properties.

Who/what needs it, uses it, or is affected by it?

This question begins to touch on significance, which is addressed directly in the last question.

What effects did it have on the surrounding events/people?

For example, Eli Whitney's cotton gin was used by southern cotton farmers. However, it affected everyone involved in the cotton industry, as well as 19th century plantation slaves.

What events led up to it? What events occurred because of it?

This could also include previous or later versions of an object or place.

For what purposes or reasons?

Is there more than one purpose or reason?

An object, event, or place can be used by two different groups for two different reasons. For example, many European knights went on Crusade in order to get remission of their sins. But poorer Europeans often went on Crusade for the salary paid to them by the knights; the Crusades let them feed their families.

Does the purpose or reason change at different times?

Before/after a war, before/after a revolution, before/after a famine or catastrophe, in modern/ancient times . . .

Is the purpose or reason dependent on any other conditions?

Location, time of the year, whether a country is at war or peace, supply and demand . . .

What is its significance? Why do we remember it?

What did it change?

For example, Columbus was not the first person to "discover" the Americas, but his voyage changed the way Europeans viewed the lands to the west and sparked the eventual colonization of North America.

Did it create/become a major turning point?

The Battle of Saratoga is often considered the turning point of the American Revolution—Americans began winning the war from this point on.

Did later phenomena use it or depend on it?

Many later declarations of the rights of citizens, including the Declaration of Independence, used language and ideas drawn from the Magna Carta.

STEP THREE: **Analyze**

Student instructions for Step Three:

> Go back to the paragraphs about the *Turtle* now. Using the list of questions below, try to determine which of the questions about function are answered in the passage. If the question is not addressed in the paragraphs, draw a line through it. If it is, write the answer to the question briefly in the margin next to the question.

HOW TO HELP THE STUDENT WITH STEP THREE

The student's list should resemble the following. These answers are simply examples. Variation is acceptable (for example, while I have crossed out "Was its behavior predictable or unpredictable?" the student could argue that, in the paragraphs presented, the *Turtle* behaved predictably). As long as the student can defend his answers, accept them. The purpose of the exercise is to make the student aware of function in a historical definition.

How did it work, behave, or unfold?

Will a descriptive sequence help the reader understand how it worked? Yes.

What would the sequence describe? How the *Turtle* submerged and how it worked underwater

~~Was its behavior predictable or unpredictable?~~

Did it work/behave differently under different circumstances? Yes [for example, above water, when it was at "near-neutral buoyancy," when near the surface].

~~At different times?~~

Can its behavior or sequence be divided into phases? When floating, when underwater

What separates the phases? Position in the water

Was there a cause or trigger for the event? The operator submerging the boat by flooding it

~~What was the time frame for its behavior or significance?~~

Where did the behavior take place? In the water

Who/what needed it, used it, or was affected by it?

What effects did it have on the surrounding events/people? It inspired Robert Fulton.

What events led up to it? The British blockade of New York harbor

What events occurred because of it? Modern submarine designers, crafts used in the Civil War, foundation of the Naval Torpedo station

For what purposes or reasons? For war

~~Is there more than one purpose or reason?~~

~~Did the purpose or reason change at different times?~~

~~Was the purpose or reason dependent on any other conditions?~~

What is its significance? Why do we remember it?

What did it change? Boats could now be used underwater.

Did it create/become a major turning point? Yes—the beginning of the use of submarines

Did later phenomena use it or depend on it? Yes—modern submarine design, Robert Fulton's experiments

WEEK 20: EXPLANATON BY DEFINITION IN HISTORY: GENUS

The student has now learned how to answer two of the three questions in a historical definition:

What is it? [Shared and unique properties]

How does it work? [Function]

There's only one question left.

Where does it belong? [Genus]

This week, he will learn about genus, and then practice putting together a composition that answers questions about both function and genus.

NOTE TO INSTRUCTOR: Next week, the student will be required to research and write a definition in history, choosing his own topic. Be sure to make some time to gather resources/visit the library.

Day One: Understand Genus in History

 Focus: Answering the question "Where does it belong?"

STEP ONE: Understand genus (Student Responsibility)

When you answer the question "Where does it belong?" for a historical phenomenon, you must first think about its properties and the way it functions. Then, think about other objects, events, places, or groups of people that share these properties or function. Then, ask yourself, "What larger group does this belong to? What other objects or phenomena have these properties, or function in this way?"

You began to do this back when you examined properties. When you made your Qualities Diagram, you thought about the *largest* group that your subject belonged to, and then tried to identify a smaller group as well. That assignment was intended to help you focus in on the unique qualities of your subject—the properties that *no other* historical phenomena shared.

333

When you think about genus, you focus in more on the properties that your subject has in common with other events, places, objects, or people groups.

Think back to last week's example, the *Titanic*. I placed the *Titanic* in the large group "boats," and then put it into the smaller group "ocean liners." I then pointed out that I would want to pay special attention to the *Titanic*'s size, since that was the property that set the *Titanic* apart from other ocean liners.

But if I were to write a paragraph defining the genus of the *Titanic*, I would want to point out all of the features that the *Titanic* had in common with other luxury ocean liners of its time:

gourmet meals and private rooms for first-class passengers

a steerage class

running water and bathtubs

a "promenade deck" where passengers could stroll

use of radios ("wireless telegraphs") in the control room

a crow's nest lookout

coal-fueled

and so on.

Take a minute to review what you learned about genus when you wrote a scientific definition:

What's the purpose of identifying *genus*?

Grouping your object (or phenomenon) together with others forces you to think about *why* you're defining it—what the ultimate point of your essay will be. When you write about volcanoes, are you focusing in on a volcano as just one of the many things that happen at the edges of the earth's plates—simply another example of what shifts in the earth's crust bring about? Or will you present the volcano as one of the most destructive forces in nature—an explosive phenomenon that destroys everything it touches?

Like the questions you've asked about properties and function, questions about genus force you to think more deeply about what you're writing. (And that's why writing is such hard work—because you have to *think* in order to do it well.)

If I group the *Titanic* together with other ocean liners, my composition will tend to focus in on how luxurious the ship was—because the *Titanic* had every feature of an ocean liner, except bigger, better, and fancier. But if I group the *Titanic* with other ocean-going boats, I might end up writing more about its size and speed—because size and speed are what an ocean-going boat needs in order to get across the Atlantic or Pacific.

NOTE TO INSTRUCTOR: The student may be confused by the overlap between properties and genus. If so, explain that dividing a historical definition into properties, function, and genus and then writing a separate paragraph on each is a training exercise—a way to teach student writers how to cover all the important areas in a historical definition. As the student becomes more mature as a writer, she will naturally begin to combine the answers to the questions about properties, function, and genus into a single integrated composition. Different ways of organizing the parts of historical definitions are covered during late high school/early college rhetoric studies.

STEP TWO: **Examine the questions about genus (Student Responsibility)**

The questions about genus in history are similar to the questions you studied for scientific definitions. Read through the questions again slowly and carefully.

What other objects, events, people, or places can it be grouped with?
What are the qualities that lead you to group them together?
What name can you give this group?
In what significant ways is it different from the others in its group?

Here's how those questions might be answered for the *Titanic:*

What other objects, events, people, or places can it be grouped with? *Other ocean liners, particularly the other ocean liners built by the White Star Line company*
What are the qualities that lead you to group them together? *Built to carry hundreds of passengers across the ocean from Europe to America; powered by coal-fired steam engines; included living quarters, bathrooms, and dining rooms for the passengers*
What name can you give this group? *Ocean liners* OR *White Star ocean liners*
In what significant ways is it different from the others in its group? *Larger; more luxurious; fewer life boats*

STEP THREE: **Read (Student Responsibility)**

Read the following two paragraphs carefully. The Krak des Chevaliers is a castle that was built by Crusaders in the twelfth century, just east of the Mediterranean Sea.

★

STEP FOUR: **Analyze**

Student instructions for Step Four:

Using the list of questions below, try to determine which of the questions about genus are answered in the passage. If the question is not addressed in the paragraphs, draw a line through it. If it is, write the answer to the question in your workbook next to the question itself.
What other objects, events, people, or places can it be grouped with?
What are the qualities that lead you to group them together?
What name can you give this group?
In what significant ways is it different from the others in its group?
When you are finished, show your answers to your instructor.

HOW TO HELP THE STUDENT WITH STEP FOUR

The student's answers should resemble the following. If necessary, show the student the answers; then, ask her to write her own answers without looking at the instructor guide.

What other objects, events, people, or places can it be grouped with?   Castles built in the Middle East during the Crusades OR castles built to guard the Homs Gap

What are the qualities that lead you to group them together?   Purpose for which they were built OR Structure OR Who built them AND/OR Castles with a bent entrance, castles that protect conquered territory and resist attack

What name can you give this group?   Crusader castles OR Crusader castles in the Middle East OR Castles in Syria OR Castles guarding the Homs Gap

In what significant ways is it different from the others in its group?   Location on a natural strongpoint, size, concentric rings around the keep

Days Two through Four:
Take Notes on Function and Genus,
Write about Function and Genus

 Focus: Researching and writing about the questions "How does it work?" and "Where does it belong?"

Over the next three days, the student will take notes about function and genus and write a brief composition answering the questions about both. She will write about the *Dred Scott* case, an important court case that took place just before the Civil War.

Instead of dividing the work up into days, I have listed the steps below. You and the student together decide whether it makes more sense to take notes over two days and write on the third, or to take notes on one day and spend two days writing. (Or some other division.)

The steps are:

Step One: Review the questions about function and genus

Step Two: Read

Step Three: Take notes

Step Four: Organize your notes

Step Five: Write

Step Six: Introduction and conclusion

Step Seven: Title and Works Cited page

Step Eight: Proofread

Note that court cases are italicized. When Dred Scott, the person, is mentioned, the name will be in plain (Roman) type. When the court case is mentioned, it will be referred to as *Dred Scott.*

STEP ONE: **Review the questions about function and genus (Student Responsibility)**

NOTE TO INSTRUCTOR: Although the student completes this step independently, check to make sure that she is actually reading out loud rather than skimming quickly through the questions silently.

Read the following questions about function and genus out loud, paying close attention to each one.

Function: How does it work?

How did it work, behave, or unfold?

Will a descriptive sequence help the reader understand how it worked?

What would the sequence describe?

Was its behavior predictable or unpredictable?

Did it work/behave differently under different circumstances?

At different times?

Can its behavior or sequence be divided into phases?

What separates the phases?

Was there a cause or trigger for the event?

What was the time frame for its behavior or significance?

Where did the behavior take place?

Who/what needed it, used it, or was affected by it?

What effects did it have on the surrounding events/people?

What events led up to it?

What events occurred because of it?

For what purposes or reasons?

Is there more than one purpose or reason?

Did the purpose or reason change at different times?

Was the purpose or reason dependent on any other conditions?

What is its significance? Why do we remember it?

What did it change?

Did it create/become a major turning point?

Did later phenomena use it or depend on it?

Genus: Where does it belong?

What other objects, events, people, or places can it be grouped with?

What are the qualities that lead you to group them together?

What name can you give this group?

In what significant ways is it different from the others in its group?

STEP TWO: **Read**

Student instructions for Step Two:

Read through the following passages without stopping to take notes.

★

Now that you've read through the sources, go through the questions one more time. Using the list below, cross out the questions that you won't be able to answer for the *Dred Scott* case.

When you've finished, check your work with your instructor.

HOW TO HELP THE STUDENT WITH STEP TWO

Although there is some room for interpretation, the student's answers should resemble the following. Explanations are provided in brackets, along with the last name of the relevant source. If the student can't decide whether or not to cross out a question, direct them to the particular source named. If necessary, give the student the answer. The purpose of this assignment is to give the student a manageable number of questions to answer, not to force the student into a guessing game.

Function: How does it work?
How did it work, behave, or unfold?
Will a descriptive sequence help the reader understand how it worked?
　　What would the sequence describe? Series of events leading to the decision; Hossell, Skog

　　~~Was its behavior predictable or unpredictable?~~ [These questions are not useful for events, only for objects and people]
　　　　~~Did it work/behave differently under different circumstances?~~
　　　　　　~~At different times?~~
Can its behavior or sequence be divided into phases? Previous decisions, this decision, after the decision. [Also acceptable to cross this one out, however.]
　　　　What separates the phases?
Was there a cause or trigger for the event? Scott's lawsuit; Hossell
What was the time frame for its behavior or significance? 1824–1857 OR 1846–1857; Hossell, Skog, Cromwell
　　Where did the behavior take place? Virginia, Illinois, Wisconsin, the U.S. and territories; all sources
　　Who/what needed it, used it, or was affected by it? African-Americans/all Americans; all sources
　　What effects did it have on the surrounding events/people? Kept African-Americans from citizenship; all sources
　　　　What events led up to it? Earlier decisions
　　　　What events occurred because of it? "Firestorm of criticism, protest and resistance," one of the steps that led to the Civil War, etc.; Greenberg, Berkin
　　~~For what purposes or reasons?~~ [Although the event *led* to several different other events, the sources do not explain how people "used" it. There is one statement that it still plays a "key role" in court cases, but there are no details about *how* it plays a key role, so this statement is best used to support "Did later phenomena use it or depend on it?" below]

~~Is there more than one purpose or reason?~~

~~Did the purpose or reason change at different times?~~

~~Was the purpose or reason dependent on any other conditions?~~

What is its significance? Why do we remember it?

What did it change? Status of African-Americans; all sources

Did it create/become a major turning point? Yes, led to Constitutional Amendments and the Civil War; Greenberg, Berkin

Did later phenomena use it or depend on it? Yes, later court cases; Berkin

Genus: Where does it belong?

What other objects, events, people, or places can it be grouped with? *Winny vs. Whitesides* OR Amendments to the constitution; Skog, Cromwell, Berkin

What are the qualities that lead you to group them together? All had to do with slavery

What name can you give this group? Lawsuits by slaves, legal decisions about slavery

In what significant ways is it different from the others in its group? Opposite to *Winny vs. Whitesides*, also opposite to the amendments meant to correct it

STEP THREE: **Take notes**

Just as you did when you took notes to write definitions in science, organize your notes as you take them. On your own paper, write each question that you didn't cross out. Then, look for answers to the questions in the passages.

As you learned in Week 18 when you wrote about Alfred Noyes, you can choose to do this in one of two ways:

1) Go through the sources one time each, placing each relevant bit of information from each source beneath the appropriate question as you go.
2) Pick the first question and go through all five sources, looking for answers. Do the same for the second question, and then the third, and so on.

There is a lot of information in these passages. Try not to be overwhelmed by it all. Some questions, such as "What name can you give this group?" will only need one answer or note. Some questions, such as "What events led up to it?" will require several notes.

A descriptive sequence is particularly helpful in historical events. You may find it helpful to number the different events that took place in the *Dred Scott* case, like this:

Will a descriptive sequence help the reader understand how it works?
1. Dred Scott was sold as a slave to Dr. John Emerson (Hossell)
2.
3.

. . . and so on.

When you answer the questions "Who/what needed it, used it, or was affected by it? What effects did it have on the surrounding events/people?" you might want to organize your notes like this:

Who was affected by it?	What effects did it have?
Dred Scott	died still a slave (Hossell)

You might also want to number and place in chronological order the events leading up to the decision.

When you are finished, show your work to your instructor.

HOW TO HELP THE STUDENT WITH STEP THREE

The student's notes should resemble the following. This is a fairly comprehensive list; it is not necessary for the student to have as many notes as below.

Function: How does it work?

How did it work, behave, or unfold?

Will a descriptive sequence help the reader understand how it worked? What would the sequence describe?

1. Dred Scott was sold as a slave to Dr. John Emerson (Hossell)
2. Emerson and Scott traveled to places where slavery was illegal, such as Illinois and Wisconsin (Hossell)
3. After Emerson died, Scott filed suit for his freedom (Hossell)
4. The case went to the Supreme Court in 1857 (Hossell)
5. The court decided 7-2 that Scott and his family were still slaves (Skog, p. 8)
6. The decision was met with "a firestorm of criticism, protest and resistance" (Greenberg)

Can its behavior or sequence be divided into phases?

Before the *Dred Scott* case (Slaves in free territories could be considered free)
During the *Dred Scott* case
After the *Dred Scott* case (Slaves were not free even if they were in free territories, and also could not become citizens of the United States)

What separates the phases?

The Supreme Court's decision

Was there a cause or trigger for the event?

The death of John Emerson, after which Dred Scott filed his lawsuit (Hossell)

What was the time frame for its behavior or significance?

Winny vs. *Whitesides* was tried in 1824 (Cromwell, p. 15)

The *Dred Scott* decision was made in 1857 (Skog, p. 7)

Scott's case was decided "11 years after he first filed suit claiming he was a free man" (Skog, p. 7), so he filed suit in 1846.

Where did the behavior take place?

NOTE TO INSTRUCTOR: The student may choose to include the information about other slavery cases tried in other states (the first three notes), but this is optional.

Winny v. Whitesides took place in Missouri (Cromwell, p. 15)

Winny had been taken from the slave state of Kentucky to the Indiana Territory and then to the Missouri Territory (Cromwell, p. 15)

Courts in Missouri, Kentucky, and Louisiana also freed slaves who were in free territories (Cromwell, p. 15)

Scott was taken from the slave state of Virginia to the free states of Illinois and Wisconsin (Hossell)

The decision was made at the Supreme Court.

Who/what needed it, used it, or was affected by it?
What effects did it have on the surrounding events/people?

Who/what was affected by it?	What effects did it have?
Dred Scott	died still a slave (Hossell)
All American blacks	could not become U.S. citizens (Hossell, also Skog, p. 8)
U.S. territories that banned slavery	Their laws were pronounced unconstitutional (Hossell, also Skog, p. 8)
Lower courts in the U.S.	Supreme Court overruled their "once free, forever free" rulings (Cromwell, pp. 16–17)

What events led up to it?

1. The Missouri Compromise of 1820 made slavery illegal in "certain federal territory north of Missouri's border" (Skog, p. 7)
2. In 1824, the slave Winny "won her freedom from her owner" in *Winny v. Whitesides*, when the court decided "'once free, forever free'" (Cromwell, p. 15)
3. Other courts in Missouri, Kentucky, Louisiana "had often freed slaves who had lived in free states or territories" (Cromwell, p. 15)
4. "Congress had taken different actions regarding slavery" (Skog, p. 6) In 1854, "Congress reversed that decision" made in the Missouri Compromise (Skog, p. 7)

What events occurred because of it?

The case "divided the nation" (Hossell)

It showed "the Supreme Court was firmly committed to the defense of slavery" (Greenberg p. 2)

It was decided that "slaves were still slaves even when they lived in free territories" (Hossell)
It was decided that "no one of African descent could become a citizen of the United States. Ever!" (Berkin)
It was decided that laws against slavery "were unconstitutional" (Hossell)
"Firestorm of criticisms, protest and resistance" (Greenberg)
Led to the Thirteenth, Fourteenth, and Fifteenth Amendments of the Constitution (Berkin)

What is its significance? Why do we remember it?
What did it change?

Made all African Americans non-citizens (Berkin)
Took authority to declare slaves free away from lower courts (Cromwell, p. 17)
Made laws banning slavery unconstitutional (Hossell, also Skog, p. 8)

Did it create/become a major turning point?

The "*Dred Scott* decision and its aftermath were important steps on the road that led to the Civil War" (Greenberg)
The decision "is widely regarded as 'the worst ever by the Supreme Court'" (Greenberg)
Revealed "racism underlying the decision" (Berkin)

Did later phenomena use it or depend on it?

Thirteenth, Fourteenth, Fifteenth Amendments were passed "to correct the constitutional defects" of the decision (Berkin)
"*Dred Scott* case and the amendments designed to correct the constitutional defects that led to it still play a key role in dozens of cases . . . each year" (Berkin)

Genus: Where does it belong?
NOTE TO INSTRUCTOR: Two different sets of options are given.

What other objects, events, people, or places can it be grouped with?

The *Winny vs. Whitesides* case (Cromwell, p. 15)
"In other cases, courts in Missouri, Kentucky, and Louisiana had often freed slaves who had lived in free states or territories" (Cromwell, p. 15)
OR
Missouri Compromise of 1820 (Skog, p. 7)
Decision of 1854 reversed the Missouri Compromise (Skog, p. 7)
Thirteenth, Fourteenth, Fifteenth Amendments to the Constitution (Berkin)
"dozens of cases in the nation's courts each year" (Berkin)

What are the qualities that lead you to group them together?

All deal with slaves "who had lived in free states or territories" (Cromwell, p. 15)

OR

All were legal decisions about slavery

What name can you give this group?

Lawsuits by slaves

OR

Legal decisions about slavery

In what significant ways is it different from the others in its group?

NOTE TO INSTRUCTOR: This question will require the student to draw deductions from the source material. If necessary, prompt the student using the answers below.

It was an opposite decision to *Winny vs. Whitesides* and the other lawsuits brought by slaves.

OR

It was a Supreme Court decision (Missouri Compromise, decision of 1854 were Congressional decisions; amendments were voted on by states; "dozens of cases" took place in lower courts)

NOTE TO INSTRUCTOR: If the student only lists one or two other events in this group, the answer "How is it different?" will change. For example, if the student listed:

Missouri Compromise of 1820 (Skog, p. 7)
Thirteenth, Fourteenth, Fifteenth Amendments to the Constitution (Berkin)

the answer might be

Dred Scott was pro-slavery; the others limited or banned slavery

STEP FOUR: **Organize your notes**

Student instructions for Step Four:

Read back through the notes that you took on the passages. Before you begin to write, do two things:

1. You may not have found good or complete answers to some of the questions. If so, you can decide not to answer them; remember, you don't need to address *every* question in your composition. Cross out any questions that you decide not to answer now.

2. Decide what order you'll answer the questions in. Put your notes in that order now. If you need help doing this, ask your instructor.

HOW TO HELP THE STUDENT WITH STEP FOUR

If the student has trouble organizing his notes, suggest that he follow one of these patterns:

> **Events that led up to the case**
> **Descriptive sequence of the case**
> **Events that occurred because of the case**
> **Significance of the case**
> **Genus of the case**

OR

> **Descriptive sequence**
> **Events that led up to the case**
> **Effects on the surrounding events/people**
> **Significance**
> **Genus**

STEP FIVE: **Write (Student Responsibility)**

NOTE TO INSTRUCTOR: The student does not need to turn in his essay until he has finished proofreading. A sample composition is found at the end of this lesson.

> Now you are ready to write your composition.
> Using your notes, write at least four paragraphs and 200 words about the *Dred Scott* case. (If you want to write a longer composition with more paragraphs, you can, but don't go beyond 500 words!) In the next step, you will add an introduction and conclusion to this composition.
> Cite at least three of your sources as you write. Quote directly from at least one of the sources.
> Be sure that you answer some of the questions about function *and* some of the questions about genus.
> You do not need to show your essay to your instructor until you have proofread it in Step Eight.

STEP SIX: **Introduction and conclusion**

Student instructions for Step Six:

> You must write both an introduction and a conclusion to your composition.
> Your introduction and conclusion cannot *both* be one sentence long. If you write a one-sentence introduction, you must write a longer conclusion, and vice versa. Remember: a one-sentence introduction or conclusion can be added to the first or last paragraph of your composition, but a two- or three-sentence introduction or conclusion can stand on its own as an independent paragraph.
> Below, you will find some guidance and additional information. Pick one type of introduction and another type of conclusion. When you've finished writing your introduction and conclusion, insert them into your composition.

If you need help, ask your instructor.

Introduction by Summary: State one or two vital facts about the case—or sum up its significance. Your goal is to pique the reader's interest, rather than give away all of the important details about *Dred Scott*.

Introduction by History: This should give historical background that comes *before* the events in the composition. Use the information below to write two or three sentences that give a broader history of the *Dred Scott* case.

★

Introduction by Anecdote: Use the following information to visualize the day of the *Dred Scott* decision. Write your own anecdote to describe the court scene as if you were there.

★

Conclusion by Summary: Write one or more sentences summing up the significance of the case. (You should already have covered the important facts in the body of the composition.)

Conclusion by Personal Reaction: Would history have been different if the *Dred Scott* case had never happened? Or: How would you have felt if you had been in the courtroom on the day of the case? Or: What do you personally feel about the Supreme Court's decision?

Conclusion by Question: Ask if the reader agrees with the significance of the case, or what the reader's reaction was to the case. OR: Ask an open-ended question about how history might have turned out without the *Dred Scott* case.

HOW TO HELP THE STUDENT WITH STEP SIX

The student has been given detailed guidance. If he struggles, tell him to go back and reread the instructions from Week 6. You can also let him read one or two of the following samples; then, require him to write a different kind of introduction or conclusion.

The student's work may resemble the following:

Introduction by Summary:

> In the late 1850s, the Supreme Court considered a case that would divide the nation and pave the way for the Civil War.

Introduction by History:

> The slavery conflict between the North and South dates back centuries before the *Dred Scott* case was decided. The large plantations of the South depended on slave labor. However, the small farms and industries of the North were successful without slavery.

Introduction by Anecdote:

> The old Senate chamber was not a pleasant place. It was cold, cramped, and dim. But on March 6, 1857, the awkward room was overflowing with onlookers waiting to hear the Supreme Court's decision on the *Dred Scott* case.

Conclusion by Summary:

> The famous *Dred Scott* decision in 1857 pitted the North and South against one another, and paved the way for the Civil War.

Conclusion by Personal Reaction:

> If I had been sitting in the courtroom on March 6 of 1857, listening to the results of the *Dred Scott* case, I would have been horrified by the Supreme Court's decision. It was racist and simply wrong.

Conclusion by Question:

> Were the North and South already on the path to civil war, or did the *Dred Scott* case turn the United States in a new and destructive direction?

STEP SEVEN: **Title and Works Cited page**

Student instructions for Step Seven:

> Read the following titles of books about the *Dred Scott* case. Notice that each title has the topic, and then a colon (:), followed by a descriptive phrase.
> *Dred Scott V. Sandford: A Slave's Case for Freedom and Citizenship*
> The *Dred Scott* Case: Slavery and Citizenship
> *Dred and Harriet Scott: A Family's Struggle for Freedom*
> The *Dred Scott* Decision: Law or Politics?

> The first part of each title is known as the *main title*. The phrase after the colon is the *subtitle*.
> Model your title on the examples above. Your main title can be either "The *Dred Scott* Case" or "*Dred Scott.*" (Or, referring to the man himself, "Dred Scott.") Place a colon after your main title. For your subtitle, write a descriptive phrase that sums up the main point or the most important section of your composition.
> Title a separate piece of paper "Works Cited." List your sources in alphabetical order.

HOW TO HELP THE STUDENT WITH STEP SEVEN

Although this step should be concluded independently, you may need to use the comprehensive Works Cited below to check the format of the student's final Works Cited page.

Berkin, Carol, et al. *Making America: A History of the United States, Vol. 1: To 1877*, brief 5th ed. Boston: Wadsworth, 2011.

Cromwell, Sharon. *Dred Scott v. Sandford: A Slave's Case for Freedom and Citizenship*. Mankato, Minn.: Compass Point Books, 2009.

Greenberg, Ethan. *Dred Scott and the Dangers of a Political Court*. Lanham, Md.: Lexington Books, 2009.

Hossell, Karen Price. *The Emancipation Proclamation.* **Chicago: Heinemann Library, 2006.**

Skog, Jason. *The Dred Scott Decision.* **Mankato, Minn.: Compass Point Books, 2006.**

STEP EIGHT: **Proofread**

Student instructions for Step Eight:

> Before you hand your paper to your instructor, follow these proofreading steps.
>
> 1) Make sure that your paper is at least 225 words in length.
> 2) Check for the required elements: title and subtitle separated by a colon, Works Cited page, introduction and conclusion (at least one of these should be longer than 1 sentence), at least three sources cited, and at least one direct quote.
> 3) Read your paper out loud, listening for awkward or unclear sections and repeated words. Rewrite awkward or unclear sentences so that they flow more naturally.
> 4) Listen for information that is repeated more than once. Eliminate repetition of ideas.
> 5) Read through the paper one more time, looking for sentence fragments, run-on sentences, and repeated words. Correct fragments and run-on sentences. Listen for unnecessary repetition. (You will have to repeat the words "slavery" "slaves" "court" etc. multiple times. But listen for other nouns and verbs that you could vary.) If you used a modifier (adverb, adjective, or prepositional phrase acting as an adjective or adverb) more than twice, find another word.
> 6) Check your spelling by looking, individually, at each word that might be a problem.
> 7) Check the formatting of your footnotes and your Works Cited page.
>
> When you're finished proofreading, show your paper to your instructor.

HOW TO HELP THE STUDENT WITH STEP EIGHT

Evaluate the paper using the following rubric:

Week 20 Rubric

Organization:

1   The composition should be at least 225 words in length. It should have at least four paragraphs.
2   At least three sources should be cited; at least one citation should be a direct quote.
3   The composition must answer questions *both* about function *and* about genus.
4   The composition must have both an introduction and a conclusion. Only one of these can be a summary. Either the introduction or the conclusion *must* be longer than one sentence.
5   The composition should have a title, centered at the top of the first page. This title should include the name of the case, followed by a colon and a descriptive phrase about the essay.

Mechanics:

1   Each sentence should make sense on its own when read aloud.
2   There should be no sentence fragments or run-on sentences.
3   All words should be spelled correctly.
4   The first line of each paragraph should be properly indented.
5   Verb tense should be consistent throughout.
6   Footnotes and the Works Cited page should be properly formatted.
7   When referring to the person, "Dred Scott" should not be italicized, but when referring to the case, *"Dred Scott"* should be italicized.
8   With the exception of important nouns such as "slaves," "slavery," "Supreme Court," etc., most nouns should not be repeated more than twice. Modifiers should not be used more than twice.

The student's composition might resemble the following. Notice that the fifth paragraph deals with genus by comparing *Dred Scott* to other court cases and pointing out its differences.

THE *DRED SCOTT* CASE: A TRIGGER FOR THE CIVIL WAR

The old Senate chamber was not a pleasant place. It was cold, cramped, and dim. But on March 6, 1857, the awkward room was overflowing with onlookers waiting to hear the Supreme Court's decision on the *Dred Scott* case.

Before the Civil War, slavery was illegal in some parts of the United States and legal in other parts. The Missouri Compromise of 1820 made slavery illegal in parts north of Missouri. There were other territories as well where slavery was not allowed.

In 1824, a slave named Winny sued her owner for freedom because she was taken into territory where slavery was illegal. The court made the decision "once free, forever free," and Winny won her freedom.[1] Other slaves were freed by courts in Missouri, Kentucky and Lousiana because they had been taken to live in free territories.

Years later, a slave named Dred Scott was sold as a slave to Dr. John Emerson in Virginia. Emerson and Scott traveled to places where slavery was illegal, such as Illinois and Wisconsin. After John Emerson died, Scott sued for his freedom. The case went to the Supreme Court eleven years later, in 1857. The court decided that Scott was still a slave. The Supreme Court also declared that no man or woman "of African descent" could be a citizen of the United States.[2]

Other court cases, including *Winny v. Whitesides* as well as many others, had granted freedom to the slave. But the *Dred Scott* case did not. Instead, the case reversed the decisions of other courts—and divided the nation. Protests and a "firestorm of criticism" followed.[3]

Eventually, the Civil War was fought between the North and South to settle the issue of slavery. Were the North and South already irreparably divided, or did the *Dred Scott* case put the U.S. on the path to war?

---

[1] Sharon Cromwell, Dred Scott v. Sandford: *A Slave's Case for Freedom and Citizenship* (Compass Point Books, 2009), p. 15.

[2] Carol Berkin et al., *Making America: A History of the United States, Vol. 1: To 1877*, brief 5th ed. (Wadsworth, 2011), p. 311.

[3] Ethan Greenberg, Dred Scott *and the Dangers of a Political Court* (Lexington Books, 2009), p. 2.

WORKS CITED

Berkin, Carol, et al. *Making America: A History of the United States, Vol. 1: To 1877*, brief 5th ed. Boston: Wadsworth, 2011.

Cromwell, Sharon. Dred Scott v. Sandford: *A Slave's Case for Freedom and Citizenship*. Mankato, Minn.: Compass Point Books, 2009.

Greenberg, Ethan. Dred Scott *and the Dangers of a Political Court*. Lanham, Md.: Lexington Books, 2009.

WEEK 21: EXPLANATION BY DEFINITION PROJECT IN HISTORY

This week, the student will chose her own historical object, event, place, or people group and will write a 500-word explanation by definition that covers properties, function, and genus.

As in Week 15, try to create overlap between this independent writing assignment. If the student can write on a topic related to her history studies, the time spent on this composition can be drawn from her history study time as well.

In this week's work, a number of skills covered in the first twenty weeks of this course are revisited. If necessary, give her additional time to go back and review.

The assignment has been broken down into steps, with suggested amounts of time for each. These are *suggestions only*. Change, adapt, and even skip steps if appropriate. The overview is:

Step One: Review the *topos*	20–30 minutes
Step Two: Brainstorm a topic	45–60 minutes
Step Three: Pre-reading	Time for library visit, plus 1–3 hours for reading
Step Four: Take notes	2–4 hours
Step Five: Draft the composition	2–4 hours
Step Six: Finalize the composition	1–3 hours

Make sure that the student reads through the **entire lesson** before beginning to work.

Although the student does not need to show her work after each step, help tips have been provided for every one. You can always show the student my examples if she can't figure out what to do next.

You may also require that she show her work whenever you think it is appropriate.

STEP ONE: **Review the *topos* (20–30 minutes)**

Student instructions for Step One:

> Before you start to look for a topic, review the questions you'll be trying to answer.
> On a sheet of paper, copy down the following *topos* and place it into the Reference section of your Composition Notebook.

HOW TO HELP THE STUDENT WITH STEP ONE

The student's completed chart should resemble the following:

Explanation by Definition: Historical Object, Event, Place, or People Group

Definition: An explanation of properties, function, and genus

Procedure   Remember

1. Answer the following questions: 1. Not all questions need to be answered.

Shared and Unique Properties   2. Answers to genus and properties may overlap.
What did it look like?
How did it behave?   3. Always try to explain significance.
What did it resemble?
What was it made of?
What sort of structure did it have?
What was its extent in space?
Where did it take place or exist?
What was its extent in time?
Did it repeat or continue into modern times?
    How has it changed over time?
What large group of other phenomena can it be assigned to?
What smaller group of other phenomena can it be assigned to?
What qualities does it share with *no other* phenomena?

Function
How did it work, behave, or unfold?
    Will a descriptive sequence help the reader understand how it worked?
        What would the sequence describe?
    Was its behavior predictable or unpredictable?
    Did it work/behave differently under different circumstances?
        At different times?
    Can its behavior or sequence be divided into phases?
        What separates the phases?
    Was there a cause or trigger for the event?
    What was the time frame for its behavior or significance?
    Where did the behavior take place?
Who/what needed it, used it, or was affected by it?
    What effects did it have on the surrounding events/people?
    What events led up to it?
    What events occurred because of it?
For what purposes or reasons?
    Is there more than one purpose or reason?
    Did the purpose or reason change at different times?
    Was the purpose or reason dependent on any other conditions?
What is its significance? Why do we remember it?
    What did it change?
    Did it create/become a major turning point?
    Did later phenomena use it or depend on it?

Genus

What other objects, events, people, or places can it be grouped with?

What are the qualities that lead you to group them together?

What name can you give this group?

In what significant ways is it different from the others in its group?

STEP TWO: **Brainstorm a topic (20–30 minutes)**

Student instructions for Step Two:

Once again, it's time to brainstorm!

Back in Week 8, you learned to ask four questions for topics in history: When? Where? What? Who? Each one of these questions points you in the direction of a historical event, object, place, or group of people—the four things you've been studying how to define.

When? Event

Where? Place

What? Object

Who? Group of people

As you prepare to research your historical definition, you'll adapt the brainstorming techniques you used in Week 8 to help you find a topic. (If you don't remember that lesson, turn back to Week 8 and read through the instructions for Day One now.)

Follow these instructions:

1. Write the words EVENT, PLACE, OBJECT, and GROUP OF PEOPLE along the long side of a piece of paper.

   Under the heading EVENT, write at least three words or phrases describing events that happen over a period of time—battles, wars, revolutions, cultural eras (for example, the Great Depression).

   Under the heading PLACE, write at least three geographical designations: countries, cities, rivers, mountains, even continents.

   Under the heading OBJECT, write down at least three *things* that people have used in history. These should be the sorts of objects that historians study and archaeologists dig up; they can be very small (compasses or sextants used in navigation, say) or very large (windmills or blimps).

   Under the heading GROUP OF PEOPLE, write down at least three different people groups or nations (e.g., "nomads" or "The French" or "peasants").

2. Circle one name or phrase in each column that seems potentially the most interesting to you. Now, choose three of the four circled names or phrases for further investigation. You should end up with a total of three brainstorming maps.

   a. If you chose the circled term from the EVENT column, write it in the middle of a second blank sheet of paper. Now ask yourself: Where did it take place? Who was involved? What objects were important to/used in the event? Try to come up with at least two answers for each question. For a brief event, such as the Battle of Hastings, there may be only one "where" answer. (However, if you were to investigate, you would find out that different phases of the battle took place on different parts of the slope and crest of Senlac Hill, so you could put "Slope of hill" and "Crest of hill" as different locations.)

   Use different colored pens or pencils to write the answers in a brainstorming map around your central term.

   b. If you chose the circled term in the PLACE column, ask yourself: When was this place important? What objects were central to the place, or used in/

nearby/in order to explore/conquer/farm/sail on it? What group of people is identified with it?

c. If you chose the circled term in the OBJECT column, ask yourself: Who built or used it? When was it used? Where?

d. If you chose the circled term in the GROUP OF PEOPLE column, ask yourself: Where did they live and/or flourish? What is the best-known event in their past? What object is most identified with them, or most important to them?

3. Because you are writing a definition, you do not need to complete the final brainstorming step of defining the subject area. It's already defined: you're writing a definition! But these brainstorming maps should give some idea of which object or phenomenon is best suited to an explanation by definition. Pick the map that turned out the best—the one that you found the most information on, or that you found the most interesting.

HOW TO HELP THE STUDENT WITH STEP TWO

Even if the student already has some idea of the topic she'd like to research, encourage her to go through this brainstorming process. Every time the student goes through the entire sequence of steps in writing a paper, the process will seem easier and more natural.

In addition, brainstorming for an explanation by definition paper is slightly different from general brainstorming, so the student will benefit from the practice.

Remember that the student will probably need to use the Internet for help in brainstorming. If necessary, review the instructions in Week 8 and Week 15.

Here is an example of how instructions #1 and #2.c might look, completed. If necessary, you can show these brainstorming maps to the student (but then she has to make her own).

This is my original brainstorming map:

Here's the map I did for #2.c, when I decided to find out more about spinning wheels. I entered "spinning wheel" and "who used it" into Google. I discovered that spinners were almost all female, primarily poor, and that James Hargreaves, who invented the spinning jenny (which replaced the spinning wheel), named the spinning jenny for his wife, who spent far too much time spinning yarn.

When I searched for "spinning wheel" and "when," I discovered that the first spinning wheels were found in Asia in the 11th century. That actually gave me an answer for "place" as well, so I put both of those facts on my brainstorming map, as well as the information that the spinning wheel was most common before the Industrial Revolution.

Now I only needed one more answer for "spinning wheel" and "where." When I entered these terms, "Europe" kept coming up. I'm not researching at this point, just brainstorming, so that's what I put on my map. Here's the finished product:

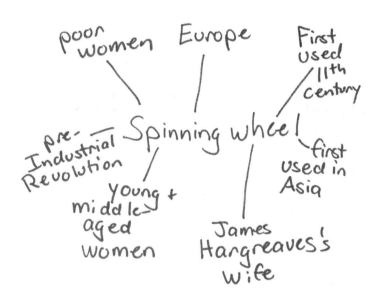

This map gives me many different combinations of terms to search when I go to the library in Step Three.

STEP THREE: Pre-reading (Time for library visit, plus 1–3 hours for reading)

Student instructions for Step Three:

> Now you'll use your brainstorming map to help you locate titles for pre-reading.
> You should aim to end up with at least three sources that give you valuable information about your topic. Follow the same sequence as in Week 15:
>
> 1. Make an initial list of titles to look for, using your local library's online catalog. Search for several different terms from your brainstorming map.
> 2. Take your brainstorming map with you and visit the library. Locate your chosen titles. Glance at the titles on either side on the shelf to see if they look useful. Pull six to eight books off the shelf and examine them. Use the indices to make sure that each book addresses your topic. Remember: you need information

about properties *and* function. You can determine an appropriate genus yourself.
3. Try to bring home at least four books that relate to your subject.
4. Read the chapters or sections of each book that relate to your topic. Don't take notes yet; instead, use bookmarks or Post-It Notes to mark pages that you might want to use.

HOW TO HELP THE STUDENT WITH STEP THREE

By this point, library and online books searches should be fairly familiar to both you and the student. If you need a refresher, review the instructions in Week 15.

STEP FOUR: **Take notes (2–4 hours)**

Student instructions for Step Four:

> Using proper form, take notes from at least three of your books. The number you will take will vary; try not to take more than 20 notes from any one book.
> Take notes in the way suggested in last week's work: As you take your notes, organize them by the question that they answer. This will be easier if you go through the Explanation by Definition in History chart first and cross out the questions that don't apply to your particular topic.
> Be sure that your notes answer at least four of the questions under Properties, and at least three to four of the questions under Function.
> Whenever you find a piece of information that might help you place your subject into a group, list it under Genus. You'll probably want to put the *same* information into either Properties or Function; it's perfectly fine to duplicate your notes for Genus. You *must* discuss Genus in your final composition.

HOW TO HELP THE STUDENT WITH STEP FOUR

For the purposes of this exercise, the student will need to organize her notes as she takes them, rather than taking notes on a single source and organizing them later.

Although this takes a little more time at the beginning, because the student has to constantly refer back to the questions as she takes notes, it saves time when the student begins to write, because an additional "Organize your notes" step is unnecessary.

This is the same process that the student followed in last week's work.

You may need to reinforce the final paragraph in the instructions: that notes taken for Genus (information that helps put the subject into a group) will probably be copied directly from the notes on Properties and Function. It's fine to have the same note reproduced, word for word, in the Genus section and in another section as well. The goal is to have at least one paragraph in the final composition that addresses Genus by 1) listing other events, objects, places, or peoples that can be grouped together with the subject of the composition and 2) pointing out how the subject of the composition differs from them.

NOTE TO INSTRUCTOR: As in Week 15, you may allow the student to take notes first and then divide them into answers to the listed questions. However, continue to encourage the student to try different methods of researching and writing.

STEP FIVE: **Draft the composition (2–4 hours) (Student Responsibility)**

Using your ordered notes, write your composition.

When you wrote your first original description in Week 15, I told you to follow this order:

First, describe the properties of your subject (in any order that you choose).

Then, describe the function. Finally, identify the genus.

For this composition, I'm not going to assign you any particular order. Instead, make sure that you address at least four of the questions for properties and at least four of the questions for function.

You must also spend at least two to three sentences placing your subject into a group and explaining how it is different from the other members of that group. You might find it useful to see an example; here is how I would have addressed genus in the *Dred Scott* composition from last week.

Other court cases, including *Winny v. Whitesides* as well as many others, had granted freedom to the slave. But the *Dred Scott* case did not. Instead, the case reversed the decisions of other courts—and divided the nation.

In three sentences, I defined the group to which *Dred Scott* belonged (other court cases about slaves) and then said how it was different (it did not grant freedom, it reversed the other decisions, it divided the nation).

You should have at least four paragraphs.

Quote directly from at least two of your sources. Make sure to footnote all direct quotes and anything which is not common knowledge.

Check your *topoi* chart one more time to make sure that you have included the required elements.

Since your complete composition, including introduction and conclusion, should be at least 500 words long, aim to have at least 450 words in this initial draft.

STEP SIX: **Finalize the composition (1–3 hours)**

Student instructions for Step Six:

1. Review the Introductions and Conclusions chart in the Reference section of your Composition Notebook. Choose one kind of introduction and another kind of conclusion. Write your introduction and conclusion. Make sure that you have at least 500 words total.
2. Choose a main title and a subtitle, separating the two with a colon. If necessary, look back at Week 20, Step Seven to review the format.
3. Assemble your Works Cited page.
4. Proofread, using the seven steps outlined in last week's assignment (Step Eight).

When your composition is finished, show it to your instructor.

HOW TO HELP THE STUDENT WITH STEP SIX

Check the student's composition, using the following rubric.

Week 21 Rubric

Organization:

1 The entire composition should be at least four paragraphs and at least 500 words in length.
2 The composition should answer at least four of the questions about function and four of the questions about properties. The student should be able to tell you which questions she answered.
3 At least two to three sentences should address genus by placing the subject into a group and explaining how it differs from others in that group.
4 The composition should have both an introduction and a conclusion. The introduction and conclusion should be of different types.
5 The composition should have a title, centered at the top of the first page. This title should include the name of the case, followed by a colon and a descriptive phrase about the essay.
6 At least two sources should be quoted.
7 All sources mentioned in footnotes should be placed on a Works Cited page.

Mechanics:

1 Each sentence should make sense on its own when read aloud.
2 There should be no sentence fragments or run-on sentences.
3 All words should be spelled correctly.
4 The first line of each paragraph should be properly indented.
5 Verb tense should be consistent throughout.
6 Footnotes and the Works Cited page should be properly formatted.
7 With the exception of important nouns, most nouns should not be repeated more than twice. Modifiers should not be used more than twice.

WEEK 22: INTENSIVE COPIA REVIEW AND PRACTICE

The student has spent most of the past few weeks researching and writing. Now it's time for a change of pace. This week, he will review all of the copia skills learned so far, master a new kind of sentence transformation, and then practice by transforming a piece of classic prose.

Day One: Copia Review, Part I

 Focus: Reviewing skills in sentence transformation

The student should read the examples and complete the exercises below. If he needs review, instruct him to go back to the lesson listed and reread the explanations.

Remember: the transformed sentences might sound better than the original—and they might sound a lot worse. The student won't know until he tries the transformations and then reads the sentences out loud. Writing always involves trial and error!

STEP ONE: Transforming nouns into descriptive adjectives and vice versa

Full explanation found in Week 1, Day 4. The sentences in this exercise are taken from *The Portrait of a Lady,* by Henry James.

Student instructions for Step One:

> Example:
> The <u>old-world</u> quality in everything that she now saw had all the charm <u>of strangeness</u>.
>
>   ADJ   N   N PREP OP
>   old-world quality → quality of old-worldness
>
>   N   PREP   OP   ADJ   N
>   charm of strangeness → strange charm
> The quality <u>of old-worldness</u> in everything she now saw had a <u>strange</u> charm.

Remember that it may sometimes it may be necessary to alter the wording of the sentence slightly (above, I did not write "had all the strange charm"). Also, your prepositional phrases will probably all include the preposition "of." This is the most natural preposition to use, and there's no need for you to struggle to find different prepositions instead.

Exercise:
On your own paper, rewrite the following sentences by changing descriptive adjectives to nouns in prepositional phrases *or* vice versa. You will need to locate the descriptive adjectives and nouns to be transformed—but if you can't find them, ask your instructor.
A *sally* is a clever remark.

HOW TO HELP THE STUDENT WITH STEP ONE

If the student struggles with these exercises, give him a hint by reading the underlined words in each sentence; those are the adjectives and nouns to be altered.

Ah, we too are a <u>lovely</u> group!
Ah, we too are a group of loveliness!

He had a <u>narrow, clean-shaven</u> face, with features evenly distributed and an expression <u>of</u> <u>placid acuteness</u>.
He had a face of narrowness and clean-shavenness, with features evenly distributed and a placidly acute expression.
NOTE TO INSTRUCTOR: When the noun "acuteness" becomes an adjective, the adjective "placid" (describing "acuteness") has to become an adverb. Adjectives cannot modify other adjectives; only adverbs can modify adjectives. You may need to explain this to the student.

It was an <u>awkward</u> beginning for a <u>clever</u> man.
It was a beginning of awkwardness for a man of cleverness.

For this <u>extravagant</u> sally his <u>simple</u> visitors had no answer.
For this sally of extravagance his visitors of simplicity had no answer.

That she was a <u>brave</u> musician we have already perceived.
That she was a musician of bravery we have already perceived.

Isabel sat there a long time, under the charm of their <u>motionless grace</u>.
Isabel sat there a long time, under their motionlessly graceful charm.

A <u>cold, cruel</u> rain fell heavily.
A rain of coldness and cruelty fell heavily.

The father caught <u>his son's</u> eye at last and gave him <u>a mild, responsive</u> smile.
The father caught the eye of his son at last and gave him a smile of mildness and responsiveness.

STEP TWO: **Transforming infinitives into participles and vice versa**

Full explanation found in Week 2, Day 4. The sentences in this exercise are taken from *Things Fall Apart,* by Chinua Achebe.

Student instructions for Step Two:

> **Example:**
> The headmaster blew the whistle <u>to call</u> the assembly to order.
>
> INF   PART
> to call → calling
>
> The headmaster blew the whistle, <u>calling</u> the assembly to order.
>
> The horse started galloping wildly away.
>
> PART   INF
> galloping → to gallop
>
> The horse started to gallop wildly away.

> **Exercise:**
> Rewrite the following sentences on your own paper, changing infinitives to participles and vice versa. Remember that you may need to add a comma when you change an infinitive into a participle, or delete a comma when a participle becomes an infinitive.

HOW TO HELP THE STUDENT WITH STEP TWO

If the student struggles with these exercises, give him a hint by reading the underlined words in each sentence; those are the participles and infinitives to be altered.

The next morning the crazy men actually began <u>to clear</u> a part of the forest and <u>to build</u> their house.
The next morning the crazy men actually began clearing a part of the forest and building their house.

The troublesome nanny-goat sniffed about, <u>eating</u> the peelings.
The troublesome nanny-goat sniffed about to eat the peelings.

At such times, in each of the countless thatched huts of Umuofia, children sat around their mother's cooking fire <u>telling</u> stories.
At such times, in each of the countless thatched huts of Umuofia, children sat around their mother's cooking fire to tell stories.

At night the messengers came in <u>to taunt</u> them and <u>to knock</u> their shaven heads together.

At night the messengers came in taunting them and knocking their shaven heads together.

That night the Mother of the Spirits walked the length and breadth of the clan, <u>weeping</u> for her murdered son.
That night the Mother of the Spirits walked the length and breadth of the clan to weep for her murdered son.

The elders sat in a big circle and the singers went round <u>singing</u> each man's praise as they came before him.
The elders sat in a big circle and the singers went round to sing each man's praise as they came before him.

She broke them into little pieces across the sole of her foot and began <u>to build</u> a fire.
She broke them into little pieces across the sole of her foot and began building a fire.

As soon as he heard of the great feast in the sky his throat began <u>to itch</u> at the very thought.
As soon as he heard of the great feast in the sky his throat began itching at the very thought.

STEP THREE: **Changing main verbs into infinitives**

Full explanation found in Week 2, Day 4. Remember: when the student changes a main verb to an infinitive, he will then need to add another main verb—which adds new meaning to the sentence.

The sentences in this exercise are adapted from *The Red Badge of Courage,* by Stephen Crane. The original sentences all contain main verbs plus infinitives; I have changed Crane's infinitives to main verbs and cut out Crane's original main verbs. When the student is finished, show him Stephen Crane's actual sentences (in bold type below).

To help the student with these sentences, I've underlined the verbs that need to be changed back to infinitives.

Student instructions for Step Three:

> **Example:**
> He <u>remained</u> on his guard.
>
> MAIN VERB   INF
>   remained   →   to remain
>
> He resolved to remain on his guard.
> He continued to remain on his guard.
> He hoped to remain on his guard.

Exercise:

Rewrite the following sentences on your own paper, changing each underlined verb to an infinitive and adding a new main verb.

HOW TO HELP THE STUDENT WITH STEP THREE

Stephen Crane's original sentences are in bold below. If the student struggles, refer him back to the list of main verbs that often take infinitives in Week 2, Day 4.

Ma, I'm <u>enlisting</u>.
Ma, I'm going to enlist.

She <u>milked</u> the brindle cow.
She continued to milk the brindle cow.

The army had done little but sit still and <u>keep</u> warm.
The army had done little but sit still and try to keep warm.

He <u>proved</u> mathematically to himself that he would not run from a battle.
He tried to mathematically prove to himself that he would not run from a battle.

Previously he <u>had</u> never <u>wrestled</u> too seriously with this question.
Previously he had never felt obliged to wrestle too seriously with this question.

He <u>admitted</u> that as far as war was concerned, he knew nothing of himself.
He was forced to admit that as far as war was concerned, he knew nothing of himself.

He sprang from the bunk and <u>paced</u> nervously to and fro.
He sprang from the bunk and began to pace nervously to and fro.

Day Two: Copia Review, Part II

 Focus: Reviewing skills in sentence transformation

The student should continue to read the examples and complete the exercises below.

STEP ONE: Transforming indirect objects into prepositional phrases and vice versa

A fuller explanation is found in Week 3, Day 4.

Student instructions for Step One:

> **Example:**
>   S   V   IO   DO
>   The fastidious gardener gave his poodle a pedicure.
>
> →   S   V   DO   PREP OP
>   The fastidious gardener gave a pedicure to his poodle.
>
> **Exercise:**
>   In the following sentences, change indirect objects to prepositional phrases. In sentences
> that do not have indirect objects, find the prepositional phrase that can be transformed into an
> indirect object and rewrite the sentence.

HOW TO HELP THE STUDENT WITH STEP ONE

The words that should be transformed are underlined in the sentences below. If necessary, point them out to the student.

IO (transform into prepositional phrase)

The wolf gave <u>Romulus and Remus</u> her milk.

The wolf gave her milk to Romulus and Remus.

PREP   OP (transform into direct object)

The woodpecker also brought food <u>to the twins</u>.

The woodpecker also brought the twins food.

IO (transform into prepositional phrase)

The starving Esau sold <u>Jacob</u> his birthright in exchange for a bowl of soup.

The starving Esau sold his birthright to Jacob in exchange for a bowl of soup.

PREP   OP   OP (transform into indirect object)

From debtor's prison, Paul Bunyan wrote letters to his friends and family.

From debtor's prison, Paul Bunyan wrote his friends and family letters.

IO (transform into prepositional phrase)

The waters of the River Styx almost granted Achilles immortality.

The waters of the River Styx almost granted immortality to Achilles.

IO (transform into prepositional phrase)

The bear gave her cub the newly caught salmon.

The bear gave the newly caught salmon to her cub.

STEP TWO: **Transforming active verbs into passive verbs and vice versa**

Full explanation is found in Week 3, Day 4. When the student changes a passive verb into an active verb, he will need to provide a subject; he may find a subject in a prepositional phrase following the verb, or he may have to create a new subject.

When he changes an active verb into a passive verb, he will need to put the subject into a prepositional phrase that modifies the verb.

The sentences in this exercise are adapted from Bobbie Kalman's *Peru: The People and Culture.*

Student instructions for Step Two:

> **Example:**
>
> As the Inca Empire grew, neighboring cultures and peoples were absorbed.
>
> | PASSIVE VERB | | NEW SUBJECT | ACTIVE VERB |
> |---|---|---|---|
> | were absorbed | → | it | absorbed |
>
> As the Inca Empire grew, it absorbed neighboring cultures and peoples.
>
> **Exercise:**
>
> Read the following sentences. If the verb is active, change it to passive. If it is passive, change it to active and invent a new subject.

HOW TO HELP THE STUDENT WITH STEP TWO

If the student has trouble distinguishing between active and passive verbs, point out the subjects and verbs as marked below. Then ask, "Is the subject actively *doing* the verb, or passively *receiving the action* of the verb?" You may need to remind the student to place the subject of active verbs into a prepositional phrase following the verb.

S   AV

The founder of the Inca dynasty, Manco Capac, led his people to the site of the present-day city of Cuzco.

The people were led to the site of the present-day city of Cuzco by the founder of the Inca dynasty, Manco Capac.

S   AV

The Incas expanded their empire across Peru.

The empire was expanded across Peru by the Incas.

S   PV

They were conquered by the Spanish in 1532.

The Spanish conquered them in 1532.

S   AV

The Incas made a lasting impression during the short period when they flourished.

A lasting impression was made by the Incas during the short period when they flourished.

S   PV

Inca society was based on sharing.

The Incas based their society on sharing.

S   PV

Older people were given tasks such as collecting firewood.

The Incas gave the older people tasks such as collecting firewood.

S   PV

After a lifetime of working, elderly Incas were provided with food and clothing.

The Incas provided the elderly people with food and clothing after a lifetime of working.

STEP THREE: **Added and intensified adjectives**

A fuller explanation can be found in Week 4, Day 4. The sentences in this exercise are adapted from *The Call of the Wild*, by Jack London. When the student is finished, he should compare his sentences to Jack London's originals, in bold type below.

Student instructions for Step Three:

> **Examples:**
>> **Added Adjective**
>>> They did not see the <u>instant</u> transformation.
>>> → They did not see the <u>instant and terrible</u> transformation.

Intensified Adjective

He broke from a sad contemplation.

→ He broke from a mournful contemplation.

Exercise:

Rewrite the following sentences by intensifying each underlined adjective *and* adding a second adjective. You will also need to add a comma or the word "and." Use a thesaurus if you need to.

The first sentence has been done for you as an example. Notice that the generic adjective "scary" has been changed to the intensified adjective "terrifying," and another adjective, "irresistible," has been added. The second adjective does not have to be a synonym for the first, but it should be consistent with the meaning of the sentence.

When you are finished, show your work to your instructor, who has the original versions of the sentences for you to compare to your own.

HOW TO HELP THE STUDENT WITH STEP THREE

The student's chosen adjectives may be very different from Jack London's original sentences, but as long as they make sense, accept them.

They were mere skeletons, draped loosely in draggled hides, with blazing eyes and slavered fangs. But the hunger-madness made them <u>scary</u>.
But the hunger-madness made them <u>terrifying, irresistible.</u>

When he flung himself against the bars, <u>shaking</u>, they laughed at him and taunted him.
When he flung himself against the bars, <u>quivering and frothing</u>, they laughed at him and taunted him.

He sprang back, <u>growling</u>, fearful of the unseen and unknown.
He sprang back, <u>bristling and snarling</u>, fearful of the unseen and unknown.

The hair hung down, <u>not nice</u>, or matted with dried blood where Hal's club had bruised him.
The hair hung down, <u>limp and draggled</u>, or matted with dried blood where Hal's club had bruised him.

Thirty or forty huskies ran to the spot and surrounded the combatants in an <u>interested</u> circle.
Thirty or forty huskies ran to the spot and surrounded the combatants in an <u>intent and silent</u> circle.

Then they became friendly, and played about in the <u>nice</u> way with which fierce beasts belie their fierceness.
Then they became friendly, and played about in the <u>nervous, half-coy</u> way with which fierce beasts belie their fierceness.

Buck hurried on, swiftly and stealthily, every nerve <u>working</u>, alert to the multitudinous details which told a story—all but the end.
Buck hurried on, swiftly and stealthily, every nerve <u>straining and tense</u>, alert to the multitudinous details which told a story—all but the end.

Also, they held it a mercy, since Dave was to die anyway, that he should die in the traces, <u>happy</u>.
Also, they held it a mercy, since Dave was to die anyway, that he should die in the traces, <u>heart-easy and content</u>.

Buck staggered over against the sled, <u>tired</u>, sobbing for breath.
Buck staggered over against the sled, <u>exhausted</u>, sobbing for breath, <u>helpless</u>.

Day Three: Copia Review, Part III

 Focus: Reviewing skills in simile, metaphor, and descriptive phrases

In 322 BC Aristotle wrote in *De Poetica,* "The greatest thing by far is to be a master of metaphor. It is the one thing that cannot be learned from others; it is also a sign of genius, since a good metaphor implies an eye for resemblance."

So, if metaphor can't be learned, how can the student become a master (and genius)? Through practice. Today, she will be practicing both metaphor and simile.

STEP ONE: **Identifying metaphor and simile**

Student instructions for Step One:

> If you need to review metaphor and simile, look back at Week 5, Day 4, and Week 6, Day 4. Underline the metaphors and similes in the following sentences. Mark each metaphor with an *M* and each simile with an *S*. Draw an arrow from the metaphor or simile to the word it describes by comparison.

HOW TO HELP THE STUDENT WITH STEP ONE

Sometimes it may be difficult to determine exactly where metaphors begin and end in a sentence. As long as the student can identify some part of the metaphor and identify the word that the metaphor describes, accept his answer.

The **fog** comes / on little cat feet.
   (Carl Sandburg, "The Fog")

Sometimes a **piece** of sun / burned like a coin in my hand.
   (Pablo Neruda, "Clenched Soul")

NOTE TO INSTRUCTOR: The student could also draw an arrow to "sun"

Lost in the forest, I broke off a dark **twig** / and lifted its whisper to my thirsty lips.
   (Pablo Neruda, "Lost in the Forest")

He was very tall and strong, with a **face** as big as a ham.
   (Robert Louis Stevenson, *Treasure Island*)

I took **him** by the waist as if he had been a sack of bran, and, with one good heave, tumbled
him overboard.
   (Robert Louis Stevenson, *Treasure Island*)

I remember observing the contrast the neat, bright doctor, with his **powder** as white as snow, and

his bright, black eyes and pleasant manners, made with the coltish country **folk**, and above all,

with that filthy, heavy, bleared scarecrow of a **pirate** of ours.
   (Robert Louis Stevenson, *Treasure Island*)

His broad, permanently scowling **face** was composed of three downward curves, something

like the insignia of a sergeant's stripes.
   (Gregory David Roberts, *Shantaram*)

My **mind** was muddy water, and one idea splashed up from it.
   (Gregory David Roberts, *Shantaram*)

Arms, legs, and heads crushed in on one another as we hunkered down in terror while the

mortars tore up the rocky **ground** outside as if it was papier-mâché.
   (Gregory David Roberts, *Shantaram*)

STEP TWO: **Transforming words into metaphors or similes**

Student instructions for Step Two:

The sentences below all originally contained figurative language. Change the underlined word(s) to metaphors or similes as directed. When you are finished, show your work to your instructor, who has the original sentences for you to compare with yours.

The key to writing good metaphor and simile is originality. Instead of using familiar phrases such as "hot as fire" or "as light as a feather," use your own experiences. What incredible heat have you experienced? Maybe you'd write "as hot as asphalt in August." Don't be afraid to try unusual, surprising, or even awkward metaphors and similes—that's what practice is for.

Exercise, Part 1: Substituting metaphors for words and phrases

Invent and then substitute a metaphor for each of the words or phrases underlined.

Example:

Her face was radiant. → Her face was a brown moon that shone on me.
(Maya Angelou, *I Know Why the Caged Bird Sings*)

★

Exercise, Part 2: Substituting similes for adverbs

Invent and then substitute a simile for each of the underlined adverbs.

Example:

He laughed harshly. → He laughed like the screech of a rusty hinge.
(James Whitcomb Riley, "The Nine Little Goblins")

HOW TO HELP THE STUDENT WITH STEP TWO

The student will be writing original metaphors, and similes for the sentences below. When she is finished, let her compare her sentences with the originals below. Ask her which metaphor or simile she thinks is better and why.

Exercise, Part 1: Substituting metaphors for words and phrases

Wisps of cotton form endless patterns.
(Leslie Parrott, *The First Drop of Rain*)

But most miraculously did we escape, how we can scarcely say, the swell passed under, and we all but capsized, as we slid from the back of the savage roaring beast.
(*Maryland Colonization Journal*)

In the evening, a brilliant display of fireworks suddenly illuminated the heavens. It was a <u>veritable kaleidoscope, a true stage set for an opera</u>.
    (Gustave Flaubert, *Madame Bovary*)

I was trying to fight down the fear that <u>prowled in my empty belly, and leapt up with sharp claws at my heart in its cage of ribs</u>.
    (Gregory David Roberts, *Shantaram*)

There is <u>ripple after ripple of sunlight</u> in her hair.
    (Oscar Wilde, *An Ideal Husband*)

I am <u>a ship without a rudder in a night without a star</u>.
    (Oscar Wilde, *An Ideal Husband*)

Exercise, Part 2: Substituting similes for adverbs

[Alessandro] would have drawn near to her <u>as quickly as iron to the magnet</u>.
    (Helen Hunt Jackson, *Ramona*)

Down he sat / <u>A little slowly, as a man in doubt</u>.
    (Elizabeth Barrett Browning, "Aurora Leigh")

The horse darted away <u>like a telegram</u>.
    (Mark Twain, *Roughing It*)

At first, Mowgli would cling <u>like the sloth</u>, but afterward he would fling himself through the branches <u>almost as boldly as the gray ape</u>.
    (Rudyard Kipling, "Mowgli's Brothers")

In vain he kick'd, and swore, and writhed, and bled, / And howl'd for help <u>as wolves do for a meal</u>.
    (Lord Byron, "Don Juan")

Sleep she <u>as sound as careless infancy</u>.
    (Shakespeare, *Merry Wives of Windsor*)

Keimer stared <u>like a pig poisoned</u>.
    (Benjamin Franklin's *Autobiography*)

STEP THREE: **Substituting descriptive phrases for single words**

Student instructions for Step Three:

You can also substitute a descriptive phrase for a single word. Back in Week 13, you learned that Erasmus substituted phrases for the noun "letter," like this:

S	V	DO
letter	pleased	me

S	V	DO
words from your pen	brought	joy

S	V	DO
pages I received from you	sent	light

S	V	IO	DO
pearls of wisdom	gave	me	pleasure

The very last phrase, "pearls of wisdom," is a metaphor. But the other two phrases substituted for "letter" are not. They are simply descriptions of what a letter is.

In today's last exercise, you'll think up descriptive phrases to substitute for words or simple phrases. Here's an example for you to look at, from Ernest Hemingway's classic story *The Old Man and the Sea:*

Nothing showed on the surface of the water but <u>a sea creature</u>.

→ Nothing showed on the surface of the water but <u>the purple, formalized, irides-cent, gelatinous bladder of a Portuguese man-of-war.</u>

The second sentence is what Hemingway actually wrote. Instead of the simple phrase "sea creature," he wrote a specific, colorful description of the sea creature itself.

In the sentences below, substitute a descriptive phrase for the underlined words. You can use a metaphor if you think of a good one, but think carefully about what the underlined words *represent.* Is there another way to describe or define it?

This will be a challenging assignment. Do your best, and if you draw a total blank, ask your instructor.

HOW TO HELP THE STUDENT WITH STEP THREE

The bolded sentences are those originally written by the authors.

If the student has trouble, use the suggested prompts. As a last resort, show her the answer and then ask her to try to think of another phrase to substitute.

Beneath all that silence and placidity <u>the great whale</u> was writhing and wretching in agony!
Beneath all that silence and placidity <u>the utmost monster of the seas</u> was writhing and wrenching in agony!
(Herman Melville, *Moby Dick*)
Prompts: "Where does a whale live? What is a word for a frightening creature?"

In the fourth seat at my left sat <u>Abraham Lincoln</u>.

In the fourth seat at my left sat <u>a new member from Illinois, the only Whig from that</u>
<u>State, a tall, awkward, genial, good fellow, the future President of the United States,</u>
Abraham Lincoln.

    (William Eleroy Curtis, *The True Abraham Lincoln*)

Prompts: "What was Abraham Lincoln's title? What did he look like?"

<u>A cat</u> would then roll about on the ground, emitting large wads of hair and horrible screams
and air-rending hisses.

<u>A large, writhing ball of fur</u> would then roll about on the ground, emitting large wads
of hair and horrible screams and air-rending hisses.

    (William Jordan, *A Cat Named Darwin*)

Prompt: "What does a cat look like when it's rolling around on the ground?"

"The Home Secretary," he said between gasps as he drank the <u>coffee</u>, "is indiscreet in his correspondence and is generally a most careless man."

"The Home Secretary," he said between gasps as he drank the <u>scalding hot liquid</u>, "is
indiscreet in his correspondence and is generally a most careless man."

    (Edgar Wallace, *The Four Just Men*)

Prompts: "What temperature is coffee? And it isn't a solid; it is a . . ."

Men, women, and children were <u>fishermen</u>.

Men, women, and children were <u>farmers of the sea</u>.

    (Norman G. Owen, *The Emergence of Modern Southeast Asia: A New History*)

Prompts: "Where did fishermen work? What kind of work did they do there?

Day Four: Varying by Equivalence

 Focus: Turning positives into negatives and vice
versa

STEP ONE: Understand varying by equivalence (Student Responsibility)

    Have you ever asked someone if she was sad, and received the reply: "Well, I'm not
happy"? This is a literary technique, called *varying by equivalence*.

    Imagine that you're cooking and need to add three eggs to a recipe. You've got four in a
carton, so subtract one egg, put it back in the fridge, and use the rest. How many eggs will you
end up using?

four, minus one

But imagine now that you've only got two eggs. To make your brownies, you'll need to run next door and borrow an egg from a friend. How many eggs will you put into the batter?

two, plus one

"Four minus one" and "two plus one" are *equivalent*. Both of them come out to the same number: three. But they have slightly different shades of meaning. "Four minus one" means that you've got a leftover egg to eat for breakfast. "Two plus one" means that you've got to give an egg back to your friend as soon as you go shopping.

When you write, you can use *equivalent expressions* to say the same thing in two different ways. Study the chart below:

Positive Statements	Negative Statements
He was in the first place	He was not among the last
There is much deceit	There is no lack of deceit
Her hearing is excellent	She is not at all deaf
I approve	I am unable to disapprove

Each positive statement can be phrased as a negative—and vice versa. This is called *varying by equivalence.*

Varying by equivalence can make your writing more colorful, exact, and even funny. In the play *Hamlet*, Shakespeare writes, "They have a plentiful lack of wit." He means, "They are not witty." By rephrasing this negative expression into a positive one, he delivers a much more effective (and entertaining) insult.

Stating something first positively and then negatively—or vice versa—is a strategy often used by speechwriters. Does this sound familiar?

"Ask not what your country can do for you—ask what you can do for your country."

That comes from a speech that President John F. Kennedy made in January of 1961. First, he told us what *not* to ask. Then, he told us *what* to ask. The negative came first; then, the positive.

One caution: Be careful when you vary by equivalence that you do not change the meaning of the sentence. For example, if you are given the positive phrase "first place," you can rewrite it as "not among the last"—after all, the first-place winner is certainly not among the last to cross the finish line. But if you are given the negative statement "He was not among the last," you can't just rewrite it as "He was in the first place." "Not among the last" might mean second, or third, or fourth. You'd need some more information before writing "He was among the winners!"

STEP TWO: **Practice changing positives into negatives and vice versa**

Student instructions for Step Two:

Fill in the chart below, changing positives into negatives and vice versa. You don't have to get too creative (although you can if you want)—this is just to get you comfortable with the idea.

HOW TO HELP THE STUDENT WITH STEP TWO

Although there is certainly room for variation, the student's answers might resemble those below. If necessary, use the answers to prompt the student.

You may need to point out that "positive" doesn't mean "good"—it means that the positive statement doesn't have a negation (not, no, never) in it.

Positive:	Negative:
The weather was cold	The weather was not the least bit warm
He was stupid	He was not intelligent
I hope you are well	I do not wish horrible things upon you
She paid attention to him	She didn't completely ignore him
They sang horribly	They didn't sing well
The ship was sinking	The ship was no longer floating
I only found dirty socks	I could not find even one clean sock
The pigeons were everywhere	There was no scarcity of pigeons

STEP THREE: Add to the Sentence Variety chart (Student Responsibility)

Add the following principle and illustration to the Sentence Variety chart.

positive statement ⟵⟶ negative statement   Her eyesight is excellent.
She is not at all shortsighted.

I am never unhappy.
I am always filled with joy.

STEP FOUR: Use the skill of varying by equivalence

Student instructions for Step Four:

The sentences below are adapted from Jane Austen's classic novel *Pride and Prejudice*. On your own paper, rewrite each underlined word, phrase, or statement so that positives become negatives and negatives become positives—just as Jane Austen first wrote them.

When you are finished, ask your instructor to show you Austen's original sentences. How close were you?

HOW TO HELP THE STUDENT WITH STEP FOUR

Austen's original sentences are in bold type below.

This assignment is meant to be challenging. However, do not allow the student to become unnecessarily frustrated; if, after a good honest try, she can't figure out how to rewrite one or more of the sentences, show her the originals and ask her to explain the differences between Austen's statements and the restatements in her workbook.

Bingley was <u>not contented</u>; his sisters declared that they were <u>not merry</u>.
Bingley was quite uncomfortable; his sisters declared that they were miserable.

His apparent partiality <u>was no longer present</u>, his attentions <u>did not continue</u>, he was <u>Elizabeth's admirer no more</u>.
His apparent partiality had subsided, his attentions were over, he was the admirer of someone else.

It was <u>seldom</u> that she could turn her eyes on Mr. Darcy himself.
It was not often that she could turn her eyes on Mr. Darcy himself.

<u>At once</u> her mother gave her to understand that the probability of their marriage was <u>not at all unpleasant</u> to her.
It was not long before her mother gave her to understand that the probability of their marriage was exceedingly agreeable to her.

In spite of her <u>lack of liking</u>, she <u>was completely aware of</u> the compliment of such a man's affection.
In spite of her deeply-rooted dislike, she could not be insensible to the compliment of such a man's affection.

My <u>not negative</u> opinion, once lost, is lost <u>for not a brief period of time</u>.
My good opinion once lost is lost for ever.

She was a <u>never wavering</u> talker.
She was a most determined talker.

Conceal the <u>less than mirthful</u> truth as long as it is possible.
Conceal the unhappy truth as long as it is possible.

WEEK 23: OUTLINING AND REWRITING, PART I

Over the next two weeks, the student will refresh her outlining skills. She'll also be given a new assignment. After outlining and discussing an essay, she'll try her hand at rewriting the essay—using her outline, but not looking at the original.

Why?

Rewriting a classic essay is yet another way to build up the student's writing. When the American statesman Benjamin Franklin was a young man, he realized that his writing "fell far short in elegance of expression, in method, and in perspicuity" (by which he meant "clearness of expression"). In his *Autobiography,* Franklin tells us what he did to improve his writing skills. The *Spectator* was a popular newspaper, containing essays and opinion pieces, published in Britain beginning in 1711.

> About this time I met with an odd volume of the *Spectator.* It was the third. I had never before seen any of them. I bought it, read it over and over, and was much delighted with it. I thought the writing excellent, and wished, if possible, to imitate it. With this view I took some of the papers, and making short hints of the sentiment in each sentence, laid them by a few days, and then, without looking at the book, tried to complete the papers again, by expressing each hinted sentiment at length, and as fully as it had been expressed before, in any suitable words that should come to hand. Then I compared my *Spectator* with the original, discovered some of my faults, and corrected them . . . By comparing my work afterwards with the original, I discovered many faults and amended them; but I sometimes had the pleasure of fancying that, in certain particulars of small import, I had been lucky enough to improve the method or the language, and this encouraged me to think I might possibly in time come to be a tolerable English writer, of which I was extremely ambitious.
>
> —*The Autobiography of Benjamin Franklin,* Part I,
> "Parentage and Boyhood"

Day One: Read

Focus: Reading and understanding a comparison-contrast essay

STEP ONE: **Read (Student Responsibility)**

Read through the following excerpt from the essay "A Brother of St. Francis," by the Irish writer Grace Rhys. Rhys was born in 1865 and wrote novels, short stories, and essays. This essay was originally published as part of the collection of essays *About Many Things* (London: Methuen, 1920).

The title refers to St. Francis of Assisi, the Italian monk who founded the Franciscan Order. St. Francis is traditionally identified with love for animals and the care of nature.

Some of Rhys's vocabulary and references may be challenging for you. On this first reading, don't worry if you don't understand some of the words or sentences. Just read slowly and carefully all the way through to the end.

STEP TWO: **Discuss**

Student instructions for Step Two:

> Go back through the essay now and underline any vocabulary words, sentences, or references that you didn't understand on your first reading. When you're finished, discuss the essay with your instructor.

HOW TO HELP THE STUDENT WITH STEP TWO

Although the theme of the essay is easy to understand, the style is intentionally challenging. A copy of the essay is below, with difficult vocabulary and obscure references underlined. Use the information following the essay to discuss these with the student.

The student has been instructed to underline anything she doesn't understand. If she has not underlined one or more of the words/phrases below, you might want to ask her what they mean anyway—just to be sure that she is following the essay's argument.

A Brother of St. Francis

by Grace Rhys

When talking to a wise friend a while ago I told her of the feeling of horror which had invaded me when watching a hippopotamus.

"Indeed," said she, "you do not need to go to the hippopotamus for a sensation. Look at a pig! There is something <u>dire</u> in the face of a pig. To think the same power should have created it that created a star!"

Those who love beauty and peace are often tempted to <u>scamp their thinking</u>, to avoid the <u>elemental terrors</u> that bring night into the mind. Yet if the fearful things of life are there, why not pluck up heart and look at them? Better have <u>no Bluebeard's chamber</u> in the mind. Better go boldly in and see what hangs by the wall. <u>So salt, so medicinal is Truth, that even the bitterest draught may be made wholesome to the gentlest soul.</u> So I would recommend anyone who can bear to think to leave the flower garden and go down and spend an hour by the pigstye.

There lies our friend in the sun upon his straw, blinking his clever little eye. Half friendly is his look. (He does not know that I—Heaven forgive me!—sometimes have bacon for breakfast!) Plainly, with that gashed mouth, those dreadful cheeks, and that sprawl of his, he belongs to an older world; that older world <u>when first the mud and slime rose and moved, and, roaring, found a voice</u>; aye, and no doubt enjoyed life, and in harsh and fearful sounds praised the Creator at the sunrising.

To prove the origin of the pig, let him out, and he will celebrate it by making straight for the nearest mud and diving into it. So strange is his aspect, so unreal to me, that it is almost as if the sunshine falling upon him might dissolve him, <u>and resolve him</u> into his <u>original element</u>. But no; there he is, perfectly real; as real as the good Christians and philosophers who will eventually eat him. While he lies there let me reflect in all charity on the disagreeable things I have heard about him.

He is dirty, people say. Nay, is he as dirty (or, at least, as complicated in his dirt) as his brother man can be? Let those who know the dens of London give the answer. Leave the pig to himself, and he is not so bad. He knows his mother mud is cleansing; he rolls partly because he loves her and partly because he wishes to be clean.

He is greedy? In my mind's eye there rises the picture of <u>human gormandisers</u>, fat-necked, with half-buried eyes and toddling step. How long since <u>the giant Gluttony was slain</u>? or does he still keep his <u>monstrous table d'hote</u>?

The pig pushes his brother from the trough? Why, that is a commonplace of our life. There is a whole school of so-called philosophers and <u>political economists</u> busied in <u>elevating the pig's shove into a social and political necessity</u>.

He screams horribly if you touch him or his share of <u>victuals</u>? I have heard a polite gathering of the best people turn senseless and rave at a mild suggestion of <u>Christian Socialism</u>. He is bitter-tempered? God knows, so are we. He has <u>carnal desires</u>? The worst sinner is man. He will fight? Look

to the underside of war. He is cruel? Well, boys do queer things sometimes. For the rest, read the blacker pages of history; not as they are <u>served up for the schoolroom by private national vanity</u>, but after the facts.

If a cow or a sheep is sick or wounded and the pig can get at it, he will worry it to death? <u>So does tyranny with subject peoples.</u>

He loves to lie in the sun among his brothers, idle and at his ease? Aye, but suppose this one <u>called himself a lord pig</u> and lay in the sun with a necklace of gold about his throat and jewels in his ears, having found means to drive his brethren (merry little pigs and all) out of the sun for his own benefit, what should we say of him then?

No; he has none of our cold cunning. He is all simplicity. I am told it is possible to love him. I know a kindly Frenchwoman who takes her pig for an airing on the sands of <u>Saint-Michel-en-Grève</u> every summer afternoon. Knitting, she walks along, and calls gaily and endearingly to the delighted creature; he follows at a word, gambolling with flapping ears over the ribs of sand, pasturing on shrimps and seaweed while he enjoys the salt air. Clearly, then, the pig is our good little brother, and we have no right to be disgusted at him. Clearly our own feet are planted in the clay.

<u>scamp their thinking</u>: "to scamp" means to do something carelessly or in a hurry, not thoroughly, so this means "avoiding thinking things through carefully"

<u>elemental terrors</u>: primitive, basic, irrational fears

<u>no Bluebeard's chamber in the mind</u>: In the well-known fairy tale "Bluebeard," a French nobleman marries wife after wife, kills each one, and keeps the bodies in a small chamber in his castle. He gives the key to his most recent wife and tells her not to open the door—which, of course, she does, and finds out the very worst about her new husband. So a "Bluebeard's chamber" is a subject that you don't really want to think about or investigate because of what might happen. A more familiar metaphor might be "can of worms."

<u>So salt, so medicinal is Truth, that even the bitterest draught may be made wholesome to the gentlest soul</u>: "Salt" and "medicinal" are both words describing something that's sharp or offensive at first to the taste, but actually improves whatever it is applied to—so, if you are willing to look at a difficult truth directly, it will actually improve your life, even if you are weak or "gentle."

when first the mud and slime rose and moved, and, roaring, found a voice: Grace Rhys is referring here to the relatively new theory of evolution. Notice that she combines this with a reference to the Genesis account of the Creator. Her point is that the pig, either way, is related to
the earth.

and resolve him into his original element: Return him back to being mud or slime again instead
of a living creature

human gormandisers: Someone who eats too much, too fast

the giant Gluttony was slain: This is a reference to Jack the Giant Killer, an English folk tale
in which a young boy delivers the medieval countryside from a number of different horrible
giants. Rhys means: We may think that we have long ago conquered our greed, but it is still
alive and well in modern times.

monstrous table d'hote: A table d'hote is when a hotel has just a few fixed menus, all at the
same price—you can't order just one item. Instead, you have to have *all* of the courses (and eat
them all).

political economists: Scholars who study how laws and governments affect buying, selling, and
wealth

elevating the pig's shove into a social and political necessity: These scholars are saying that
greed, oppressing the poor in order to get more, and accumulating wealth at the expense of
others is an inevitable part of any nation's existence—rather than something to be repented of
and changed.

victuals: food

Christian Socialism: A political movement in which socialism (the sharing out of all wealth
evenly) is based on the teachings of Jesus. Rhys is saying that "the best people turn senseless
and rave" at a mention of it because they are greedy and desperate to keep control of their own
wealth, like a pig is desperate to keep control of his food. Christian Socialism was a major religious movement in nineteenth-century Britain.

carnal desires: bodily appetites

served up for the schoolroom by private national vanity: Rhys is referring to popular British
children's histories that "whitewash" British history by leaving out all of the flaws and faults of
the British empire.

So does tyranny with subject peoples: Unjust governments oppress the sick, powerless, and poor who are subject to them

called himself a lord pig: Rhys is comparing the pig to dictators who satisfy all their own longings for luxury at the expense of their people.

Saint-Michel-en-Grève: A seaside town in Brittany, on the northwest French coast

STEP THREE: **Reread (Student Responsibility)**

Now that you have discussed the essay, go back through and read it from beginning to end a second time, just as carefully.

Day Two: Outlining

 Focus: Creating a two-level outline

STEP ONE: **Summarize**

Student instructions for Step One:

> Before you begin outlining the paragraphs of the essay, make sure that you understand its overall form and meaning.
> In order to do this, you'll need to answer three questions:
> 1) What technique does Grace Rhys use in the essay?
> 2) What is she telling us about pigs?
> 3) What is she telling us about ourselves?
> If you're able to answer, write one sentence answering each question on your own paper.
> If not, ask your instructor for help.

HOW TO HELP THE STUDENT WITH STEP ONE

> The student's answer should resemble the following.

In "A Brother of St. Francis," Grace Rhys uses comparison and contrast. She tells us not to despise pigs, because people and pigs behave very much alike. She also tells us that we have to rise above animal behavior.

If she has difficulty answering the questions, use the following additional questions to help her come up with her sentences. The answer to the third question is implied in the essay, not actually stated outright in this excerpt, so the student may have particular trouble with 3.

1) What do we call it when someone points out the similarities and differences between two things?
2) Should we despise pigs or not? Why?
3) Does Grace Rhys think that it is OK for humans to behave like pigs? What is she telling us to rise above?

STEP TWO: **Two-level outline**

Student instructions for Step Two:

> Now, write out a two-level outline of the essay. Make use of the helps in the copy below. The paragraphs are divided into groups, separated by the sign ◉ ; assign a Roman numeral to each group.
>
> If you need more assistance, ask your instructor how many subpoints belong to each Roman numeral.
>
> If you *still* need help, tell your instructor.

HOW TO HELP THE STUDENT WITH STEP TWO

The student's outline should resemble the following.

I. Introduction
    A. Anecdote
    B. Command to the reader
II. The pig
    A. Appearance
    B. Origin OR Mud
III. Comparison of pig and man
    A. Dirt
    B. Greedy
    C. Pushy
    D. Screams and fights
    E. Worries the wounded
    F. Lazy OR Lies around while others work
IV. Conclusion
    A. Conclusion by personal reaction OR The pig
    B. Command OR Ourselves

If necessary, tell the student how many subpoints belong to each main point; this will help her begin to figure out the structure of the essay.

If the student needs additional help, use the questions and directions below.

I. These three paragraphs are the first part of the essay—the first thing the reader sees. You've practiced writing the first part of a composition. When you learned how to do that, back in Week 6, what was it called?

> **A.** The first two paragraphs are an example of a type of introduction that you have studied and practiced. Look at your introduction reference page. Which introduction does this most closely resemble?

> **B.** After beginning with an anecdote, the author addresses the reader directly. What does she want the reader to do? What could we call this kind of communication? It isn't a statement or a question; it is a . . .

II. The next two paragraphs are all about one thing. What is it?

> **A.** What aspect of the pig does the first paragraph describe?

> **B.** What part of the pig's experience does the second paragraph describe?

III. The next six paragraphs all do exactly the same thing. What does each one do?

> **A.** What characterizes both the pig and the dens of London?

> **B.** What character quality does the pig and the gormandizer share?

> **C.** What piggish behavior is also spoken of by the philosophers and political economists?

> **D.** What behaviors do pigs and people share?

> **E.** What do both pigs and tyrants do?

> **F.** What do both pigs and dictators do?

IV. The author began with an introduction. What does she end with? (You learned about this in Week 6 also.)

> **A.** What type of conclusion is the first part of the paragraph?

> **B.** How are the last two sentences different from the story? What sort of statement is the author directing at the reader? [NOTE TO INSTRUCTOR: This is actually a variation on the Conclusion by Question—Rhys is telling the reader *how* to react to the information.]

Day Three: Rewriting

 Focus: Rewriting a classic essay from an outline

Today, the student will use the outline created in Day Two to rewrite Grace Rhys's essay in her own words.

Since this is the first time the student has tried to rewrite someone else's writing, give all necessary help—as noted below.

STEP ONE: **Reread (Student Responsibility)**

Read "A Brother of St. Francis" again, carefully, from beginning to end.

STEP TWO: **Understand the model (Student Responsibility)**

NOTE TO INSTRUCTOR: Although this step is the student's responsibility, you will need to make sure that she has read the text slowly and carefully.

Before you start writing, take another look at the structure of "A Brother of St. Francis." A sample outline of the passage is on the left; a description of the elements of the essay is on the right. Read through both of them carefully.

I.	Introduction	Two-part introduction
	A. Anecdote	Personal anecdote
	B. Command to the reader	Direct statement to reader
II.	The pig	Description of the main subject
	A. Appearance	Major aspect
	B. Mud	Second major aspect
III.	Comparison of pig and man	Comparison of main subject and another subject
	A. Dirty	Six aspects compared
	B. Greedy	
	C. Pushy	
	D. Screams and fights	
	E. Worries the wounded	
	F. Lies around while others work	
IV.	Conclusion	Two-part conclusion
	A.The pig	Conclusion by personal reaction
	B. Ourselves	(Final statement)

Let's look at each one of these elements in turn.

First, notice that Rhys's introduction and conclusion have the same structure. Each one starts with a story (her conversation with her friend in the introduction, a story *about* another friend in the conclusion) and then ends with a direct statement to the reader. This is another version of the Introduction by Anecdote; at the end of her story, Rhys exhorts the reader to think carefully, to consider the pig without fear.

Second, Rhys goes on to introduce her main subject, the *thing* to which she will compare another *thing*: the pig. She introduces the pig by describing in detail two major aspects of the pig: its appearance, and its habits. (Those might sound familiar to you from your biographical sketch *topos*.)

Third, Rhys compares six details about a pig's behavior with details about the same behavior in humans. This is the main part of the essay—the comparison and contrast. (There is more comparison than contrast—she finds pigs and people to be very similar!)

Finally, Rhys writes a conclusion which is very effective because it has different content, but the same structure as the introduction. She uses the form of a Conclusion by Personal Reaction by first telling a story that she's heard, and then explaining to the reader what she's learned by taking her own advice and considering the pig—that we too have "feet of clay" (meaning that we too are tempted to behave like animals).

STEP THREE: **Rewrite**

Student instructions for Step Three:

> Now that you've got a little more understanding about the structure of Grace Rhys's essay, use your outline to write your own version of her piece without glancing back at it even once.
>
> This is not an exercise in memorization! You are not supposed to reproduce her words exactly. Remember, Franklin said that his effort was to express the ideas in the original piece "as fully as it had been expressed before, in any suitable words that should come to hand." You can and should use your own words. I'm also going to give you a break: your essay doesn't need to be "as fully" expressed as the original. It can be shorter. Use these guidelines for each section.

Section	Rhys's word count	Your word count
I.	172 words	At least 70 words
II.	183 words	At least 70 words
III.	342 words	At least 125 words
IV.	110 words	At least 50 words

> Just to help you out, here's my stab at rewriting the introductory anecdote without looking back:

> Not long ago, I was talking to a friend about my fear of hippopotamuses. She said, "Forget about the hippopotamus. Look how terrifying pigs are!" She was right. I didn't want to think carefully about a pig.

> Compare this with the original opening paragraphs.

> When talking to a wise friend a while ago I told her of the feeling of horror which had invaded me when watching a hippopotamus.
>
> "Indeed," said she, "you do not need to go to the hippopotamus for a sensation. Look at a pig! There is something dire in the face of a pig. To think the same power should have created it that created a star!"

> As you can see, I used my own words, and left out the whole observation that stars and pigs were created by the same power. But I retell the same conversation that Grace Rhys does.
>
> Since you've never tried to do this before, it may seem difficult and unnatural. If you have no idea at all what to write, ask your instructor for help.

HOW TO HELP THE STUDENT WITH STEP THREE

This step has two purposes: 1) to give the student a chance to practice a sophisticated type of comparison and contrast without also forcing her to come up with and organize her own topic, and 2) to stretch the student's use of illustration, vocabulary, and theme just a little bit past the comfortable point. Neither purpose requires the student to have total recall of the original essay. If necessary, continually reassure the student that she can invent her own sentences and even examples and anecdotes, if she can't remember the original.

This exercise will feel unnatural and difficult to some students. Since it is the first attempt at rewriting, do your best to keep the student from becoming frustrated. You may give the student three levels of assistance on this challenge.

First, if the student has drawn a total blank and seems unable to write, allow her to reread a single section of the original essay. Then, while it is fresh in her mind, ask her to rewrite just that section without looking at the original.

Second, allow the student to reread a single section of the original essay. Then, ask her to paraphrase each sentence in her own words, using her own vocabulary, **while** looking at the original. Then, ask her to rewrite just that section **without** looking at the original.

Third, allow the student to reread a single section of the original essay. Then, allow her to read the same section of my paraphrase below.

The student's composition might resemble the following:

[I]   Not long ago, I was talking to a friend about my fear of hippopotamuses. She said, "Forget about the hippopotamus. Look how terrifying pigs are!" She was right. I didn't want to think carefully about a pig.

It is easy for us to avoid thinking about unpleasant subjects such as pigs. The idea brings up all sorts of things we don't want to contemplate, like a Bluebeard's chamber in our minds. But it can do us a great deal of good to consider truth carefully, even if truth is unpleasant to us. It can act like medicine to even the gentlest soul.

[II]   Look carefully at a pig. He lies on his straw in the sunshine, looking friendly. But he looks as though he came right out of the mud, as though he belongs to a much older time. He has jowly, saggy cheeks, a strange gashed mouth, and a tiny blinking eye. If you let him out, he goes straight back to the mud and wallows in it. That just shows that he came out of the dirt.

[III]   Pigs may seem dirty, and they may enjoy wallowing in the mud. But the slums of London are just as dirty as a pigstye.

Pigs are greedy about their food, but lovers of gourmet food are just as bad. They eat too much food, far too quickly.

Pigs push other pigs away from their food troughs. But people push the weak and poor away in order to grab wealth for themselves, too.

If you touch a pig's food, he screams horribly at you; but people can scream at each other during parties, if someone suggests that they give up their goods. Pigs fight with each other, but the history of the world is the history of wars, despite the attempt of some children's histories to ignore human wars.

Pigs attack the wounded, but tyrants also attack those among their subjects who are at a disadvantage.

Pigs lie lazily in the sun, but dictators often spend their days doing nothing but lazing around, while their subjects do all the work.

[IV]   Pigs can be wonderful pets. I heard of a woman who takes her pig for a walk, just like a dog, and he runs along the beach enjoying the surf and keeping her company. We should not be disgusted by pigs. They are our little brothers, and we are very much like them.

You can evaluate the student's essay using the following rubric:

Week 23 Rubric

Organization:

1 The composition should have four sections.
2 The first section should be at least 70 words long and contain both an anecdote and a command or statement.
3 The second section should be at least 70 words long and should describe the pig's appearance and also mention the mud he wallows in.
4 The third section should contain six comparisons of pigs and human beings. It should be at least 125 words long. The comparisons can be in separate paragraphs or grouped together.
5 The last section should be at least 50 words long. It should contain both a story and a statement about the theme of the essay.

Mechanics:

1 Each sentence should make sense on its own when read aloud.
2 There should be no sentence fragments or run-on sentences.
3 All words should be spelled correctly.
4 The first line of each paragraph should be properly indented.
5 Verb tense should be consistent throughout.

STEP FOUR: Compare

Student instructions for Step Four:

> Read your essay out loud.
> Then, read the original essay out loud.
> You don't have to make any huge conclusions about how they compare. Just listen to how each essay sounds.

HOW TO HELP THE STUDENT WITH STEP FOUR

There is no need to draw the student into a discussion about differences. The purpose at this point is simply to begin to train her ear to hear the differences in sound between the two compositions. Your task is just to make sure that she reads both compositions *out loud*.

Day Four: Copia Exercise

Sentence Transformation

 Focus: Practicing skills in sentence transformation

STEP ONE: **Review (Student Responsibility)**

Read carefully through your Sentence Variety chart and pay close attention to the examples. You should have nine different types of transformation on the chart.

STEP TWO: **Transform**

Student instructions for Step Two:

Pick five sentences from your rewrite of "A Brother of St. Francis." Using five of the techniques on the Sentence Variety chart, transform each sentence. Read the original sentences and the transformed sentences out loud to your instructor. Decide together which sentences sound best.

Insert the best sentences back into your composition. Does this improve the sound of your essay?

If you have trouble finding sentences to transform, make use of the following tips as you look through your work.

To transform descriptive adjectives into nouns, look for adjectives that come right before the nouns they modify. Or, look for prepositional phrases beginning with "of" and see if they can be turned into descriptive adjectives.

To transform active verbs into passive, look for sentences with action verbs and direct objects.

Look for sentences with indirect objects to transform into objects of a preposition.

To transform a participle into an infinitive, look for an -ing word following an action verb.

To transform a main verb into an infinitive, pick a strong verb and see whether you are able to add one of the following verbs to it:

VERBS THAT ARE OFTEN FOLLOWED BY INFINITIVES

agree	aim	appear	arrange	ask	attempt
beg	begin	care	choose	consent	continue
dare	decide	deserve	dislike	expect	fail
forget	get	hesitate	hope	hurry	intend
leap	like	love	ought	plan	prefer
prepare	proceed	promise	refuse	remember	start
strive	try	use	wait	want	wish

To intensify an adjective, look for descriptive adjectives that either come before a noun or follow a linking verb.

To change a word into a phrase, metaphor, or kenning, look for strong and interesting nouns.

To change a positive statement to a negative statement, look for a strong statement. Then use your thesaurus to find antonyms for the nouns and verbs in the statement.

If you have trouble, ask your instructor for help.

HOW TO HELP THE STUDENT WITH STEP TWO

Answers will obviously vary. Below, you can find examples of my own transformations, done on sentences from the sample composition. The original sentences are in italics, followed by the transformed sentence in bold type.

If you and the student together are unable to locate five good sentences for transformation in the student's composition, you could (as a last resort) assign the student the sentences below.

Even if she does not need the examples below, the student may find it interesting to read them after her own work is finished.

descriptive adjectives ⟷ nouns

Pigs fight with each other, but the history of the world is the history of wars, despite the attempt of some children's histories to ignore human wars.
Pigs fight with each other, but world history is war history, despite the attempt of some histories for children to ignore human wars.

passive verb ⟷ active verb

But people push the weak and poor away in order to grab wealth for themselves, too.
But the weak and poor are pushed away by people who want to grab wealth for themselves, too.

indirect object ⟶ object of the preposition

no appropriate sentence

infinitives ⟷ participles

Pigs may seem dirty, and they may enjoy wallowing in the mud.
Pigs may seem dirty, and they may like to wallow in the mud.

main verb ⟶ infinitive

Pigs push other pigs away from their food troughs.
Pigs love to push other pigs away from their food troughs.

adjective ——————► intensified adjective

Pigs can be wonderful pets.
Pigs can be stupendous pets.

adjective ——————► added adjective

Pigs can be wonderful pets.
Pigs can be wonderful and loyal pets.

word ——————► phrase describing what the word is or does
    metaphor
    kenning

We should not be disgusted by pigs.
We should not be disgusted by the creature that wallows in the dirt.
We should not be disgusted by the muddy pink pillows with legs.
We should not be disgusted by pork-bearers.

positive statement ◄——————► negative statement

We should not be disgusted by pigs.
We should be delighted by pigs.

Look carefully at a pig.
Do not avoid gazing upon pigs!

Week 24: Outlining and Rewriting, Part II

Day One: Read

 Focus: Reading and understanding an essay of definition

STEP ONE: **Read (Student Responsibility)**

Read through the following slightly condensed essay "A Few Words on Christmas," by Charles Lamb. Lamb was an English writer who lived 1775–1834 (which means that when he died, Charles Dickens was twenty-two years old). He is best known for *Tales from Shakespeare,* a children's book retelling the stories of Shakespeare's plays. Lamb co-wrote *Tales from Shakespeare* with his younger sister, Mary.

This essay was first published in *The London Magazine* in 1822.

Like last week's essay, this essay might contain some challenging vocabulary and unfamiliar references. Don't worry if you don't understand every sentence; just read slowly and carefully through to the end.

STEP TWO: **Discuss**

Student instructions for Step Two:

Go back through the essay now and underline any vocabulary words, sentences, or references that you didn't understand on your first reading. When you're finished, discuss the essay with your instructor.

HOW TO HELP THE STUDENT WITH STEP TWO

Like last week's essay, this one is intentionally challenging in its language and references (although the structure is straightforward).

A copy of the essay is below, with difficult vocabulary and obscure references underlined. Use the information following the essay to discuss these with the student.

The student has been instructed to underline anything she doesn't understand. If she has not underlined one or more of the words/phrases below, you might want to ask her what they mean anyway—just to be sure that she is following the essay's argument.

A Few Words on Christmas

by Charles Lamb

Close the shutters, and draw the curtains together, and pile fresh wood upon the hearth! Let us have, for once, an <u>innocent *auto de fé*</u>. Let the <u>hoarded corks</u> be brought forth, and branches of <u>crackling laurel</u>. Place the wine and fruit and the hot chestnuts upon the table. And now, good folks and children, bring your chairs round to the blazing fire. Put some of those rosy apples upon your plates. We'll drink one glass of bright sherry "to our absent friends and readers," and then let us talk a little about Christmas.

And what is Christmas?

Why, it is the happiest time of the year. It is the season of mirth and cold weather. It is the time when Christmas-boxes and jokes are given; when mistletoe, and red-berried laurel, and soups, and sliding, and school-boys, prevail; when the country is illuminated by fires and bright faces; and the town is radiant with laughing children. Oranges, as rich as the <u>fruit of the Hesperides</u>, shine out in huge golden heaps. Cakes, frosted over (as if to rival the glittering snow) come forth by thousands from their ovens: and on every stall at every corner of every street are the roasted apples. . . .

And *this* night is Christmas Eve. Formerly it was a serious and holy vigil. Our <u>forefathers observed it strictly till a certain hour</u>, and then <u>requited their own forbearance</u> with cups of ale and Christmas candles, with placing the *yule log* on the fire, and <u>roaring themselves thirsty</u> till morning. Time has altered this. We are neither so good as our forefathers were—nor so bad. <u>We go to bed sober; but we have forgotten their old devotions</u>. Our conduct looks like a sort of compromise; so that we are not worse than our ancestors, we are satisfied not to be better: but let that pass. . . .

One mark and sign of Christmas is the *music*; <u>rude enough</u>, indeed, but generally gay, and speaking eloquently of the season. Music, at festival times, is common to most countries. In Spain, the serenader twangs his guitar; in Italy, the musician <u>allures</u> rich notes <u>from his Cremona</u>; in Scotland, the bagpipe drones out its miserable noise; in Germany, there is the horn, and the pipe <u>in Arcady</u>. We too, in our turn, have our <u>Christmas "*Waits*,"</u> who <u>witch</u> us at early morning, before cock-crow, with strains and welcomings which belong to night. They wake us so gently that the music seems to have commenced in our dreams, and we listen to it till we sleep again. Besides this, we have our songs, from the young and the old, <u>jocose</u> and fit for the time. What old gentleman of sixty has not his stock—his one, or two, or three frolicksome verses. He sings them for the young folks, and is secure of their applause and his own private satisfaction. His wife, indeed, perhaps says "Really, my dear Mr. Williams, you should *now* give over these, <u>&c.</u>"; but he is more resolute from opposition, and gambols through his <u>"Flowery Meads of May," or "Beneath a shady bower,"</u> while the children hang on his thin, trembling, untuneable notes in delighted and delightful amazement . . .

Leaving now our *eve* of Christmas, its jokes, and songs, and warm hearths, we will indulge ourselves in a few words upon CHRISTMAS DAY. It is like a day of victory. Every house and church is as green as spring. The laurel, that never dies—the holly, with its armed leaves and scarlet berries—the mistletoe, under which one sweet ceremonial is (we hope still) performed, are seen. Every brave shrub that has life and verdure seems to come forward to shame the reproaches of men, and to show them that the earth is never dead, never parsimonious . . .

Hunger is no longer an enemy. We feed him, like the ravenous tiger, till he pants and sleeps, or is quiet. Everybody eats at Christmas. The rich feast as usual; but the tradesman leaves his moderate fare for dainties. The apprentice abjures his chop, and plunges at once into the luxuries of joints and puddings. The school-boy is no longer at school. He dreams no more of the coming lesson or the lifted rod; but mountains of jelly rise beside him, and blanc-mange, with its treacherous foundations, threatens to overwhelm his fancy; roods of mince pies spread out their chequered riches before him . . . Even the servant has his "once a year" bottle of port; and the beggar his "alderman in chains."

Oh! merry piping time of Christmas! Never let us permit thee to degenerate into distant courtesies and formal salutations. But let us shake our friends and familiars by the hand, as our fathers and their fathers did. Let them all come around us, and let us count how many the year has added to our circle. Let us enjoy the present, and laugh at the past. Let us tell old stories and invent new ones—innocent always, and ingenious if we can. Let us not meet to abuse the world, but to make it better by our individual example. Let us be patriots, but not men of party. Let us look *of the time*—cheerful and generous, and endeavour to make others as generous and cheerful as ourselves.

an innocent *auto de fé:* The *auto de fé*, or "act of faith," was originally a public ceremony held during the Inquisition during which men and women convicted of heresy would carry out public acts of penance. Sometimes, if the prisoners had been condemned to death, it would end with a burning at the stake. Eventually, *auto de fé* just came to stand for burning at the stake—which is how Lamb uses it. Point out to the student what a strange beginning this is for a Christmas essay!

hoarded corks: Hoarded bottles of wine, sealed with corks. This is an example of *metonymy*, using part of something (the cork in the bottle) to stand for the whole thing (the bottle itself).

crackling laurel: Wreaths made out of the plant bay laurel, used in ancient Greece to represent victory and triumph, were also used in England as traditional Christmas decorations.

fruit of the Hesperides: The Hesperides were nymphs who, in Greek myths, kept a mysterious garden where golden apples grew. The apples gave immortality. (One of them, stolen by the goddess of discord, also helped start the Trojan War, a story that the student can look up online by searching for "Judgment of Paris.")

forefathers observed it strictly till a certain hour: In some ancient Church traditions, a vigil was kept until midnight, when Mass was celebrated and Christmas began.

requited their own forbearance and roaring themselves thirsty: Having observed the Christmas vigil by staying sober until after mass, the "forefathers" then celebrated the arrival of Christmas by getting roaring drunk.

We go to bed sober but we have forgotten their old devotions: Lamb realizes that getting drunk after Mass is not a good thing; it is better that he and his friends "go to bed sober." However, although they have given up this indulgence (which makes him "better" than his forefathers), they have also given up the observance of the vigil and Mass, making Christmas both more sober and more secular.

rude enough: Not "uncivil," but rather unrefined, uncultured, common, rough—songs for the "common man" as opposed to elegant High Church choir performances.

allures: Draws out

from his Cremona: From his violin. The Italian town of Cremona is known for the manufacture of fine stringed instruments; Antonio Stradivari was born and made his Stradivarius violins there.

in Arcady: An area of southern Greece

Christmas "Waits": Town pipers in Britain. Until 1835, many British towns had bands of "waits" who were responsible for providing music for public events. After 1835, they only tended to form around Christmas in order to play carols, and these volunteer bands became known as "Christmas waits."

witch: Bewitch, entrance

jocose: Merry, joking

&c: An old way to write etc. (et cetera)

"Flowery Meads of May," or "Beneath a shady bower": Traditional English folk songs

parsimonious: Miserly, covetous

abjures his chop: Gives up his usual cheap piece of meat (because he's getting a better piece) blanc-mange, with its treacherous foundations: A gelatine dessert that is halfway between a cake and a pudding in consistency

roods: An Old English (and long obsolete) unit of measurement. One rood was about 1/4 of an acre (a lot of mince pies, in other words).

"alderman in chains": A slang term for a turkey garnished with sausage links

patriots but not men of party: Celebrating their country and its traditions, but not promoting any one particular political party

STEP THREE: **Reread (Student Responsibility)**

Now that you have discussed the essay, go back through and read it from beginning to end a second time, just as carefully.

Day Two: Outlining and Analyzing

 Focus: Understanding the structure of the essay

STEP ONE: **Two-level outline**

Student instructions for Step One:

Begin today's work by writing out a two-level outline of the essay.
Use this model:

I.
II.
III.
  A.
  B.
IV.
  A.
  B.
V.

Write your outline on your own paper, or use your word processor. If you are writing on paper, leave plenty of room after each major point and subpoint—you'll be returning to this sheet of paper in the second and third steps of today's work.

See if you can figure out where to divide the essay into major points and subpoints. If you need help, ask your instructor.

When you are finished, check your outline with your instructor.

HOW TO HELP THE STUDENT WITH STEP ONE

The student's two-level outline should resemble the following (note that extra space should have been left after each major point and subpoint, so that the student has room to work on Steps Two and Three):

I. Introduction
II. Definition of Christmas
III. Christmas Eve
    A. Christmas Eve customs
    B. Music
IV. Christmas Day
    A. Decorations OR Visual signs
    B. Food
V. Conclusion

If necessary, show the student the copy of the essay below, with the placement of major points and subpoints marked.

I.

    Close the shutters, and draw the curtains together, and pile fresh wood upon the hearth! Let us have, for once, an innocent *auto de fé*. Let the hoarded corks be brought forth, and branches of crackling laurel. Place the wine and fruit and the hot chestnuts upon the table. And now, good folks and children, bring your chairs round to the blazing fire. Put some of those rosy apples upon your plates. We'll drink one glass of bright sherry "to our absent friends and readers," and then let us talk a little about Christmas.

II.

    And what is Christmas?

    Why, it is the happiest time of the year. It is the season of mirth and cold weather. It is the time when Christmas-boxes and jokes are given; when mistletoe, and red-berried laurel, and soups, and sliding, and school-boys, prevail; when the country is illuminated by fires and bright faces; and the town is radiant with laughing children. Oranges, as rich as the fruit of the Hesperides, shine out in huge golden heaps. Cakes, frosted over (as if to rival the glittering snow) come forth by thousands from their ovens: and on every stall at every corner of every street are the roasted apples. . . .

III.

III.A.   And *this* night is Christmas Eve. Formerly it was a serious and holy vigil. Our fore-fathers observed it strictly till a certain hour, and then requited their own forbearance with cups of ale and Christmas candles, with placing the *yule log* on the fire, and roaring themselves thirsty till morning. Time has altered this. We are neither so good as our forefathers were—nor so bad. We go to bed sober; but we have forgotten their old devotions. Our conduct looks like a sort of compromise; so that we are not worse than our ancestors, we are satisfied not to be better: but let that pass. . . .

III.B.   One mark and sign of Christmas is the *music*; rude enough, indeed, but generally gay, and speaking eloquently of the season. Music, at festival times, is common to most countries. In Spain, the serenader twangs his guitar; in Italy, the musician allures rich notes from his Cremona; in Scotland, the bagpipe drones out its miserable noise; in Germany, there is the horn, and the pipe in Arcady. We too, in our turn, have our Christmas "*Waits*," who witch us at early morning, before cock-crow, with strains and welcomings which belong to night. They wake us so gently that the music seems to have commenced in our dreams, and we listen to it till we sleep again. Besides this, we have our songs, from the young and the old, jocose and fit for the time. What old gentleman of sixty has not his stock—his one, or two, or three frolicsome verses. He sings them for the young folks, and is secure of their applause and his own private satisfaction. His wife, indeed, perhaps says "Really, my dear Mr. Williams, you should *now* give over these, &c."; but he is more resolute from opposition, and gambols through his "Flowery Meads of May," or "Beneath a shady bower," while the children hang on his thin, trembling, untuneable notes in delighted and delightful amazement . . .

IV.

IV.A.   Leaving now our *eve* of Christmas, its jokes, and songs, and warm hearths, we will indulge ourselves in a few words upon CHRISTMAS DAY. It is like a day of victory. Every house and church is as green as spring. The laurel, that never dies—the holly, with its armed leaves and scarlet berries—the mistletoe, under which one sweet ceremonial is (we hope still) performed, are seen. Every brave shrub that has life and verdure seems to come forward to shame the reproaches of men, and to show them that the earth is never dead, never parsimonious. . . .

IV.B   Hunger is no longer an enemy. We feed him, like the ravenous tiger, till he pants and sleeps, or is quiet. Everybody eats at Christmas. The rich feast as usual; but the tradesman leaves his moderate fare for dainties. The apprentice abjures his chop, and plunges at once into the luxuries of joints and puddings. The school-boy is no longer at school. He dreams no more of the coming lesson or the lifted rod; but mountains of jelly rise beside him, and blanc-mange, with its treacherous foundations, threatens to overwhelm his fancy; roods of mince pies spread out their chequered riches before him . . . Even the servant has his "once a year" bottle of port; and the beggar his "alderman in chains."

V.

Oh! merry piping time of Christmas! Never let us permit thee to degenerate into distant courtesies and formal salutations. But let us shake our friends and familiars by the hand, as our fathers and their fathers did. Let them all come around us, and let us count how many the year has added to our circle. Let us enjoy the present, and laugh at the past. Let us tell old stories and invent new ones—innocent always, and ingenious if we can. Let us not meet to abuse the world, but to make it better by our individual example. Let us be patriots, but not men of party. Let us look *of the time*—cheerful and generous, and endeavour to make others as generous and cheerful as ourselves.

If the student still needs help, you may also ask the following prompting questions.

I. What function does this paragraph perform?

II. What does this paragraph define?

III. The next two paragraphs both describe aspects of same day. What day?

    III.A. What sort of rituals does this paragraph describe?

    III.B. What aspect of the Christmas celebration does this paragraph discuss?

IV. What day do the next two paragraphs describe?

    IV.A. What aspect of Christmas Day does Lamb describe here?

    IV.B. What element of the Christmas celebration does this paragraph focus on?

V. What function does this paragraph perform?

STEP TWO: **Three-level outline**

Student instructions for Step Two:

Now go back to the sections of the essay covered by the Roman numerals III and IV on your outline. Each of those major points has subpoints.

Beneath each subpoint, find the correct number of supporting details, as indicated below. Insert them into your outline. Ask for help if necessary; when you are finished, show your outline to your instructor.

III.
    A. (2 supporting details)
    B. (3 supporting details)
IV.
    A. (2 supporting details)
    B. (4 supporting details)

HOW TO HELP THE STUDENT WITH STEP TWO

The student's outline should resemble the following. If necessary, use the model and the explanations that follow to help the student locate the correct supporting details.

III. Christmas Eve
    A. Christmas Eve customs
        1. Formerly, serious and holy vigil OR Our forefathers
        2. Now, sober but no devotions OR Us
    B. Music
        1. In other countries
        2. The waits in England
        3. Our own songs

IV. Christmas Day
    A. Decorations
        1. Houses and churches
        2. The plants used
    B. Food
        1. Rich and tradesmen
        2. Apprentices
        3. School-boy
        4. Servant and beggar

EXPLANATIONS

Note that there is more than one "correct" way to outline any given piece of essay—and the more conversational an essay is, the more likely it is to contain asides and observations that don't fit neatly onto an outline. Outlining is merely a tool to uncover the progression of thought in a piece. Do not allow the student to get too hung up on finding the "right" answers.

The student may find it helpful to look at the model four-level outlines once she has finished her own work.

III.A.

This paragraph contrasts two different types of behavior on Christmas Eve—the serious vigil (and overdrinking) by our forefathers, and "our" (Lamb and his contemporaries) own sober observance with no vigil. Each type of behavior makes up a supporting detail on the outline.

The details *about* each behavior would belong on a four-level outline and might look like this:

A. Christmas Eve customs
1. Formerly, serious and holy vigil
    a. Observed strictly
    b. Then celebrated with ale and yule log
2. Now, sober but no devotions
    a. We are neither as good or as bad
    b. We are satisfied to be neither worse nor better

III.B.

This paragraph divides Christmas music into three clear categories: foreign countries, English "waits," and personal songs. The four-level outline would include the specific countries mentioned, plus the details about the Christmas Waits and the personal songs.

B. Music
1. In other countries
    a. Spanish guitars
    b. Italian violins
    c. German horns
    d. Arcadian pipes
2. The waits in England
    a. They come at early morning
    b. We listen and fall back asleep
3. Our own songs
    a. Sung by young and old
    b. Merry and fit
    c. Each old gentleman has his own

IV.A.

The paragraph about the decorations is divided into two sets of observations; one, about the houses and churches; the second, about the plants used to decorate them.

A. Decorations OR Visual signs
    1. Houses and churches
        a. Green as spring
    2. The plants used
        a. Laurel
        b. Holly
        c. Mistletoe

IV.B.

This passage could conceivably be outlined as:
  B. Food
    1. The rich
    2. Tradesman
    3. Apprentice
    4. School-boy
    5. Servant
    6. Beggar

However, the structure of Lamb's sentences, plus background knowledge about English social classes, suggests that he is thinking of four different types of people: the well-to-do; the young and upwardly mobile (apprentices); children; and the poor. Each class of person indulges in a different way in the food of the season.

STEP THREE: Analysis

Student instructions for Step Three:

You'll finish today's work by looking at the remaining three paragraphs of the essay: the introduction, the definition, and the conclusion. Rather than outlining these paragraphs, you will try to identify the elements of introductions, conclusions, and definitions that they include. Carry out the instructions below.

1. Reread the first paragraph of Charles Lamb's essay. Examine the types of introductions on your Introductions chart. Which type of introduction does Lamb use? Write the name of the type on your outline, following the Roman numeral I.

2. Reread the last paragraph of the essay. Examine the types of conclusions on your Conclusion chart. What type of conclusion is closest to Lamb's? Write the name of the type on your outline, following the Roman numeral V.

3. Turn to the chart that describes Explanation by Definition: Historical Object, Event, Place or People Group. Read through the questions. Then, look carefully at the two paragraphs (the first is only one line long) that belong to Roman numeral II. In your opinion, does Lamb define Christmas by focusing on its properties, its function, or its genus? Write your answer on your outline, following the Roman numeral II.

When you are finished, show your work to your instructor.

HOW TO HELP THE STUDENT WITH STEP THREE

The student's finished outline should resemble the following:

I. Introduction
　　Introduction by Anecdote
II. Definition of Christmas
　　Function
III. Christmas Eve
　　A. Christmas Eve customs
　　　　1. Formerly, serious and holy vigil
　　　　2. Now, sober but no devotions
　　B. Music
　　　　1. In other countries
　　　　2. The waits in England
　　　　3. Our own songs
IV. Christmas Day
　　A. Decorations OR Visual signs
　　　　1. Houses and churches
　　　　2. The plants used
　　B. Food
　　　　1. Rich and tradesmen
　　　　2. Apprentices
　　　　3. School-boy
　　　　4. Servant and beggar
V. Conclusion
　　Conclusion by Personal Reaction

Go over the following explanations with the student:

I. Introduction
Introduction by Anecdote
Lamb is describing an imaginary scene of Christmas celebration—to quote the definition of an Introduction by Anecdote from the student's chart, an "invented scene based on your knowledge of the subject." The only difference between this anecdote and others the student has seen is that Lamb chooses to tell his scene using the first person, including himself (and the reader) in it.

V. Conclusion
Conclusion by Personal Reaction
Lamb addresses Christmas personally, giving a personal statement and telling *himself* how to react—but he includes the reader by using the first person, just as in the introduction. Notice that Lamb and Grace Rhys both construct their essays so that the conclusions mirror

the introductions.

II. Definition of Christmas
   Function
Because Christmas is a recurring event, the description of its function will sound a little bit different from other definitions of function the student has seen.

Lamb defines Christmas almost exclusively by talking about how it unfolds—the behaviors that characterize it (present-giving, jokes, sliding, baking). He also talks about who is affected by it (school-boys and laughing children specifically, but "bright faces" has a much wider implication). He also mentions events that occur because of it—cakes come out of the ovens, oranges shine out in huge golden heaps, roasted apples appear.

Day Three: Rewriting

 Focus: Rewriting a classic essay from an outline

Today, the student will use the outline created in Day Two to rewrite Charles Lamb's essay in his own words. Continue to give the student all necessary help.

STEP ONE: **Reread (Student Responsibility)**

Read "A Few Words on Christmas" again, carefully, from beginning to end.

STEP TWO: **Understand the model (Student Responsibility)**

NOTE TO INSTRUCTOR: Although this step is the student's responsibility, you will need to make sure that she has read the text slowly and carefully.

Before you start writing, take another look at the structure of "A Few Words on Christmas." A sample outline of the passage is on the left; a description of the elements of the essay is on the right. Read through both of them carefully.

I. Introduction	Introduction by anecdote in first person
Introduction by Anecdote	plural, including both writer and reader
II. Definition of Christmas	
Function	Definition of the phenomenon
III. Christmas Eve	Division of phenomenon into two phases
A. Christmas Eve customs	Aspects of the first phase
1. Formerly, serious and holy vigil	using comparison and contrast
2. Now, sober but no devotions	

B. Music

    1. In other countries

    2. The waits in England

    3. Our own songs

IV. Christmas Day   Aspects of the second phase

A. Decorations OR Visual signs

    1. Houses and churches

    2. The plants used

B. Food

    1. Rich and tradesmen

    2. Apprentices

    3. School-boy

    4. Servant and beggar

V. Conclusion   Conclusion by personal reaction in first

    Conclusion by Personal Reaction   person plural, including both writer and

                                                   reader

Let's look at each one of these elements in turn.

First: Just like Grace Rhys, Charles Lamb is careful to make his introduction and his conclusion resemble each other. Both of them are personal (a personal anecdote, and a personal opinion), and both of them are written in the first person plural.

Second, Lamb gives a brief definition of the event he is about to talk about.

Third, Lamb goes on to divide the event into two phases: Christmas Eve and Christmas Day. He then goes on to discuss important aspects of each phase. In his paragraphs about Christmas Eve, he also uses comparison and contrast—he contrasts old Christmas Eve customs with new Christmas Eve customs, and he also compares the music in England to the music in other countries.

STEP THREE: **Rewrite**

Student instructions for Step Three:

Now rewrite Lamb's essay, in your own words, using *only* your outline. Don't look at the essay itself as you write!

Like your Rhys essay, your version of "A Few Words on Christmas" can be shorter than the original. Use these guidelines as a minimum word count for each section:

Section	Lamb's word count	Your word count
I	94	35
II	111	50
III	328	120
IV	222	75
V	128	50

If you get completely stuck, ask your instructor for help.

When your composition is finished, show it to your instructor.

HOW TO HELP THE STUDENT WITH STEP THREE

As in last week, continually remind the student that she can invent her own sentences, examples and anecdotes if necessary.

Remember that you can give the student three levels of assistance:

First, if the student has drawn a total blank and seems unable to write, allow her to reread a single section of the original essay. Then, while it is fresh in her mind, ask her to rewrite just that section without looking at the original.

Second, allow the student to reread a single section of the original essay. Then, ask her to paraphrase each sentence in her own words, using her own vocabulary, **while** looking at the original. Then, ask her to rewrite just that section **without** looking at the original.

Third, allow the student to reread a single section of the original essay. Then, allow her to read the same section of my paraphrase below.

The student's composition might resemble the following:

[I]   Let's gather around the blazing fire now to celebrate Christmas. Draw the curtains, bring out the special bottles of wine and the plates of fruit. Pull your chairs up to the crackling flames, settle in, and let's drink a toast.

[II]   What is Christmas?

Christmas is the time when children are happiest and schoolboys rejoice. At Christmas, faces are brighter. It is the season of sledding, of eating warm soup, a time of presents and laughter. At Christmas, cakes come out of the oven shining white like snow. Oranges glitter in huge heaps, and apples roast on every corner.

[III]   The first part of Christmas is Christmas Eve. Once, our forefathers kept watch until midnight, and then lit the Yule log and drank ale to celebrate. We no longer keep watch until midnight—and we go to bed sober. We are no worse than our ancestors, but we are also no better.

Christmas music marks the season. In other countries, musicians play their own instruments to celebrate. In England, the Christmas carollers visit us during the night and sing. Their songs are almost like dreams, and we listen and then go back to sleep. We sing our own songs, too. Every old man remembers his favorite songs and sings them to the children who will listen, even though wives tell them to stop.

[IV]   And then, on Christmas Day itself, every house and church is green with wreaths and decorations. Laurel branches, red-berried holly, and mistletoe abound, and people kiss beneath the mistletoe. It seems as though the earth is alive and growing again.

Everyone feasts. Rich people eat as always, but tradesmen and apprentices eat much better food than usual. School-boys dream of puddings, jelly, and acres of mince pies. Servants drink port, and even beggars have turkey to eat.

[V]   Let us all enjoy Christmas. Let us shake hands and rejoice. Tell stories that are innocent or ingenious. Be generous, and be cheerful. Enjoy the present and make the best of the past; work to make the world a better place. And let us do our best to make others as happy as ourselves.

You can evaluate the student's essay using the following rubric:

Week 24 Rubric

Organization:

1 The composition should have five sections.
2 The first section should be at least 35 words long and should be the retelling/description of a Christmas feasting scene around the fire, written in the first person plural.
3 The second section should be at least 50 words long and should define Christmas by listing different activities, foods, and moods that characterize the season.
4 The third section should be at least 120 words long and should describe both Christmas Eve customs in the past and present, and different kinds of Christmas music. It should mention both "Christmas waits" or Christmas carollers, and old gentlemen who sing to children.
5 The fourth section should be at least 75 words long and should describe both the plants used in Christmas decorations, and the kinds of food eaten at Christmas.
6 The last section should be at least 50 words long. It should be an exhortation, written in the first person plural, about how we should all behave because of Christmas.

Mechanics:

1 Each sentence should make sense on its own when read aloud.
2 There should be no sentence fragments or run-on sentences.
3 All words should be spelled correctly.
4 The first line of each paragraph should be properly indented.
5 Verb tense should be consistent throughout.

STEP FOUR: **Compare**

Student instructions for Step Four:

> Read your essay out loud.
> Then, read the original essay out loud.
> You don't have to make any huge conclusions about how they compare. Just listen to how each essay sounds.

HOW TO HELP THE STUDENT WITH STEP FOUR

As with last week's assignment, you simply need to make sure that the student reads both compositions *out loud*. This will allow her to listen to the difference in sound between the two versions of the essay.

Day Four: Copia Exercise
Figurative Language

 Focus: Practicing skills in figurative language

STEP ONE: Examine plain and figurative language (Student Responsibility)

Charles Lamb was a writer of his time. In the eighteenth century, metaphors, similes, and other word pictures were an essential part of any good writer's vocabulary. Lamb's essays and stories are packed with figurative language—so much so that we might find them hard to read. In modern times, good writers usually write straightforward, clean prose, with word pictures used sparingly—for emphasis, not as a regular way of expression.

Neither one of these ways of writing is good or bad; they are simply different. Modern writing (spare, clean, and bare) can be improved with a few techniques from the eighteenth century. And, if you ask me, Charles Lamb's writing would be much improved with a little more sparsity and cleanliness.

Today, you'll take a series of sentences from Charles Lamb's ornate essay and change them around. For each, you'll first rewrite the sentence in plain, straightforward prose, with no word picture. You'll then turn your plain sentence back into an expression with a metaphor or simile—but one drawn from your world, that makes sense to you.

Here's how I would handle Lamb's strange first metaphor, about the *auto de fé*. (What a bizarre metaphor for an essay about Christmas!)

Let us have, for once, an innocent *auto de fé*.
Let us have a welcoming, warm Christmas fire in the hearth.
Let us have, for once, an innocent sea of fire and brimstone.
Let us have, for once, a harmless wildfire.

First, I turned Lamb's metaphor back into a straightforward statement. Then I thought to myself: What is made out of fire, but isn't an innocent fire burning in a living room fireplace? Wildfires—forest fires—burn wood, but aren't innocent. And hell is pictured as a sea of fire and brimstone. I tried substituting both of those for "warm Christmas fire in the hearth."

I don't think either of my metaphors is very good, by the way. But I also think Lamb's is weird and unnecessary. If I were writing this essay, I'd choose the straightforward statement in place of the other three.

STEP TWO: **Transform Charles Lamb's sentences**

Student instructions for Step Two:

> On your own paper, rewrite each of the following sentences twice—once as a plain statement with no figurative language, and once with a metaphor or simile of your own choosing. Read all three sentences and, for each, pick your favorite. What sounds best to your ear—the plain statement, Lamb's figurative language, or your own imaginative effort?
>
> When you are finished, show your sentences to your instructor.

HOW TO HELP THE STUDENT WITH STEP TWO

Sample transformations are seen below. In brackets after each of Lamb's sentences are the qualities that the student should consider when choosing a new metaphor; if the student needs help, read the implied qualities to him.

Oranges, as rich as the fruit of the Hesperides, shine out in huge golden heaps. [So delicious that they are unreal; able to make you live forever and cure all ills; supernaturally wonderful]

Oranges, rich and juicy and delicious, shine out in huge golden heaps.

Oranges, as rich as the elixir of youth, shine out in huge golden heaps.

Oranges, as irresistible as the fruit of the tree of the knowledge of good and evil, shine out in huge golden heaps.

Cakes, frosted over (as if to rival the glittering snow) come forth by thousands from their ovens. [White and hard to the touch, shining, encouraging you to grab them]

Cakes, frosted over with white shiny icing, come forth by thousands from their ovens.

Cakes, frosted over (as if rolled in the most beautiful of diamonds) come forth by thousands from their ovens.

Cakes, frosted over (as if glowing with their own internal light) come forth by thousands from their ovens.

It is like a day of victory. [Victory is pretty straightforward]

It is a day in which everyone feels triumphant.

It is like a day on which independence is declared.

It is like the moment at which a war is won.

Every house and church is as green as spring. [Green is also straightforward—but here carries the sense of new life, birth, fertility, new beginnings]

Every house and church has wreaths and greenery hung all over it.

Every house and church is as green as a mossy glen filled with baby rabbits.

Every house and church is as green as new grass.

Hunger is no longer an enemy. [Something to be welcomed, not done away with]
We are glad to be hungry.
Hunger is a long-anticipated guest.
Hunger is our favorite uncle, finally come to stay.
Hunger is no longer a threatening storm, but a welcome gentle rain.

We feed him, like the ravenous tiger, till he pants and sleeps, or is quiet. [It overcomes us, wanted to devour us, is dangerous but becomes not dangerous]
We feed our hunger until we are no longer hungry.
We give him everything, like an invading robber who takes all of our belongings and finally goes away.
We feed him, like famine, until his demands are finally satisfied.

Mountains of jelly rise beside him. [Quantity—more jelly that you could possibly ever use, want, or need]
He has a lot of jelly.
A tidal wave of jelly rises beside him.
A blizzard of jelly sweeps over him.

Roods of mince pies spread out their chequered riches before him. [Quantity—a ridiculously huge amount of pie]
A lot of mince pies are in front of him.
An ocean of mince pies laps at his feet.
A vast mine of mince pies opens in front of him.

WEEK 25: INDEPENDENT COMPOSITION: MODELED ON A CLASSIC ESSAY

This week, the student will try a different technique: writing an essay based on one of the two models examined in the past two weeks. Using the frame provided by either Grace Rhys or Charles Lamb, the student will fill it with original content. The finished composition will need to be at least 450 words in length (usually, about two double-spaced typed pages of text).

As I've been doing for these independent writing projects, I will give a suggested amount of time to spend on each step, rather than breaking the tasks down into four days. Remember: these are only *suggested* times. You and the student can decide how many days to devote to the assignment—three days, four days, or even more if necessary. Remember that it's perfectly fine for the student to switch topics after beginning to work.

Here's an overview of the steps:

Step One: Understand the assignment	20–30 minutes
Step Two: Brainstorm a topic	45–60 minutes
Step Three: Pre-writing	2–3 hours
Step Four: Draft the composition	3–6 hours
Step Five: Sentence revision	1 hour
Step Six: Proofread and title	30–60 minutes

Although the student is not required to show his work after each step, you may ask to see it at any time.

This assignment will require the student to draw on techniques from several different *topoi* and combine them into one essay. It should begin to become clear to him that the *topoi* are merely tools—they have been taught as forms to follow, but the more familiar and comfortable the student becomes with them, the more likely he will be to use them in flexible ways, mixing elements from each to form new essays and compositions.

Be sure to read through the entire week before offering the student help on any one step. You'll be able to give better assistance if you understand where the student is headed.

STEP ONE: Understand the assignment, 20–30 minutes (Student Responsibility)

Read through the following two assignments and choose one of them. Be sure to read all the way to the end of Step One before you decide.

1) Comparison Essay, Based on Grace Rhys's "A Brother of St. Francis"

Your task: Compare two different things, showing that one is better than its reputation and the other is worse.

You can follow Rhys closely and compare human beings to another animal (not a pig). You can show that human beings are no better than this animal—or you can concentrate on showing that the animal is far, far nobler and more interesting than people. You can compare human beings to something else that isn't an animal. Or you can compare two things that are different from each other—any two things.

Your limitation: You have to have the same basic intention as Grace Rhys. Of the two subjects that you pick to compare, one of them has to have a much more positive, important, or valued character than the other. And you have to show that the less valued subject is nobler than most people think, while the more valued subject is less wonderful than its reputation. (For example, imagine that you're going to write about food. Compare Cracker Jack and broccoli. Show that Cracker Jack has many wonderful qualities—and that broccoli is not as great as people think.)

The structure of your essay must follow this pattern:

Two-part introduction
    Personal anecdote
    Direct statement to reader
Description of the main subject
    Major aspect of main subject described
    Second major aspect of main subject described
Comparison of main subject and another subject
    Three to six aspects of both subjects compared
Two-part conclusion
    Conclusion by personal reaction
    Final statement

2) Definition and Description Essay, Based on Charles Lamb's "A Few Words on Christmas"

Your task: Define and describe a special event that you have experienced.

You can describe a yearly holiday (although not Christmas). You can describe a family tradition—a visit to the State Fair, a yearly beach vacation. Or you can describe an event that you loved and remember fondly—a special trip that you took with your parents, the greatest birthday party you ever had, the time you won a competition.

Your limitation: Your essay has to be positive; it has to show the *wonderfulness* of the event, and it has to invite/exhort/encourage others to experience it or plan a similar experience.

The structure of your essay must follow this pattern:

Introduction by anecdote
    Written in the first person plural, including both writer and reader
Definition of the event

      Division of the event into two phases
           Description of aspects of the first phase, using comparison and contrast
           Description of aspects of the second phase
      Conclusion by personal reaction
           Written in the first person plural, including both writer and reader

GENERAL INSTRUCTIONS FOR BOTH ESSAY TYPES

Choose a topic that won't require you to do a lot of extra research and reading. Your focus in this essay should be on reproducing the structure of one of these classic essays, but pouring your own ideas and experiences into it. If you do need to quote and footnote a piece of information, you may—but it is fine to write this essay with no footnotes whatsoever.

Even if the model feels unnatural and strange to you, concentrate on expressing your own experiences and ideas, using your own vocabulary. Sticking to the framework of the model will expand your abilities by forcing you to develop an idea in a new way—one you would probably never have come up with on your own.

STEP TWO: **Brainstorm a topic (45–60 minutes)**

Student instructions for Step Two:

To find a topic, you'll need to brainstorm—but your brainstorming will look a little different, depending on which model you choose.

If you find that you're completely stuck on your topic, switch to the other model and try brainstorming that one instead.

You can ask your instructor for help if you need it.

1) For Comparison Essay, Based on Grace Rhys's "A Brother of St. Francis"

a) First, jot down as many things as you can think of on a sheet of paper. To get you started, think about the following categories:

> *Kinds of animals*
> *Types of food*
> *Pastimes and entertainments*
> *Sports*
> *Hobbies*
> *Books and movies*
> *Famous historical events*
> *Kinds of jobs (or careers)*

b) Next, draw a line down the middle of a piece of paper. On one side, write "Positive." On the other, write "Negative." Under the heading "Positive," write down the names of everything you came up with that has a positive reputation or connotation (it won an Oscar, it is cute and fluffy, it's good for you, it has prestige). On the other side of the paper, write down everything that has a negative reputation or connotation (it lost millions at the box office, it's a predator, only losers are associated with it). If something is neutral, leave it off the list.

Here an example of how a few categorizations might work:

POSITIVE	**NEGATIVE**
Lemurs	*Vultures*
Being a doctor	*Being a garbage collector*
The Civil Rights movement	*The Black Hole of Calcutta*

c) Using your lists, choose two things to compare. The *negative* subject will be your main subject (like Rhys's pig). The *positive* subject will be the thing that you compare it to (in Rhys's essay, human beings).

2) Definition and Description Essay, Based on Charles Lamb's "A Few Words on Christmas"

a) Begin by writing down the names of as many holidays and special occasions as you can.

b) Write down brief phrases or sentences describing special events in your past (trips, events, family outings) that stand out in your memory.

c) Look back through your list. Try to remember, right off the top of your head, three or four specific, colorful descriptive details about each one. Choose the event or holiday that is the most well-defined and vivid in your mind.

HOW TO HELP THE STUDENT WITH STEP TWO

The student's instructions are very specific, but if she needs additional help, you may show her part of the sample answers below. Additional suggestions for help are also included.

1) For Comparison Essay, Based on Grace Rhys's "A Brother of St. Francis"

a) *Kinds of animals:* **Lion, vulture, armadillo, louse, scorpion, whale, dolphin**
Types of food: **Broccoli, Twinkies, Captain Crunch, popcorn, ice cream, steak, salad**
Pastimes and entertainments: **Video games, ice skating, reading, Wii, Minecraft**
Sports: **Hockey, baseball, boxing, judo, wrestling, football, dressage**
Hobbies: **Sewing, models, reading, hiking, stamp collecting, gardening, model trains**
Books and movies: **The Lord of the Rings, The Babysitters Club series**
Famous historical events: **Civil Rights movement, Vietnam War, War of 1812**
Kinds of jobs (or careers): **Lawyer, doctor, fast food worker, custodian, cashier, librarian**

If she still struggles, send her to a dictionary, encyclopedia, or Wikipedia. Tell her to just skim through the pages, looking for names and objects that belong to the categories given in the lesson.

b) The second step is to divide these into "negatives" and "positives." Remind the student that her answers aren't necessarily "right" or "wrong," since whether or not something is admirable or prestigious depends on your point of view. In some families, being a lawyer is the height of achievement; other families might have a tradition of speaking of lawyers as slimy and dishonorable. And a third family might have no particular opinion about lawyers whatsoever. (For that matter, if you're a pork farmer you probably don't think of pigs as either terrifying or disgusting.) The goal is for the student to be able to argue convincingly, from her own point of view, that a "negative" subject has "positive" value. So if the subject is negative for the student, it's negative.

Having said that, here's how my list above might break down for *some* students, with the "neutral" subjects omitted entirely.

POSITIVE	*NEGATIVE*
Lion	Vulture
Whale	Louse
Dolphin	Scorpion
Broccoli	Twinkies
Steak	Captain Crunch
salad	reading
Minecraft	hockey
dressage	*The Babysitters Club* series
gardening	Vietnam War
reading	fast food worker
Lord of the Rings	custodian
Civil Rights movement	
lawyer	
doctor	
librarian	

c) The student will find it easier to compare if the two subjects are of the same type. Good pairings, for example, might be

Main subject	*Compared to . . .*
Twinkies	broccoli
lawyer	fast-food worker
Minecraft	reading
louse	lion

2) Definition and Description Essay, Based on Charles Lamb's "A Few Words on Christmas"

a) Exact lists will depend on the student's familiar traditions. My sample list might be:

Halloween, Thanksgiving, Fourth of July, Memorial Day, Easter, Valentine's Day, New Year's Day

b) Examples might be:

Trip to the State Fair last year, our family's annual summer beach vacation, going to Disney World two years ago, our visit to Alaska to see our cousins

c) I might answer:

Thanksgiving: Mom always makes the stuffing that takes nearly a week because she makes the bread herself and then dries it and picks her own sage and cooks her own giblets. We always have cinnamon rolls for breakfast. We used to watch the Christmas parade but we got frustrated because it was all Broadway scenes and no actual floats, so now we watch It's a Wonderful Life. I make pumpkin pies, lemon and chocolate chess pies, and an apple pie.

Trip to the State Fair last year: Emily won a blue ribbon for the mosaic she entered in arts and crafts! Deep-fried Oreos—they were really greasy and drippy. Confectioners' sugar from the funnel cakes blew all over us when it got windy. There were Angora goats with long wool and twisty horns.

STEP THREE: **Pre-writing (2–3 hours)**

Student instructions for Step Three:

Before you start working on your actual essay, you need to go through each required element and make sure that your topic is going to work for you. Plus, giving yourself time to do pre-writing will make the drafting of the composition much simpler, and will allow you to concentrate on making your prose read smoothly and beautifully.

For an essay based on your own personal thoughts and reactions, the pre-writing step is like the note-taking step when you write an essay based on research. It gives you the raw material to turn into a composition. You should never plunge directly into drafting an essay without giving yourself plenty of notes to work with, rearrange, and juggle.

Follow the directions below for the essay of your choice.

1) Comparison Essay, Based on Grace Rhys's "A Brother of St. Francis"

Keep in mind your task: You must compare two things, showing that one is better than its reputation, and the other is worse.

On your own paper, jot down phrases and sentences that address the following questions and suggestions. You may find it helpful to glance back at Rhys's original essay in Week 23 as you work.

Two-part introduction
  Personal anecdote. *What story will you retell or invent in order to introduce your main subject—your negative subject? This story should highlight the negative aspects of the subject—why people think poorly of it.*
  Direct statement to reader. *Exhort the reader to re-examine or re-think his or her original reaction.*
Description of the main subject

Major aspect of main subject described. *This does not have to be specifically either negative or positive, but it should be something that is absolutely characteristic of your subject—something that makes it what it is. You can use the Explanation by Definition chart in your* topoi *reference section to help you brainstorm.*

Second major aspect of main subject described. *Same instructions as above—but this could be a slightly less central property or aspect of the subject—perhaps personal appearance or something else that will draw the reader into a deeper consideration of what the subject is.*

Comparison of main subject and another subject

Three to six aspects of both subjects compared. *In order to prepare for this step, you'll need to borrow techniques that you first practiced in Week 5, when you learned about comparison and contrast. Jot down as many aspects of each subject as you can think of, and then circle those that are similar. Remember, your goal is to show the similarity between the two subjects, just as Rhys showed the similarities between pigs and people by highlighting their behavior.*

Two-part conclusion

Conclusion by personal reaction. *This should be a story or anecdote that—in contrast to the opening story—highlights something that is good, positive, or lovable about the main subject.*

Final statement. *Can you explain what difference it will make to the reader if he or she can change the way he or she thinks about the main subject? Or can you make a statement about he or she should* view the main subject?

2) Definition and Description Essay, Based on Charles Lamb's "A Few Words on Christmas"

Keep in mind your task: You must define and describe a special event that you have experienced.

On your own paper, jot down phrases and sentences that address the following questions and suggestions. You may find it helpful to glance back at Lamb's original essay in Week 24 as you work.

Introduction by Anecdote

Written in the first person plural, including both writer and reader. *Can you imagine a scene that takes place during the event? What do you see, smell, hear, taste, feel? Now, can you invite the reader to join you in sensing the same things?*

Definition of the event. *What characterizes the event? What behaviors take place during it? What do you see, hear, smell, feel, taste, or do during the event? How long does it last? Who takes part in it? Try to answer these and any other useful questions from your Explanation by Definition chart. The most central qualities of the event belong here. Others that you come up with can be addressed in the "Description of aspects of the second phase" below.*

Division of the event into two phases. *Some holidays, like Christmas, have both an "eve" and a "day." But even if your event doesn't fall into this pattern, you can divide it into a before/after, before/ during, or during/after. What divisions work best? What characterizes each part of the division?*

Description of aspects of the first phase, using comparison and contrast. *Do different people observe/celebrate this part of the event in different ways? Are these people separated by age, experience, gender, nationality? What makes them different, and how are their reactions different?*

Description of aspects of the second phase. *Here, you should describe at least two of the aspects you came up with but did not use in the Definition of the Event, above. If necessary, spend a little more time brainstorming, using the Explanation by Definition questions.*

Conclusion by Personal Reaction

Written in the first person plural, including both writer and reader. *This should not be a scene or a story; more of an exhortation to the reader to join you in making the most of this event or another like it in the future. Remember to use "we" and "us" as you make your notes. What part of the event would benefit others the most? How would it change them?*

HOW TO HELP THE STUDENT WITH STEP THREE

If the student needs more assistance, allow her to read my model answers below. I have chosen my own topics, but have tried to give examples of the sorts of answers you can expect from a student at this stage.

Encourage the student to answer the questions fully. The more writing she does now, the less frustrating she'll find the actual essay composition. This exercise is designed, in part, to teach the student the value of pre-writing. Working with words already set down, no matter how rough and incomplete, is always easier than facing down a blank page.

1) Comparison Essay, Based on Grace Rhys's "A Brother of St. Francis"

Comparing: Twinkies and broccoli

Two-part introduction
    Personal anecdote. *The time when I was younger that my mother served broccoli-cheese casserole and I couldn't make myself swallow it. Smell: greenness, kind of gassy. See: the broccoli was like a tangle of seaweed and the edges were brown. Feel: it was mushy and stringy at the same time. And then I had a Twinkie for dessert. The whole time I was eating it, the rest of my family was telling me how bad it was for me, but it was the most delicious thing I ever tasted.*
    Direct statement to reader. *You may think of broccoli as wonderfully good for you—but let's not forget about Twinkies. They make us happy, and that's just as valuable to our well-being as vitamins and minerals.*
Description of the main subject
    Major aspect of main subject described. *Creamy white filling inside the golden sponge cake. It's like a surprise or a treasure. Like an egg, except the yellow is on the outside and the white is on the inside—so like an inside-out egg. Like a present that you open.*
    Second major aspect of main subject described. *Experience of eating it*
Comparison of main subject and another subject
    Three to six aspects of both subjects compared. *Chemicals: people say that Twinkies are nothing but chemicals, but broccoli is sprayed by chemicals too—and if it isn't, you get those fat green worms that sometimes get cooked up with it and served to you! Nutrition: broccoli may have vitamins and minerals but a Twinkie has a whole gram of protein AND twenty milligrams of calcium! (I looked that up.) Calories: Twinkies may be fattening, but a single Twinkie is only 150 calories—and most people have to eat broccoli smothered in white sauce and cheese just to get it down, so that's got even more calories than a single Twinkie. Long shelf life: People say that Twinkies are like styrofoam because they last forever. But why is it better to have something in your refrigerator, like broccoli, that goes all brown and mushy within days—and then you feel like you have to eat it anyway?*

Two-part conclusion

Conclusion by personal reaction. *Going to the State Fair and eating a deep-fried Twinkie, and how that sort of expressed for me the entire experience—it was crisp and creamy, sweet and tangy, it smelled like fall time and celebration, eating it just made me feel that I was having a holiday and that everything was going to be OK.*

Final statement. *Appreciating the Twinkie will free you from guilt and let you enjoy an indulgent treat. It might even change the way you think about broccoli if you realize that you can eat food because you enjoy it, not because you have to.*

2) Definition and Description Essay, Based on Charles Lamb's "A Few Words on Christmas"

My event: The Virginia State Fair

NOTE TO INSTRUCTOR: I intentionally chose an event that is not a holiday. It is perfectly fine for the student to choose Thanksgiving or some other yearly holiday—that will make following Lamb's model much simpler. I wanted to show you what answers might look like for an event that's not quite so similar to Christmas.

Introduction by Anecdote

Written in the first person plural, including both writer and reader. *I am walking through the entrance tunnel into the State Fair of Virginia. Ahead of me I can see the oak trees of the old fairground. I can hear cows mooing up on the hill where the agricultural tent is. I can smell sausages and peppers, popcorn, and funnel cake. All around me, people are chattering happily. The sun is out, and the blue fall sky is brilliant. In the distance, I can see the equine show rings and just barely see horses moving inside them.*

Definition of the event. *Agriculture and animals: barns of horses, tents of cows and sheep and goats, long rows of rabbits and chickens. Shining rows of farm equipment, feed displays. I can smell the animals—it is a good smell, a mix of sheep and horse, hay, and grain. People are busy washing, grooming, and caring for animals. Some of them are obviously full-time farmers. Others are high school students. They seem purposeful and happy.*

Division of the event into two phases. *Morning: we visit the animal tents and watch the animal competitions. Afternoon: the midway, refreshment booths, and game booths.*

Description of aspects of the first phase, using comparison and contrast. *Last year, the State Fair of Virginia was almost cancelled when it went bankrupt. It was rescued at the last minute, but many of the animal displays couldn't be brought back in time. Instead of six or eight large barns and animal tents, there were barely two. There was a lot of empty rutted ground in place of the sheep and goats, almost no rabbits or poultry, just a few horses. It was sad and a letdown. In contrast, in other years, there was a full animal display and it felt much more special, much more festive.*

Description of aspects of the second phase. *The food: steaming hot funnel cakes, with confectioners' sugar dusted over them and getting all over us; fried Oreos, like chocolate-filled dumplings; sausages and onions and peppers, with thick salty fries; pizza dripping with hot steaming cheese; gyros, wrapped in foil, smelling savory and covered with sauce. The display buildings:*

elaborate, detailed, hand-made quilts, some of them colorful and complicated, others white-on-white with careful stitching. Tons of booths selling stuff: candy, jewelry, jams, woodcrafts, baskets, plants. Rides: rusty and tottering, held together with wire and propped up with firewood—I'm afraid to go on them!

Conclusion by Personal Reaction

Written in the first person plural, including both writer and reader. *If you don't live in the country, going to the State Fair reminds you of [This should not be a scene or a story; more of an exhortation to the reader to join you in making the most of this event or another like it in the future. Remember to use "we" and "us" as you make your notes. What part of the event would benefit others the most? How would it change them?]*

STEP FOUR: Draft the composition (3–6 hours)

Student instructions for Step Four:

> Using your pre-writing notes and keeping an eye on the model that you're following, write your composition. Remember: you're aiming for at least 450 words. Your composition must include the elements listed in Step One, but you can decide where your paragraphs should end and begin.

HOW TO HELP THE STUDENT WITH STEP FOUR

Sample compositions are found below. If the student needs help, you may allow her to read one or both of them.

1) Comparison Essay, Based on Grace Rhys's "A Brother of St. Francis"

I will never forget sitting at the kitchen table, staring down at a broccoli-and-cheese casserole. I knew I needed to choke it down. After all, broccoli is good for you, right? But it had a green, gassy smell. The broccoli looked like a tangle of browning seaweed. I could barely swallow it.

Afterwards, my mother allowed me to have a special treat: a Twinkie. "It's terrible for you," she said. My brother agreed. "Twinkies have so many chemicals in them that they'll last on the shelf for years," he told me. I didn't care. When I unwrapped that plastic covering and sank my teeth into it, I was the happiest that I'd been all day. Broccoli may be good for you—but don't forget the value of Twinkies. A Twinkie can make you happy. And that's just as important for your health as the vitamins in a stalk of broccoli.

Consider the Twinkie. It's like an inside-out egg, but the treasure at the center isn't a yellow yolk surrounded by white; it's a white, creamy, delicious filling, surrounded by golden cake. The middle of a Twinkie is the reward for biting down through the cake.

You can eat a Twinkie plain, but that's not all you can do with this snack food. Slice it and serve it on ice cream to make a Twinkie Sundae. Dip it in chocolate and roll it in peanuts for a

Twinkie Surprise. Coat it in batter, fry it, and sprinkle it with confectioners' sugar for a Deep Fried Twinkie. Drizzle caramel on it and make a Coated Twinkie.

Maybe a Twinkie has a lot of chemicals in it, but think about how much chemical spray it takes to keep broccoli worm-free. You might try to wash that off, but some of it remains—so when you eat broccoli, you're eating chemicals.

Broccoli has plenty of vitamins and minerals in it—but a Twinkie has nutritional value too. One Twinkie has a whole gram of protein in it, as well as twenty milligrams of calcium.

Broccoli might be low in calories, but a Twinkie has only 150 calories in it. Most people eat broccoli covered in butter, white sauce, and cheese—because it's the only way broccoli tastes good. Broccoli with butter and cheese has at least 150 calories in it, so in a way, a Twinkie has fewer calories than your average broccoli dish.

I have never had a plate of broccoli that made me happy. But last fall, I had a deep-fried Twinkie at the State Fair. It was crisp on the outside, warm and gooey and creamy on the inside, and it was dusted with cinnamon sugar. That Twinkie tasted like a party to me. It made me feel like fall time had come. Eating the Twinkie make me happy.

You too should learn to appreciate the Twinkie. Indulge in a Twinkie and feel happiness, instead of grimly stuffing down a plate of broccoli just because it's good for you. A Twinkie is good for your mind and your soul, not just for your body.

2) Definition and Description Essay, Based on Charles Lamb's "A Few Words on Christmas"

Let's walk together into the Virginia State Fair, past the ticket booths, through the gates, and down into the entrance tunnel. As we walk up towards the gate, we can see the oak trees of the old fairground. Their limbs are dark against the blue fall sky, and they still have leaves. Cows are mooing up on the hill to our right. Take a deep breath; do you smell the sausages and peppers, the funnel cakes and the fried Oreos? Join in the happy chatter all around. Everyone around us is looking forward to the fair.

What is the State Fair? First of all, it is a celebration of agriculture. There are barns of horses, groomed and waiting to go into the show ring. Tents filled with wooden stalls are home to cows, sheep, and goats of all sizes and colors. The tents smell good—like animals, hay, and grain. Farmers and high school students spend their days caring for the animals, washing and brushing them, making sure that they are comfortable and fed. Outside the tents, rows of combines and tractors, green and bright blue, shine in the sun.

This part of the State Fair is all about farming—the animals and their owners, the show rings where the animals are judged, and all the equipment you need to raise livestock and grow crops. It used to cover over half of the fairgrounds, with hundreds of different breeds and kinds of animals and dozens of different farms represented. But this past year, the State Fair went bankrupt and was almost cancelled. At the last minute, the Fair was rescued and went ahead—but it was too late to bring back the old animal displays. Instead of six or eight barns and tents of animals, barely two tents were filled. Instead of sheep and goats, there was only empty, rutted ground. There were no long rows of exotic poultry and unique rabbits.

But down on the midway, where the food booths and sale buildings stand, there was still plenty going on. There were steaming hot funnel cakes with sugar dusted over them, booths for cotton candy and caramel popcorn, and plenty of chocolatey fried Oreos. There were sausages with onions and peppers, pizzas dripping with hot steaming cheese, and savory gyros wrapped in foil. Booths sold candy, jewelry, jam, wooden crafts, and woven baskets. Display buildings held entries of quilts, canned goods, pies, breads, and other handmade items.

For those us of us who don't live in the country, the State Fair reminds us of how farmers live every day. We can see what's important to rural communities, how much effort goes into raising livestock and crops, and what wonderful foods are produced. If we do live in the country—maybe even run farms ourselves—the State Fair reminds us to be proud of how we live and what we make.

STEP FIVE: **Sentence revision (1 hour)**

Student instructions for Step Five:

> Read back through your composition now. If you have not already used at least one metaphor and at least one simile, find a place for both of these now. Add them in.
>
> Once you have made sure that your essay contains both a metaphor and a simile, look back at your Sentence Variety chart. You must use at least *two* additional techniques (not including metaphor and simile!) to transform at least two of your original sentences.
>
> Your goal here is to make your sentences sound more lyrical and beautiful, not to make them more awkward. Read your original and transformed sentences out loud to make sure that you have improved them.
>
> If you have difficulty finding sentences to transform, look back at the guidelines given to you in Week 23, Day Four.

HOW TO HELP THE STUDENT WITH STEP FIVE

You may need to help the student locate sentences to be transformed. For your reference, here are the guidelines:

To transform descriptive adjectives into nouns, look for adjectives that come right before the nouns they modify. Or, look for prepositional phrases beginning with "of" and see if they can be turned into descriptive adjectives.

To transform active verbs into passive, look for sentences with action verbs and direct objects.

Look for sentences with indirect objects to transform into objects of a preposition.

To transform a participle into an infinitive, look for an -ing word following an action verb.

To transform a main verb into an infinitive, pick a strong verb and see whether you are able to add one of the following verbs to it:

VERBS THAT ARE OFTEN FOLLOWED BY INFINITIVES

agree	aim	appear	arrange	ask	attempt
beg	begin	care	choose	consent	continue
dare	decide	deserve	dislike	expect	fail
forget	get	hesitate	hope	hurry	intend
leap	like	love	ought	plan	prefer
prepare	proceed	promise	refuse	remember	start
strive	try	use	wait	want	wish

To intensify an adjective, look for descriptive adjectives that either come before a noun or follow a linking verb.

To change a word into a phrase, metaphor, or kenning, look for strong and interesting nouns.

To change a positive statement to a negative statement, look for a strong statement. Then use your thesaurus to find antonyms for the nouns and verbs in the statement.

The student may also need help inserting a metaphor into the composition. Similes ("like" or "as" statements) are relatively easy; one of my sample compositions already contains a simile:

Consider the Twinkie. It's like an inside-out egg.

and the second simile is easy to insert.

> **Instead of sheep and goats, there was only empty, rutted ground.**
> becomes
> **Instead of sheep and goats, there was only empty, rutted ground, like a parking lot after a concert has ended.**
> or, in a more scholarly vein,
> **Instead of sheep and goats, there was only empty, rutted ground, like the village green of the Lost Colony after its disappearance.**

However, a metaphor requires to you to speak *directly* of one thing in terms of another, so the student may need some help going through the intermediate steps. If necessary, remind her to *first* think of a simile:

The cheese dripping off a piece of pizza looks like lava oozing down the side of a volcano.

and then to use the same language about the pizza that you would use about lava and a volcano:

There were sausages with onions and peppers, pizzas covered with a pyroclastic flow of melted cheddar, and savory gyros wrapped in foil.

STEP SIX: **Proofread and title (30–60 minutes)**

Student instructions for Step Six:

Proofread your paper, using the following steps.

1) Make sure that your paper is at least 450 words in length.
2) Check to make sure that all of the elements listed in the model are also in your paper.
3) Read your paper out loud, listening for awkward or unclear sections and repeated words. Rewrite awkward or unclear sentences so that they flow more naturally.
4) Listen for information that is repeated more than once. Eliminate repetition of ideas.
5) Read through the paper one more time, looking for sentence fragments, run-on sentences, and repeated words. Correct fragments and run-on sentences. Listen for unnecessary repetition. If you used a modifier more than twice, find another word.
6) Check your spelling by looking, individually, at each word that might be a problem.

When your paper is completely proofread, give it a title—once again, following the example of your models.

Grace Rhys titled her essay using a descriptive phrase/metaphor for the pig: "A Brother of St. Francis." If you wrote an essay modelled after Rhys's work, title it by thinking of a descriptive phrase/metaphor that applies to your main subject.

Charles Lamb titled his essay very literally: it is "A Few Words on" the topic of Christmas. If you wrote a composition like Lamb's, give it the same kind of title—but you have to think of a different way to say "a few words."

Once you've titled your essay, give it to your instructor for evaluation.

HOW TO HELP THE STUDENT WITH STEP SIX

The student may struggle with the titling of the essay. For the first essay, tell him that he can simply pick a descriptive phrase out of his composition, if necessary; for example, I could title my Twinkie composition "A Treat that Makes You Happy" or "Good for Your Mind and Soul." You could also encourage the student towards a more metaphoric title: "Treasure on the Inside" or "An Inside-Out Egg."

For the second essay, you may need to send him to the thesaurus to look up synonyms for "a few" and "words." I could have titled my essay, "Some Thoughts on the State Fair," "Brief Musings on the State Fair," or "A Short Description of the State Fair."

Read through the student's transformed sentences with him. He may need to transform more than two in order to find two sentences that are improvements on the original. The goal is for the final composition to contain two transformed sentences.

When the student is finished, check his composition using the following rubric.

Week 25 Rubric

Organization:

1 The composition should be at least 450 words in length.
2 It should contain each of the elements listed in the appropriate model.
3 The composition should contain at least one simile and one metaphor.
4 The title should be centered at the top of the page and should follow the appropriate model.
5 At least two of the sentences should have been transformed, using the copia skills learned up to this point.
6 No piece of information should be repeated.

Mechanics:

1 Each sentence should make sense on its own when read aloud.
2 There should be no sentence fragments or run-on sentences.
3 All words should be spelled correctly.
4 The first line of each paragraph should be properly indented.
5 No single word or phrase should be repeated unnecessarily.

WEEK 26: EXPLANATION BY TEMPORAL COMPARISON IN HISTORY

Day One: Introduction to Temporal Comparisons

 Focus: Understanding how to compare something to itself at different points in time

This week, the student will return to the idea of comparison and contrast—with a twist.

STEP ONE: **Understand the concept of temporal comparison (Student Responsibility)**

Look at the following photos:

Now, look back at these two portraits, taken from Week 18 of this course.

Alfred Noyes, Poet, Dies at 77;
Noted for 'The Highwayman'

Alfred Noyes in study of his home on the Isle of Wight

What do the two sets of pictures have in common? Both of them show the same place or person at different points in time. The first set of photos shows a store building in Porter County, Indiana, in 1917—before and after a tornado blew through the town. The portraits show the author Alfred Noyes. The first portrait is of Noyes as a middle-aged writer; the second is of Noyes as an old man, shortly before his death.

You can use writing to present the same sort of "before and after" depictions of objects, events, places or people. When you describe the properties of one thing at two different points in time, you are writing a *temporal comparison*. You are comparing something to itself at another point in time.

Look at this example of temporal comparison, from a two-volume biography of Mary, Queen of Scots.

> She came into England at the age of twenty-five, in the prime of womanhood, the full vigour of health, and the rapidly ripening strength of her intellectual powers. She was there destined to feel in all its bitterness that "hope delayed maketh the heart sick." Year after year passed slowly on, and year after year her spirits became more exhausted, her health feebler, and her doubts and fears confirmed, till they at length settled into despair. Premature old age overtook her, before she was past the meridian of life; and for some time before her death, her hair was white. . . .Yet, during the whole of this long period . . . Mary retained the innate grace and dignity of her character, never forgetting that she had been born a queen.

> —H. G. Bell, *Life of Mary Queen of Scots*, Vol II (Edinburgh: William Brown, 1890), p. 181.

This contrasts the qualities of the young Mary (in her prime, in full health, her intellect strengthening) with the older Mary (exhausted spirits, feeble health, despairing, white-haired). It also tells you what stayed the same: "the innate grace and dignity of her character."

A comparison in time highlights how a single object, event, place, or person has *changed*, through pointing out both the things that have shifted over time. It can also point out what things have stayed the same.

STEP TWO: **Analyze paragraphs of temporal comparison**

Student instructions for Step Two:

Now you'll look in more detail at how a brief temporal comparison is constructed.

For each of the comparisons below, fill out the chart by writing down all the ways in which the historical phenomena differ at earlier and later dates. If you need help, ask your instructor.

The first chart has been started for you.

1) This paragraph is about the famous II Army Corps of the United States; the Corps fought against the Confederate States during the American Civil War.

★

2) This compares the ancient Olympics with the modern version.

★

3) These three paragraphs compare conditions before and after the nineteenth-century Industrial Revolution.

★

HOW TO HELP THE STUDENT WITH STEP TWO

The student's charts should resemble the following. The answers in brackets are optional.

II Army Corps before	II Army Corps after
Most famous in the army Stormed Bloody Lane at Antietam Took 4,000 casualties at Gettysburg Broke the Bloody Angle at Spotsylvania [Strongest fighting unit]	Fought out and used up Shot to pieces Weakest fighting unit

Ancient Olympics	Modern Olympics
14 events 300 competitors 40,000 spectators	300 events 10,000 athletes 200 countries The whole world watches

Before the Industrial Revolution	During and After the Industrial Revolution
Families made their own furniture, clothes, shoes Crafts were handmade Process was slow, few items produced Items were expensive Only people with money could buy them [Made goods by hand in small shops or homes] Traditional life in the countryside [Workers less dependent on will of employer]	New devices and machines replaced labor More goods produced Lower prices Bigger machines gave rise to factories Goods made in factories and on assembly lines Goods more affordable to greater number of people Moved to cities Specialized economic life Workers dependent on will of employer

STEP THREE: Understand the place of a brief temporal comparison in the Description of a Person

Student instructions for Step Three:

Look again at the paragraph about Mary Queen of Scots. Read it carefully and then read through the list of qualities that the writer compares and contrasts.

She came into England at the age of <u>twenty-five</u>, in the <u>prime of womanhood</u>, the full <u>vigour of health</u>, and the rapidly ripening <u>strength of her intellectual powers</u>. She was there destined to feel in all its bitterness that "hope delayed maketh the heart sick." Year after year passed slowly on, and year after year her spirits became more exhausted, her <u>health feebler</u>, and her <u>doubts and fears</u> confirmed, till they at length settled into despair. <u>Premature old age</u> overtook her, before she was past the meridian of life; and for some time before her death, her <u>hair was white</u>. . . Yet, during the whole of this long period . . . Mary retained the innate <u>grace and dignity</u> of her character, never forgetting that she had been born a queen.

—H. G. Bell, *Life of Mary Queen of Scots*, Vol II (Edinburgh: William Brown, 1890), p. 181.

Age   (twenty-five, prime of womanhood, premature old age)
Health   (vigour of health, health feebler)
Intellect   (strength of intellectual powers, doubts and fears)
Appearance (hair was white)
Character   (grace and dignity)

Now, examine the Description of a Person from your list of *topoi*.

Description of a Person

Definition: A description of selected physical and non-physical aspects of a person

Procedure	Remember
1. Decide on which aspects will be included. They may include:	1. Descriptions can be "slanted" using appropriate adjectives.
Physical appearance	2. An overall metaphor can be used to organize the description and give clues about character.
Sound of voice	
What others think	
Portrayals	
Character qualities	
Challenges and difficulties	
Accomplishments	
Habits	
Behaviors	
Expressions of face and body	
Mind/intellectual capabilities	
Talents and abilities	
Self disciplines	
Religious beliefs	
Clothing, dress	
Economic status (wealth)	
Fame, notoriety, prestige	
Family traditions, tendencies	

In comparing the young Mary to the older Mary, the writer mentions her physical appearance, her character qualities, challenges and difficulties she faced (premature aging, decline in her health), and her intellectual capabilities.

This paragraph about Mary Queen of Scots is one part of a longer description of Mary. As you can see, the writer chooses aspects of Mary and then compares them at different points in time. The paragraph of temporal comparison becomes a small part of a longer composition— a Description of a Person.

On your Description of a Person chart, add a third point under the heading "Remember." The point should be:

3. The description can include one or more paragraphs of temporal comparison (the comparison of aspects at different points in time)

HOW TO HELP THE STUDENT WITH STEP THREE

The student's updated chart should look like this:

Description of a Person

Definition: A description of selected physical and non-physical aspects of a person

Procedure	Remember
1. Decide on which aspects will be included. They may include:	1. Descriptions can be "slanted" using appropriate adjectives.

Physical appearance
Sound of voice
What others think
Portrayals
Character qualities
Challenges and difficulties
Accomplishments
Habit
Behaviors
Expressions of face and body
Mind/intellectual capabilities
Talents and abilities
Self disciplines
Religious beliefs
Clothing, dress
Economic status (wealth)
Fame, notoriety, prestige
Family traditions, tendencies

2. An overall metaphor can
be used to organize the description
and give clues about character.
**3. The description can
include one or more paragraphs
of temporal comparison (the
comparison of aspects at different
points in time).**

STEP FOUR: Understand the place of a brief temporal comparison in an Explanation by Definition

Student instructions for Step Four:

A brief temporal comparison can also be used in an explanation by definition, as a way of exploring any of the three areas that a definition involves—properties, function, genus.

Look back at the three charts you made in Step Two. On the lines below, jot down the questions that are answered about properties, function, and/or genus in each chart.

II Army Corps: _____

Olympics: _____

Industrial Revolution: _____

When you are finished, check your answers with your instructor. Ask for help if you need it.

Finish up today's work by adding the following to the Explanation by Definition: Historical Object, Event, Place, or People Group chart, in the "Remember" column:

4. The definition can include one or more paragraphs of temporal comparison (the comparison of properties, function, and/or genus at different points in time)

HOW TO HELP THE STUDENT WITH STEP FOUR

The student should have jotted down one or more of the following questions. Where there are multiple answers, it isn't necessary for her to have located *all* of the questions listed below, but you should point out which questions she has missed.

Only the questions were required. The relevant information in each paragraph/chart is included in parentheses. If necessary, use it to prompt the student.

Additional answers are acceptable as long as the student can defend her answers.

For Army Corps paragraph:

Properties: How did it behave? (**list of the Army Corps' accomplishments**)
Function: Did it work/behave differently at different times? (**yes: earlier in the war/later in the war**)
Genus: What other objects, events, people, or places can it be grouped with?
(**fighting units**)
In what significant ways is it different from the others in its group?
(**first strongest, then weakest**)

For the Olympics:
Properties: What was its extent in space? (**smaller vs. much larger**)
Did it repeat or continue into modern times? How has it changed over time?
(**Yes; the size has changed**)

For the Industrial Revolution (the student should have found at least three of the following):
Function: Will a descriptive sequence help the reader understand how it worked? (**Machines replaced labor, bigger machines gave rise to factories, more people moved to cities to work in the factories**)
What effects did it have on the surrounding events/people? (**More people could buy things, people moved to cities, working conditions changed**)
What events led up to it? (**Families making their own furniture, clothes, shoes; slow, few items, expensive; only people with money could buy them**)
What events occurred because of it? (**Machines replaced labor, more goods were produced, they were cheaper; factories appeared; people moved to cities and became dependent on their employers**)
For what purposes or reasons? (**Because of the invention of new devices and machines**)
What is its significance? What did it change? (**It changed the way people lived and work; it changed the prices and availability of goods**)
Did it create/become a major turning point? (**Yes; it changed lifestyles**)

The student's *topos* chart should now look like this:

Explanation by Definition: Historical Object, Event, Place, or People Group

Definition: An explanation of properties, function, and genus

Procedure	Remember

1. Answer the following questions

1. Not all questions need to be answered

2. Answers to genus and properties may overlap

Shared and Unique Properties

3. Always try to explain significance

What did it look like?
How did it behave?
What did it resemble?
What was it made of?
What sort of structure did it have?
What was its extent in space?
Where did it take place or exist?
What was its extent in time?
Did it repeat or continue into modern times?
          How has it changed over time?
What large group of other phenomena can it be assigned to?
What smaller group of other phenomena can it be assigned to?
What qualities does it share with *no other* phenomena?

4. The definition can include one or more paragraphs of temporal comparison (the comparison of properties, function, and/or genus at different points in time)

Function

How did it work, behave, or unfold?
          Will a descriptive sequence help the reader understand
                    how it worked?
                    What would the sequence describe?
          Was its behavior predictable or unpredictable?
          Did it work/behave differently under different circumstances?
                    At different times?
          Can its behavior or sequence be divided into phases?
                    What separates the phases?
          Was there a cause or trigger for the event?
          What was the time frame for its behavior or significance?
          Where did the behavior take place?
Who/what needed it, used it, or was affected by it?
          What effects did it have on the surrounding events/people?
          What events led up to it?
          What events occurred because of it?
For what purposes or reasons?
          Is there more than one purpose or reason?
          Did the purpose or reason change at different times?
          Was the purpose or reason dependent on any other conditions?
What is its significance? Why do we remember it?
          What did it change?
          Did it create/become a major turning point?
          Did later phenomena use it or depend on it?

Genus

What other objects, events, people, or places can it be grouped with?
What are the qualities that lead you to group them together?
What name can you give this group?
In what significant ways is it different from the others in its group?

Day Two: Writing Brief Temporal Comparisons, Part I

> Focus: Using visual observation to compare changes over time

Over the next two days, the student will practice writing several kinds of brief temporal comparisons.

STEP ONE: **Observe a set of portraits**

Student instructions for Step One:

> Look carefully at these two photographs. The first shows the British statesman Winston Churchill in 1895, at the age of twenty-one; he is wearing the uniform of a British cavalry officer (his unit was called the 4th Queen's Own Hussars). The second shows Churchill in 1943, during an interview in Canada; he is sixty-nine years old and is partway through his first term as Prime Minister of the United Kingdom.

> On a piece of notebook paper, make two columns. At the top of one column, write "Young Churchill." At the top of the other, write "Old Churchill." As you examine the photographs, jot down words and phrases that describe them.
>
> Since you're relying entirely on visual observation, you can only address the following aspects in the Description of a Person directly:
>
> > Expressions of face and body
> > Clothing, dress

But you can also *speculate* about other things based on your interpretation of Churchill's appearance: his stance, his expression, the look in his eyes, etc. As you take notes, choose one or more of the following and write down words and phrases that you think *might* describe them for both the young and the old Churchill.

> Character qualities
> Mind/intellectual capabilities
> Talents and abilities

If you have difficulty, ask your instructor for help.

You should end up with 6–10 observations in each column, Show your work to your instructor when you are finished.

HOW TO HELP THE STUDENT WITH STEP ONE

The student's two columns might look something like this:

Young Churchill	Old Churchill
Steady gaze, looking right at camera	Looking down away from camera
Thick smooth hair	Thin hair, losing hair in front
Smooth jaw	Mouth turning down at corners
Round heavy chin	Lines on face
	Sagging jowls
Thick straight eyebrows	Thinning eyebrows
Military uniform with lots of trim	Dark suit with pinstripes
Straight shoulders	Hunched shoulders
Trim and fit	Heavy, belly
Determined	Tired
Confident	Defensive

If the student has trouble coming up with the required number of observations, ask the following questions:

> *What is the young Churchill looking at? How would you describe his gaze?*
> *How does Churchill's hair change?*
> *What two different adjectives would you choose to describe Churchill's mouth in the first photograph, and then in the second photograph?*
> *Look carefully at his eyebrows in both photographs. How are they different?*
> *How does his clothing change?*
> *Look at his shoulders. What adjective would you use to describe them in the first photo? How about in the second?*
> *How about Churchill's weight and fitness? Can you choose two adjectives that describe these aspects in the first photo, and then two different adjectives for the second?*
> *If you were to describe Churchill's mood in the first photograph, what two adjectives would you pick?*
> *In the second photograph, Churchill is leading a country that is fighting the Second*

World War. How do you think he feels? What two adjectives would you use to describe his mood?

STEP TWO: **Write about a set of portraits**

Student instructions for Step Two:

> Using your lists and referring back to the portraits, write one or two brief paragraphs contrasting the young Churchill to the older Churchill. Aim to have between 50 and 100 words.
>
> Your paragraphs will probably flow more smoothly if you write a paragraph about young Churchill and then another about the older Churchill (the subject-by-subject method of comparison). However, you can also do a point-by-point comparison, where you compare the physical appearance of the two versions of Churchill, then the character of young vs. old, then the expressions of each, and so forth. If you do this, you have to try to avoid repeating "The young Churchill . . . the old Churchill" over and over again.
>
> When your description is finished, show it to your instructor.

HOW TO HELP THE STUDENT WITH STEP TWO

The student's description might resemble one of the following:

> As a young man, Winston Churchill was trim and fit, with a confident, determined gaze. He had straight shoulders, thick smooth hair, and a round, heavy chin. He wore the uniform of a British cavalry officer.
>
> By the time he was nearly seventy, Churchill had grown much heavier. His face was lined, and his jowls sagged. As Prime Minister, he wore a dark pinstriped suit. His shoulders were hunched, and his eyes had become tired and defensive.

> In his portrait at the age of 21, the young Winston Churchill wears a military uniform. He stares straight at the camera. His shoulders are straight, and he is slim and fit. He looks both confident and filled with determination.
>
> In contrast, the older Churchill avoids looking at the camera. He looks tired and defeated. He slumps in his chair and his belly strains his pinstriped suit.

> At 21, Winston Churchill was fit and thin, with thick smooth hair. By the time he was nearly seventy, he had gained weight and his hair and eyebrows had thinned. The young Churchill wore his military uniform proudly; the older Churchill wore a pinstripe suit. He had been confident and determined as a young man, with a straight level gaze; as an older man, Churchill seemed exhausted and defensive, with hunched shoulders and evasive eyes.

Use the following rubric to check the student's description:

Week 26, Part I Rubric

Organization:

1 The description should be between 50 and 100 words in length.
2 It may be either one paragraph or two.
3 The description should compare the same aspects for both the young and old Churchill.
4 The description should make some attempt to speculate about the character of the subject as well as his physical appearance.
5 The description may be organized either subject by subject (first the young Churchill, then the old Churchill) or point by point.

Mechanics:

1 Each sentence should make sense on its own when read aloud.
2 There should be no sentence fragments or run-on sentences.
3 All words should be spelled correctly.
4 The first line of each paragraph should be properly indented.
5 Verb tense should be consistent throughout.
6 "The young" and "the old" should not be repeated more than twice each.

STEP THREE: **Produce a slanted version of the description**

Student instructions for Step Three:

> In the first level of this course (Week 17), you learned that a personal description can be slanted, or biased. The words that you choose as you write your description can incline the reader to like or dislike, respect or despise the subject.
>
> Read the following description of the Mughal emperor Akbar, written by his son Jahangir:
>
> > In his august personal appearance he was of middle height, but inclining to be tall; he was of the hue of wheat; his eyes and eyebrows were black, and his complexion rather dark than fair; he was lion bodied, with a broad chest, and his hands and arms long . . . His august voice was very loud, and in speaking and explaining had a peculiar richness.[28]
>
> Jahangir greatly admired his father; you can tell this by the words he chooses. With your pencil, underline the words "august," "wheat," "lion-bodied," "broad," "long," and "richness." These are nouns and adjectives with positive connotations. If Jahangir had written that his father was "of the hue of clay" or that he was "jackal-bodied," you would have an entirely different picture of Akbar.

---

28. John F. Richards, *The Mughal Empire* (Cambridge University Press, 1995), pp. 44–45.

Compare Jahangir's words with the following description of the emperor Nero, written by the Roman historian Suetonius:

> He was well-proportioned, but his body was spotted and malodorous. . . . His features were pretty rather than pleasing, with eyes that were blue, but dull. His neck was heavy and his stomach hung over his skinny legs.[29]

If Suetonius had described Nero's features as "fine-cut," his neck as "strong," and his legs as "trim," you would take away an entirely different (and much more positive) impression of the emperor.

Using your thesaurus, rewrite your brief description so that the reader gets a positive impression of the young Churchill and a negative impression of the older Churchill—or vice versa. Remember that the same quality can often be described with negative *or* positive words. Here are a few options to get you started—but be sure to choose some words of your own as well.

POSITIVE	NEGATIVE
determined	obstinate
solid	corpulent
cheeks	jowls
confident	arrogant

When you are finished, show your work to your instructor.

HOW TO HELP THE STUDENT WITH STEP THREE

The student's rewritten description might resemble the following:

> As a young man, Winston Churchill was dapper and dandified, with an arrogant, obstinate gaze. He had straight shoulders, glossy slicked-back hair, and a round, fatty chin. He wore the gaudy uniform of a British cavalry officer.
>
> By the time he was nearly seventy, Churchill had grown more solid. His face was distinguished and lined. As Prime Minister, he wore an elegant dark pinstriped suit. His shoulders were set forward, and his eyes had become tired and humble.

If necessary, remind the student to use her thesaurus!

When she is finished, ask her to read back through the Description of a Person in her *topoi* index. Point out that she has just reviewed the first skill listed in the "Remember" column.

---

29. Eric R. Varner, *Mutilation and Transformation: Damnatio Memoriae and Roman Imperial Portraiture* (Brill, 2004), p. 47.

Day Three: Writing Brief Temporal Comparisons, Part II

Focus: Using written descriptions to compare changes over time

STEP ONE: **Read about a place at two different points in time (Student Responsibility)**

Read the following brief descriptions of Lake Chad, a lake which has varied enormously in size and depth for centuries.

★

STEP TWO: **Observe contrasts**

Student instructions for Step Two:

On a piece of notebook paper, make two columns. At the top of one column, write "Lake Chad Before 1960s." At the top of the other, write "Lake Chad Now." Go back through the paragraphs above and jot down words and phrases that describe Lake Chad in the appropriate columns.

You should end up with six to ten observations in each column. Show your work to your instructor when you are finished.

HOW TO HELP THE STUDENT WITH STEP TWO

The student's observations should resemble the following but do not have to be as extensive; there should be at least six observations in each column.

Lake Chad Before 1960s	Lake Chad Now
As large as Lake Erie in North America	5% (1/20th) of its 1960 size
23,500 sq. km/10,000 sq. miles	Dust from the dry bed blows everywhere
One of the largest on earth	1350 sq. km./839 square miles
Much open water	Small area in south of original basin
Narrow/no belts of vegetation	Collapsed fisheries, salty soil
15 feet deep	Invasive plants cover 50% of surface
Dotted with islands	1.5 m [4.9 ft] deep
Inhabitants live on fish	Edged by swampy vegetation and reeds
	Water plants float in center

Many small sandy islands
Fewer fish
More farmland around the edges

STEP THREE: **Write about a place at two different points in time**

Student instructions for Step Three:

Using your chart, write the same sort of description as in the last assignment—one or two paragraphs contrasting Lake Chad before the 1960s with Lake Chad today. You have a little bit more information than you did for the Churchill assignment, so aim for 75–125 words.

For the purposes of this assignment, it isn't necessary for you to footnote your information. Try not to use the exact words of your sources, but the information in the source paragraphs is definitely general knowledge.

As with the last assignment, you will probably find it easier to write first about Lake Chad before the 1960s, and then cover the same aspects for Lake Chad now. But you can also write point by point (size then, size now; depth then, depth now; vegetation then, vegetation now; etc.) as long as you can avoid repeating "then" and "now" or similar phrases over and over again.

When you are finished, show your work to your instructor.

HOW TO HELP THE STUDENT WITH STEP THREE

The student's paragraph(s) may resemble the following:

Lake Chad was once ten thousand square miles across, one of the largest lakes on earth. Its open water was 15 feet deep, dotted with islands. Little vegetation grew at its border, and its inhabitants lived on the fish they caught in the lake.

Now, the lake has shrunk to just 5% of its old size; it is only 839 square miles and 4.9 feet deep. The water remains only in the south of the original lake bed, and dried mud from the rest of the basin blows all over the world. Water plants grow around its edges and have even invaded the lake itself, covering half of the surface and floating in the very center.

Before the 1960s, Lake Chad was 23,500 square kilometers and 15 feet deep; now, it is only 1350 square kilometers and barely five feet deep. Once one of the largest lakes on earth, Lake Chad now only occupies a small southern area of its original lake bed. The inhabitants around the lake used to live primarily on fish, but now they farm around the edges of the lake and support themselves with agriculture too. The lake once had large open spaces and only narrow borders of vegetation, but now it is edged by reeds, and marsh plants grow over half of its surface.

Check the student's work using the following rubric.

Week 26, Part II Rubric

Organization:

1 The description should be between 75 and 125 words in length.
2 It may be either one paragraph or two.
3 The description should compare the same aspects for Lake Chad both before the 1960s and today.
4 The description may be organized either subject by subject or point by point.
5 The description should not use the exact same phrasing as the sources, but footnotes are not necessary.

Mechanics:

1 Each sentence should make sense on its own when read aloud.
2 There should be no sentence fragments or run-on sentences.
3 All words should be spelled correctly.
4 The first line of each paragraph should be properly indented.
5 Verb tense should be consistent throughout.
6 Adverbs such as "then" and "now" or phrases such as "before the 1960s" and "in modern times" should not be repeated.

STEP FOUR: Add vivid metaphors and/or similes

Student instructions for Step Four:

When you first began writing descriptions of places in the first level of this course (Week 10), you learned that effective descriptions use figurative language—vivid metaphors and interesting similes.

Here are examples of both, drawn from Charles Dickens's classic novel *Oliver Twist*.

> The snow lay on the ground, frozen into a hard thick crust; so that only the heaps that had drifted into by-ways and corners were affected by the sharp wind that howled abroad: which, <u>as if expending increased fury on such prey as it found</u>, caught it savagely up in clouds, and, whirling it into a thousand misty eddies, scattered it in air.

> The old smoke-stained storehouses on either side rose heavy and dull from the dense mass of roofs and gables, <u>and frowned sternly upon</u> water too black to reflect even their lumbering shapes.

In the first example, Dickens uses a simile (introduced by *as if*) to compare the wind to a bird of prey. In the second, he uses a metaphor—he speaks of the storehouses as though they were old angry men staring down into the water.

Go back to your description and try to invent one simile and one metaphor. Insert them into your description. Does it sound more interesting—or does the new language sound forced? You won't always improve a piece of writing by including metaphors and similes, but you won't know until you make the experiment.

HOW TO HELP THE STUDENT WITH STEP FOUR

Sample metaphors and similes are in bold type below.

Lake Chad was once ten thousand square miles across, **lying like a gigantic jewel in the dry African lands**. It was one of the largest lakes on earth. Its open water was 15 feet deep, **peppered** with islands. Little vegetation grew at its border, and its inhabitants lived on the fish they caught in the lake.

Now, the lake has shrunk to just 5% of its old size; it is only 839 square miles and 4.9 feet deep. The water remains only in the south of the original lake bed, and dried mud from the rest of the basin blows all over the world, **the ash of a sunburnt land.** Water plants grow around its edges **like a spreading green plague** and have even invaded the lake itself, covering half of the surface and **seizing possession of** the very center.

If the student has difficulty finding the appropriate metaphor or simile, suggest that she focus on the following:

1. What the larger version of Lake Chad must have looked like from the sky: something spilled, something precious and valuable.
2. The contrast between the larger and smaller versions of the lake: as though something stole, thieved, consumed, or blotted part of it out.
3. The wide openness of the larger lake—like a prairie or some other vast open space.
4. The water plants: invaders, a conquering army, usurpers, interlopers
5. The appearance of the many small islands throughout the lake: like something scattered or dropped.

When the student is finished, ask her to read the Description of a Place from her *topoi* list. Point out to her that she has just reviewed the second element in the Remember column.

Day Four: Introduction to Longer Temporal Comparisons

 Focus: Understanding the use of temporal comparison as an organizing theme

A temporal comparison can be a useful element in a longer composition, but it can also stand on its own as an independent piece. Today, the student will look at an essay-length temporal comparison and analyze its elements.

STEP ONE: **Read (Student Responsibility)**

The following essay, "By Post to Peace," was written by Karl Krueger and first appeared in *The Rotarian* (January 1938, pp. 38–39). It describes how the postal system changed from its beginnings up until 1938. Read it carefully.

STEP TWO: **Outline**

Student instructions for Step Two:

There is more than one way to outline this passage "correctly." Your assignment is to pay particular attention to the comparisons in the passage by making an outline on your own paper that fits the model below. You may copy the points in bold type directly into your own outline. If a point is in italics, it is telling you the *type* of information that you need to use to fill in the outline.

    I. Introduction
        A. The mail in 1938
            1. *One kind of mail*
            2. *Another kind of mail*
            3. *A characteristic of the mail*
        B. *An aspect of the mail system's history*
            1. *Observation about length of time*
            2. *Founder*
    II. Ancient mail systems
        A. *Type of early postal system*
        B. *Type of early postal system*
        C. *Type of early postal system*
        D. *Type of early postal system*
        E. Other postal systems
    III. Medieval mail systems
        A. *One kind of system*
        B. *Another kind of system*
            1. *A place where it was*

    2. *A place where it was*
   C. *Another feature of the medieval systems*
  IV. Heinrich von Stephan's changes
   A. *Overall title for things he noticed*
    1. *One type of thing he noticed*
    2. *Another type of thing he noticed*
   B. *Thing he spearheaded*
    1. *First detail about what he spearheaded*
    2. *Second detail about what he spearheaded*
   C. *Result*
    1. *First detail of result*
    2. *Second detail of result*
    3. *Third detail of result*
    4. *Fourth detail of result*
  V. *Current condition*
   A. *One type of detail about current condition*
   B. *Another type of detail about current condition*

  If you need help, ask your instructor. When you're finished with your outline, show it to your instructor.

HOW TO HELP THE STUDENT WITH STEP TWO

The goal of the exercise is to familiarize the student with the form of an extended temporal comparison. Try to avoid frustration with the outlining exercise. If the student cannot figure out what to put for a particular point or subpoint, give her the answer.

  The finished outline should resemble the following (of course, variations and differences are always acceptable if the student can defend them).

I. Introduction
  A. 1938 [current] mail system
    1. 3-cent stamp OR Mail in the Americas OR Domestic mail
    2. 5-cent stamp OR Mail between the continents OR International mail
    3. Safety of the system
  B. The origin of the mail system
    1. Has been going for 65 years
    2. Begun by Henrich von Stephan
II. Ancient mail systems
  A. Southwest Asia
  B. Persian Empire
  C. Roman postal system
  D. References in the Bible
  E. Other postal systems
III. Medieval mail systems
  A. Private postal systems

    B. Public postal systems
        1. In Europe
        2. In England
    C. Treaties provided for mail delivery
IV. Heinrich von Stephan's changes
    A. Noticed "inscrutables" of the postal service
        1. Different rates
        2. Different routes
    B. Suggested an International Congress
        1. Met in 1874 in Switzerland
        2. Formed the International Postal Union
    C. Led to agreement on four items
        1. Uniform postage rates and weights
        2. Classifications
        3. Payments to railroads and steamships in other countries
        4. System of registration and compensation
V. How the postal service now works
    A. Price
    B. Delivery

STEP THREE: **Analyze**

Student instructions for Step Three

> During this step, your instructor will carry on a dialogue with you.

HOW TO HELP THE STUDENT WITH STEP THREE

Carry on the following dialogue with the student:

INSTRUCTOR: This essay begins with an introduction. What does that introduction briefly describe?

> Student: The current mail system

INSTRUCTOR: In the margin next to the first main point, write down, "Brief summary of current state." Now let's look at the second Roman numeral. All of the points in this section describe the postal system at what point in time?

> Student: Ancient times

INSTRUCTOR: Exactly. This describes the postal system at its earliest state of development. In the margin, write "Early stage of development." Now for the third point. What point of development does it describe?

Student: The middle ages

INSTRUCTOR: In the margin, write "Later stage of development." Notice that we're not up to the current day—1938, at the writing of this essay—yet. First, the writer has to describe a transition period. During the changes that Heinrich von Stephan made, the postal system made a transition into its modern form. In the margin next to IV, write "Transition to current form." Now, you probably have a good idea what the last section describes.

Student: Current form

INSTRUCTOR: Write that next to the fifth Roman numeral

Brief summary	**I. Introduction**
of current state	**A. 1938 [current] mail system**
	1. Mail in the Americas
	2. Mail between the continents
	3. Safety of the system
	B. The origin of the mail system
	1. Has been going for 65 years
	2. Begun by Henrich von Stephan
Early stage of	**II. Ancient mail systems**
development	**A. Southwest Asia**
	B. Persian Empire
	C. Roman postal system
	D. References in the Bible
	E. Other postal systems
Later stage of	**III. Medieval mail systems**
development	**A. Private postal systems**
	B. Public postal systems
	1. In Europe
	2. In England
	C. Treaties provided for mail delivery
Transition to	**IV. Heinrich von Stephan's changes**
current form	**A. Noticed "inscrutables" of the postal service**
	1. Different rates
	2. Different routes
	B. Suggested an International Congress
	1. Met in 1874 in Switzerland
	2. Formed the International Postal Union
	C. Led to agreement on four items
	1. Uniform postage rates and weights
	2. Classifications

> 3. **Payments to railroads, steamships in other countries**
> 4. **System of registration and compensation**

Current form   **V. How the postal service now works**
       A. Price
       D. Delivery

STEP FOUR: Write down the pattern of the *topos* (Student Responsibility)

Finish up today's lesson by copying the following onto a blank sheet of paper in the Reference section of your Composition Notebook. You'll come back to this *topos* next week and examine it further.

Temporal Comparison: History

Definition: A comparison between the earlier and later stages of the same historical phenomenon

Procedure	Remember

1. Begin with a brief introduction to the phenomenon
    a. May include a summary of its current state
    b. Can briefly mention important aspects
2. Describe at least one earlier stage of its development.
    a. Properties
    b. Function
    c. Genus
3. Describe the transition to its current form
    a. May involve a chronological narrative of historical events
    b. May involve a historical sequence
4. Describe the current form of the phenomenon.
	1. Can include more than one earlier stage of development

WEEK 27: TEMPORAL COMPARISONS IN HISTORY AND SCIENCE

Day One: Take Notes for a Temporal Comparison

 Focus: Taking notes on a subject at two points in time

Today the student will prepare to write his own version of a longer temporal comparison in history. The assigned topic: how the city of Chicago changed from the early 1800s to the early 1900s.

STEP ONE: Review the *topos*

Student instructions for Step One:

> Before you begin your note-taking, review the form of the comparison by reading carefully through the Temporal Comparison: History *topos* in your reference notebook.
>
> With the definition in mind, read through the following excerpt from a longer temporal comparison in history, written by an educator who went back to her old primary school for a visit.

★

> Notice that Rita Brause begins by introducing you to the phenomenon of her school (in the original, the introduction is much longer) and then goes on to describe both earlier and later stages in its development. However, instead of describing the school as she knew it, talking about its transition, and then describing it again as it is in the present day, she goes back and forth between the earlier and later versions of the school, like this:
>
> | | | |
> |---|---|---|
> | Entrance lobby in my day | compared to | Entrance lobby now |
> | Drapes in my day | compared to | Drapes now |
> | Chandeliers in my day | compared to | Chandeliers now |
>
> and so on. When she finishes making her comparisons, she then begins to write about *why* the transition to the current form of the school happened ("I attribute this to the changed roles . . ."). I didn't include this part of the essay because it is full of academic language—the writer is a professor at Fordham University.

What should you take away from this? When you're writing a temporal comparison, you can either organize your thoughts subject by subject or point by point—just as when you're doing a regular Explanation by Comparison/Contrast. In a subject-by-subject comparison, Rita Brause would spend a page or two describing her school as it was when she attended it, and then spend another page or so describing all the same aspects about the school in the present day. In her point-by-point comparison, she goes back and forth, describing each aspect of the school then and now.

On your Temporal Comparison: History chart, write

2. Can either be organized point by point or subject by subject

in the Remember column.

HOW TO HELP THE STUDENT WITH STEP ONE

Make sure that the student's *topoi* chart now looks like this:

Temporal Comparison: History

Definition: A comparison between the earlier and later stages of the same historical phenomenon

Procedure	Remember

1. Begin with a brief introduction to the phenomenon
    a. May include a summary of its current state
    b. Can briefly mention important aspects
2. Describe at least one earlier stage of its development.
    a. Properties
    b. Function
    c. Genus
3. Describe the transition to its current form
    a. May involve a chronological narrative of historical events
    b. May involve a historical sequence
4. Describe the current form of the phenomenon.
	1. Can include more than one earlier stage of development
	2. Can either be organized point by point or subject by subject

STEP TWO: **Read (Student Responsibility)**

Read through the following excerpts about the city of Chicago both before and after the Great Fire of 1871 without stopping to take notes.

★

STEP THREE: **Take notes**

Student instructions for Step Three:

> Spend the rest of your work time today taking notes about Chicago.
>
> You'll find it easier to write your composition if you organize your notes as you take them. Use three different headings, either on three sheets of paper or as three columns on a single page:
>
> Chicago in the Early 1800s
Chicago in the Late 1800s/Early 1900s
What Led to the Change?
>
> Now, go back through the passages and take notes from each source. Just as you did with the Dred Scott piece, you can do this in one of two ways:
>
> 1) Go through the sources one time each, placing each relevant bit of information from each source beneath the appropriate question as you go.
>
> 2) Pick the first heading and go through all four sources, looking for answers. Do the same for the second heading, and then the third.
>
> Take at least two notes from each passage, and at least twelve notes in total. When you are finished, show your work to your instructor.

HOW TO HELP THE STUDENT WITH STEP THREE

The student's notes might resemble the following. She should have at least two notes from each source, and at least 10 notes altogether.

Chicago in the Early 1800s

In 1848, no railroads, canals, gas, water transport, omnibuses, or cars (Plumbe, pp. 12–13)

No sewers, sidewalks, paved streets (Plumbe, p. 12)

No gas or water system (Plumbe, p. 12)

No telegraph or telephones (Plumbe, p. 13)

"wolves were occasionally seen prowling about" (Plumbe, p. 13)

Population of less than 5,000 in 1840 (Plumbe, p. 15)

Railroad construction and roads built in 1850s (Plumbe, p. 13)

Chicago in the Late 1800s/Early 1900s

Population of over 1 million in 1890 (Plumbe, p. 15)

"creator of the first skyscrapers" (Cremin & Penn, p. 7)

"up through the 1890s, city experienced a period of unprecedented economic growth and expansion" (Cremin & Penn, p. 7)

"national capital of such iconic industries as animal slaughtering, meat packing, and shipping" (Cremin & Penn, p. 7)

Monadnock Building showed "Chicago's ability to be an innovator in the field of architecture" (Cremin and Penn, p. 7)

"had an infrastructure of urban services that was the marvel of the world" (Miller, p. 177)

thousands of streets, lamps, streetcar lines, waterworks, sewers, canals, parks (Miller, p. 177)

City "extended its boundaries into Lake Michigan by using refuse from the disaster as land-fill" (Campbell, p. 128)

What Led to the Change?

Fire "broke out in a busy neighborhood of Chicago in a cattle barn" owned by the O'Learys (Campbell, p. 127)

Fire burned for 30 hours and destroyed "18,000 buildings across 2000 acres" (Campbell, p. 128)

Destroyed "homes, churches, factories, warehouses, and municipal buildings" (Campbell, p. 128)

"Chicago rebuilt quickly after the fire" (Cremin & Penn, p. 7)

"Within hours of the fire's end, a massive rebuilding effort was under way" (Campbell, p. 128)

"began creating a new city upon the still-smoldering ashes of the old" (Cremin & Penn, p. 7)

"A year later, $40 million worth of new buildings" (Campbell, p. 128)

"The fire leveled the central business district but did not destroy integral parts of Chicago's great Prairie Exchange Engine" (Miller, p. 177)

Day Two: Write a Temporal Comparison in History

Focus: Writing about a subject at different points in time

STEP ONE: **Write**

Student instructions for Step One:

Using your notes, write the rough draft of a composition that compares Chicago in the early 1800s to Chicago in the late 1800s/early 1900s and later. Follow the pattern of the Temporal Comparison: History on your *topoi* chart:

1) Begin with a brief introduction to the city of Chicago. You can decide whether this will describe Chicago in the present day (this might require you to look up a few more facts) or in the 19th century.

2) Describe Chicago in the early 19th century.

3) Describe the Great Fire briefly, including a short chronological narrative of historical events.

4) Describe Chicago in the late 19th/early 20th century more fully.

For this essay, use the subject-by-subject rather than point-by-point approach.

Your composition must be at least 150 words in length, and should be divided into at least two or three paragraphs.

Cite at least three sources, using at least one direct quote.

You can show your draft to your instructor if you need help, but you do not *have* to show your work until after you've proofread it in Step Three.

HOW TO HELP THE STUDENT WITH STEP ONE

The student's composition might resemble the following.

I decided to introduce the composition by talking about the city of Chicago today, so I looked up a few facts about population and size online. The student could also begin with a brief description of Chicago in the early 19th century.

> Today, the city of Chicago has nearly three million people. Among American cities, only New York and Los Angeles cover more ground. But Chicago's beginnings were much more humble. In 1835, the city had fewer than 3500 inhabitants. There were no sewers or water system, no sidewalks or paved streets, and no telegraphs or telephones. The edges of the city were so wild that wolves were sometimes seen there![1]
>
> The construction of new railroads began to bring more people to Chicago. But Chicago's biggest changes came after 1871. In October, 1871, a fire broke out in a cattle barn and burned through the city for thirty hours. The buildings were already dry because of a drought, and winds drove the fire to burn even faster. Two thousand acres of the city were destroyed, and 18,000 buildings burned down.[2]
>
> But as soon as the fire burned out, the people of Chicago began to rebuild.[3] New skyscrapers were designed and built. Streets, water systems, canals, parks, and streetcar lines were planned and constructed.[4] The city even used trash from the destroyed buildings to fill in part of Lake Michigan and create more land to build on.[5] By 1890, Chicago had over one million people. It was a leader in meat packing and shipping, and its infrastructure was "the marvel of the world."[6]

---

[1] George Edwards Plumbe, *Chicago: The Great Industrial and Commercial Center of the Mississippi Valley* (The Civic-Industrial Committee of the Chicago Association of Commerce, 1912), pp. 12–13.

[2] Ballard C. Campbell, ed., *Disasters, Accidents and Crises in American History* (Infobase Publishing, 2008), pp. 127–128.

[3] Campbell, p. 128.

[4] Donald L. Miller, *City of the Century: The Epic of Chicago and the Making of America* (Simon & Schuster, 1996), p. 177.

[5] Campbell, p. 128.

[6] Miller, p. 177.

The student may find it helpful to read the following example of how a point-by-point comparison might be developed.

Notice that when point-by-point comparisons are made, the description of the transitional point generally *follows* the comparisons, becoming one of the last elements of the composition.

Throughout the 19th century, Chicago rapidly changed. The population grew from less than five thousand in 1840 to over one million in 1900. It grew from a small town where "wolves were occasionally seen prowling about" to a bustling metropolis with thousands of cars and buses.[1] In the early 1800s, there were no canals, sewers, or waterworks, but less than a century later, a great system of them existed.

Chicago was already becoming prosperous when the Great Fire of 1871 nearly destroyed it. a fire broke out in a cattle barn and burned through the city for thirty hours. The buildings were already dry because of a drought, and winds drove the fire to burn even faster. Two thousand acres of the city were destroyed, and 18,000 buildings burned down.[2]

However, the resilient citizens "began creating a new city upon the still-smoldering ashes of the old."[3] Instead of the former wooden buildings, the world's first skyscrapers were built. Although the central business district was destroyed by the fire, the stockyards and packing plants survived. The industries of meat packing and shipping continued to thrive. The fire did not end the growth of Chicago, but helped it develop even more quickly.

---

[1] George Edwards Plumbe, *Chicago: The Great Industrial and Commercial Center of the Mississippi Valley* (The Civic-Industrial Committee of the Chicago Association of Commerce, 1912), pp. 12–13.

[2] Ballard C. Campbell, ed., *Disasters, Accidents and Crises in American History* (Infobase Publishing, 2008), pp. 127–128.

[3] Dennis H. Cremin & Elan Penn, *Chicago: A Pictorial Celebration* (Sterling Publishing Co., 2006), p. 7.

STEP TWO: **Title and Works Cited age**

Student instructions for Step Two:

> Choose a title for your essay. Include the main subject (Chicago) as well as a phrase describing the time frame that you cover in your composition.
> Title a separate piece of paper "Works Cited." List the sources used in alphabetical order.

HOW TO HELP THE STUDENT WITH STEP TWO

The student should have chosen a descriptive title that includes the main topic as well as a reference time. Examples might be:

Chicago Before and After the Great Fire
Chicago in the Early 19th and Early 20th Centuries
How Chicago Changed from the Early 1800s to the Early 1900s
A Comparison of Chicago Before 1850 and After 1871

If the student struggles, read her one of the titles as an example, and then have her write her own.

Use the comprehensive Works Cited page below to check the student's final Works Cited page.

Campbell, Ballard C., ed. *Disasters, Accidents and Crises in American History.* New York: Infobase Publishing, 2008.

Cremin, Dennis H. and Elan Penn. *Chicago: A Pictorial Celebration.* New York: Sterling Publishing Co., Inc., 2006.

Miller, Donald L. *City of the Century: The Epic of Chicago and the Making of America.* New York: Simon & Schuster, 1996.

Plumbe, George Edwards. *Chicago: The Great Industrial and Commercial Center of the Mississippi Valley.* Chicago: The Civic-Industrial Committee of the Chicago Association of Commerce, 1912.

STEP THREE: **Proofread**

Student instructions for Step Three:

> Proofread your paper, following these guidelines.
> 1) Make sure that your paper is at least 150 words in length and at least two paragraphs.
> 2) Check for the required elements: descriptive title, introduction to Chicago, description of Chicago in the early 1800s, description of the city after the fire, description of the fire as the transition point; also a Works Cited page, at least three sources cited, and at least one direct quote.
> 3) Read your paper out loud, listening for awkward or unclear sections and repeated words. Rewrite awkward or unclear sentences so that they flow more naturally.
> 4) Listen for information that is repeated more than once. Eliminate repetition of ideas.
> 5) Read through the paper one more time, looking for sentence fragments, run-on sentences, and repeated words. Correct fragments and run-on sentences. Listen for unnecessary repetition. If you used a modifier (adverb, adjective, or prepositional phrase acting as an adjective or adverb) more than twice, find another word.
> 6) Check your spelling by looking, individually, at each word that might be a problem.
> 7) Check the formatting of your footnotes and your Works Cited page.
> When you're finished proofreading, show your paper to your instructor.

HOW TO HELP THE STUDENT WITH STEP THREE

Check the student's final composition, using the following rubric.

Week 27 Rubric, Temporal Comparison In History

Organization:

1   The composition should be at least 150 words in length. It should have at least two or three paragraphs.
2   At least three sources should be cited; at least one citation should be a direct quote.
3   The composition should contain an introduction to current Chicago, a description of Chicago in the early 1800s, an explanation of the Great Fire of 1871 that includes a brief chronological narration, and a description of Chicago after the fire.
4   The composition should have a title, centered at the top of the first page. This title should include the subject "Chicago" as well as a reference to time.

Mechanics:

1   Each sentence should make sense on its own when read aloud.
2   There should be no sentence fragments or run-on sentences.
3   All words should be spelled correctly.
4   The first line of each paragraph should be properly indented.
5   Verb tense should be consistent throughout.
6   Footnotes and the Works Cited page should be properly formatted.
7   Most common nouns should not be repeated more than twice. Modifiers should not be used more than twice.

Day Three: Introduction to Temporal Comparison in Science, Part I

 Focus: Understanding the first kind of temporal comparison in science

All things in nature change over time. In fact, a large part of science is the study of why, and how, things change.

A temporal comparison in science describes the changes that have happened to a scientific object or phenomenon over time. There are two major kinds of temporal change in science: regular changes that are part of repeating life cycles, and changes that are *not* part of regular growth and development.

STEP ONE: Read: Temporal comparison of changes due to repeating life cycles (Student Responsibility)

> Read through the following five paragraphs carefully. The author is providing you with an Explanation by Definition; in the course of the essay, he will answer a series of questions about properties and function.

★

STEP TWO: Analyze: Temporal comparison of changes due to repeating life cycles

Student instructions for Step Two:

> Using your Explanation by Definition: Natural Object or Phenomenon chart, go back through the composition. In the spaces provided below, write which question(s) each paragraph of the essay answers.
>
> When you are finished, show your work to your instructor.

HOW TO HELP THE STUDENT WITH STEP TWO

The student's answers should resemble the following. He should have at least one question for each paragraph, but does not necessarily need to include all possible answers.

Paragraph 1: What is it made of? What sort of structure does it have?
Paragraph 2: How does it work or behave? Can its behavior be divided into phases? Is there a cause or trigger for its behavior? Where does the behavior take place?
Paragraph 3: How does it work or behave? Can its behavior be divided into phases? Is there a cause or trigger for its behavior? Where does the behavior take place?
Paragraph 4: How does it work or behave? Can its behavior be divided into phases? Is there a cause or trigger for its behavior? Where does the behavior take place? Is it dependent on anything else?
Paragraph 4: What sort of structure does it have? How does it behave?

STEP THREE: Discuss

INSTRUCTOR: Which paragraphs of the essay compare the frog to itself at different points in time?

Student: Paragraphs 2, 3, and 4

INSTRUCTOR: In the first and last paragraphs, the writer is describing the properties of a frog. Which paragraphs describe the functions of a frog?

Student: Paragraphs 2, 3, and 4

INSTRUCTOR: Why do you think that the writer uses temporal comparison in these three paragraphs?

Student: The functions change as the tadpole grows.

NOTE TO INSTRUCTOR: If necessary, prompt the student by asking, "Do newly hatched tadpoles and older tadpoles breathe in the same way? Do they swim in the same way? Do they eat the same things?"

INSTRUCTOR: Because the way a frog functions *changes* as it grows, the author chooses to describe the functions of breathing, swimming and eating by comparing them at different stages of a frog's life. Does he use subject-by-subject or point-by-point comparison?

Student: Point-by-point

INSTRUCTOR: Notice that the essay does not give you a detailed **sequence.** Rather than describing how a tadpole becomes a frog, the author simply explains how a tadpole breathes at two different times, how a frog swims at two different times, and what a frog eats at two different times. Look at the two diagrams in your workbook. The first shows how an essay containing a sequence would be developed. The second illustrates how a definition using temporal comparison is developed. These are two different strategies that you can put to use when you're writing about science.

STEP FOUR: **Add to the *topos***

Student instructions for Step Four:

> In the "Remember" column of your Explanation by Definition: Natural Object or Phenomenon chart, add the following:

> **3. Temporal comparison (describing the same thing at two different points in time) can be used to develop your answers**

HOW TO HELP THE STUDENT WITH STEP FOUR

Check to see that the student has added the bolded point to his *topoi* chart.

Explanation by Definition: Natural Object or Phenomenon

Definition: An explanation of properties, function, and genus

1. Answer the following questions:
Essential Properties and Accidental Properties
What does it look like?
How does it behave?
What senses come into play as you observe it?
What do those senses reveal?
Is your observation passive (watching/listening) or active (experimenting/collecting/probing)?
What sorts of measurements (temperature, quantity, time, etc.) are necessary to your observation?
What does it resemble?
What is it made of?
What sort of structure does it have?
What is its extent in space?
What is its extent in time?
Which properties are essential?
Which are accidental?
Function
How does it work or behave? . . .

1. Not all questions need to be answered.

2. Selection of genus can be based on either properties or function.

3. Temporal comparison (describing the same thing at two different points in time) can be used to develop your answers.

Day Four: Writing a Temporal Comparison in Science, Part I

 Focus: Writing temporal comparisons of changes due to repeating life cycles

Like frogs, stars have a regular life cycle: birth, youth, maturity, age, death. Today, the student will write a brief temporal comparison, describing a star at two different points in time: youth and old age.

STEP ONE: **Read (Student Responsibility)**

Read carefully through the following paragraphs of information.

STEP TWO: **Chart**

Student instructions for Step Two:

Divide your own paper into two columns. At the top of the left-hand column, write "Young star." At the top of the right-hand column, write "Old star."

Go back through the paragraphs from Step One and write descriptive information about young stars in the left column; information about old stars goes in the right column. Remember that you are not writing details about *sequences*. You don't need to write down information about *how* a star moves from youth into old age; this will not be part of your final composition.

For the purposes of this assignment, don't worry about noting down the source for each piece of information.

The beginning of your chart might look like this:

Young star	Old star
Orbited by a disk of gas and dust	Red giants Shed outer layers become glowing rings of gas ("planetary nebulae")

Aim to have at least five pieces of information under each heading.
When you are finished, show your work to your instructor.

HOW TO HELP THE STUDENT WITH STEP TWO

The student's finished chart might resemble the following, with a minimum of five pieces of information in each column:

Young star	Old star
Orbited by a disk of gas and dust	Red giants
Hotter on the inside than on the outside	Shed outer layers become glowing rings of gas ("planetary nebulae")
Internal temperature 15 million K	Varies in temperature and brightness.
Nuclear reactions in the interior transform hydrogen to helium	Surface temperature drops
Consist mainly of hydrogen	Luminosity and radiation increases
Rotate faster	Surface area of star expands
Corona (outermost atmosphere) emits X-rays	Energies are uneven
Blue light, hot	

STEP THREE: **Write**

Student instructions for Step Three:

> Using the information in your chart, write a point-by-point comparison of a young star and an old star.
>
> You will probably find it helpful to begin by locating parallel pieces of information. For example, in the chart above, "Orbited by a disk of gas and dust" and "Shed outer layers become glowing rings of gas" are parallel—both of them describe the relationship of the star to outlying layers of gas. You should discuss these two points in the same paragraph.
>
> The composition can be brief; aim for at least a hundred words. You'll probably want to divide the composition into at least two paragraphs. Avoid one-sentence paragraphs, though!
>
> Your biggest challenge will be to avoid repeating "young star" and "old star" over and over again. Try to think of ways to vary your sentence structure.
>
> When your work is finished, show it to your instructor.

HOW TO HELP THE STUDENT WITH STEP THREE

The student's composition should resemble the following:

> Young stars are characterized by hot blue light, while old stars give off reddish light that earns them the name "red giants." In their youth, stars have an internal temperature of 15 million K; as they age, they vary in temperature and in brightness, and the energy they produce is uneven. The surface temperature of an older star drops, but because the star expands, its surface area increases. This means that the star actually grows brighter. Young stars also rotate more quickly than old stars of the same type.

Young stars are often located at the center of a disk of gas and dust. Old stars are also surrounded by rings of gas, but these rings—incorrectly known as "planetary nebulae"—are actually formed from the outer layers that the aging star sheds.

You can use the following rubric to check the student's finished work.

Week 27 Rubric, Temporal Comparison In Science

Organization:

1 The description should be at least 100 words long, with at least two paragraphs.
2 It should be organized as a point-by-point comparison.
3 It should *not* include a descriptive sequence about how a young star turns into a red giant; it should instead describe the young star, and also describe the same aspects of an old star.

Mechanics:

1 Each sentence should make sense on its own when read aloud.
2 There should be no sentence fragments or run-on sentences.
3 All words should be spelled correctly.
4 The first line of each paragraph should be properly indented.
5 Verb tense should be consistent throughout.
6 "The young" and "the old" should not be repeated more than twice each.

WEEK 28: TEMPORAL COMPARISONS IN SCIENCE

Day One: Introduction to Temporal Comparison in Science, Part II

 Focus: Understanding the two kinds of temporal comparison in science

STEP ONE: **Write down the pattern of the *topos* (Student Responsibility)**

In last week's work, you began to learn about the different ways that a temporal comparison in science can be constructed. These comparisons often occur as part of a longer composition, but could also stand alone as brief independent essays.

By way of review, copy the following onto a blank sheet of paper in the Reference section of your Composition Notebook.

Temporal Comparison: Science

Definition: A comparison between the earlier and later stages
of the same natural object or phenomenon

Procedure

1. Compare aspects of the subject
at different stages of a regular life cycle

Remember

1. Often occurs as part of a
longer composition
2. Can either be organized point by
point or subject by subject

STEP TWO: **Read: Temporal comparison of natural changes (Student Responsibility)**

Read through the following two excerpts carefully. The first describes the Great Red Spot, a storm in Jupiter's atmosphere so large that it can be seen from Earth. The second describes a glacier which once covered the land that is now Wisconsin.

★

STEP THREE: **Analyze: Temporal comparison of natural changes**

Student instructions for Step Three:

How is the Great Red Spot of Jupiter different from a frog?

I'm sure that plenty of differences come to your mind. But here's the one I want you to think about: Frogs go through the same transformation again and again. Millions of tadpoles have breathed with gills and eaten pond scum, before turning into frogs that breathe air and eat animal life. The descriptions in "Queer Things about Frogs" could apply to almost any tadpole-to-frog transformation.

But the Great Red Spot of Jupiter goes through a unique series of changes. Nothing except the Great Red Spot itself can be described in exactly this way.

Read carefully through the chart below:

Earlier Great Red Spot	**Current Great Red Spot**
1. Developed deep red color 1880s	1. 15,000 miles east to west
2. 25,000 miles east to west	

Ongoing Changes

1. Color fluctuates
2. Moves 1,250 miles north-south
3. Moves in longitude

You will see that the author describes the Great Red Spot at two different points in time—in its earliest form, when it had just developed its deep red color and was 25,000 miles across; and in its current form, when it has shrunk to 15,000 miles across. The author also adds an additional set of descriptions: The Great Red Spot changes color and location constantly. These changes are *cyclical*. They happen over and over again—but they happen only to the Great Red Spot, not to *all* atmospheric phenomena on Jupiter.

Now, look closely at the description of the Wisconsin glacier. Can you fill in the chart below? If you need help, ask your instructor.

HOW TO HELP THE STUDENT WITH STEP THREE

The student's chart should resemble the following:

Earlier Form of Glacier	**Later Form of Glacier**
1. What it did:	1. What it did:
a) Advanced, pushing everything out of its way	a) Ground to a halt
b) Picked up massive amounts of dust, dirt, debris	b) Retreated to Canada
2. What it was like:	2. What it was like:
a) Reached thickness of nearly two miles	a) Melting into streams and rivers
b) Towered 1600 feet in air	b) Cut into furrows and lines

What Caused the Change
1. Warmer, drier weather

Give the student as much help as necessary, since the answers may not be obvious.

When the student has finished the chart, point out the author's use of both metaphor and simile. The simile is:

Beads of water coalesced into tiny streams like nervous perspiration from a sentient being awaiting its imminent demise.

The author then builds on this simile by using metaphoric language that refers to both the glacier and the sun and wind as sentient (thinking, aware) beings:

Each spring the brow of the great glacier began to glisten.
The snout of the glacier began to drip.
During the heat of the summer the hungry sun and thirsty wind caused tiny streams to form atop the glacier.
[T]he once invincible glacier, its surface now deeply lined, retreated to Canada . . .

STEP FOUR: **Add to the pattern of the *topos***

Student instructions for Step Four:

> Add the following to your Temporal Comparison: Science chart, under "Procedure."
>
> > 2. Compare aspects before and after a natural change unique to the subject
> >   a. May include description of changes that occur in a regular cycle
> >   b. May include explanation of why the change occurs
>
> Notice that points *a* and *b* are optional; the comparison of Jupiter includes *a* but not *b*, while the excerpt on the Wisconsin glacier contains *b* but not *a*.

HOW TO HELP THE STUDENT WITH STEP FOUR

Check to make sure that the student's *topos* chart now includes the following:

Temporal Comparison: Science

Definition: A comparison between the earlier and later stages
of the same natural object or phenomenon

Procedure   Remember

1. Compare aspects of the subject   1. Often occurs as part of a
at different stages of a regular life cycle   longer composition
2. Compare aspects before and after a   2. Can either be organized point
natural change unique to the subject   by point or subject by subject
    a. May include description of changes
    that occur in a regular cycle
    b. May include explanation of why
    the change occurs

Day Two: Writing a Temporal Comparison in Science, Part II

Focus: Writing temporal comparisons of natural changes

Today, the student will write a brief temporal comparison that compares the Washington volcano Mount St. Helens (including nearby Spirit Lake) to itself before and after it erupted on May 18, 1980.

STEP ONE: **Read (Student Responsibility)**

Read the following excerpts carefully.

★

STEP TWO: **Chart**

Student instructions for Step Two:

Divide your own paper into three columns. At the top of the left-hand column, write "Before." In the middle column, write "After." At the top of the right-hand column, write "Cause."

Go back through the paragraphs from Step One and write descriptive information about Mount St. Helens and Spirit Lake before the eruption in the left column. In the center column, write information about the mountain and lake *after* the eruption. In the right-hand column, write information about the cause of the change (the eruption).

The beginning of your chart might look like this:

Before	After	Cause
9,677 feet high	Summit and north flank collapsed	Giant landslide

Aim to have at least five notes in the Before column, eight to nine notes in the After column, and five notes in the Cause column.

HOW TO HELP THE STUDENT WITH STEP TWO

The student's chart might resemble the following, with at least five of the included notes in each of the Before and Cause columns, and at least eight notes in the After column.

Before	After	Cause
9,677 feet high	Summit and north flank collapsed	Giant landslide
Regular cone covered with snow	150 square miles of trees knocked down	Lateral blast
Same shape as Mount Fuji	Bridges and houses destroyed	Rocks and melting ice created mudflows
Spirit Lake, blue and crystal-clear, picture perfect	Bleak and gray landscape	
	Spirit Lake, filled with floating and sunken trees	Greatest volcanic eruption in 48 states in recorded history
	8,364 feet (1,313 feet shorter)	
Wildlife; birds, deer and elk, squirrels, bears	1 cubic mile lost	
	1500 foot crater formed, shape of 1x2 mile amphitheater	World's largest recorded avalanche
Forest, wildflowers such as lupine and fireweed	230 square miles devastated, 15 miles north to Green River	Superheated gases carried volcanic rock into the lake
	Spirit Lake filled with dirt, trees, rocks, carcasses	
Hikers and campers	Spirit Lake, bottom 300 feet higher	
	Water temperature 100 degrees	
	Fish, food chains, habitats gone.	
	Water 22 times as alkaline, contained manganese, iron, phosphate, sulfate, chloride.	

STEP THREE: **Write**

Student instructions for Step Three:

> Using the information in your chart, write a subject-by-subject comparison of Mount St. Helens and Spirit Lake before and after the eruption.
>
> Include a brief explanation of the cause of the change (that would be the eruption itself). This explanation does not need to be a descriptive sequence or a chronological narrative; it should simply tell the reader that the eruption occurred and should include a few helpful descriptive details. The explanation can either come in the middle of the composition or at the end.
>
> The composition should have at least three paragraphs and should be at least 125 words in length (it can be longer).
>
> When your work is finished, show it to your instructor.

HOW TO HELP THE STUDENT WITH STEP THREE

The student's finished composition might resemble the following:

> Before May 18, 1980, Mount St. Helens was 9,677 feet high. Its cone was covered by snow, and it strongly resembled Mount Fuji in Japan. Birds lived on its slopes, as did deer and elk. Squirrels hunted nuts, and bear fished in the nearby streams. Not far away, beautiful Spirit Lake was blue and as clear as crystal. Hikers and campers enjoyed the mountain and the lake.
>
> Then, on May 18, a lateral blast blew away the top and the north side of the mountain. A giant landslide carried dirt and rock down the mountain, in the world's largest recorded avalanche. Mudflows carried debris and dead animals into Spirit Lake. Volcanic rock fell into the water.
>
> After the eruption, Spirit Lake was filled with trees, dirt, and decaying animal bodies. The temperature of the water had risen to 100 degrees, and the water had been poisoned with phosphate, sulfate, and chloride. The lake was 300 feet shallower, and the fish were dead. Mount St. Helen's was more than 1300 feet shorter. Its slopes were bleak and gray, covered with fallen trees. The mountain had lost 1 cubic mile of its mass, and its top was now a crater 1500 feet deep, shaped like an amphitheater 2 miles wide.

Note that the student could also place the brief description of the eruption itself at the end of the composition.

You can use the following rubric to check the student's finished work.

Week 28 Rubric, Second Temporal Comparison In Science

Organization:

1 The description should be at least 125 words long, with at least three paragraphs.
2 It should be organized as a subject-by-subject comparison.
3 It should include a brief description of the eruption itself, either in the middle of or at the end of the composition.

Mechanics:

1 Each sentence should make sense on its own when read aloud.
2 There should be no sentence fragments or run-on sentences.
3 All words should be spelled correctly.
4 The first line of each paragraph should be properly indented.
5 Verb tense should be consistent throughout.

Day Three: Sentence Transformations in Science Writing

 Focus: Practicing skills in sentence transformation

Most of the student's sentence transformations have been done using examples from history or literature. Today, he'll work on transforming sentences from science essays.

As an additional challenge, the student will be asked to identify *what* transformations are possible for each sentence.

STEP ONE: **Review (Student Responsibility)**

Read carefully through the nine types of transformation on your Sentence Variety chart. Then, review the following instructions for transformation carefully.

To transform descriptive adjectives into nouns, look for adjectives that come right before the nouns they modify. Or, look for prepositional phrases beginning with "of" and see if they can be turned into descriptive adjectives.

To transform active verbs into passive, look for sentences with action verbs and direct objects.

Look for sentences with indirect objects to transform into objects of a preposition.

To transform a participle into an infinitive, look for an -ing word following an action verb.

To transform a main verb into an infinitive, pick a strong verb and see whether you are able to add one of the following verbs to it:

VERBS THAT ARE OFTEN FOLLOWED BY INFINITIVES

agree	aim	appear	arrange	ask	attempt
beg	begin	care	choose	consent	continue
dare	decide	deserve	dislike	expect	fail
forget	get	hesitate	hope	hurry	intend
leap	like	love	ought	plan	prefer
prepare	proceed	promise	refuse	remember	start
strive	try	use	wait	want	wish

To intensify an adjective, look for descriptive adjectives that either come before a noun or follow a linking verb.

To change a word into a phrase, metaphor, or kenning, look for strong and interesting nouns.

To change a positive statement to a negative statement, look for a strong statement. Then use your thesaurus to find antonyms for the nouns and verbs in the statement.

STEP TWO: **Transform**

Student instructions for Step Two:

In each of the following sentences, identify the element that can be transformed. (There may be more than one transformation possible.) Then, rewrite the sentence on your own paper, using the guidelines on your Sentence Variety Chart.

All of the sentences below are original, taken directly from the listed sources.

HOW TO HELP THE STUDENT WITH STEP TWO

For each sentence, I have described likely transformations and given an example. Other transformations may be possible (for example, many positive statements can be converted to negative and vice versa). Accept any reasonable answers.

However, make sure that the student identifies at least five different kinds of transformation—rather than just changing all the positives to negatives, or making all of the descriptive adjectives into metaphors, or making all the active verbs passive, etc.

If the student needs help, tell him *which* transformation he needs to carry out.

From J. Arthur Thomson, *The Outline of Science, Vol. 1: A Plain Story Simply Told* (New York: G. P. Putnam's Sons, 1922).

Blue, green, yellow, red, and white combine to give a glorious display of colour.
Transformations: Infinitive to participle, adjective to intensified or added adjectives, noun to descriptive adjective

Blue, green, yellow, red, and white combine, giving a glorious and vibrant display of color.
Blue, green, yellow, red and white combine, giving a dazzling display of color.
Blue, green, yellow, red and white combine to give a glorious color display.

Play, we repeat, gives us a glimpse of the possibilities of the mammal mind.
Transformations: Indirect object to object of the preposition, descriptive adjective to noun
Play, we repeat, gives a glimpse to us of the possibilities of the mind of mammals.

The elephant at the Belle Vue Gardens in Manchester used to collect pennies from benevolent visitors.
Transformations: Infinitive to main verb, adjective to added adjective, descriptive adjective to noun.
The elephants at the Belle Vue Gardens in Manchester often collected pennies from visitors of benevolence.
The elephants at the Belle Vue Gardens in Manchester would collect pennies from benevolent and generous visitors.

When a visitor gave the elephant a halfpenny it used to throw it back with disgust.
Transformations: Indirect object to object of preposition, infinitive to main verb
When a visitor gave a halfpenny to the elephant, it threw it back with disgust.

From P. W. Atkins, *The Periodic Kingdom: A Journey into the Land of the Chemical Elements* (New York: Basic Books, 1995).

Magnesium was culled from its compounds by Davy in 1808, calcium in 1808 (also by Davy), and strontium in 1808 (Davy again).
Transformations: Passive verb to active verb
Davy culled magnesium, calcium, and strontium from their compounds in 1808.

By investigating the properties of X rays emitted by atoms, Moseley was able to count the positive charges of a nucleus.
Transformations: Infinitives to participles, infinitive to main verb, noun to descriptive adjective [note that in compounds like X ray, no hyphen is used in the noun form, but a hyphen is used in the adjective form]
By investigating X-ray properties emitted by atoms, Moseley could count the positive charges of a nucleus OR positive nuclear charges.

Stars do not burn smoothly from their inception to their death.
Transformations: Negative statement to positive statement
Stars burn unevenly from their inception to their death.

The internal structure of atoms was determined by a succession of experiments in the late nineteenth and early twentieth centuries.
Transformations: Passive verb to active verb, noun to descriptive adjective
A succession of experiments in the late nineteenth and early twentieth centuries determined internal atomic structure.

From Rachel Carson, *Silent Spring* (Boston: Houghton Mifflin, 1994).

Under primitive agricultural conditions the farmer had few insect problems.
Transformations: Descriptive adjectives to nouns, adjectives to intensified or added adjectives
Under primitive conditions of agriculture, the farmer had few problems with insects.
Under ancient and primitive agricultural conditions the farmer had few and inconsequential insect problems.
Under primeval agricultural conditions the farmer had negligible insect problems.

When the public protests, confronted with some obvious evidence of damaging results of pesticide applications, it is fed little tranquilizing pills of half truth.
Transformations: Metaphor to word, passive verb to active verb
When the public protests, confronted with some obvious evidence of damaging results of pesticide applications, scientists feed it little tranquilizing pills of half-truth.
When the public protests, confronted with some obvious evidence of damaging results of pesticide applications, it is given calming half-truths.

There is a cheaper and better way to remove crabgrass than to attempt year after year to kill it out with chemicals.
Transformations: Infinitives to participles
There is a cheaper and better way to remove crabgrass than attempting year after year to kill it out with chemicals.
There is a cheaper and better way to remove crabgrass than to attempt killing it out with chemicals, year after year.

As many examples show, the poison is carried in by rains and runoff from surrounding land.
Transformations: Passive verb to active verb
As many examples show, rains and runoff carry the poison in from surrounding land.

Day Four: Copia Exercise
Negative and Positive Modifiers

 Focus: Understanding negative and positive modifiers

STEP ONE: Understand the purpose of negative and positive modifiers (Student Responsibility)

Back in Week 22, you learned the technique of *varying by equivalence*. You learned that a positive statement can be rewritten as a negative, or vice versa.

Positive Statements	Negative Statements
They have a plentiful lack of wit.	They are not witty.
His attentions were over.	His attentions did not continue.
The prospect was exceedingly agreeable.	The prospect was not at all unpleasant.

Varying by equivalence can also be done for individual words in a sentence—particularly adjectives and adverbs. Look how Erasmus changed the positive adverb *greatly* as he varied his sentences.

Your letter pleased me greatly.
Your letter pleased me in no small measure.
Your letter pleased me in no small scale.

In the last two sentences, Erasmus transforms a single adverb into a phrase expressing the same meaning—but expressed negatively.

Usually, a positive adverb or adjective is the first one to come to your mind when you're writing. A negative restatement usually highlights some important comparison or contrast. The following three sentences are from Bill Bryson's bestseller *A Short History of Nearly Everything*:

He was a bright but not outstanding student.
Meteorites are not abundant and meteoritic samples not especially easy to get hold of.
Putting things in order is not the easiest of tasks.

Why didn't Bryson just write the following?

He was a bright, mediocre student.
Meteorites are scarce, and meteoritic samples hard to get hold of.
Putting things in order is a hard task.

Because, in each case, he was drawing a contrast between the negatively-phrased modifier and something else. In the first sentence, Bryson plays against the assumption that a bright student is *always* an outstanding student, by highlighting the reader's assumption that bright and out-standing are always parallel.

The second sentence comes right after a paragraph in which a scientist has been trying to figure out where to find very ancient rocks, which he wants to use in an effort to find the exact age of the Earth. The problem, says Bryson, is that "very ancient rocks" are extremely hard to get to. What did the scientist do?

> The assumption he made—rather a large one, but correct, as it turned out—was that many meteorites are essentially leftover building materials from the early days of the solar system, and thus have managed to preserve a more or less pristine interior chemistry. Measure the age of these wandering rocks and you would have the age also (near enough) of the earth.[30]

Much easier than digging miles down into the earth for layers of ancient rock, right? Well . . .

> As always, however, nothing was quite as straightforward as such a breezy description makes it sound. Meteorites are not abundant and meteoritic samples not especially easy to get hold of. [31]

The reader is expecting the scientist's solution to solve a problem—the lack of abundant, easily accessible ancient rocks. Bryson chooses the negative phrases "not abundant" and "not especially easy to get hold of" in order to highlight the difficulties that still exist. In comparison with ancient rocks, meteorites are *still* hard to get your hands on.

How about the third sentence? It is the introduction to a paragraph about biological classification which explains how a certain scholar took *forty years* to figure out a classification system:

> Putting things in order is not the easiest of tasks. In the early 1960s, Colin Groves of the Australian National University began a systematic survey of the 250-plus known species of primate. Oftentimes it turned out that the same species had been described more than once—sometimes several times—without any of the discoverers realizing that they were dealing with an animal that was already known to science. It took Groves four decades to untangle everything, and that was with a comparatively small group of easily distinguished, generally noncontroversial creatures. Goodness knows what the results would be if anyone attempted a similar exercise with the planet's estimated 20,000 types of lichens, 50,000 species of mollusk, or 400,000-plus beetles.[32]

Given how huge the task is, "not the easiest of tasks" is an ironic understatement, meant to contrast with the enormity of the job.

As you can see, choosing to use a negative or a positive modifier has to do with the feel or tone that you want to convey to the reader. The opposing meanings can be very subtle, and you may not always be able to express exactly why an author chooses one method over another. For now, just try to be aware of the differences that a change in modifiers might produce.

One more thing to keep in mind: Rephrasing a modifier might require a whole phrase, like this:

> He had a <u>secret</u> desire to be a superhero.
> He had a desire, <u>not known to anyone,</u> to be a superhero.

---

30. Bill Bryson, *A Short History of Nearly Everything: Special Illustrated Edition* (Broadway, 2010), p. 156.
31. Ibid.
32. Bryson, *A Short History*, p. 363.

Or, a modifer can be changed with a single word.

> He had a <u>secret</u> desire to be a superhero.
> He had an <u>unrevealed</u> desire to be a superhero.

STEP TWO: **Practice changing positive modifiers into negatives and vice versa**

Student instructions for Step Two:

> Fill in the chart below, changing positives into negatives and vice versa. You don't have to get too creative (although you can if you want)—this is just to get you comfortable with the idea. Remember that if you insert a phrase in place of a single word, you may also need to add punctuation.
> If you have trouble finding a way to rephrase the sentence, follow these three steps:
> 1) Look up the adverb or adjective in the thesaurus.
> 2) Find the *antonyms* to the adverb or adjective.
> 3) Use an antonym (to transform a negative to a positive), or else put a negative in front of an antonym (to transform a positive to a negative)

HOW TO HELP THE STUDENT WITH STEP TWO

Although there is certainly room for variation, the student's answers might resemble those below. If necessary, use the answers to prompt the student.

You may once again need to point out that "positive" doesn't mean "good"—it means that the positive statement doesn't have a negation (not, no, never) in it.

These are a little more challenging than the student's previous exercise in varying by equivalence.

Positive:	Negative:
He was usually in a hurry.	He was, not surprisingly, in a hurry.
The gift was generous.	The gift was in no way stingy
She ran away rapidly.	**She ran away, in a non-leisurely fashion.**
Her speech was eloquent.	Her speech was not at all inarticulate.
The thunder was terrifying.	The thunder was in no way reassuring.
The dog ate greedily.	**The dog ate without moderation.**

STEP THREE: **Add to the Sentence Variety chart (Student Responsibility)**

Add the following principle and illustration to the Sentence Variety chart. Note that the first example is of an adjective, while the second is an adverb.

positive modifier ⟷ negative modifier   He was cheerful this morning.
                                           He was not unhappy this morning.

                                           She drove quickly.
                                           She drove in no way slowly.

STEP FOUR: **Practice sentence variety**

Student instructions for Step Four:

The sentences below are adapted from Bill Bryson's bestselling nature book *A Walk in the Woods: Rediscovering America on the Appalachian Trail* (New York: Broadway Books, 1998). On your own paper, rewrite each underlined modifier so that positives become negatives and negatives become positives—just as Bill Bryson first wrote them. If you change a phrase to a word or vice versa, you may have to insert additional punctuation and/or conjunctions (and, but, or, nor, for, yet).

When you are finished, ask your instructor to show you Bryson's original sentences. How close were you?

HOW TO HELP THE STUDENT WITH STEP FOUR

Bryson's original sentences are in bold type below. The student's answers should resemble the originals but do not have to be identical.

A sign announced that this was an exceptional footpath, the not unknown Appalachian Trail.
A sign announced that this was no ordinary footpath, but the celebrated Appalachian Trail.

Black bears, not frequently, attack.
Black bears rarely attack.

All bears are agile, in no way stupid, and not inconsiderably strong, and they are always hungry.
All bears are agile, cunning, and immensely strong, and they are always hungry.

With a grizzly, you should make for a less than short tree, since grizzlies abhor climbing.
With a grizzly, you should make for a tall tree, since grizzlies aren't much for climbing.

With black bears, however, playing dead is <u>less than productive</u>, since they will <u>not cease</u> chewing on you until you are considerably past caring.
With black bears, however, playing dead is futile, since they will continue chewing on you until you are considerably past caring.

The bears were <u>unmistakably</u> startled, but <u>calmed</u> by the flash.
The bears were clearly startled but not remotely alarmed by the flash.

If I did happen upon a bear, I would be quite <u>without resources</u>.
If I did happen upon a bear, I would be quite helpless.

Week 29: Preparing To Write About A Longer Work Of Fiction

Over the next two weeks, the student will work on applying story analysis skills to a longer work of fiction.

The work is a classic retelling of the Robin Hood legend by the well-known writer Mary MacLeod (1861–1951), originally published in 1906 in a longer collection called *A Book of Ballad Stories*. The retelling is a little more than 13,000 words long; it could be classified as a "novella" (shorter than a full-length novel but longer than a short story).

There is one contradiction in the novella. The very first line says that Robin Hood lived "in the days of Richard I" (Richard Lionheart ruled England 1189–1199). But later on, the king of England is called "Edward"—probably Edward I, who ruled 1272–1307 (although it could also refer to Edward II, 1307–1327, or Edward III, 1327–1377).

Why the difference? Apparently, in her introduction, Mary MacLeod is referring to the sixteenth-century tradition that Robin Hood lived during the days of the Crusades; this was first suggested by the Renaissance historian John Mair in 1521. But her retelling is based on older versions of the Robin Hood folk tales. These earliest tales place Robin Hood during the reign of a "King Edward."

In all likelihood, the stories do come from 1272 or later, rather than from the time of Richard Lionheart.

Instead of dividing this week's work into days, I have given the student a simpler assignment: First, read *The Legend of Robin Hood* all the way through without stopping—just read for fun. Then, read back through it a second time, making a few notes as she goes.

Follow the steps below. You and the student can divide the reading and note-taking up into as many different days as necessary.

STEP ONE: **Read (Student Responsibility)**

Get comfortable and read *The Legend of Robin Hood* from beginning to end. You can do this over two days or more if necessary.

Enjoy the stories.

Don't forget to eat a cookie.

STEP TWO: **Take notes**

Student instructions for Step Two:

> Now, go back and reread *The Legend of Robin Hood* from the beginning, one more time. As you read, write down the following information for each chapter.
>
> 1) What is the title of the chapter?
> 2) Who is the main character?
> 3) What is the most important thing that happens to the main character in the chapter?
> 4) Who are the other important characters?
> 5) What is one important thing that happens to each of them?
>
> To help you, here are my answers for the first chapter.
>
> **1) Chapter One, Robin Hood and the Knight**
> **2) Robin Hood**
> **3) He gives money, clothes, and help to a poor knight**
> **4) Little John, Sir Richard Lee**
> **5) Little John goes with Sir Richard Lee; Sir Richard Lee becomes prosperous again**
>
> Your answers might be slightly different—which is fine. Just be able to explain *why* you chose the answers you did. For example, even though so much of the chapter is about the knight Richard Lee, I chose Robin Hood as the main character because the chapter begins *and* ends with him.
>
> When you're finished with your chapter notes, show them to your instructor.

HOW TO HELP THE STUDENT WITH STEP TWO

Model answers follow. It is fine for the student's answers to vary slightly, as long as he can explain the reasoning behind his choices.

You may need to remind him that he doesn't have to identify *every* character in the chapters; he should only pick out the characters who cause things to change, or who go through changes themselves.

1) Chapter One, Robin Hood and the Knight
2) Robin Hood
3) He gives money, clothes, and help to a poor knight
4) Little John, Sir Richard Lee
5) Little John goes with Sir Richard Lee; Sir Richard Lee becomes prosperous again

1) Chapter Two, Little John and the Sheriff of Nottingham
2) Little John
3) He goes to work for the Sheriff of Nottingham
4) Sheriff of Nottingham, Robin Hood
5) Sheriff has to take an oath to Robin Hood, Robin Hood gets the better of the sheriff

1) Chapter Three, How Robin Hood was Paid His Loan
2) Robin Hood
3) He gets his loan repaid
4) Sir Richard Lee
5) He repays the loan

NOTE: Although part of the chapter is about Richard Lee, the chapter centers around the repayment of the loan to Robin Hood, so that Robin Hood's expectations shape the action of this chapter's story.

1) Chapter Four, The Golden Arrow
2) Robin Hood
3) Wins the gold arrow at the tournament
4) Little John, Sheriff of Nottingham, Richard Lee
5) Little John is wounded in the knee, the sheriff puts on the tournament to catch Robin Hood, Richard Lee takes the outlaws into his castle

1) Chapter Five, How the Sheriff Took Sir Richard Prisoner
2) Sir Richard
3) Taken prisoner by the sheriff
4) Sheriff of Nottingham, Robin Hood
5) Sheriff dies, Robin Hood rescues Richard Lee

NOTE: Robin Hood could also be the main character, since he rescues Sir Richard, but Sir Richard goes through a greater change—from freedom, to imprisonment, to freedom again.

1) Chapter Six, How the King Came to Sherwood Forest
2) King Edward
3) Finds Robin Hood
4) Robin Hood
5) Agrees to go back to court with the king

1) Chapter Seven, How Robin Hood Went Back to the Greenwood
2) Robin Hood
3) Goes back to the greenwood
4) King Edward
5) Makes peace with Richard Lee and with Robin Hood

1) Chapter Eight, Robin Hood and the Butcher
2) Robin Hood
3) Tries to be a butcher
4) Sheriff of Nottingham
5) Tricked by Robin Hood into going to Sherwood Forest

1) Chapter Nine, The Jolly Tanner
2) Arthur-a-Bland
3) Joins Robin Hood's band
4) Robin Hood, Little John
5) Robin Hood meets his match when he fights Arthur, Little John meets his relative again

1) Chapter Ten, How Robin Hood Drew His Bow for the Last Time
2) Robin Hood
3) Dies
4) Sir William, Little John
5) Sir William leads the king's fight against Little John, Little John buries his master

WEEK 30: WRITING ABOUT A LONGER WORK OF FICTION

Day One: Think

 Focus: Understanding how individual sections of episodic fiction work

Last week, the student took notes in order to remember the main events of *The Legend of Robin Hood*. Today, he will use those notes and the story itself to write brief answers to a series of questions.

STEP ONE: **Review (Student Responsibility)**

Read quickly back through your notes now, to remind yourself of the characters and events in the story.

Then, read the following definitions from Level 1 of this course carefully.

protagonist: the character who wants to get, become, or accomplish something
antagonist: the character, force, or circumstance that opposes the protagonist

hero/heroine: a central character with admirable qualities
villain: an antagonist with evil motives

conflict: the clash between protagonist and antagonist
story climax: the point of greatest tension or conflict
pivot point: the moment at which the main character changes goals, wants, or direction

STEP TWO: **Understand the form of episodic fiction**

Student instructions for Step Two:

The Legend of Robin Hood is a work of **episodic fiction.** Read the definition out loud now:

episodic fiction: a series of self-contained stories, connected

by common characters and/or an overall plot

In episodic fiction, each chapter or story has its own protagonist and antagonist and its own conflict. These characters and conflicts work together to produce the larger story.

You are probably most familiar with episodic fiction from television. Most television series use the techniques of episodic fiction. Each TV show, or "episode," can be watched on its own—but each one also adds to the overall story that the TV series is telling as a whole. In some episodic TV, such as the series *Lost*, the overall story (the one told by *all* the episodes together) is so important that individual episodes may not make very much sense unless you've watched all the episodes before; the episodes are more like chapters in a regular novel. In other series, particularly comedies, the overall structure is much weaker. The characters and their stories do develop over time, but you can perfectly well watch an episode from the middle of the second or third or fourth season and understand it without difficulty. Comedy series, such as *I Love Lucy* or *Seinfeld*, are more likely to have stronger episodes and a weaker overall structure.

The classic children's novels *Five Children and It*, *Homer Price*, *The Moffats* and *Pippi Longstocking* all use an episodic structure. So does James Herriot's bestselling *All Creatures Great and Small*.

Add the definition of episodic fiction to your Literary Terms chart now.

HOW TO HELP THE STUDENT WITH STEP TWO

Check to see that the student has added the new definition to the literary terms chart.

STEP THREE: Identify the literary elements of each episode

Student instructions for Step Three:

Tomorrow, you and your instructor will discuss the overall structure and interpretation of the entire *Legend of Robin Hood*. Today, you'll prepare by identifying the protagonist, antagonist, and conflict in individual chapters.

When you identified the main character in each chapter (last week), you were naming the protagonist (with two exceptions . . . see the hints below!). Now, ask yourself the following series of questions:

1) What does the protagonist want to do, become, or get?

2) What force or person is blocking the protagonist's goal? (This is the antagonist)

3) At what event, or in what way, or in what scene do the protagonist and the antagonist clearly clash with each other?

4) How is the clash resolved? (Or is it left unresolved?)

To help you out, I've done the first chapter below.

1) Robin Hood wants to help Sir Richard Lee and then be paid back.

2) Nothing keeps him from helping, but Richard Lee gets involved with the tournament, and that keeps him from getting back to Robin Hood.

3) They don't clash, but Robin Hood is still waiting at the end of the chapter.

4) Unresolved.

Using your own paper, follow my model for the remaining chapters. Don't worry too much about getting the "right" answer. The purpose of this exercise is to get you thinking more critically about the structure of the individual stories; there may be more than one "correct" way to analyze each one.

If you need help, ask your instructor. A few additional hints are below.

When you're finished, show your work to your instructor.

HINTS

Chapter Two, "Little John and the Sheriff of Nottingham": Although the chapter ends with the sheriff sleeping in the greenwood, the *real* conflict isn't between the sheriff and Little John. Who is much more active than the sheriff in opposing the protagonist?

Chapter Three, "How Robin Hood was Paid His Loan": This is really a continuation/resolution of the first chapter, with some of the same answers.

Chapter Four, "The Golden Arrow": Remember that Robin Hood is the protagonist, so the clash and resolution will involve Robin Hood, not supporting characters.

Chapter Five, "How the Sheriff Took Sir Richard Prisoner": In this chapter, something strange happens. The main character of the chapter is *not* the same as the protagonist. Remember, the protagonist has a want or goal that makes the action of the chapter unfold. Which character would that be? (Also, this chapter has the most obvious clash between protagonist and antagonist of *any* chapter!)

Chapter Six, "How the King Came to Sherwood Forest": The *antagonist* is the same as in Chapter Five.

Chapter Seven, "How Robin Hood Went Back to the Greenwood": In this chapter, a *circumstance* is the antagonist—not a person.

Chapter Eight, "Robin Hood and the Butcher": You will find the answers to questions 2–4 much simpler to find if you look for a want or goal that is not explicitly stated in the chapter—just implied.

Chapter Nine, "The Jolly Tanner": This chapter has the same antagonist as Chapters Five and Six.

Chapter Ten, "How Robin Hood Drew His Bow for the Last Time": As in Chapter Five, the main character is not the protagonist—he does not set the events of the chapter in motion. Who does that? Also, notice that there are *two* resolutions to this final chapter.

HOW TO HELP THE STUDENT WITH STEP THREE

The student's work should resemble the following. If necessary, use the answers below to prompt the student.

Chapter Two, "Little John and the Sheriff of Nottingham"
1) Little John wants to pay the sheriff back for his treachery and greed
2) The other servants, particularly the steward and the cook
3) When Little John breaks into the buttery, the steward and the cook both try to stop him
4) The cook joins Little John and Robin Hood

Chapter Three, "How Robin Hood was Paid His Loan"

1) Robin Hood wants his loan paid back

2) Sir Richard Lee gets delayed at the tournament

3) They don't clearly clash, but Robin Hood keeps waiting

4) Richard Lee arrives to repay the loan, and then Robin Hood forgives the debt and gives him presents

Chapter Four, "The Golden Arrow"

1) Robin Hood wants to go and win the Golden Arrow

2) The sheriff is determined to capture Robin Hood

3) The sheriff's men ambush Robin Hood and his men

4) Robin Hood and his men take refuge in Richard Lee's castle

Chapter Five, "How the Sheriff Took Sir Richard Prisoner"

1) The Sheriff of Nottingham wants to take Sir Richard prisoner

2) Robin Hood sets out to rescue Sir Richard

3) Robin Hood and the sheriff meet in battle

4) The sheriff gets decapitated

NOTE: You may need to point out to the student that Robin Hood becomes the *antagonist* in this chapter. If the student has "protagonist" and "hero" confused in his mind, he may have trouble with this idea. Remind him that "antagonist" and "protagonist" are simply names describing the roles characters play in the unfolding of the plot, not to be interpreted as "bad guy" and "good guy."

Chapter Six, "How the King Came to Sherwood Forest"

1) King Edward wants to capture Robin Hood

2) Robin Hood is very hard to find

3) The king punches Robin Hood when he misses the target

4) Robin Hood recognizes the king and asks for mercy

Chapter Seven, "How Robin Hood Went Back to the Greenwood"

1) Robin Hood tries to live at court OR Robin Hood decides to go back home to the greenwood

2) His companions desert him and his money melts away OR The king wants him to stay/ return after seven days

3) The clash happens over time as he loses his money and his friends OR When he tells the king he wants to go back and the king says he must return

4) Robin returns to the greenwood

Chapter Eight, "Robin Hood and the Butcher"

1) Robin decides he wants to be a butcher OR Robin decides that he wants to trick the sheriff

NOTE: The true motivation of Robin Hood is to trick the sheriff, but this isn't explicitly stated in the chapter, so do not require the student to come up with this answer. However, "Robin decides that he wants to trick the sheriff" leads to much clearer and simpler answers for the next three questions, so if the student struggles with answers 2–4, tell him this answer to 1) and then ask him to try the next three questions again.

2) The other butchers
3) The butchers invite Robin to dinner OR Robin takes the sheriff into the greenwood
4) Robin distracts the butchers with food and drink OR The sheriff has to give Robin Hood his gold

Chapter Nine, "The Jolly Tanner"
1) Arthur-a-Bland wants to visit the greenwood
2) Robin Hood challenges him to a duel with his staff.
3) The two fight for hours but are evenly matched
4) Arthur-a-Bland joins Robin and Little John in the greenwood

Chapter Ten, "How Robin Hood Drew His Bow for the Last Time"
1) Sir William sets out to capture Robin Hood
2) Robin Hood and his archers resist
3) The two armies meet and fight a long battle
4) The battle is a draw but Robin Hood dies

Day Two: Discuss

 Focus: Understanding the overall structure of episodic fiction

Today, you will carry on a conversation with the student. As you talk about *The Legend of Robin Hood,* the student will write observations on the lines in his workbook. These will be used to help construct the week's brief essay.

STEP ONE: **Identify the overall plot structure**

INSTRUCTOR: Let's start by looking at the first three chapters as a whole. The author begins with an introduction—telling you who the main characters are, and giving you a little bit of information about each one. Where does the actual *story* begin? What are the words that introduce the first legend about Robin Hood?

Student: "It happened one day."

INSTRUCTOR: In this first story, Robin Hood is the protagonist. What supporting character does he meet?

Student: Sir Richard Lee

INSTRUCTOR: Robin Hood gives Sir Richard Lee enough money to buy back his land. What does Richard Lee promise to do?

Student: To return the money within a year

INSTRUCTOR: In what chapter does Richard Lee return to pay the money?

Student: Chapter Three

INSTRUCTOR: So the story of Robin Hood's loan to Richard Lee begins in Chapter One and ends in Chapter Three. Between the beginning and the end of that story, two other stories are sandwiched in. What are the two stories-within-the-story?

Student: Richard Lee helps the yeoman at the tournament, and Little John goes to serve the Sheriff of Nottingham.

INSTRUCTOR: Why do you think that the author places the story of Richard Lee and the yeoman *inside* the story of Robin Hood's loan to Richard Lee? What is similar about those two stories?

Student: Richard Lee is helping the yeoman, just as Robin Hood helped him.

INSTRUCTOR: Write that in your workbook.

First story-within-a-story: Richard Lee helps the yeoman just like Robin Hood helped him.

INSTRUCTOR: Robin Hood has become a model—someone whose behavior other men can copy. Now, let's think about the second story—the story of Little John and the sheriff. Is the sheriff better off or worse off at the end of the second story?

Student: Worse off

INSTRUCTOR: What has he lost?

Student: His silver dishes, his cook, and three hundred and three pounds

INSTRUCTOR: In the first story, the poor knight Richard Lee becomes more prosperous, and uses his wealth to help others. In the second story, the rich Sheriff of Nottingham becomes poorer. The two men change places. Write that in your workbook now.

Second story-within-a-story: Richard Lee becomes more prosperous and the sheriff becomes poorer. The two men change places.

INSTRUCTOR: Although the different episodes within *The Legend of Robin Hood* have different protagonists, Robin Hood is the protagonist of the entire story. Can you tell, from these first three interlocking episodes, what Robin Hood wants—what his goal is?

Student: He wants to make the poor richer and the rich poorer OR He wants to make men more equal

NOTE TO INSTRUCTOR: If necessary, prompt the student by asking, "Does Robin Hood want everyone in society to stay right where they are? What does he want change about them?"

INSTRUCTOR: Write that in your workbook now.

Robin Hood's goal: To make men in society more equal [or a similar answer]

INSTRUCTOR: Let's look at how the other three questions you answered for each episode might be answered for the entire story. If Robin Hood's goal is to make men in society more equal, what person—or people—blocks him?

Student: Both Sheriffs of Nottingham, the king, and Sir William

NOTE TO INSTRUCTOR: Help the student identify all four of the characters in the answer by asking, "Who opposes Robin Hood in Chapters Four and Five? How about in Chapters Six and Ten? How about in Chapter Eight? How about in Chapter Ten only?"

INSTRUCTOR: Write that in your workbook.

Who opposes him? Both Sheriffs of Nottingham, the king, and Sir William

INSTRUCTOR: The sheriffs, the king, and Sir William are all *officials*—people with recognized jobs to do within English society, and the authority to carry them out. What is Robin Hood?

Student: An outlaw

INSTRUCTOR: So you could say that Robin Hood's attempts to make men more equal are opposed by the forces of law and order within English society. Write that in your workbook now.

What force opposes him? Law and order within English society

INSTRUCTOR: What happens to Robin Hood when he tries to enter into English society and be part of that law and order, in Chapter Seven? He loses two things. What are they?

Student: He loses his money and he loses his companions.

INSTRUCTOR: Robin Hood can only try to change English society as long as he stays outside of it. Add that to your notes.

What force opposes him? Law and order

Robin Hood can only try to change English society as long as he stays outside of it.

INSTRUCTOR: As soon as Robin Hood tries to become part of English society, he loses all of his power. He only gets it back when he goes into the greenwood. So how would you answer the third question? At what event, or in what way, or in what scene do the protagonist and the antagonist clearly clash with each other?

Student: When Robin Hood goes to court in Chapter Seven

NOTE TO INSTRUCTOR: The battle in Chapter Ten is the most obvious physical clash. But in Chapter Ten, Robin Hood is just fighting against one of the characters who opposes him. In Chapter Seven, he clashes with something much larger—the entire structure of English society. If necessary, read this explanation to the student.

INSTRUCTOR: Write that in your workbook now.

The clash between protagonist and antagonist: When Robin Hood goes to court in Chapter Seven

INSTRUCTOR: How is the clash resolved?

Student: Robin Hood has to leave the court and go back to the greenwood.

INSTRUCTOR: Write that into your workbook.

Resolution: Robin Hood has to leave the court and go back to the greenwood.

INSTRUCTOR: Would you say that this is a victory for Robin Hood—or a defeat?

NOTE TO INSTRUCTOR: Allow the student to come up with his own answer for this question. You may wish to discuss the following points with him:
—The resolution is a victory in that Robin Hood is able to keep on helping the poor and stealing from the rich—he is able to escape from the restrictions English society would put on him and go back to his goal of making men more equal. The court does not force him to become an official part of the society he continues to oppose.
—The resolution is a defeat in that Robin Hood is unable to change English society. Instead, he has to leave it in order to remain powerful. It is, in a way, too strong for him.
—You also could say that the struggle between Robin Hood and English society ends in a draw. In the final battle in Chapter Ten, neither side wins. They simply fight to the point of exhaustion and then retreat.

STEP TWO: **Discuss identity and concealment**

INSTRUCTOR: Throughout *The Legend of Robin Hood,* characters disguise themselves and are mistaken for others. See if you can find seven instances of a character taking another name or another identity. Write a sentence describing each one.

NOTE TO INSTRUCTOR: The instances are:

> **Little John becomes Reynold Greenleaf** (Chapter Two)
> **Robin Hood is called "the master hart"** (Chapter Two)
> **The Sheriff of Nottingham has to dress like an outlaw** (Chapter Two)
> **Robin Hood and his men disguise themselves in order to go to the tournament** (Chapter Four)
> **The king and his men put on monks' habits** (Chapter Six)
> **The king and his knights put on Lincoln green** (Chapter Seven)
> **Robin Hood pretends to be a butcher** (Chapter Eight)

Prompt the student, if necessary, by telling him the chapter and giving him the name of the character who assumes another identity.

INSTRUCTOR: We've already talked about how Robin Hood has to live outside of the law and order of English society. Every time characters move from the realm of the outlaw into the society of law and order, or vice versa, they change clothes, names, and identities. Are any of the changes permanent?

> Student: No.

INSTRUCTOR: The story seems to be telling you that people can't really move from one world to another. What do you think is the most successful transformation, or change of identity?

NOTE TO INSTRUCTOR: Answers will vary. The goal here is to encourage the student to express his *own* opinion—even if that opinion is only one sentence long! Make sure that the student tells you *why* the transformation seems to be successful.
Sample acceptable answers might be:

> The king becomes a monk so successfully that Robin Hood doesn't recognize him until the very end of the chapter.

> Robin Hood's transformation into a butcher works, because he manages to get the sheriff to come with him into the greenwood.

Days Three and Four: Write

Over the next two days, the student will use his notes from last week and this week to construct an original critical essay of at least 375 words.

The student will complete the following five steps. You and the student should decide together how many steps to finish per day.

Step One: Write a brief narrative summary
Step Two: Write about the overall structure of *The Legend of Robin Hood*
Step Three: Write about identity and concealment
Step Four: Write an introduction and conclusion
Step Five: Proofread

You may ask to see the student's work at any point, but he does not have to show you his essay until you have finished Step Five.

The student instructions follow. If he needs help, you may show him one or more paragraphs of the sample composition provided.

STEP ONE: **Write a brief narrative summary**

Begin your work by writing a brief narrative summary of *The Legend of Robin Hood*. Summarizing a work of episodic fiction can be challenging. Follow these instructions:

1. Start off by explaining that *The Legend of Robin Hood* is episodic fiction. You don't have to use the phrase "episodic fiction," but if you do, be sure to define it for the reader.
2. Summarize briefly the events that happen in at least three of the stories. These can be one-sentence summaries, or a little longer—that's up to you. You will probably find your reading notes from last week very useful!
3. Describe briefly the importance of two or three important secondary characters.

You may do all of this in one paragraph, or you may spread it out over two or more. This part of the composition should be at least 120–125 words in length.

STEP TWO: **Write about the overall structure of *The Legend of Robin Hood***

Using your notes from Day Two, write at least two paragraphs about the overall plot structure of *The Legend of Robin Hood*. In the first paragraph, explain what Robin Hood wants, what opposes him, what the primary clash of the story is, and how it is resolved. In the second paragraph, explain whether or not Robin Hood was successful, and why you came to that conclusion.

This part of your composition should also be at *least* 120–125 words. Remember, your entire composition will need to be at least 375 words.

STEP THREE: **Write about identity and concealment**

Now, write at least one paragraph about the ways in which the characters conceal their identities or disguise themselves. Begin with a sentence explaining that disguises are something that many characters use. Then, give at least two good examples.

Keep an eye on your word length. By now, your paper should be very close to 350 words or longer.

STEP FOUR: **Write an introduction and conclusion**

Write a brief opening paragraph (it can be a single long sentence or more) that identifies the book by its title and tells the reader who the author is. Your introduction should also say, very briefly, what Robin Hood sets out to do in the book, and whether or not he succeeds.

(Sometimes writers get stuck because they start writing with the introduction. In most cases, a good introduction is one of the last things you add to the essay!)

Then, write a concluding paragraph that gives your personal opinion about *The Legend of Robin Hood*. What parts did you enjoy, and why? What parts did you dislike? Why? What did you wish the author had done differently? What did the author do well?

STEP FIVE: **Proofread**

When you have finished Step Four, put your essay away for a few hours or overnight before proofreading.

Then, follow these proofreading steps.

1) Check to make sure that all five required elements are present.

2) Make sure that your finished essay is at least 375 words long.

3) Make sure that you have quoted from *The Legend of Robin Hood* at least once. Since your copy of the story is not an independent publication, you do not need to footnote your quote.

4) Read your paper out loud, listening for awkward or unclear sections and repeated words. Rewrite awkward or unclear sentences so that they flow more naturally.

5) Listen for information that is repeated more than once. Eliminate repetition of ideas.

6) Read through the paper one more time, looking for sentence fragments, run-on sentences, and repeated words. Correct fragments and run-on sentences. Listen for unnecessary repetition.

7) Check your spelling by looking, individually, at each word that might be a problem.

When you are finished proofreading, give your essay to your instructor.

The student's essay might resemble the following:

In Mary MacLeod's retelling of the Robin Hood folktales, *The Legend of Robin Hood*, Robin Hood tries to change English society—but he is unable to do so.

The Legend of Robin Hood is made up of a series of stories about Robin Hood's adventures. In one story, Robin Hood gives a poor knight named Sir Richard Lee enough money to help him become prosperous again. In another story, Robin Hood disguises himself in order to enter an archery tournament put on by the Sheriff of Nottingham. In a third, he pretends to be a butcher so that he can get the Sheriff's gold. Robin Hood's companions, Little John and Will Scarlet, accompany him on his adventures, and Sir Richard Lee becomes one of Robin Hood's allies. Sir Richard even allows Robin Hood to hide in his castle when the Sheriff of Nottingham tries to capture him. This angers the Sheriff so much that he arrests Sir Richard—but Robin Hood manages to set his friend free.

The Legend of Robin Hood tells the story of a man who is trying to make the rich and poor of England more equal. When Robin Hood gives money to Sir Richard Lee and takes it from the Sheriff of Nottingham, he is trying to change English society. But to do this, he has to stay an outlaw. In Chapter Seven, Robin Hood is invited to the royal court by King Edward himself. He goes—but the longer he stays, the more money and companions he loses. Finally, the story tells us, Robin Hood thinks to himself that he will "die with sorrow" if he stays any longer with the king. He returns to the greenwood and to his life as an outlaw.

Ultimately, Robin Hood fails to change English society. Although his men manage to fight off the army that the king sends to arrest him, Robin is defeated by the forces of law and order. At the end of the story, he dies, and England remains unchanged.

Throughout *The Legend of Robin Hood*, characters disguise themselves and change their identities. Robin Hood pretends to be a butcher in order to trick the Sheriff of Nottingham into coming to the greenwood. The king and his men disguise themselves as monks so that they can find Robin Hood. And Robin Hood and his men all have to change their clothes so that they can take part in the Sheriff's archery tournament.

Although the adventures are fun to read, I found *The Legend of Robin Hood* to be a sad and, in the end, depressing story. Robin Hood dies of an illness and is buried, and nothing has really changed. I wished that Mary MacLeod had included stories about Maid Marian, as well. Instead, she chose to tell only about the adventures of Robin Hood and his "merry men."

Check the student's work using the following rubric.

Week 30 Rubric

Organization:

1   The essay should be at least 350 words long.
2   The essay should include the following required elements:
   a)   An introduction identifying the title and author and summarizing Robin Hood's wants/goals
   b)   A narrative summary that explains the episodic nature of the stories, summarizes at least three of them briefly, and introduces at least two important secondary characters
   c)   At least two paragraphs explaining what Robin Hood wants, what opposes him, what the story's primary clash is, and how it is resolved. The student should also explain whether or not Robin Hood succeeded.
   d)   At least one paragraph describing ways in which characters disguise themselves, with at least two examples
   e)   A conclusion giving the student's personal opinion about *The Legend of Robin Hood*
3   The student should quote directly from the story at least once.

Mechanics:

1   Each sentence should make sense on its own when read aloud.
2   There should be no sentence fragments or run-on sentences.
3   All words should be spelled correctly.
4   The first line of each paragraph should be properly indented.
5   Verb tense should be consistent throughout.
6   Direct quotes should be properly formatted.

WEEK 31: COMBINING THE *TOPOI* IN HISTORY

In the two levels of this course so far, the student has learned how to construct six different basic types of essay—chronological narratives, descriptions, biographical sketches, sequences, comparisons and contrasts, and explanations by definition. The student has examined the elements that belong to each form, and how they differ for history compositions and science compositions.

Learning about the *topoi* is an important starting place, but when good, mature writers put together their own essays, they rarely follow any one of the *topoi* exactly. Instead, they combine, adding and subtracting elements to produce a piece of writing that flows smoothly forward.

Compare learning to write and learning to draw. When a beginner starts to study drawing, she might start out working on basic shapes, and then go on to perspective drawings. Then she might practice drawing landscapes; then, still life scenes; after that, drawings of animals; after that, people.

These are all valuable skills. And once the student becomes an artist, she'll probably spend some time using those skills just as you practiced them. If she does a portrait, she'll use everything learned when she practiced drawing people. She'll probably draw some landscapes, and perhaps a few still life scenes.

But she might also strike out on her own and draw a landscape that has a person or two in it, plus an animal in the distance—or perhaps just a half-glimpsed animal. Or she might combine elements of still life and portraits together.

Over the next three weeks, the student will prepare for the final project by examining how elements from different *topoi* can be combined together into a single effective essay. In both history and science, the student will examine a classic piece of writing, identify the techniques and forms that the writer uses, and then practice writing a brief composition.

Day One: Analyze the Model

 Focus: Understanding how writers combine elements

STEP ONE: Review the *topoi* (Student Responsibility)

NOTE TO INSTRUCTOR: You may want to make sure that the student completes this step slowly and carefully!

Before you begin today's work, read carefully through the following *topoi* in your Composition Reference Notebook. Don't just skim through them; pay attention to each element!

Chronological Narrative of a Past Event
Description of a Place
Description of a Person
Biographical Sketch
Sequence: History
Explanation by Comparison/Contrast
Explanation by Definition: Historical Object, Event, Place, or People Group
Temporal Comparison: History

To help keep your attention on the material, I recommend that you read the *topoi* out loud.

STEP TWO: Read (Student Responsibility)

Read carefully through the following excerpt from "Julius Caesar Crossing the Rubicon," by the nineteenth-century historian and writer Jacob Abbott.

STEP THREE: Understand how *topoi* can be combined

Student instructions for Step Three:

During this step, your instructor will carry on a dialogue with you. Keep your *topoi* chart next to the essay as you work.

HOW TO HELP THE STUDENT WITH STEP THREE

You will guide the student into recognizing the different elements that are present in the essay, using the dialogue below. A copy of the student's completed work follows.

INSTRUCTOR: The overall form of this essay is *chronological narrative of a past event*. Write that just above the title. Abbott covers, in chronological order, the major events that lead up to Caesar's crossing of the Rubicon. Notice just a few of the time words that Abbott uses: At the beginning of the fifth paragraph, circle the time word *as*. Both the seventh and the ninth paragraphs begin with *In the meantime;* circle both of them. The thirteenth paragraph begins with *while;* circle it. *In the course of the day* and *for some time* come in the next two paragraphs; circle both. Now, find two places where Abbott uses dialogue to hold the reader's interest. Read them out loud to me.

> Student: "We can retreat *now*, but once across that river, we must go on." "An omen! a prodigy! Let us march to where we are called by such a divine intimation. The die is cast."

INSTRUCTOR: Write the word *dialogue* in the margin next to each one. Notice that Abbott uses this dialogue right at the crisis point of the essay—when Caesar is deciding whether or not to cross the Rubicon. Now, look at the first four paragraphs of the essay. What do these four paragraphs describe? Hint: it is mentioned in the first line of each paragraph.

> Student: The Rubicon

INSTRUCTOR: Abbott could have begun his essay with a description of a place. Instead, he decides to use a brief *explanation by definition* of the Rubicon. He starts by listing a few properties of the Rubicon. He answers the questions, "What was its extent in space?" by describing its size. What words does he use for its size?

> Student: *Little, small and insignificant*

INSTRUCTOR: Underline those words now. He also answers the question "Where did it take place or exist?" Where was the stream?

> Student: *In the north of Italy*

INSTRUCTOR: Underline that phrase. He also answers the question "What was its extent in time?"—in other words, when did the Rubicon exist?

> Student: *In ancient times*

INSTRUCTOR: Underline those words as well. The most important part of this definition is the explanation of the Rubicon's function. Abbott answers the questions "Who/what needed it, used it, or was affected by it?" "For what purposes or reasons? What is its significance? Why do we remember it?" Look at the third paragraph. Why was the Rubicon important?

Student: It was the boundary between the north and the south of Rome.

INSTRUCTOR: Underline the word "boundary." What were generals not allowed to do?

Student: Cross the Rubicon with an army

INSTRUCTOR: That is why we remember the Rubicon—because it was the "sign and symbol of civil restriction to military power." Write "Explanation by Definition" in the left margin, next to the first four paragraphs. The author uses a short form of one *topos* as an introduction to his essay. Now, look over at your Explanation by Comparison/Contrast chart. Abbott inserts two brief but interesting comparisons/contrasts into his definition. They are both in the same paragraph. Which paragraph are they in?

Student: The second paragraph

INSTRUCTOR: The first contrast is between the Rubicon's importance and its size. Its importance was huge; its size was tiny. What is the second contrast between?

Student: The Rubicon in history and the Rubicon in nature

INSTRUCTOR: Write "Comparison/Contrast" in the right margin next to the second paragraph. Abbott also borrows from the Description of a Person *topos*. In several places, he describes aspects of Julius Caesar—his accomplishments and behaviors, and his fame, notoriety, and prestige. Next to the fifth paragraph, write the words *accomplishments* and *fame*. Then, glance down to the end of the essay. The last two paragraphs describe the events that lead up to the crossing of the Rubicon. The two paragraphs before that talk about Caesar's character qualities and intellectual capabilities—he is "conscious of the vast importance of the decision," but he doesn't think about the "vast public interests" involved. He is only thinking of himself. Write the word "character" in the margin next to those paragraphs.

INSTRUCTOR: As you can see, Jacob Abbott uses bits and pieces from several different *topoi* to develop and finish his chronological narrative. Your goal is to be so comfortable with the forms you've studied that you can do the same as you write.

Chronological Narrative of a Past Event

Julius Caesar Crossing the Rubicon

by Jacob Abbott

There was a little stream <u>in ancient times,</u> <u>in the north of Italy,</u> which flowed eastward into the Adriatic Sea, called the Rubicon. This stream has been immortalized by the transactions which we are now about to describe.

The Rubicon was a very important boundary, and yet it was in itself so <u>small and insignificant</u> that it is now impossible to determine which of two or three <u>little</u> brooks here running into the sea is entitled to its name and renown. In history the Rubicon is a grand, permanent, and conspicuous stream, gazed upon with continued interest by all mankind for nearly twenty centuries; in nature it is an uncertain rivulet, for a long time doubtful and undetermined, and finally lost.

The Rubicon originally derived its importance from the fact that it was the <u>boundary</u> between all that part of the north of Italy which is formed by the valley of the Po, one of the richest and most magnificent countries of the world, and the more southern Roman territories. This country of the Po constituted what was in those days called the hither Gaul, and was a Roman province. It belonged now to Caesar's jurisdiction, as the commander in Gaul.

All south of the Rubicon was territory reserved for the immediate jurisdiction of the city. The Romans, in order to protect themselves from any danger which might threaten their own liberties from the immense armies which they raised for the conquest of foreign nations, had imposed on every side very strict limitations and restrictions in respect to the approach of these armies to the capital. The Rubicon was the limit on this northern side. Generals commanding in Gaul were never to pass it. To cross the Rubicon with an army on the way to Rome was rebellion and treason. Hence the Rubicon became, as it were, the visible sign and symbol of civil restriction to military power.

As Caesar found the time of his service in Gaul drawing toward a conclusion, he turned his thoughts more and more toward Rome, endeavoring to strengthen his interest there by every means in his power, and to circumvent and thwart the designs of Pompey. He had agents and partisans in Rome who acted for him and in his name. He sent immense sums of money

Comparison/ Contrast

Explanation by Definition

accomplish- ments fame

to these men, to be employed in such ways as would most tend to secure the favor of the people. He ordered the Forum to be rebuilt with great magnificence. He arranged great celebrations, in which the people were entertained with an endless succession of games, spectacles, and public feasts. When his daughter Julia, Pompey's wife, died, he celebrated her funeral with indescribable splendor. He distributed corn in immense quantities among the people, and he sent a great many captives home, to be trained as gladiators to fight in the theatres for their amusement. In many cases, too, where he found men of talents and influence among the populace, who had become involved in debt by their dissipations and extravagance, he paid their debts, and thus secured their influence on his side. Men were astounded at the magnitude of these expenditures, and, while the multitude rejoiced thoughtlessly in the pleasures thus provided for them, the more reflecting and considerate trembled at the greatness of the power which was so rapidly rising to overshadow the land.

It increased their anxiety to observe that Pompey was gaining the same kind of influence and ascendency, too. He had not the advantage which Caesar enjoyed in the prodigious wealth obtained from the rich countries over which Caesar ruled, but he possessed, instead of it, the advantage of being all the time at Rome, and of securing, by his character and action there, a very wide personal popularity and influence. Pompey was, in fact, the idol of the people . . . [and] considered himself as standing far above Caesar in fame and power . . .

In the meantime, the period was drawing near in which Caesar's command in the provinces was to expire; and, anticipating the struggle with Pompey which was about to ensue, he conducted several of his legions through the passes of the Alps and advanced gradually, as he had a right to do, across the country of the Po toward the Rubicon, revolving in his capacious mind, as he came, the various plans by which he might hope to gain the ascendency over the power of his mighty rival and make himself supreme.

He concluded that it would be his wisest policy not to attempt to intimidate Pompey by great and open preparations for war, which might tend to arouse him to vigorous measures of resistance, but rather to cover and conceal his designs, and thus throw his enemy off his guard. He advanced, therefore, toward the Rubicon with a small force. He established his headquarters at Ravenna, a city not far from the river, and employed himself in objects of local interest there in order to avert as much as possible the minds of the people from imagining that he was contemplating any great design. Pompey sent to him to demand the return of a certain legion which he had lent him from his own army at a time when they were friends. Caesar complied with this demand without any hesitation, and sent the legion home. He sent with this legion, also, some other troops which were properly his own, thus evincing a degree of indifference in respect to the amount of the force retained under his command which seemed wholly inconsistent with the idea that he contemplated any resistance to the authority of the government at Rome.

In the meantime, the struggle at Rome between the partisans of Caesar and Pompey grew more and more violent and alarming. Caesar, through his friends in the city, demanded to be elected consul. The other side insisted that he must first, if that was his wish, resign the command of his army, come to Rome, and present himself as a candidate in the character of a private citizen. This the constitution of the state very properly required. In answer to this requisition, Caesar rejoined that, if Pompey would lay down his military commands, he would do so too; if not, it was unjust to require it of him . . .

To a large part of the people of the city these demands of Caesar appeared reasonable. They were clamorous to have them allowed. The partisans of Pompey, with the stern and inflexible Cato at their head, deemed them wholly inadmissible and contended with the most determined violence against them. The whole city was filled with the excitement of this struggle, into which all the active and turbulent spirits of the capital plunged with the most furious zeal, while the more considerate and thoughtful of the population . . . trembled at the impending danger.

Pompey himself had no fear. He urged the Senate to resist to the utmost all of Caesar's claims, saying if Caesar should be so presumptuous as to attempt to march to Rome he could raise troops enough by stamping with his foot to put him down.

It would require a volume to contain a full account of the disputes and tumults, the manoeuvres and debates, the votes and decrees, which marked the successive stages of this quarrel . . . A thousand plans were formed, and clamorously insisted upon by their respective advocates, for averting the danger. This only added to the confusion, and the city became at length pervaded with a universal terror.

While this was the state of things at Rome, Caesar was quietly established at Ravenna, thirty or forty miles from the frontier.

He was erecting a building for a fencing school there, and his mind seemed to be occupied very busily with the plans and models of the edifice which the architects had formed. Of course, in his intended march to Rome, his reliance was not to be so much on the force which he should take with him, as on the cooperation and support which he expected to find there. It was his policy, therefore, to move as quietly and privately as possible, and with as little display of violence, and to avoid everything which might indicate his intended march to any spies which might be around him, or to any other persons who might be disposed to report what they observed, at Rome. Accordingly, on the very eve of his departure, he busied himself with his fencing school, and assumed with his officers and soldiers a careless and unconcerned air, which prevented any one from suspecting his design.

In the course of the day, he privately sent forward some cohorts to the southward, with orders for them to encamp on the banks of the Rubicon. When night came, he sat down to supper as usual and conversed with his friends in his ordinary manner, and went with them afterward to a public entertainment. As soon as it was dark and the streets were still, he set off secretly from the city, accompanied by a very few attendants. Instead of making use of his ordinary equipage, the parading of which would have attracted attention to his movements, he had some mules taken from a neighboring bakehouse and harnessed into his chaise. There were torch-bearers provided to light the way. The cavalcade drove on during the night, finding, however, the hasty preparations which had been made inadequate for the occasion. The torches went out, the guides lost their way, and the future conqueror of the world wandered about bewildered and lost, until, just after break of day, the party met with a peasant who undertook to guide them. Under his direction they made their way to the main road again, and advanced then without further difficulty to the banks of the river, where they found that portion of the army which had been sent forward encamped and awaiting their arrival.

Caesar stood for some time upon the banks of the stream, musing upon the greatness of the undertaking in which simply passing across it would involve him. His officers stood by his side. "We can retreat *now*," said he, "but once across that river, we must go on."

dialogue

He paused for some time, conscious of the vast importance of the decision, though he thought only, doubtless, of its consequences to himself. Taking the step which was now before him

character

would necessarily end either in his realizing the loftiest aspirations of his ambition, or in his utter and irreparable ruin.

There were vast public interests, too, at stake, of which, however, he probably thought but little. It proved, in the end, that the history of the whole Roman world, for several centuries, was depending upon the manner in which the question now in Caesar's mind should turn.

There was a little bridge across the Rubicon at the point where Caesar was surveying it. While he was standing there, the story is, a peasant or shepherd came from the neighboring fields with a shepherd's pipe—a simple musical instrument made of a reed and used much by the rustic musicians of those days. The soldiers and some of the officers gathered around him to hear him play. Among the rest came some of Caesar's trumpeters, with their trumpets in their hands. The shepherd took one of these martial instruments from the hands of its possessor, laying aside his own, and began to sound a charge—which is a signal for a rapid advance—and to march at the same time over the bridge. "An

dialogue

omen! a prodigy!" said Caesar. "Let us march where we are called by such a divine intimation. The die is cast."

So saying, he pressed forward over the bridge, while the officers, breaking up the encampment, put the columns in motion to follow him.

Day Two: Prepare to Write

 Focus: Reading sources for an essay in history

Now that the student has examined how an accomplished author combines *topoi* and uses elements from different forms, she will start preparing to do the same in a historical essay of her own.

Her essay will be about Joan of Arc.

STEP ONE: **Read (Student Responsibility)**

Today, you only have one step to perform. Before you start thinking about which *topoi* you will use, read through the following sources carefully, without stopping to take notes.

★

NOTE TO INSTRUCTOR: Although today's work can be completed independently, you may need to encourage the student to read carefully. She has been given much more material than she will actually take notes on, so also encourage her not to be intimidated by the amount of information.

Days Three and Four: Take Notes for a History Composition

 Focus: Taking notes

Over the next two days, the student will take notes on the sources about Joan of Arc. She will then spend the first half of next week writing her essay.

There are only three assigned steps: settling on *topoi* to include, preparing to take notes, and then the note-taking itself. Because the sources are lengthy, the student will undoubtedly need more than one day to work through the note-taking process. I strongly suggest that she get started on her note-taking on Day Three, but you and the student can decide how much work should be completed on each day.

STEP ONE: Choose tentative *topoi* and elements

Student instructions for Step One:

To take notes effectively, you'll need to make a tentative decision about the *topoi* that you'll include in your essay.

Look back through the following *topoi* in your Composition Reference Notebook. Keeping in mind the sources that you read in Day Two, choose at least three *topoi* that you might be able to use in an essay about Joan of Arc. Four is even better.

Remember that you don't have to include *every* element in the chosen *topoi*; you can just incorporate one or two aspects into your final paper.

Chronological Narrative of a Past Event
Description of a Place
Description of a Person
Biographical Sketch
Sequence: History
Explanation by Comparison/Contrast
Explanation by Definition: Historical Object, Event, Place, or People Group
Temporal Comparison: History

Once you've made your choice, show your selections to your instructor. Ask for help if you need it.

HOW TO HELP THE STUDENT WITH STEP ONE

The following *topoi* are best suited to the provided sources. Once the student has shown you the *topoi* she intends to use, use the information below to help her narrow down her topics. This information will also be helpful for Step Two.

Chronological Narrative of a Past Event

Any events between Joan of Arc's childhood and her execution could be placed into a chronological narrative.

Before the student begins taking notes, explain to her that she does not need to (and probably shouldn't try) to take notes on and then write a narrative covering the *whole* period. She should choose one part of Joan's life to focus on, such as:

From Joan of Arc's call by the voices to her arrival at Chinon

OR

From the point where she joins Charles to her capture

OR

From the point of Charles's coronation to the execution of Joan of Arc

Description of a Place

Both details and a picture of medieval Chinon, where Joan met Charles, are available to the student.

Description of a Person

The aspects of Joan that could be highlighted are:

Physical appearance

What others think

Portrayals

Character qualities

Habits

Behaviors

Religious beliefs

Clothing, dress

Economic status

Fame, notoriety

The aspects of Charles that could be highlighted are:

What others think

Character qualities

Habits

Behaviors

Talents and abilities

Clothing, dress

Economic status

Fame, notoriety, prestige

Family traditions, tendencies

Biographical Sketch

The difference between a chronological narrative of past events and a biographical sketch is that a sketch would focus much more on Joan's life, and less on the war between France and England and the Dauphin's shortcomings. A sketch might include just the following five events:

Joan hears voices

Joan goes to Chinon

Joan becomes a general of the French army

Joan is captured by the English

Joan is tried and put to death

along with important supporting details.

The sketch could include any of the aspects listed above.

Explanation by Comparison/Contrast

The sources would allow the student to compare:

Chinon and Domremy

The Dauphin and Joan of Arc (contrast in decisiveness, leadership, conviction)

Joan and other peasant girls of her day

Explanation by Definition: Historical Object, Event, Place, or People Group

The source material isn't suited to a full explanation by definition, but at least one element could be borrowed:

Temporal comparison between Domremy in Joan's childhood and after its destruction by the English

STEP TWO: **Prepare to take notes**

Student instructions for Step Two:

At the top of a sheet of notebook paper, or at the beginning of a new word processing document, enter the name of the first *topos* that you intend to use. Then, write a brief phrase or sentence describing the person, historical period, place, or other phenomenon that the *topos* will cover. You might also find it useful to jot down the aspects you might want to include.

For example, if the first *topos* you decided to include was "Chronological Narrative of a Past Event," you might then write, "Joan of Arc's life, from Hearing Voices to Leading the French Army" or "The French War with the English, from Joan's Arrival in Chinon to her Capture by the English." If you chose "Description of a Person," you could then write "The Dauphin Charles—What Others Think, Character Qualities, Behaviors, Notoriety."

The heading on your paper should help you keep in mind, as you go through your sources and take notes, exactly what kinds of information you're looking for. Otherwise, you may end up taking too many notes that you don't need (and won't use.)

Do the same for the rest of your selected *topoi*, using a different page for each heading.

HOW TO HELP THE STUDENT WITH STEP TWO

If necessary, use the information from Step One to help the student narrow her topics.

STEP THREE: **Take notes**

Student instructions for Step Three:

> Spend the rest of your time taking notes on the sources about Joan of Arc.
>
> Remember to pick and choose only those facts and details that will support the *topoi* you've chosen. You do not need to write down *every* fact and detail—that would give you far too much information! Having too much information can be paralyzing when you sit down to write.
>
> Aim to have at least six to eight notes about each *topos*, but do not take more than fifteen notes for any single *topos*.
>
> As before, you can choose which note-taking method suits you best:
>
> 1) Go through the sources one time each, placing each relevant bit of information from each source on the appropriate page of notes as you go. OR
>
> 2) Pick the first *topos* and go through all four sources, looking for answers. Do the same for the second *topos*, and then the third, and so on.
>
> NOTE: The excerpt from *The History of the Renaissance World* is from the manuscript—at the time of this writing, the book had not yet been typeset, so there are no page numbers for you to reference. When there are no page numbers for a source, use this notation:
>
> (Bauer, n.p.)
>
> which simply means: This piece of information came from Bauer, no page number.
>
> I have provided you with what might be the first four or five notes on a sample *topos*, below. Follow this model.
>
> If you need help, ask your instructor. When you are finished, show your work to your instructor.
>
> Description of a Person
> The Dauphin Charles—What Others Think, Character Qualities, Behaviors, Notoriety
>
> Had fits of "pathological apathy" (Bauer, n.p.)
> Sometimes played out "deep long-term strategies" as a king (Bauer, n.p.)
> "Weak in body and mind, idle, lazy, luxurious and cowardly" (Lowell, p. 55)
> The "puppet" of his courtiers (Lowell, p. 55)

HOW TO HELP THE STUDENT WITH STEP THREE

There are many different ways in which this information could be organized, but the sample notes below show what the student's notes might look like.

If the student needs help, allow her to look at one or more of the models below; then ask her to take her own notes without looking back at my sample answers.

When finished, she should have no fewer than five to six notes and no more than fifteen for each *topos*.

Chronological Narrative of a Past Event
From Joan of Arc's call by the voices to her arrival at Chinon

She first heard the voices around 1424, "about noonday, in the summer season." They told her to be good and to go to church (Patten, p. 115)
She had been fasting (Gower, p. 160)
The voices told her to go to France and help the Dauphin (Patten, p. 116)
Sometimes she also saw a bright light (Gower, p. 160)
She thought the voices were angels (Gower, p. 160)
Joan went to the soldier Robert de Baudicourt, but he didn't listen (Patten, pp. 116–117)
Finally he let her go and see the king at Chinon (Patten, p. 119)
She arrived on March 6, 1429, and recognized the king (Patten, pp. 119–120)

Chronological Narrative of a Past Event
From the point of Charles's coronation to the execution of Joan of Arc

Charles was crowned in Reims "following the tradition established by the Frankish king Clovis" (Bauer, n.p.)
The "mysterious momentum of the French army" faded (Bauer, n.p.)
Joan led the attack on Paris but she was badly wounded (Bauer, n.p.)
Charles retreated to the other side of the Loire (Bauer, n.p.)
Joan was taken prisoner when she was attacking the city of Compiegne (Bauer, n.p.)
Charles did not try to ransom her (Bauer, n.p.)
She was put on trial for heresy, February 21, 1431 (Bauer, n.p.)
She was asked about her voices, and said that they were sent by God and were "very noble" and "always quite clear" (Gower, p. 159)
She was condemned and then executed on May 30, 1431 (Bauer, n.p.)

Description of a Place: Chinon

Built "upon a meadow beside the river Vienne" (Lowell, p. 53)
The castle of Chinon sits on a high ledge behind the town (Lowell, p. 53)
The castle itself has "thick walls, huge towers, and deep moats," with "lofty rooms" and "large mullioned windows" (Lowell, pp. 53–54)
The moat was hewn into the rock and crossed by a drawbridge (Lowell, p. 54)
The streets were narrow and covered with cobbles, and ditches ran through them (picture from Gower)
The second and third floors of the houses overhung the dark, winding streets (picture from Gower)

Description of a Person
Joan—Physical appearance, what others think, portrayals,
character qualities, religious beliefs, clothing and dress

Brought up to be "industrious, to sew and spin" (Patten, pp. 113–114)

Watched sheep and cattle when young, helped take care of the flock (Patten, p. 114)

"good industrious girl" and "kind, simple, industrious, pious" (Patten, p. 114)

Often praying and in church (Patten, p. 114)

Also "merry and fond of playing" (Patten, p. 114)

After her mission started, wore men's clothing—"doublet, hose, surcoat, boots, and spurs" and a sword (Patten, p. 118)

Showed "an intense and ever-increasing devotion to things holy" (Gower, p. 6)

A passion for prayer, for visiting churches (Gower, p. 6)

"passed many an hour in a kind of rapt trance before the crucifixes and saintly images" (Gower, p. 6)

Also enjoyed playing: swift at foot racing, graceful in the "village dance" (Gower, p. 7)

Wore "rough red serge" and a cap (Gower, p. 12)

All portraits are "spurious" and painted after the fact (Gower, p. 12)

Dark hair (Gower, p. 12)

Believed that God spoke to her in the voices of angels (Gower, p. 160)

Believed God had called her "to raise the siege of Orleans" and to take Charles to Rheims (Lowell, p. 57)

Description of a Person
The Dauphin Charles—What Others Think, Character Qualities, Behaviors, Notoriety

Had fits of "pathological apathy" (Bauer, n.p.)

Sometimes played out "deep long-term strategies" as a king (Bauer, n.p.)

Withdrawn and indecisive (Bauer, n.p.)

"Weak in body and mind, idle, lazy, luxurious and cowardly" (Lowell, p. 55)

The "puppet" of his courtiers (Lowell, p. 55)

"at times frivolous and splendor-loving, at times gloomy and solitary" (Lowell, p. 55)

Spent most of his money "in luxurious living" or gave it to his favorites (Lowell, p. 55)

Extravagant, and so often "wretchedly poor" (Lowell, p. 56)

Reluctant to see Joan (Lowell, p. 57)

Biographical Sketch: Joan of Arc

Joan hears voices

She was "between twelve and thirteen" when "a Voice came to her from God for her guidance" (Patten, p. 115)

She had been fasting (Gower, p. 160)

The voices told her to save France by helping the Dauphin (Patten, p. 116)

Sometimes she also saw a bright light (Gower, p. 160)

She thought the voices were angels (Gower, p. 160)

Joan goes to Chinon

Joan went to the soldier Robert de Baudricourt, but he didn't listen (Patten, pp. 116–117)

Finally he let her go and see the king at Chinon (Patten, p. 119)

She travelled with the soldier Bertrand de Poulangy (Gower, p. 11)

She arrived on March 6, 1429, and recognized the king (Patten, pp. 119–120)

She stayed in the tower called Coudray (Lowell, p. 54)

She was not able to see the king until she had been examined by "certain clerks and priests" to make sure that she was not a witch (Lowell, p. 46)

Charles tried to trick her, but she said that she knew who he was "by the counsel of her voices" (Lowell, p. 57)

Joan becomes a general of the French army

She led a successful attack on the English army at Orleans (Bauer, n.p.)

After this, the French had victory after victory and Charles was coronated in Reims (Bauer, n.p.)

The attack on Paris failed and Joan was wounded (Bauer, n.p.)

The momentum of the army "had faded" (Bauer, n.p.)

Joan is captured by the English

She led an attack based at the French city of Compiegne (Bauer, n.p.)

While she was outside, the governor shut the gates and she was trapped (Bauer, n.p.)

The Dauphin did not try to ransom her (Bauer, n.p.)

She was treated as a heretic, not a prisoner of war (Bauer, n.p.)

Joan is tried and put to death

The trial lasted from February 21 to May 30, 1431 (Bauer, n.p.)

She was questioned about her voices and said that they came from God and helped her "to live well" (Gower, p. 159)

She said that the voices were "sent to me by God" and were the voices of angels (Gower, p. 160)

She was executed hastily at Rouen (Bauer, n.p.)

Explanation by Comparison/Contrast
Qualities of the Dauphin and Joan of Arc

Dauphin	Joan of Arc
"Idle, lazy, luxurious" (Lowell, p. 55)	Industrious (Patten, p. 113)
"Weak in body and mind" (Lowell, p. 55)	"energy and conviction" (Bauer, n.p.)
"withdrawn generalship" (Bauer, n.p.)	"at the head of the Dauphin's army" (Bauer, n.p)
"frivolous and splendor-loving" (Lowell, p. 55)	"intense and ever-increasing devotion to things holy" (Gower, p. 6)
"child of a crazy father and a licentious mother" (Lowell, p. 55)	"daughter of an honest farmer" (Patten, p. 114)

WEEK 32: COMBINING THE *TOPOI* IN HISTORY AND SCIENCE

This week, the student will draft and finalize a history composition combining *topoi*. He will then make a start at understanding how science writers also combine *topoi*.

Days One and Two: Write

 Focus: Combining *topoi* into
a history composition

Over the next two days, the student will write a composition of at least 300 words that uses elements from at least three different *topoi*. Longer is fine, 300 is a bare minimum.

The assignment has six steps.

Step One: Draft the main *topos*
Step Two: Add other *topoi*
Step Three: Provide an introduction and conclusion
Step Four: Construct the Works Cited page
Step Five: Title
Step Six: Proofread

The student should read through all six steps before beginning to write.

Together, you and the student should decide how much time to spend on each step.

For all the steps below, if the student needs additional help, you may allow him to read one or more of the models I provide.

STEP ONE: **Draft the main *topos***

Student instructions for Step One:

In the model you examined at the beginning of Week 31, Jacob Abbott used the Chronological Narrative of a Past Event as the "skeleton" for his essay—the primary organizational form. He then inserted shorter forms and selected elements of other *topoi* into it.

Before you start to write, decide which of the *topoi* you've taken notes on will serve as your "skeleton." Choose one that has plenty of notes to go with it. (The Chronological Narrative of a Past Event and the Biographical Sketch will probably be the simplest *topoi* to use, but the Description of a Person might be a possibility as well.)

Using your notes and referring to your reference chart, write a draft of the main *topos*.

Be sure to look back at your chart, reminding yourself of the elements that should belong in the *topos*.

Aim for at least 150 words; try to get closer to 200 words if possible. Be sure to cite at least *two* sources and to include at least one direct quote.

When you cite your sources, you do not need to cite the names of the chapters (given in quotation marks for your reference), just the book titles.

HOW TO HELP THE STUDENT WITH STEP ONE

You may need to remind the student to look back at the chart in the Reference Section of his notebook. This will help him to include all of the required elements.

The student's work might resemble one of these:

The following *topos* is an example of the Chronological Narrative of a Past Event, using the notes taken for "From the point of Charles's coronation to the execution of Joan of Arc." Notice the use of dialogue in the last paragraph, as suggested in the *topos* chart.

> Charles arrived in the city of Reims and was crowned King of France there, just as the medieval Frankish king Clovis had been. But as soon as he was crowned, the momentum that the French army had gained started to fade.[1]
>
> Joan's leadership also began to fade. She was badly wounded when she led the French army in an attack on Paris, which was controlled by the English. Not long after that, Joan led an attack on the city of Compiegne. There, she was taken prisoner by the English.[2]
>
> Charles did not even try to ransom Joan. In February of 1431, she was put on trial for heresy. She explained that voices had told her to help Charles get France back from the English. She insisted that the voices were "very noble and "always quite clear." "I think it was sent to me by God," she said at her trial. "When I heard it for the third time I recognised it as being the voice of an angel."[3] But she was condemned as a heretic and was put to death on May 30, 1431.

---

[1] Susan Wise Bauer, *The History of the Renaissance World: From the Rediscovery of Aristotle to the Conquest of Constantinople* (W. W. Norton, 2013), n.p.

[2] Ibid.

[3] R. S. Gower, *Joan of Arc* (Charles Scribner's Sons, 1893), p. 159.

The following *topos* is an example of a Biographical Sketch of Joan of Arc. As suggested on the *topos* chart, it includes aspects from the Description of a Person chart as well.

Joan of Arc began to hear voices just after she had turned twelve years old. The first time she heard the voices, she had been fasting. She had always been pious, with a passion for prayer and for visiting churches. She spent hours praying before crucifixes and the images of saints. [1] She believed that these voices were angelic and came from God. The voices told her to save France from the English by helping the Dauphin, Charles, get his throne back.

Joan travelled to Chinon, where the Dauphin was staying. She was not allowed to see him until she had been examined by clerks and priests who needed to make sure that she was not a witch. After they had spoken to her, they allowed her to see Charles. When she came into his presence, he tried to trick her into believing that he was not the king—but she recognized him anyway. She told him that the "counsel of her voices" had pointed him out. [2]

There are no portraits of Joan, so we do not know what she looked like. All we know is that she had dark hair. Before she became the leader of Charles's army, she dressed in red serge with a cap, like other young French women. But when she began to fight, she wore men's clothing—doublet, hose, boots, spurs, and a sword. [3]

Joan successfully attacked the city of Orleans, and then led the French in victory after victory. Because of Joan of Arc, Charles was able to be crowned in the French city of Reims, according to custom.

But after Joan was wounded at Paris, the French army began to lose its momentum. [4] She was captured at the city of Compiegne by the English, who treated her as a heretic instead of a prisoner of war. She was put on trial and interrogated about the voices that she heard. She insisted that the voices came from God and helped her to "live well." [5] But she was condemned and put to death at Rouen on May 30, 1431.

---

[1] William Patten, ed., *The Junior Classics, Vol. 7: Stories of Courage and Heroism* (P. F. Collier & Son, 1912), p. 114.

[2] Francis C. Lowell, *Joan of Arc* (Houghton, Mifflin and Co., 1897), pp. 46 and 57.

[3] R. S. Gower, *Joan of Arc* (Charles Scribner's Sons, 1893), p. 12; Patten, p. 118.

[4] Susan Wise Bauer, *The History of the Renaissance World: From the Rediscovery of Aristotle to the Conquest of Constantinople* (W. W. Norton, 2013), n.p.

[5] Gower, p. 159.

STEP TWO: **Add other *topoi***

Student instructions for Step Two:

> Look back over your notes and decide which *topoi* or elements you will add to your composition. If necessary, glance back at the essay by Jacob Abbott that began Week 31. Notice how he borrows aspects from Description of a Person, Comparison/Contrast, and Definition in order to flesh out his Chronological Narrative of a Past Event.
>
> Decide where the *topoi* or elements will be located in your composition. Draft the *topoi* or elements and insert them into your essay. You must add elements from at least two different *topoi*. You may need to rearrange paragraphing or slightly rewrite some of your existing sentences so that the new elements fit into your composition smoothly. (If your original composition was a Description of a Person, it's perfectly fine to use elements from another Description of a Person as one of your additional *topoi*—so if you described Joan, you could add descriptions of Charles or vice versa.)
>
> You should aim to have a total of at least 250 words by the end of this step; longer is better!

HOW TO HELP THE STUDENT WITH STEP TWO

A description of a place, description of a person, or comparison/contrast can be inserted into either a chronological narrative or a biographical sketch. In addition, elements from a chronological narrative can be inserted into a biographical sketch (for example, if the student focused on Joan of Arc in the biographical sketch, he could now add a series of events involving the Dauphin) and vice versa (aspects of Joan's personality could be added to a chronological narrative).

The student's work might resemble one of the following. The added text is in bold.

Comparison/Contrast of the Dauphin and Joan and aspects of the Description of a Person (Joan), both added to the original Chronological Narrative. Notice that I have changed the paragraphing and replaced pronouns with proper names in order to make the new elements fit in smoothly:

> Charles arrived in the city of Reims and was crowned King of France there, just as the medieval Frankish king Clovis had been. But as soon as he was crowned, the momentum that the French army had gained started to fade.[1]
>
> Joan's leadership also began to fade. She was badly wounded when she led the French army in an attack on Paris, which was controlled by the English. Not long after that, Joan led an attack on the city of Compiegne. There, she was taken prisoner by the English.[2]
>
> Charles did not even try to ransom Joan. **His true character now became obvious. Joan was hard-working and filled with energy, but Charles was lazy, idle, and weak. Joan was devoted to holy things, but Charles only cared about luxury and frivolous pastimes. While Joan had served as the**

head of his army, Charles had withdrawn from leadership.[3]

In February of 1431, Joan was put on trial for heresy. She explained that voices had told her to help Charles get France back from the English. She insisted that the voices were "very noble and "always quite clear." "I think it was sent to me by God," she said at her trial. "When I heard it for the third time I recognised it as being the voice of an angel."[4] **Joan had always been deeply pious. Even as a child, she was often praying and in church. She spent hours sitting before crucifixes and images in "a kind of rapt trance."[5] She never gave up her belief that God had spoken to her and had called her to raise the siege of Orleans.[6]**

Joan of Arc was condemned as an heretic and was put to death on May 30, 1431.

_____

[1] Susan Wise Bauer, *The History of the Renaissance World: From the Rediscovery of Aristotle to the Conquest of Constantinople* (W. W. Norton, 2013), n.p.

[2] Ibid.

[3] Ibid.; Francis C. Lowell, *Joan of Arc* (Houghton, Mifflin and Co., 1897), p. 55.

[4] R. S. Gower, *Joan of Arc* (Charles Scribner's Sons, 1893), p. 159.

[5] Gower, p. 6.

[6] Lowell, p. 57.

Description of a Place and Description of a Person (Charles), both added to the original Biographical Sketch. Notice that I had to insert a transitional sentence ("Now Charles was king") to introduce the Description of a Person smoothly.

Joan of Arc began to hear voices just after she had turned twelve years old. The first time she heard the voices, she had been fasting. She had always been pious, with a passion for prayer and for visiting churches. She spent hours praying before crucifixes and the images of saints.[1] She believed that these voices were angelic and came from God. The voices told her to save France from the English by helping the Dauphin, Charles, get his throne back.

Joan travelled to Chinon, where the Dauphin was staying. **Chinon was a medieval town with narrow, dark cobbled streets, overhung by the second and third floors of the houses that crowded them. The town itself had been built on a meadow next to the Vienne River, but the Dauphin was lodging at the castle that sat on a high ledge behind it. The castle was thick-walled, surrounded by a deep moat that had been hacked into the rock, and could only be reached by a drawbridge.[2]**

Joan was not allowed to see the Dauphin until she had been examined by clerks and priests who needed to make sure that she was not a witch. After they had spoken to her, they allowed her to see Charles. When she came into his presence, he tried to trick her into believing that he was not the king—but she recognized him anyway. She told him that the "counsel of her voices" had pointed him out.[3]

There are no portraits of Joan, so we do not know what she looked like. All we know is that she had dark hair. Before she became the leader of Charles's army, she dressed in red serge with a cap, like other young French women. But when she began to fight, she wore men's clothing—doublet, hose, boots, spurs, and a sword.[4]

Joan successfully attacked the city of Orleans, and then led the French in victory after victory. Because of Joan of Arc, Charles was able to be crowned in the French city of Reims, according to custom.

Now Charles was king, but he was withdrawn, indecisive, and apathetic.[5] He was lazy and cowardly, controlled by his courtiers, and he spent so much money on luxurious living that he was often broke. He had fits of gloom and began to withdraw.[6]

After Joan was wounded at Paris, the French army began to lose its momentum.[7] She was captured at the city of Compiegne by the English, who treated her as a heretic instead of a prisoner of war. She was put on trial and interrogated about the voices that she heard. She insisted that the voices came from God and helped her to "live well."[8] But she was condemned and put to death at Rouen on May 30, 1431.

---

[1] William Patten, ed., *The Junior Classics, Vol. 7: Stories of Courage and Heroism* (P. F. Collier & Son, 1912), p. 114.

[2] Francis C. Lowell, *Joan of Arc* (Houghton, Mifflin and Co., 1897), pp. 53–54.

[3] Lowell, pp. 46 and 57.

[4] R. S. Gower, *Joan of Arc* (Charles Scribner's Sons, 1893), p. 12; Patten, p. 118.

[5] Susan Wise Bauer, *The History of the Renaissance World: From the Rediscovery of Aristotle to the Conquest of Constantinople* (W. W. Norton, 2013), n.p.

[6] Lowell, pp. 55–56.

[7] Bauer, n.p.

[8] Gower, p. 159.

STEP THREE: **Provide an introduction and conclusion**

Student instructions for Step Three:

> Choose an introduction and a conclusion from your Introductions and Conclusions chart. You may pick any introduction and conclusion—but make sure that they don't repeat the same information.
>
> To write an introduction by history that uses a brief scene or an introduction by anecdote that uses an invented scene, you may need to reread the sources from Week 31. You may also find the additional excerpts below helpful (although you may need to look up some of the terms used.)

Each introduction and conclusion should be at least two sentences long and should be placed in separate paragraphs, not incorporated into the existing paragraphs of the composition.

Remember that your final word count must be over 300.

★

HOW TO HELP THE STUDENT WITH STEP THREE

The student's introduction and conclusion might resemble the following (obviously, the content will depend on the forms the student has chosen to include in the composition). If necessary, you may let the student read one or more of the model answers.

1. Introduction by Summary

Joan of Arc was a simple, devout peasant girl from a humble family. But she managed to change the course of French history by helping the Dauphin Charles regain the French throne.

The Dauphin Charles would have lost France to the English without the help of Joan of Arc. However, he allowed her to be captured and put to death without raising a finger to save her.

2. Introduction by History

a. Information about past attitudes towards the subject

In the years that she fought for Charles, Joan of Arc was both loathed and loved. The men who followed her believed that she was a saint, sent by God to help them. But the English and French who fought against her called her a witch and a heretic.

b. Description of how some aspect of the subject has changed or developed over time

In 1431, Joan of Arc was condemned as a heretic and burned alive. But just twenty-five years later, she was declared innocent. In 1904, she was given the title *Venerable*; in 1908, she was beatified; and finally, in 1920, Joan of Arc was declared to be a saint.

c. Brief scene from history

In the Market Square of Rouen, a young girl stands next to a pyre of wood, surrounded by soldiers. Some of them are weeping. Others look impatient—and hungry.

The young girl is Joan of Arc, and in just a few minutes, she will climb to the top of the pyre and be burned to death for heresy.

3. Introduction by Anecdote

   a. A story drawn from personal experience

   A few years ago, I visited the French village of Rouen. There, in the middle of the deserted market square, was a square metal plate marking the spot where Joan of Arc was burned at the stake. It was an eerie, silent reminder of the great injustice that took place here.

   b. An invented scene, based on your knowledge of the subject
   [This introduction uses information from the paragraphs by Jules Michelet and from the beginning of the Patten source.]

   The year is 1422. Two little girls run, hand in hand, through a meadow near the French village of Domremy. Both of them are carrying flowers. The younger girl, Haumette, intends to put her flowers on the Fairy Tree at the meadow's edge. But the older girl, ten-year-old Joan, has another purpose. She wants to take her flowers into the nearby church and lay them in front of the image of her favorite saint.

1. Conclusion by Summary

   Without Joan's help, the Dauphin Charles might never have gotten his throne back from the English. Joan's courage and her conviction that God was speaking through her helped Charles keep his country. In return, he left her in English captivity, and did nothing to save her from execution.

2. Conclusion by Personal Reaction

   a. Personal statement

   Joan not only convinced the heir to the throne of France to follow her, but she also managed to get his battle-hardened officers and soldiers to obey her as their general. When I remember how shy and uncertain I was at the age of seventeen, I am amazed by Joan's courage and her confidence.

   b. Your opinion about the material

   Joan's trial and execution for heresy obviously had nothing to do with her religious beliefs. The English, and the French who were loyal to the English, wanted to get rid of the Dauphin's strongest general. In my opinion, the trial was all about politics and was a terrible misuse of the Church's power.

c. Your own experience with the subject

I have found Joan's story fascinating ever since I first read about her, in a picture book, when I was only eight or nine. Since then, I have read at least ten biographies of Joan of Arc. Each one made me marvel more and more at the amazing accomplishments of this young girl.

3. Conclusion by Question

If Joan had not come to fight for the Dauphin, would France now be part of the British Empire? And if Charles had taken the time and effort to rescue Joan from her captors, what further victories would she have led the French army into?

STEP FOUR: **Construct the Works Cited page**

Student instructions for Step Four:

> At the top of a separate sheet of paper, center the words "Works Cited." In proper form, list the sources you used to write your essay.

HOW TO HELP THE STUDENT WITH STEP FOUR

The proper format for all sources is found below.

Bauer, Susan Wise. *The History of the Renaissance World: From the Rediscovery of Aristotle to the Conquest of Constantinople.* New York: W. W. Norton, 2013.

Gower, R. S. *Joan of Arc.* New York: Charles Scribner's Sons, 1893.

Lowell, Francis C. *Joan of Arc.* Boston: Houghton, Mifflin and Co., 1897.

Michelet, Jules. *Joan of Arc.* Ann Arbor, Mich.: University of Michigan Press, 1967.

Patten, William, ed. *The Junior Classics, Vol. 7: Stories of Courage and Heroism.* New York: P. F. Collier & Son, 1912.

Stanley, Diane. *Joan of Arc.* New York: HarperCollins, 2002.

STEP FIVE: **Title**

Student instructions for Step Five:

Give your composition a title that describes the primary *topos* you decided to use.

For example, if I wrote a chronological narrative of past events that covered the events of Joan of Arc's call by the voices, up to her arrival at Chinon, I might title it:

The Beginning of Joan of Arc's Mission

or

Joan of Arc: From Call to Acceptance by the King

or

How Joan of Arc Went to War

Notice that the first title simply names the period of Joan's life that the composition covers. The second uses Joan's name as the title, inserts a colon, and then describes the period of her life that will be discussed by putting it into a subtitle. The third describes the overall result—what happened at the end of the chronological narrative.

Your instructor has other sample titles for you to look at, should you be completely unable to come up with an idea.

HOW TO HELP THE STUDENT WITH STEP FIVE

If necessary, show the student some of the following sample titles and encourage her to use them as models.

Joan of Arc at War
Joan of Arc Leads the French Armies
Joan of Arc: Her Life as a General
Joan of Arc: From Joining the French Army to Her Death
Joan of Arc: Warrior Maiden
The Dauphin Charles: A Reluctant King
Joan of Arc's Extraordinary Life
The Flawed Rule of the Dauphin Charles

STEP SIX: **Proofread**

Student instructions for Step Six:

Before you hand your composition to your instructor, go through the following proofreading steps very carefully.

1) Check to make sure that you have used elements from at least three different *topoi*, plus an introduction and a conclusion.

2) Make sure that your finished essay is at least 300 words long. Longer is better!

3) Make sure that you have quoted from at least one source and cited at least two sources.

4) Read your paper out loud, listening for awkward or unclear sections and repeated

words. Rewrite awkward or unclear sentences so that they flow more naturally.

    5) Listen for information that is repeated more than once. Eliminate repetition of ideas.

    6) Read through the paper one more time, looking for sentence fragments, run-on sentences, and repeated words. Correct fragments and run-on sentences. Listen for unnecessary repetition.

    7) Check your spelling by looking, individually, at each word that might be a problem.

When your paper is ready, give it to your instructor.

HOW TO HELP THE STUDENT WITH STEP SIX

Check the student's work, using the following rubric.

Week 32 Rubric

Organization:

1   The essay should be at least 300 words long. Longer is better!
2   The essay should include the following required elements:
    1) An introduction and conclusion that are both separate paragraphs, at least two lines long, and that do not repeat the same information
    2) Elements from at least three different *topoi*
    3) A title that explains the main point or most important content of the composition
    4) A separate Works Cited page
3   The student should quote directly from at least one source and should cite at least two.

Mechanics:

1   Each sentence should make sense on its own when read aloud.
2   There should be no sentence fragments or run-on sentences.
3   All words should be spelled correctly.
4   The first line of each paragraph should be properly indented.
5   Verb tense should be consistent throughout.
6   Direct quotes should be properly formatted.
7   Footnotes and Works Cited page should be properly formatted.

Day Three: Analyze the Model

> Focus: Understanding how writers
> combine elements

STEP ONE: **Review the *topoi* (Student Responsibility)**

NOTE TO INSTRUCTOR: You may want to make sure that the student completes this step slowly and carefully.

Before you begin today's work, read carefully through the following *topoi* in your Composition Reference Notebook. Don't just skim through them; pay attention to each element!

Chronological Narrative of a Scientific Discovery
Scientific Description
Sequence: Natural Process
Explanation by Comparison/Contrast
Explanation by Definition: Natural Object or Phenomenon
Temporal Comparison: Science

To help keep your attention on the materal, I recommend that you read the *topoi* out loud.

STEP TWO: **Read (Student Responsibility)**

Read carefully through the following essay, "Dr. William Harvey," by A. Dickson Wright. It was first published in *New Scientist* magazine, June 6, 1957.

You may not be familiar with a "blue pencil," referred to in the conclusion of the essay. In the days before computers, a blue pencil was traditionally used by copy editors to mark mistakes and corrections on written pages, because blue would not show up when it was photocopied. Blue pencils are no longer used, but to "blue pencil" something still means "to correct it."

STEP THREE: **Understand how *topoi* can be combined**

Student instructions for Step Three:

During this step, your instructor will carry on a dialogue with you. Keep your *topoi* chart next to the essay as you work.

HOW TO HELP THE STUDENT WITH STEP THREE

You will guide the student into recognizing the different elements that are present in the essay, using the dialogue below. A copy of the student's completed work follows.

INSTRUCTOR: What do you think is the overall form of this essay—the main *topos* that acts as the skeleton of the whole composition?

> Student: Chronological narrative of a scientific discovery

NOTE TO INSTRUCTOR: There are also strong aspects of a biographical sketch in this essay, but the discovery of circulation is more central. If the student cannot come up with the above answer, go through the dialogue below and then return to the question. If she does provide the correct answer, go through the dialogue anyway to point out the elements.

INSTRUCTOR: The first two paragraphs of the essay tell you about two specific circumstances that existed before Harvey's discovery of circulation. In the first paragraph, underline the words "school of wild conjecture which had dominated medical thought for 1500 years." That's the first circumstance. The second circumstance was the misunderstanding of how the heart actually worked. What three erroneous things were believed about the heart's function?

> Student: Arteries contained gases or foul vapors, blood was at fever heat, there were small openings between the two sides of the heart.

INSTRUCTOR: Underline those three things in the second paragraph. In the margin beside the first two paragraphs, write "Circumstances before the discovery." If you look at your *topoi* chart, you'll see this in the "Remember" column beneath "Chronological Narrative of a Scientific Discovery." The author of this essay spends less time talking about the steps or events that led to the discovery, and more time describing how the discovery changed medicine. But he still describes the steps in chronological order. In the fourth paragraph, circle the words "first" and "till." In the sixth paragraph, circle the phrases "Twenty years were to pass" and "As the years went by." Then, go down to the paragraph that begins, "Harvey thus opened up a wonderful prospect." Circle the phrase "at last began." In the next paragraph, circle the phrase "In recent years." The author of this essay is using the form of a chronological narrative of scientific discovery—but his focus is on how that scientific discovery changed the practice of medicine over time. Go back to the beginning of the essay now and and write "Chronological narrative of a scientific discovery" above the title.

INSTRUCTOR: Now let's look at the rest of this essay. The author borrows elements from at least *five* additional *topoi*! How many of them can you point them out?

NOTE TO INSTRUCTOR: The borrowed *topoi* are:

Biographical sketch
Sequence: Natural process
Scientific description
Temporal comparison: Science
Explanation by definition: Natural object or phenomenon (function)

They are marked on the copy of the essay that follows. To help the student, you may ask the following questions:

"Which paragraphs list the important events in William Harvey's life? Those paragraphs borrow from the biographical sketch."

"Which paragraph describes, step by step, the natural cycle of circulation that repeats again and again? That paragraph is a sequence, describing a natural process."

"Which paragraph describes each part of the circulatory system and tells what it is made of? That paragraph is a scientific description. (Notice the difference between this description and the sequence in the third paragraph!)"

"What sentences tell you about the differences between old understandings of the circulatory system and Harvey's understanding? Those sentences are making use of a temporal comparison."

"On your Explanation by Definition: Natural Object or Phenomenon chart, you'll see that a descriptive sequence can be used to explain *function*. Where you have marked Sequence: Natural Process, you could also mark Explanation by Definition. You could also write Explanation by Definition next to the paragraphs that explain who made use of the new understanding of the circulatory system—how it changed medicine."

INSTRUCTOR: What kind of conclusion does the author use?

Student: Conclusion by question

INSTRUCTOR: What kind of introduction does he use? Hint: It tells you exactly why William Harvey's discovery was so important.

Student: Introduction by summary

INSTRUCTOR: Write both of those labels on the essay.

Chronological narrative of a scientific discovery
Dr. William Harvey

by A. Dickson Wright

by A. Dickson Wright

Introduction
by summary

The outstanding figure in the history of British medicine is undoubtedly Dr. William Harvey, whose name is a household word to every doctor throughout the world and who yet seems to be little known to the public at large. Medicine might almost be divided into the pre- and post-Harveian epochs. What was it, then, that he did to transform medicine? Quite briefly, he was the first to quit the <u>school of wild conjecture which had dominated medical thought for 1500 years</u> and in its place to establish the experimental method. This method involved three things: first, a line of thought leading to a crucial experiment; second, the performance of the experiment; and third, the deduction therefrom.

temporal
comparison

Circum-
stances
before the
discovery

This method led him to discover the circulation of the blood, a thing which had mystified the medical world till his time. <u>The arteries were supposed to contain gases or foul vapours, and the heart, which is partitioned into two cavities, was supposed to supply the blood to the body at fever heat.</u> The blood was also supposed to pass from one side of the heart to the other, and when it was pointed out that there were no apertures, the retort was that the openings were too small for the human eye to see. . . . There are no openings normally between the two sides of the heart, yet up to Harvey's time this was thought to be so.

Sequence:
Natural
process

Explanation
by
Definition

Harvey demonstrated that at each beat of the heart a spray of blood left the two sides of the heart, one directed towards the lungs and the other to the body generally. As soon as the blood left the heart, the heart muscle slackened and the heart valves closed to prevent the return of the blood, so that it had to pursue its way through the lungs and the body. Having completed the passage the blood returned to the heart by the veins, but to the opposite side of the heart from that which it originated, and then the figure-of-eight circulation was repeated again. It was a wonderful and simple method, the blood being aerated on one side of the heart and the aerated blood sent to the body from the other. The amount discharged from each side had to be equal, or there would be piling up of blood on one side or the other.

William Harvey first started to speak in public of this discovery in the year that Shakespeare died (1616) and he waited for twelve years till he published his book entitled *Exercitatio*

Anatomica de Motu cordis et Sanguinis in Animalibus (Anatomical exercise on the Motion of the Heart and Blood in Animals). The year of publication was 1628, the place Frankfurt and Latin the language, and in this remarkable book of 72 pages he announced his discovery, backing it with beautifully conceived experiments which he made on various animals—the deer of King Charles's forests, rabbits, frogs, toads, snakes, snails, and even the translucent shrimp.

The publication of this book provoked a storm in the world of medicine such had never been seen before. Abuse was spewed over Harvey in every language of the world: he came to be regarded as a quack, and his private practice faded away. Nevertheless he maintained a dignified silence and persevered with his research. He was willing to demonstrate his experiments to any who wished to see. . . .

Twenty years were to pass before Harvey made his first written answer to the critic (Riolan, anatomist of Paris) and this was couched in the kindest and most courteous terms. As the years went by agreement grew and grew, and when he died of a stroke at Roehampton . . . the old man of nearly eighty years was the beloved and respected leader of medicine in [England]. Every doctor of eminence joined his funeral procession. . . .

The life that ended on 3 June 1657 . . . had begun on 1 April 1578, in Folkestone. Harvey's parents were well-to-do citizens of that town, and Harvey enjoyed the best education obtainable. He went to King's School Canterbury, at the age of ten . . . then to Cambridge at the age of fifteen. After four years there studying the arts, he went to Padua, near Venice, to study medicine. . . .

Biographical sketch

Returning to Cambridge with his Padua degree . . . Harvey received his Cambridge degree in medicine at the age of 24. With this wonderful education behind him, he married the daughter of Queen Elizabeth's doctor. Nothing was lacking to make a successful career, and this followed with great speed—physician to St. Bartholomew's Hospital, to James I, and to Charles I.

Harvey's closing years were saddened by the Civil War, which broke out when he was 64. In spite of his age, as physician to King Charles he followed him to the wars. He was at the battle of Edgehill, which was a victory for Charles, and looked after the young princes who were to become Charles II and James II. While he was away at the wars the mob looted his house in London, and some of his writings were lost for ever. . . .

The great importance of Harvey's discovery was that it

revolutionised the concept of how life was maintained in the human body through the constant irrigation of the tissues by a vast network of blood vessels, varying from the main artery with a calibre of two thumbs down to the finest blood vessels (capillaries), the diameter of which is one-tenth of a human hair. The aggregate length of these vessels is immense, estimated at thousands of miles, and yet they are filled with only twelve pints of blood. The heart provides the power, beating without cessation, and in a life of seventy years makes 3,500 million beats. The blood circulates at a remarkable speed, completing the circuit of the whole body in twelve seconds, or passing through the 100 miles of blood vessels in the brain in two seconds.

The construction of such a system would provide a nightmare for an engineer.

Harvey thus opened up a wonderful prospect; the anatomists found that the anatomy they had taught had to be corrected to fit in with the new concept. The physician at last began to think with logic and reason, and the treatment of every disease was benefited by the new discovery. The harmful ritualistic practice of bleeding was exposed as useless. The surgeon benefited by preventing loss of blood at operations.

In recent years the surgery of the heart and circulation has developed at an amazing speed, though in the field of research there are thousands of questions still to be answered. Many other circulations besides that of the blood have been discovered in the 100,000 miles of tubes which our bodies are estimated to contain. One might say that the body consists of tubes and life consists of circulations.

Yet if Harvey returned to the world today, 350 years after his discovery, and became acquainted with all our advances, and if in one of his hands was placed the little book of 72 pages which he published in 1628, and in the other a blue pencil, he could read the book through without once using the pencil.

Of what other scientific book could this be said?

Day Four: Prepare to Write

 Focus: Reading sources for an essay in science

Now that the student has examined how an accomplished author combines *topoi* and uses elements from different forms in a science essay, he will start preparing to do the same in a composition of his own.

STEP ONE: **Read (Student Responsibility)**

Today, you only have one step to perform. Before you start thinking about which *topoi* you will use or what your exact topic will be, read through the following sources carefully, without stopping to take notes.

NOTE TO INSTRUCTOR: Although today's work can be completed independently, you may need to encourage the student to read carefully. He has been given much more material than he will actually take notes on, so also encourage him not to be intimidated by the amount of information.

WEEK 33: COMBINING THE *TOPOI* IN SCIENCE

Days One and Two: Take Notes for a Science Composition

 Focus: Taking notes

Over the next two days, the student will take notes for a science composition, just as he did for last week's Joan of Arc essay. He will then spend the second half of the week writing his essay.

There are only three assigned steps: settling on *topoi* to include, preparing to take notes, and then the note-taking itself. Because the sources are lengthy, the student will undoubtedly need more than one day to work through the note-taking process. I strongly suggest that he get started with the note-taking on Day One, but you and the student can decide how much work should be completed on each day.

STEP ONE: Choose tentative *topoi* and elements

Student instructions for Step One:

To take notes effectively, you'll need to make a tentative decision about the *topoi* that you'll include in your essay.

Look back through the following *topoi* in your Composition Reference Notebook. Keeping in mind the sources that you read last week, choose at least three *topoi* that you might be able to use in an essay about Pasteur and/or Pasteur's accomplishments. Four is even better.

Remember that you don't have to include *every* element in the chosen *topoi;* you can just incorporate one or two aspects into your final paper.

Chronological Narrative of a Scientific Discovery
Scientific Description
Biographical Sketch
Sequence: Natural Process
Explanation by Comparison/Contrast
Explanation by Definition: Natural Object or Phenomenon

533

Temporal Comparison: Science

Once you've made your choice, show your selections to your instructor. Ask for help if you
need it.

HOW TO HELP THE STUDENT WITH STEP ONE

The following *topoi* are best suited to the provided sources. Once the student has shown you
the *topoi* he intends to use, you can use the information below to help him narrow down his
topics. This information will also be helpful for Step Two.

Chronological Narrative of a Scientific Discovery

Pasteur has multiple innovations to his name, and three different discoveries are described
in the source materials: the anthrax vaccine, the process of pasteurization, and the rabies
vaccine.

Both the process of pasteurization and the rabies vaccine are described with enough detail
to construct a full chronological narrative. There is less information about the anthrax vaccine;
a narrative about anthrax would need to be a smaller part of the final composition, added to a
more detailed "skeleton" or organizing *topos*.

Biographical Sketch

The sources do not contain enough information about Pasteur's youth, personal life, and
education for a full biographical sketch organized around the major events of his life. However,
a sketch could be organized around his work/accomplishments. In chronological order, those
would be:
Pasteurization (1858)
Anthrax vaccine (1882)
Rabies vaccine (1885)
Opening of the Pasteur Institute (1888)

Sequence: Natural Process

The process by which microorganisms enter into living matter and spoil it can be
described in some detail. You may need to point out to the student that the discovery of vaccines, and the ways in which vaccines produce immunity, are not "natural processes" that
repeat in cycles. These sequences are created by human intervention; you would describe them
under the heading of "explanation by definition" instead.

Explanation by Comparison/Contrast

The following comparisons and contrasts are possible; some would be very brief (only a sentence or two), others more lengthy:

> contrast of general understanding of germs/infection before and after Pasteur
> contrast milk, wine, beer, etc. before and after pasteurization
> Pouchet's theory of microorganisms vs. Pasteur's theory
> contrast of vaccinated sheep vs. nonvaccinated sheep
> contrast of dogs/rabbits inoculated with rabies by injection vs.
>   dogs/rabbits inoculated by trepanning
> comparison/contrast of three subjects who got the rabies vaccine (Joseph Meister,
>   J. B. Jupille, and Louise Lepelletier)
> comparison of spores and bacteria to seeds and growing plants

These topics overlap with "temporal comparison: science" below, since temporal comparison is a very specific type of comparison/contrast.

Explanation by Definition: Natural Object or Phenomenon

Possible topics for definition include:

> Pasteurization
> Microorganisms
> The disease of rabies
> The rabies vaccine

Temporal Comparison: Science

The following comparisons/contrasts are temporal in nature:

> behavior of bacteria spores vs. behavior of vegetative bacteria
> contrast of general understanding of germs/infection before and after Pasteur
> contrast milk, wine, beer, etc. before and after pasteurization

STEP TWO: **Prepare to take notes**

Student instructions for Step Two:

> As you did for your last writing assignment, write the name of each *topos* that you've selected at the top of a new page (whether notebook paper or word processing document). Then, write a brief phrase or sentence describing exactly what that *topos* will cover. For example, if the first *topos* you decided to include was "Chronological Narrative of a Scientific

Discovery," you might then write "The Rabies Vaccine."

The heading on your paper should help you keep in mind, as you go through your sources and take notes, exactly what kinds of information you're looking for. Otherwise, you may end up taking too many notes that you don't need (and won't use).

HOW TO HELP THE STUDENT WITH STEP TWO

If necessary, use the information from Step One to help the student narrow his topics.

STEP THREE: **Take notes**

Student instructions for Step Three:

Spend the rest of your time taking notes on the sources.

Remember to pick and choose only those facts and details that will support the *topoi* you've chosen. You do not need to write down *every* fact and detail—that would give you far too much information! Having too much information can be paralyzing when you sit down to write.

Aim to have at least five or six to eight notes about each *topos*, but do not take more than fifteen notes for any single *topos*. (Some comparisons and sequences might have only three to four pieces of information in them.)

As before, you can choose which note-taking method suits you best:

1) Go through the sources one time each, placing each relevant bit of information from each source on the appropriate page of notes as you go. OR

2) Pick the first *topos* and go through all four sources, looking for answers. Do the same for the second *topos*, and then the third, and so on.

I have provided you with what might be the first four or five notes on a sample *topos*, below. Follow this model.

If you need help, ask your instructor. When you are finished, show your work to your instructor.

Chronological Narrative of a Scientific Discovery:
The Rabies Vaccine

Before Pasteur, "no one understood why people caught diseases" or "the spread of germs" (Miles, p. 4)

"Even doctors didn't think germs could cause infection or disease" (Zamosky et al., p. 7)

Pasteur produced vaccine in 1884 (Feinstein, p. 105)

Tested by placing "spinal cord tissue from the sick animals in direct contact with the brains of the healthy animals" (Feinstein, pp. 105–106)

Then, vaccinated Joseph Meister in 1885 after he was attacked by rabid dog (Feinstein, p. 106)

HOW TO HELP THE STUDENT WITH STEP THREE

There are many different ways in which this information could be organized, but the sample notes below show what the student's notes might look like.

If the student needs help, allow him to look at one or more of the models below; then ask him to take his own notes without looking back at my sample answers.

When finished, the student should have no fewer than five to six notes and no more than fifteen for each *topos*. (Comparisons and sequences may have fewer elements than five.)

NOTE TO INSTRUCTOR: The production of the rabies vaccine is, technically, more difficult to understand than pasteurization. Students at this level vary widely in their grasp of basic scientific principles. If the student grows frustrated with the attempt to understand how the rabies vaccine works, suggest that he investigate pasteurization instead; the process doesn't require as much background knowledge.

Chronological Narrative of a Scientific Discovery:
The Rabies Vaccine

Before Pasteur, "no one understood why people caught diseases" or "the spread of germs" (Miles, p. 4)

"Even doctors didn't think germs could cause infection or disease" (Zamosky et al., p. 7)

"Mad dogs" were "the terror of the countryside" (Keim and Lumet, p. 161)

Dr. Roux recommended "cauterisation with hot irons" and "butter of antimony" (Keim and Lumet, p. 162)

Pasteur discovered saliva that had "microbes" of rabies, but that had "lost all their virulence" (Keim and Lumet, p. 163)

This was "attenuated" (or weakened) virus (Keim and Lumet, p. 166)

"Inoculation with attenuated virus rendered dogs resistant" to rabies "and prevented the disease from appearing in those that had been bitten" (Keim and Lumet, p. 167)

Pasteur produced vaccine in 1884 (Feinstein, p. 105)

Tested by placing "spinal cord tissue from the sick animals in direct contact with the brains of the healthy animals" (Feinstein, pp. 105–106)

Then, vaccinated Joseph Meister in 1885 after he was attacked by rabid dog (Feinstein, p. 106)

After this he treated J. B. Jupille, a week after he was bitten (Keim and Lumet, pp. 171–172)

He treated 2,682 people who had been bitten between October 1885 and December 1886, and only 31 died (Keim and Lumet, p. 175)

More people came to Pasteur and he opened the Pasteur Institute in 1888 (Feinstein, p. 107)

Chronological Narrative of a Scientific Discovery:
Pasteurization

Before Pasteur, "yogurt and other dairy products" spoiled in just a day or two (Haven, p. 77)

Pasteur "discovered that microscopic organisms floated everywhere in the air, unseen" (Haven, p. 77)

He found that it was "not the air itself but the floating particles in it that carried bacteria which induced the decomposition" (Gehrmann, p. 96)

These organisms "fell by chance onto food and all living matter" and then multiplied (Haven, p. 77)

Pasteur knew that heat would kill microorganisms, particularly in acids (Gaynes, p. 152)

Boiling a liquid one to three times would destroy the bacteria (Gehrmann, p. 96)

Some bacteria required "fractional sterilization . . . a killing of decomposition bacteria by several short period heatings far enough apart to allow the spores to sprout into vegetative cells that can be easily killed" (Gehrmann, p. 96)

This is called pasteurization (Gehrmann, p. 96)

The heating of milk has to be "very carefully regulated" to a temperature between 130–140 degrees F (Gehrmann, p. 96)

Two methods are used for milk—the flash method and the holding method (Gehrmann, p. 96)

Pasteurization kills strep, tuberculosis, typhoid, cholera, dysentery (Gehrmann, p. 96)

Biographical Sketch: Pasteur's Accomplishments

Pasteurization (1858)

Pasteur found that it was "not the air itself but the floating particles in it that carried bacteria which induced the decomposition" (Gehrmann, p. 96)

These organisms "fell by chance onto food and all living matter" and then multiplied (Haven, p. 77)

Pasteur knew that heat would kill microorganisms, particularly in acids (Gaynes, p. 152)

Boiling a liquid one to three times would destroy the bacteria (Gehrmann, p. 96)

This is called pasteurization (Gehrmann, p. 96)

Anthrax vaccine (1882)

    In the 1870s, anthrax was killing sheep and cattle in France (Zamosky et al., p. 7)

    Robert Koch discovered the bacterium that killed them (Zamosky et al., p. 7)

    Pasteur developed a vaccine and demonstrated how effective it was (Zamosky et al., p. 7)

Rabies vaccine (1885)

    Pasteur discovered saliva that had "microbes" of rabies, but that had "lost all their virulence" (Keim and Lumet, p. 163)

    This was "attenuated" (or weakened) virus (Keim and Lumet, p. 166)

    "Inoculation with attenuated virus rendered dogs resistant" to rabies "and prevented the disease from appearing in those that had been bitten" (Keim and Lumet, p. 167)

Pasteur produced vaccine in 1884 (Feinstein, p. 105)

Then, vaccinated Joseph Meister in 1885 after he was attacked by rabid dog (Feinstein, p. 106)

He treated 2,682 people who had been bitten between October 1885 and December 1886, and only 31 died (Keim and Lumet, p. 175)

Opening of the Pasteur Institute (1888)

More people came to Pasteur and he opened the Pasteur Institute in 1888 (Feinstein, p. 107)

Sequence: Natural Process
How Microorganisms Spoil Living Matter

Microscopic organisms float in the air and fall onto food, etc. (Haven, p. 77)

Multiply when they find "decaying substance to use as nutrient" (Haven, p. 77)

Generate spores which "resist all destructive action much better than the growing bacteria" (Gehrmann, p. 96)

Spores then sprout (Gehrmann, p. 96)

Explanation by Comparison/Contrast
Joseph Meister, J. B. Jupille, and Louise Lepelletier

Meister	Jupille	Lepelletier
Alsatian	Shepherd	Young girl
Aged nine	Aged fifteen	
First person successfully vaccinated	Second vaccinated	
June 6, 1885	October 29, 1885	December, 1885
Fourteen wounds	Badly bitten a week before	Bitten 37 days before
No symptoms	Immune	Died

Explanation by Comparison/Contrast
Spores and Bacteria/Seeds and Growing Plants

Spores and seeds	Bacteria and growing plants
Resting state	Vegetative state
Preserves life in winter and drought	Growing active plant
Hardier	More easily killed

Explanation by Definition: Natural Object or Phenomenon
Microorganisms

1. Properties

    Can only be seen with a microscope

    Extent in space: Floats "everywhere in the air, unseen" (Haven, p. 77)

2. Function

    "entered human flesh during operations and through cuts to cause infection and disease" (Haven, p. 77)

    "fell by chance onto food and all living matter" (Haven, p. 77)

    Killed by applying heat (Gaynes, p. 152)

    Cause decomposition (Gehrmann, p. 96)

    Two phases: spore and growing bacteria (resting and vegetative (Gehrmann, p. 96)

    Vegetative phase: "begin their destructive activities at once when they get into suitable food material" (Gehrmann, p. 96)

    Spore phase: "resting and do not cause any change until they sprout" (Gehrmann, p. 96)

    Sprouting phase takes several hours to several days according to temperature (Gehrmann, p. 96)

3. Genus

    no notes

Temporal Comparison: Science
Behavior of Bacteria Spores vs. Behavior of Vegetative Bacteria

(All from Gehrmann, p. 96)

Spores	Vegetative
Resting	Growing
Do not cause change until they sprout	Begin to destroy at once
Kept from growing by cold	Killed by heat
Resist destruction	Easier to kill

Days Three and Four: Write

 Focus: Combining *topoi* into
a science composition

Over the next two days, the student will write a composition of at least 300 words that uses elements from at least three different *topoi*. Longer is fine; 300 is a bare minimum.

Like last week's Joan of Arc essay, this assignment has six steps.

Step One: Draft the main *topos*
Step Two: Add other *topoi*
Step Three: Provide an introduction and conclusion
Step Four: Construct the Works Cited page
Step Five: Title
Step Six: Proofread

The student should review through the instructions for all six steps before beginning to write.

Together, you and the student should decide how much time to spend on each step.

For all the steps below, if the student needs additional help, you may allow him to read one or more of the models I provide.

STEP ONE: **Draft the main *topos***

Student instructions for Step One:

In the essay about William Harvey that you examined last week, the author used the Chronological Narrative of a Scientific Discovery as the "skeleton" for his essay—the primary organizational form. He then inserted a compact biographical sketch as well as selected elements of other *topoi* into it.

Before you start to write, decide which of the *topoi* you've taken notes on will serve as your "skeleton." Choose one that has plenty of notes to go with it. (The Chronological Narrative of a Scientific Discovery and the Biographical Sketch will probably be the simplest *topoi* to use.)

Using your notes and referring to your reference chart, write a draft of the main *topos*.

Be sure to look back at your chart, reminding yourself of the elements that should belong in the *topos*.

Aim for at least 150 words; try to get closer to 200 words if possible. Be sure to cite at least *two* sources and to include at least one direct quote.

HOW TO HELP THE STUDENT WITH STEP ONE

You may need to remind the student to look back at the chart in the Reference Section of his notebook. This will help him to include all of the required elements.

The student's work might resemble one of these:

The following is an example of the Chronological Narrative of a Scientific Discovery, using the notes taken about pasteurization. Notice the inclusion of the background paragraph explaining circumstances that existed before the discovery, as suggested in the *topos* chart.

> Before the work of Louis Pasteur, yogurt, milk, cheese, and butter spoiled in less than two days—so that no one could eat these foods unless they lived within a day's journey of the cow.[1] No one really understood why dairy products, as well as meat, wine, and beer, rotted so quickly.
>
> Louis Pasteur found the answer. He discovered that the air was filled with microorganisms called bacteria that fell onto the food and started decomposition. He also learned that the bacteria were very sensitive to heat. Boiling a liquid, either once or up to three times, would destroy the bacteria in it.[2]
>
> The process of heating liquids in order to kill the bacteria became known as pasteurization, after Louis Pasteur. Pasteurization kills the bacteria that cause strep, tuberculosis, typhoid, cholera, and dysentery. Milk is one of the most important foods that needs to be pasteurized. Two methods are used for milk—the flash method, and the holding method—but both have to be "very carefully regulated."[3]

---

[1] Kendall Haven, *100 Greatest Science Discoveries of All Time* (Greenwood Publishing, 2007), p. 77.

[2] Adolph Gehrmann, "Pasteurization," in *The American Food Journal* 12:1 (January, 1917), p. 96.

[3] Ibid.

The following is an example of a Biographical Sketch of Louis Pasteur, focusing in on his accomplishments and achievements. These are listed chronologically, one of the suggestions on the *topoi* chart.

> In the 1850s, Louis Pasteur discovered how to remove dangerous bacteria from milk and other foods. He theorized that bacteria, floating in the air, fell onto food and then grew there. Since heat kills microorganisms, he knew that boiling the milk would destroy the bacteria in it. This process became known as pasteurization.[1]

Pasteur also discovered a vaccine for anthrax. In the 1870s, thousands of sheep and cattle were dying from the disease anthrax, all across France. A scientist named Robert Koch had identified the bacterium that caused anthrax; Louis Pasteur developed a vaccine that made sheep immune to the disease. [2]

Ten years later, Pasteur began looking for a solution to an even more deadly disease—rabies. He found a weakened form of the rabies virus. Dogs who were inoculated with this weakened virus were resistant to rabies. Even more importantly, if someone had been bitten and infected with rabies, injection with the weakened virus "prevented the disease from appearing." [3] The first patient to receive the vaccination, Joseph Meister, was nine years old. He had been bitten by a mad dog, but did not come down with the disease. [4]

In 1888, not long before his death, Louis Pasteur opened a full clinic known as the Pasteur Institute. So many people had come for his rabies vaccination that he needed a full-time office to treat them. At the end of his life, Pasteur was buried at the Institute. [5]

---

[1] Adolph Gehrmann, "Pasteurization," in *The American Food Journal* 12:1 (January, 1917), p. 96.

[2] Lisa Zamosky, Thomas B. Ciccone and Ronald Edwards, *Louis Pasteur* (Compass Point Books, 2009), p. 7.

[3] Albert Keim and Louis Lumet, *Louis Pasteur*, trans. Frederic Tabor Cooper (Frederick A. Stokes, 1914), p. 167.

[4] Stephen Feinstein, *Louis Pasteur: The Father of Microbiology* (Enslow Publishers, 2008), p. 106.

[5] Robert P. Gaynes, *Germ Theory: Medical Pioneers in Infectious Diseases* (ASM Press, 2011), p. 169.

STEP TWO: **Add other *topoi***

Student instructions for Step Two:

Look back over your notes and decide which *topoi* or elements you will add to your composition. If necessary, glance back at A. Dickson Wright's essay in Week 32. Notice how he borrows aspects from a Sequence: Natural Process as well as Scientific Description, Explanation by Definition, and Temporal Comparison to flesh out his combination of chronological narrative and biographical sketch.

Decide where the *topoi* or elements will be located in your composition. Draft the *topoi* or elements and insert them into your essay. You must add elements from at least two different *topoi*. You may need to rearrange paragraphing or slightly rewrite some of your existing sentences so that the new elements fit into your composition smoothly.

You should aim to have a total of at least 250 words by the end of this step; longer is better!

HOW TO HELP THE STUDENT WITH STEP TWO

A sequence, comparison/contrast, or temporal comparison can be inserted into either a chronological narrative or biographical sketch. Elements from a biographical sketch can also be inserted into a chronological narrative, as can elements from an explanation by definition.

The student's work might resemble one of the following. The added text is in bold.

Sequence: Natural Process and Temporal Comparison (bacteria spores vs. vegetative bacteria), both added to the original Chronological Narrative. Notice that I have changed the paragraphing and replaced pronouns with proper names in order to make the new elements fit in smoothly:

> Before the work of Louis Pasteur, yogurt, milk, cheese, and butter spoiled in less than two days—so that no one could eat these foods unless they lived within a day's journey of the cow.[1] No one really understood why dairy products, as well as meat, wine and beer, rotted so quickly.
>
> Louis Pasteur found the answer. He discovered that the air was filled with microorganisms called bacteria that fell onto the food and started decomposition. **These microorganisms, which feed on decaying substances, produce spores that are very hard to kill. The spores then sprout into growing, active bacteria.** [2]
>
> **Spores and growing bacteria both live in foods. But the spores, which are like seeds, do not cause any change in the food. They are hard to destroy, and do not grow into vegetative bacteria until they are warmed. Vegetative bacteria, on the other hand, are alive and destructive. They begin to work just as soon as they find "suitable food material," but they are also much easier to kill than spores.** [3]
>
> Pasteur learned that the **growing** bacteria were very sensitive to heat. Boiling a liquid, either once or up to three times, would destroy the bacteria in it.[4]
>
> The process of heating liquids in order to kill the bacteria became known as pasteurization, after Louis Pasteur. Pasteurization kills the bacteria that cause strep, tuberculosis, typhoid, cholera, and dysentery. Milk is one of the most important foods that needs to be pasteurized. Two methods are used for milk—the flash method, and the holding method—but both have to be "very carefully regulated."[5]

---

[1] Kendall Haven, *100 Greatest Science Discoveries of All Time* (Greenwood Publishing, 2007), p. 77.

[2] Adolph Gehrmann, "Pasteurization," in *The American Food Journal* 12:1 (January, 1917), p. 96.

[3] Ibid.

[4] Ibid.

[5] Ibid.

Aspects from the Explanation by Definition and the Explanation by Comparison/Contrast (Meister, Jupille, and Lepelletier), both added to the original Biographical Sketch. Notice that I have had to make some changes in paragraphing and wording to incorporate the new text smoothly into the composition.

In the 1850s, Louis Pasteur discovered how to remove dangerous bacteria from milk and other foods. He theorized that bacteria, floating in the air, fell onto food and then grew there.

This bacteria, which could only be seen with a microscope, caused decomposition in the food. It went through two phases: spores (resting) and vegetative (growing). In its spore phase, the bacterium did not cause any changes; but once it began to grow, it began to destroy the food.[1]

Since heat kills microorganisms, Pasteur knew that boiling milk would destroy the bacteria in it. This process became known as pasteurization.[2]

Pasteur also discovered a vaccine for anthrax. In the 1870s, thousands of sheep and cattle were dying from the disease anthrax, all across France. A scientist named Robert Koch had identified the bacterium that caused anthrax; Louis Pasteur developed a vaccine that made sheep immune to the disease.[3]

Ten years later, Pasteur began looking for a solution to an even more deadly disease—rabies. He found a weakened form of the rabies virus. Dogs who were inoculated with this weakened virus were resistant to rabies. Even more importantly, if someone had been bitten and infected with rabies, injection with the weakened virus "prevented the disease from appearing."[4] The first patient to receive the vaccination, Joseph Meister, was nine years old. He had been bitten by a mad dog, but did not come down with the disease[5]

After Meister, Pasteur treated an older patient, a fifteen-year-old shepherd named J. B. Jupille. Unlike Meister, Jupille had been bitten a full week before he was treated. He received his injections on October 29, 1885, more than four months after Joseph Meister. But, like Meister, he did not come down with the disease.

Pasteur had a very different outcome with a little girl named Louise Lepelletier. She was treated 37 days after she was bitten, much later than either Meister or Jupille. Unlike Meister and Jupille, she did not respond. Lepelletier died, despite Pasteur's treatment.[6]

In 1888, not long before his death, Louis Pasteur opened a full clinic known as the Pasteur Institute. So many people had come for his rabies vaccination that he needed a full-time office to treat them. At the end of his life, Pasteur was buried at the Institute.[7]

---

[1] **Adolph Gehrmann, "Pasteurization," in *The American Food Journal* 12:1 (January, 1917), p. 96.**

[2] Ibid.

[3] Lisa Zamosky, Thomas B. Ciccone and Ronald Edwards, *Louis Pasteur* (Compass Point Books, 2009), p. 7.

[4] Albert Keim and Louis Lumet, *Louis Pasteur*, trans. Frederic Tabor Cooper (Frederick A. Stokes, 1914), p. 167.

[5] Stephen Feinstein, *Louis Pasteur: The Father of Microbiology* (Enslow Publishers, 2008), p. 106.

[6] **Keim and Lumet, pp. 171, 174.**

[7] Robert P. Gaynes, *Germ Theory: Medical Pioneers in Infectious Diseases* (ASM Press, 2011), p. 169.

STEP THREE: **Provide an introduction and conclusion**

Student instructions for Step Three:

> Choose an introduction and a conclusion from your Introductions and Conclusions chart. You may pick any introduction and conclusion—but make sure that they don't repeat the same information.
>
> To write an introduction by history that uses a brief scene or an introduction by anecdote that uses an invented scene, you may need to reread the sources from Week 32. You may also ask your instructor to show you the sample introductions and conclusions provided for the Joan of Arc essay; this may help you to come up with introductions and conclusions for this composition.
>
> Each introduction and conclusion should be at least two sentences long and should be placed in separate paragraphs, not incorporated into the existing paragraphs of the composition.
>
> Remember that your final word count must be over 300.

HOW TO HELP THE STUDENT WITH STEP THREE

Allowing the student to read the sample introductions and conclusions from Step Three of Week 32, Days One and Two, may be helpful.

STEP FOUR: **Construct the Works Cited page**

Student instructions for Step Four:

> At the top of a separate sheet of paper, center the words "Works Cited." In proper form, list the sources you used to write your essay.

HOW TO HELP THE STUDENT WITH STEP FOUR

The proper format for all sources is found below.

Feinstein, Stephen. *Louis Pasteur: The Father of Microbiology.* Berkeley Heights, N.J.: Enslow Publishers, 2008.

Gaynes, Robert P. *Germ Theory: Medical Pioneers in Infectious Diseases.* Washington, D.C.: ASM Press, 2011.

Gehrmann, Adolph. "Pasteurization." In *The American Food Journal*, Vol. 12, No. 1 (January, 1917), p. 96.

Haven, Kendall. *100 Greatest Science Discoveries of All Time.* Westport, Conn.: Greenwood Publishing, 2007.

Keim, Albert and Louis Lumet. *Louis Pasteur*, trans. Frederic Taber Cooper. New York: Frederick A. Stokes, 1914.

Miles, Elizabeth. *Louis Pasteur.* Chicago: Heinemann-Raintree, 2009.

Zamosky, Lisa, Thomas B. Ciccone and Ronald Edwards. *Louis Pasteur.* Mankato, Minn.: Compass Point Books, 2009.

STEP FIVE: Title

Student instructions for Step Five:

> Give your composition a title that describes the primary *topos* you decided to use.
> For example, if I wrote a chronological narrative of scientific discovery that dealt with Louis Pasteur's discovery of an anthrax vaccine, I might title it:
>
> Louis Pasteur and the Anthrax Vaccine
>
> or
>
> How Louis Pasteur Discovered a Vaccine for Anthrax
>
> or
>
> Louis Pasteur: Discoverer of the Anthrax Vaccine

Notice that the first title simply couples the scientist and the result of his discovery together. The second describes a process—the steps that Pasteur went through to get to that result. The third uses Pasteur's name as the title, inserts a colon, and then describes his role in discovering the vaccine in the subtitle.

> Your instructor has other sample titles for you to look at, should you be completely unable to come up with an idea.

HOW TO HELP THE STUDENT WITH STEP FIVE

If necessary, show the student some of the following sample titles and encourage her to use them as models.

> The Discovery of Pasteurization
> Pasteurization: Louis Pasteur's Greatest Accomplishment
> The Accomplishments of Louis Pasteur
> The Answer to Rabies: How Louis Pasteur Created the Rabies Vaccine
> Louise Pasteur and the Problem of Rabies

STEP SIX: **Proofread**

Student instructions for Step Six:

> Before you hand your composition to your instructor, go through the following proof-reading steps very carefully.
>
> 1) Check to make sure that you have used elements from at least three different *topoi*, plus an introduction and a conclusion.
> 2) Make sure that your finished essay is at least 300 words long. Longer is better!
> 3) Make sure that you have quoted from at least one source and cited at least two sources.
> 4) Read your paper out loud, listening for awkward or unclear sections and repeated words. Rewrite awkward or unclear sentences so that they flow more naturally.
> 5) Listen for information that is repeated more than once. Eliminate repetition of ideas.
> 6) Read through the paper one more time, looking for sentence fragments, run-on sentences, and repeated words. Correct fragments and run-on sentences. Listen for unnecessary repetition.
> 7) Check your spelling by looking, individually, at each word that might be a problem.
>
> When your paper is ready, give it to your instructor.

HOW TO HELP THE STUDENT WITH STEP SIX

Check the student's work, using the following rubric.

Week 33 Rubric

Organization:

1 The essay should be at least 300 words long. Longer is better!
2 The essay should include the following required elements:
   1) An introduction and conclusion that are both separate paragraphs, at least two lines long, and that do not repeat the same information.
   2) Elements from at least three different *topoi*.
   3) A title that explains the main point or most important content of the composition.
   4) A separate Works Cited page.
3 The student should quote directly from at least one source and should cite at least two.

Mechanics:

1 Each sentence should make sense on its own when read aloud.
2 There should be no sentence fragments or run-on sentences.
3 All words should be spelled correctly.
4 The first line of each paragraph should be properly indented.
5 Verb tense should be consistent throughout.
6 Direct quotes should be properly formatted.
7 Footnotes and Works Cited page should be properly formatted.

WEEKS 34 THROUGH 36: FINAL PROJECT

At the end of Level 1 of this course, the student carried out an independent project that drew on all the skills practiced over the year. Now that she's at the end of Level 2, she will do the same.

Over the course of this year, the student has added new *topoi* to her arsenal of writing tools. She's also practiced more advanced note-taking and research skills; learned to brainstorm for her subject; and begun to see how different *topoi* can fit together to create a more interesting and complex composition.

Instead of two weeks (like last year), the student should take at least three weeks to work on this project. Instead of beginning with the *topoi* list, she'll start with brainstorming. And instead of a minimum of two *topoi* in her paper, she will need to use at least three.

Over the course of the three weeks (or more), the student should complete the following twelve steps:

Step One: Create brainstorming maps	1–2 hours
Step Two: Resource collection	3 hours . . . or possibly more
Step Three: Pre-reading, Part I	2–3 hours
Step Four: Choose tentative *topoi* and elements	1 hour
Step Five: Pre-reading, Part II	3–4 hours
Step Six: Take notes	3–4 hours
Step Seven: Draft the main *topos*	3–4 hours
Step Eight: Add other *topoi*	2–3 hours
Step Nine: Provide an introduction and conclusion	60–90 minutes
Step Ten: Title	20 minutes
Step Eleven: Construct the Works Cited page	30 minutes
Step Twelve: Proofread	2 hours

You should hold VERY loosely to the suggested times. Reading takes time. Writing, which is thinking on the page, takes even more time. The goal of this final project is for the student to take all of the things she has learned to do over the past two years and put them to use in one project. She should take as much time as necessary to meet this goal.

The student can choose to spend more time on the project and stretch it out over additional weeks. She can take additional time to illustrate her final composition with drawings, graphs, charts, maps and diagrams—or not. But however the student approaches this final composition, it must:

1. Include at least three of the *topoi* in her reference chart.
2. Be at least 1250 words in length (that's five to seven typed, double-spaced pages).
3. Make use of at least four sources.
4. Include footnotes and a Works Cited page.

The directions below assume that a library visit will be part of the process. As this instructor manual has mentioned before, using e-books (including those at books.google.com) is an acceptable alternative, as long as the e-books are not self-published (which usually means unedited, un-fact-checked, and unreliable).

General rubrics are provided for your use in Appendix VIII.

Many of the steps below should be completed independently. If the student seems confused, make sure that she has gone back and read the recommended lessons carefully.

STEP ONE: **Create brainstorming maps (1–2 hours) (Student Responsibility)**

Turn back to Week Eight, and read carefully through the instructions for Day One (brainstorming in history) and Day Two (brainstorming in science). Following the instructions, create two brainstorming maps for history and two for science.

Go through this process even if you think you already know what you want to write about. Every brainstorming map that you create forces your brain to make new connections; you may find a new perspective on a subject you think you already understand, or discover a topic that's even more interesting than the one you've already picked. And, if you discover during Step Two that resources for your original idea are few and far between, you'll already have a couple of alternative topics lined up.

STEP TWO: **Resource collection (3 hours . . . or possibly more)**

Student instructions for Step Two:

This will be your most time-consuming task, because it requires you to visit the library and collect your resources.

Before you can settle on the *topoi* you'll include in your composition, you need to have some idea of what information is out there and available to you.

Your goal is to end up with six sources that tell you something helpful about your general subject area. But you should start out by reading a couple of encyclopedia articles on your subject.

In Level One of this course, I told you not to use Wikipedia. Here's what I said:

You may not use Wikipedia. Wikipedia is not professionally edited or fact-checked. Anyone can post anything on Wikipedia. Usually, other users will identify and remove mistakes—but if you happen to use Wikipedia five minutes after someone has posted bad information (which people sometimes do just for fun), you won't realize that you're writing down false facts.

That's still true. But I'm going to relax my anti-Wikipedia stance for this step, and allow you to start off by consulting Wikipedia entries that relate to your subject.

Why? Because this is only the first pre-reading stage. Your goal right now is just to figure out what terms and phrases you should search for in your first library visit. Don't plan on using *anything* you find on Wikipedia in your composition. But if Wikipedia can point you towards phrases and words that will help you search for resources that have been professionally edited and fact-checked, you'll get a jump on your research.

Once you're armed with keywords and phrases to search for (remember, you haven't settled on the form of your composition yet—so you don't know whether a chronological narrative, an explanation by definition, a biographical sketch, or some other *topos* will best suit your subject), prepare for a library visit by making an initial list of titles to look for, using your local library's online catalog. If you need a refresher, reread the instructions for Week 8, Days Three to Four.

If you're unable to find more than one or two books, you should choose another subject area definition and try using its keywords for your search. And if *none* of your subject area definitions are giving you good keywords for searching, you might consider choosing another brainstorming map.

You should finish making up your preliminary list of titles before you visit the library. Once you're there, ask the reference librarian for help finding the books, if necessary. Glance on either side of the titles to see whether nearby books might also have something interesting to say about your subject area.

Pull at least 10–12 books off the shelf and take them to a place where you can examine them more closely. Using the index, make sure that at least one of the keywords in your subject area appears in the book.

Try to bring home at least six books that relate to your subject.

HOW TO HELP THE STUDENT WITH STEP TWO

If a library visit is not possible, help the student locate the appropriate e-books.

Be sure to glance over the books that the student selects. They should not be too long and complicated; at least two of them should have brief *summaries* of information. If all of the books are detailed, book-length studies, the student will have difficulty choosing only the important details needed for the relatively brief composition. (She will probably not think that 1250 words is brief. In the world of nonfiction, it is.)

STEP THREE: **Pre-reading, Part I (2–3 hours)**

Student instructions for Step Three:

> In the last two writing assignments, you began your research by just reading—not taking notes, or looking for facts, but just reading.
>
> Read the chapters or sections of each book that relate to your topic. Don't take notes yet—you don't know what information you'll need. But be sure to use bookmarks (torn slips of notebook paper are fine) or Post-It Notes to mark pages where you find interesting information.

HOW TO HELP THE STUDENT WITH STEP THREE

Make sure that the student doesn't skimp on this step! Familiarity with the available sources is *central* to Steps Four and beyond—if the student picks *topoi* that won't be supported by her research, she will grow increasingly frustrated as she tries to follow the next few instructions. Check to make sure that there are actually bookmarks or Post-It notes in the student's books. Ask her to tell you, in her own words, what she's learning about her subject.

STEP FOUR: Choose tentative *topoi* and elements (1 hour) (Student Responsibility)

Now that you've read through your resources, you should have some idea of what *topoi* might fit your subject material. Do the books about your topic contain plenty of chronological events? How about biographical details and personal descriptions? Descriptive sequences of natural cycles?

Just as you did in your last two assignments, settle on *topoi* that you might want to use to organize your paper. Since your paper will need to include at least three *topoi*, choose at least four. Five would be safer. Inevitably, when you start taking notes, you discover that you had less information than you thought in at least one area!

Before you go on to the next step, read through the *topoi* you've chosen carefully. Reading out loud always helps you to concentrate.

STEP FIVE: Pre-reading, Part II (3–4 hours) (Student Responsibility)

Now return to your bookmarked/Post-It marked pages and reread them carefully.

You're still not taking notes. Remember: in the last two assignments, you read your sources first, before even *thinking* about note taking. The more familiar you are with your material, the simpler the note-taking process will be.

As you read, keep your chosen *topoi* in mind. If you realize that one of your *topoi* won't work, cross it off your list. If you find material that would support another *topos*, add it.

STEP SIX: Take notes (3–4 hours)

Student instructions for Step Six:

Just as you did in the last two assignments, write the name of each *topos* at the top of a sheet of notebook paper (or word processing document). Add an explanatory phrase that describes the content the *topos* will cover. (If you need to review, look back at Week 31, Days Three and Four, Step Two).

Then, take your notes.

Remember to pick and choose only those facts and details that will support the *topoi* you've chosen. You do not need to write down *every* fact and detail—that would give you far too much information! Having too much information can be paralyzing when you sit down to write.

Aim to have at least eight or nine notes about each *topos*, but do not take more than twenty notes for any single *topos*.

Choose which note-taking method suits you best:

1) Go through the sources one time each, placing each relevant bit of information from each source on the appropriate page of notes as you go. OR

2) Pick the first *topos* and go through all four sources, looking for answers. Do the same for the second *topos*, and then the third, and so on.

HOW TO HELP THE STUDENT WITH STEP SIX

Check to make sure that the student has in fact created separate pages for each *topos* (at least four), and that each page has at least eight or nine notes, but no more than twenty notes on it.

The exception: where a sequence or comparison genuinely has fewer pieces of information, but is still complete. In that case, reassure the student that she doesn't have to somehow pad out her notes.

STEP SEVEN: **Draft the main *topos* (3–4 hours) (Student Responsibility)**

Which one of your pages contains the most notes? That's the *topos* that should probably be the "skeleton," the primary organizational form, of your composition.

Decide which *topos* will be at the center of your composition. Using your notes and referring to your reference chart, write a draft of the main *topos*.

Be sure to look back at your chart, reminding yourself of the elements that should belong in the *topos*.

STEP EIGHT: **Add other *topoi* (2–3 hours) (Student Responsibility)**

Look back over your notes and decide which *topoi* or elements you will add to your composition.

Decide where the *topoi* or elements will be located in your composition. Draft the *topoi* or elements and insert them into your essay. You must add elements from at least two different *topoi*. You may need to rearrange paragraphing or slightly rewrite some of your existing sentences so that the new elements fit into your composition smoothly.

STEP NINE: **Provide an introduction and conclusion (60–90 minutes) (Student Responsibility)**

Choose an introduction and a conclusion from your Introductions and Conclusions chart. You may pick any introduction and conclusion—but make sure that they don't repeat the same information.

Each introduction and conclusion should be at least two sentences long and should be placed in separate paragraphs, not incorporated into the existing paragraphs of the composition.

STEP TEN: **Title (20 minutes) (Student Responsibility)**

Choose a title for your paper. This should be more descriptive than simply the name of the person, object, or phenomenon you're writing about. Remember that you can use the following format:

Name [of person, object, phenomenon]: Why it's important

OR

Name [of person, object, phenomenon]: What happened to it

STEP ELEVEN: **Construct the Works Cited page (30 minutes)**

At the top of a separate sheet of paper, center the words "Works Cited." In proper form, list the sources you used to write your essay.

HOW TO HELP THE STUDENT WITH STEP ELEVEN

You can check the format of any particular resource by going to worldcat.com, typing in the name of the resource, clicking on the title, and then clicking on the "cite" button. Then, click on "Turabian," the general style used in this book.

STEP TWELVE: **Proofread (2 hours)**

Student instructions for Step Twelve:

Before you hand your composition to your instructor, go through the following proofreading steps very carefully.

1) Check to make sure that you have used elements from at least three different *topoi*, plus an introduction and a conclusion.

2) Make sure that your finished essay is at least 1250 words long.

3) Make sure that you have cited at least four sources.

4) Read your paper out loud, listening for awkward or unclear sections and repeated words. Rewrite awkward or unclear sentences so that they flow more naturally.

5) Listen for information that is repeated more than once. Eliminate repetition of ideas.

6) Read through the paper one more time, looking for sentence fragments, run-on sentences, and repeated words. Correct fragments and run-on sentences. Listen for unnecessary repetition.

7) Check your spelling by looking, individually, at each word that might be a problem.

8) Check the formatting of your footnotes and your Works Cited page.

9) Read your title out loud. Does it give the reader a good sense of what your composition will cover?

When your paper is ready, give it to your instructor.

HOW TO HELP THE STUDENT WITH STEP TWELVE

Check the student's work, using the rubric below. Then, check the elements of the *topoi* included by using the general rubrics in Appendix VIII. The student must be able to identify for you the *topoi* she has used.

Final Project, Basic Rubric

Organization

1 At least three *topoi* should be used.
2 The composition should be at least 1250 words long.
3 There should be an introduction and conclusion, both in separate paragraphs.
4 At least four sources should be cited.
5 The paper should have a title that conveys a sense of the paper's content.

Mechanics

1 Each sentence should make sense on its own when read aloud.
2 There should be no sentence fragments or run-on sentences.
3 All words should be spelled correctly.
4 The first line of each paragraph should be properly indented.
5 Verb tense should be consistent throughout.
6 Direct quotes should be properly formatted.
7 Footnotes and Works Cited page should be properly formatted.

Appendix I

TOPOI

Chronological Narrative of a Past Event

Definition: A narrative telling what happened in the past and in what sequence

Procedure

1. Ask *Who did what to whom?*
   (Or, *What was done to what?*)
2. Create main points by placing the answers in chronological order.

Remember

1. Select your main events to go with your theme.
2. Make use of time words.
3. Consider using dialogue to hold the reader's interest.

Chronological Narrative of a Scientific Discovery

Definition: A narrative telling what steps or events led to a discovery, and in what sequence

Procedure

1. Ask, *What steps or events led to the discovery?*
2. Ask, *In what sequence did these steps or events happen?*
3. Create main points by placing the answers in chronological order.

Remember

1. May need a background paragraph explaining the circumstances that existed before the discovery.
2. Make use of time words.
3. If possible, quote directly from the scientist's own words.

Description of a Place

Definition: A visual description of a physical place

Procedure	Remember
1. Ask, *What specific purpose should this description fulfill?*	1. Make use of space and distance words and phrases.
2. Choose a point of view.	2. Consider using vivid metaphors and similes.

Scientific Description

Definition: A visual and structural description of an object or phenomenon

Procedure	Remember
1. Describe each part of the object or phenomenon and tell what it is made from.	1. Consider using figurative language to make the description more visual.
2. Choose a point of view.	2. Consider combining points of view.

Description of a Person

Definition: A description of selected physical and non-physical aspects of a person

Procedure	Remember
1. Decide which aspects will be included. They may include:	1. Descriptions can be "slanted" using appropriate adjectives.
Physical appearance	2. An overall metaphor can be used to organize the description and give clues about character.
Sound of voice	
What others think	
Portrayals	
Character qualities	
Challenges and difficulties	
Accomplishments	
Habits	
Behaviors	
Expressions of face and body	
Mind/intellectual capabilities	
Talents and abilities	
Self disciplines	
Religious beliefs	
Clothing, dress	
Economic status (wealth)	
Fame, notoriety, prestige	
Family traditions, tendencies	

Biographical Sketch

Definition: A chronological summary of the important events in a person's life combined with description of aspects of the person

Procedure	Remember
1. Decide on the life events to list in the chronological summary.	1. The main focus can be on the subject's work/accomplishments.
2. Choose aspects from the Description of a Person chart to include.	a. Listed chronologically
	b. Listed by subject/topic

Sequence: Natural Process

Definition: A step-by-step description of a cycle that occurs in nature

Procedure	Remember
1. Describe the natural process chronologically, step by step.	
2. Decide which other elements to include.	
a. Introduction/summary	
b. Scientific background	
c. Repetition of the process	

Sequence: History

Definition: A step-by-step description of a process, machine, or cycle in history

Procedure	Remember
1. Provide an introductory description	
2. Describe the functioning of the process, step by step	
3. Decide which other elements to include.	
a. Introduction	
b. Historical background	
c. Results/consequences	

Explanation by Comparison/Contrast

Definition: A comparison of similarities and differences

Procedure	Remember
1. Decide which aspects of the subjects are the same, and which are different.	1. Use both methods to give variety.
2. Choose a method for comparing and contrasting.	
a. Point-by-point	
b. Subject-by-subject	

Explanation by Definition: Natural Object or Phenomenon

Definition: An explanation of properties, function, and genus

Procedure

1. Answer the following questions:

Essential Properties and Accidental Properties

What does it look like?

How does it behave?

What senses come into play as you observe it?

What do those senses reveal?

Is your observation passive (watching/listening) or active (experimenting/collecting/probing)?

What sorts of measurements (temperature, quantity, time, etc.) are necessary to your observation?

What does it resemble?

What is it made of?

What sort of structure does it have?

What is its extent in space?

What is its extent in time?

Which properties are essential?

Which are accidental?

Function

How does it work or behave?

Will a descriptive sequence help the reader understand how it works? What would

Remember

1. Not all questions need to be answered.
2. Selection of genus can be based on either properties or function.
3. Temporal comparison (describing the same thing at two different points in time) can be used to develop your answers.

the sequence describe?

Is its behavior predictable or unpredictable?

Does it work/behave differently under different
circumstances?

At different times?

Can its behavior be divided into phases?

What separates the phases?

Is there a cause or trigger for its behavior?

What is the time frame for its behavior?

Where does the behavior take place?

Who/what needs it or uses it?

Is anything dependent on it?

Is it dependent on anything else?

Who/what affects its working/behavior?

For what purposes?

Is there more than one purpose?

Does the purpose change at different times?

Is the purpose dependent on any other
conditions?

Genus

What other objects or phenomena can it be
grouped with?

What are the qualities that lead you to group
them together?

What name can you give this group?

In what significant ways is it different from
the others in its group?

Explanation by Definition: Historical Object, Event, Place, or People Group

Definition: An explanation of properties, function, and genus

Procedure

1. Answer the following questions:
   Shared and Unique Properties
   What did it look like?
   How did it behave?
   What did it resemble?
   What was it made of?
   What sort of structure did it have?
   What was its extent in space?
   Where did it take place or exist?
   What was its extent in time?
   Did it repeat or continue into modern times?
      How has it changed over time?
   What large group of other phenomena
      can it be assigned to?
   What smaller group of other phenomena
      can it be assigned to?
   What qualities does it share with no other
      phenomena?

   Function
   How did it work, behave, or unfold?
      Will a descriptive sequence help the
         reader understand how it worked?
         What would the sequence describe?
      Was its behavior predictable or unpredictable?
      Did it work/behave differently under
         different circumstances?
         At different times?
      Can its behavior or sequence be divided
         into phases?
         What separates the phases?
      Was there a cause or trigger for the event?
      What was the time frame for its behavior
         or significance?
      Where did the behavior take place?

Remember

1. Not all questions need to be
   answered.
2. Answers to genus and properties
   may overlap.
3. Always try to explain significance.
4. The definition can include one
   or more paragraphs of temporal
   comparison (the comparison of
   properties, function, and/or genus
   at different points in time).

Who/what needed it, used it, or was
    affected by it?
    What effects did it have on the surrounding
        events/people?
    What events led up to it?
    What events occurred because of it?
For what purposes or reasons?
    Is there more than one purpose or reason?
    Did the purpose or reason change at
        different times?
    Was the purpose or reason dependent
        on any other conditions?
What is its significance? Why do we remember it?
    What did it change?
    Did it create/become a major turning point?
    Did later phenomena use it or depend on it?

Genus

What other objects, events, people, or places
    can it be grouped with?
What are the qualities that lead you to group
    them together?
What name can you give this group?
In what significant ways is it different from
    the others in its group?

Temporal Comparison: History

Definition: A comparison between the earlier and later stages
of the same historical phenomenon

Procedure

1. Begin with a brief introduction to
   the phenomenon.
      a. May include a summary
         of its current state
      b. Can briefly mention
         important aspects
2. Describe at least one earlier stage
   of its development.
      a. Properties
      b. Function
      c. Genus
3. Describe the transition to its
   current form.
      a. May involve a chronological
         narrative of historical events
      b. May involve a historical
         sequence
4. Describe the current form of
   the phenomenon.

Remember

1. Can include more than one
   earlier stage of development
2. Can either be organized point by
   point or subject by subject

Temporal Comparison: Science

Definition: A comparison between the earlier and later stages
of the same natural object or phenomenon

Procedure

1. Compare aspects of the subject
   at different stages of a regular life cycle.
2. Compare aspects before and after
   a natural change unique to the subject.
      a. May include description of changes
         that occur in a regular cycle
      b. May include explanation of why
         the change occurs

Remember

1. Often occurs as part of a
   longer composition
2. Can either be organized point by
   point or subject by subject

Appendix II

LITERARY TERMS

hero/heroine: a central character with admirable qualities

protagonist: the character who wants to get, become, or accomplish something

antagonist: the character, force, or circumstance that opposes the protagonist

villain: an antagonist with evil motives

conflict: the clash between protagonist and antagonist

simile: a comparison that uses "like," "as," or similar words

metaphor: a comparison that speaks of one thing in terms of another

synecdoche: a kind of metaphor that uses a part to represent the whole

inversion (plot): an unexpected revelation that reverses the meaning or action of the story

surprise story: a story that uses inversion to change the reader's point of view

supporting character: a character who helps, supports, or hinders the protagonist or antagonist

genre: a particular type or form of literature; works that use similar forms or have similar purposes

fantasy: a genre in which stories are set in a world that doesn't exist

stanza: a group of lines in a poem

onomatopoeia: when a word sounds like its meaning

alliteration: when words begin with the same sound or sounds

meter: the rhythmical pattern of a poem

foot: a set of syllables that follows a certain pattern of stress and unstress

rhyme scheme: a pattern of repeating rhyme marked with letters of the alphabet

sonnet: a 14-line poem written in iambic pentameter

ballad: a poem that tells a story, usually a heroic or tragic one

pivot point: the moment at which the main character changes goals, wants, or direction

story climax: the point of greatest tension or conflict

foreshadowing: giving the reader clues about what will happen later in the story

episodic fiction: a series of self-contained stories, connected by common characters and/or an overall plot

Appendix III

SENTENCE VARIETY CHART

descriptive adjectives ⟷ nouns

an eloquent man
a man of eloquence

passive verb ⟷ active verb

The king ruled his kingdom.
The kingdom was ruled by its king.

indirect object ⟶ object of the preposition

The mother gave the baby a bottle.
The mother gave a bottle to the baby.

infinitives ⟷ participles

The truth needs saying.
The truth needs to be said.

main verb ⟷ infinitive

I usually plan ahead.
I usually need to plan ahead.
I usually manage to plan ahead.

adjective ⟶ intensified adjective

The sun was bright.
The sun was incandescent.

adjective ⟶ added adjective

He leaped into the cold water.
He leaped into the cold and murky
water OR
He leaped into the cold, murky water.

word   ⟶   phrase describing what the word   letter   ⟶   words from
                             is or does   your pen
                             metaphor   letter   ⟶   pearls of wisdom
                             kenning   sea   ⟶   whale road

positive statement ⟷ negative statement   Her eyesight is excellent.
                                                          She is not at all shortsighted.

                                                          I am not at all unhappy.
                                                          I am filled with joy.

positive modifier ⟷ negative modifier   He was cheerful this morning.
                                                          He was not unhappy this morning.

                                                          She drove quickly.
                                                          She drove in no way slowly.

Appendix IV

INTRODUCTIONS & CONCLUSIONS

Introductions

1. Introduction by Summary
   One or more sentences that tell the reader what the composition is about and what its most central conclusion will be

2. Introduction by History
   a. Information about past attitudes towards the subject
   b. Description of how some aspect of the subject has changed or developed over time
   c. Brief scene from history

3. Introduction by Anecdote
   a. A story drawn from personal experience
   b. An invented scene, based on your knowledge of the subject

Conclusions

1. Conclusion by Summary
   Write a brief summary of the most important information in the passage, including specific details.

2. Conclusion by Personal Reaction
   a. Personal statement
   b. Your opinion about the material
   c. Your own experience with the subject

3. Conclusion by Question
   Ask the reader to react to the information.

Appendix V

TIME & SEQUENCE WORDS

For chronological narratives

Words for events that happen before any others
First
At first
In the beginning
Before

Words for events that happen at the same time
When
At that point
At that moment
While

Words for an event that happens very soon after a previous event
When
As soon as
Soon
Shortly/shortly afterwards
Presently
Before long
Not long after
Immediately

Words for an event that happens after a previous event—but you're not exactly sure whether a long or short period of time elapsed first
Next
Afterward
After
After some time
Subsequently
Following/ following that
Furthermore
Then

Words for an event that happened long after another event
Eventually
Later/ later on
Finally

Words for an event that happened after another event—AND was caused by the previous event
As a result
As a consequence
Since
Because
Seeing that

573

SPACE AND DISTANCE WORDS/ PHRASES
For descriptions

Orientation
To (on) the right (side)
To (on) the left (side)
Above
Below
To/From the north/south/east/west of
On the one side/On the other side
In/at the middle of
In/at the center of
Around

Close relationship
By
Near (by)
Close (by)
Next to
At

Distant relationship
At a (in the) distance
Off
Far off (away)
Around (round)
About
Beyond
Further (farther)
Further away (on)
Until

Vertical relationship
Above
Below
Beyond
On
Up/upon
Over
Under
Up from (to/into)
Down
Down from (on/to/into)
Higher/higher than
Lower/lower than

Horizontal relationship
Back
Forward
Past
Before
In front of
From
Across
On (to/onto/on and on)
Into
Out (of)
By
Between
On either side (of)
Opposite

Interlocking relationship
Through
Into
In
Inside
With
Within
Without
Outside (outside of/outside)
Filled with
Around
Surrounding/surrounded by

Indeterminate relationship
Where
There
With
Without
A distance from
On the one/other side
On and on

Appendix VI

POINTS OF VIEW

FOR PLACE DESCRIPTIONS

1. From above (impersonal)
2. From inside
3. From one side or angle
3. Moving through or around

FOR SCIENTIFIC DESCRIPTIONS

1. Removed from the object or phenomenon
2. Present with the object or phenomenon

APPENDIX VII

WEEKLY RUBRICS

Week 2 Rubric
Sequence: History

Organization:

1 The entire composition should be at least 290 words in length.
2 There should be at least three paragraphs.
    a. One paragraph describing the machine/object.
    b. One paragraph describing its function, step by step.
    c. At least one additional paragraph, containing one or more of the following:
        i. An introduction of 40 words or more
        ii. Historical background (invented is fine) of the machine's development
        iii. Results/consequences (invented is fine) of the machine's use

Mechanics:

1 Each sentence should make sense on its own when read aloud.
2 There should be no sentence fragments or run-on sentences.
3 All words should be spelled correctly.
4 The first line of each paragraph should be properly indented.
5 Verb tense should be consistent throughout (past tense for the historical background and present tense for the descriptive paragraphs is acceptable).

Week 4 Rubric
Chronological Narrative And Sequence: History

Organization:

1   The entire composition should be at least 250 words in length.
2   The events of the Gold Rush should be in chronological order.
3   There should be at least five paragraphs.
    a.   At least four paragraphs should describe the major events of the Gold Rush.
    b.   One paragraph should describe the process of panning for gold.
        i.   One sentence should describe the pan itself.
        ii.   The other sentences should describe, step by step, the panning process.
4   There should be at least one line of dialogue.

Mechanics:

1   Each sentence should make sense on its own when read aloud.
2   There should be no sentence fragments or run-on sentences.
3   All words should be spelled correctly.
4   The first line of each paragraph should be properly indented.
5   Verb tense should be consistent throughout (past tense for the historical background and present tense for the descriptive paragraphs is acceptable).
6   Specific information should be properly footnoted.
7   A Works Cited page should be attached.

Week 5 Rubric
Explanation By Comparison/Contrast

Organization:

1   The entire composition should be 100–300 words in length. NOTE: The student has not been assigned a dictated length. The student's focus should be on the form of the composition, which should take at least 100 words to develop properly.
2   There should be three paragraphs.
  a. The first paragraph should describe *only* similarities.
  b. The second paragraph should describe differences, going back and forth between beavers and platypuses as it compares them fact for fact.
  c. The third paragraph should describe differences, first covering all the facts for platypuses, and then covering similar facts for beavers.

Mechanics:

1   Each sentence should make sense on its own when read aloud.
2   There should be no sentence fragments or run-on sentences.
3   All words should be spelled correctly.
4   The first line of each paragraph should be properly indented.
5   Verb tense should be consistent throughout.

Week 7 Rubric
Explanation By Comparison/Contrast In History

Organization:

1   The entire composition should be at least seven paragraphs in length.
2   At least four aspects/categories of the brothers should be discussed.
3   For each aspect discussed, the student should first cover similarities, and then should explain differences, first for one brother and then the other. (Note that the bicycle category has *only* similarities).
4   The composition should contain both an introduction and a conclusion. At least one of these must be a separate paragraph of two sentences or more.
5   The conclusion and introduction should not *both* be summaries.
6   All direct quotes should be footnoted.
7   All sources mentioned in footnotes should be placed on a Works Cited page.

Mechanics:

1   Each sentence should make sense on its own when read aloud.
2   There should be no sentence fragments or run-on sentences.
3   All words should be spelled correctly.
4   The first line of each paragraph should be properly indented.
5   Verb tense should be consistent throughout.
6   No noun or verb should be used more than twice (with the exception of state-of-being verbs, linking verbs, and the verb "said").
7   No modifier or prepositional phrase acting as a modifier should be used more than once.

Week 9 General Rubric

Organization:

1 The entire composition should be around 500 words in length.
2 The required elements of the selected *topoi* should be present.
3 The composition should contain both an introduction and a conclusion. At least one of these should be a separate paragraph of two sentences or more.
4 The conclusion and introduction should not *both* be summaries.
5 The composition should contain at least two direct quotes.
6 All direct quotes should be footnoted.
7 All sources mentioned in footnotes should be placed on a Works Cited page.
8 The composition should have a title, centered at the top of the first page. This title should include both the event/person/place/process and a word or phrase describing or defining the purpose of the paper.

Mechanics:

1 Each sentence should make sense on its own when read aloud.
2 There should be no sentence fragments or run-on sentences.
3 All words should be spelled correctly.
4 The first line of each paragraph should be properly indented.
5 Verb tense should be consistent throughout.
6 No noun or verb should be used more than twice (with the exception of the name of the paper's subject, state-of-being verbs, linking verbs, and the verb "said").
7 No modifier or prepositional phrase acting as a modifier should be used more than once.
8 Footnotes and the Works Cited page should be properly formatted.

Week 10 Rubric

Organization:

1   The entire composition should have at least three paragraphs: narrative summary (first paragraph) and at least two paragraphs covering the analytical elements. It can be as long as five paragraphs.
2   The analysis should cover all four of the required topics:
    a. Two to three sentences about the story-within-a-story structure
    b. Two to three sentences about the way the central story fools Mr. Nuttel *and* the reader
    c. How word choice makes the ghost story more effective
    d. How Saki uses irony in the choices of the names
3   The composition should contain at least two direct quotes.

Mechanics:

1   Each sentence should make sense on its own when read aloud.
2   There should be no sentence fragments or run-on sentences.
3   All words should be spelled correctly.
4   The first line of each paragraph should be properly indented.
5   Verb tense should be consistent throughout.
6   No noun or verb should be used more than twice (with the exception of state-of-being verbs, linking verbs, and the verb "said").
7   No modifier or prepositional phrase acting as a modifier should be used more than once.

Week 11 Rubric

Organization:

1 The entire composition should have at least five paragraphs but can be as long as seven to eight paragraphs.
2 The introduction should include the titles of both stories and authors, and should summarize the most compelling similarity or difference between the stories. It should be the first independent paragraph of the paper.
3 The comparison and contrast section of the paper should be at least three paragraphs in length. It should compare and contrast three elements:
   a. story structure
   b. story climax
   c. language

Each comparison and contrast should begin by describing similarities and then should describe differences.
4 The paragraph[s] on language should contain direct quotes from both stories.
5 The conclusion should be the last paragraph of the paper. It should give the student's personal opinion about the stories.

Mechanics:

1 Each sentence should make sense on its own when read aloud.
2 There should be no sentence fragments or run-on sentences.
3 All words should be spelled correctly.
4 The first line of each paragraph should be properly indented.
5 Verb tense should be consistent throughout.
6 No noun or verb should be used more than twice (with the exception of state-of-being verbs, linking verbs, and the verb "said").
7 No modifier or prepositional phrase acting as a modifier should be used more than once.
8 "However" and "but" should not be used more than twice each. "One the one hand" and "on the other hand" should not be used more than once.

Week 12 Rubric

Organization:

1 The entire composition should be two paragraphs and at least 150 words in length.
2 The first paragraph should describe what a volcano is. The second should describe a volcanic eruption.
3 All three sources should be cited.
4 All sources mentioned in footnotes should be placed on a Works Cited page.
5 The composition should have a title, centered at the top of the first page. This title should *not* be simply "Volcano" or "Volcanic Eruption." (See Step Three.)
6 At least one metaphor or simile should be included.

Mechanics:

1 Each sentence should make sense on its own when read aloud.
2 There should be no sentence fragments or run-on sentences.
3 All words should be spelled correctly.
4 The first line of each paragraph should be properly indented.
5 Verb tense should be consistent throughout.
6 No noun or verb should be used more than twice (with the exception of state of being verbs, linking verbs, and the verb "said").
7 No modifier or prepositional phrase acting as a modifier should be used more than once.
8 Footnotes and the Works Cited page should be properly formatted.

Week 13 Rubric

Organization:

1 The entire composition should be two paragraphs and at least 150 words in length.
2 The first paragraph should describe how a Venus' flytrap works. The second should describe what creatures use a Venus' flytrap and for what purposes.
3 All three sources should be cited.
4 All sources mentioned in footnotes should be placed on a Works Cited page.
5 The composition should have a title, centered at the top of the first page. This title should *not* be simply "Venus' Flytraps." (See Step Three.)
6 At least one metaphor or simile should be included.

Mechanics:

1 Each sentence should make sense on its own when read aloud.
2 There should be no sentence fragments or run-on sentences.
3 All words should be spelled correctly.
4 The first line of each paragraph should be properly indented.
5 Verb tense should be consistent throughout.
6 No noun or verb should be used more than twice (with the exception of state-of-being verbs, linking verbs, and the verb "said").
7 No modifier or prepositional phrase acting as a modifier should be used more than once.
8 Footnotes and the Works Cited page should be properly formatted.

Week 15 Rubric

Organization:

1   The entire composition should be at least six paragraphs and at least five hundred words in length.
2   The first two to three paragraphs should describe the properties of the object or phenomenon and should answer at least three of the questions about properties.
3   The next two to three paragraphs should describe function and should answer at least two of the questions about function.
4   The next one to two paragraphs should place the object or phenomenon into a group and explain what qualities define the group. It can also say how the object differs from the others in the group, but this is optional.
5   The composition should have both an introduction and a conclusion. One of these should be a separate paragraph. The introduction and conclusion should be of different types.
6   The composition should have a title, centered at the top of the first page. This title should *not* be simply the name of the object or phenomenon.
7   At least two sources should be cited.
8   All sources mentioned in footnotes should be placed on a Works Cited page.

Mechanics:

1   Each sentence should make sense on its own when read aloud.
2   There should be no sentence fragments or run-on sentences.
3   All words should be spelled correctly.
4   The first line of each paragraph should be properly indented.
5   Verb tense should be consistent throughout.
6   No noun or verb should be used more than twice (with the exception of state-of-being verbs, linking verbs, and the verb "said").
7   No modifier or prepositional phrase acting as a modifier should be used more than once.
8   Footnotes and the Works Cited page should be properly formatted.

Week 16 Rubric
Brief Poem Essay

Organization:

1 The entire composition should be at least five paragraphs and 250 words in length, but can be longer.
2 The introduction should include the names of both poems and a major similarity or difference between them.
3 One paragraph should describe similarities. At least three additional paragraphs should describe differences.
4 Each poem should be quoted directly at least once.
5 The conclusion should be either a conclusion by personal reaction or a conclusion by question.
6 The title should be centered at the top of the page. It should include the names of both poems.

Mechanics:

1 Each sentence should make sense on its own when read aloud.
2 There should be no sentence fragments or run-on sentences.
3 All words should be spelled correctly.
4 The first line of each paragraph should be properly indented.
5 Verb tense should be consistent throughout.
6 No noun or verb should be used more than twice (with the exception of state-of-being verbs, linking verbs, and the verb "said").
7 No modifier or prepositional phrase acting as a modifier should be used more than once.
8 Poem citations should be properly formatted.

Week 18 Rubric
Biographical Sketch And Critical Analysis

Organization:

1   The entire composition should be at least five paragraphs and 500 words in length, but can be longer.
2   The composition should include an introduction, a chronological narrative of events in the life of Alfred Noyes, at least two different paragraphs describing at least two different aspects of Noyes's life, a brief critical analysis, and a conclusion.
3   The critical analysis should be at least three paragraphs in length. It should include a plot summary of "The Highwayman," a paragraph discussing the structure of the poem, and a final paragraph describing either Noyes's use of the color red or else the reversals in the poem.
4   The composition should include at least one direct quote from "The Highwayman" and at least one direct quote from another source.
5   The title should include the name of Alfred Noyes and a phrase describing him.
6   The introduction should summarize why Noyes is important.
7   The conclusion should either summarize Noyes's importance or give a personal reaction to Noyes or his work. If the conclusion summarizes, it should not be identical to the introduction.
8   No single piece of information or quote should be repeated from one section to the next.

Mechanics:

1   Each sentence should make sense on its own when read aloud.
2   There should be no sentence fragments or run-on sentences.
3   All words should be spelled correctly.
4   The first line of each paragraph should be properly indented.
5   Verb tense should be consistent throughout. The narrative summary may be in either the past or the present tense.
6   No modifier or prepositional phrase acting as a modifier should be used more than twice.
7   Poem citations, footnotes, and works cited should be properly formatted.

Week 19 Rubric
Properties Of A Historical Phenomenon

Organization:

1 The entire composition should be at least two paragraphs and 120 words in length, but can be longer.
2 The composition should be organized in one of the following ways:
  Paragraph I. The Inca empire (where, when, etc.)
  Paragraph II. The Inca people (appearance, behavior, etc.)
      OR
  Paragraph I. Incan people in the past
  Paragraph II. Incan influence in modern times
3 At least five of the questions about properties should be addressed.
4 The composition should include at least three sentences discussing the property or properties that the student identified as unique to the Inca.
5 The composition should include at least one direct quote and should cite at least three sources.
6 The composition should include at least one simile or metaphor.
7 The title should include the word "Inca" plus another descriptive word or phrase.

Mechanics:

1 Each sentence should make sense on its own when read aloud.
2 There should be no sentence fragments or run-on sentences.
3 All words should be spelled correctly.
4 The first line of each paragraph should be properly indented.
5 Verb tense should be consistent throughout.
6 No modifier or prepositional phrase acting as a modifier should be used more than twice.
7 Footnotes and the Works Cited page should be properly formatted.

Week 20 Rubric

Organization:

1   The composition should be at least 225 words in length. It should have at least four paragraphs.

2   At least three sources should be cited; at least one citation should be a direct quote.

3   The composition must answer questions *both* about function *and* about genus.

4   The composition must have both an introduction and a conclusion. Only one of these can be a summary. Either the introduction or the conclusion *must* be longer than one sentence.

5   The composition should have a title, centered at the top of the first page. This title should include the name of the case, followed by a colon and a descriptive phrase about the essay.

Mechanics:

1   Each sentence should make sense on its own when read aloud.

2   There should be no sentence fragments or run-on sentences.

3   All words should be spelled correctly.

4   The first line of each paragraph should be properly indented.

5   Verb tense should be consistent throughout.

6   Footnotes and the Works Cited page should be properly formatted.

7   When referring to the person, "Dred Scott" should not be italicized, but when referring to the case, *"Dred Scott"* should be italicized.

8   With the exception of important nouns such as "slaves," "slavery," "Supreme Court," etc., most nouns should not be repeated more than twice. Modifiers should not be used more than twice.

Week 21 Rubric

Organization:

1 The entire composition should be at least four paragraphs and at least 500 words in length.
2 The composition should answer at least four of the questions about function and four of the questions about properties. The student should be able to tell you which questions she answered.
3 At least two to three sentences should address genus by placing the subject into a group and explaining how it differs from others in that group.
4 The composition should have both an introduction and a conclusion. The introduction and conclusion should be of different types.
5 The composition should have a title, centered at the top of the first page. This title should include the name of the case, followed by a colon and a descriptive phrase about the essay.
6 At least two sources should be quoted.
7 All sources mentioned in footnotes should be placed on a Works Cited page.

Mechanics:

1 Each sentence should make sense on its own when read aloud.
2 There should be no sentence fragments or run-on sentences.
3 All words should be spelled correctly.
4 The first line of each paragraph should be properly indented.
5 Verb tense should be consistent throughout.
6 Footnotes and the Works Cited page should be properly formatted.
7 With the exception of important nouns such as "slaves," "slavery," "Supreme Court," etc., most nouns should not be repeated more than twice. Modifiers should not be used more than twice.

Week 23 Rubric

Organization:

1   The composition should have four sections.
2   The first section should be at least 70 words long and contain both an anecdote and a command or statement.
3   The second section should be at least 70 words long and should describe the pig's appearance and also mention the mud he wallows in.
4   The third section should contain six comparisons of pigs and human beings. It should be at least 125 words long. The comparisons can be in separate paragraphs or grouped together.
5   The last section should be at least 50 words long. It should contain both a story and a statement about the theme of the essay.

Mechanics:

1   Each sentence should make sense on its own when read aloud.
2   There should be no sentence fragments or run-on sentences.
3   All words should be spelled correctly.
4   The first line of each paragraph should be properly indented.
5   Verb tense should be consistent throughout.

Week 24 Rubric

Organization:

1　The composition should have five sections.
2　The first section should be at least 35 words long and should be the retelling/description of a Christmas feasting scene around the fire, written in the first person plural.
3　The second section should be at least 50 words long and should define Christmas by listing different activities, foods, and moods that characterize the season.
4　The third section should be at least 120 words long and should describe both Christmas Eve customs in the past and present, and different kinds of Christmas music. It should mention both "Christmas waits" or Christmas carollers, and old gentlemen who sing to children.
5　The fourth section should be at least 75 words long and should describe both the plants used in Christmas decorations, and the kinds of food eaten at Christmas.
6　The last section should be at least 50 words long. It should be an exhortation, written in the first person plural, about how we should all behave because of Christmas.

Mechanics:

1　Each sentence should make sense on its own when read aloud.
2　There should be no sentence fragments or run-on sentences.
3　All words should be spelled correctly.
4　The first line of each paragraph should be properly indented.
5　Verb tense should be consistent throughout.

Week 25 Rubric

Organization:

1   The composition should be at least 450 words in length.
2   It should contain each of the elements listed in the appropriate model.
3   The composition should contain at least one simile and one metaphor.
4   The title should be centered at the top of the page and should follow the appropriate model.
5   At least two of the sentences should have been transformed, using the copia skills learned up to this point.
6   No piece of information should be repeated.

Mechanics:

1   Each sentence should make sense on its own when read aloud.
2   There should be no sentence fragments or run-on sentences.
3   All words should be spelled correctly.
4   The first line of each paragraph should be properly indented.
5   No single word or phrase should be repeated unnecessarily.

Week 26, Part I Rubric

Organization:

1   The description should be between 50 and 100 words in length.
2   It may be either one paragraph or two.
3   The description should compare the same aspects for both the young and old Churchill.
4   The description should make some attempt to speculate about the character of the subject as well as his physical appearance.
5   The description may be organized either subject by subject (first the young Churchill, then the old Churchill) or point by point.

Mechanics:

1   Each sentence should make sense on its own when read aloud.
2   There should be no sentence fragments or run-on sentences.
3   All words should be spelled correctly.
4   The first line of each paragraph should be properly indented.
5   Verb tense should be consistent throughout.
6   "The young" and "the old" should not be repeated more than twice each.

Week 26, Part II Rubric

Organization:

1   The description should be between 75 and 125 words in length.
2   It may be either one paragraph or two.
3   The description should compare the same aspects for Lake Chad both before the 1960s and today.
4   The description may be organized either subject by subject or point by point.
5   The description should not use the exact same phrasing as the sources, but footnotes are not necessary.

Mechanics:

1   Each sentence should make sense on its own when read aloud.
2   There should be no sentence fragments or run-on sentences.
3   All words should be spelled correctly.
4   The first line of each paragraph should be properly indented.
5   Verb tense should be consistent throughout.
6   Adverbs such as "then" and "now" or phrases such as "before the 1960s" and "in modern times" should not be repeated.

Week 27 Rubric, Temporal Comparison In History

Organization:

1 The composition should be at least 150 words in length. It should have at least two or three paragraphs.
2 At least three sources should be cited; at least one citation should be a direct quote.
3 The composition should contain an introduction to current Chicago, a description of Chicago in the early 1800s, an explanation of the Great Fire of 1871 that includes a brief chronological narration, and a description of Chicago after the fire.
4 The composition should have a title, centered at the top of the first page. This title should include the subject "Chicago" as well as a reference to time.

Mechanics:

1 Each sentence should make sense on its own when read aloud.
2 There should be no sentence fragments or run-on sentences.
3 All words should be spelled correctly.
4 The first line of each paragraph should be properly indented.
5 Verb tense should be consistent throughout.
6 Footnotes and the Works Cited page should be properly formatted.
7 Most common nouns should not be repeated more than twice. Modifiers should not be used more than twice.

Week 27 Rubric, Temporal Comparison In Science

Organization:

1 The description should be at least 100 words long, with at least two paragraphs.
2 It should be organized as a point-by-point comparison.
3 It should *not* include a descriptive sequence about how a young star turns into a red giant; it should instead describe the young star, and also describe the same aspects of an old star.

Mechanics:

1 Each sentence should make sense on its own when read aloud.
2 There should be no sentence fragments or run-on sentences.
3 All words should be spelled correctly.
4 The first line of each paragraph should be properly indented.
5 Verb tense should be consistent throughout.
6 "The young" and "the old" should not be repeated more than twice each.

Week 28 Rubric, Second Temporal Comparison In Science

Organization:

1 The description should be at least 125 words long, with at least three paragraphs.
2 It should be organized as a subject-by-subject comparison.
3 It should include a brief description of the eruption itself, either in the middle of or at the end of the composition.

Mechanics:

1 Each sentence should make sense on its own when read aloud.
2 There should be no sentence fragments or run-on sentences.
3 All words should be spelled correctly.
4 The first line of each paragraph should be properly indented.
5 Verb tense should be consistent throughout.

Week 30 Rubric

Organization:

1   The essay should be at least 350 words long.
2   The essay should include the following required elements:
   1) An introduction identifying the title and author and summarizing Robin Hood's wants/goals
   2) A narrative summary that explains the episodic nature of the stories, summarizes at least three of them briefly, and introduces at least two important secondary characters
   3) At least two paragraphs explaining what Robin Hood wants, what opposes him, what the story's primary clash is, and how it is resolved. The student should also explain whether or not Robin Hood succeeded.
   4) At least one paragraph describing ways in which characters disguise themselves, with at least two examples
   5) A conclusion giving the student's personal opinion about *The Legend of Robin Hood*
3   The student should quote directly from the story at least once.

Mechanics:

1   Each sentence should make sense on its own when read aloud.
2   There should be no sentence fragments or run-on sentences.
3   All words should be spelled correctly.
4   The first line of each paragraph should be properly indented.
5   Verb tense should be consistent throughout.
6   Direct quotes should be properly formatted.

Week 32 Rubric

Organization:

1   The essay should be at least 300 words long. Longer is better!
2   The essay should include the following required elements:
    1) An introduction and conclusion that are both separate paragraphs, at least two lines long, and that do not repeat the same information
    2) Elements from at least three different *topoi*
    3) A title that explains the main point or most important content of the composition
    4) A separate Works Cited page
3   The student should quote directly from at least one source and should cite at least two.

Mechanics:

1   Each sentence should make sense on its own when read aloud.
2   There should be no sentence fragments or run-on sentences.
3   All words should be spelled correctly.
4   The first line of each paragraph should be properly indented.
5   Verb tense should be consistent throughout.
6   Direct quotes should be properly formatted.
7   Footnotes and Works Cited page should be properly formatted.

Week 33 Rubric

Organization:

1   The essay should be at least 300 words long. Longer is better!
2   The essay should include the following required elements:
    1) An introduction and conclusion that are both separate paragraphs, at least two lines long, and that do not repeat the same information.
    2) Elements from at least three different *topoi*.
    3) A title that explains the main point or most important content of the composition.
    4) A separate Works Cited page.
3   The student should quote directly from at least one source and should cite at least two.

Mechanics:

1   Each sentence should make sense on its own when read aloud.
2   There should be no sentence fragments or run-on sentences.
3   All words should be spelled correctly.
4   The first line of each paragraph should be properly indented.
5   Verb tense should be consistent throughout.
6   Direct quotes should be properly formatted.
7   Footnotes and Works Cited page should be properly formatted.

Final Project, Basic Rubric

Organization

1   At least three *topoi* should be used.
2   The composition should be at least 1250 words long.
3   There should be an introduction and conclusion, both in separate paragraphs.
4   At least four sources should be cited.
5   The paper should have a title that conveys a sense of the paper's content.

Mechanics

1   Each sentence should make sense on its own when read aloud.
2   There should be no sentence fragments or run-on sentences.
3   All words should be spelled correctly.
4   The first line of each paragraph should be properly indented.
5   Verb tense should be consistent throughout.
6   Direct quotes should be properly formatted.
7   Footnotes and Works Cited page should be properly formatted.

Appendix VIII

GENERAL RUBRICS

Mechanics Rubric: All
1. Each sentence should make sense on its own when read aloud.
2. Possessive forms should be written properly.
3. Verb tense should be consistent throughout.
4. Subjects and verbs must be in agreement.
5. Antecedents of pronouns should be clear.
6. Unnecessary repetition of the same nouns, adjectives, and proper names should be avoided.
7. The titles of poems or short stories should be in quotation marks.
8. Direct quotes should be incorporated into full sentences and should be properly punctuated.
9. Poem quotes should be properly formatted and attributed.
10. Secondary sources should be properly footnoted:

    First name, last name, *Title of book* (Publisher, year of publication), p. xx.
11. The Works Cited page should be separate and should be properly formatted. Entries should be alphabetized and single spaced, with double spaces separating entries. "Works Cited" should be centered at the top.

    Last name, first name. *Title of book*. City of publication: Publisher, year.
12. Compositions of more than one page should have page numbers.
13. Typed compositions should be double-spaced.
14. All compositions should be titled. Title should be descriptive and should be centered at the top of the first page.

Summary of Narrative Fiction
Organization
1. Events should be in chronological order.
2. If two or more events are listed in a single sentence, they should have a cause and effect relationship.
3. Each event of major importance should be in the summary (if it were missing from the original passage, the narrative would no longer make sense).

Summary of Descriptive Fiction
Organization
1. If two or more details are listed in a single sentence, they should be related.
2. Details of conversations should not be listed.
3. Any events should be connected to the description by a time word.

Chronological Narrative of Past Events:
Organization
1. Events should be in chronological order.
2. Time words should be used to create transitions.
3. A clear theme should be used to sort through and choose events.
4. Dialogue may be used.

Chronological Narrative of Scientific Discovery
Organization
1. Events should be in chronological order.
2. The paragraph giving "background information" should be the first or second paragraph in the composition.
3. Time words should be used.
4. If possible, the scientist's own words should be quoted.

Description of a Place
Organization
1. The description should use appropriate adjectives and verbs to convey the purpose of the description.
2. Space and distance words and phrases should be used.
3. Point of view should remain consistent: from above, from inside, from one side or angle, OR moving through/around.
4. A vivid metaphor or simile should be used when possible.

Scientific Description
Organization:
1. The description should make use of one or both points of view: removed, present.
2. Present point of view descriptions should incorporate at least three of the five senses: sight, sound, smell, taste, feeling.
3. Removed point of view descriptions should describe each part of the object or phenomenon and tell what it is made of.
4. At least one metaphor or simile may be used.
5. The description should cover each part of the object or phenomenon.

Description of a Person
Organization
1. The description should include at least five, but no more than eight of the aspects listed on the Description of a Person chart.
2. The description may be slanted in a positive or negative direction.
3. A governing metaphor may be used to organize the description.

Biographical Sketch
Organization
1. The sketch should include selected aspects from the Description of a Person chart.
2. The focus may be on:
     a. Life events, listed chronologically
     b. The subject's work/accomplishments, listed chronologically
     c. The subject's work/accomplishments, listed by subject/topic

Sequence: Natural Process
Organization
1. Each step in the process should be described in order.
2. Ideas or images from the source material should be footnoted. Scientific facts do not need footnotes.
3. One or more of the following must be included:
     a. Introduction/summary
     b. Scientific background
     c. Repetition of the process

Sequence: History
Organization
1. The sequence should begin with a clear description of the parts that make up the the process, machine, or cycle.
2. Next, the sequence should provide a clear step-by-step description of how it works.
3. The sequence may include one or more of the following:
     a. Introduction
     b. Historical background
     c. Results or consequences

Explanation by Comparison/Contrast
Organization
 1. The explanation should compare and contrast two or more subjects.
 2. The explanation should cover both the similarities and differences between the subjects.
 3. One of the following methods should be used:
    a. Point-by-point comparison
    b. Subject-by-subject comparison
    c. A combination of the two methods

Explanation by Definition: Natural Object or Phenomenon
Organization
 1. The definition should address and answer questions from at *least* one of the following categories:
    a. Essential and Accidental Properties
    b. Function
    c. Genus
 2. The definition may also describe the same thing at two different points in time.

Explanation by Definition: Historical Object, Event, Place, or People Group
Organization
 1. The definition should address and answer questions from at *least* one of the following categories:
    a. Shared and Unique Properties
    b. Function
    c. Genus
 2. The definition may also compare the properties, function, and/or genus of the subject at two different points in time.

Temporal Comparison: History
Organization
 1. The comparison should describe the similarities and differences between the earlier and later stages of the *same* historical phenomenon.
 2. The comparison should contain the following four elements, in order:
    a. Brief introduction to the phenomenon
    b. Description of one or more earlier stages of its development
    c. Description of transition to its current form
    d. Description of current form
 3. The comparison can be organized in one of the following ways:
    a. Point-by-point comparison
    b. Subject-by-subject comparison

Temporal Comparison: Science

Organization

1. The comparison should describe aspects of the same subject at two different points in time.
    a. The different points in time might occur as part of a regular life cycle.
    b. The different points in time might occur as part of a natural change unique to the subject.
2. The comparison may also include explanations of why the changes occur.
3. The comparison can be organized in one of the following ways:
    a. Point-by-point comparison
    b. Subject-by-subject comparison